Forging Modernity

Forging Modernity

Why and How Britain Developed the Industrial Revolution

Martin Hutchinson

The Lutterworth Press

THE LUTTERWORTH PRESS

P.O. Box 60
Cambridge
CB1 2NT
United Kingdom

www.lutterworth.com.
publishing@lutterworth.com

Hardback ISBN: 978 0 7188 9686 7
Paperback ISBN: 978 0 7188 9689 8
PDF ISBN: 978 0 7188 9687 4
ePub ISBN: 978 0 7188 9688 1

British Library Cataloguing in Publication Data
A record is available from the British Library

First published by The Lutterworth Press, 2023

Copyright © Martin Hutchinson, 2023

All rights reserved. No part of this edition may be reproduced,
stored electronically or in any retrieval system, or transmitted
in any form or by any means, electronic, mechanical,
photocopying, recording, or otherwise, without
prior written permission from the Publisher
(permissions@lutterworth.com).

Contents

List of Illustrations	vii
Acknowledgements	ix
Note on Money	xi

1	Introduction: What this Book Is About	1
2	The Competitors: Europe's Potential Industrializers in 1600	25
3	Britain in 1600 and Early Changes, 1600-48	64
4	The Restoration Renaissance, 1649-88	95
5	Iron, Steam and Finance, 1689-1720	137
6	The Industrial Revolution Takes a Whig Nap, 1721-60	183
7	The Tory-Assisted Take-off, 1761-83	216
8	Pitt, Rotary Steam Engines and War, 1784-1806	276
9	Liverpool's Policies Lead to Modernity, 1807-30	321
10	Epilogue: The Victorians and After	376

Bibliography	401
Index	413

List of Illustrations

All illustrations are in the public domain unless otherwise stated

1.	Machine de Marly	12
2.	Philip III of Spain	27
3.	Henry IV of France	36
4.	Rudolf II of Habsburg, Holy Roman Emperor	45
5.	Prince Maurice of Nassau	55
6.	John Winchcombe	73
	Image courtesy of Newbury Town Council (CC BY-SA 4.0)	
7.	Francis Bacon, Viscount St. Alban	85
8.	Lucius Cary, 2nd Viscount Falkland	92
9.	Edward Hyde, Earl of Clarendon	103
	Image courtesy of the Wellcome Library (CC BY 4.0)	
10.	Sir Robert Clayton's House	112
11.	Prince Rupert	123
12.	Sir Dudley North	127
13.	Newcomen engine	160
	Image courtesy of Jernkontoret	
14.	Sir Ambrose Crowley's Greenwich house.	164
15.	Exchange Alley	179
16.	Lombe's Mill	197
17.	Bridgewater Canal	212
18.	James Brindley	214
19.	Granville Leveson Gower, 2nd Earl Gower	220
20.	Gurney's Bank	233
21.	Trent and Mersey Canal	245
	Image courtesy of Elliott Brown (CC BY-SA 2.0)	
22.	Roger Newdigate	249
23.	Josiah Wedgwood	252
24.	John Wilkinson	258

25.	Sir Richard Arkwright	262
26.	Matthew Boulton	266
27.	The House of Commons	277
28.	Watt rotary engine	293
	Image courtesy of David Maciulaitis (CC BY 2.0)	
29.	Bramah Hydraulic Press	309
30.	Henry Maudslay	310
31.	Robert Banks Jenkinson, 2nd Earl of Liverpool	322
32.	Fish Dinner at the Brunswick Hotel	334
33.	Gas lighting	337
34.	Humphrey Davy	341
35.	Power loom	346
	Image courtesy of the Wellcome Library (CC BY 4.0)	
36.	St. Rollox chemical	352
37.	The collier	367
	Image courtesy of Rawpixel (CC BY-SA 4.0)	
38.	Opening Liverpool and Manchester Railway	372
39.	Goldsworthy Gurney.	374

Acknowledgements

Intellectually, I must own my debt to the late Professor Alfred D. Chandler's[1] course in Business History and the following Business History seminar at Harvard Business School in the academic year 1972-1973. Chandler's course focussed mostly on the growth of the great US businesses in the late nineteenth and early twentieth centuries, and the development of their business strategies and organization structures. He taught me that the history of business is the history of businesses, and that examining those businesses' strategies and their success or failure can be highly informative. He also left me with a burning interest in the 'prequel' to US industrial success, the Industrial Revolution in Britain, which by writing this book I have finally been able to satisfy.

In writing this book, I am immensely grateful to Professor Kevin Dowd of the University of Durham, my esteemed collaborator on *Alchemists of Loss: How Modern Finance and Government Intervention Crashed the Financial System* (Chichester: Wiley, 2010). Kevin has read the book in draft and given me immensely helpful feedback, as he did for my previous book, *Britain's Greatest Prime Minister: Lord Liverpool*. In this case, he also provided me with valuable advice on several topics covered by the book, especially in the financial sector. Most particularly, he arranged for an immensely distinguished group of British and American scholars to advise me on information sources relating to country banking, which I believe to have been the critical

---

1. Alfred D. Chandler, Jr (1918-2007). Massachusetts Institute of Technology, 1950-63, Johns Hopkins University, 1963-70, Harvard Business School, 1970-89. *Strategy and Structure: Chapters in the History of American Enterprise* (Boston: MIT Press, 1962), *The Visible Hand: The Managerial Revolution in American Business* (Cambridge, MA: The Belknap Press, 1977).

source of finance for Industrial Revolution entrepreneurs and businesses generally.

For their most kind and helpful advice on country banking information sources, I am very grateful to Professor Mark Billings of Exeter University, Kurt Schuler, senior fellow of the Center for Financial Stability in New York City, George Selgin, director of the Center for Monetary and Financial Alternatives at the Cato Institute, Washington, DC, and Professor Lawrence H. White of George Mason University, Fairfax, VA.

I am also grateful to James A. Dorn of the Cato Institute for his advice and encouragement in this work.

As always, I am immensely grateful to my son, Rumen M. Hutchinson, both personally and for his professional help with the preparation of this book and the design of the cover.

Note on Money

It is now half a century since Britain went decimal, so I should include a note on the currency system and coinage of the Industrial Revolution period from 1600 to 1830. I should also give some hint to readers of the modern equivalent of the various wage, price and budgetary sums mentioned in the text, in sterling and in other currencies of the time.

The British currency consisted of pounds, shillings (shortened to 's' in the text) and pennies (shortened to 'd' from the Roman 'denarii'), with twelve pennies to the shilling and 20 shillings to the pound. Between 1604 and 1817, no gold pound coins (sovereigns) were minted; the common gold coin was the guinea, worth a variable number of shillings. Coins such as shillings, sixpences, crowns and half-crowns were minted in silver; twopenny pieces, pennies and fractions thereof in copper.

The pound was from 1717 fixed in value against both silver and gold by Sir Isaac Newton[1] as Master of the Mint; this became a gold standard as silver became scarcer and increased in value. Convertibility under this standard was suspended in 1797 and resumed formally in 1821 at £3 17s 10½d per troy ounce of 22-carat gold, or £4.25 (in decimals) per ounce of pure gold. After 1821, silver was no longer legal tender for sums of more than £2.

Roderick Floud, in 'The Changing Value of Money',[2] sets out three different ways in which we can compare money items in the distant past to those today. We can multiply an 1820 price by the change of a price index from 1820 to today, by the change of a wage index or by

---

1. Isaac Newton (1642-1727). Kt 1705, FRS 1672. MP for Cambridge University, 1689, 1701. *Principia Mathematica* (1687), *Opticks* (1704). Warden of the Mint, 1696-99, Master of the Mint, 1699-1727.
2. Roderick Floud, 'The Changing Value of Money', *History Today*, Vol. 69, no. 3 (March 2019).

the change in Gross Domestic Product. Using Floud's example of the £10,000 annual income of Jane Austen's Mr Darcy from 1813 (*Pride and Prejudice* was published in that year), we get modern equivalents for Mr Darcy's income of £620,000 today (March 2019, when the article appeared) inflating by prices, £7,305,000 today inflating by wages and about £40 million inflating by GDP (which Floud uses not for earnings but for public construction, state budgets, etc.).

Floud prefers the wage index to the price index – we buy different things today, for example, relatively less food. I disagree; we are all richer than 200 years ago and inflating by wages overinflates an 1813 income as if today's technology had been available then. GDP indexing overinflates even more. Mr Darcy was rich, but not the richest man in England; the Marquess of Stafford's income was about £100,000. Mr Darcy is not quite equivalent to a modern CEO, as Floud suggests; Pemberley is a much nicer home than the CEO's, but Mr Darcy's plumbing, transportation and medical care were pathetic by modern standards.

There is an easier way: to use the gold standard. Gold was worth £4.25 per troy ounce in 1821-30; it is worth about £1,500 per ounce today. By this measure, Mr Darcy's £10,000 a year in paper-money 1813 is worth about £8,000 gold standard pounds (gold traded around 25% above par in 1813) or £2,820,000 today. That's between Floud's price and wage calculations; it shows what a good long-term store of value gold is. I suggest therefore that to get a modern (2022) equivalent you should multiply 1812-14 prices and wages by 282 and 1819-30 prices and wages by 353. The 353 conversion multiple also works for the world between 1717 and 1793.

Before 1717, say in 1600, we need to use a higher multiple, reflecting the higher bullion content of English coinage. The James VI and I gold sovereign of 1603-4 weighed 11.15 grams of 0.875 purity (21-carat) gold and so would have been worth 1.333 1817 sovereigns at bullion value; an appropriate conversion value for 1600 pounds to 2022 would thus be 470:1.

As for foreign money, where a sterling equivalent was needed, I have used representative exchange rates for the period concerned. For 1600, exchange rates can be calculated as follows:

Spain: The Spanish *peso* or 'piece of eight' was a silver coin containing 27.5 grams of silver of 0.9306 fine, and thereby valued at around 0.2 English pounds (the 1600 pound contained about 142 grams or 4.565 troy ounces of sterling silver of 0.925 fine). The ducat was a gold coin of similar value.

France: In 1600, the French currency was the *livre tournois* – the Tours pound – which became nationally accepted, as distinct from other

Note on Money

regional variants, with about 0.28 troy ounces (8.71 grams) of silver, or about fifteen livres to the English pound. The livre was devalued by over a third by the time of the Revolution, to about 25 to the pound sterling; this was also the approximate exchange rate of the 1815-30 French franc.

Holy Roman Empire: The official currency of the Holy Roman Empire in 1600 was the *Reichsthaler*, established by the Leipzig Convention of 1566 at one ninth of a Cologne Mark, or 25.98 grams of silver; it was worth about 0.19 English pounds. To add complexity the Reichsthaler was primarily used as an accounting unit and for foreign exchange transactions; the main circulating currency was the *Gulden* (also known as the florin) which exchanged within the Empire at two thirds of a Reichsthaler, or 0.13 English pounds.[3]

Netherlands: The *rijksdaalder*, used as a unit of account, was in 1600 worth 0.2 English pounds sterling, divided into 50 *stuivers*. The guilder of 20 stuivers was used as a transaction currency (the guilder was worth 0.08 English pounds).

---

3. This is an over-simplification of a very complex reality, with strong regional variations. If it makes you feel better, Sir Isaac Newton confessed in a letter to the Lords of the Treasury of 12 April 1720 that he did not fully understand the Holy Roman Empire's currency system either.

1

Introduction: What this Book Is About

This book sets out the process by which a small group of islands off the Eurasian Continent catalysed a revolution in human welfare that has permitted the global population to increase by almost ten times while everybody became unimaginably richer. The Industrial Revolution was the most important transition for mankind since the development of agriculture, and much more unequivocally positive in its effects on living standards. It is a story of superior economic policies, political and scientific ideas, over a period of some 180 years, that enabled islands with only minor special advantages to develop in a unique way that turned out incalculably beneficial for humanity.

I shall begin by showing what preconditions, in terms of both resources and policies, were essential for the development of an industrial society from a mediaeval one. I have listed a total of sixteen such factors, all of which contributed significantly; one could argue that one or other such factor was unnecessary, but we have only a few 'control experiments' so can demonstrate only that societies without several such factors did not make this development. (I shall assume that the 'game' begins in the early seventeenth century, so that certain necessities such as printing, settled agriculture and ocean-going transportation already exist and are available throughout Europe.) I shall show why the preconditions are needed to create any industrial economy, regardless of where it is created. By applying this template to societies other than Britain, I shall show in what respects they were lacking. I shall then examine the development of British policies and society, to show how the necessary conditions for industrialization were developed and enhanced.

Factors Needed to Move from a Mediaeval Society to an Industrial One

Individual Freedom

British society at the time of the Industrial Revolution differed from all contemporary Continental societies except the Netherlands in one overwhelmingly important respect: almost all its people were fully free. That freedom derived from the period after a pandemic, the Black Death.

Before the Black Death the Norman Conquest of England had sharply compromised the living standards and embryonic freedoms of the then-indigenous Saxons. The Normans appropriated the large land-holdings and imposed serfdom, the more severe French version of feudalism. Most of the Saxon population existed in an unfree status for the following centuries, providing labour and possibly military service to their feudal lord, and receiving no cash compensation. As England became more settled and its wealth increased, more land was cleared and cultivated. However, population increase among the serfs kept them mired in serfdom, even though the non-rural sectors of the economy were developing a cash economy with free exchange.

Then the Black Death from 1348 wiped out at least a third of the population. The result was a severe labour shortage. In response, the ruling classes who controlled Parliament passed the Statute of Labourers 1351, prohibiting working people's wages from being increased. These restrictions were initially somewhat effective, but over generations, with people moving, new employers emerging and new job types appearing, they became a dead letter – the Peasants Revolt of 1381 showed the former serfs asserting their new autonomy. By the fifteenth century, wage restrictions had effectively disappeared – the descendants of the serfs freed themselves and worked for the much higher wages now available. This period was in retrospect known as 'Merrie England'. For many of the former serfs, if not for those embroiled with their former masters in the Wars of the Roses, it was indeed 'Merrie'!

This liberation happened across Europe for similar demographic reasons, but England and the future Netherlands saw workers liberated more fully than in France, Spain or the Holy Roman Empire. Thus, even though living standards declined again with increasing population after 1500, the greater freedom of English labour, maintained even through the impoverished early seventeenth century, was an important contributor to the Industrial Revolution.

English working men were free to move about the country, provided they could support themselves – only the 1601 Poor Law, which provided

Introduction: What this Book Is About

a minimal subsistence for the indigent on a parish basis, forced those seeking relief to return to their home parish. They were also free to work in any occupation they chose and to make any arrangement they could negotiate with their employer.

These freedoms were essential to the genesis of the Industrial Revolution, and a leading reason why it happened first in Britain. The Holy Roman Empire, for example, full of industrious and well-schooled German engineers, was still bedevilled by serfdom and feudal obligations in the eighteenth century because the Thirty Years' War (1618-48) had re-immiserated much of its populace. Consequently, German industrialization was mostly delayed until after 1850.

Rule of Law

As well as individual freedom, the rule of law was necessary for industrialization. Laws should be clearly and unambiguously stated, equitably applied and universally applicable, and the arbitrary misuse of them by a king or bureaucrat should be prevented. In mediaeval societies, kings and other powerful nobles often acted above the law, subverting the lives, rights and property of ordinary people. In the eighteenth century, that was still the case in France and Spain, but not in the Holy Roman Empire, the Netherlands or Britain.

The development of English law reflected a perception that the power of the king had limits. Sir John Fortescue's[1] 1470 work, *The Difference between an Absolute and Limited Monarchy*, describes how the English monarchy was bound by law, rather than absolute like the French one. In practice, it was possible for an English King like Henry VIII[2] to flout the law.

The Civil War and the Interregnum, together with the legalism of the seventeenth century and the 1689 Bill of Rights, established the rule of law as a bedrock constitutional principle. Legal scholars and Members of Parliament played an important role in resurrecting shadowy mediaeval or Saxon liberties and establishing a solid legal structure that provided effective opposition to the early Stuart Kings.

---

1. Sir John Fortescue (1394-1479) Kt. MP for Tavistock, 1421-25, Totnes, 1426 and 1432, Plympton Erle, 1429, and Wiltshire, 1437. Chief Justice of the King's Bench, 1442-60. He held the nominal title of Chancellor of England during Henry VI's exile and readeption, 1463-71.
2. Henry VIII (1491-1547). King of England, 1509-47.

Sir William Blackstone's[3] *Commentaries on the Laws of England* (1765-69) codified English common law and made it available to ordinary people. Eighteenth-century Britain was a highly, even excessively, legalistic society, and the courts were often abominably slow and expensive. However, the existence of a rock-solid legal system was universally accepted and an enormous protection for entrepreneurs whose success conflicted with existing vested interests.

Scientific Revolution

To design and produce the complex machinery necessary for an industrial society, the Scientific Method was essential. Without it, *ad hoc* advances might have occurred but the kind of sustained scientific advance over a prolonged period that produced James Watt's[4] steam engine, Arthur Woolf's Cornish Engine and the first workable locomotives would have been impossible.

The Scientific Method, propounded by, amongst others, Francis Bacon[5] in his *Novum Organum Scientiarum* (1620), showed the practical technologists of the seventeenth, eighteenth and nineteenth centuries how they could perfect their machines using an iterative method of practical experimentation refined by theoretical reasoning, leading to further practical experimentation. This powerful methodology produced more sustained advances than had previously been possible and provided an intellectual paradigm that would prove key to the Industrial Revolution.

The Scientific Method and the quickened pace of scientific advance to which it led explain well why the Industrial Revolution occurred in Western Europe in the eighteenth and nineteenth centuries. Western European countries other than Britain had equal access to Bacon's treatise (which was written in Latin and published in the Netherlands). They also had access to the research other great scientists of the time,

---

3. William Blackstone (1723-1780). Kt 1770. Tory MP for Hindon, 1761-68, and Westbury, 1768-70. Vinerian Professor of English Law, Oxford, 1759-66. Justice of King's Bench, 1770-80. *Commentaries on the Laws of England* (1765-69).

4. James Watt (1736-1819). Invented steam condenser, 1765. Partnership with Matthew Boulton, 1775, with whom he developed the first truly economically superior steam engines.

5. Francis Bacon (1561-1626). Kt 1603, Baron Verulam, 1618, Viscount St Alban, 1621. MP for Bossiney, 1581, Weymouth and Melcombe Regis, 1584, Taunton, 1586, Liverpool, 1589, Middlesex, 1593, Ipswich, 1601 and 1604, and Cambridge University, 1614. Attorney-General, 1613-17, Lord Chancellor, 1617-21.

Introduction: What this Book Is About

only a minority of whom were British. Countries outside Europe, such as China, Japan, the Mughal and the Ottoman Empires, accessed Bacon's work only indirectly, and their intellectual climate was less well equipped to take advantage of its paradigm.

As well as the Scientific Method itself, it was also necessary for a society's business and professional class, within the overall Baconian paradigm, to be oriented towards practical experimentation and results rather than theoretical knowledge. N.A.M. Rodger, the naval historian, in discussing the progress of ship design in the eighteenth century,[6] illustrates the difference between British approaches and those of its naval rival, France. Among others, no less a mathematician than Leonhard Euler[7] advised the French navy on ship design, focussing on the fashionable subject of hydrodynamics, but omitting consideration of skin friction, which at sailing ship speeds contributed almost the entire resistance to motion. Thus, Euler's work was useless. Conversely, British shipwrights focussed on the practical problems faced by sailing ships under normally rough conditions over prolonged periods at sea, and came up with copper-bottoming, which after its adoption by the British navy gave Britain a decisive naval advantage.

Rodger's explanation of Britain's greater ability to make important practical advances in ship design applies equally to the practical advances in manufacturing technology and techniques that formed the Industrial Revolution. Then, as now, few industrial advances took place at the cutting edge of scientific knowledge; instead, they rested on the application of well-established scientific knowledge to practical problems and situations.

Rights and Security of Private Property

Building a business using a new technology requires the investment of much capital, with a high risk of failure and a relatively long payback. Its risks are not only unquantifiable but also un-assessable; it differs qualitatively from sending a trading ship on a long voyage.

---

6. N.A.M. Rodger, *The Command of the Ocean: A Naval History of Britain, 1649-1815* (New York: W.W. Norton, 2004), p. 410.

7. Leonhard Euler (1707-83). Swiss mathematician, physicist, astronomer, logician and engineer, the most eminent mathematician of the eighteenth century. Pioneered topology and analytic number theory; introduced the concept of a function and the modern notation for trigonometric functions, the base of natural logarithms e and the imaginary number i. Also discovered that $e^{i\pi} + 1 = 0$.

(An insurance company can provide insurance against shipwreck by insuring large numbers of similar voyages, but each new technological investment is unique; there is no way to find insurance against its possible failure.) To enter such a venture, generally absorbing most of his capital, an entrepreneur must have highly secure property rights, against expropriation by a government, a powerful noble, his workforce or a fellow citizen armed with a good lawyer and a friendly judge.

Rock-solid property rights are generally not possible in an absolutist regime, or in one with an uncertain legal code. They are the most important single requirement for industrial capitalism to come into existence, even more important than wholly free markets. A lengthy period of well-defined, well-enforced property rights, without the intervention of military, political or financial factors is essential for industrialization to occur.

When examining societies for their potential for industrialization, we should examine their potential for a long period of solid property rights, without externally imposed interruptions. Geography, making a society relatively immune from military incursions, is an additional important factor. Property must be secure against marauding armies and domestic agitators, who can destroy property and render long-term plans nugatory. Industrial investment requires a much greater physical security than farming, where the loss of a year's crop can be repaired in the following year.

Britain was lucky in this respect. Its Civil War was not especially destructive, and occurred early in the pre-industrialization process, before major investments were at stake. Then Britain enjoyed two centuries of domestic peace, protected by the Royal Navy, with only brief and unsuccessful Jacobite rebellions in 1715 and 1745 and a small abortive French attack in 1798. With stable governments firmly committed to maintaining order, violent unrest was also minor before the 1830s.

Contrast this with the experience of the other European competitors for industrialization. Spain had one major domestic incursion, the War of the Spanish Succession, before falling victim to Napoleon in 1808. France had a civil war (the Fronde) in 1648-53, then a lengthy period of domestic peace until both domestic and foreign military chaos after 1789. The Netherlands was invaded by France in 1672-78 but was then tranquil until modest domestic revolts in 1783-87 and the French Revolutionary invasion of 1795. The Holy Roman Empire fared worst of all, suffering the immensely damaging Thirty Years' War between 1618 and 1648, then being the scene of most of the conflicts over the following century, before succumbing to French invasion and domestic

Introduction: What this Book Is About

chaos after 1792. Lack of domestic tranquillity was a significant obstacle to industrialization in most European countries, with the Holy Roman Empire worst off.

In Britain, it was also necessary for 'Luddism' to be resisted. The first major outbreak of machine-breaking occurred in 1779, in the early stages of the adoption of water-powered machinery in the textile sector, which threatened traditional 'cottage' textile operations. One Ned Ludd, a weaver from Anstey, Leicestershire, allegedly smashed two stocking frames, but this was only a small part of a substantial outbreak that included the destruction of one of Richard Arkwright's[8] mills in Birkacre, Lancashire.

The authorities suppressed the disturbances on public order grounds, but there were further disturbances over the next four decades, particularly during the economically difficult decade of the 1790s. The most serious outbreaks came in 1812, after Napoleon's Milan Decree had cut off most of Britain's export markets, throwing many textile operators out of work, after an exceptionally poor harvest in 1811 had raised the price of grain to exceptional levels.

The government's answer to the riots was the Destruction of Stocking Frames etc. Act 1812, which made the destruction of industrial machinery a capital felony. The Second Earl of Liverpool,[9] Leader of the House of Lords in Spencer Perceval's[10] government, introduced the bill in the House of Lords (and Lord Byron used his maiden speech in the upper chamber to oppose it). Nobody was executed under the specific provisions of the Act (which expired automatically two years later) but it acted as an effective deterrent to machine-breaking activity, which died down thereafter.

Perceval, Liverpool and their colleagues knew that the labour-saving machinery of the Industrial Revolution was improving living standards rapidly, even though some traditional workers, such as framework knitters, handloom weavers and 'croppers' were being made redundant by the innovations. Since those groups contained over 100,000 workers, the social disruption and hardship was considerable.

---

8. Richard Arkwright (1732-92). Kt 1786. Invented the spinning frame, known as the 'father of the modern factory system'. High Sheriff of Derbyshire, 1787.

9. Robert Banks Jenkinson (1770-1828), 2nd Earl of Liverpool from 1808. MP for Rye, 1790-1803. Foreign Secretary, 1801-4, Leader of the House of Lords, 1803-6, 1807-27, Home Secretary, 1804-6, 1807-9, Secretary for War and the Colonies, 1809-12, Prime Minister, 1812-27.

10. Spencer Perceval (1762-1812). Attorney-General, 1802-6, Chancellor of the Exchequer 1807-12, Prime Minister 1809-12.

This attitude was not universal – for example, the Russian Empress Catherine the Great,[11] in her 1767 *Nakaz*, or Instruction, decreed that 'no machines should ever be introduced into Russia, because they may result in a reduction in the number of working people'.[12]

Finally, for an industrialist to establish a long-lasting industrial enterprise, he must be sure that his rights to the enterprise and its output can be made legally watertight. Not only must his property right in that enterprise be sound, but he must also know that his intellectual property, the know-how and scientific insight that went into the facility's construction, is safe from being copied by others, either domestically or worldwide. Copyright and patent law are relatively late additions to the corpus of law in most societies, but at least their beginnings must be established for industrialization to occur.

In addition to statutory protections for intellectual property rights, there must be provisions to enforce them legally without excessive cost or delay. Boulton[13] and Watt's lawsuits to uphold Watt's steam engine patents were critical to this in Britain; there must be adequate mechanisms for such enforcement wherever industrialization is to occur. However, Boulton's 1775 use of Parliament to extend Watt's patent for 31 years, like Thomas Savery's[14] use of Parliament in 1698 to extend his over-general patent for 35 years, shows how these mechanisms could be abused.

Good Climate for Savers

Conventional development economists at this point will murmur something about 'sophisticated capital markets'. Actually, sophisticated capital markets, while in existence, were irrelevant to Britain's industrialization or even antithetic to it before the share boom of the 1880s. The short-term thinkers and globalist trade financiers in the City of London never financed the early industries.[15] The amounts required

---

11. Sophie of Anhalt-Zerbst (1729-96). Married Peter III of Russia (1728-62), 1745. As Catherine, Empress-Consort of Russia, 1762, Empress of Russia, 1762-96.

12. I am indebted to Linda Colley, *The Gun, the Ship, and the Pen* (New York: Liveright Publishing, 2021), p. 75, for this reference.

13. Matthew Boulton (1728-1809). Founded Boulton & Watt, 1775. Founder member, Birmingham Lunar Society, 1765.

14. Thomas Savery (1650-1715). Inventor, promoter. Original 14-year 1698 patent on his steam pump was extended by Parliament to 1733.

15. Possibly with one notable exception: the Hollow Sword Blade Company's probable financing of Newcomen's engine – see Chapter V.

Introduction: What this Book Is About

were too small for profitable 'merchant banking' and the payoffs were too distant, while the technology was mostly incomprehensible to the classics graduates who dominated the merchant banks' leadership.

The principal source of financing for the early industrialists was their savings and the savings of those around them, whether family, partners or occasionally 'angel' investors. Even quite poor men with engineering or technological skills could get financing through local networks of investors with country banks as intermediaries. For this to take place, the country's economic climate had to be favourable to savers, allowing them to generate and retain liquid surpluses, both before venturing into entrepreneurship and from the fruits of early success.

A favourable climate for savers included several elements. In addition to rock-solid property rights, the money unit had to be stable in value – inflationary paper currencies or coinage debasement attacked savers' holdings directly. Initially, savings could be held in bullion or plate – Tudor and Stuart households held much of their net worth on the dinner table – or in land, although the illiquidity of land holdings made them unattractive as sources of industrial capital. As the financial system developed, it needed to include either rock-solid banks or long-term instruments with complete security paying a reliable real yield. In Britain after 1751, government Consols ('Consolidated Annuities', created by Pelham) filled this need admirably.

The savings instruments available had to extend beyond the gentry and urban middle classes, so that working people could also build up modest pools of capital that were secure and not held in coin, vulnerable to theft. The true innovation, after industrialization was under way, came with the Savings Bank Act 1817, which provided specialised 'Trustee Savings Banks' for working-class savers, whose funds were invested only in government bonds, and were thus secure against financial crises affecting the conventional banking system.

Finally, there should not be excessive 'progressiveness' in the tax system, allowing the government to gouge huge percentages out of large savings holdings, thus discouraging their formation. Only with all these elements in place is a climate of saving encouraged, and liquid pools of wealth built up that can finance industrialization.

Small-scale Localism

The capitalism of the Industrial Revolution was notably localist. With new companies small and banking atomized, there was little pull towards big cities. The Whig Supremacy, one-party rule of 1714-60 was concentrated in the Whig stronghold of London, with most opportunities in the centralized financial sector of London itself, the plundering run from London by the East India Company or in the slave colonies of the Americas. The Whigs had little political strength in the provinces (other than 'rotten boroughs' available for cash) and little interest in what went on there.

When party dominance changed with the accession of George III[16] in 1760, political power became devolved to the Tory small towns and rural areas. This coincided with a doubling from the previous decade of patent applications in the 1760s[17] and the emergence of numerous wealthy provincial industrialists, notably, Josiah Wedgwood[18] (pottery), Arkwright (textiles), John Wilkinson[19] (iron manufactures) and Matthew Boulton (metal goods and eventually steam engines). Infrastructure during this period was provincial also, with James Brindley's[20] 'Grand Cross' system of canals in the Midlands, backed and partly financed by the Staffordshire magnate, the second Earl Gower.[21]

With new enterprises and sources of finance spread around Britain, innumerable approaches to problems could be tried and solutions applied on a small scale to different sectors. The result was an unprecedented effervescence of innovation, which over time led to unprecedentedly rapid growth.

The localist approach was not inevitable; in the seventeenth century Louis XIV's France showed the attraction to monarchs and the defects for the populace of centralized state-directed enterprise. It produced

---

16. George III (1738-1820). King of Great Britain, 1760-1820, from 1801 King of the United Kingdom of Great Britain and Ireland.

17. B.R. Mitchell (ed.), *British Historical Statistics* (Cambridge: Cambridge University Press, 2011), Table VIII-23, pp. 438-39.

18. Josiah Wedgwood (1730-95). Founder of Wedgwood & Co., 1759.

19. John Wilkinson (1728-1808). Ironmaster. Invented cylinder-boring machine, 1774.

20. James Brindley (1716-72). Engineer, designer of the Bridgewater Canal and the Liverpool and Manchester Canal. Postulated 'Grand Cross' scheme to link by canal the Mersey, Trent, Severn and Thames rivers, completed after his death.

21. Granville Leveson-Gower (1721-1803). 2nd Earl Gower from 1754, 1st Marquess of Stafford from 1786. KG 1771. Bedfordite/Tory MP for Bishop's Castle, Westminster and Lichfield, 1744-54. Lord Privy Seal, 1755-57, 1784-94, Master of the Horse, 1757-60, Lord Chamberlain, 1763-65, Lord President of the Council, 1767-79, 1783-84.

Introduction: What this Book Is About

magnificent feats of engineering such as the Machine de Marly, a gigantic hydraulic system completed in 1684, consisting of fourteen water wheels, each 38 feet in diameter, that powered more than 250 pumps to bring water 500 feet up a hillside from the River Seine to the Louveciennes Aqueduct. Considered the most complex machine of the century, it took three years to build for the purpose of supplying the ornamental fountains at Versailles, which used more water than the city of Paris. No useful industrial development resulted from this magnificent contraption, although its frequent breakdowns employed a staff of 60 to keep it running for over 130 years.[22]

Independent Localized and Competitive Banking System

England's banking system during the Industrial Revolution was remarkably open and competitive. The market speculation over the 1689-1720 period, as the national debt built up in ways very lucrative for the Whig-allied promoters, had concentrated the financial system on banks and securities dealers in London. After 1750, as no more 'bubbles' occurred and risk-free interest rates had stabilized at around 3%, numerous 'country banks' appeared based in provincial towns. By the Bank of England Act 1708, no bank, other than the Bank of England, could have public stockholders or more than six partners; the result was a proliferation of small banks, with six or fewer partners and no more than one or two branches – by 1790 there were more than 300 such banks and by 1813 more than 800.

These country banks were located in every town of any significance; their partners were local attorneys, traders and businessmen. Consequently, there was no centralization of capital availability. Instead, debt was available locally, from people whose wealth and social class was not out of touch with the entrepreneurs themselves. These banks financed primarily trade, but also the small-scale infrastructure projects, such as canals, that resulted from economic growth. As industrial companies arose, they financed their short-term capital needs for receivables and inventory, and indirectly brokered some of their long-term capital needs.

Thus, there was no control of which entrepreneurs obtained funding – not by the government, nor by the fashionable elite and higher education institutions. The country bankers were certainly neither fashionable nor highly educated. Moreover, any entrepreneur had a choice of several

---

22. See: http://www.marlymachine.org/ (accessed 3 August 2021).

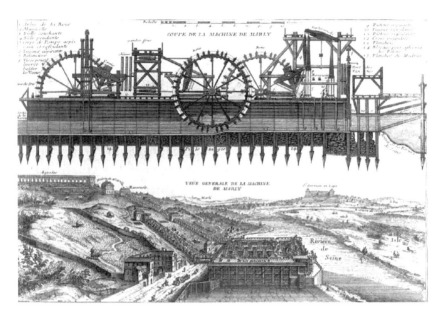

The Machine de Marly, which fed Louis XIV's fountains – how not to industrialize. Engraving by Nicolas de Fer

country banks available within a day's horse ride. This atomization of credit fragmented the capital market for small business.

Given the small-scale needs of early industry, before the coming of the more capital-intensive railroads, the English financial system of 1760-1826 proved ideal to finance it. Later, legislative and economic changes promoted bank consolidation, but by then large-scale industrialization was already in full swing.

Surplus of Investible Capital and a System to Deploy It

The largest privately held asset in mediaeval societies was arable land, which had a market value because crops could be grown on it and sold for cash. Under the European feudal system, land was mostly held subject to rights of superior feudal lords, to whom in many cases it reverted at the tenant's death. It could not be bought and sold freely, and so could not be used as security for mortgage borrowings. This problem bedevilled the emergence of free markets on the Continent, most notably in the Holy Roman Empire, in parts of which serfdom persisted until the early nineteenth century. With the society's largest asset not realizable or mortgageable, industrialization was impossible.

Introduction: What this Book Is About

In England, this problem was solved by Edward Hyde, Earl of Clarendon[23] after the Restoration, through the Tenures Abolition Act 1660, passed immediately after Charles II[24] returned from exile. This abolished the Court of Wards and Liveries, and tenancies in capite and by knights-service, and purveyance. By doing so, it eliminated many feudal dues and service obligations that had been due to the Crown. More importantly, it eliminated the feudal restrictions on land holding, making land an asset that could be freely bought, sold and mortgaged. It thereby freed up enormous amounts of capital that could be used to finance industrialization (as well as overseas plantations, speculation, gambling and other less desirable investments). By creating a free market in land, it gave Britain an advantage that France, Spain and the Holy Roman Empire all lacked, even a century later.

Apart from landholdings, and the earnings from empire, the British economy benefited greatly from the middle of the eighteenth century from the surplus of investible capital derived from its large and liquid government bond market. Government bonds, from 1751 mostly in the form of the highly liquid three-per-cent Consols, were a safe store of value, albeit one that fluctuated with the vicissitudes of war and peace. Fluctuations in Consols prices produced massive profits for investors in the post-war periods 1782-92 and 1813-24, which acted as a catalyst for industrialization. While downward fluctuations in Consols prices early in wars, notably during the difficult 1790s, had a contrary depressing effect upon trade, industrialization and the economy, the large, liquid pool of capital in Consols, more than 100% of GDP from 1780 onwards, allowed merchants and industrialists to accumulate on a safe and remunerative basis the capital they needed for expansion.

Small-scale Shareholder Capitalism

Another key driver of the Industrial Revolution was shareholder capitalism. There were few public companies, and the South Sea Bubble of 1720 had deterred retail investors from investing in them. The most prominent of them, the East India Company, was described by Adam

---

23. Edward Hyde (1609-74). Baron Hyde from 1660, 1st Earl of Clarendon from 1661. MP for Wootton Bassett, 1640, and Saltash, 1640-42. Chancellor of the Exchequer, 1643-46, Lord Chancellor, 1658-67.

24. Charles II (1630-85). King of Great Britain *de jure*, 1649-85, *de facto*, 1660-85.

Smith[25] as a 'nuisance in every respect'. It was corrupt, bureaucratic and at the time Smith wrote had just, through incompetence in performance of its administrative duties, brought on the Bengal famine of 1770, one of the worst in India's history. Public companies with broad shareholdings played no significant role in the Industrial Revolution until the advent of the railways, half a century later.

Large companies and the public debt market could be dangerous in contributing to market bubbles, which diverted capital from productive enterprise and, when they burst, destroyed it. Since the Industrial Revolution required long-term, illiquid investment that would achieve returns only once new technologies had been adopted and perfected, diversion of the country's capital into short-term bubbles and their bailouts would have seriously retarded its progress.

Post-Restoration Britain suffered two such bubbles, for debt finance in the 1690s and in the stock and government finance markets in 1720, both of which were encouraged by misguided policy. Under the financially prudent administration of Sir Robert Walpole,[26] the country learned to avoid such bubbles, and the next general bubble did not occur until 1825 and was dealt with capably by Liverpool as prime minister.

There was another form of shareholder capitalism that was central to the Industrial Revolution: the free association of small pools of capital in small businesses. Normally, when an individual entrepreneur developed a new industrial technique, he had insufficient capital to deploy it, so he assembled a small group of partners to produce the capital required. Since the partners formed a small group, they were not subject to influence by government or outside bodies, beyond adherence to the minimal regulations of the time. Likewise, country bank partners made decisions based on their own views and interests.

The small-scale shareholder capitalism of the Industrial Revolution put shareholder interests first, not through economic theory, but because the people that ran the companies and banks were themselves

---

25. Adam Smith (1723-90). Scottish economist. Professor of Moral Philosophy, University of Glasgow, 1753-63. Commissioner of Customs in Scotland, 1778-90. Rector of the University of Glasgow, 1787-89. *The Theory of Moral Sentiments* (1759), *The Wealth of Nations* (1776).

26. Robert Walpole (1676-1745). KB from 1725, KG from 1726, 1st Earl of Orford from 1742. MP for Castle Rising, 1701-2, and King's Lynn, 1702-42. Secretary at War, 1708-10, Treasurer of the Navy, 1710-11, Paymaster of the Forces, 1714-15, 1720-21, First Lord of the Treasury and Chancellor of the Exchequer, 1715-17, 1721-42, Prime Minister, 1721-42.

Introduction: What this Book Is About 15

proportionately major shareholders of the institutions concerned. Most country banks and embryonic industrial companies had to put shareholder returns first to survive; there was no spare cash available for quixotic social or environmental goals, and any investments or loans made for idiosyncratic non-market purposes were a danger to the institution's survival. The capitalism of the early Industrial Revolution was pluralist capitalism in its purest form.

Fiscal Prudence and Sound Money

To replace royal revenues from eliminated feudal dues, the Tenures Abolition Act 1660 also imposed an excise duty on tea, coffee, sherbet and chocolate. By shifting state revenues to these new sources, the Act performed a vital service for the country's fiscal future. Instead of being fixed, as were previous taxes, customs and excise duties on these newly consumed products (as well as on tobacco and sugar, produced in Britain's American and West Indian colonies) increased with the increase in national wealth, trade, 'luxury' and consumption of these expensive imported goods. The burden of this system fell primarily on the wealthier classes; the revenues it produced were naturally buoyant as wealth and trade increased.

The Restoration fiscal reforms, after hiccups during the Anglo-Dutch Wars, stabilized the financial system until 1688. Then the almost continuous wars of 1689-1713 and intermittent warfare after 1739 required the establishment of a long-term government debt system. Thereafter, the government generally ran a surplus in peacetime, although the frequent wars caused debt to increase to a maximum of 260% of GDP in 1819.

Following the Napoleonic wars, Liverpool was faced with a gigantic public debt and budget expenditure that greatly exceeded income. His solution was twofold. He cut public spending (other than debt service) by 69% in the three years 1814-17, pulling the budget back into balance in 1818. Then, instead of inflating Britain's way out of trouble through the 'repression' of low interest rates and high inflation, he went the other way, putting Britain back onto the Gold Standard in 1821, thereby bringing about a 40% price deflation.

This made the 'real' debt burden even greater, but it made London the unquestioned entrepot of commerce and finance, its currency universally used for financing transactions, bringing incalculable long-term economic benefits. The debt-to-GDP ratio was below 200% in 1827 when Liverpool left office, and down to 30% by 1914.

In the sixteenth century, successive governments, notably that of Henry VIII, had attempted to increase revenue by debasing the coinage, but after the Restoration, it was realized that this damaged trade and reduced confidence in the government. Consequently, from 1662 Charles II's government produced a silver coinage with a milled edge, that could not be clipped by users without the damage being immediately apparent. A further recoinage in 1696 led by Newton increased the supply of domestic coinage and stabilized its value. Then in 1717 Newton put Britain on a bi-metallic gold/silver standard which, as silver prices rose, became the Gold Standard. This was suspended in 1797, during the lengthy Revolutionary/Napoleonic wars with France but was restored by Liverpool's government in 1821.

From 1717, therefore, Britain had a sound money of unquestioned value, that unlike other countries' currencies was not subject to debasement. The adverse hyperinflationary experience of the newly independent United States with 'continentals' in 1776-81 and of the French Republic with *assignats* in 1792-96, together with similar, if milder, such experiences in other countries such as Austria in 1759-1811, convinced British policymakers that state-issued paper money led to dangerous inflation. In 1797-1821, when Britain was off the Gold Standard, it relied for currency on banknotes issued by the Bank of England and the country banks, avoiding state issuance of inconvertible paper money.

Agricultural Revolution

In order for there to be an Industrial Revolution, there first needs to be an Agricultural Revolution, whereby agricultural productivity rises to the point at which an increasing proportion of the population can devote itself to non-agricultural activities.

In eastern Europe, serfdom persisted, and agricultural productivity was so low that, even with almost the entire population on the land, only a modest surplus was produced. Furthermore, landholding was intimately connected with rule; a family could not sell its estate without losing its social and political position. In those conditions, there was no workforce available to industrialize and no surplus wealth available to invest in industrial activities. Famines were also frequent, further tying people to the land to ensure their survival.

Even where formal serfdom had disappeared, as in Ireland, over-population and low agricultural productivity could prevent urbanization and industrialization. Only where new crops and new methods of cultivation had taken hold, as in Britain, the Netherlands and some of

Introduction: What this Book Is About

France, was there both a surplus population and surplus wealth available to allow the possibility of industrialization. The saleability of land also produced greater social mobility, preventing successful industrialists from being socially ghettoized, while producing pockets of wealth that could be used to finance industrial ventures, canals, railroads and so on. Even the great canal developer, the third Duke of Bridgewater,[27] could only invest because his landholdings, being saleable, were also mortgageable.

Expensive Labour

Contrary to intuitive belief, high real wages favoured industrialization because they maximized the cost benefits of labour-saving and powered devices. Countries such as Austria that by the eighteenth century had relatively low wages had little relative cost advantage from machinery, which in its first iterations added only modestly to productivity. Having begun to mechanize, competitive forces then led to further mechanization, in a virtuous circle that increased the depth of industrialization.

Robert Allen's magisterial study of the Industrial Revolution goes into this in detail,[28] revealing that London labourers earned about 3.5 times the minimum necessary for subsistence in 1790, about the same as in Amsterdam, as against 1.7 times subsistence in Florence, 1.3 times subsistence in Vienna, and just the subsistence level in Delhi and Beijing. Measured by the 'respectability ratio' based on a different and broader basket of goods, London's ratio for stonemasons was 2.2, compared with 2.0 in Antwerp, 1.2 in Florence and Paris and 0.9 in Vienna and Valencia.

This wage differential had not always existed. According to Allen's calculations wages in much of Western Europe had been high and close to equal between countries around 1500, largely through the population decline brought by plague 150 years earlier. Increasing population and New World silver impoverished the working classes, while enriching the elite, until 1650. Then real wages in Britain and the Netherlands turned around and began to rise again, while wages in southern Europe tended to decline still further. By the early nineteenth century real wages in

---

27. Francis Egerton (1736-1803). 3rd Duke of Bridgewater from 1748. Built Bridgewater Canal, extended to Liverpool, 1759-65.
28. Robert G. Allen, *The British Industrial Revolution in Global Perspective* (Cambridge: Cambridge University Press, 2009), Figs 2.3 and 2.6.

Vienna were a quarter of those 400 years earlier, while in England real wages continued to increase as industrialization took hold.

The principal losers from the industrialization process were those whose occupations used un-mechanized methods: for example, hand-loom weavers and framework knitters. Since travel was expensive and slow and labourers were often insensitive to technological changes and new opportunities, the labour market did not arbitrage efficiently. This produced pockets of poverty and unrest where labour had become uncompetitive and was exploited.

British manual workers were better off than their Continental European contemporaries and far better off than Asians, who were in many cases (e.g. Indian textile sector workers) affected by the same technological wage-suppressing forces and without the intellectual, financial or technological means to change their livelihoods.

In the Middle Ages, government policy had acted to suppress wage rates rather than raise them – the Statute of Labourers 1351 being a prime example. After 1620 the policy of removing 'surplus' labour from Britain to the American colonies proved a prime example of a policy that tended to increase real wages at home. As discussed below, Liverpool in introducing the Corn Laws in 1815 proclaimed that high wages were a benefit to industrial innovation. Only after 1830, as cheap-labour-linked statesmen such as Peel became dominant, did government policy on wages become more equivocal, although the outflow of Britons to the colonies remained strong until the 1950s, helping shore up wages.

Freedom from Destitution for the Poor

For industrialization to occur, the working class had to be raised somewhat above the subsistence level. If they were not, as in early nineteenth century Austria, Italy and southern Ireland, they became naturally risk-averse, prone to political agitation (since they had nothing to lose) and unlikely to engage in the self-improvement that led to industrial advance. In addition, impoverished working people were especially hostile to industrialization, since the temporary periods of unemployment caused by the business cycle could cause them to fall into starvation.

For a pre-industrial society to raise living standards above the level of Malthusian subsistence, workers needed reasonable freedom from destitution in their old age. The late marriage and moderate fertility control necessary for living standards to improve appear to have been facilitated by old age security, which meant that large families were no longer necessary to prevent destitution in old age.

Introduction: What this Book Is About

In many Catholic countries, including mediaeval England, the monasteries provided a limited level of provision for the poor. This fell away at the Reformation, but in England the Poor Law of 1601 and its successors provided old-age subsistence, locally financed and provided and generally in the form of modest cash payments. Much of this benefit was reversed by the Whigs' Poor Law Amendment Act 1834, which established workhouses and the detestable principle of 'less eligibility', that is, workhouse conditions worse than those of the lowest paid labourer. Still, until 1834 the English working classes could be significantly less concerned about their old age than most of their Continental contemporaries.

Intensive Commercial Economy

In the early seventeenth century, the British economy did not differ significantly from those of other European countries, being heavily dominated by agriculture, beset by internal trade barriers and with only certain sectors fully commercial. Yet, beginning in the 1650s during the Interregnum and accelerating with the return of stable government after 1660, the economy began to acquire a complexity and commercial spirit that was matched in Europe only in the Netherlands.

The best qualitative description of this intensive development of the British economy was given in Daniel Defoe's[29] *A Tour Through the Whole Island of Great Britain*. Written between 1724 and 1727, before industrialization got going, Defoe's account is full of descriptions of the specialist trades carried on in individual towns and the commerce to which those trades led. Defoe himself was from a commercial background and commercially oriented in his outlook. Defoe's work makes it clear that specialization, mechanization and in-depth knowledge of each branch of trade was already highly developed, as were the trading and sales operations in each branch of industry.

This pre-industrialization development of the British commercial economy accounted for the high level of British wages. By providing jobs for the literate and numerate, it increased the penetration of those skills in the British population. Directly, it provided a major impetus for industrialization, in developing an entrepreneurial and commercial

---

29. Daniel Defoe (1660-1731). Whiggish writer, journalist and merchant. *An Essay upon Projects* (1697), *Robinson Crusoe* (1719), *A Journal of the Plague Year* (1722), *Moll Flanders* (1724), *A Tour Through the Whole Island of Great Britain* (1724-27), *The Complete English Tradesman* (1726).

approach to business which sought new ways of improving profitability and seized new opportunities as they became available.

There were legal pre-conditions for an intensive commercial economy to occur. A state ought to avoid promoting monopolies and raising barriers to competition, as in the policies of France's Louis XIV and Jean-Baptiste Colbert, and those of Britain's James VI and I.[30] It also needed to avoid splintering its economy by allowing substantial barriers to domestic trade and internal tariffs. Here the Holy Roman Empire was at a disadvantage; because it consisted of several hundred quasi-independent states, there were few substantial markets within which a vibrant commercial economy could arise. France and Spain also had domestic tariffs, but they were deliberate policy decisions rather than side-effects of a constitutional reality.

Availability of Cheap Energy

The makers of the Industrial Revolution were aware of environmental and resource issues, to which they were alerted by market signals. The most important example of this was the move to increased use of coal.

Traditionally, wood was the principal fuel used for domestic heating and cooking, the principal energy source (as charcoal) for producing iron and the principal material used for both furniture and shipbuilding. With Britain having only a modest surface area, much of which was cleared and used for agriculture, it was inevitable that limitations in the wood supply would appear, indicated by price. This problem first became acute in the late sixteenth century, at which point coal began to be shipped from Newcastle to London for domestic consumption. By 1700 most Londoners and citizens of some provincial towns (with nearby coal deposits) used coal for heating and cooking. As a result, the British coal industry was strongly developed around Newcastle and in other places with coal deposits and local demand. British coal production increased tenfold between 1500 and 1700.[31]

Britain's cost advantages through widely available coal were increased in 1709 by Abraham Darby's[32] perfection of a method of smelting pig

---

30. James VI and I (1567-1625). King James VI of Scotland, 1567-1625, and King James I of England, 1603-25.

31. Allen, *The British Industrial Revolution in Global Perspective*, Table 4.1.

32. Abraham Darby (1678-1717). Founder of Coalbrookdale ironworks, 1709, where he perfected coke-fired iron smelting process. Son Abraham Darby II (1711-63) and grandson Abraham Darby III (1750-89) were also involved in the business, themselves making several advances.

Introduction: What this Book Is About 21

iron using coal-derived coke instead of wood-derived charcoal. This made Coalbrookdale Iron Works and other blast furnaces located near coalfields cost-competitive with Swedish and other sources of iron. The increased demand for coal led to the development of a canal network, which enabled coal to be supplied cheaply to towns and factories that were not close to mines.

The wide availability of cheap coal led to the development of steam technology. The early steam engines of Thomas Newcomen[33] were highly inefficient in fuel use and so were only cost-effective where coal was cheap and readily available. Later, cheap coal made even the primitive engines of the Stockton and Darlington Railway cost-effective in moving heavy goods in an area of great coal availability. Eventually, the Watt engine and more efficient engines for manufacturing were developed from the Newcomen engine, and, once the first railways had been developed, engine technology improved quickly until steam was competitive everywhere.

The makers of the Industrial Revolution took an environmental/ resources problem – the increasing shortage of wood – and solved it through technological innovation and, by so doing, increased the productivity of industry. They were motivated by the price mechanism; there was no central authority directing them to make the revolutionary changes they made. The adoption of coal in domestic use and industry was the result of a few technological advances, followed by millions of individual decisions.

Profitable Overseas Empire

Industry and industrialization were enhanced in countries with large overseas empires, such as Spain and Britain, in two ways:

First, the empire and trading links associated with it produced gold, silver or cash crops that could be taxed and sold either domestically or in Continental Europe. Spain's bullion shipments increased to a high level around 1525 and stayed there for a century. Britain and the Netherlands benefited from East Indian production of tea and coffee, effectively Anglo-Dutch duopolies in Europe after around 1650. From the Americas, tobacco and sugar became important cash crops, grown with slave labour and producing substantial government revenues. Strategically, those revenues could remove the acute financing problems

---

33. Thomas Newcomen (1664-1729). Devised first true steam engine around 1712, which was in use for around 90 years in large-scale applications such as mine pumping.

that beset early modern governments. The existence of large 'cash crop' economies and mining ventures in the Americas and Indies enabled large fortunes to be built, which could be deployed into commercial and industrial ventures.

The other great advantage from overseas empires and extensive international trade was large-scale sources of raw materials, which could be obtained from the lowest-cost producers worldwide. The most significant example of this, which exploded in importance after the country's political independence but when it was still highly dependent on Britain economically, was the cotton grown in the southern United States, which was the central input into the Lancashire textile and garment industry. Theoretically, since the US was already independent, other countries could have competed with Britain for this cotton or the US could have developed a textile and garment industry for itself. In practice, despite the efforts of Francis Cabot Lowell[34] and other American manufacturers, most U.S. cotton continued to be transported to Britain until late in the nineteenth century.

* * *

We cannot impose too severe a judgement on the policies of seventeenth and eighteenth century governments. After all, none of us can see what lies in the future. For example, Philip II of Spain benefited from huge windfall gains from transatlantic silver deposits. However, by devoting those gains to religious and dynastic wars and thus repeatedly leading his country into bankruptcy, he blew Spain's chance of Industrial Revolution 200 years later. Smaller war expenditures and a greater devotion to the economic well-being of his people might have led Spain in a different and better long-term direction.

As full industrialization neared, and the benefits to Britain and the Netherlands of a prosperous commercial economy became clear, we can be more critical of states that did not move in the same direction. After 1750, Louis XV of France and Charles III of Spain (the latter a reformer, but along French lines) could have seen that a more expansionary economic policy, with internal trade barriers removed, markets and trade stimulated, and wealth spread more broadly among their people, would have led to better results even in the short term.

Before Watt's first rotary steam engine in 1783, it was apparent to only a few policymakers even in Britain that powered industrialization was

---

34. Francis Cabot Lowell (1775-1817). Founded Boston Manufacturing Company, 1814.

Introduction: What this Book Is About

the way ahead – Gower, canal pioneer and member of most Cabinets from 1767 to 1794, was one such. Only after Watt's invention did the economically capable leaders, William Pitt the Younger[35] and Lord Liverpool become aware that Britain's economic potential was being permanently transformed.

The next chapter examines Britain's principal European competitors for a potential Industrial Revolution – France, Spain, the Holy Roman Empire and the Netherlands – and considers why they missed out on leading the world into industrialization. It takes as a starting point the societies in 1600, when the Renaissance, the invention of printing and transoceanic exploration had already happened. It does not examine the major Asian civilizations of that period – China, Japan, the Mughal Empire and the Ottoman Empire – partly because to do so would require a familiarity with the finer points of those civilizations that I do not possess. For whatever reason, possibly simple chronological happenstance,[36] industrialization was initially a European phenomenon.

The remaining chapters, divided into convenient chronological periods, examine the emergence of the Industrial Revolution in Britain up to 1830. There is an Epilogue discussing the Victorian period and after, by which time it was neither a revolution nor purely British.

In each chapter, several themes are followed. Political developments are examined as they relate to industrialization, coming to the conclusion that industrialization was most facilitated in periods when the political Tory party was dominant. Relevant legislation is noted and in some cases discussed in detail. I hope to demonstrate that the political and legislative background in Britain was mostly uniquely favourable to industrialization's emergence.

A second theme covers the societal changes that affected industrialization, including demographic developments, including those arising from increased cultivation of potatoes. Other important societal changes included the development of financial markets and imperial developments, which affected the financing of industrialization and the supply of entrepreneurs.

A third theme is scientific development, both in Britain and elsewhere. Normally, scientific developments were not quickly implemented

---

35. William Pitt (1759-1806). MP for Appleby and Cambridge University, 1781-1806. Chancellor of the Exchequer, 1782-83, Prime Minister and Chancellor of the Exchequer, 1783-1801, 1804-06.

36. If industrialization had been destined to occur after AD 750 instead of after AD 1750, it would not have occurred first in Europe.

industrially (one exception was gas lighting) but the changes in scientific approach in Britain, with a growing professionalism and depth of knowledge, were reflected in an increasing capacity for industrial innovation.

A fourth emphasis is on the key innovations that changed the way business was conducted. These may be infrastructural, like James Brindley's canal system, individual inventions, such as those of Newcomen or Watt, or groups of inventions, such as in textiles. Occasionally an entirely new industry appeared, such as machine tools, gas lighting, chemicals or railways, which made a wide range of changes to industry and society.

Finally, I look at the careers of each era's entrepreneurs. Some, like Wedgwood and Arkwright, are well known and ended up very rich; others, though building substantial businesses, ended up in the poorhouse. By discussing multiple businesses, their strategies and success, I hope to shed light on how industrialization developed. Through these examinations I hope to demonstrate that developments in marketing, control systems, organization, finance and logistics were as important to industrialization as changes in production and new power sources.

The Industrial Revolution was a unique event in world history and continues to fascinate; I hope this book reflects that fascination.

2

The Competitors: Europe's Potential Industrializers in 1600

I shall not discuss why industrialization happened in Europe, rather than somewhere else, notably China, Japan, India or the Ottoman Empire, all of which had high-level civilizations when the process was beginning. One well-known study of the question[1] suggests that the process was almost random, and due to the prevalence of fossil fuels (specifically, coal) in Britain and the surplus funds generated by exploitation of the Americas. Coal and the Americas were certainly important, but China had access to both factors. It is today the world's largest producer of coal, while the Americas, although further from China than from Europe, were as easy to reach for fifteenth century sailing ships because they could have sailed from China or Japan to California without losing sight of land.

That strongly suggests that there were factors within Chinese civilization itself, in the period when the technology to industrialize might have been available, that prevented China from industrializing. While Song Dynasty China was intellectually vibrant, albeit with a bias against the more useful arts, by the fifteenth century rapid population growth and intellectual stagnation had made China a defensive society that repelled Western contacts rather than attempting to take advantage of them. For example, the famous voyages of Admiral Zheng He in

---

1. Kenneth Pomeranz, *The Great Divergence: China, Europe, and the Making of the Modern World Economy* (Princeton, NJ: Princeton University Press, 2000).

1405-33 appear to have had the purpose of demonstrating China's greatness rather than discovering new lands.

For Japan, the problem is industrialization's timing. From 1600 to 1868, Japan was ruled by the Tokugawa shogunate, a central policy of which was resisting contact with the outside world, to promote political stability. Japan developed major corporations during this period – the Mitsui (1673) and Sumitomo (1615) trading houses both date to the seventeenth century – and economic growth was considerable, but from 1635 foreign trade was severely restricted so Japan would have had to develop industrialization without outside intellectual or technological input.

The Mughal civilization in India at its peak was far richer than any European country – its government's revenues under Emperor Jahangir (1605-27) were equivalent to £100 million, compared to less than £1 million for Britain's James VI and I.[2] However, Jahangir had the largest collection of precious stones ever assembled, which suggests that little productive use was made of the wealth. Mughal civilization declined rapidly in the early eighteenth century, enabling Britain to take over parts of Mughal territory from 1765 onwards; there is little evidence of any significant attempts at powered industrialization, although the Mughal territories also had large coal deposits. Bengal was described by Adam Smith as the clearest example of a declining society, with increasing impoverishment and starvation in years of bad harvest.

The Ottoman Empire in 1600 ruled much of Croatia, some of Slovenia and the remainder of south-eastern Europe and was thereby a European power. However, from 1600 on it was in mild decline, economically, intellectually and militarily. Economically, it suffered badly from the Dutch and British East India Companies setting up direct trading routes to East Asia; much highly lucrative business for spices, tea and coffee was thereby lost to the Ottomans (and to Venice, their Mediterranean partners). There were few notable technological advances emerging from the Ottoman Empire after 1600, and they appear to have made little use of the Scientific Method.

Hereafter, I shall confine my attention to Britain's European competitors, who had access to the same intellectual capital and similar social conditions. I shall examine why only one European country launched the Industrial Revolution, rather than it being launched simultaneously in several countries with similar resources and intellectual development.

---

2. William Dalrymple, *The Anarchy: The Relentless Rise of the East India Company* (London: Bloomsbury, 2019), p. 14.

The Competitors: Europe's Potential Industrializers in 1600

I shall show that it was only partly due to resources and pre-existing technology but was more fundamentally caused by a particular intellectual climate and national policy, which arose in Britain over the 180 years from 1649. That climate and policy were not present elsewhere in Europe to the same extent, except in the Netherlands, with which I deal below.

To gauge the relative position of Europe's countries approaching industrialization, we should start by looking at the competitors, at some date before but close to when the process began. Since the British policy transition began with the Interregnum of 1649-60 (although some policies were in place previously), I shall examine the major countries in Europe in 1600, with some reference to developments in each country over the next two centuries. In 1600, the five principal competing states in Europe that might have moved towards industrialization were Spain, France, the Holy Roman Empire, the Netherlands and England[3].

Philip III of Spain, a fashion icon who brought peace but not much prosperity. Painting by Antoine du Succa.

Spain in 1600

Spain was the most powerful European country in 1600. Its reigning king, Philip III (1598-1621) was pious but not especially intelligent or diligent. However, his overall policy of winding down the wars started by his father Philip II (1556-98) steered Spain away from the recurring bankruptcies of that reign. Philip III subcontracted control of the Spanish bureaucracy to Francisco Gomez de Sandoval y Rojas, first Duke of Lerma, in

---

3. Britain did not exist until the union of Crowns in 1603; I have tried to be consistent in using 'England' before that date and 'Britain' after it, except for legislative purposes, where Union only occurred in 1707.

office until 1618, who was highly corrupt, allegedly amassing a fortune of 43 million ducats.[4]

Spain was almost universally Catholic. Philip III's wife Margaret of Austria, sister of the hard-line Catholic, Holy Roman Emperor Ferdinand II (1619-37) was devout and politically active, so the influence of the intolerant Spanish Church was strong. Apart from the activities of the Spanish Inquisition, this was exemplified by the expulsion of 300,000 Moriscos (Moors who had nominally converted to Christianity) between 1609 and 1614. While popular with the native Spanish, this resulted in a sharp decline in agricultural and small business output in the regions affected. Overall, Philip III's reign was one of economic stagnation and the beginnings of decline.

Since around 1525, Spain had enjoyed a large, if fluctuating, income from the silver bullion mined in the New World, most particularly at Potosi, in modern Bolivia. As well as causing long-term European inflation, this made the King of Spain potentially the richest monarch in Europe. After its arrival in Spain, bullion flowed to the rest of Europe through Spain's military expenditure and consumption of European imports. It did not remain there. From 1500 to 1800, there was a structural differential between the gold/silver exchange ratio in Europe and in Asia; in 1600 an ounce of gold was worth twelve ounces of silver in Europe, but only six ounces of silver in Asia, a huge and long-lasting arbitrage opportunity. Hence, Spain's silver bullion was primarily used to pay for European imports of spices and luxury goods from Asia. Imports from Asia greatly exceeded exports to Asia but, in addition, it was highly profitable to export silver bullion and coins to Asia and return gold to Europe – the arbitrage trade added to the natural European trade deficit to drain the silver from Europe.

Spain's income from the New World potentially gave it similar fiscal advantages to those enjoyed by Britain from tobacco and sugar excises 150 years later. Annual silver production from the New World mines peaked in the quinquennium 1621-25 at 15.6 million pesos.[5] By that time fraud and theft were considerable, so only 8.9 million pesos of that amount were landed at Seville, down from a high of 11.6 million

---

4. In 1600 forty-three million ducats, if a true figure, was worth around ten million pounds sterling – a fortune much larger than that of any early industrialist.

5. Stanley J. Stein and Barbara H. Stein, *Silver, Trade and War: Spain and America in the Making of Early Modern Europe* (Baltimore: Johns Hopkins University Press, 2000), Table I, p. 24.

The Competitors: Europe's Potential Industrializers in 1600   29

pesos in 1591-95. Taking an average of the two latter figures, the annual revenues from the New World mines arriving through Seville peaked during Philip III's reign at about ten million pesos (£2 million).

The Spanish treasury did not have the right to all this revenue. The mines were mostly owned by various members of the Spanish nobility, the only people with sufficient liquidity to finance their development. The treasury was theoretically entitled only to a 'silver import tax' on the bullion landed at Seville. In addition to this, the Spanish treasury had full rights to taxation only from Castile. Overall, in 1600 Spain's annual royal revenue was around 8.5 million ducats[6] (£1.7 million). Its debts were ten times that amount – 85 million ducats (£17 million). The Spanish government's revenue was four times England's level of around £400,000 in 1600, from an Iberian Union[7] domestic population of around double that of England, but its debts were a much larger multiple of England's, and their management caused frequent cash-flow crises.

The silver flow was never enough to support Spain's geopolitical ambitions and became even more inadequate when output from the New World mines fell 40% after 1625 while leakage increased. Inevitably, state cash flow became straitened, at which point, the first time as early as 1523, the treasury resorted to a *secuestro* of the incoming bullion, paying through short-term loans carrying an artificially low interest rate of around 5%. Over time, the number of *secuestros* increased, as did the leakage of bullion no longer imported by the official route through Seville.

Philip II and his father Charles V/I (Charles V of the Holy Roman Empire, 1520-56, and Charles I of Spain, 1516-56) consistently overspent their income on costly wars. Charles had a vision of a universal Catholic monarchy controlled by the Habsburgs, including both Spain and the Holy Roman Empire. Pursuing and defending this vision against Protestantism and rival states was ruinously expensive. Then Philip II undertook a 40-year attempt to maintain control of the Netherlands, a fifteen-year war with England and an expensive proxy war that led to outright war backing the Catholic League against Henry IV in the French Wars of Religion. He ended the French war by the Treaty of Vervins of May 1598, shortly before his death, but left the Dutch and English wars for his son to sort out.

---

6. Paul C. Allen, *Philip III and the Pax Hispanica, 1598-1621: The Failure of Grand Strategy* (New Haven: Yale University Press, 2000), p. 2.

7. Spain and Portugal were united as the Iberian Union from 1580 to 1640.

Despite his substantial income, Philip II declared bankruptcy four times in his 42-year reign, damaging the fortunes of the Fugger family early in his reign, then moving on to Genoese bankers. Philip III inherited his father's debts; he wound down his wars (peace was signed with Britain in 1604 and a twelve-year truce with the Netherlands in 1609) but expanded court spending and allowed greater corruption among his ministers. At the end of his reign, an initially successful participation in support of the Habsburg-ruled Holy Roman Empire in the Thirty Years' War (the 1620 Battle of the White Mountain was a notable triumph) augured further fiscal trouble in the future.

Spain and Portugal not only created the first transatlantic empires, they were also the first major Western traders in African slaves. (The slave trade was common throughout the Mediterranean region before and after 1400, with Christian slaves being shipped to North Africa and Moslem North African slaves shipped to Europe.) Under Henry the Navigator (1394-1460), who was half English through his mother, a daughter of John of Gaunt,[8] Portugal had pioneered the exploration down the African coast by sea. The first cargo of African slaves was shipped to Europe in 1444 and Portugal later established a network of African trading posts, exchanging European textiles and weapons for African slaves, spices and precious metals.[9]

Spanish and Portuguese transatlantic exploration after 1492 broadened and deepened the slave trade. African slaves were not much used in the Potosi silver mines, because they found the climate and altitude intolerable; there the Spanish rulers used Amerindian slaves primarily. However, African slaves were better adapted to the work and climate in the sugar plantations of coastal areas of Mexico and Brazil. Hugh Thomas estimates that in the first quarter of the seventeenth century, the total number of slaves exported from Africa was around 200,000, (i.e. 8,000 per annum) of which 100,000 went to Brazil, 75,000 to Spanish America, 12,500 to São Tomé and only a few hundred to Europe. The trade was controlled from Seville, as was most Iberian transatlantic trade, although Portuguese Jewish *conversos* were generally the largest traders.

Slave-produced crops were only modest revenue providers to Spain and Portugal compared to bullion shipments and East Indian spices.

---

8. John of Gaunt (1340-99). Third son of Edward III. Father of Henry IV. Duke of Aquitaine, 1390-99.

9. I am indebted to Hugh Thomas, *The Slave Trade: The Story of the Atlantic Slave Trade, 1440-1870* (New York: Simon & Schuster, 1997), for the very full explanation of the Atlantic trade's origins and development.

Thomas estimates that in the late sixteenth century, the value of the slave trade to the Portuguese crown, through taxes, customs and so on was 280,000 *cruzados*[10] (£47,000), compared with two million (£330,000) for the East Indian trade.

Spain's bullion revenues and fiscal difficulties produced three major barriers to progress towards industrialization. First, Spain became the main provider of bullion to the rest of Europe, maintaining forces abroad and importing manufactured goods from the rest of Europe for consumption domestically and by the wealthy settlers in the New World. Seville had a monopoly on this trade (until 1717, when its monopoly was transferred to Cadiz) and its entrepot business was highly profitable. This trade pattern hollowed out Spanish industries such as wool production that had been internationally competitive, shipping to the Bruges market, before bullion shipments began. Thus, economic activity that might have developed into industrialization was reduced and links to potential markets lost.

Second, the Spanish monarchy's repeated defaults left interest rates very high and the domestic banking system underdeveloped. If the state could only borrow at 10-15%, private borrowers were forced to pay correspondingly more, while domestic banks were impoverished by their repeated losses on state lending. Since many of the Genoese banks had representatives in Madrid, they were able to capture domestic Spanish banking business at high interest rates, thereby suppressing embryonic Spanish competition.

Third, the flow of revenues from bullion, even those not wasted by the state, were used for conspicuous aristocratic consumption and did not generate private businesses and financial savings pools, in the way that British tobacco and sugar revenues were to do. New World silver mining was carried on by private entrepreneurs under licence from the state, but their activities remained concentrated in the New World. Exploiting political connections for profit, as Lerma spectacularly proved, was far more lucrative than economically productive, domestic, private sector activity. Likewise, the highly profitable Seville (later Cadiz) entrepot business was an oligopoly, which did not finance or encourage competition. Even the raw materials for silver mining, such as mercury, were supplied by the German Fuggers. Over these centuries, the wealthy Spanish aristocracy never developed the entrepreneurial

---

10. Around 1600 the cruzado contained 22.9 grams of silver of 0.917 fine. Hence, it was worth just under five sixths of a peso or thaler, or 0.167 English pounds.

and infrastructure-building activities of their British counterparts, with corresponding loss to Spanish economic development.

These effects worsened as Spanish bullion income declined after 1625. Spain had European responsibilities that were extremely expensive to defend, and the involvement of Philip IV (1621-65) in the Thirty Years' War made matters worse. In the latter stages of that war Spain's treasury took to large-scale selling of state offices, which increased corruption and weakened private property rights still further, since purchasers of offices resorted to extortion to recoup their investment. Further defaults followed in 1647, 1652, 1661 and 1666. The late seventeenth century saw severe political and economic decline, with Spain's population falling by one million by 1700. Charles II, the king over this period, 1665-1700, was a sickly and mentally defective product of the Habsburg penchant for in-breeding (Philip II and Philip IV had both married their Austrian Habsburg nieces, while Philip III married his first cousin once removed, also an Austrian Habsburg).

After 1700, the first dozen years of Habsburg-Bourbon conflict over the Spanish succession subjected Spain to a war on her own territory. The succession of Bourbon rulers Philip V (1700-46), Ferdinand VI (1746-59) and Charles IV (1788-1808), while an improvement on their Habsburg predecessors, were generally ineffectual, and Spain was dragged into several unnecessary wars by the French relatives of the new royal house. Only Charles III (1759-88) proved capable, in the 'enlightened despot' manner of his contemporaries, Maria Theresa of Austria and Frederick II of Prussia, expanding the country's university system and promoting scientific achievement.

Even under Charles III, Spanish industry expanded on the Colbertian French pattern (see below) rather than the English pattern, with royal monopoly industries set up in porcelain and crystal, little entrepreneurial vigour and continued internal tariffs between the various formerly separate kingdoms within Spain, which remained barriers to trade. For fiscal reasons, the government's financial and economic position remained beleaguered and defensive. While Spain had economic thinkers, they remained mercantilist before the nineteenth century; the most notable was Luis Jerónimo de Uztáriz y Hermiaga (1670-1732) whose book *Theorica, y Practica de Comercio y de Marina* (Theory and Practice of Commerce and Maritime Affairs), published in 1724, combined elements of the thought of Jean-Baptiste Colbert and Thomas Mun.

Spain's colonies in Latin America grew substantially in the eighteenth century, despite the declining output of their silver mines, and an affluent settler population developed. That population's demand for European goods continued to be satisfied by imports from other countries through the monopoly ports of Seville and later Cadiz or, increasingly, by British, French and Dutch smugglers.

Scientifically, Spain had been a European leader in the sixteenth century. As one notable example, Jerónimo de Ayanz y Beaumont (1553-1613) developed a steam-powered pump for the silver mines in Seville, for which he was granted a royal patent in 1606. His device placed the water in tanks and then, heating it by a coal fire, used the steam to pump the water out of the mine. His invention, not a true engine because it lacked moving parts, appears similar in principle to those of the Marquess of Worcester and Thomas Savery (see Chapters 4 and 5 below) but decades earlier than either. Like many prototypes, it was probably not very effective and thus led to no further developments.[11]

After 1625, Spain's declining political and economic position caused scientific activity to fall back. Few of the period's scientific advances emerged from Spain, although the country remained competitive in chemistry, with eighteenth-century Spanish chemists discovering the elements tungsten and platinum. Spanish society generally lacked both the pools of entrepreneurially-inclined savings that might have led to industrial advances and the pre-industrial economic base of commerce on which such advances could build.

In 1600, Spanish property rights were limited and the law, while voluminous, was heavily tilted towards the privileges of the traditional aristocracy. Property rights were further damaged by the repeated *secuestros* of silver bullion by the state; since property rights were insecure even in the state's most important dealings with the elite, they could have little solidity for lesser folk. This did not change significantly during the seventeenth century, and the periods of semi-anarchy under Charles II and war thereafter made things worse. After 1713 the 'Bourbon reforms' produced a gradual improvement, with the reign of Charles III seeing especial progress. Still, Charles IV's reign, dominated by his wife's favourite Manuel Godoy (1767-1851), saw wars and regression, and after 1808 civil war and French occupation severely damaged both legal and property rights.

Spanish savers benefited from the bullion in a silver coinage, mostly in the form of *reales* of one eighth of a peso. This coinage was debased, beginning as early as 1600 under Philip III with the *real de vellon* less than half silver, and debasement continued until a currency reform of

---

11. See website: https://spanishtechnologyproject.weebly.com/jeronimo-de-ayanz.html (accessed 18 May 2022).

1737 which set the value of a *real de vellon* at one twentieth of a peso. In the New World Spanish 'pieces of eight', still coined from fine silver, became a near-universal coinage throughout the eighteenth century, being much used in the future United States, but in Spain itself there was a 2.5 to one devaluation. Overall, Spanish savers over the seventeenth and eighteenth centuries were poorly treated, although not as badly in the late eighteenth century as in the Holy Roman Empire or France. Moreover, the lack of a secure banking system or secure government bonds meant that savings had to be kept in cash or invested in land – not a recipe for their growth or efficient redeployment.

In 1600, Spain was a relatively benign society for the very poor, because of the continued dominance and wealth of the Catholic Church, which through its monasteries provided relief from destitution. The wars and unrest after 1665, followed by the anti-Catholicism of the late eighteenth century (the Jesuits were expelled in 1767) and the attempts to remove some of the Church's benefices reduced that protection. Moreover, increased fertility rates expanded the Spanish population by 50% during the eighteenth century, from eight million to twelve million, putting pressure on wages since there was little economic growth and land was fully (if inefficiently) used in large landholdings.

Agricultural labour productivity was relatively low and static, around that of France in 1750 and little more than half that in Britain or the Netherlands. Real wages declined for both skilled and unskilled workers from 1500 to 1850, and by the second half of the eighteenth century were less than half those in Britain and the Netherlands. Literacy was the lowest in Western Europe, with only 20% of the population able to sign their name in 1800.[12]

Spanish energy costs were among the highest in Europe. Spain had limited coal deposits, though its first mine was opened in Asturias in 1593, and its forests were denuded by Philip II's 'Armada' shipbuilding programmes between 1570 and 1600. Consequently, energy in the second half of the eighteenth century was around 50% more expensive than in the Netherlands, 15% more expensive than in Paris and double the cost in most of Britain.[13]

Spain had the most profitable of all New World empires after 1500. This profitability continued at a diminished level until the eighteenth century. Like other early modern empires, it rested on exploitation of

---

12. Allen, *The British Industrial Revolution in Global Perspective*, p. 60 (agricultural productivity), pp. 44-45 (wages), p. 53 (literacy).

13. Ibid., pp. 99-102.

The Competitors: Europe's Potential Industrializers in 1600

non-European labour; in Spain's case through a tribute system that provided the Peruvian mines with slave labour, supplied by the local Inca aristocracy, for 250 years (though the Mexican mines used mostly waged labour). There was little African slavery, primarily because African labour was not viable in the chilly high-altitude environment of the Peruvian mines. However, because of the underdeveloped Spanish domestic economy, New World-derived profits did not generate much useful entrepreneurial capital at home.

Overall, Spain's hugely profitable empire gave it the opportunity to develop economically, had it invested the money in education instead of warfare, avoided repeated state bankruptcies, removed internal tariffs and allowed the empire's demand to generate a vibrant commercial and agricultural economy at home, thereby raising wage rates. It would also have needed to improve its societal structure and protection of property rights, while avoiding savings-destroying inflation and currency debasement. Even then, it would have suffered from high-cost energy, but that could possibly have been overcome. Nevertheless, its lack of industrialization and overall impoverishment over the years between 1600 and 1800 must mostly be attributed to the policy failures of Spain's rulers.

France in 1600

France in 1600 was undergoing a period of capable government, of an approach unusual in French history. From 1562 to 1598, an intermittent religious/dynastic war, the French Wars of Religion, had taken place under the three weak sons of Henry II (1547-59): Francis II (1559-60), Charles IX (1560-74) and Henry III (1574-89), backed by their formidable mother Catherine de Medici. The Catholic League was led primarily by the Guise family and backed by Philip II of Spain. The Huguenot (Calvinist) faction was led by Henry de Bourbon (1553-1610), from 1572 onwards king of Navarre (a southern province, mostly annexed by Spain in 1512), and had some backing from German Protestants and Elizabeth I[14] of England. Catherine and her Catholic sons vacillated between the factions, though acquiescing to the 1572 Massacre of St Bartholomew, in which the Guise supporters massacred some 35,000 Huguenots.

Henry de Bourbon was a distant cousin to the three sons of Henry II, but their next male heir and married to their sister Marguerite. He succeeded to the French throne and ruled as Henry IV (1589-1610),

---

14. Elizabeth I (1533-1603). Queen of England, 1558-1603.

Henry IV of France. He was France's best King; policy was reversed after his death. Painting by Frans Pourbus the Younger.

ending the religious war by converting to Catholicism in 1593 and passing the Edict of Nantes providing for toleration of the Huguenots and giving them certain political rights in 1598. In 1600, after the annulment of his marriage to Marguerite, who had proved barren, he married the usefully wealthy Marie de Medici (from a different branch of the family than Catherine de Medici) who provided him with two sons and several daughters and acted as Regent during the first few years of Louis XIII's reign (1610-43), after Henry was assassinated in 1610.

Despite the French Wars of Religion, after 1600 religious conflict was only moderately damaging, as the Huguenots represented only 10-15% of the population and were until 1685 guaranteed toleration. Their political power was removed by Louis XIII and his minister Cardinal Richelieu (in power from 1624 until his death in 1642) after the 1628 Siege of La Rochelle. Then, in 1685, under Louis XIV (1643-1715), the Edict of Nantes was revoked. The ensuing persecution led to the emigration of 180,000 Huguenots and the loss to France of much of its business and skilled artisan class.

Henry IV's ordinary revenues in the 1590s were about eleven million livres tournois and total royal revenues were about 25-30 million livres[15] at the end of a long period of war and depression, so French revenues totalled £1.7-2.0 million in 1600 compared to £400,000 in England, where the population was only 30% that of France. Since Henry did not control all of France until 1598, a war with Spain broke out in 1595,

---

15. Vincent J. Pitts, *Henri IV of France: His Reign and Age* (Baltimore: Johns Hopkins University Press, 2012), p. 184.

The Competitors: Europe's Potential Industrializers in 1600

and payments to opposition nobles to join Henry had totalled between 20 million and 32 million livres, the financial position remained tight. Fortunately, from 1596 Maximilien de Bethune, duc de Sully (1560-1641) took control of French state finances, and order was gradually restored.

Henry was unique among France's pre-1789 monarchs in attempting to improve the lot of ordinary people: 'If God gives me life, I will make it so that no ploughman in my realm will lack the means to have a chicken in his pot on Sunday.'[16] Sully on his behalf removed many internal taxes, centralized tax collecting, removed tax farmers, freed up agricultural markets and undertook a broad-ranging programme of public works. He also established the French silk industry around Lyons, which became an important export sector in the centuries ahead.

The high quality of Henry IV's government compared with its European contemporaries or French successors is illustrated by the story of William Lee (1563-1614), an English clergyman who in 1589 invented a stocking frame that enabled woollen stockings to be knitted more quickly. He was unable to gain a patent in England, allegedly because Elizabeth I, like Russia's Catherine the Great two centuries later, feared the effect of new machinery on employment. However, when Lee moved to France, Henry IV granted him a patent and allowed him to set up in Rouen. Alas, after Henry's death Lee was forced to give up his work and died in poverty in Paris, although his brother took the invention back to England and established it as the keystone of the East Midlands framework knitting industry.[17]

Henry IV attempted to set up a French East India Company, along the lines of the recent British and Dutch companies and established France's first North American colonies in Canada at Port Royal in 1605 and Quebec in 1608. By 1610, with its economy recovered from the wars, France appeared to be heading soundly towards industrialization, provided Henry IV's and Sully's enlightened economic policies continued to be followed.

In the event, those policies were reversed by their successors. Richelieu, who believed an impoverished peasantry would be less likely to rebel, centralized power in the monarchy, censored the press and persecuted opponents, while reducing the rights of private property. He also raised

---

16. Hardouin de Péréfixe de Beaumont, *Histoire du roi Henri le Grand* (1661), quoted in Pitts, *op. cit.* p259.

17. Lee's history is given in Paul Mantoux, *The Industrial Revolution in the Eighteenth Century* (London: Jonathan Cape, 1928), pp. 195-96.

taxes on salt and land to fund his military campaigns, impoverishing the peasants further, while ensuring at the Estates General of 1614 that the Church remained exempt from taxation.

As well as persecuting Huguenots, Louis XIV expanded state expenditure and pursued a mercantilist economic policy to finance it. One of the most important ministers in his government was Jean-Baptiste Colbert (1619-83), who was Controller-General of Finances from 1665 until 1683. Colbert favoured a positive balance of trade, i.e. an excess of exports over imports. His preferred policy to achieve this was import substitution, developing domestic industries to replace foreign capabilities. For example, a 1665 decree encouraged domestic glass manufacturing to replace imports of Venetian glass and was followed by a 1672 decree forbidding such imports altogether, as the domestic capability had become established. Colbert attempted to encourage output by promoting state-licensed monopolies or oligopolies in many areas, while he also prescribed both qualities and measures of goods, preventing a free market from growing up. With many trades closed to outsiders, those without established wealth or political connections were unable to build businesses, again reducing competition.

Colbert's policies of import substitution indeed increased royal revenues, but any benefit from this was dissipated by Louis XIV in endless wars. Colbert also engaged in partial repudiation of royal debts, without any attempt to institutionalize the royal finances; consequently, interest rates remained high and no bond market like that in the Netherlands (and in Britain after 1694) could grow up. While he attempted to increase internal trade, he could not abolish internal customs duties because of the royal need for revenue, so the French economy, despite its greater size than Britain's, remained atomized and inefficient.

France's eighteenth-century economic problems were worsened by the efforts of the Scottish gambler, financier and proto-Keynesian economist John Law (1671-1729). Law, an early believer in paper money, obtained the ear of the Regent Philippe d'Orleans (1715-23) and in 1716 set up the Banque Générale Privée, which took over much of France's public debt, and was nationalized in 1718 as the Banque Royale. The Banque Royale issued immense amounts of paper money, supposedly secured by France's landholdings in the Mississippi basin; then in 1720 went bankrupt. Unlike Britain's contemporary South Sea Company (SSC), which had financed itself by share issues, the Banque Royale had issued banknotes, which consequently absorbed much of the savings of the French middle classes. Also, unlike the South Sea Company, investors in the Banque Royale enjoyed no even partial bailout after its collapse; indeed, records of individuals' holdings of French public debt were burnt, to prevent further repercussions.[18] Consequently, much of France's private capital was lost in the bankruptcy and its public credit was ruined.

France's economic policies did not improve significantly after 1720. A contemporary of Law, the Irish-born Richard Cantillon (1685?-1734) in his *Essai* published in 1730 postulated the law of supply and demand, discussed the effect of money supply on prices, suggested that oversupply of money as in Law's case would cause a ruinous financial crash and proposed that trade balances could be improved by offering better quality products. Regrettably, although Cantillon had made considerable money from Law's Mississippi Company, selling early, he was then forced into exile and was killed in 1734 when his house in London was burned to the ground.

If the French had followed Cantillon, they might have got somewhere. However, French economic thought for the remainder of the eighteenth century was dominated by the Physiocrats, led by François Quesnay (1694-1774) and Anne Robert Jacques Turgot (1727-81). The Physiocrats believed that the source of economic wealth was land and agricultural labour, and that agricultural products should therefore be priced as high as possible. All industrial and non-agricultural labour, products and services were 'unproductive appendages' to the agricultural sector. While the Physiocrats' belief in private property was helpful, as was their encouragement of self-interest, their overall belief system was detrimental to developing the resources, technology and skills needed for industrial take-off.

Meanwhile, the economic policies of Louis XV (1715-74) and Louis XVI (1774-92), after an interval of stability under Cardinal André-Hercule de Fleury (1653-1743, chief minister to Louis XV from 1726 until 1743), involved oppressively high taxation, governed by the costs of repeated unsuccessful wars against Britain and imposed unequally, with the nobles exempt from many taxes and the Church exempt from all of them. Those policies ended in near bankruptcy, resulting in the Estates General being called in 1789 for the first time since 1614, leading to the French Revolution. In 1800, France was the world's most economically unequal significant economy, with a Gini coefficient of 73.3 compared

---

18. A. Carlos, L. Neal and K. Wandschneider, 'The Origins of National Debt: The Financing and Re-financing of the War of the Spanish Succession', paper presented at the IEHA annual meeting, Helsinki, 2006, p. 13.

to Britain's 58.9 and the Netherlands' 51.9, despite ten years' rule by liberals and radicals.[19]

After 1800, French economic thought improved. Jean-Baptiste Say (1767-1832) was the first true French classical/free market economist; his 1803 *Treatise on Political Economy* stated the principles of free choice of labour and security of property rights from the state, as well as Say's Law, that supply creates its own demand. Selected as a member of the *Tribunat* in 1799, his reluctance to compromise with Napoleon led to his removal in 1804. He was forced into private life, where he demonstrated the soundness of his theories by setting up a cotton-spinning factory successfully, employing 500 people. Meanwhile, France remained astonishingly mechanically backward; a government survey found only 48 steam engines in the entire country in 1816, fewer than the 110 Britain had installed before the expiry of the Savery patent in 1733.[20]

After the war ended, Say came to Britain, where he mixed mostly in Whig and Radical circles. He wrote a highly prescient survey of the British economy, *De l'Angleterre et des Anglais* (1815). However, he did not appreciate the full productivity benefits of industrialization, believing that the immense burden of Napoleonic war debt and associated taxes would make British labour uncompetitive once peace fully returned.

Under the benign government of Louis XVIII, Say was in 1819 one of the founders of the *École spéciale de commerce et d'industrie*, the world's first business school. The Restoration, Orleanist and Second Empire French governments of 1815-70 were at least moderately receptive to the ideas of Say and Frédéric Bastiat (1801-50). French industrialization got under way in those years, although Britain had by then established a lengthy lead.

While many French economic policies deterred an Industrial Revolution, the country's intellectual climate was moderately favourable to it. Richelieu had founded the Académie Française in 1636 and René Descartes (1596-1650) had made important philosophical and scientific advances, albeit mostly while living in the Netherlands. France continued to be a European scientific leader throughout the eighteenth century, with Antoine Lavoisier's (1743-94) discoveries in chemistry especially important.

---

19. Source: Gapminder, http://gapm.io/ddgini (accessed 5 February 2021).

20. The statistic for France can be found in Margaret Jacob, *The First Knowledge Economy: Human Capital and the European Economy, 1750-1850* (Cambridge: Cambridge University Press, 2014), p. 71.

The Competitors: Europe's Potential Industrializers in 1600   41

French innovations important to the modern world continued – mayonnaise, modern dental tools, the hot-air balloon – but they were not turned into substantial businesses, often being developed in the public sector. For example, the *fardier à vapeur* (steam wagon) of Captain Nicolas-Joseph Cugnot (1725-1804) was developed for the French Army; the full-sized model of 1770 moved at 2.25mph but was very unstable and required the fire to be relit every fifteen minutes. The Montgolfier brothers' hot-air balloon of 1783 worked well and got their father, a paper manufacturer, elevated to the aristocracy, but because of its lack of power or steering had few practical applications beyond very dangerous joy-riding. Overall, the highly theoretical approach of French intellectuals and the lack of a commercially-oriented artisan class prevented the country from making more progress before 1789.

France saw no improvement in property rights for the mass of the population between the death of Henry IV and 1789 – indeed they deteriorated overall under the stresses of French national finances. The Catholic Church owned around 40% of all wealth and paid no taxes, although it made a voluntary contribution of about 5% of its theoretical tax liability. The nobility was also partly exempt from the onerous land tax, while other taxes continued to be 'farmed' as they had been in James VI and I's Britain, resulting in innumerable abuses. Law courts existed, but laws varied by region and the courts treated noblemen and commoners unequally, so that the commoner's property was ill-protected against arbitrary seizure.

The climate for savers was also poor. The currency had been debased during the Wars of Religion, although it was stabilized during the reigns of Henry IV and Louis XIII. Then, from 1701, France began to issue paper money, which inevitably lost its value before being swept into the bankruptcy of Law's Banque Royale in 1720. Stability was restored under Fleury in 1726, with the livre devalued by about one third from Henry IV's time to make 24 livres equal to £1. A further issue of paper money was introduced in 1776 and the notorious *assignats* in 1789, which were subjected to hyperinflation, as was the successor money introduced by the Directory in 1796. Napoleon re-introduced a gold coinage in 1799, but France defaulted on his debt in 1815. There was no system of long-term French government bonds similar to British Consols and by the 1780s the government's debt of 110 million livres was in default. Hence, there were no reliable government instruments in which middle-class savers could invest before 1815.

Wage costs in France around 1750 lay between those in Spain and Britain, with skilled labourers earning close to British levels in Paris but wages in the provinces considerably lower. Literacy was much lower than in Britain at only 35% in 1800, which both reflected and caused lower social mobility among the lower strata in French society.

While the Catholic Church still played a substantial role in alleviating destitution in 1600, its role was less than in other countries where the Church remained dominant without a substantial alternative faith, and less than in mediaeval times. Its charitable role also declined after the rule of Richelieu, who added fiscal burdens to ordinary people while relieving the Church and its members. With France having such high inequality, life was hard for the peasantry, and their willingness to take business risks was correspondingly muted.

Because of Colbert's policies, French industry tended towards monopoly in the seventeenth and eighteenth centuries and lost the competitive commercial spirit it had been developing under Henry IV. Scientific invention continued at a high level but was not married to commercial innovation. As Lord Liverpool noted in 1820, when trade with France was freed in 1787-92, its volume was around that with Spain or Portugal, far less than expected given France's size.[21]

France had considerable coal reserves, but they were expensive to mine and of mediocre quality – hence this was a barrier against early industrialization. Conversely, with its many excellent rivers, the country was an early pioneer in mill technology and water-powered industrialization occurred in several places. One early example was the Lodève water-powered textile factory, granted a monopoly on the manufacture of French military uniforms by Fleury, a native of the town. However, it lost its monopoly and much of its prosperity at the Revolution.

France had a large overseas empire, inaugurated by Henry IV in Canada. Its emphasis in Canada was on the fur trade rather than settlements; thus, the colony's size and profitability were limited. The foundation of Louisiana in 1699 brought opportunities for further expansion, but the collapse of the Mississippi Scheme in 1720 slowed that expansion considerably. In the West Indies, the Compagnie des îles d'Amérique founded Guadeloupe and Martinique in 1635, giving France a 20-year head start over Britain in that region, and this was followed by Haiti in 1664, which grew to be the richest sugar colony in the Caribbean. However, the French West India Company, founded by Colbert in 1664 to monopolize the slave and sugar businesses, was nationalized ten years later.

---

21. T.C. Hansard, *The Parliamentary Debates New Series: Commencing with the Accession of George IV*, Vol. 1, cols 565-94, 26 May 1820.

The Competitors: Europe's Potential Industrializers in 1600

In the East, Colbert founded a French East India Company in 1669, sixty years after Henry IV's abortive attempt, with capital of fifteen million livres (£800,000), larger than the Dutch East India Company's initial capital 67 years earlier. It established colonies on Réunion and Mauritius and established itself near Madras; however, by 1719 it was close to bankruptcy. After the Seven Years' War and the loss of French settlements in India, the company was nationalized in 1769.

By 1700 France had a more important position in slave-enabled sugar growing than Britain, although only a limited position in tobacco. In Africa, France set up a trading post in Senegal in 1624. Overall, France had as large and profitable an empire as Britain in the late seventeenth century, but lack of naval success thereafter caused its growth to be slower and imposed high costs. After 1720, colonial revenues, important in the seventeenth century, formed a declining source of net revenue to finance any French industrialization.

France's surplus of investible capital built up rapidly under Henry IV. Moreover, France's empire produced additional resources, greater than Britain's before 1700. However, the fiscal and policy follies pursued by France's rulers after 1610 meant that little of those resources were in hands that might become industrial entrepreneurs, or even finance them. Resources were heavily concentrated in the Church and the traditional aristocracy, while the commercial middle classes were impoverished by the 1720 crash and the working classes were ground down by the tax system. Thus, little beyond dilettante scientific experimentation took place.

Finally, France was almost completely free from marauding armies after 1600 and Henry IV's Edict of Nantes ensured that religious conflict remained localized. There was only one serious outbreak of unrest, the Fronde, between 1648 and 1653. Then, after 1789, radical upheaval followed by two decades of Continental war made industrial progress almost impossible.

In 1600, France appeared the most likely of any European country to industrialize. It was large, with excellent resources, and Henry IV and Sully's policies were pushing the country towards a wealthy peasantry and vibrant commercial economy like that of the Netherlands 50 years later or Britain a century later – a pre-condition to industrialization. Had Henry IV lived, or Sully been allowed to continue in office until his death in 1641, such a society might have come into being and French progress towards industrialization might have become unstoppable.

In the event, poor social and fiscal policies under Richelieu, poor economic policies under Louis XIV and Colbert, the financial crisis of

44 *Forging Modernity*

1720 and the unsuccessful wars of the eighteenth century combined so that in 1800 France was economically a long way behind Britain. This affected France's strategic position; under Napoleon she was never as strong relative to Britain as she appeared. For his ill-fated campaign of 1815 Napoleon raised only 17.5 million francs[22] – equivalent to £700,000, less than 3% of the £27 million raised by Nicholas Vansittart[23] in one bond issue four days before Waterloo. Economically at least, the denouement was not 'a damned near-run thing' but inevitable.

Holy Roman Empire in 1600

The Holy Roman Empire was a masterpiece of fuzzy logic design, in existence 400 years before there were mathematicians capable of analysing it. Its boundaries were fuzzy – areas like Burgundy, Switzerland and northern Italy were partial participants in it, generally without representation in its representative body the Imperial Diet (or Reichstag). The sovereignty of its participant states was fuzzy, varying on their size and precise relationship with the centre. Its decision-making was fuzzy, with different issues being decided by the emperor alone, by a group of the major rulers, or by the Imperial Diet. Its foreign policy was fuzzy, with different parts of the Empire varying in their enthusiasm for military campaigns and participation therein, depending on their view of the opponent's threat to their region. Finally, its taxation was fuzzy, with different areas having different taxation obligations and only the Habsburg hereditary lands (most of which were not part of the Empire) providing substantial sources of revenue for its Habsburg rulers.

The Holy Roman Empire in 1600 consisted of some 1,800 states, some of which were ecclesiastic, and many the tiny landholdings of Imperial Knights. Its emperor was elective with seven electors, the king of Bohemia (roughly the modern Czech Republic), the electors of the Palatinate, Saxony and Brandenburg, and the archbishops of Mainz, Cologne and Trier. Bavaria replaced the Palatinate in 1623, the Palatinate was restored by the 1648 Treaty of Westphalia and Hanover was added in 1692. The Imperial Diet, originally similar to the French Estates General

---

22. Andrew Roberts, *Napoleon the Great* (London: Allen Lane, 2014), p. 745.
23. Nicholas Vansittart (1767-1851). 1st Baron Bexley from 1823. MP for Hastings, 1796-1802, Old Sarum, 1802-6, Helston, 1806-12, East Grinstead, 1812, and Harwich, 1812-23. Chancellor of the Exchequer, 1812-23, Chancellor of the Duchy of Lancaster, 1823-28. British bond issue announced in the Budget of 14 June 1815.

The Competitors: Europe's Potential Industrializers in 1600

but in permanent session at Regensburg from 1663, consisted of three colleges, the College of Electors, the College of Princes (rulers of principalities within the Empire) and the College of Cities (independent cities within the Empire). The College of Princes was then divided into ecclesiastical and secular colleges, with Imperial Knights and lesser nobility represented collectively in the secular college, while Princes had individual votes.

Imperial revenues in 1612 totalled 5.4 million Gulden[24] (about £700,000, less than twice Britain's revenues, on four times the population). Since the Imperial constitution failed to provide properly for the central government, most of that revenue came from taxation within the Habsburgs' directly ruled lands; impoverishment became an increasing problem for Holy Roman Emperors over the next 200 years.

Holy Roman Emperor Rudolf II as Vertumnus. He was a glorious intellectual eccentric. Painting by Giuseppe Arcimboldo.

The Empire's constitution, with its representative Imperial Diet, was supposed to embody 'German freedoms'. Since it included a myriad of checks and balances, it was examined by the United States' Founding Fathers in drawing up the 1787 U.S. constitution – they regarded the British House of Commons as altogether too powerful. In practice, however, the constitution of the Holy Roman Empire rendered it incapable of decisive action and provided inadequate resources to fund the Empire's increasingly expensive military forces. After the 1648 Treaty of Westphalia, the emperor derived most of his power from the Habsburg lands ruled directly, in Austria, Hungary, Italy, the future Slovenia and Croatia and, to a lesser extent, Bohemia. Nevertheless, in principle and in practice, the Holy Roman Empire was 'free' in a way that the absolutist states of France, Spain and Russia were not.

---

24. Peter H. Wilson, *Heart of Europe: A History of the Holy Roman Empire* (Cambridge, MA: The Belknap Press, 2020), p. 450, gives that figure for 1612, the year of Rudolf II's death.

The Empire as it existed in 1600 had primarily been designed by Maximilian I (1493-1519), who had established domestic peace through two successive reform initiatives in 1495 and 1500 but never solved the conundrum of the Empire's revenue-raising ability. He died insolvent in Innsbruck, despite his close relationship with the Fugger bank. His dynastic project was remarkably successful, as he was succeeded as emperor by his grandson Charles V (1519-56), who also inherited Spain through one of Maximilian's cleverly arranged dynastic marriages. Charles V temporarily alleviated the Empire's financial problems through silver shipments from the New World, but gradually yielded control of the Empire to his more religiously tolerant younger brother Ferdinand I (1556-64), who took over as emperor on Charles' retirement in 1556, while Charles's Catholic-absolutist son Philip II succeeded to the Spanish throne. The two Habsburg families remained close through genetically damaging intermarriage for the next century.

By 1600, the emperor was Ferdinand I's grandson Rudolf II (1576-1612), a free-thinking and intellectually active, if somewhat ineffectual, emperor, subject to severe depression, whose thirteen-year Long Turkish War (1593-1606) ended in stalemate, raising Imperial debt to 32 million Gulden (£4.1 million) by 1612, although his administration was relatively economical. Rudolf moved the Imperial capital from Vienna to Prague in 1583, which enjoyed an artistic and intellectual Golden Age (his brother and successor Matthias [1612-19] moved it back after his death).

Rudolf II was the foremost art collector of his age; during the latter stages of the Thirty Years' War his collection was scattered, although some works remain in Prague Museum. He also had a keen interest in astronomy, being a major patron of Tycho Brahe (1546-1601) and Johannes Kepler (1571-1630), both of whom he attracted to Prague. The other fashionable sciences Rudolf patronized have a less solid reputation today: astrology, alchemy and necromancy. This reflected the intellectual climate of the time. Astrologers and alchemists were present in most of the courts of Europe, for example one of Elizabeth I's key advisors, another visitor to Prague, was John Dee (1527-1608). As for necromancers, the Holy Roman Empire of the late sixteenth and early seventeenth century saw the highest number of witch burnings in history, showing the 'science' to be unpopular with the Church but very fashionable.

Although the Holy Roman Empire's alchemists achieved several advances in chemistry over the next century, all Rudolf's favoured sciences except astronomy proved to be dead ends, doing nothing for the long-term growth of the Holy Roman economy or for the scientific reputation of the Holy Roman Empire and its successor states. Without

The Competitors: Europe's Potential Industrializers in 1600   47

Francis Bacon's Scientific Method or the luck of Newton's work coinciding with the monarch's efforts, which made Britain's foundation of the Royal Society under Charles II a watershed, Rudolf II's scientific efforts, intelligent, whole-hearted and expensive though they were, led to no bright future.

The Empire's biggest problem was religious division. Martin Luther (1483-1546) had posted his 'Ninety-five Theses' in Wittenberg in 1517, after which Protestantism, both Lutheran and eventually Calvinist, spread unevenly through the Empire. This caused considerable conflict, which appeared to be settled in 1555 by the Peace of Augsburg on the principle of *cuius regio, eius religio* – the religion of each state, Catholic or Lutheran (but not at that stage Calvinist), being set by that of its ruler.

Rudolf II was fairly religiously tolerant but the more conventional Matthias was a rigid Catholic. Conflict broke out in 1618, when Bohemia rebelled against its even more rigidly Catholic King Ferdinand (King of Bohemia, 1617-19, Holy Roman Emperor Ferdinand II, 1619-37), Matthias' cousin and heir, and elected the Calvinist Frederick V, Elector Palatine (1596-1632) as its king. Following Matthias' death, the subsequent Imperial election of Ferdinand II deepened the conflict. Ferdinand II's position was secured, and Frederick ejected from Bohemia by Spanish troops after the 1620 Battle of White Mountain.

There followed 30 years of war throughout the German parts of the empire, in which the Catholics were generally but not exclusively successful, while the Protestants received outside help from King Gustavus Adolphus of Sweden (1611-32) and France's Cardinal Richelieu. (Despite Frederick's marriage to James VI and I's daughter Elizabeth, he did not receive significant British help and was deprived of his Electorate in 1623.) The war did major long-term economic damage; it has been estimated that one quarter of the Empire's population were killed by it and the accompanying famines and diseases.[25]

The 1648 Treaty of Westphalia established the modern system of nationality, in which nations selected their own rulers without interference from outside. Regardless of the ruler's religious preferences, it established the religion of each state within the Empire as being that held in 1624, considered a 'normal' year. By increasing the sovereignty of the Empire's 1,800 constituent states, it also weakened central control. A side-effect was to assist the rise of *homo economicus*, who had already been highly visible in the Empire in 1500 (for example,

---

25. Jan de Vries, *The Economy of Europe in an Age of Crisis, 1600-1750* (Cambridge: Cambridge University Press, 1976), p. 4.

the Fugger banking family) but had been suppressed by more than a century of religious strife. Had the Empire enjoyed good policy and a good economic structure after 1648, an Industrial Revolution was still a possibility, since the eighteenth-century wars were nowhere near as damaging as the Thirty Years' War. However, the Empire's structural weaknesses prevented much further progress.

Ferdinand II's son and successor Ferdinand III (1638-57) was more tolerant than his father, ending the Thirty Years' War. His son and successor Leopold I (1658-1705, elected over French opposition) moved towards absolutism as ruler over the Habsburg hereditary lands, which he substantially enlarged. After the 1683 Battle of Kahlenberg Mountain, relieving the Ottoman siege of Vienna, Leopold successfully rolled back the long-standing Ottoman Turkish threat with the help of Poland's King John III Sobieski (1674-96) and Prince Eugene of Savoy (1663-1736). By the 1699 Treaty of Karlowitz, the Habsburgs gained control of almost all Hungary, giving the family more territory outside the Empire than in it. Alas, Leopold I then embroiled the Empire in the War of Spanish Succession (1701-15).

Leopold's two sons Joseph I (Emperor 1705-11) and Charles VI (Emperor 1711-40) gained further victories over the Turks through Prince Eugene but were primarily concerned with the succession, since both men had only daughters, who were not permitted to accede to the throne. Then, Maria Theresa (Archduchess of Austria/Queen of Hungary, 1740-80) succeeded to the Austrian throne. After a short and financially straitened interval of Imperial rule by the Bavarian Prince-Elector Charles VII (1742-45) of the Wittelsbach family, her husband Francis of Lorraine (1708-65) became Holy Roman Emperor Francis I (1745-65).

Maria Theresa's succession clashed with the ambitions of Frederick II of Prussia (1740-86) to produce two wars, the Austrian Succession from 1740 to 1748 and the Seven Years' War of 1756 to 1763, both fought largely in the German provinces of the Empire. Both Maria Theresa and her son Joseph II (1765-90) were reformers, with Joseph introducing full religious toleration in 1782 and beginning the process of reforming the Empire's prevalent feudal land tenure. Then, under Joseph's brother Leopold II (Emperor 1790-92) and Leopold II's son Francis (Holy Roman Emperor Francis II, 1792-1806, Austrian Emperor Francis I, 1804-35), the French Revolutionary and Napoleonic wars, again taking place largely in Empire territory, further slowed economic progress.

The Holy Roman Empire was a major pioneer in scientific advance, but many of its advances came in alchemy. The Empire produced two

The Competitors: Europe's Potential Industrializers in 1600

major alchemical figures: Johann Joachim Becher (1635-82), the inventor of the 'phlogiston' theory of combustion (which postulated that burning substances lost negative-mass phlogiston rather than taking in oxygen), who was patronised by both Leopold I and Britain's Prince Rupert of the Rhine, and Hennig Brand (c. 1630-1692), the discoverer of phosphorus.[26]

In other scientific areas, Otto von Guericke (1602-86) was the first demonstrator of atmospheric pressure and the physics of the vacuum, conducting a famous demonstration to the Reichstag in 1654 with a team of horses unable to separate two halves of a sphere with a vacuum inside. Later, Gottfried Leibniz (1646-1716), the true inventor of modern calculus and scientific polymath, was born in Saxony and a life-long resident of the Empire, receiving patronage from several of its Electors. In the following century, Leonhard Euler (1707-83), born in Switzerland, spent many years at the court of Frederick II of Prussia and the Saxony-born Carl-Friedrich Gauss[27] carried on the German mathematical/scientific tradition. Still, the departure for Britain of the Hanoverian William Herschel[28] suggests that aristocratic and royal patronage were also available in Britain, where commercial opportunities were more abundant.

Overall, while the Empire was a scientific leader in the seventeenth century and to a lesser extent in the eighteenth century, the problem restricting industrialization was not the amount and quality of scientific advance, but the lack of commercialization thereof.

Probably the Empire's biggest barrier to early industrialization was its system of land tenure, both at the aristocratic and peasant levels. Fully free labour existed for only about 6-8% of the rural population, unlike in Britain where serfdom had disappeared in the high-wage fourteenth and fifteenth centuries. East of the Elbe, a feudal system was still in operation, with peasants tied to the land and labouring only for their feudal lord without cash income. West of the Elbe, the system varied between different states within the Empire, but freedom of movement and conversion of feudal work obligations into cash rents were by no means universal; most peasants existed in a hybrid system.

---

26. Brand's discovery in 1669 was the subject of a famous 1771 painting by Joseph Wright of Derby (1734-97).
27. Carl Friedrich Gauss (1777-1855). Creator of many theorems in mathematics and physics.
28. William Herschel (1738-1822). Knight of the Royal Guelphic Order from 1816. FRS 1781. Copley Medal, 1781. Discovered Uranus, 1781.

For landlords, the system also had disadvantages. Land holdings were 'owned' by families not in freehold, as in Britain, but under a feudal tenure system that gave landlords significant judiciary rights over their lands but provided for the lands to revert to the feudal superior if the landlord had no heirs. Land could not easily be sold or mortgaged; hence, the major potential source of capital for industrialization was tied up. Klemens von Metternich[29] outlined the need to reform this system,[30] but by his time in office after 1809 the chance for an industrial lead was gone.

With this ownership system, there was little incentive for agricultural productivity (northern Italian agricultural productivity was the lowest in Western Europe)[31] and land was a largely sterile asset. Writing in 1826, the German agricultural economist Johann Heinrich von Thünen (1783-1850) produced a mathematically elegant theory of concentric rings, whereby remote areas were left to grain production and ranching; this well described the agriculturally static economy of central and eastern Europe, where productivity was only marginally greater than needed to avoid starvation and surpluses were small. Naturally, in such an environment, industry did not arise spontaneously. This limitation applied to a lesser extent further west.

As in France and Spain, another major obstacle to economic advance in the Empire was its internal tariffs. With around 1,800 jurisdictions within the Empire, tariffs between constituent states effectively acted as external trade borders, and proliferated after the 1648 Treaty of Westphalia eliminated the possibility of central control of small-state revenue generation. The former Empire did not move towards a single market for goods and services until after the German *Zollverein* (customs union) of 1833. Even the Habsburg lands, of Austria, Hungary and elsewhere had internal tariffs well into the nineteenth century. In the eighteenth century there were 32 toll houses on the Rhine and 35 on the Elbe, with each riverine state imposing tolls on goods that crossed through its territory.[32]

---

29. Klemens von Metternich (1773-1859). Prince from 1813. Ambassador to Saxony, 1801-3, to Prussia, 1803-6, to France, 1806-9. Foreign Minister of the Austrian Empire, 1809-48, Chancellor, 1821-48.
30. Metternich's reform proposals are set out in Wolfram Siemann, *Metternich: Strategist and Visionary* (Cambridge, MA: The Belknap Press, 2019), for example, an 1844 paper on Hungary's needs, p. 656.
31. Allen, *The British Industrial Revolution in Global Perspective*, p. 60.
32. Wilson, *Heart of Europe*, p. 469.

Another influential German economist, Friedrich List (1789-1846), saw the value of protectionism for large states such as the German confederation and the United States but recognized that removing internal tariffs was critical to economic growth. He was a major inspiration behind the *Zollverein*.

Karl Marx (1818-83) was brought up in the former Empire, in what had been the electoral bishopric of Trier but was by then ruled by Prussia. Since he grew up before the *Zollverein* in a place suffering from the effects of an Industrial Revolution in which it was not participating, Marx unsurprisingly found free-market capitalism unattractive. Unlike in France or Britain, there was no significant free-market economist in the Empire's successor states until the rise of Carl Menger (1840-1921), the founder of the Austrian school.[33]

Those subjects of the Holy Roman Empire not mired in serfdom had solid property rights, within the limits of the Empire's landholding system. While there was little theoretical backing for property rights from German economists, in practice they were well protected. The first copyright law came as late as 1837, in Prussia, while patent law came even later, the Imperial Patent Law being established only in 1877.

For the period the Empire had a strong legal system, albeit an over-regulated one – the *Reinheitsgebot* ('purity order'), established in Ingolstadt in the Duchy of Bavaria in 1516, setting strict conditions for beer production and ingredients, being one example. The plethora of small states created inter-state competition, so extreme systems of autocracy did not flourish. The Empire had a functioning system of courts that provided the middle and artisan classes (though not the serfs) with the possibility of redress against the powerful, both within a state and from other states – they were much more protected than in France or Spain.

Around 1600, savers in the Empire were treated relatively well, with a stable silver Reichsthaler coinage for half a century from 1566. The Thirty Years' War brought disruption, with the Imperial general Albrecht von Wallenstein issuing over 20 million Gulden of base coinage in the 1620s. After a period of post-Westphalian calm, in the eighteenth century savers fared worse, with the Conventionsthaler replacing the Reichsthaler at a devaluation of 10% in 1754, and the Gulden defined as half of a Conventionsthaler, a 33% devaluation from its previous value.

---

33. Menger's first significant economic work, *Principles of Economics*, was published in 1871.

Then, from 1759, the Habsburg monarchy transitioned to a Gulden paper money issued by the Vienna Stadt Banco, initially convertible into silver, which gradually depreciated in value as inflation increased (fluctuating between 16% and 31% a year between 1770 and 1816) with even nominal silver convertibility being abolished in 1797. Finally, after crises caused by the Napoleonic wars, Austria declared bankruptcy on 20 February 1811. The Stadt Banco's notes, amounting to 1.06 billion Gulden (nominally over £100 million) were converted to new notes, the Wiener Währung, at one fifth of their value. Further war expenditures then caused the Wiener Währung to trade at one fifth of their silver value by 1816, although two years later, by establishing a new bank, Austria was able to redeem at least some of the Wiener Währung and undertake to issue no further paper money.

Savers in the Holy Roman Empire had a solid existence until 1618, were assaulted by the Thirty Years' War, but then enjoyed a century of tranquillity until the 1750s. Thereafter, high inflation and paper money issues destroyed the value of savings over the next 60 years. Once again, one cannot wonder that the young Karl Marx, with his middle-class family's savings subjected to this regime, was disillusioned by capitalism; indeed, the above statistics of the Empire's monetary profligacy were compiled by Marx himself.[34]

Inflation combined with feudal land ownership systems to depress wage rates in the Empire between 1600 and 1800. In the fifteenth century, wages in Vienna were as high as in London or Paris, but they declined by half in terms of silver over the next 400 years, and, by 1800, wages in Vienna and northern Italy were barely above subsistence level, and conditions in Hungary and eastern Germany were as bad. In northern Germany wages remained higher – they could hardly have done otherwise with the high-wage Austrian Netherlands in the Empire until 1792 – but even here currency difficulties depressed them in the late eighteenth century. Literacy was around French levels in Germany, at 35% in 1800, but relatively low in Austria at 21%, little above the Spanish level. Thus, the forces leading potential industrializers to substitute machinery for human labour were weak and the number of artisans with sufficient intellectual training to make mechanical improvements was limited.[35]

---

34. Karl Marx, article in the *New-York Daily Tribune*, 22 March 1854, in K. Marx and F. Engels, *Collected Works* (Moscow: Progress Publishers, 1980), vol. 13.
35. Allen, *The British Industrial Revolution in Global Perspective*, pp. 44-45 (wages), p. 53 (literacy).

The Empire had three methods of ensuring that its poorest citizens did not fall into destitution. First, those who remained serfs had an implied obligation of subsistence from their masters; they were thus better off than the poorest Irish. Second, in Catholic parts of the Empire, monasteries remained active, and the social system was sufficiently traditional that indigent locals could rely on their support. Third, in the Protestant Empire, particularly towards the West, embryonic Poor Laws along British lines grew up over the seventeenth and eighteenth Centuries, again providing a 'safety net'. Overall, the poor were generally better off in the Empire than in France or Spain.

Around 1500, the Holy Roman Empire had an intensive commercial economy by contemporary standards. The Hanse towns, not all of which lay within the Empire, were highly competitive trading entrepots, with outposts in other countries, such as that in London. The Fugger merchant, banking and mining dynasty in Augsburg was led by Jakob Fugger 'the Rich' (1459-1525), who died worth 2.13 million guilders (about £280,000)[36] after financing Charles V's campaign in the Imperial election of 1519. The Fuggers were not only the richest family in Europe, surpassing the Medicis (albeit without the papal ambitions); they were also pioneers in banking, mining and commercial practices. After Jakob's death the Fuggers made the foolish decision, presumably lured by Spain's New World silver mines, to continue a heavy participation in Spanish state financing; this proved unprofitable and the family's fortunes and prominence declined following Philip II's repeated bankruptcies.

The religious schism in the early sixteenth century, the wars to which it led and the Empire's lack of a transoceanic empire or trade links reduced the competitiveness of the Hanse towns and caused the Empire's merchant communities to lose ground relative to their Dutch and British competitors. The Thirty Years' War was especially damaging, because of its length and pervasiveness. In addition, the myriad domestic tariffs prevented large-scale commercial activity from dominating the Empire's domestic market, which remained atomised.

The Holy Roman Empire had ample sources of coal, in the Ruhr region and in the east of Brandenburg (now in Poland). Furthermore, Ruhr coal was well situated for transportation, being near the Rhine. The Empire also had substantial resources of iron ore, some in the Ruhr

---

36. Equivalent to at least £600,000 by 1600, given the New World influx of silver after 1525 and the inflation it generated.

region close to coal deposits, others in the modern Czech Republic, where Metternich made use of them for an iron works in the 1830s. The Empire was thus as well supplied with resources for the early Industrial Revolution as Britain.

Since it faced major military enemies, was located at the centre of Europe, and had limited access to sea coasts and limited resources, the Empire never developed a large naval or merchant marine force. It missed out on the transoceanic empires and trading routes that Spain, France, the Netherlands and Britain all developed. This became a considerable disadvantage in the eighteenth century, since there were no colonial revenue sources or trade flows to boost the Imperial coffers, while there were large military needs that drained them. Joseph II set up an Austrian East India Company in 1775, 170 years after the Netherlands and England; being so late into the game, it failed at it and was wound up in 1785. The lack of an overseas empire was a serious disadvantage to the Holy Roman Empire in the early years of industrialization, since the capital and new markets that such an empire would have brought were unavailable.

Finally, the Holy Roman Empire was at a considerable disadvantage to Britain, France or the Netherlands in its lack of large-scale investible capital. The aristocracy were generally impoverished by the late eighteenth century, unable to sell or mortgage their lands; there was no flow of money from overseas investments and the merchant communities were in relative decline. The lack of finance availability was an important barrier to success for any industrial ventures within the Empire. Only after the 1833 *Zollverein* and extensive land reform was this problem solved.

In summary, the Holy Roman Empire was large, well endowed with natural resources, with an active scientific culture, and politically sufficiently non-absolute and governed by the rule of law that non-aristocrats could potentially flourish. Its failure to industrialize early was determined by its old-fashioned feudal systems of land tenure and agricultural labour, its myriad of internal tariffs, its rulers' relative poverty and its lack of a transoceanic Empire. Politically, its statesmen made some mistakes, notably in monetary policy, but the largest problem was a constitutional structure so immobile that it prevented substantial reform without a consensus that could never be achieved. The result was a miserable period of non-industrialization until the 1833 *Zollverein*, after which with growing Prussian dominance Germany's natural economic strengths emerged.

The Competitors: Europe's Potential Industrializers in 1600

The Netherlands in 1600

In 1600, the Netherlands consisted of the northernmost seven provinces of the former Dukedom of Burgundy, which had been absorbed into the Habsburg dominions in 1478 through Maximilian I's marriage to their heiress. While the ten southern Low Countries provinces (the future Belgium) remained predominantly Catholic, the Netherlands leaned towards Protestantism, rising in revolt when William the Silent (Stadtholder of Holland, Zeeland and Utrecht, 1559-67, 1572-84) rebelled in 1567 against Philip II's attempt to maintain Catholic hegemony.

Prince Maurice of Nassau was an excellent general and quietly effective ruler. Painting by Jan van Ravesteyn.

In 1600 the Netherlands, ruled by William the Silent's son Prince Maurice of Orange (Stadtholder of Holland and Zeeland, 1585-1625, of Utrecht, Guelders and Overijssel, 1590-1625, of Groningen, 1620-25) was mired in its Eighty Years' War of independence from Spain. This lasted until a twelve-year truce between 1609 and 1621, then continued as part of the Thirty Years' War until the 1648 Treaty of Münster, which recognized the independence of the Netherlands but not of what became modern Belgium, which devolved to Austria.

The Netherlands in 1600 had enjoyed a decade in the 1590s, the 'Ten Glory Years', that was successful both economically and militarily. It was rapidly evolving into a successful commercial society like Britain a century later, albeit with a population of only 1.5 million in 1600 (1.8 million in 1700). It had inherited solid institutions from Philip the Good (Duke of Burgundy, 1419-1467), who had conquered the future Netherlands in 1433 and established a representative States General which evolved into the Netherlands' principal governing body, declaring independence from Spain by the 1581 Act of Abjuration.

Philip the Good had also left the Netherlands a central chamber of accounts and, from 1579, it had a budget system that provided for annual budgeting and equal taxation in each of the Netherlands' provinces and prohibited internal tariffs. As a republic with a non-hereditary Stadtholder, the Netherlands in 1600 was less 'absolutist' than any other state in Europe and, indeed, the next two centuries saw two separate periods without a Stadtholder.

Netherlands' state revenues were around 5.5 million guilders[37] (£455,000) in the three years 1598 to 1600, greater than English revenues and with one third of the population. Netherlands' state revenues rose rapidly during the next two decades to a three-year average of fifteen million guilders (£1.24 million) in 1624-26, roughly double the British revenues of that period and nearly double the revenues of the Holy Roman Empire, which had twelve times the population. Just as the Holy Roman Empire was hampered by its lack of Imperial revenue, so the Dutch Republic became powerful for its modest size, battling Spain and financing projects of infrastructure and national expansion.

Prince Maurice was the Netherlands' most successful general and Stadtholder of all the Netherlands' seven provinces except Friesland, which was ruled by his cousin Willem-Louis of Nassau (1560-1620). He captured various key fortresses and towns during the Ten Glory Years and won the Battle of Nieuwpoort in 1600, introducing the new tactics of volley fire and cooperation between infantry and cavalry, as well as paying the army on time and feeding it efficiently. He was an inspiration to his nephew Marshal Turenne of France (1611-75) and to Gustavus Adolphus of Sweden.

Prince Maurice was succeeded as Stadtholder by his half-brother Frederick Henry (Stadtholder, 1625-1647), who was succeeded by his son William II (Stadtholder, 1647-50), who married the British King Charles I's[38] daughter Mary (1631-60). On William II's death, there was a 'First Stadtholderless Period' until his son William III[39] was elected Stadtholder in 1672. William III married the future British King

---

37. Jan de Vries and Ad van der Woude, *The First Modern Economy: Success, Failure and Perseverance of the Dutch Economy, 1500-1815* (Cambridge: Cambridge University Press, 1997), Holland Excise Revenues table, p. 104. Holland's excise revenues were 2.2 million guilders; these represented two thirds of Holland's revenues and Holland's revenue quota was 57.7% of the Netherlands' total. Thus, Netherlands' revenues can be roughly calculated at 5.5 million guilders (2.2/(.667x.577)).

38. Charles I (1600-49). King of England, Scotland and Ireland, 1625-49.

39. William III (1650-1702). Stadtholder of the United Provinces, 1672-1702, King, with Mary, of Great Britain, 1689-1702.

The Competitors: Europe's Potential Industrializers in 1600   57

James II's[40] daughter Mary[41] in 1678 and, at William's insistence by the request of prominent English Protestants, invaded Britain in 1688 to depose James II.

After William III's death, the Netherlands continued without a Stadtholder until the hereditary Prince of Orange William IV, a cousin of William III who had married the British King George II's[42] eldest daughter Anne (1709-59) in 1734, was elected Stadtholder in 1747, the office being made hereditary. His son William V (Stadtholder 1751-95) was, after a Regency by Anne during his minority, the last Stadtholder of the Dutch Republic before its conquest by France in 1795. Then, after France's defeat William V's son Prince William VI of Orange Nassau (King of the Netherlands, 1815-40) was elected Sovereign Prince of the Netherlands in December 1813 and proclaimed himself King William I in 1815, transforming the Netherlands into a monarchy.

In 1600, the Netherlands was beginning its seventeenth-century economic expansion. It benefited from an immigration of some 100,000 mostly skilled migrants from the Catholic provinces still held by Spain – this depressed the commercial success of Antwerp and correspondingly raised that of Amsterdam and other Dutch cities. Then, in the 1590s, with Dutch shipbuilding and Mediterranean trade expanding, the states of Holland and Zeeland launched a state-backed expedition to find the Northeast Passage, following the English Muscovy Company 40 years earlier. A private sector expedition of four ships was launched to the East Indies in 1595, returning the following year with enough spices to turn a decent profit; a further expedition of eight ships in 1598 made 400% on the capital invested.

The English heard of these successes and formed the private sector East India Company (EIC) in 1600. In 1602 the Dutch formed the mixed public-private Dutch East India Company (VOC), with a much larger capital than the EIC of 6.44 million guilders (£541,000) and a 21-year monopoly on trade to the Indies east of the Cape of Good Hope and west of Manila.

The VOC proved extremely successful, pursuing a strategy that combined commerce with military force, and paying dividends of 40% of invested capital by the 1620s. It established a monopoly over imports to Europe of many spices from the East Indies, forcing out Portuguese traders and in one incident in 1623 massacring the members of an East

---

40. James II (1633-1701). King of Great Britain, 1685-88.
41. Mary II (1662-94). Queen, with William, of Great Britain, 1689-94.
42. George II (1683-1760). King of Great Britain, 1727-60.

India Company post in Amboyna. It also established monopolies on trade with China and Japan, which proved lucrative in the short term, although the 1644 change of dynasty in China and Japan's gradual move to greater isolationism after 1670 reduced its long-term revenues. The VOC remained highly successful and profitable, albeit with gradually increasing competition from French and British counterparts until around 1730, after which its profitability declined. It suffered badly in the Fourth Anglo-Dutch War (1780-84) and was wound up in 1799.

In 1621, encouraged by the VOC's early success, and by the end of the twelve-year truce with Spain, the Dutch formed the Dutch West India Company (GWC), with eventual capital of 2.8 million guilders (£235,000), of which one million guilders was provided by the States-General and the VOC and the remainder by municipalities and Dutch and foreign private shareholders. The GWC's grand design was to seize the Portuguese colonies in Africa and the Americas, and thereby to dominate the sugar and slave trades. Initially, its main success was in raiding, most notably seizing a Spanish silver ship. Then, in 1630, it captured Recife, in Brazil, which proved to be unprofitable because of the cost of defending it. The company was recapitalized twice, in 1647 and 1674 and settled to a profitable slave-trading business based in modern Ghana, with sugar colonies in the West Indies, although it lost market share to French and British ventures after 1660. Britain finally conquered the Dutch sugar colonies in the Fourth Anglo-Dutch War, after which the GWC's remaining assets were nationalized. Nevertheless, from 1650 through most of the eighteenth century, the GWC was profitable, trading slaves and sugar and adding to the available capital for Dutch industrialization.

The Netherlands in the early seventeenth century was a centre of financial innovation. The VOC, being larger than any previous joint-stock company, established the Amsterdam Stock Exchange in 1602 as an entrepot for its stock and bond issues; the Exchange acquired a dedicated building in 1611. This was the world's first stock exchange; it led London by about 80 years and helped the Netherlands finance other new businesses and become a vibrant commercial economy. Trading techniques proliferated, notoriously during the famous 'tulip bubble' of 1636-37, and the 'Dutch auction' was invented, in which prices are lowered until a bid is received.

The year 1609 saw the establishment of the Exchange Bank of Amsterdam, which acted as a central bank for the province of Holland, which under the agreement of 1579 as modified was normally responsible for 57.7% of consolidated Dutch tax revenue. This enabled a public debt

The Competitors: Europe's Potential Industrializers in 1600

market to grow up, initially bearing interest at 8.33% annually, already a better rate than the Netherlands' competitors. Over the next 40 years interest rates declined and by 1650 Holland was borrowing at 4% annually.

The *Rampjaar* ('disaster year') of 1672 was a crisis year for the Netherlands: France invaded and the Netherlands was forced to flood much of the country to form the Dutch Water Line and cut Holland off from the French invaders. The year is generally held to mark the end of Dutch economic supremacy; after it the costs of military defence and high taxes that burdened the populace made economic growth sluggish. Late in the seventeenth century, with continuous wars to be financed, taxation became burdensome; by 1700, according to one modern estimate, the Netherlands' tax revenues per capita were 10.6 grams of gold, compared to 5.1 grams in Britain.[43]

After 1688, renewed wars increased Dutch expenditure again and taxation rose further, even though as in England public debt was used to finance the increased expenditure. By 1713, total Dutch public debt had reached 378 million guilders (£32 million) compared to Britain's debt the same year of £36 million, with three times the population. As a result, debt service charges exceeded the state's normal income and a class of rentiers diverted investment from more productive purposes.

In 1600 the Netherlands was already a leader in the sciences, because of its intellectual and religious openness. It also became a centre of international publishing, printing works of Bacon, Hobbes and Locke from Britain, for example. René Descartes lived there from 1629 to 1649 and did most of his important work there. Hugo Grotius (1583-1645) would play a major part in the establishment of international law, while Baruch Spinoza (1632-77) would become one of the century's leading philosophers. Later in the century, Christiaan Huygens (1629-95), astronomer and inventor of the pendulum clock, and Antonie van Leeuwenhoek (1632-1723), in microscopy and biology, made important contributions. After 1672, Dutch pre-eminence declined; only Dante Gabriel Fahrenheit (1686-1736), who moved to Holland and invented the eponymous temperature scale, was notable.

Private property rights were well protected in the Netherlands, better than anywhere else in Continental Europe. The country also had a well-established rule of law, its provisions solidified by Grotius; its

---

43. Roderick Floud, Jane Humphries and Paul Johnson (eds), *Cambridge Economic History of Modern Britain: Volume 1: 1700-1870* (Cambridge: Cambridge University Press, 2014), Table 1-11, p. 34.

bourgeois culture ensured that at least the middle classes could get legal redress if needed. With a solid government bond market and an early stock market, the Netherlands had a good savings climate until 1672, although a real estate bubble in the 1660s later proved troublesome. While the lack of economic dynamism and high taxation increased the society's inequality after 1672, all these protections remained through the eighteenth century until the French conquest of 1795. Then, inflation and an 1810 debt default (as France took over full control) made savings insecure. Before 1795 the Netherlands was the most successful European country in satisfying this group of criteria for industrialization but failed thereafter.

During its Golden Age, the Netherlands was a leader in economic thought. Pieter de la Court (1618-85) was a successful cloth trader and an economic thinker during the First Stadtholderless Period; his 1662 work, *Interest van Holland*, celebrated republicanism and, more significantly, the benefits of free trade. After 1672, Dutch leadership in this area declined; one example of 'brain drain' was Bernard Mandeville (1670-1733), philosopher, political economist and satirist, who moved to Britain in his twenties and never returned to the Netherlands.

The development of the Netherlands' commercial economy after 1600 raised wage rates, which for labourers in 1675 were 25% higher than in Britain and far higher than elsewhere in Europe.[44] Slowing Dutch economic growth caused wages to stagnate, so that after 1700 Dutch and British wage rates were about equal; then, Dutch troubles after 1780 caused real wage rates to decline so that by 1825 they were 15% below those of Britain, although still higher than elsewhere in Europe. For skilled labour, the picture was similar; Dutch wage rates were higher than British in 1675, about equal by 1775 and lower after 1800. Literacy was also very high in the Netherlands; at 68% in 1800 well ahead of anywhere else in Europe including Britain (53%). The Netherlands thus satisfied the industrialization requirements that wage rates should be high, encouraging the substitution of machines for manpower, and that literacy should be high, increasing the adaptability to new working methods.

The Netherlands provided cash payments to the poor in the seventeenth and eighteenth centuries, probably the highest poor relief in Europe at around 3% of GDP in 1760 compared to 2.2% of GDP in England in

---

44. Allen, *The British Industrial Revolution in Global Perspective*, pp. 44-45 (wages), p. 53 (literacy).

The Competitors: Europe's Potential Industrializers in 1600   61

1790.[45] The system fell apart after the French conquest of 1795 and the debt default of 1810 and poor relief payments were much lower after Dutch self-government returned, around 1.5% of GDP in 1820. Thus, before 1795, working-class Netherlanders were well protected against destitution and could afford to take risks.

The Netherlands had a highly intensive commercial economy from around 1600. The commercial middle class gained political power, particularly in the First Stadtholderless Period of 1650 until 1672. Because of the Netherlands' widespread trade, consumer purchasing patterns were far broader than anywhere else in Europe, at least before 1672, and relatively low interest rates and a developed banking system caused small businesses to proliferate.

In energy and transportation, the Netherlands developed unique solutions, deployed mostly during the seventeenth century that both raised its industrial development above other countries and hindered it from taking the next steps that might lead to a true Industrial Revolution. Since 1500, it had engaged in massive programmes of land reclamation that vastly expanded its arable land era. Given these and the country's topography, it was both simple and relatively cheap to develop a system of waterways, connecting with the river network, that could be used for the transport of goods and people at a cost and efficiency Britain only achieved after James Brindley's Grand Cross canal system. In later years this canal network made the Netherlands a laggard in railway development, having to import engineers from England, using a non-standard track gauge that required special locomotives and constructing its first line, from Amsterdam to Haarlem, only in 1839.

The Netherlands had limited coal and timber supplies, although coal was available from either Britain across the North Sea or the Ruhr, relatively nearby up the Rhine. Therefore, it used domestic peat for heating and other uses, a limited and inefficient energy source. Iron ore, however, was available, from the Walloon region of what became southern Belgium.

The Netherlands in the seventeenth century developed a huge inventory of wind power, a technology superior to water power, given the Netherlands' flat topography, although the windmills themselves were expensive to maintain. The first wind-powered sawmill was constructed

---

45. Bas van Bavel and Auke Rijpma, 'How Important Were Formalized Charity and Social Spending before the Rise of the Welfare State?: A Long-run Analysis of Selected Western European Cases, 1400-1850', *Economic History Review*, Vol. 69, no. 1 (2016), p. 171.

in 1594, while technological advances included the Archimedes screw for water pumping, patented in 1654, and the 'Hollander' paper-making windmill in 1674.[46] Industrial windmills were concentrated in the Zaan region (north of Amsterdam) and were used for sawing, oilseed pressing, paper-making, cutting tobacco, paint preparation and hemp processing. The number of Zaan region windmills rose from 128 in 1630 to 584 in 1731, although there was then a modest decline to 482 in 1795, reflecting the slowing in the overall Dutch economy.

The plethora of wind power and windmill expertise hampered the development of steam power and steam-powered industry, because even with expensive Dutch labour and the high cost of windmill maintenance, the cost saving from the early steam engines was insufficient compared to windmill-powered industry. This limited the Netherlands' industrialization before 1795; then economic disruption and destruction of capital hampered it further, with industrialization occurring first in the Walloon region of Belgium and major industrialization in the Netherlands only after 1850.

Through the VOC and the Dutch West Indies Company, the Netherlands had a highly profitable empire in the seventeenth and eighteenth centuries in relation to its size. This brought a massive surplus of investible capital, although after 1700 there were insufficient opportunities to invest it and the Netherlands became an exporter of capital, like late-nineteenth-century Britain. Thus, unlike in Spain, France and the Holy Roman Empire, shortage of investible capital did not constrain potential Dutch industrialization.

Invasion by foreign armies and domestic unrest were both significant retardants of Dutch economic development. The country was at war with Spain until 1648. Several wars with England were primarily naval, then the French invasion of 1672 severely disrupted the Dutch economy. Lengthy wars from 1688 to 1713 drained the Dutch economy, but mostly took place in the Austrian Netherlands (Belgium) rather than in the Netherlands itself. Then a long period of peace provided opportunities until 1780, after which the Fourth Anglo-Dutch War severely disrupted Dutch trade, followed by domestic unrest until 1787. Finally, the 1795 French invasion, followed by heavy taxes, domestic conflict and an 1810 debt default, prevented progress until 1815.

Politically, the Netherlands was well set up for early industrialization, although it lacked scale. Its economy also developed the intensive commercial nature considered necessary to industrialization well before

---

46. De Vries and van der Woude, *The First Modern Economy*, pp. 300, 345-47.

competitor economies such as Britain's. Its workforce was expensive, with high literacy, so substitution of capital for labour was both possible and potentially profitable. It lacked coal and iron ore reserves but could have imported them at moderate cost.

Apart from size, the Netherlands' disadvantages before 1795 were twofold: a lack of economic dynamism after 1700 and an alternate energy source (windmills) that made early steam engines economically unattractive. Then it suffered 20 years of foreign occupation and impoverishment, from 1795 to 1815, during which markets were disrupted and entrepreneurial investments in technology were impossible. After 1815 the Netherlands was relatively poor with limited incentives to develop beyond its canal and windmill technology, so industrialization was delayed until the later nineteenth century.

* * *

In summary, therefore, Spain, France, the Holy Roman Empire and the Netherlands all had significant obstacles to developing an Industrial Revolution before Britain. If Britain had not existed, France and the Holy Roman Empire, under their improved post-1815 governance structures, might have developed a spontaneous Industrial Revolution within the next century, but the Netherlands had locked itself into windmill technology, while Spain was impoverished and in decline. The chapters ahead will demonstrate how better policies, rather than superior natural resources or better access to scientific advances, were the key drivers of Britain's lead in industrialization.

3

Britain in 1600 and Early Changes, 1600-48

The Starting Point: Britain in 1600

The British Isles in 1600 consisted of one large kingdom, England, a smaller dependent state, Wales, united with England in 1536, a troubled semi-independent nation, Ireland, first invaded by Henry II in 1171, and a fully independent nation, Scotland, ruled by its own king, James VI, since 1567. Scotland would join nominally with England by the union of the two Crowns in 1603; it would not join in full political union until 1707.

England in 1600 was ruled by the aged Elizabeth I, a truly remarkable woman, who had ruled so much by the force of her personality that she had made life very difficult for any successor. The decades-long war with Spain and the Irish rebellion had exhausted the Treasury, and there were no solid structures for obtaining popular consent to the taxes needed to rectify the problem. The country had suffered a rapid population increase, by 70% from 2.4 million in 1500 to 4.1 million in 1600[1] with persistent inflation, so living standards had declined considerably. England was also in the early stages of looking

---

1. Mitchell (ed.), *British Historical Statistics*, Table I-1 gives an estimate for 1600, based on extrapolating parish register birth rates backwards from 1801, and one for 1541, the earliest date given (parish registration of births became a legal requirement in 1538). I have extrapolated Mitchell's 1541 figure back 41 years linearly using the 1541-61 change.

for overseas trading posts further away than Europe, but without the means to pay for much international expansion.

Most dangerous, the succession to Elizabeth seemed likely to be disputed, as she had resisted providing assurances that James VI of Scotland, her first cousin twice removed but her nearest relative, should succeed her. Certainly, Philip III of Spain had hopes that his elder half-sister, Isabella Clara Eugenia (1566-1633), ruler with her husband Archduke Albert (1559-1621) of the Spanish Netherlands, might succeed Elizabeth; she was a descendant of John of Gaunt, the patriarch of the Lancastrian line.

The other parts of the future Britain were considerably poorer than England. Wales was almost entirely agricultural; while it had produced the Tudor dynasty, it would produce no more significant national leaders until David Lloyd George.[2] However, Wales was never a major source of upheaval and was generally Royalist during the Civil War.

Scotland was an independent country, at war intermittently with England until the 1547 Battle of Pinkie. It had moved sharply to Calvinist Presbyterianism, led by John Knox (1514-72) during the long minority and absence in France of Queen Mary (1542-87). On Mary's deposition in favour of the infant James VI in 1567, the Protestant party had taken full control of Scotland's administration, but in adulthood James' relationship with Elizabeth was fairly amicable, since both recognized that he was her most plausible Protestant successor. After 1603, Scotland was to become a source of opposition to royal rule and instigator of the Civil War, later providing support for Parliament. It remained disaffected under the later Stuarts; its economy only integrated with England's after the 1707 Act of Union.

England's relationship with Ireland was only mildly exploitative until the Reformation, but England's turn to Protestantism was not shared by Ireland, after which the traditional Irish leadership became disaffected, and were subjected under Elizabeth to repeated campaigns of conquest and subjection, culminating in the English victory at Kinsale in 1602. Thereafter, England and Scotland subjected Ireland to aggressive colonization, primarily led by English and Scottish Presbyterians, which was most successful in Ulster. The Irish rebellion of 1641, combined with the English Civil War, led to Cromwell's seizure of Catholic landholdings in the 1650s. That produced an Ireland impoverished and

---

2. David Lloyd George (1863-1945). 1st Earl Lloyd George of Dwyfor, 1945. Prime Minister, 1916-22.

subjected to quasi-colonial rule, with most Irish land held by absentee Protestant grandees.

Scotland and Wales were to play significant roles in the Industrial Revolution, but Ireland outside Ulster remained primarily agricultural and increasingly impoverished.

The sixteenth century was miserable for the English working classes. The repeated plagues of the previous centuries had depopulated the country, leaving a surplus of arable land for the populace it needed to support; consequently, the purchasing power of English labourers and craftsmen had reached a high point around 1475-1500. Robert C. Allen calculated London labourers' wage rates at about 4.1 times the purchasing power necessary for subsistence in 1500, declining to around 2.9 times the subsistence purchasing power in 1600 and a nadir of about 2.8 times the subsistence purchasing power in the 1630s. In terms of a more generous 'respectability' basket of goods (for example, including the purchase of bread, meat, dairy products, beer, soap, lamp oil, candles and fuel), the decline is similar, from 1.5 times the purchasing power of a 'respectable' basket in 1475 to 1.0 times that ratio around 1625. Skilled workers' wages – Allen used masons as an example – showed a similar decline from 2.5 times the 'respectability' basket in 1475 to 1.7 times that basket in 1625.[3]

The period of high working-class earnings in late fifteenth-century England was not fully matched in other countries, where even in Western Europe the peak in wages was generally 10-20% lower than in England, and this had important structural consequences. In England, the move from feudalism, whereby service obligations were translated into cash payments, land holdings became outright freeholds and rural labourers became economically 'free' had begun in the thirteenth century, but working-class prosperity in the fifteenth century pushed it much further. It would be completed by legislation in 1660, discussed below.

During that halcyon fifteenth-century period of 'Merrie England', population pressure was especially low, so land prices were low and labourers' wages were high, far above Malthusian subsistence level. With parliamentary representation of at least the upper fringe of the skilled working class established by the 'Model Parliament' of 1295 and its 40s-freehold franchise, the British social system was already more open and 'democratic' than those of France or Spain. It was also slowly

---

3. Allen, *The British Industrial Revolution in Global Perspective*, Figs 2.2, 2.3 and 2.6.

becoming market-based, so when new better-paid opportunities arose for those working on the land, they were increasingly free to pursue them.

Working-class living standards declined during the sixteenth century by about 25-30% and would bottom out at one third below their late-mediaeval peak early in Charles I's reign. The same decline had occurred in most other countries of Europe; for the European working classes, the sixteenth-century Renaissance and opening to the New World had been thoroughly miserable. Only after 1650 did the British working classes' experience begin to differ from those elsewhere in Europe.

The increased openness of British society did not vanish. Sixteenth-century inflation lowered working-class living standards, but also lowered the real cost of a 40s freehold, entitling its owner to a vote, so that more of the upper working class were included in the franchise. Furthermore, the increase in Parliament's power effected by Henry VIII's use of Parliament to pass the Reformation statutes, led to a political system with strong elements of instability, but also relatively broad representation.

England also differed from Spain and France in 1600 by being a limited monarchy, where in principle even the monarch was bound by the laws. Sir John Fortescue in *The Difference between an Absolute and Limited Monarchy* (*c.* 1470) had written:

> there be two kind of kingdoms, of which that one is a Lordship, called in Latin 'Dominium Regale' and the other is called 'Dominium Politicum et Regale'. And they differ, in that the first may rule his people by such Laws as he makyth himself, and therefore he may set upon them Tallies, and other Impositions, such as he wills himself, without their Assent. The second may not rule his people, by other Laws than such that they assent to; and therefore he may set upon them no impositions without their own Assent.[4]

Fortescue gave the example of the kings of France, who in Louis IX's time (1226-70) levied no taxes without the three estates' consent, but during the Hundred Years War became absolute, levying taxes without consent with the nobility exempted, so that:

> the Commons be so impoverished and destroyed, that they may scarcely live. They drink water, they eat apples with

---

4. Sir John Fortescue, *The Difference between an Absolute and Limited Monarchy*, (London: W. Bowyer, 1714), pp. 1-2.

Bread right brown made of Rye. They eat no Flesh, but if it be seldom, a little Lard or Entrails or Heads of Beasts slain for the Nobles, and merchants of the Land. … Their wives and children go barefoot; they may in none other way live.[5]

In England, on the other hand:

Blessed be God, this Land is ruled under a better Law, and therefore the people thereof be not in such penury, nor thereby hurt in their Persons, but they be wealthy and have all things necessary, to the sustenance of Nature. Wherefore they be Mighty, and able to Resist all the adversaries of this Realm, and to best other Realms, that do or will do them wrong.[6]

Fortescue was writing at the peak of the late-mediaeval surge in English living standards. Still, the principle that Parliament must consent to royal tax levies was immensely important in the run-up to the Civil War, causing British history to diverge radically from French and Spanish history, greatly benefiting both ordinary people and economic progress.

By 1600, England was already diverging from its Continental neighbours in the breadth and depth of its merchants' global interests. The first major joint-stock company, the Muscovy Company, was granted in 1555 by royal charter to carry on trade with Muscovy (part of today's Russia) for which trade the company had a monopoly. A predecessor organization the 'Company of Merchant Adventurers to New Lands', part-founded by Sebastian Cabot (1474-1557), a survivor of his father John Cabot's 1497 voyage to Newfoundland, had in May 1553 sent a small flotilla headed by Richard Chancellor (c. 1521-56) to find a northeast passage to 'Cathay'. Having failed to do so, Chancellor had travelled overland to Moscow, and cleared a substantial trade profit, while opening relations with the Russian Czar Ivan IV 'the Terrible' (1547-84).

The Muscovy Company was not initially successful; Chancellor was lost at sea on its first voyage. Its second chief trader, Anthony Jenkinson (1529-1611) (an ancestor of Lord Liverpool) made four voyages to Russia, an additional overland trip to Persia and returned with trading agreements, maps and an invitation from Ivan IV to Queen Elizabeth I

---

5. Ibid., p. 17.
6. Ibid., pp. 23-24.

for an alliance. The company continued in existence with its monopoly of Russian-British trade until 1698, but its revenues and profits lessened with the period of instability in Russia that followed Ivan IV's death in 1584, and with increasing Dutch competition after 1600.

Interest in the potential for trading to the East Indies arose from the profits of a net £140,000 from a Portuguese East India carrack, the *Madre de Deus*, seized at the Battle of Flores in 1592, and from news of the successful 1595-96 and 1598-99 Dutch voyages to the East Indies. With the precedent of the Muscovy Company available, it was natural for London merchants to seek a royal charter for an East India Company (EIC). This was granted for a fifteen-year period on 31 December 1600, the company having capital of £68,373, less than a tenth of that of the Dutch East India Company established two years later.

In the Americas before 1600, there had been a huge amount of gallant English seafaring, but not a lot to show for it. Sir Francis Drake (*c*. 1540-96) who had circumnavigated the world between 1577 and 1580, was dead, Sir Walter Raleigh's (1552-1618) attempted colonization of Virginia had failed and no other significant colonization attempts had been made. Portugal, Spain and, embryonically, France had trans-atlantic settlements, but Britain did not.

Whereas England in the late sixteenth century was a leader in global exploration, its scientific track record was less impressive. Probably its leading scientist was John Dee, whose mathematical studies were accompanied by true international celebrity as an alchemist, including a period at the court of Emperor Rudolf II. William Gilbert (1544-1603) in his *De Magnete*, published in 1600, made significant advances in the understanding of magnetism and electricity, a term which he defined. The early seventeenth century was to prove scientifically more productive.

Private property rights were not especially strong in 1600 in England. To some extent, that is what the Civil War would be about: a contest between property owners, one class of whom believed that royal favour should allow them to enrich themselves, while the other believed that property gave rights independent of the king and the government. In a three-stage process including the Civil War, the Restoration settlement and the 1688 Revolution, the latter view was to win. In 1600 it was by no means dominant; the feudal belief that property rights derived from the king, or through him from the local landowner was still strong.

The rule of law was still not secure, although the erosion of traditional and mediaeval rights that had already taken place in Spain and France had not gone as far. Elizabeth, like her father and her sister, resorted to arbitrary power from time to time, especially if national security or religion were involved. Ordinary people could get a hearing through the law courts, but the chances of success against a politically powerful antagonist were slim. Fortescue had not been wrong in 1470 when he claimed that England was governed by laws, not by absolute monarchs, but other countries, notably the Netherlands, were ahead of England in this respect by 1600.

England's savings climate had improved considerably under Elizabeth I. Whereas Henry VIII had debased the coinage, reducing the value of savings by as much as three quarters, Elizabeth's financial advisor Sir Thomas Gresham[7] perceived that coinage debasement had adversely affected confidence in England's ability to pay its debts. He therefore had ended it. In 1560 he removed the debased currency from circulation and issued a new coinage with high fineness. Since Gresham took in debased currency for exchange only based on its silver content (unlike in Liverpool's recoinage of 1816), the Crown gained an additional £50,000 from this recoinage, at the expense of savers. For the remainder of Elizabeth's reign and that of James VI and I, the coinage remained sound, although the continued inflow of silver from the New World caused hidden inflation which reduced further the value of savings. Nevertheless, although England had no reliable banks in 1600, savers were after 1560 better treated than in most Continental jurisdictions.

The financial services sector would be crucial to the Industrial Revolution. The London financial market in 1600 was considerably less developed than those of Genoa, Venice or Amsterdam, in which banks already existed. In 1600, both scriveners and goldsmiths performed financial transactions on an *ad hoc* basis, but their approach was different.

Scriveners, who had formed a guild in 1373, were professional drafters of legal documents, usually licensed as notaries public. Being knowledgeable of the legal forms that would be accepted by a court, and of adequate substance and professional standing, scriveners could hold money on behalf of customers, make payments and so on. In the Middle Ages, their first clients for such types of banking services had been farmers of larger holdings, who, after driving their flocks of sheep to market in London, would deposit the sale proceeds of those sheep with these reliable intermediaries.

---

7. Thomas Gresham (1519-79). Kt 1559. Merchant, financier. Founded Royal Exchange, 1565.

Britain in 1600 and Early Changes, 1600-48

Scriveners had lost some of their importance with the invention of printing but still acted for clients in conveyancing, property management in general and inheritance. (Attorneys also existed but were involved mainly in more complex legal matters.) A new Scriveners' Company was incorporated in 1617 and, because land turnover was high, scriveners enjoyed prosperous decades until 1642. John Milton (1562-1647), father of the poet John Milton,[8] was a scrivener, and made enough money to keep his son in his old age, scrivening being more profitable than writing epic poems about Paradise. As the legal system became more professionalized after 1660, scriveners' business declined, with only their notary functions surviving.

In financial matters, scriveners acted as 'cash keepers' for clients' holdings of cash and valuables, and as loan brokers helping clients to invest in mortgage loans, using their document search expertise at the Mayor's Court in London to ensure that property parcels were owned by the borrower and free of other encumbrances. They only rarely took deposits, and most of the loans they made directly were funded by their own resources rather than client monies. Given their activities, their client base was primarily rural landed gentry, not London merchants or the very rich aristocracy. It should be noted that they made few transfers of money between the country and London; their clients brought cash and valuables with them for storage when they came to 'town' with or without flocks of sheep.[9]

Goldsmiths' client base was primarily the very rich and the Court, for whom they designed and produced gold and silver 'plate', itself an important store of value, as well as the London mercantile community. Like scriveners, they also acted as 'cash keepers', providing storage for plate, coinage and other valuables, and would melt down plate and pay the value of the resulting bullion when their clients needed money. The largest of them acted as substantial, theoretically short-term financiers of the state and engaged in foreign exchange dealings with merchants in London and Continental financial centres. Goldsmiths made fewer private mortgage loans than scriveners, since they lacked a detailed

---

8. John Milton (1608-74). Secretary for Foreign Tongues, 1649-60. *L'Allegro* and *Il Penseroso* (1632), *Eikonoklastes* (1649), *Paradise Lost* (1667).

9. The activities of seventeenth-century scriveners and goldsmiths are described in Frank Melton, *Sir Robert Clayton and the Origins of English Deposit Banking, 1658-1685* (Cambridge: Cambridge University Press, 1986), pp. 16-40.

knowledge of land holdings, but their Court and mercantile contacts brought them considerable short-term lending business. Goldsmiths' business expanded with the Civil War and Interregnum, as noble families sought to have their plate melted down for cash; they were in a stronger position relative to scriveners by 1660. Clarendon remarks that by the time he was Lord Chancellor, in the early 1660s, the scriveners' 'money business' had been taken over by a group of five to six eminent goldsmiths, whose professional holdings of gold gave customers additional security in their solidity as proto-banks.[10]

There was considerable destitution in England in the last years of Elizabeth's reign. Living standards had declined, the monasteries had been abolished in the 1530s and 1540s, removing their traditional function in helping the poor, and the wars with Spain had brought economic difficulties and unemployment. The Poor Law of 1601 was to provide considerable alleviation of this problem.

Like other European countries, England already had substantial entrepreneurs in the sixteenth century. In textiles, the Winchcombe family of Newbury were for three generations among the country's largest wool cloth manufacturers, England's principal export industry. The first 'Jack of Newbury', who died in 1520, was described by Thomas Fuller, writing around 1660, as 'the most considerable clothier (without fancy or fiction) England ever beheld'.[11] While 'Jack of Newbury' is reported to have provided 100 men for the royal forces at Flodden in 1513, his son John Winchcombe[12] may have been the clothier to which Fuller refers, with '100 looms in his house, each managed by a man and a boy'. This John Winchcombe also provided men for Henry VIII's armies and manufactured over 6,000 cloths per annum in the 1540s, with Stephen Vaughan writing from Holland to the Council in 1544, 'If your honours send hither Winchcombe's kerseys they will, with great gains, make great heaps of money.'[13]

---

10. Edward, Earl of Clarendon, *The Life of Edward Earl of Clarendon*, 3 vols (Oxford: Clarendon Printing House, 1759), vol. 3, p. 597.
11. Thomas Fuller (1608-61) DD. *History of the Worthies of England* (London: J.G.W.L. and W.G., 1662), p. 98.
12. John Winchcombe (1489-1557). MP for Great Bedwyn and Cricklade, 1545-47.
13. Entry for John Winchcombe, of Bucklebury and Thatcham, Berks., in S.T. Bindoff (ed.), *The History of Parliament, 1509-58* (Woodbridge: Boydell & Brewer, 1982) (available online). Kerseys are coarse-ribbed woollen cloths for work clothes. Stephen Vaughan (1502-49). Governor, Merchant Adventurers, Bergen-op-zoom, 1538-45.

Winchcombe invested in land, gained a coat of arms and was close to Edward Seymour[14] and Thomas Gresham. Alas, the scale of his operations was so alarming to the authorities that a 1555 statute during the retrogressive reign of Mary I forbade weavers to have more than one woollen loom in their house, on penalty of 20s a week.[15] While the available technology gave Winchcombe no manufacturing economies of scale, as an exporter he had considerable marketing economies of scale, being able to ship substantial quantities and gaining a reputation with foreign buyers for reliable quality.

John Winchcombe was 'the most considerable clothier England ever beheld'. Painting by the School of Federico Zuccaro.

Thus, England had the beginnings of a commercial economy by 1600, especially in London and large prosperous towns. While the country's exports did not extend far beyond traditional cloth and woollen goods, local specialties existed in other areas. Nevertheless, as in the woollen example quoted above, neither law nor custom produced a free market. The Statute of Artificers 1563, which codified earlier legislation, established the control of trade guilds over most trades, and prevented competition in those trades by those who had not served a seven-year apprenticeship. Employees had to get permission to transfer between employers, and many wages and prices were fixed by the statute, which caused difficulties as inflation continued.

The statute indicates clearly that England in the late sixteenth century was not yet a proto-capitalist economy. It still retained the thought-patterns and restrictions of the Middle Ages, both among the legislators and statesmen and among the merchants who pushed for the statute to be enacted. The statute was finally repealed in 1814 but it had fallen

---

14. Edward Seymour (1500-52). 1st Duke of Somerset from 1547. Lord Protector of the Realm, 1547-49.
15. The Weavers Act 1555 (2 and 3 Philip and Mary c. 11), quoted in Mantoux, *The Industrial Revolution in the Eighteenth Century*, p. 35.

largely into disuse before then – for one thing, it was held not to apply to trades that had not existed in 1563.

England had only a small surplus of investible capital in 1600 but was already deploying it effectively, capitalizing the East India Company in that year. In this respect, therefore England ranked alongside the Netherlands and France, and ahead of Spain and the Holy Roman Empire, where the financial difficulties of the state hampered capital market development.

Occupying a large part of an island, provided Scotland could be kept friendly, England by 1600 had become relatively safe from foreign predators. Domestic unrest was another matter; the country had suffered several such episodes during the sixteenth century and was to suffer a major civil war in the next generation. However, the Civil War when it came was far less devastating to Britain than the Thirty Years' War, fought in the same period, was to the Holy Roman Empire.[16] Here, too, Britain had an advantage over its competitors.

Finally, most other countries in Western Europe had access to substantial coal reserves similar to England's. By 1600 England was beginning to use those coal reserves more intensively than other countries. England's wood resources had already become somewhat scarce and expensive, raising the cost of firewood in urban areas substantially, although for naval needs the shortage was alleviated by supplies from Scandinavia and later the American colonies. Ruth Goodman[17] explains that the principal difficulty was the rapid expansion of London's population, which rose from 75,000 to 250,000 during the sixteenth century. This caused London firewood prices to soar, as the available woodland for 'coppicing' within a day's journey from London became exhausted.

Fortunately, a solution existed, in the 'sea coal' from around Newcastle, which, being close to river and sea routes, could be shipped from Newcastle to London more cheaply than closer coal available only by overland routes. Newcastle coal had been used in London since

---

16. Modern estimates suggest 200,000 killed by war or disease in England, compared with about five million in Germany in the Thirty Years' War (where the population declined by about seven million).

17. Ruth Goodman, *The Domestic Revolution: How the Introduction of Coal into Victorian Homes Changed Everything* (New York: Liveright Publishing, 2020). The subtitle suggests she is discussing Victorian domestic arrangements, but her analysis relates to the period after 1570, and the transition was mostly completed by the late seventeenth century. Her coal shipment figures are on p. 88, in metric tons (one metric ton equals approximately 2,205lbs).

Britain in 1600 and Early Changes, 1600-48   75

the twelfth century by blacksmiths and lime burners (preparers of quicklime for the building trades). Beginning around 1570, high wood prices caused London households to switch from wood-burning to coal-burning for their domestic fuel needs.

Ruth Goodman relates in detail how this change required a host of modifications in living styles, from cooking methods to house design – chimneys were not necessary for wood-burning households but were essential for coal-burning, and had to be retrofitted, an expensive operation. Goodman reports that shipments of coal from Newcastle to London were 15,000 metric tons annually in the mid-sixteenth century, but rose to 27,000 metric tons in 1581-82, 68,000 metric tons in 1591-92, 144,000 metric tons in 1605-6 and 288,000 metric tons in 1637-38. By the years 1660-64, annual shipments of coal from Newcastle to London averaged 181,000 chaldrons, equivalent to 478,000 metric tons.[18]

Naturally, this extensive use by such a large city of 'sea coal' led to further development of the coal mining industry. New coal deposits were found, and ways of extracting coal more efficiently and safely were devised, for example, 'long wall' mining in which the entire coal seam was exposed. Other sources of supply were developed, for example, in Scotland, which provided a higher-quality hotter-burning coal than that from Newcastle. Already by 1660, therefore, Britain's coal industry was far ahead of its competitors. Britain did not have significantly more access to coal than several other countries, but since its coal industry was more developed and sold higher volumes, its coal was cheaper and more readily available for potential industrial uses. This was to prove an inestimable advantage in industrialization.

Overall, the England of 1600 was not especially well positioned to develop an Industrial Revolution. While the London mercantile community was outward-looking and seeking new markets, and the country had developed considerable expertise in ocean voyaging and warfare, the overall business climate remained bound by tradition and guild restrictions, extended as recently as 1563. The governing class was corrupt and oriented towards exploitation of monopolies and special favours rather than entrepreneurship, or open trade in general. The country was relatively poor, with a population considerably smaller than all its competitors except the Netherlands, and its living standards had

---

18. Mitchell (ed.), *British Historical Statistics*, Table IV-1, p. 240, gives the figure in chaldrons, a unit of coal volume in 1660 equivalent to 2.6 Imperial tons of 2,240lbs. For consistency with the previous figures, I have converted to metric tons, which differ from the Imperial ton by only 1.6%.

declined substantially over the previous century. In only one respect was it unique: the move to coal usage in London's homes was not matched elsewhere and would lead the coal industry to develop the necessary scale for industrialization. However, that provided only one small piece of the changes that would be necessary for industrialization to occur.

Early Progress, Britain 1600-48

Economic policy under the first two Stuarts remained corrupt and oriented towards the exploitation of monopolies, without significant understanding of the free market, as already existed in the Netherlands. However, there was a new aggressiveness in development of overseas markets and settlements that was to bear great fruit later. Moreover, several legislative and intellectual developments, aside from the political turmoil of the period, provided significant steps towards an industrial future.

The first of these steps, at the end of Elizabeth's reign, was the Poor Law 1601. As in other European countries, relief of the indigent had before the Reformation been concentrated in monasteries and other Church bodies. After the Reformation settlement had begun to remove the monasteries, Thomas Cromwell's (1485-1540) Poor Law 1536 provided for public works schemes for 'vagabonds' and provisionally an income tax to finance them; it became a dead letter after Cromwell's fall. The rising population and declining living standards of the late sixteenth century made the problem of poverty worse, and several attempts were made to address it until finally in 1601 definitive legislation was passed.[19]

The Poor Law 1601 for the first time compelled local parishes to pay a tax 'rate' based on property value for the support of the poor in the parish, and provided a system of 'overseers', themselves monitored by Justices of the Peace, to distribute the funds collected. The use to which funds were put was left to each parish and, in some cases, money was used to provide food, clothing or shelter, or to establish workfare schemes for the able-bodied poor. The great majority of the money raised was paid in 'outdoor' allowances, either regularly to the 'impotent' poor – the old, mentally ill and disabled – or on a one-off basis to the able-bodied who had lost work or whose work, perhaps in a time of dearth, was unable to support them. The normal allowance for full-time recipients was 6d per week initially, but generally rose to 1s per week after 1660.

---

19. Paul Slack, *The English Poor Law, 1531-1782* (Cambridge: Cambridge University Press, 1990), gives details on the law, its costs and administration.

Even at the latter level, equivalent to about £18 per week in 2020 money, the allowance was below the subsistence level in most years but was a substantial help towards avoiding outright starvation.

The Poor Law system was instituted only gradually, with many parishes reluctant to impose a tax on their residents (or administratively unable to do so). However, by 1660 over 4,000 parishes had the system in place, and by 1696 it effectively fully covered England, although coverage in Wales was not completed until late in the eighteenth century. Scotland instituted a similar system in the 1690s, however, there were administrative difficulties because the 'civil parish' was less well defined than in England. Ireland did not institute such a system until the 1830s, when the English 1834 Poor Law Amendment Act was mirrored by a similar act for Ireland in 1838.

The principal problem with the Poor Law, once it was fully in place, was the tendency for its costs to escalate. Slack gives a Board of Trade estimate of a cost of £400,000 in 1660, equivalent to 0.8% of national income, but this cost increased steadily over the following century, to an average of £2.0 million in 1783-85, or 2% of national income.[20] This reflected both a greater expenditure per head of population, in cash or in terms of wheat purchasing power, and a gradually increasing number of the impoverished covered, perhaps as high as 15% of the population in the 1780s. Expenditure varied greatly according to the quantity of the annual harvest and trade conditions generally; in the difficult, early wartime years after 1793 they took a further leap upwards.

Various attempts were made over the years to reduce the costs of poor relief. These took the form of attempts to deny it to the able-bodied poor, restrictions on the ability of the poor to move between parishes (in the eighteenth century, according to Slack, as much as one fifth of the population in many parishes was 'unsettled' so not entitled to relief) and, in 1723, an attempt to replace this system of 'outdoor relief' with 'workhouses'.

The genius of the Poor Law was its localism and flexibility. First, it placed both the tax obligation and the relief responsibility at a parish level, keeping it close to individual problems. Second, it provided relief mostly in cash, rather than forcing the destitute to move to workhouses and have their lives controlled by unsympathetic overseers. While mobile poor people could fall through the cracks (though there were cases where an established home parish paid relief even to recipients living elsewhere), the system's localism made it as user-friendly as

---

20. Ibid., p. 22.

possible, greatly reducing the risk of destitution for the poor. By so doing, it increased their ability to try new things, take risks and together create a new industrial world.

Liverpool, as prime minister responsible, among other things, for overpopulated and non-industrialized Ireland, would note in 1824 the problem of destitution there without the benefit of a Poor Law:

> You should also recollect that Ireland has no poor-laws. I here contrast the condition of the colonial slave with that of the unemployed peasant, or the broken-down small farmer of Ireland. The former is sure of food and clothing and derives even some advantages from the caprices of his master; but the poor peasant in Ireland, where there is no system of parochial relief, when unemployed, is a vagrant without a home or any chance of relief, save that which he derives from casual charity. ... When the serf is separated from the soil, when he is looked upon as a free being dependant on his own exertions, it is a wise policy to make some provision for his wants, when those exertions are unable to supply them, and in this view I consider that the establishment of the poor-laws in this country were productive of more good than evil. From such a resource, however, the poor of Ireland derive no benefit, as she has no general poor-rates.[21]

Monopolies, Good and Bad

The continued orientation of economic policy towards the exploitation of monopolies had important economic consequences. In Britain as in the rest of Europe, most major new business opportunities arose from monopolies granted by the king for a period of years. Sometimes this made sense – the East India Company and other companies formed to carry out economically perilous long-distance trade had plenty of competition from other countries in 1600, together with perils from the weather, inadequate marine technology and international marauders. There was little danger in 1600 of a new monopoly on trade to the East Indies degenerating into a comfortable well-padded sinecure. As the trade developed, the companies grew bigger and the risks decreased,

---

21. Hansard, *Parliamentary Debates New Series*, Vol. 11, cols 267-68, 8 April 1824.

Britain in 1600 and Early Changes, 1600-48

the danger of corruption and sloth became far greater – Adam Smith was not wrong in his strictures on the East India Company of 1770. However, for a new long-distance trading business struggling against large odds, national monopolies made sense, which is why they were used in all European countries that attempted to enter this business.

Inevitably, in the corrupt courts of Elizabeth I and, more particularly, James VI and I and Charles I, the monopoly privilege was abused to reward royal favourites with monopolies that damaged economic welfare. The practice took off in the last cash-strapped years of Elizabeth I and then became ubiquitous under James, who although keeping the country at peace discovered that the Crown's ordinary revenues were insufficient to support his Court and administration and that parliamentary grants were difficult to obtain and still did not always cover his costs. (His fiscal problem derived from the rise in prices, which had more than doubled since 1500 – many royal revenues and parliamentary grants were expressed in fixed amounts and so did not rise with inflation.)

By the Parliament of 1621, the problem of monopolies had achieved major political salience. It had become the practice to grant patents in order to farm out certain judicial functions previously performed by state officials, such as the licensing of inns and alehouses – patentees would pay a fee to the Crown and make the money back by charging for licences. Patents of monopoly were granted (again, for a fee to the Crown) providing the sole right to use a particular form or method of trade or industry – they often became intertwined with particular 'projects' at a time when the economy was diversifying. Parliament revived the ancient power of impeachment, pursuing Sir Giles Mompesson and Lord Chancellor Bacon, who was blamed for organizing the sale of patents and monopolies.

Mompesson was a typical, if extreme, example of an early Stuart entrepreneur; his career shows the opportunities that such entrepreneurs thought worth exploiting. He was born into a family of long-established but modest Wiltshire gentry, married a well-connected wife and entered Parliament in 1614 as MP for Great Bedwyn. He then enjoyed a stroke of good fortune when the half-brother of his wife's sister's husband George Villiers (1592-1628) was taken up as 'favourite' by James VI and I and rapidly promoted to become first Duke of Buckingham. With Buckingham as his ally, and Bacon as Attorney General and later Lord Chancellor providing legal coverage, Mompesson had access to numerous money-making ventures, that could be exploited by a man with high energy and little scruple.

His first scheme in 1616 was to obtain a patent for the licensing of inns (where travellers stayed overnight) – in return for taking on this duty he was paid £100 per annum and allowed to keep 20% of the licence fees. His energy was such that he not only sold 1,200 licences to innkeepers for £5 and £10 each but prosecuted 4,000 other innkeepers who refused to pay. He even extended the scheme illegally to taverns (with no overnight lodging), in one case begging a room for the night and then fining the tavern owner next morning since he had acted as an innkeeper.

As well as licensing inns, Mompesson obtained a commission to sell timber valued at up to £25,000 from the Crown Estates, thereby raising £7,000. Then he became surveyor of the New River Company, the recently completed 20-mile aqueduct from Islington to the Lea River, at a salary of £200 per annum, and obtained a monopoly patent for the manufacture of gold and silver thread, which enabled him to harass the London goldsmiths who were his competitors. Finally, he obtained a licence to reclaim all 'lost' Crown lands, keeping those worth less than £200 per annum – the large London charities were his targets here.

After impeachment by Parliament in 1621, Mompesson fled into exile, escaping from the parliamentary sergeant-at-arms, and was fined £10,000 *in absentia*. He returned to England finally in 1628 and engaged in a coal mining venture in the Forest of Dean, which was overthrown by rioters in 1631. He was a Royalist during the Civil War, compounded to retain his estates for only £561 in 1649, and died sometime between 1651 and 1663.[22]

Mompesson's career was typical of his time, though his over-ambition, excess of energy and alienation of important interests like the London goldsmiths led to his impeachment.

Another entrepreneur typical in his manipulation of the patent system and royal favours, but atypical in that he was responsible for a significant industrial advance, was Sir Robert Mansell.[23] Mansell, of

---

22. Sir Giles Mompesson (1583-1651/63). Kt 1616, degraded 1621. MP for Great Bedwyn, 1614-21. His will was written in 1651 but not proved until 1663; he died between those dates. Details in A. Thrush and J.P. Ferris, *The History of Parliament: The House of Commons, 1604-29* (Cambridge: Cambridge University Press, 2010), available at: https://www.historyofparliamentonline.org/volume/1604-1629/member/mompesson-giles-1584-1651 (accessed 19 September 2022).

23. Sir Robert Mansell (c.1570-1652). Kt 1596. MP for King's Lynn, 1601, Carmathenshire, 1604-14, Glamorgan, 1624-25 and 1628, and Lostwithiel,

Britain in 1600 and Early Changes, 1600-48

Welsh origin, began his career as a naval officer, rising to Vice Admiral of England. Then, in 1615, he obtained a monopoly for the manufacture of glass, for which he promised the royal finances an annuity of £3,000 per annum. Mansell bought a glass works at Vauxhall in London and over the next few years set up several others in different places, none very successful, until in 1617, having set up a glass works at Newcastle, he came up with a process whereby glass could be made in a coal-fired furnace.

Mansell expanded production rapidly, until by 1624, output from his coal-fired Newcastle works was 6,000-8,000 tons per annum. Like Mompesson, Mansell was attacked for his monopoly in the 1621 Parliament. However, he managed to preserve it until 1642, when it was finally cancelled by the Long Parliament. Regrettably, from his point of view, by 1621 he had spent £28,000 in setting up his glass works and that, together with the fees payable to the Crown and the legal fees and bribes needed to preserve his monopoly patent (which with coal-firing, involved some reward for genuine innovation), meant the overall enterprise was only marginally profitable, although glassware from the Mansell monopoly may still be found today.

Three years after Mompesson's impeachment, Parliament enacted the Statute of Monopolies 1624. This made all past patents and monopolies null and void. It provided for limited-term future monopolies for:

> any letters patents and grants of privilege, for the term of fourteen years and under, hereafter to be made, of the sole working or making of any manner of new manufactures within this realm to the true and first inventor and inventors of such manufactures, which others at the time of making such letters patents and grants shall not use, so as also they be not contrary to the law nor mischievous to the state by raising prices of commodities at home, or hurt of trade, or generally inconvenient: the same fourteen years to be accounted from the date of the first letters patents or grants of such privilege hereafter to be made, but that the same shall be of such force as they should be if this Act had never been made, and of none other. (s. 6)

By this wording Parliament did not create the world's first working patent system – the Venetian Patent Statute of 1474 had contained its

---

1626. Captain RN, Cadiz expedition, 1596, Vice-Admiral of the Narrow Seas, 1603. Treasurer of the Navy, 1604-18. Glass monopoly, 1615-42.

main elements – but it focussed British economic activity on technological innovation rather than on arbitrarily assigned royal monopolies. The prohibition against royal monopolies was evaded by Charles I, who defended his monopoly grants in the conciliar courts which he controlled, but after the Restoration the patent system as we know it came into being. In the reign of Queen Anne,[24] the law officers of the Crown established as a condition of grant that: 'the patentee must by an instrument in writing describe and ascertain the nature of the invention and the manner in which it is to be performed' – in other words, provide a specification of the invention. Puckle's 'machine' gun[25] in 1718 was the first invention to provide such a specification.

Dudd Dudley (1600-83), whose career would prove important to Britain's industrial future, was another user of patents, both before and after 1624. He was the illegitimate son of Edward Sutton, fifth Baron Dudley, a wealthy but spendthrift and over-indebted nobleman. Since the baron was devoted to Dudley's mother Elizabeth Tomlinson, by whom he had eleven children, and was still in funds during Dudley's youth, Dudley was educated at Balliol College, Oxford and then sent to manage his father's iron works at Pensnett Chase, near Dudley (at that time fuelled by charcoal, the universal technology, but becoming increasingly in short supply in several districts). Dudley experimented and began fuelling the iron works' smelting process with the coal derivative coke. Although this process was never entirely successful (the local coal contained impurities), Lord Dudley obtained a monopoly for it in 1620.[26]

Dudley expanded operations to the nearby Cradley works, producing only three tons a week of iron but passing quality tests at the Tower of London. Alas, the Cradley works was destroyed by a flood in May 1623, after which Lord Dudley ran out of money. Dudd Dudley persisted, obtaining a further patent in 1638 for smelting metals with coal, but was unable to exploit it.[27] Dudley served as an army officer in the Bishops' War of 1639 and became a Royalist colonel in the Civil War, being

---

24. Anne (1665-1714). Queen of Great Britain, 1702-14.
25. This was supposed to fire round bullets at Christians and square ones at Turks but there is no evidence that the gun was ever used in battle.
26. Grace's Guide to British Industrial History says 22 February 1620.
27. Dudley's experiments in coal-based smelting are set out in P.W. King, 'Dud Dudley's Contribution to Metallurgy', *Historical Metallurgy*, Vol. 36, no. 1 (2002).

Britain in 1600 and Early Changes, 1600-48

taken prisoner at the Siege of Worcester in 1646 and again (by Andrew Yarranton, whom we will meet again in Chapter 4) in 1648.

Dudley's coke-based pig iron production was the first in England. It failed for three reasons: the coal was somewhat unsuitable; the shaky finances of early seventeenth century aristocrats (whose borrowing costs and terms were extortionate); and the fact that wood for charcoal was not yet as scarce and expensive as it later became, so the economics were marginal – he was undercut in price by fierce charcoal-based competition.

The adverse economic effects of royal monopolies were illustrated by the New Soap patent of 1632. Under this, Charles I granted a fourteen-year monopoly to the Society of Soapmakers of Westminister, prohibiting any other soap manufacture, in return for a payment of £4 per ton of soap sold through the patent. Various trials were arranged, and certificates were issued that the New Soap 'washyth whiter'. By a 1636 decree of the Star Chamber, soap manufacture was prohibited except by the New Soap proprietors in Westminster, or in Bristol, which was limited to 600 tons per annum, while soap pans of other manufacturers were destroyed. The result was considerable destruction of wealth, and a greatly reduced consumption of the now expensive and scarce soap, doubtless worsening further the mood of a labouring class oppressed by 150 years of declining wages. The New Soap patent contributed to reformers' calls that only genuine innovations should be patentable.

As Sir Edward Coke (1552-1634)[28] wrote in *Institutes of the Lawes of England*: To be patented,

> new manufacture must have seven properties. First, it must be for twenty-one years or under. Secondly, it must be granted to the first and true inventor. Thirdly, it must be of such manufactures, which any other at the making of such letters patent did not use. ... Fourthly, the privilege must not be contrary to law. ... Fifthly, nor mischievous to the state, by raising the prices of commodities at home. In every such new manufacture that deserves a privilege, there must be *urgens necessitas et evidens utilitas*. Sixthly, nor to the hurt of trade. ... Seventhly, nor generally inconvenient.

---

28. Coke, Sir Edward, *Institutes of the Lawes of England*, 4 vols (Clarke, 18th edn, 1797 [1628-44]), Part Three, ch. 85, 'Against Monopolists', p.184.

84   *Forging Modernity*

Coke's doctrine has remained the core of patent law to this day; it was key to industrial innovation.

Rule of Law

In the early seventeenth century a succession of great lawyers Coke,[29] John Selden[30] and Sir Matthew Hale[31] played a vital role for industrialization in establishing the rule of law on a rigorous basis. They delved back into Saxon and mediaeval history, finding 'liberties' in that period that had often only doubtfully existed and codified them. As all three inclined to Parliament's side in the disputes with the Crown, their objective was to cement more tightly the subjection of the king to existing laws, which had been pointed out by Fortescue, but frequently ignored by Henry VIII and others. In reality, James VI and I was a legalistic pedant while Charles I was generally quite scrupulous (though some of his advisors, notably Strafford,[32] skirted the edge of the constitutionally permissible).

Coke and Selden's work was legitimized by the Civil War and formed a rock of the Restoration settlement that followed it. Although Hale served both the Protectorate and the post-Restoration governments in senior judicial roles, his greatest effect came through his writings, which codified common law and are cited today in both Britain and the United States. The work of all three men was to have great long-term importance in helping men of humble backgrounds to know the precise law and trust the courts, and thereby prevent rip-offs by the well connected.

---

29. Edward Coke (1552-1634). Kt 1603. MP for Aldeburgh, 1589, Norfolk, 1593, Liskeard, 1621, Coventry, 1624, Norfolk, 1625-26, Buckinghamshire, 1628. Solicitor General, 1592-94, Attorney General, 1594-1606, Chief Justice of Common Pleas, 1606-13, Chief Justice of King's Bench, 1613-16.
30. John Selden (1584-1654). MP for Lancaster, 1624, Great Bedwyn, 1626, Ludgershall, 1628, and Oxford University, 1640. Legal scholar, political philosopher and author.
31. Matthew Hale (1609-76) Kt 1660. MP for Gloucestershire, 1654, and Oxford University, 1659. Justice of the Common Pleas, 1653-59, Chief Baron of the Exchequer, 1660-71, Lord Chief Justice, 1671-76. Author of *The History and Analysis of the Common Law of England* (1713).
32. Thomas Wentworth (1593-1641). 1st Viscount Wentworth from 1629, 1st Earl of Strafford from 1640. MP for Yorkshire, 1614, 1621, 1625 and 1628, and Pontefract, 1624. Lord Deputy of Ireland, 1633-40, Lord Lieutenant of Ireland, 1640-41.

Scientific Method

The most important scientific advance of the early seventeenth century was made, not by a professional scientist but by a lawyer. This was the Scientific Method, codified by **Francis Bacon**. Most of the Industrial Revolution's technological advances were made by practical men, without great use of the latest scientific theories, even those as far-ranging as Isaac Newton's. Their advances, and those of the scientists who after 1660 were pushing forward the boundaries of knowledge at an increasing pace, all depended on Bacon's fundamental intellectual paradigm: the Scientific Method.

Francis Bacon, Viscount St. Alban. He propounded the Scientific Method and aided rapid American colonization. Painted by John Vanderbank.

Bacon propounded the Scientific Method in his 1620 treatise, *Novum Organum Scientiarum* ('New Instrument of Science'), intended to form part of a larger work covering the whole of human knowledge. Previous scientists, whether in the ancient world or in China, had relied upon theorising about the universe to make intellectual advances. Bacon was the first to propose forming a hypothesis based on existing empirical knowledge about a subject, undertaking a series of experiments to test the hypothesis and refining the hypothesis based on those experiments' results.

Bacon's method of induction involved building a theory of general axioms based on particular cases observed by the senses and then attempting to test that theory through further experimentation. Each set of axioms could then be built upon to create more general axioms, building the scientific edifice on a solid foundation of experimental observation. This iterative combination of intellectual reasoning and experimentation was immensely powerful in accelerating the pace of scientific advance from Bacon's time onwards.

Bacon was also the inspiration for the foundation in 1662 of Britain's Royal Society, which especially in its early years acted as a forcing house for the Scientific Method as well as a clearing house for scientific and technological advances from all over Europe. Through Bacon's methodology, the broader push towards practical experimentation and away from received authority that it represented, and the additional resources that were devoted to science from his time onwards, scientific advance quickened markedly from the middle seventeenth century, providing an increasing flow of new knowledge through which new technologies could be created.

The early seventeenth century was more scientifically fertile in other respects. In 1614 the Scottish mathematician John Napier (1550-1617) published *Mirifici Logarithmorum Canonis Descriptio* which introduced the world to logarithms, a mathematical advance which even as recently as my childhood, just before pocket calculators, was essential for complex calculations. Without Napier's advance, the engineering calculations underlying the Industrial Revolution would have been impossible. Napier published in Latin, making his studies accessible all over Europe, but made his tables less immediately useful by calculating 'natural logarithms' to base e.[33] The quickest adoption of Napier's logarithms was in Britain, where Henry Briggs (1561-1630) published tables of base-ten logarithms in 1617 and 1624 that allowed them to be used easily for ordinary calculations.

In 1628, William Harvey (1578-1657), a leading physician who later protected the young Charles II at the Battle of Edgehill, published his *Exercitatio Anatomica de Motu Cordis et Sanguinis in Animalibus*, describing the movement of the human heart and the circulation of the blood. Knowing that the work was important, he arranged to have it published at Frankfurt, where the annual book fair would ensure its wide circulation. By this work, Harvey made the first substantial advance in medical knowledge since Galen (*c.* 133-200). Harvey's discovery was the beginning of medical advances that immeasurably lengthened and improved peoples' lives in the years after the Industrial Revolution.

Agriculture and Fen Drainage

The revolution in agriculture in Britain gathered speed in the first half of the seventeenth century. The benefit of this to industrialization takes two forms. First, by eliminating customary feudal tenure, land becomes an asset that can be bought, sold and readily mortgaged, with the potential to finance industrialization. Second, it is necessary to improve

---

33. The base of natural logarithms, $e = 2.71828$, defined rigorously half a century later by the Swiss mathematician Jacob Bernoulli (1654-1705).

Britain in 1600 and Early Changes, 1600-48

agricultural productivity to spur population growth and a healthier workforce and thus, when the Industrial Revolution arrives, facilitate factory urbanization, employing large numbers of people away from the land.

Both these processes took a leap forward in the early seventeenth century, primarily through the rapid progress of the enclosure movement. While formal parliamentary enclosure, using Acts of Parliament to dispossess traditional common-land rights, did not occur much before the late eighteenth century, less formal means of enclosure, by which traditional rights were bought out, peaked during the seventeenth century, mostly during the first half.

Approximately 24% of England's arable land is estimated to have been enclosed in the seventeenth century, compared to only 2% in the sixteenth, 13% in the eighteenth and 11% in the nineteenth.[34] Two economic factors propelled the acceleration in enclosures after 1600: inflation and rapid population increase. Inflation led to enclosures because traditional lease systems provided for a peppercorn rent, often set centuries earlier, paid annually by the tenant, with a lump-sum paid upfront. As prices rose the annual rent became uneconomic for the landlord, who consequently sought shorter leases at market rents, that could be renewed at higher levels if inflation had devalued the rent payments. Population increases resulted in the subdivision of small landholdings and the increase in landless labourers; both made it attractive for smallholders to be bought out by their landlords, while landless labourers either worked for larger landholders or migrated into towns to find work.

Enclosure did not itself increase the productivity of arable land or labour but led to the quicker adoption of new farming techniques when they came along, mostly after 1650. The best available data suggests that land productivity increased by 0.46% per annum between 1550 and 1650, as more labour was available per acre, while labour productivity increased by only 0.1-0.2% annually during that period. Labour productivity growth then accelerated to 0.4% per annum after 1670, as population plateaued, while land productivity increased by only 0.18% per annum in the second half of the seventeenth century.[35] Enclosure was inevitably unpopular (for example, there was a substantial revolt against

---

34. Mark Overton, *Agricultural Revolution in England: The Transformation of the Agrarian Economy, 1500-1850* (Cambridge: Cambridge University Press, 1996), p. 148.

35. Ibid., Table 3.10, p. 85.

the local gentry at Newton, Northamptonshire in 1607) but it led to more productive agriculture and a workforce available for industrialization.

During this period there was an additional attempt to add to the stock of farming land by draining the Fens, a low-lying area of marsh and wetlands in Cambridgeshire, Norfolk and Lincolnshire similar to much of the Netherlands and totalling 1,500 square miles. Francis Russell, fourth Earl of Bedford (1587-1641), spent £100,000 of his own money in the 1630s draining the Great Level of the Cambridgeshire Fens, renamed the Bedford Level in his honour, which caused substantial rioting by those fishermen and wildfowlers who earned their living in the area. Wind pumps were used to keep the land drained. Even though royal and other investor monies were then brought in, the inevitable Civil War disruption meant that work was only finished in 1653, twelve years after Bedford's death. Unfortunately, the peat underlying most of the surface shrank as it dried and was exposed to air, making the land sink, so by the end of the century most of the farmland produced by Bedford's scheme was again under water. Successful fen drainage was not finally possible until steam pumps were brought in during the 1820s.

The Birth of the Colonies

Of all economic developments in the early seventeenth century, the most notable was an explosion in the size and scope of British overseas trade and possessions. The profits from this activity mostly came later, but the investment of resources and people devoted to them during this half century was truly remarkable, far ahead of Britain's competitors.

The East India Company's first voyage, headed by James Lancaster (1554-1618), set out in 1601 and captured a 1,200-ton Portuguese carrack, which provided sufficient money to set up trading posts at Bantam on Java and the Spice Islands (today, the Moluccas). It returned to England in 1603, where Lancaster was knighted by James VI and I. The voyage was also notable for Lancaster's successful experimental use of lemon juice as a treatment for scurvy, a remedy that the Admiralty was finally to make general in 1795.

The EIC continued to send vessels over the following decades, some of which were lost, with its initial business focusing on spices from Bantam. In 1608 an EIC ship successfully called at Surat, in India's Gujarat province, and four years later Sir Thomas Roe on behalf of James VI and I signed a trade treaty with the Mughal Emperor Jahangir, under which the EIC established trading posts at Masulipatnam on the Bay of Bengal and at Surat.

Britain in 1600 and Early Changes, 1600-48

In Indonesia, the EIC remained second to the Dutch VOC (the Dutch massacre of English and Japanese traders at Amboyna in 1623 did not help matters), although its Bantam trading post remained open until 1689. The Portuguese, who had been established in the East Indies a century earlier, gradually lost their position, with the Dutch taking Malacca from Portugal in 1641. The EIC attempted to expand into China and Japan over the following decades, but without great success.

The EIC's Indian business prospered. The Mughal rulers were happy to allow their people to export Indian textiles in exchange for silver (English woollens never sold well in Indian climates). The EIC's available capital expanded steadily, reaching £3 million by the 1630s. However, domestic English troubles thereafter affected the EIC; Charles I, desperate for money, allowed its monopoly to lapse, and Cromwell, opposed in principle to monopolies, refused to reinstate it. Even though by 1647 the EIC had 24 'factories' and 90 Western employees in India, in 1657 the entire company was valued at just £14,000.[36] In Asia by 1650, Britain had established a substantial foothold in terms of trade, albeit less so in physical presence, but had yet to receive major net economic benefits from exploiting it.

In North America and the Caribbean, more substantial progress had been made. There was still little money coming in from British settlements, but the country's North American and Caribbean foothold was very substantial. Jamestown, Virginia, had been colonized in 1607, with the addition of the first African slaves in 1619. Plymouth, Massachusetts, had been colonized in 1620. More significantly, a very well-backed settlement had been established at Boston in 1630, including the first American college, Harvard, founded in 1636.

By 1650, the settler population of the future United States has been estimated at 50,368, including about 400 African-Americans in Virginia, of which 18,408 were in Massachusetts (Plymouth and the future states of New Hampshire and Vermont), 18,731 were in Virginia, 4,504 in the Catholic-founded colony of Maryland, 4,924 in the separatist Connecticut and Rhode Island, 4,116 in the Dutch colony of New Amsterdam and 185 in the Swedish colony in Delaware.[37] There was especially rapid expansion of the North American settler population

---

36. David Veevers, 'Before Empire', *History Today*, Vol. 70, no. 10 (2020).

37. US Census Bureau, *Historical Statistics of the United States, Colonial Times to 1970*, 'Chapter Z: Colonial and pre-Federal Statistics, Series Z 1-19', p. 1168, available at: https://www.census.gov/library/publications/1975/compendia/hist_stats_colonial-1970.html (accessed 4 October 2020).

in the 1640s, when disgruntled Cavaliers fled from the authoritarian Puritan regime being established at home. The colonies' main export was tobacco from Virginia, whose exports had exceeded one million pounds' weight in each of the years 1637-1640 (figures are not available between 1640 and the Restoration) – with under 400 slaves imported there before 1650, the principal labour force was by indentured servitude of British convicts and the impoverished.

In the West Indies, Bermuda was colonized from 1612 and Barbados from 1627, which began to export sugar in the 1640s after experimenting with tobacco, indigo and other crops. Again, the primary workforce was British and Irish indentured servants. However, a British workforce did not do well in the Caribbean climate, and the young Reverend George Downing[38] claimed in 1645 that over 1,000 African slaves had been brought that year to Barbados.[39] With the Bahamas colonized in the 1640s, the total population of the British-controlled West Indies was over 40,000 by 1650, with 37,000 British-born and 6,000 African-born slaves in Barbados alone.[40]

Although the revenues from North America and the Caribbean were not great before 1650 (partly because of the political trouble at home), the level of investment and manpower there was already very substantial indeed. The growth in population of Britain's transatlantic colonies to almost 100,000 by 1650 gave them a potential importance far greater than British investment in India to that time, and greater than the Dutch had achieved despite their huge investment in their East and West India Companies. Britain's transatlantic population also dwarfed that of France, whose transatlantic population in 1650, from a much larger domestic base, was only around 2,000 in Canada and 5,000 in the Caribbean, mostly on Martinique.

Britain in the early seventeenth century had discovered the formula for developing large and profitable overseas colonies. This was not by accident; Bacon, while Lord Chancellor (1617-21), had told James VI and I that substantial forced emigration of British indentured servants

---

38. George Downing (1623-84). 1st Bart from 1663. MP for Edinburgh, 1654, Carlisle, 1656 and 1659, and Morpeth, 1660-81. Scoutmaster-General, 1649-57. Resident, Envoy and Ambassador to Holland, 1658-60, 1661-65, 1670-72. Commissioner for Trade, 1660-72, Secretary to the Treasury, 1667-71, Commissioner for Customs, 1671-84.

39. Hugh Thomas, *The Slave Trade*, p. 196.

40. Britannica, *Barbados* (accessed 4 October 2020).

Britain in 1600 and Early Changes, 1600-48 91

brought double benefits: 'the avoidance of people here, and in making use of them there'.[41] This policy of massive population transfer appears to have caused real wages in Britain to end their century-long decline around 1630, marking an important step in Britain's transformation into a high-wage economy in relation to its competitors. Overall transatlantic population transfer intensified during the disturbed years of the 1640s, but a higher proportion of those leaving England were the dispossessed rather than the indigent.

Slave workforces were self-limiting, because the slaves never developed capital of their own, with which they could start businesses. Relying on voluntary emigration limited growth, because early settlement was hard, and even with Britain's religious differences there were not that many people who wished to emigrate to a near-wilderness. Sending domestic minor malefactors of both sexes as indentured servants built up the transatlantic population of British stock, who, furthermore, could accumulate capital and start businesses once their indentures ran out. In the long run, competition from slave labour and the inhospitable climate limited the potential of using indentured servants to encourage growth in the West Indies colonies, but indentured servants provided spectacular growth potential in North America, enabling British settlements there to outrun all competitors.

The Oxfordshire School of Economic Thought

Finally, the period immediately before the Civil War saw the first buds of a school of thought that was to produce two flowerings later in the century: the Tory party; and what I have called the Oxfordshire School of Economic Thought. To see those buds, we must visit the idyllic Oxfordshire village of Great Tew, in the 1630s, before the disputes between King Charles I and his Parliaments descended into Civil War. In that decade, the manor house at Great Tew was occupied by **Lucius Cary, second Viscount Falkland**,[42] a wealthy aristocrat who inherited large Oxfordshire estates on the death of his father in 1633.

Falkland was a remarkable man; **Edward Hyde, first Earl of Clarendon**, wrote later that: 'all mankind could not but admire and

---

41. Quoted in Thomas, *The Slave Trade*, p. 177.
42. Lucius Cary (1610-43). 2nd Viscount Falkland (Scotland) from 1633. MP for Newport (Isle of Wight) 1640-42. Secretary of State, 1642-43, Lord Privy Seal, 1643. Killed at First Battle of Newbury, 1643.

Lucius Cary, 2nd Viscount Falkland was the inspiration for the Tories and the Oxfordshire School. Painted by Cornelis Janssens van Ceulen.

love him'.[43] At Great Tew, he assembled a circle of theological and political thinkers which Hyde, one of their number, described as 'a college situate in a purer air'.[44] Apart from Falkland and Hyde, the group included John Selden, Edward Sheldon (who became Archbishop of Canterbury after the Restoration), the poets Abraham Cowley, Sir John Suckling and Thomas Carew and Edmund Waller, a politically moderate poet and politician who served in Parliament intermittently for 60 years from 1625 to 1685.

The Great Tew circle, following the doctrines of Richard Hooker (1554-1600) propounded a rationalist approach to religion and opposed the somewhat intolerant and corrupt government of Charles I, although they remained Royalist. They were opposed to the absolutist rule of Charles I and Strafford and to the narrow quasi-Catholic Anglicanism of Archbishop William Laud[45] but remained strongly committed both to the Church of England and to the king as leader of the country. They differed from time to time on religion and other matters, but consciously took the view of Cicero and Erasmus that such differences should not mar an underlying friendship and might lead to truth.

Economics was peripheral to the Great Tew group (although their limited economic ideas were to have lasting influence, as shown later), but they strongly opposed the royal monopolies that hampered the economy under the early Stuarts and supported freedom of domestic

---

43. Sir James A.R. Marriott, *The Life and Times of Lucius Cary, Viscount Falkland* (London: Methuen, 1907), p. 75.
44. Ibid., p. 81.
45. William Laud (1573-1645). Dean of Gloucester, 1616-21, Bishop of St David's, 1621-26, Bishop of Bath and Wells, 1626-28, Bishop of London, 1628-33, Archbishop of Canterbury, 1633-45. First Lord of the Treasury, 1635-36.

trade. The shenanigans of Mompesson and the New Soap proprietors were anathema to them. Since Great Tew's thinkers objected to the state-imposed restrictions of the Tudor and early Stuart monarchy, they had an early belief in the value of freeing up trade, at least domestically, and removing restrictions on property transfer. Clarendon would develop these ideas during his time as Lord Chancellor between 1660 and 1667.

When crisis came in 1640, Falkland (whose viscountcy was Scottish, without a seat in the Lords) and Edward Hyde led an important moderate group in the Long Parliament's House of Commons. They began by supporting major reforms but ended up opposing John Pym's Grand Remonstrance of November 1641. (The Grand Remonstrance passed by only eleven votes and, by destroying the central principles of Charles' government, made rapprochement with the Crown impossible. According to Clarendon's later *History of the Rebellion*, Oliver Cromwell[46] had planned to emigrate to New England if it failed – there's an interesting alternate history novel in that thought!)

Falkland and Hyde then joined Charles' administration, Falkland as Secretary of State. When the nation descended into civil war, he fought for the king at the Battle of Edgehill but became discouraged by the Royalist lack of success and the worsening relations between the two sides. Consequently, before the Battle of Newbury in September 1643, Falkland told his friends he 'foresaw much misery to his own country and did believe he should be out of it ere night'. He was killed in that day's battle. His influence lived on, both as a romantic example of the perfect Cavalier gentleman and as an intellectual mentor to Hyde, who although two years older was from a less rich and elevated background, so saw Falkland as his mentor as well as friend.

As a romantic hero, Falkland was much admired by the Victorians; Sir John Marriott in his 1907 biography described him as 'combining in no ordinary degree the intellectual luxuriance of the Greek and the moral austerity of the Puritan'.[47] His principal importance to later generations was the intellectual impetus which he and the Great Tew circle gave to his friend Hyde, who, as Lord Chancellor Clarendon, implemented after 1660 policies in economics and other areas very different to those of the 1630s.

* * *

---

46. Oliver Cromwell (1599-1658). MP for Huntingdon, 1628-29, and Cambridge, 1640-49. Colonel, 1643, Lt General, 1645. Lord Protector, 1653-58.
47. Marriott, *op. cit.* p. 1.

With its depressed living standards for the labouring classes, economically illiterate government and worsening political and religious strife, Britain in the first half of the seventeenth century did not look destined for a glorious future. Entrepreneurial investments that were undertaken, such as those of Mompesson and Bedford, were either scams or aristocratic boondoggles that ultimately failed. Nevertheless, in its intellectual activity both scientific and political-economic, its astonishingly rapid colonial development, its growing coal industry and even some aspects of its policy, Britain had hidden underlying advantages that would emerge after 1649.

4

The Restoration Renaissance, 1649-88

The Interregnum

As discussed above, the early Stuart regime was hostile to both free markets and innovation. Much economic activity took the form of royal monopolies, obtained through political manipulation at Court. Since the political class was relatively closed and contained few business-oriented people, economic advances were few. Below the elite level, economic activity was constrained by laws designed to protect vested interests and prevent 'creative destruction'. The result was an economy that was largely static, with population increases pressing against available resources, and average working-class incomes declining. This had already begun to change somewhat in the 1630s period of 'personal rule' with real wages ending their decline around 1630.

After the king's defeat in 1646 and still more after his execution in 1649, different groups became involved in government and the political system opened up. The Presbyterians who formed the parliamentary party were socio-economically similar to the parliamentary majority that had drafted the 1624 Statute of Monopolies; they included the wealthy merchants and service providers of the City of London as well as country gentry who had previously been excluded from the tight circle at the Court. They were, generally, commercially minded, committed to the rights of private property and, being involved in trade either locally or through London, relatively open to free-market-oriented reforms. The more conservative of this group were excluded from government by 'Pride's Purge' of the Rump Parliament in 1648, which by excluding Royalists and many moderates tilted control towards the radicals.

The radicals in the Rump Parliament and the 'Council of State' (dominated by the New Model Army) that controlled it were mostly from a lower social class than the Presbyterians. Apart from their extremism in religious matters, many were democratically oriented 'Levellers' seeking an overthrow of traditional society and its replacement with a 'Godly' quasi-democracy. The Levellers were not especially commercial and were less respectful of property rights than the Presbyterians, with proto-socialist ideas of common ownership widespread. Both this group and to a lesser extent the Presbyterians were somewhat hostile to scientific enquiry, believing it to be contrary to Scriptural doctrine.

Finally, there was Cromwell himself. Already, in 1649, through his control of the Army, he was the most important individual in government; after 1653 he took overall control. Although he was religiously in sympathy with the radicals and opposed to the conservative Presbyterians, he was a staunch upholder of property rights (except those of Royalists and Catholics) and socially traditionalist.

The new forces running Britain after 1649 produced new policies. Monopolies were no longer favoured and competition was welcomed both domestically and internationally. While colonial development was already strong before 1649, there was a new aggression to Britain's colonial and trade policy which would bear great fruits. Entrepreneurship was no longer left to those of noble birth and connections at court; instead, the fields of innovation were increasingly open to those with ordinary backgrounds. The new openness reflected that of the contemporary Netherlands, a country which greatly influenced the leaders of Interregnum Britain.

The most important innovation which the 1649-53 Commonwealth took from the Netherlands was secure property rights. Fortescue, writing in 1470, had already pointed out that the English monarchy differed from the French one in being subject to laws, but the Tudors and the early Stuarts had demonstrated repeatedly that the monarchy was still sufficiently arbitrary to infringe property rights, by granting monopolies to favourites, for example. The rulers of the Commonwealth saw that the Netherlands' prosperity had been gained by its openness to trade and security of property rights and sought to establish similar openness and security in England.

Property rights were not initially sacrosanct for religious minorities, as Cromwell was to demonstrate in Ireland, but in England Cromwell and then Clarendon, in designing the Restoration settlement, established them as a primary freedom. For example, William Penn, from a

The Restoration Renaissance, 1649-88

Commonwealth background (and the founder of Pennsylvania) wrote in 1675, fourteen years before John Locke's *Two Treatises of Government* (1689):

> The First of these Three Fundamentals is Property, that is, Right and Title to your own Lives, Liberties and Estates: In this, every Man is a Sort of Little Soveraign to himself: No Man has Power over his Person, to Imprison or hurt it, or over his Estate to Invade or Usurp it: Only your own Transgression of the Laws, (and those of your own making too) lays you open to Loss; which is but the Punishment due to your Offences, and this but in Proportion to the Fault committed. So that the Power of England is a Legal Power, which truly merits the Name of Government. That which is not Legal, is a Tyranny, and not properly a Government. Now the Law is Umpire between King, Lords and Commons, and the Right and Property is One in Kind through all Degrees and Qualities in the Kingdom: Mark that.[1]

A second innovation that the Interregnum Parliaments took from the Netherlands was a more comprehensive tax system. The early Stuarts had suffered from a chronic lack of revenue, with Parliament granting them only 'customary' revenues and feudal fees that had fallen far behind inflation. In the 1630s, Charles I had resorted to extra-parliamentary sources of income, notably the notorious 'Ship Money' to boost revenues. Some of these expedients had worked; customs revenues alone were £500,000 per annum in 1641 because of the growth of trade and a new tariff schedule. Overall, royal revenue had increased to about £900,000 per annum in 1640 from £400,000 in 1600. That was a considerable success, although less than it appears because of continued inflation; it was around half the revenues per capita of the Netherlands.

The Parliamentarians during the Civil War had full powers of taxation in the areas they controlled, and no scruples about using them. On top of customs duties, they imposed excise duties on domestic consumption, thereby taxing the poor as well as the comfortably off. A second source of revenue was a primitive land tax, effectively an

---

1. William Penn, *England's Present Interest Discovered, with Honour to the Prince, and Safety to the People*, pamphlet, 1675. William Penn (1644-1718). Son of Admiral Sir William Penn (1621-70), the conqueror of Jamaica in 1655. Colonial proprietor of Pennsylvania from 1681.

income tax on agricultural income; this would become the central basis of revenue collection in the centuries ahead. Finally, after 1646, the Parliamentarians imposed fines and distraints on royal and Royalist property; this produced considerable additional one-off revenues. Overall, revenues from 1642 to 1660 totalled £83 million, an average of £4.37 million per annum, much of this being one-off seizures. By 1658-60, the Interregnum regime had also accumulated considerable debts, so when its administrative capability fell apart after Cromwell's death, a partial default on debts was inevitable.

The central economic legislation of the Commonwealth was the Navigation Act 1651, modified versions of which were to remain in force until 1849. Its principles reflected the prevailing mercantilism, the masterwork of which had been propagated by Thomas Mun[2] in the 1620s and privately circulated (although not published until 1664). Mun, the son of a substantial mercer, made his career in the City of London, ending up as a director of the East India Company. In his mercantilist classic, *England's Treasure by Forraign Trade*, he argued that England should run a trade surplus and thereby build up 'treasure'.

Looked at in the light of the economic conditions prevailing when he wrote it, Mun's masterpiece was prescient. Early modern states like James VI and I's Britain faced a permanent shortfall of cash. Inflation from the influx of gold and silver from Latin America had wiped out the value of traditional levies, such as feudal dues, while early modern states also lacked the bureaucratic efficiency needed to impose an income tax, in Britain a product of the 1790s. In Mun's time there were no real capital markets. At the same time, warfare was becoming more expensive. Hence 'treasure' was indeed the principal need of the seventeenth-century monarch; it was far more important than trade.

The Navigation Act followed Mun's principles by banning foreign ships from transporting goods from Asia, Africa or America to England or its colonies; only ships with an English owner, master and a majority English crew were acceptable. It allowed European ships to ship their own country's products to Britain but banned shipment to England in European ships of any goods from a third country in Europe. It was aimed primarily at the Dutch, who at that time had the greatest share of the European carry trade, essentially banning Dutch ships from

---

2. Thomas Mun (1571-1641). Director, East India Company, 1615-41. Author of *A Discourse of Trade, from England unto the East Indies* (1621) and *England's Treasure by Forraign Trade* (1664).

The Restoration Renaissance, 1649-88 99

shipping goods to England (there being few goods produced specifically in the Netherlands that were competitive in the English market).

The Navigation Act became increasingly important as the trade for tobacco from Virginia, sugar from the Caribbean and tea and coffee from Asia increased. By funnelling the produce of British colonies through British shipping and British ports, where excise duty could be charged, they created a great money machine for the Treasury as colonial output increased. Many continental Europeans seeking tobacco and sugar found it attractive to buy through Britain, since the Navy became increasingly effective against smuggling, and for tobacco there were few other high-quality sources available.

The Navigation Act was renewed and extended at the Restoration in 1660, extending the 'enumerated products' that could only be carried in British ships from tobacco to sugar, indigo and ginger; the cocoa bean was added in 1670. It also tightened the rule that the crew be majority English to a three-quarters requirement, although 'any of His Majesty's subjects' in Scotland, Ireland or the colonies could now count towards the requirement.

Overall, Mun's economic principles were highly profitable to British rulers during the seventeenth century. They developed colonies in North America and the Caribbean, producing addictive products, tobacco and sugar, which could be subjected to a heavy excise before being sold not only in Britain but also in continental Europe to buyers without such colonies. They also developed East Indian trade links for tea and coffee, with similar advantages. The Navigation Acts were an important linkage in the engine that provided the finance for industrialization. Had Britain adopted Adam Smith's free trade principles in the seventeenth century, the profitability of its North American and Caribbean colonies would have been much less, as foreign carriers would have shipped colonial products directly to continental Europe, evading British excises.

The other legislation of the Rump Parliament with major economic effect was much less benign: the Act for the Settlement of Ireland 1652. Cromwell had in previous years commanded forces in Ireland that quelled both Royalists and Catholic rebels against the English occupation, undertaking massacres at Drogheda and Wexford that were comparable, if smaller-scale, to the Thirty Years' War's Sack of Magdeburg by Catholic forces in 1631. Under the Act, the leaders of the Irish Army lost two thirds of their estates and the remaining Irish landowners (other than those who had actively supported Parliament) lost one third of their estates, the land being redistributed to parliamentary soldiers, the 'Adventurers' who had lent money to Parliament in 1642, and other 'settlers'.

The massacres remained a source of grievance for Irish nationalists for centuries, but the 1652 Act did far more long-lasting damage to Ireland, because of its wanton destruction of Irish Catholics' property rights. While most Rump Parliament legislation was nullified after the Restoration, most dispossessions under this Act were ratified by the 1662 Act of Settlement, which restored lands only to some of the most politically prominent Catholics. Irish Catholic land ownership, which, even after the sixteenth-century dispossessions, had been around 60% of Irish land in 1630, fell to 8% during the Protectorate and was restored only to 20% after 1660. It then fell again after William III's Irish campaign to 14% in 1691 and by the operation of various penal laws to around 5% by 1790.

The economic effect of this on Ireland was devastating. After 1660 there was little Irish-owned capital and effectively no Irish Catholic gentry or monied middle class. Consequently, with no state funding for non-denominational Irish schools until 1817, the Irish labouring class became propertyless peasants, subsisting on tiny plots of land, dominated from the eighteenth century by a potato monoculture. The result was repeated famines, the worst in 1740-41, in which a hard frost destroyed the potato crop. There was little commercial development outside Dublin and the Protestant settlements in the north, no industrial development, and from the mid-eighteenth century a population increase as fast as England's, but without England's solid economy to support it.

Thomas Malthus predicted that population would outrun resources and lead to mass starvation; he was wrong in England, where even in the impoverished year in which he wrote (1798) the vast majority of the population lived well above subsistence. In Ireland, he was to be proved only too tragically prescient in the 1840s. The roots of that tragedy lay in the Cromwellian dispossessions of almost 200 years earlier, which had destroyed the social structure of the Irish population and removed its capital base.

Oliver Cromwell took direct control of the government in April 1653, dismissing the Rump Parliament. Barebone's Parliament, which succeeded it, was nominated by the Council of State and lasted only until December 1653, after which three Protectorate Parliaments were elected, in practice, subordinate to Cromwell as Protector. The Protectorate Parliaments were far more conservative than the Rump, reflecting Cromwell's own views and the prevalence of royalism in the

The Restoration Renaissance, 1649-88

country; all three Protectorate Parliaments, for example, contained the future Sir Robert Jenkinson (1621-77), first of a notable Tory line of Oxfordshire baronets and the ancestor of Lord Liverpool. Cromwell's government was highly authoritarian, especially in its first phase of rule by regional major-generals, but gradually through its protection of property rights and social conservatism increased its acceptance among former Royalists, with even the strong Laudian Peter Heylyn[3] praising Cromwell's rule in 1657.

One reform undertaken by Cromwell that would later prove economically important was the readmission of Jews to London. Since their official expulsion in 1290, only a few Jewish merchants had remained in London, mostly posing as Spaniards. In late 1655, a Jewish delegation visited London to discuss official toleration. Cromwell felt that admission of Jews would allow London to compete more effectively with Amsterdam, which had a substantial Jewish community, so from early 1656 Jews began to immigrate to Britain, with a synagogue in Creechurch Lane in the City of London operating from at latest 1663. The Jewish community rapidly came to play a major part in Britain's commerce and later finance.

Cromwell's rule saw an acceleration of British expansion in colonies, the Navy and slavery. While Cromwell opposed the East India Company, bringing it close to bankruptcy, he was highly expansionist elsewhere, with the 1655 capture of Jamaica from Spain being a high point. Jamaica, as well as becoming a sugar producer, became an entrepot for both piracy against the Spanish possessions and shipping and for the slave trade.

During this period the modest British activity in the slave trade began to be institutionalized. The Commonwealth chartered a Guinea Company in 1651, to acquire slaves from the Gold Coast; it suffered difficulties, losing several slave cargoes to a pirate squadron commanded by Prince Rupert[4] and did not establish a profitable business before 1660.

---

3. Peter Heylyn (1599-1662). Laudian churchman and writer, publishing the Royalist newspaper, *Mercurius Aulicus*, 1643-44, compiling the global *Cosmographie* in 1652 and writing an excellent biography of Laud, *Cyprianus Anglicanus*, published in 1662.

4. Prince Rupert of the Rhine (1619-82). KG 1642, PC 1662. Son of Elizabeth of Bohemia, grandson of James VI and I, uncle of the future George I. Royalist cavalry general, 1642-46, Royalist admiral, 1648-50, Pirate admiral 1651-53. Active in development of mezzotint printing, 1654-60. FRS, 1665. Inventor of 'Rupert's Drops', glass baubles used in bulletproof glass. Admiral, 1665-67, 1672-74; St James' Day Battle, 1666, Battle of

Nevertheless, the demand for slaves in British colonies was growing rapidly; the slave population of Barbados alone expanded from 6,000 in 1650 to 80,000 by 1667, although many of those were brought by Dutch traders after the Dutch loss of Brazil in 1654.[5]

Before 1649, the British Navy had been growing but was still relatively modest. It was also badly and corruptly administered. The Spanish Armada had been beaten largely by requisitioning commercial shipping, and the early Stuarts had focussed naval building on a few prestige ships such as the *Sovereign of the Seas* (1637) – 'Barbary pirates' kidnapped natives of Devon and Cornwall to be sold into slavery on many occasions before 1642. The Navy had been moderately Presbyterian during the Civil War, so the Commonwealth, with substantial new finance available, wanted to strengthen it and bring it fully under its control.

Overall, the Commonwealth provided the Navy with £8 million between 1649 and 1660, compared to £3.5 million in the war years 1625-29 and £1 million in the 1630s decade of ship money.[6] The Navy's objectives were to defeat the modest Royalist naval forces under Prince Rupert, to stamp out pockets of Royalism in the embryonic American and Caribbean colonies and to face the strong Dutch Navy. The Commonwealth embarked on a massive programme of naval ship-building, at the height of the Dutch War (1652-54) employing over 2,000 men in the dockyards. Between 1649 and 1654 it built eighteen ships in the dockyards and 36 by contract, a total of 28,000 tons in five years.[7] Although the Navy remained poorly and corruptly administered, it began to play a vital role, protecting and developing the colonial commerce that would provide revenue for industrialization.

Cromwell's death in 1658 caused the republican regime to collapse. His son Richard Cromwell's Protectorate was succeeded by a Rump renewal, by a more conservative Council of State, by a threatened military coup and by General George Monck's[8] march on London which ended in a new Convention Parliament and the restoration of the monarchy. The

---

Texel, 1673. Director, Royal African Company, 1672-82, Founder and Governor, Hudson's Bay Company, 1670-82.

5. Thomas, *The Slave Trade*, p. 187.

6. Rodger, *The Command of the Ocean*, p. 46.

7. Ibid., p. 43.

8. George Monck (1608-70). 1st Duke of Albemarle from 1660. Major General, 1648, C-in-C, Scotland, 1650-52. Marched army from Coldstream to London, January 1660, and negotiated Restoration with Parliament. C-in-C of the Forces, 1660-70. Lord Lieutenant of Ireland, 1660-62. First Lord of the Treasury, 1667-70.

regime was already under severe financial stress because of its massive military and naval expenditure and had been forced after public outcry to reduce taxes in 1655 and 1657. Its death throes were accompanied by financial default, with the Army and Navy unpaid, the latter owing over £1.2 million in unpaid bills.[9] The Restoration was welcomed, not only by the populace tired of rule by the Army and religious extremists, but also by the state's 'men of business' who knew that by combining the monarchy's legitimacy with the Interregnum's money-raising capabilities, a stable system of government finance could be created.

Restoration Politics, 1660-88

The Restoration settlement was designed and implemented by two very intelligent men: a cynical pragmatist Charles II, long on charm but light on detail, and Clarendon, a philosophically highly sophisticated, detail-oriented statesman and founder of 'Church and King' Toryism. For seven years after the Restoration they worked well together, despite their very different temperaments. The political and economic structure they set up survived through the 'long' eighteenth century, with only minor modification after 1688, until partially dismantled after 1830. The year 1660, not 1688, marks the foundation of the constitutional structure that led to the Industrial Revolution.

The Restoration period also saw the birth of the two-party system. The names 'Whig' and 'Tory' stemmed from the Exclusion Crisis of 1678-81, with the Whigs, generally, opponents of the king and the Tories supporters. The Whigs at that time were indeed almost exclusively oppositional in their belief system, forcing

Edward Hyde, Earl of Clarendon. His Restoration Settlement opened the way for industry. Engraving by M. Bury after P. Lely.

---

9. Rodger, *The Command of the Ocean*, p. 95.

104   *Forging Modernity*

the execution of several innocent Catholic peers and shutting down all imports from France, even while Britain was at peace with the country. Only after 1688, with the support of King William III, did they adjust their approach and become the main celebrants of that Revolution (though several of the Revolution's instigators were Tory supporters of the Anglican church).

The Tories, while they did not have a party designation prior to 1680, originated in the policies of the Restoration itself. As Lord Chancellor, Clarendon set up the Restoration constitutional settlement and pushed Britain in an entirely new direction. Later, through his second son Laurence Hyde, Earl of Rochester,[10] he was the inspiration for the Tory party of 1678 onwards. Finally, his *History of the Rebellion*, published in 1703, is generally regarded as the greatest work of history written in the seventeenth century.

The influx of merchants and small landowners into the governing class in the Interregnum had greatly increased the commercial-mindedness of the English political system. No longer could royal economic policy consist of awarding monopolies in vital commodities to favoured courtiers and wondering why the economy stagnated. The Interregnum leaders were however not especially interested in scientific advances, which they regarded, rationally or subconsciously, as attempts to interfere with God's design for the universe.

The return of Charles II, Clarendon, the future James II and Prince Rupert, all interested in science and new ideas, revolutionized the creativity of the British political system. From a rather intellectually sleepy country, generally well behind the Continent's best practice, it became a leader in technological and economic innovation. The foundation of the Royal Society within months of the king's return was a leading indicator of the new intellectual and economic climate. Many of the new scientists were deeply religious men, either Anglican like Robert Boyle or Dissenting like Isaac Newton; their thirst for knowledge and adherence to Bacon's Scientific Method were universal.

The approach of the Restoration's leaders became that of the Tory party. Clarendon was dismissed in 1667 and played no further part in

---

10. Laurence Hyde (1642-1711). 1st Earl of Rochester from 1682. KG from 1685. MP for Newport, 1660, Oxford University, 1661, and Wootton Bassett, 1679. First Lord of the Treasury, 1679-84, Lord President of the Council, 1684-85, 1710-11, Lord High Treasurer, 1685-86, Lord Lieutenant of Ireland, 1700-3.

The Restoration Renaissance, 1649-88

active politics, but his two sons Henry, second Earl of Clarendon,[11] and Rochester were both important Tory politicians, helped after 1688 by being uncles of Queen Mary II and Queen Anne (their sister Anne had married James II in 1660). Both Rochester and Clarendon, the second Earl, were dismissed by James II in 1687, at which point, like many Tories, they moved into opposition to James's support for Catholicism.

The two younger Hydes ensured that their father's principles of support for the Church of England and for a constitutional monarchy became the bedrock of future Toryism. In the early eighteenth century, this belief system would sometimes lead to Jacobitism, and Henry St John, Viscount Bolingbroke,[12] refined it (in a somewhat more free-thinking direction) with his 1749 tract, *On the Idea of a Patriot King*, which was highly influential on the young George III.

Politically, the Tory party contained only a minority of the great nobility, who were generally opposed to royal authority. Its bedrock was the country squire, the 'Allworthy' and 'Western' of the Tory Henry Fielding's *Tom Jones*, as well as the Church of England itself, a numerous and powerful group. While the Tory party tended to be opposed by the great financiers of the City of London (who were to welcome William III's 'Dutch finance'), it contained most of the merchants, more prosperous shopkeepers, country bankers and industrialists outside London – the Royalist/Parliamentarian divisions of the 1640s being mirrored in the Tory/Whig divisions of the 1680s.

Economically, the Tory party believed in a global Britain, with trading links and productive colonies all over the world and without extensive ambitions on the continent of Europe – the religious element and strongest support for the anti-French wars of 1689-97 and 1702-13 was Whig. Being more open to commerce and not well represented in high finance, the Tory party was also more open to the early stirrings of industrialization, which the City of London notably did not finance

---

11. Henry Hyde (1638-1709). 2nd Earl of Clarendon from 1674. MP for Lyme Regis, 1660, and Wiltshire, 1661-74. Lord Privy Seal, 1685-87, Lord Lieutenant of Ireland, 1685-87.

12. Henry St John (1678-1751). 1st Viscount Bolingbroke from 1712, 1st Earl of Bolingbroke (Jacobite), 1715. MP for Wootton Bassett, 1701-8, and Berkshire, 1710-12. Commissioner for building 50 new churches, 1712-15. Secretary at War, 1704-8, Northern Secretary of State, 1710-13, Southern Secretary of State, 1713-14. Secretary of State to the Old Pretender, 1715-16. Founder of *The Craftsman* (1726-35). Author of *On the Idea of a Patriot King* (1749).

significantly until the 1880s. Large, established corporations such as the East India Company were predominantly Whig; innovators, entrepreneurs and scientists were mostly Tory; and the respective parties' policies reflected this division.

The transition to a new age began immediately, with the Convention Parliament's passage of the Tenures Abolition Act 1660, which eliminated many feudal dues and service obligations due to the Crown and feudal restrictions on land holding, making land in a realizable asset that could be freely bought, sold and mortgaged. This freed up enormous amounts of capital that could be used to finance industrialization (as well as overseas plantations, speculation, gambling and other less desirable investments). By creating a free market in land, it gave Britain an advantage that France, Spain and the Holy Roman Empire all lacked, even a century later.

To replace state revenues, the Act imposed an excise duty on tea, coffee, sherbet and chocolate. By shifting state revenues to these new sources, Clarendon performed a vital service for the country's fiscal future. Instead of being fixed, customs and excise duties on these newly consumed products (as well as on tobacco and sugar) would increase with the increase in consumption of these expensive imported goods. These new revenues formed the basis of Britain's taxation system until the 1840s; by 1792 customs and excise duties were producing 69% of Britain's revenue of £18.7 million, itself some fifteen times the revenue in 1661 (in pounds whose value had declined only about 20%).[13] The burden of this new system fell primarily on the luxury-consuming wealthier classes; the revenues it produced were naturally buoyant as wealth and trade increased.

After the Restoration, with both king and Parliament recognizing that a regular parliamentary-approved revenue was necessary, Parliament set the annual state revenue at £1.2 million, tight but workable in peacetime. Unfortunately, Parliament's calculation of the taxes needed to sustain this revenue was off by about 10%, and the figure did not properly take account of the costs needed to clean up the Interregnum government's debts or make allowances for any property restitution to Royalists. Accordingly, Charles II quickly ran into financial trouble and remained there throughout his reign, despite careful financial management by most of his ministers. Pleas to Parliament to alleviate the problem were generally fruitless, their prospects not improved by

---

13. Mitchell (ed.), *British Historical Statistics*, Table XI-1.

The Restoration Renaissance, 1649-88

Charles II's licentious (though not especially expensive) Court. The result was the 1672 Great Stop of the Exchequer.

At the beginning of 1672, royal finances reached a crisis. Clarendon had been gone more than four years and the ministers of the Cabal[14] who succeeded him were less competent, far less scrupulous and by this time in almost open war with each other, some openly undermining the king's policies. With the third Anglo-Dutch War imminent, it was decided to fit out a fleet and cut back on other government expenditure, including debt repayments. Accordingly, on 2 January 1672, a cessation of debt repayments was announced, initially for one year, with only interest at 6% being paid. The total of debt outstanding affected by this Great Stop was about £1.2 million.[15]

France and Spain repeatedly defaulted on their debts, but the small group of 25 lenders to the English government, mostly London's goldsmith bankers, had grown complacent under Charles II, whose repayment record was relatively good. Hence, the distress among London's goldsmith bankers was extreme, with Sir Richard Vyner, owed £416,000 partly because of the cost of supplying the crown for the royal coronation in 1661, the worst hit. The Earl of Danby,[16] who succeeded the Cabal, promised compensation to the goldsmiths, but only limited compensation was paid.

In 1677, a scheme was worked out whereby £767,000 of the government's obligations, intermittently paying 6% interest, were passed on to the goldsmith bankers' depositors, most of them merchants and the wealthy from around London, getting that portion of the obligation off the goldsmith bankers' balance sheets. Then, the whole remaining mess ended up in a prolonged court case, the Goldsmith Bankers case, in which, in 1696, Lord Somers,[17] the Whig Lord Keeper, denied the goldsmith

---

14. Sir Thomas Clifford (1630-73), Henry Bennet, 1st Earl of Arlington (1618-85), Duke of Buckingham (1628-87), Lord Ashley (1621-83) and John Maitland, 1st Duke of Lauderdale (1616-82).

15. Bruce C. Carruthers, *City of Capital: Politics and Markets in the English Financial Revolution* (Princeton, NJ: Princeton University Press, 1996). Chapter 3 has useful details on the goldsmith banker lenders in the Great Stop and their depositors.

16. Thomas Osborne (1632-1712). Bt 1647, Baron Osborne from 1673, Earl of Danby from 1674, Marquess of Carmarthen from 1689, Duke of Leeds from 1694. MP for York, 1665-73. Treasurer of the Navy, 1668-73, Lord High Treasurer, 1673-79, Lord President of the Council, 1689-99.

17. John Somers (1651-1716). 1st Baron Somers from 1697. MP for Worcester, 1689-93. Solicitor General, 1689-92, Attorney General, 1692-93,

108 *Forging Modernity*

bankers further compensation on a technicality. The goldsmith bankers appealed to the full House of Lords, where the modest Tory majority, by the Appropriation of Revenue Act 1700, gave them compensation for principal and part of the interest due.[18]

The short-term damage to the City of London was severe; the goldsmiths, who had emerged in Cromwell's time as London's leading bankers, were badly wounded. Royal borrowing declined for the remainder of Charles II's reign and that of James II; a more long-term solution to the nation's funding problems only arrived with 'Dutch finance' in the 1690s. The damage to the economy was limited: private credit remained unimpaired, and the royal budget righted itself within a few years under the energetic and capable Danby and an appropriately pacific foreign policy.

The damage to savers from the Great Stop was substantial, but less than it would have been earlier or later, for two reasons. The government had not yet institutionalized its debt financing, so losses from the Great Stop fell almost entirely on goldsmith bankers and those with businesses supplying the government, rather than extending to the population at large. Conversely, in 1662 Charles II had instituted a milled, machine-stamped silver coinage, with the phrase *Decus et tutamen* ('An ornament and a safeguard') engraved on the edge, preventing the 'clipping' of coinage that reduced the value of ordinary people's savings. He also ended the practice of repeated debasement of the coinage, so over-indulged in by Henry VIII. Citizens could hold the new milled coinage and be sure it could be exchanged at par, without suffering inflation. Hammered coinage continued to circulate in increasingly degraded form until the Great Recoinage of 1696 but solid, value-preserving coinage was from this point available.

The Exclusion Crisis of 1678-81 saw two important Acts of Parliament, one highly politically and constitutionally positive, the other negative. First, the Habeas Corpus Act 1679 allowed a detainee to petition for release from imprisonment and the petition had to be heard by a court within three days. This principle had been stated in Chapter 39 of Magna Carta, but its codification provided the poor and politically unpopular with a powerful means to avoid undue detainment. It was yet another rectification of the balance between nobility and commons and would

---

Lord Keeper of the Great Seal, 1693-97, Lord Chancellor, 1697-1700, Lord President of the Council, 1708-10. Prominent member of the Whig Junto.

18. Carruthers, *City of Capital*, pp. 122-27, gives details of the Goldsmith Bankers litigation.

The Restoration Renaissance, 1649-88

have no parallel in France or Spain for another century. Over the next three centuries, the Act was suspended on numerous occasions in times of crisis, but always for a limited period.

Second, the Trade with France Act 1678 was a gross Whig interference with freedom of trade, banning imports from France, a country with which Britain was not at war. It continued in force until it was repealed by James II's first Tory Parliament of 1685. It resulted in a substantial loss of customs revenue on imports of French products, especially wine, and in increased smuggling.

Economic Developments

Demographically, the period 1649-88 differed from previous and subsequent periods in having little population growth. Fertility was lower than before 1640 or in the eighteenth century. Overall, the English population, having increased by nearly 25% between 1600 and 1640 to 5.1 million, declined marginally between 1640 and 1700, peaking at 5.2 million in 1652 and then falling back to five million.[19] This combined with an increased vigour in the economy to produce rising living standards.

Robert C. Allen shows the purchasing power of labourers' wages steadily rising from a low of 2.8 times the subsistence level in the 1630s to four times the subsistence level in 1725, while the 'respectability' ratio of labourers' wages rose from 1.0 in the 1630s to 1.4 in 1725 – still below the high of the late fifteenth century, but not by much. Skilled workers' wages also rose, though less rapidly, from 1.7 times the respectability basket in 1625 to 2.1 times that basket in 1725, still significantly below the 1475 level.[20] The working-class misery of the pre-Civil War period was steadily alleviated. British living standards in this period were making up the gap that had opened below Dutch living standards and pulling ahead of living standards in France and the Holy Roman Empire.

The greatest initial effect of low or negative population growth showed itself in agriculture. With fewer workers and consumers available, wages rose, product prices fell and land rentals also fell. On an average taking the period 1700 to 1749 as equalling 100, an index of agricultural wages bottomed at 67 in the 1640s and then rose sharply to reach 101, slightly above its next-century levels, by the 1680s. Labour productivity

---

19. Mitchell (ed.), *British Historical Statistics*, Table I-1.
20. Allen, *The British Industrial Revolution in Global Perspective*, Figs 2.2, 2.3 and 2.6.

growth, which had been slow in the earlier seventeenth century, rose to 0.4% per annum from 1670 to 1700,[21] cumulatively a major shift that, even with no population growth, allowed a relatively prosperous surplus of labourers to move into the towns and seek commercial or manufacturing employment. For the middle rank of farmers, it also provided the modest surplus that could be devoted to educating their children; literacy among farmers is estimated to have risen from 50% in 1560 to 75% in 1700.[22] Agricultural productivity and real wages by 1688 had risen sharply, with literacy correspondingly rising also, and were creating a skilled, solvent workforce for future industrialization. Lower rents did, however, make life difficult for landowners and their mortgage bankers like Clayton & Morris (which I shall come to in the next section).

During the Restoration period the British economy first began its sustained take-off. The period saw a newly aggressive approach to international trade and colonial expansion which brought new products to British consumers, new opportunities to British entrepreneurs and new revenues to the Treasury. Throughout national life, there was a new spirit of aggression and openness to new ideas and technologies, that quickened the nation's commercial life from London through the substantial towns into the smallest villages. The result was the beginnings of a sustained, albeit gentle, upturn in GDP per capita, that was to lead seamlessly into the Industrial Revolution. This, not the post-1688 period (which saw innovations mostly in finance), was the point of take-off and, I would argue, it is this reality which has been obscured by Whig historians seeking to elevate the 1688 Revolution and denigrate Charles II and James II. It took 246 years for Charles II to get his first fair biography;[23] the intellectual neglect and contempt in those centuries extended into economic as well as political history, and into descriptions of the British economy as well as its government.

The Restoration period also saw the beginnings of improvement in Britain's infrastructure. Water transport was the key for the early

---

21. Overton, *Agricultural Revolution in England*, Table 3.1, p. 64 (wages) and Table 3.10, p. 85 (productivity).

22. Allen, *The British Industrial Revolution in Global Perspective*, Table 10.5, p. 261.

23. If you exclude Aurelian Cook's obscure 1685 hagiography, *Titus Britannicus*, Sir Arthur Bryant's *King Charles the Second* was published in 1931. Previous biographies of Charles II varied from unfriendly to libellous.

The Restoration Renaissance, 1649-88   111

Industrial Revolution – heavy industrial loads are hard to transport by horse-drawn vehicles on mud-prone roads. During this period the rivers Avon, Great Ouse, Trent and Mersey were rendered fully navigable to barges for much of their length, but Turnpike Acts were ineffective until the following period and the canal-building boom came in the middle of the next century.

The Birth of Banking

The Restoration period also saw the genesis in Britain of true deposit banking, the first practitioner of which was a scrivener. Robert Abbott (*c.* 1610-58) had established a successful scrivening business with an office in Cornhill in 1635. During the Interregnum it specialized in business with Royalists seeking to raise finance for their regime-imposed fines. When Abbott died in 1658, Robert Clayton,[24] his nephew, and John Morris (*c.* 1626-82), his apprentice, instead of winding down the business as Abbott's will provided, financed several Royalist insurrectionists – notable among them, George Monck – in the confused period that followed Cromwell's death. With the Restoration of 1660, the new bank, now named Clayton & Morris, was positioned for success and Abbott's widow and son were pensioned off.

Clayton & Morris' original headquarters burned down in the Great Fire of 1666. However, by 1672, they had built an imposing new headquarters in Old Jewry in which the bank's central staff both lived and did business, described by Macaulay[25] as 'containing a superb banqueting room wainscoted with cedar and adorned with battles of gods and giants in fresco'. To some extent, the bank's new business was an expansion and professionalization of the old: lending remained

---

24. Robert Clayton (1629-1707). Kt 1671. Whig MP for London, 1679-89, 1695 ,1701 and 1705-7, and Bletchingley, 1690, 1698, 1702. Alderman of the City of London, 1670-83, Sheriff, 1671, Lord Mayor, 1679-80. Assistant, Royal African Company, 1672-81. Director, Bank of England, 1702-7.

25. Thomas Babington Macaulay (1800-59). 1st Baron Macaulay from 1857. Whig MP for Calne, 1830-32, Leeds, 1832-34, and Edinburgh, 1839-47, 1852-56. Secretary to the Board of Control, 1832-33, Law Member of Governor-General's Council, 1834-38, Secretary at War, 1839-41, Paymaster-General, 1846-48. Wrote *Minute on Education* (1835), stating: 'A single shelf of a good European library is worth the whole native literature of India and Arabia'. This description is from *The History of England from the Accession of James the Second* (1848), Vol. 1, p. 267.

Sir Robert Clayton's house and bank headquarters. It is the birthplace of modern British banking. Engraving by Joseph Swain

concentrated in mortgage loans to the country gentry, though the clientele extended to large, albeit heavily indebted, landowners like the Duke of Buckingham.[26] On the deposit side, the bank's average deposits totalled £1.7 million by the peak years in the early 1670s, on which the bank paid interest on only a modest part, though deposits declined thereafter as agricultural incomes fell.

Clayton & Morris established a network of agents: local lawyers, scriveners or land agents, which extended over most of southern England and the Midlands but did not extend to the Duchy of Lancaster

---

26. George Villiers (1628-87). 2nd Duke of Buckingham from 1628. Master of the Horse, 1668-74.

The Restoration Renaissance, 1649-88

(whose paperwork was carried out in Preston) or to Scotland, Ireland or Wales. This had two main functions. One was to assess the value of lands proposed to be put under mortgage and the character of their mortgagees. The other was to oversee the management of mortgaged lands, sometimes acting as bailiff, to ensure that rent payments were made and were not diverted. Managing Buckingham's vast estates from 1671 and his debts of £135,308 (in 1673),[27] thereby saving His Grace from total insolvency, was a major part of the bank's work, though it also brought visibility and credibility with other clients. With this network of agents, the bank established a system of country payment – in some cases through bills of exchange, in other cases by direct couriers of cash (sometimes the traditional sheep-drovers, who travelled in groups with dogs and sheep and were not in great danger from highwaymen).

Accounts of customers' deposits were kept in a semi-public ledger which was available for inspection. However, Clayton & Morris also used their depositors' money in short-term lending (for example, pawning customers' valuables), details of which were kept separately and not shown to clients. Over the Restoration period, the bank developed the cheque, which was not negotiable and by 1675 was standardized and required for all payment orders.

Unlike the goldsmith bankers, Clayton & Morris did not invest significantly in government paper. The bank does not feature in the 1677 list of outstanding creditors from the Great Stop. Also, unlike the larger goldsmith bankers, the bank was not normally active in foreign exchange; indeed, when it attempted on an exceptional basis to provide funds in Danzig for its client Rochester, it appears to have messed up.[28]

Other private banks (such as Hoare's [1672], Child's [1671] and Coutts [1692] that still exist today) were founded by goldsmiths. Given the differences in business between the scriveners and goldsmiths from which they originated, their client bases and business mixes were also different. The goldsmith bankers never developed the national network of agents of Clayton & Morris, nor their depth of activity in the long-term mortgage business.

Morris died in 1682 and Clayton's bank declined thereafter, being wound up some time after 1698, when Clayton's nephew and heir died

---

27. Details of Clayton & Morris' operations are contained in Melton, *Sir Robert Clayton and the Origins of English Deposit Banking, 1658-1685*, Buckingham debts, p. 199.
28. The Rochester anecdote is cited in ibid., p. 113 – he described the Bank's instructions as 'heathen Greek to everybody in this place'.

of smallpox. It was not the ancestor of any modern bank. Nevertheless, its business, more than that of the early goldsmith bankers, was the ancestor of modern banking, and its business mix, origins in the quasi-legal professions and concentration on the mortgage markets and the landed gentry was to be replicated by the country bankers, the first being Smith's of Nottingham in 1688[29] but arising in large numbers after 1750. Those country banks played a major role in financing the Industrial Revolution, much more than the London houses.

Trade and Empire

During the seventeenth century, imports and consumption of five new products became very popular in Britain: sugar, tobacco, coffee, tea and chocolate. After 1660, their production, trade and consumption greatly increased British wealth and, through excise taxes, state income. After the Great Stop, with peace mostly maintained, Charles II's financial difficulties and those of James II were greatly alleviated by these new sources of revenue (as well as by modest subsidies from Louis XIV) and subsequent regimes benefited from them still more.

By the early 1680s, with peace for several years and revenues rising, Charles II would embark on his dream palace at Winchester in Tory-dominated Hampshire, designed by Sir Christopher Wren as a smaller but more architecturally interesting version of Versailles, alas left unfinished at his death.[30] James II was provided with ample revenues by the Tory-dominated 1685 Parliament and his finances, helped by continued peace, remained satisfactory to the end.

Sugar began to be used in Europe after Spanish and Portuguese colonizers began production in Brazil and the Caribbean around 1500. Sugar production used large quantities of slave labour, initially local but eventually imported from Africa. The Dutch, after their conquest of Brazil in 1621, spread sugar production more generally across the Caribbean, and both British and French colonizers developed large sugar colonies. While in Tudor times honey was the main sweetener used in Britain, the increased availability of sugar after 1650 produced a wide variety of new uses for it, in cakes, jams, tea, coffee, cocoa and

---

29. Margaret Dawes and C.N. Ward-Perkins, *Country Banks of England and Wales* (Canterbury: Chartered Institute of Bankers, 2000), Vol. 1, p. 9.
30. See: https://www.royalpalaces.com/palaces/winchester/ (accessed 13 January 2021).

The Restoration Renaissance, 1649-88

so on. Sugar imports to Britain in 1700 totalled around £600,000 annually (excluding smuggling), on which a duty of 10% was charged, or £60,000.[31] British sugar consumption continued upwards during the eighteenth century and customs revenue rose correspondingly; in 1822 Lord Liverpool estimated that the sugar duties were over £5 million per annum in 1821.[32]

The first European to consume tobacco was Christopher Columbus, and its consumption spread through Europe during the sixteenth century, grown mostly in the Spanish West Indies and Brazil. Sir John Hawkins introduced tobacco to England in 1565 and Raleigh popularized it among high-end consumers. The Jamestown colonists discovered the Native Americans growing it, and John Rolfe is believed to have introduced Trinidad tobacco seed to the colony around 1612 with a view to commercial production; already 2,300 pounds were exported to Britain in 1615-16. By 1640, over one million pounds of tobacco was exported from Britain's American colonies per year. The duties on these imports became important, such that in 1652 an Act was passed to prevent the cultivation of tobacco in England. By the middle 1670s, British duties on colonial tobacco, all of which was by law shipped to England, totalled £100,000 annually, around 8% of the Crown's total revenue. By 1700, tobacco excise duties contributed around £400,000 annually to the Crown's revenue, about 10% of the total.[33] The value of non-smuggled imports later declined and after American independence tobacco became only a modest revenue contributor, maybe £50,000 annually by 1800.

Coffee appears to have been widely drunk first in the Ottoman Empire in the fifteenth century. The first London coffee house was opened by Pasqua Rosée, probably of Turkish origin, in 1652. Thomas Garway (1632-1704), from a well-established family of City merchants, opened a coffee house, the Sultaness Head, shortly thereafter. This burned down in the Great Fire of 1666 and Garway established Garraway's Coffee

---

31. Mitchell (ed.), *British Historical Statistics*, Table IX-7, pp. 462-64.

32. *The State of the Nation at the Commencement of 1822, Considered under the Four Departments of the Finance, Foreign Relations, Home Department, Colonies and Board of Trade* (London: John Hatchard & Son, 1822), p. 167.

33. Tax History Museum, 1660-1712 The Restoration to the Peace of Utrecht, available at: https://www.taxnotes.com/tax-history-project/tax-history-museum/1660-1712 (accessed 21 September 2022).

House in Exchange Alley to replace it. Since the first coffee houses were in the City of London, they became meeting places for merchants. Garraway's, doubtless helped by Garway's family connections (one cousin was an MP), was the first such entrepot for the merchants and traders of the Royal Exchange. Later, two more specialized entrepots emerged: Jonathan's, opened around 1680, became a meeting place for dealers in securities and Lloyd's, established in 1686, quickly came to specialize in marine insurance.

Coffee houses spread rapidly in the 1670s and were meeting places for writers, actors and politicians as well as merchants. Charles II's government attempted unsuccessfully to ban them in 1676, because:

> Many Tradesmen and others, do therein mis-spend much of their time, which might and probably would otherwise be imployed in and about their Lawful Callings and Affairs; but also, for that in such Houses, and by occasion of the meetings of such persons therein, diverse False, Malitious and Scandalous Reports are devised and spread abroad, to the Defamation of His Majesties Government, and to the Disturbance of the Peace and Quiet of the Realm.[34]

Unlike tobacco and sugar, which were grown in British colonies, coffee was imported primarily for the British market with little re-exporting. Imports totalled only £36,000 in 1700, but the average tax yield between 1703 and 1705, with a special wartime tax, was £116,475.[35] Further rapid growth led to a volume of £4 million in imports and perhaps £520,000 in tax by 1800.[36]

Like coffee, tea, grown and popular in China, was drunk by a few European travellers in the sixteenth and early seventeenth centuries. It then became available in the coffee houses, the first such sale being probably by Garway in the Sultaness Head. He wrote a detailed 'Tea Circular' in 1657 advertising the new drink. Charles II's wife Catherine of Braganza popularized it among fashionable ladies and Queen Anne later drank it regularly, as celebrated by Alexander Pope:[37]

---

34. 'A proclamation for the suppression of coffee houses' by the King, (John Bill, 29 December 1675), available at https://quod.lib.umich.edu/e/eebo2/B19975.0001.001?rgn=main;view=fulltext (accessed 26 October 2022).

35. William Deringer, *Calculated Values: Finance, Politics, and the Quantitative Age* (Cambridge, MA: Harvard University Press, 2018), p. 98.

36. Mitchell (ed.), *British Historical Statistics*, Table IX-7, pp. 462-64.

37. Alexander Pope (1688-1744). Poet. *The Rape of the Lock* (1712), Canto 3.

The Restoration Renaissance, 1649-88

Here thou, great Anna, whom three realms obey
Dost sometimes counsel take – and sometimes tea.

In 1700 tea imports amounted only to £14,000 but later in the century the East India Company developed the China tea business and imported tea plants into India, so that by 1792 tea imports totalled 16.6 million pounds, worth £1,303,000 on which the duty at 13% was £170,000.[38]

Chocolate, native to Mesoamerica, was imported to Europe by the Spaniards and fashionable at the Spanish court by the late sixteenth century. Its use, primarily sweetened as a drink, spread to Britain through the coffee houses, but grinding the cocoa beans was laborious so it remained expensive. In 1729 Walter Churchman, from Bristol, patented a water-powered cocoa grinder, and chocolate increased in popularity from that point. Churchman's patent was bought by Fry, Vaughan & Co. in 1761 and became the basis for the Fry's chocolate business, which moved to a Boulton & Watt steam engine in 1795 and produced Britain's first solid chocolate bar in 1847. The volume of cocoa beans imported and taxation thereon were only modest before 1800.

The plethora of new products available to British consumers after 1660 resulted from a major long-term increase in the scope and volume of British international trade. It was during this period that Britain became a world power, and her commercial activities grew towards dominating world markets. One driver of this new aggression and success was a jump in the strength and capability of the Royal Navy, which began to take on a global role.

Charles II and the future James II were both keen yachtsmen (Charles II effectively invented yachting as a sport) and Prince Rupert, having commanded fleets both official and pirate, shared their enthusiasm for the Navy and technical knowledge of naval matters. The Restoration regime combined the larger budgets devoted to the Navy during the Interregnum with a new efficiency in naval administration, together with an understanding of and devotion to the Navy's needs at top policymaking levels.

Accordingly, James was installed as Lord High Admiral (he had nominally held that post since 1638) and an efficient Navy Board was

---

38. For tea values, see Mitchell (ed.), *British Historical Statistics*, Table IX-7, pp. 462-64; for its weight and duty in 1792, see Lord Liverpool's speech, Hansard, *Parliamentary Debates New Series*, Vol. 6, cols 682-717, 26 February 1822.

assembled to assist him. One of those appointed was Samuel Pepys[39] as Clerk of the Acts, who soon acquired a mastery of detail that made him the centre of naval administration. Administrative systems were completely reformed, for example, in the 'pursery' supply of food to ships in commission, and efficiency was thereby considerably increased.[40] There was a major scandal in 1667, when lack of funds left the Navy out of commission and subject to a Dutch attack while defenceless at anchor in the River Medway. Thereafter, the systems worked and, with a 1677 building programme of 30 ships of the line, British naval strength built up steadily both in home waters and around the world. As Rodger writes: 'Together (Charles II and James II) achieved a remarkable transformation in their Navy, creating a loyal, coherent and reasonably united body of officers and men, with an established career structure for the officers. Professional ability replaced political correctness as the criterion for advancement.'[41]

The can-do spirit of the Restoration Navy was epitomized by the career of Admiral Sir Robert Holmes (1622-92). After service in Prince Maurice's troop during the Civil War, he joined Prince Rupert's naval/ pirate squadron in 1648, where he rose to commanding the four prizes the fleet brought back to France. After the Restoration, he led a Royal Adventurers expedition to the Guinea Coast in search of a legendary 'Mountain of Gold', capturing a Dutch fort. In a second expedition, he captured three Dutch forts, including the main Dutch base in West Africa and several Dutch ships; he is generally credited with starting the Second Anglo-Dutch War. During that war, he was promoted to Rear Admiral after the Four Days' Battle of 1666, then, in his most famous exploit landed on the island of Vlieland, sacked the Dutch town of West-Terschelling and burnt 150 Dutch merchant ships in a major victory known as 'Holmes' Bonfire'. Finally, in 1672 he successfully attacked the returning Dutch Smyrna Convoy, thereby also starting the Third Anglo-Dutch War.

In India, the EIC's prospects improved markedly once Charles II was restored. Charles II acquired Bombay in 1662 as a wedding present from

---

39. Samuel Pepys (1663-1703). FRS 1665. MP for Castle Rising, 1673, and Harwich, 1679 and 1685. President of the Royal Society, 1684-86. Secretary of the Admiralty, 1673-79, 1684-89.
40. Rodger, *The Command of the Ocean*, pp. 95-111, gives details of the Restoration naval reforms.
41. Ibid., p. 131.

The Restoration Renaissance, 1649-88

Portugal for his marriage to Catherine of Braganza – the Portuguese merchants' position was declining, reflecting the limited size and old-fashioned nature of its domestic economy. Being more aggressive than the Portuguese and with a stronger position than the Dutch or later French interlopers, the EIC acquired a dominant position in European trade with India, with an average of 968,000 pieces of textiles per annum exported to Europe over the years 1680 to 1684, more than three times the average of the Dutch VOC, for a total annual value of £800,000. The EIC's major ports, Bombay (which absorbed much of the business of Surat) and Madras on the Coromandel Coast, established in 1639 as Fort St George, became entrepots for intercontinental trade and the EIC soon began to help local rulers maintain order. The EIC share price, which had bottomed at £70 in 1665 rose to a range of £360-£500 by its 1683 peak.[42]

The principal force behind the EIC was Sir Josiah Child,[43] who was a director of the EIC from 1673 and Governor or Deputy Governor from 1681 to 1690. Child, from a mercantile background, made his first fortune under the Protectorate as Victualler to the Navy, then pursued a political and mercantile career that made him worth £200,000 in the 1680s, on the diarist John Evelyn's estimate. He was also a widely read, albeit unsound, writer of economics, first propounding in 1668 the remarkably twenty-first-century economic idea that prosperity could be increased by artificially holding down interest rates: 'All countries are at this day richer or poorer in exact proportion to what they pay, and have usually paid, for the Interest of Money.'[44]

Under Child's tutelage, the EIC abandoned its previous principle of declining to back its trading with military force, so authorized by Charles II in a series of Acts that allowed the EIC to govern territory, command troops and make war and peace. In 1685 James II, using England's new global naval capability, sent a fleet of twelve ships with 600 men to confront the Mughal Emperor Aurangzeb militarily and established armed British colonies in India. In the short term, this

---

42. John Keay, *The Honourable Company: A History of the East India Company* (London: HarperCollins, 1991), pp. 170, 177.

43. Josiah Child (1630-99). Bt 1678. MP for Petersfield, 1658-59, Dartmouth, 1673, and Ludlow, 1685. Director, East India Co., 1674-76, 1678-99, Governor, EIC, 1681-83, 1686-88, Deputy Governor, 1684-86, 1688-90.

44. Quoted in T.S. Ashton, *The Industrial Revolution 1760-1830* (Oxford: Oxford University Press, 1948), p. 8.

change of policy proved disastrous; Aurangzeb's forces of some 100,000 troops overwhelmed the EIC's puny 600 and gained complete victory by 1690. In the longer term, it marked the beginning of EIC rule in India, although the forces needed to achieve this were considerably larger than that sent by James II.

These trading advances were important, both through what they led to in India and through their effect in globalizing Britain's purchasing and marketing capability. India became a substantial market for British manufactured goods, enabling Britain's producers to achieve economies of scale not available to competitors. Even so, the economic benefits of the EIC's operations were dwarfed by the benefits from Britain's American and West Indian colonies. Regrettably, those benefits depended on slavery.

The moral black spot of the Restoration regime came in Africa, where its entrepreneurial spirit was applied to the transatlantic slave trade. This had been dominated by the Portuguese and Spanish in the fifteenth and sixteenth centuries and by the Dutch in the early seventeenth century; from this point on, it was dominated by Britain. However, over the roughly 400 years of the transatlantic slave trade, with roughly eleven million slaves transported, only 2.6 million, 24%, were transported by British ships. 42% were transported in Portuguese ships, mostly to Brazil, 15% in Spanish ships, 11% in French ships, 5% in Dutch ships and 3% by American ships (post-independence). The British acceleration of the trade was nevertheless crucial in increasing its volume; 54% of the slaves were transported in the eighteenth century and 31% in the nineteenth century, with the greatest damage being done to African economies and societies during that period.[45]

British participation in the slave trade, and its use of slaves, was notably more effective than that of other countries. Despite their 200-year start, and their control over notably fertile sugar-growing countries such as Cuba and Brazil, neither Spain nor Portugal benefited hugely from their large volume of slaves transported. Only 9.1% of the slaves transported worked in mines, compared with 54.5% in sugar plantations and 18.2% in coffee plantations, with the high-altitude Potosi silver mines worked primarily by local labour. British tobacco plantations in the seventeenth century were worked mostly

---

45. Dr Neil Frankel, 'The Atlantic Slave Trade and Slavery in America', http://www.slaverysite.com/Body/facts%20and%20figures.htm (accessed 10 December 2020).

The Restoration Renaissance, 1649-88

by indentured British and Irish servants, but their Caribbean sugar plantations later contributed more to British state revenues and played a larger role in British economic development than did Spanish or Portuguese colonial output other than the silver mines. By the late seventeenth century Spain and Portugal, colonies, mines, slaves and all, were in clear economic and geopolitical decline.

British expansion in the slave trade began immediately after the Restoration, when the Company of Royal Adventurers of England Trading with Africa was incorporated by royal charter in 1663 and given the monopoly for Britain's African trade, hoping for gold as well as slaves. Its formation was impelled by Prince Rupert, who knew the African slave coast well from his pirate days, although the future James II became its President. The Royal Adventurers did indeed find gold, minting some of it into the first 'guineas', milled coins with an elephant on one side and, in its early years, gold was more important than slaving. The depredations of the Second Anglo-Dutch War (1665-67) wrecked the company's profitability and in the general financial chaos of 1672 it was wound up.

Its assets were bought at a discount by a new chartered company the Royal African Company, which again had the future James II as Governor and Prince Rupert as a director, with a monopoly of all African trade that lasted until James II's deposition in 1688. Between 1672 and 1689, the RAC exported around 90,000 slaves from Africa, of whom 25,000 went to Barbados, 23,000 to Jamaica, and the rest to Spanish colonies or British North America – the RAC sold 75,000 slaves to British North America between 1675 and 1725. Overall, the British Caribbean imported 175,000 slaves in the last quarter of the seventeenth century, a sharp increase from previous periods. The RAC made good profits in the early 1680s, both from transporting slaves and from exporting British textiles and cutlery to the African coast.[46]

The North American and Caribbean colonies continued their rapid growth and the profits generated for colonists and for the Treasury through excises grew even more rapidly. The overall settler and slave population of the future United States grew from 50,368 in 1650 to 210,372 in 1690, with growth accelerating through the period. The two greatest population centres remained Massachusetts and Virginia, with 1690 populations of 49,504 and 53,046, respectively. The total slave population leaped in the 1680s, from 6,971 in 1680 to 16,729 in 1690,

---

46. Hugh Thomas, *The Slave Trade*, pp. 198-205.

mostly in Virginia, although the great growth of tobacco output had occurred earlier, based on white indentured labour. New York was captured by Colonel Richard Nicolls (1624-72) and four British frigates on 6 September 1664, when Britain and the Netherlands were officially still at peace; it grew more slowly, with a brief Dutch re-occupation in 1673, and a population of 13,909 in 1690.[47] Pennsylvania was founded in 1681 by Sir William Penn and was dominated by the Quaker religious community.

The rapid growth of the British colonies in the future United States owed much to capable Cavalier/Tory government. In Virginia, Sir William Berkeley (1605-77), governor from 1641 until 1652 (when he was expelled by the Commonwealth) and 1660 until 1677, pursued a policy of economic diversification (he began growing rice in Virginia), free trade, friendly relations with Native Americans and autonomy from London – he was economically well ahead of his mercantilist time. Sir Edmund Andros (1637-1714) was successively governor of New York (1674-83), the Dominion of New England (1686-89), Virginia (1692-98) and Maryland (1693-94); he was ousted from New England when the Boston Puritans heard of the overthrow of James II and recalled from Virginia when a Whig faction gained power in London. Like Berkeley, he believed in good relations with the Native Americans, signing a long-lasting treaty with the Iroquois, and in free trade and economic diversification for the colonies themselves. While the later history of the American colonies was largely Whig, this early growth and prosperity was primarily Tory and Anglican.

The Commonwealth had attempted to fulfil Barbados' need for labour with indentured servants, particularly from Ireland, but the Barbados registers show four times as many deaths as marriages. With sugar profitable, the transition to slavery was rapid; by 1680 Barbados had 20,000 free whites and 46,000 enslaved Africans. In Jamaica, the climate kept the white population under 10,000, while the slave population increased to 45,000 by 1700. Bermuda had a population of 6,000 by 1690; other British settlements in the Bahamas and the Leeward Islands remained small. The economic contributions from Barbados and Jamaica, primarily through sugar production, was already substantial by 1688 and grew thereafter.

---

47. US Census Bureau, *Historical Statistics of the United States, Colonial Times to 1970*, 'Chapter Z: Colonial and pre-Federal Statistics, Series Z 1-19', p. 1168.

Prince Rupert (self-portrait). Restoration royals aided industrialization as in no other period.

In area, the largest British colony was Prince Rupert's Land, established in 1670, which occupied 1.5 million square miles, the drainage area of Hudson's Bay. Prince Rupert was excited by the possibilities for exploitation of the trade in beaver furs, so in 1670 led the foundation of the Hudson's Bay Company, of which he remained governor until his death in 1682. The company, which was granted a monopoly on all

124 *Forging Modernity*

products from its region (primarily beaver furs) established six trading posts on Hudson's Bay during the seventeenth century and gained French acquiescence to its rights by the 1713 Treaty of Utrecht.

Economic Thinkers

Cromwell's Irish clearances greatly enriched the economic and scientific polymath **Sir William Petty,**[48] the son of an impoverished Hampshire clothier. After a shipwreck in Normandy, a brief Jesuit education, and a few years in the Navy and the family clothing business, Petty studied at Utrecht, and then medicine at Leyden. He then spent time in Paris as personal secretary to Thomas Hobbes[49] before obtaining an Oxford doctorate in medicine in 1649.

While at Oxford, Petty joined a scientific society under John Wilkins[50] which later became the nucleus of the Royal Society. During the Commonwealth he became a Fellow of Brasenose College and deputy to the professor of anatomy, where he amazed his students and achieved fame by reviving a hanged woman whose corpse was brought to him for an anatomical demonstration (the woman lived another ten years). Petty took a practical approach to scientific and medical research, being strongly influenced by the Scientific Method.

In 1652, Petty became physician-general to the New Model Army in Ireland. He saw an opportunity in the Act for the Settlement of Ireland and in the many English soldiers who had received vouchers to acquire sequestered Irish land. Land sequestration was proceeding chaotically and Petty saw that an accurate survey was needed to determine what landholdings were available. Accordingly, he put together a proposal for a survey which could be completed quickly and would include a detailed map of the country, the first to be made. Petty completed the survey by May 1656, as promised, using unemployed soldiers with chains and simple surveying instruments which Petty himself designed. The

---

48. William Petty (1623-87). Kt 1661. Founder Fellow of the Royal Society, 1660. MP for West Looe, 1659. MP (Ireland) for Inistioge, 1661-66. Author of *A Treatise of Taxes and Contributions* (1662), *Political Arithmetic*, 1676 (published 1690). Great-grandfather of 1st Marquess of Lansdowne, Prime Minister of Great Britain, 1782-83.
49. Thomas Hobbes (1588-1679). Philosopher. Author of *Leviathan* (1651).
50. John Wilkins (1614-72). Warden of Wadham College, Oxford, 1648-59, Master of Trinity College, Cambridge, 1659-60. Founder (1660) and Fellow of the Royal Society, 1663. Bishop of Chester, 1668-72.

The Restoration Renaissance, 1649-88

resulting Down Survey was carried out on a scale of 40 Irish perches (840 feet) to the inch and continued in use until the nineteenth century. Petty enriched himself by buying soldiers' vouchers, thereby acquiring 50,000 acres of Irish land, as well as a £9,000 fee.

Petty entered the Third Protectorate Parliament in 1659. Charles II's Restoration caused him momentary embarrassment, but the Merry Monarch was not about to condemn someone so clever and amusing, so gave him a knighthood instead – Petty's part in founding the Royal Society doubtless helped. Petty then returned to his Irish estates, most of which he retained after the 1662 Act of Settlement, developing an iron works and a fishery in Kerry and writing extensively on the prospects to develop Ireland.

Petty's main economic works were published after his death. He rejected Hobbes' ideal of a benign Leviathan state, instead using a Baconian approach to develop economic data with which the world could be analysed. He regarded his *Political Arithmetic* as an essential instrument in developing economic policy; his thirst for quantification led to the beginnings of official economic statistics in the 1690s.

On fiscal policy, Petty recommended reducing government expenditure, except for the duty of care for the poor, sick and elderly (notably, the Poor Law 1601). He also recommended taxes on consumption rather than production, as they would be less damaging to enterprise, and proposed that taxes should be payable in forms other than scarce gold or silver.

Petty developed the first national income accounts, estimating British national income at £40 million, and the thesis that national wealth consisted of output rather than fixed assets.

He believed the natural interest rate was the rental yield on prime land, then argued against governments meddling with interest rates, pointing to the 'vanity and fruitlessness of making civil positive laws against the laws of nature'.[51]

Petty's greatest contribution to economic thought was the doctrine of laissez-faire. A century ahead of Adam Smith, he declared that government regulations were economically damaging, and that the free market should operate to produce the economically optimum result. He also warned against restrictions on trade.

---

51. *Quantulumcunque Concerning Money* (London: A & J. Churchill, 1695), p. 48.

Petty was personally influential on other men who made significant economic advances. He was a friend of John Graunt (1620-74), a prosperous City of London haberdasher (although bankrupted by the Great Fire), who worked with the Bills of Mortality for the London parishes to develop the first mortality statistics – analysing causes of death, ages at death and the probability of surviving an additional year at each age. Petty used his work to calculate the cost to society of early deaths. Petty was also influential on the economic work of Edmond Halley, Gregory King and Charles Davenant.

Petty's ideas became much more influential after the posthumous publication of his most important works. He represented a decisive break with the economic policies of the early Stuarts and gave intellectual inspiration for a free-market approach. While he failed to produce a systemization of his economic thought, he was influential on both Whig and Tory policymakers after the 1688 Revolution and contributed greatly to the environment in which industrialization became possible. Overall, his work was among the most important intellectual advances which made the British business climate after 1660 differ markedly from that of continental Europe.

Andrew Yarranton (1616-84), the captor of Dudd Dudley, also made his name during the Interregnum and looked towards an industrial future for himself. He was from a yeoman family in Worcestershire, apprenticed to a linen draper in 1632 but ran away, 'living a country life' until joining the Parliamentary Army in 1642, rising to the rank of captain. In 1646 he became a member of the Worcestershire County Committee to administer 'parliamentary justice' to local Royalists; this activity enriched him considerably, enabling him to speculate in forfeited Royalist estates.

In 1652, Yarranton set up an iron works at Astley, using iron from the Forest of Dean and local charcoal. Three years later, he undertook to make the River Salwarpe navigable from the Severn to Droitwich; after a change of sources of finance at the Restoration, five locks were built, but the project ran out of money before completion. He was also involved in abortive schemes to connect the Severn and Kidderminster with local coalfields; they also ran out of money around 1680 but were eventually realized a century later via the Staffordshire and Worcestershire Canal. Yarranton did succeed in restoring navigability to the River Avon above Evesham.

Yarranton was imprisoned intermittently after the Restoration but in 1667 was sent, together with Ambrose Crowley II, to Saxony to learn how to tinplate iron; his discoveries were sufficient for Philip Foley[52] to set up a tinplate mill at Wolverley in 1670.

In 1677, Yarranton wrote an economic treatise, *England's Improvement by Sea and Land to Outdo the Dutch without Fighting*, in which he suggested a massive programme of canal building, financed by public borrowing and expansion of credit. The canals were indeed central to industrialization, although the most useful ones were privately financed; the expansion of public credit came in the 1690s, but was spent on wars, not canals.

Sir Dudley North, a merchant, statesman and Oxfordshire School economist. Artist unknown.

The most distinguished exponent of Oxfordshire School economics during this period, anticipating Adam Smith by nearly a century, was **Sir Dudley North**.[53] From a Royalist and Tory family, he was educated at Bury St Edmunds Grammar School, after which he was apprenticed to a merchant in Turkey and in 1661 became a factor at Smyrna, rising to be local treasurer of the Levant Company. He returned to London in 1680 and resumed a mercantile business, where he found that merchants no longer dealt in cash: 'which, by almost all sorts of Merchants, was slid into Goldsmith's Hands, and they themselves paid and returned only by Bills, as if all their dealings were in Banco. He considered this a foolish, lazy Method, and obnoxious to great Accidents.'[54] He also had a sharp eye for foolish speculations; as

---

52. Philip Foley (1648-1716). Youngest of three sons of ironmaster Thomas Foley (1617-77). Whig MP for Bewdley, Stafford and Droitwich, 1679-1681, 1685-1701.
53. Dudley North (1641-91). Kt 1683. MP for Banbury, 1685. Brother of 1st Baron Guilford, Lord Keeper of the Great Seal, and great-grand-uncle of Lord North. Sheriff, City of London, 1682-83, Alderman, 1682-84. Commissioner of Customs, 1684, 1685-89, Lord of Treasury, 1684-85, Governor, Muscovy Company, 1686-91.
54. Roger North, *Life of the Honourable Sir Dudley North, Knight* (London: John Whiston, 1745), p. 148.

128   *Forging Modernity*

his biographer brother said: 'I have often heard Sir Dudley say: "Run away from great bargains." So, I doubt he would have made but an indifferent South Sea Merchant.'[55]

North was nominated for sheriff of the City of London in 1682. He was initially beaten by the Whig candidate but installed in the position by the king. In office North selected the juries that condemned the 'Whig martyrs' William Russell[56] and Algernon Sidney[57] to be executed for their involvement in the Rye House Plot to assassinate Charles II. He was then through the influence of Lord Treasurer Rochester made Commissioner of Customs, where his skill with accounts enabled him, first, to eliminate several frauds in the Customs and, then, at Rochester's request, to prove that the books for the 'farm' of the Hearth Tax revenues were fraudulent.[58] In late 1684 he was appointed a Lord of the Treasury but returned to Customs in the new reign of James II.

North, MP for Banbury, was elected Chairman of the Ways and Means Committee in the 1685 Parliament. Here he rejected the land tax proposed by the Whigs and, instead, imposed modest customs duties on tobacco and sugar, both colonial commodities whose consumption was rapidly increasing. He failed to prevent an excessively lucrative arrangement by which the goldsmith bankers could bring bullion into the Treasury and have it coined into money by weight, which at times of low bullion prices was inflationary. In a meeting with parliamentarians and Lord Treasurer Rochester:

> Sir Dudley North reasoned with them against it beyond Reply; and then the Argument was 'Let there be Money, my Lord, by God let there be Money.' ... The Country Gentlemen are commonly full of one profound Mistake, which is that, if a great deal of Money be made, they must have a share of it,

---

55. Ibid., p. 196. He is referring to the South Sea Bubble speculation.
56. William Russell (1639-83). Whig MP for Tavistock and Bedfordshire, 1660-81. Father raised to Dukedom of Bedford in 1694, after the Whigs regained power.
57. Algernon Sidney (1623-83). MP for Cardiff, 1645-53. Lord Warden of the Cinque Ports, 1648-51. Republican political philosopher. *Discourses concerning Government* (1698).
58. North, *Life of the Honourable Sir Dudley North, Knight*, p. 170. The 'farm' fraud was carried out by Francis Dashwood and his son Samuel (1643-1705), the grandfather and uncle of Sir Francis Dashwood (1708-81), politician, rake and founder of the Hellfire Club.

The Restoration Renaissance, 1649-88

such be the supposed consequence of what they call plenty of Money.[59]

Some fallacies never die!

North left office in 1687, refusing to accept James II's efforts to eliminate the Test Act in favour of Catholics, then, after the Revolution, was forced to defend himself before the Convention Parliament, where the rampaging Whigs tried to criminalize their policy differences. Shortly before his death in 1691 North published *Discourses upon Trade*, the earliest classic of free-market economics, 40 years before Cantillon and 85 years before Adam Smith's *Wealth of Nations*. This had limited circulation, but North's friendships with influential Tories and his own public career gave it considerable policy significance. It was rediscovered by the economist John McCulloch (1789-1864), who not only republished it but sent a copy to David Ricardo,[60] who responded: 'I had no idea that anyone entertained such correct opinions, as are expressed in this publication, at so early a period.'[61]

North believed that interest rates and trade should both be as free as possible and summarized England's economy as of 1691 as follows:

> In process of time, if the people apply themselves industriously, they will not only be supplied, but advance to a great overplus of Foreign Goods, which improved, will enlarge their Trade. Thus, the English nation will sell unto the French, Spanish, Turk, etc. not only the product of their own Country, as Cloath, Tin, Lead, etc., but also what they purchase of others, as Sugar, Pepper, Calicoes, etc., still buying where goods are produced, and cheap, and transporting them to Places where they are wanted, making great advantage thereby.[62]

North also anticipated Mandeville's 1714 *Fable of the Bees*:

> The main spur to Trade, or rather to Industry and Ingenuity, is the exorbitant Appetites of Men, which they will take pains

---

59. Ibid., p. 179.
60. David Ricardo (1772-1823). MP for Portarlington, 1819-23. Stockbroker and economist; his *On the Principles of Political Economy and Taxation* (1817) propounded the Doctrine of Comparative Advantage.
61. Jacob Hollander (ed.), *Letters of David Ricardo to John Ramsay McCulloch, 1816-1823* (New York: Macmillan, 1896), p. 126.
62. North, *Life of the Honourable Sir Dudley North, Knight*, p 11.

130 *Forging Modernity*

to gratifie, and so be disposed to work, when nothing else will incline them to it; for did Men content themselves with bare Necessities, we should have a poor World.[63]

North ends by condemning sumptuary laws, restrictions on trade and other government interference:

Thus we may labour to hedge in the Cuckow, but in vain; for no People ever yet grew rich by Policies, but it is Peace, Industry and Freedom that brings Trade and Wealth, and nothing else.[64]

The phrase, 'No people ever yet grew rich by Policies', should be forced recitation for every Keynesian or Marxist economist!

Portents of Industrialization

While the first true industrial progress came later, this period saw several advances that foreshadowed the changes ahead:

In 1655 **Edward Somerset, second Marquess of Worcester** (1602-67) wrote *The Century of Inventions* (published in 1663), in which he described a steam engine that could be used for pumping water, apparently similar to that built by the Spanish Jerónimo de Ayanz y Beaumont around 50 years earlier and to that which would be built and patented by Thomas Savery 40 years later. Worcester was a Royalist Catholic and an unsuccessful Civil War commander, who was imprisoned by the Council of State in 1653-54. After that time, he devoted himself to experimentation; his steam pump was described by a visitor as being able to raise four large buckets of water to a height of 40 feet in one minute.

Worcester was an aristocratic dilettante, whose *Century of Inventions* consists mainly of impracticable speculations[65] (Robert Hooke dismissed his steam pump as a perpetual motion machine) but his invention and that of Denis Papin (1647-1713), who demonstrated a steam-powered pressure cooker to the Royal Society in 1679, gave ideas to Savery.

Dudd Dudley, the other precursor of an important new technology, was sequestrated from his modest estates during the Interregnum, but got

---

63. Ibid., p. 12.

64. Ibid., p. 23.

65. For example, 'XLVI. How to make an artificial bird to fly which way, and as long as one pleaseth, by or against the wind, some times chirping, other times hovering, still tending the way it is designed for.'

The Restoration Renaissance, 1649-88

them back at the Restoration. He then returned to smelting, publishing a book in 1665, *Metallum Martis, or, Iron Made with Pit-coale, Sea-coale, etc.* Shortly afterwards, he established another iron furnace in Dudley, this one with the bellows powered by two horses. Here he was partnered by another entrepreneur **Sir Clement Clerke** (*c.* 1635-93), a Royalist with a wealthy wife granted a baronetcy at the Restoration. Dudley appears to have been forced to sell out of this marginally profitable enterprise also, but retired to a substantial house in Worcester, where he continued a career of unsuccessful 'projecting' until he died. The furnace remained in business for a decade.[66]

Clerke also developed the first British reverberatory furnaces,[67] which he applied to the smelting of iron, lead and copper, devoting his substantial estate to doing so and being thwarted of financial success on several occasions through bankruptcies and debt collectors. The most financially viable of his enterprises was lead smelting, carried on by his son Talbot Clerke (*c.* 1663-1708) at Stokeleigh near Bristol; this was solidly profitable, but descended into litigation in 1683 – although Talbot Clerke managed it for some years in the 1690s and it was still in business in 1754. The Clerkes then set up a copper smelter in Putney and an iron foundry at Vauxhall, which offered shares publicly as 'The Company for Making Iron with Pitcoal' in 1692. Their iron-from-coke process was also used at Coalbrookdale from around 1693, sixteen years before Abraham Darby set up there, taking over the forge, which had become disused in 1703.

Like Dudley, the Clerkes suffered from the disarray of seventeenth-century aristocratic finances and from lawsuits. Their lead smelting business in Bristol appears to have been solidly profitable, but iron-from-coke smelting was probably only economically viable with iron ore and the most suitable coal available locally, a combination found at Coalbrookdale, even before Darby's arrival. The cost of coke relative to charcoal was falling over time as iron smelting volumes increased and wood became scarcer; the viability of coke-based smelting may have been boosted further after 1689 by the timber-absorbing shipbuilding

---

66. P.W. King, 'Sir Clement Clerke and the Adoption of Coal in Metallurgy', *Transactions of the Newcomen Society*, Vol. 73, no. 1 (2001), pp. 33-52, gives details of Clerke's life, his interaction with Dudley and the pre-Darby smelting of pig iron and other metals using coke and coal.
67. A reverberatory furnace isolates the metal being smelted from the fuel, thus avoiding impurities, for example, sulphur from coal.

programmes of the Nine Years' War and the War of the Spanish Succession. Still, the unattractive financial results of Dudley and Clerke's pioneering did not encourage others.

Another innovation was John Dwight's (1636-1703) fine stoneware pottery, patented in 1672 and exhibited at the Royal Society in 1674. Dwight established the Fulham Pottery to manufacture his product without great success, inspiring two Dutch brothers, the Elers, who took his methods and established a pottery near Burslem, Staffordshire in 1690; this ran to 1700, again without great financial success. Its methods were copied by Aaron Wedgwood (1666-1743), who with his sons Thomas (1703-76) and 'Long John' (1705-80) became the most successful members of the Wedgwood pottery dynasty until their cousin Josiah rented a modest pottery from them in 1759.

George Ravenscroft (1632-83) was a Roman Catholic merchant who lived for a time in Venice, acquiring glass trade know-how and establishing a successful import/export business. Then, in 1673, he established a glass-making factory in London and began to make crystal with lead oxide added, obtaining a patent for this process in 1674. He perfected his process in 1676, adding a further factory in Henley-on-Thames, which had a sand deposit especially suitable for lead oxide production. His business was successful, but in 1679 he was forced to close it, probably after harassment by London's Whig mobs during that year's 'Popish Plot' frenzy. However, others copied his lead glass process, and Britain became a leader in the industry, showing that private sector initiative could achieve better results than Jean-Baptiste Colbert's dirigiste attempt to get France into the glassware business.

Most important to the future of industrialization was **Thomas Tompion** (1639-1713). Tompion was the eldest son of a blacksmith, who was apprenticed in 1664 to a London clockmaker and who opened his own establishment around 1670. He benefited from a burgeoning market for clocks, inspired by the invention of the pendulum clock in 1656 by Christiaan Huygens. Charles II commissioned him in 1676 to make two clocks for the Royal Observatory, with very long pendulums swinging in very small arcs, wound once a year; these proved highly accurate. With help from Robert Hooke, he made some of the first watches with balance springs and Hooke's anchor escapement. His finest clock was the 1690 'Mostyn Tompion', a year-duration *grand sonnerie* (a form of quarter-striking in which the hour is repeated after each quarter hour sounds) now in the British Museum. Tompion built around 5,500 watches and 650 clocks, some very complex, developing fine-tolerance engineering

The Restoration Renaissance, 1649-88

techniques and materials know-how that became essential to later machine development.

Science

The Restoration period marked the take-off of scientific innovation, with considerable encouragement from Charles II and Prince Rupert, both keen amateur experimenters. The catalyst was the formation on 28 November 1660 of what would become the Royal Society, when granted a royal charter two years later. This was to some extent an amalgamation of previous groups based at London's Gresham College and in Oxford, with origins dating back to 1645. It derived from Francis Bacon's idea of a 'House of Solomon' – a collecting house for scientific experimentation where the accumulated wisdom would generate further ideas and experimental work. The Royal Society's *Philosophical Transactions* was first published in 1665 and continues to this day.

Founding Fellows of the Royal Society included Sir William Petty, Robert Boyle and Sir Christopher Wren. Robert Hooke became its Curator of Experiments and a Fellow in 1663. The Royal Society gained the final accolade of Royal approval and social status in 1665, when Charles II, the future James II, Prince Rupert and Clarendon all became Fellows. Other Fellows included Sir Isaac Newton elected in 1672, Gottfried von Leibniz in 1673, John Flamsteed in 1677 and Edmond Halley in 1678.

Robert Boyle (1627-91), the seventh son of the first Earl of Cork, was the father of modern chemistry – his *The Sceptical Chymist* of 1661 was its foundation work. He differed from the alchemists in using Bacon's Scientific Method to pursue scientific advances, with theory driving experimentation and vice versa. He propounded Boyle's Law, that the pressure of a gas is inversely proportional to volume, a central identity in the development of steam power. He was also a keen Anglican theologian.

Sir Christopher Wren (1632-1723), the son of a dean of Windsor and the nephew of Matthew Wren (Bishop of Ely 1638-46 and 1660-67), was appointed Professor of Astronomy at Gresham College in 1657; a Wren lecture at Gresham was used to gather members for the Royal Society's inaugural meeting. He was elected Savilian Professor of Astronomy at Oxford in 1661 and carried out considerable work in astronomy, optics and the measuring sciences. Then, in 1669, he switched to architecture, becoming Surveyor of the King's Works. He was instrumental in rebuilding 51 churches destroyed by the Great Fire of London, as well as St Paul's Cathedral, completed in 1708. He was President of the Royal Society from 1680 to 1682 and a Tory MP in four Parliaments between 1685 and 1701. Dismissed from his appointments by the Whigs in 1718, he died in 1723, aged 91.

Robert Hooke (1635-1703) was less well-off than Boyle and Wren; he took an inheritance of £40 to become educated at Westminster, also in a staunchly Tory/Anglican tradition, then financed his Christ Church, Oxford education by working as a 'chemical assistant'. With Boyle's patronage, he was appointed the Royal Society's Curator of Experiments, then in 1665 made his name by publishing *Micrographia*, showing microscope-generated images of fleas and micro-organisms, as well as determining that fossils were the remnants of extinct creatures. He had already discovered Hooke's Law, that the tension of a spring is proportionate to its extension. He propounded the inverse square law of gravitation before Newton, though without Newton's mathematical analysis. He was the first to propound a wave theory of light and to demonstrate that heat expanded matter. Finally, he invented the anchor escapement, becoming a patron of Tompion.

Sir Isaac Newton (1642-1727) carried out almost all his scientific work during the Restoration period, publishing *Principia Mathematica* in 1687, although *Opticks* did not appear until 1704. Like Hooke, he was born in modest circumstances, his education at King's School, Grantham being funded by an uncle, before going to Trinity College, Cambridge as a subsizar, performing valet's duties for the titled students. After a year away from Cambridge during the Plague of 1665, during which he did much of his best theoretical work, he graduated MA in 1668 and became Lucasian Professor of Mathematics the following year. Over the next two decades, he revolutionized mechanics, gravitation and optics, invented the reflecting telescope and came up with his 'fluxions' notation of calculus some years before Leibniz, whose formulation was superior and is used today. Unlike Boyle, Wren and Hooke, he was a low-church Whig, serving in two parliaments in 1689 and 1701 and owing his later position as Master of the Mint to Whig patronage.

John Flamsteed (1646-1719), the son of a maltster, was educated at Derby School and briefly at Jesus College, Cambridge. In 1674, having written several papers in astronomy, he was appointed assistant to a committee to examine a lunar method of determining longitude. As a result of this work, in 1675, he was appointed the first Astronomer Royal and given charge of Greenwich Observatory, the foundation stone of which was laid that year. He remained Astronomer Royal until his death, also becoming Rector of Burstow in Surrey. He compiled a

The Restoration Renaissance, 1649-88   135

star catalogue, with three times as many stars as Tycho Brahe's, which was published in 1712. His *Historia Coelestis Britannica* was published posthumously in 1725; it was the first major output of Greenwich Observatory.

Edmond Halley (1658-1742) was the son of a wealthy soap maker, educated at St Paul's School and Queen's College, Oxford. He became assistant to Flamsteed, proposing to prepare a catalogue of stars in the Southern Hemisphere, for which he spent two years in St Helena between 1676 and 1678. In 1682 he made observations of Halley's Comet and predicted its return in 1759. In 1693 he published an article on life annuities, using the statistics compiled in Breslau by Casper Neumann (1648-1715); this article became the foundation of the life assurance industry. In 1698-1700 he commanded the world's first scientific voyage, to determine the variation by position of the magnetic compass, published as the *General Chart of the Variation of the Compass* in 1701. He became Savilian Professor of Mathematics at Oxford in 1703 and discovered the proper motion of the 'fixed' stars in 1718, succeeding Flamsteed as Astronomer Royal in 1720.

Outside the Royal Society, the most important scientific advances were made by the doctor **Thomas Sydenham** (1624-89). Sydenham, from a Puritan family, obtained a licence to practice from the College of Physicians in 1663 and became London's most successful practitioner of medicine. He developed new methods that regarded each disease as individual, to be distinguished by the symptoms, drawing up a complete picture of the characteristics of each. He pioneered the use of 'Jesuits' Bark' (quinine) for malaria and used opium to relieve suffering. He also worked from the maxim, 'First, do no harm', regarding with suspicion the numerous dangerous and painful remedies then used. He published several works, the most important being the *Observationes Medicae* of 1676 and was referred to in the following century as the 'English Hippocrates'. In 1600, only 5% of dying men sent for a doctor; by 1700, the majority did so; Sydenham's work bore considerable responsibility for this change.[68]

* * *

The changes in government wrought by the Civil War and the Interregnum were as important economically as politically. From 1649, commercial considerations began to play an important role in British

---

68. Ian Mortimer, *The Time Traveller's Guide to Restoration Britain* (London: Vintage, 2017), p. 406.

economic policies, then, from 1660, a new spirit of scientific innovation and business entrepreneurship took hold. Conversely, infrastructure remained poor and the financial markets primitive, so the Britain of 1688 still lacked basic building blocks for industrialization. Nevertheless, it was already quite different from any other European country, even the Netherlands, and the roots of the Industrial Revolution were planted during this period of extensive political and economic experimentation.

5

Iron, Steam and Finance, 1689-1720

The period between the 1688 Revolution and the South Sea Bubble was one of political turmoil and substantial progress towards industrialization on several fronts. The period's lengthy and expensive wars created a robust market for long-term government debt, while the mechanics by which that market was created produced an active secondary share market. The wars also caused the growth of a large armaments industry, which produced Sir Ambrose Crowley's first large-scale iron works. Following Petty's work, the English government began to collect and keep economic statistics. Finally, there were the technological beginnings of industrialization itself, in the Newcomen steam engine and the Coalbrookdale Iron Works.

Political Developments, 1689-1702

Charles II had been an almost ideal ruler for a country undergoing an intellectual, scientific and entrepreneurial efflorescence. However, while James II shared many beliefs and capabilities with his brother, he was both more rigid and less intelligent. Even though he inherited a stable Tory government and a well-disposed Parliament elected in 1685, his clumsy attempts to open the English political system to Catholics alienated the Church-and-King Tories and it all unravelled within three years.

Whigs like the slippery second Earl of Sunderland[1] to whom James II then turned for support were unreliable with a purely transactional

---

1. Robert Spencer, (1641-1702). 2nd Earl of Sunderland from 1643. KG 1687. Secretary of State for the Northern Department 1679-80, 1683-84,

relationship with a king they disliked. Sunderland (who turned Catholic in 1687, reverting to Anglicanism in 1691) made overtures to William III in the summer of 1688. The surprise birth of a male heir to the throne (James, 'the Old Pretender' 1688-1766) in June 1688 united the political classes against him, since they feared long-term Catholic rule – Louis XIV's 1685 Revocation of the Edict of Nantes and subsequent persecution of his Huguenot subjects had naturally inflamed their fears. William III walked through an open door to the throne in November 1688; his large fleet and 14,000 men were almost unnecessary.

William III was declared King of England, Scotland and Ireland jointly with his wife, Mary II, James II's daughter and the legitimate heir after James and his infant son, by the Convention Parliament, with an accompanying Bill of Rights in February 1689. Having been ruler of the Netherlands since 1672, William favoured the pro-Dutch Whigs, who had been predominant among those inviting him to invade (four of the 'Immortal Seven' whose letter invited William to invade were Whigs, with two moderates[2] and one Tory [Danby]). His principal motive for invading Britain had been to get its assistance in the Netherlands' new war with France, (the Nine Years' War) rather than James II's neutrality and close relationship with France – the Whigs were helpful in this endeavour. However, Mary II, who kept mainly in the background but still had influence, was close to her uncle Rochester and leaned towards the Tories, as did her sister Anne.

William III's early ministries were predominantly Whig, dominated by the Junto of powerful Whig politicians. The underlying Tory strength of popular opinion asserted itself in the 1690 election and from then until 1697 and again in 1700 and 1701 the finance specialist Sidney Godolphin[3] represented the moderate Tory interest as First Lord of the Treasury (not then a joint position with that of prime minister). William III came to see the advantages of party competition and after

---

Secretary of State for the Southern Department, 1680-81, 1684-88, Lord President of the Council 1685-88, Lord Chamberlain, 1695-99.

2. One of the moderates was Charles Talbot (1660-1718), 12th Earl of Shrewsbury from 1667, 1st Duke of Shrewsbury from 1694. Southern Secretary of State, 1689-90, 1695-98, Northern Secretary of State, 1694-95, Lord Chamberlain, 1699-1700, Lord Lieutenant of Ireland, 1713-14, Lord High Treasurer, 1714.

3. Sidney Godolphin (1645-1712). Baron Godolphin from 1684, Earl of Godolphin from 1706. MP for Helston, 1665-1684. Northern Secretary, 1684, First Lord of the Treasury 1684-85, 1690-97, 1700-01, Lord High Treasurer 1702-10.

Iron, Steam and Finance, 1689-1720

the first years avoided giving the Whigs complete dominance, unlike the first two Georges a generation later. The Triennial Act 1694, mandating elections every three years, helped him to keep the political pack of cards well shuffled. After the 1697 Treaty of Ryswick ended the Nine Years' War, more Tories were admitted to William's ministries, even though Mary II had died in 1694.

Whig and eighteenth century historians claimed the 1688 Revolution completely changed English government. This is not entirely the case. It increased the power of Parliament and meant that no year went by without a parliamentary session – though the demands of 'Dutch finance', whereby debt was authorized and rolled over each year were also responsible for that. The Corrupt Practices Act 1695 reflected the new power of Parliament and the importance of not having its elections suborned; in practice, while in operation until 1854, the Act was only occasionally enforced.

However, Charles II had been far from an absolute monarch, while as late as 1778-82 George III effectively ran the government through the feeble Lord North and a couple of able assistants primarily responsible to the king. The advent of William Pitt the Younger reduced royal power, the advent of the selfish and idle Prince Regent[4] in 1811 reduced it further and the Reform Act of 1832 reduced it further still, but George III changed his government in 1807, and William IV[5] attempted unsuccessfully to do so in 1835. Queen Anne, who vetoed bills until 1708, still 'touched for the King's Evil' – people suffering from scrofula would kneel before the monarch seeking his or her curing touch – the practice was only abandoned under the Hanoverians because George I thought it a Papist superstition.[6] In many respects, the true birth of modern British government was in 1660, not 1688 and its designer was Clarendon, not William III.[7]

While the Revolution changed government less than its adherents later proclaimed, it involved relatively little bloodshed (except in Ireland) or violation of property rights (again, except in Ireland). Whereas the Civil

---

4. George IV (1762-1830). Prince Regent, 1811-20. King of United Kingdom, 1820-30.
5. William IV (1765-1837). King of United Kingdom, 1830-37.
6. George I (1660-1727). Elector of Hanover, 1698-1727. King of Great Britain, 1714-27.
7. Clarendon's key innovation, as previously mentioned, was the Tenures Abolition Act 1660. The Restoration also brought the advent of primarily ministerial government.

140   *Forging Modernity*

War had led to the sequestration of Royalist estates, and later European revolutions were even more extreme in their destruction of lives and property, the 1688 Revolution, by avoiding sequestrations, established property rights more firmly in England and Scotland. John Locke's famous invocation of 'Life, Liberty and Property' was published in his *Two Treatises of Government* in 1689; from that date British governments took property rights very seriously.

Locke's own Whiggish connections (his patron had been the Whig leader the first Earl of Shaftesbury)[8] ensured that even the most radical Whigs (though not Thomas Jefferson, who never entered British politics) were entirely sound on property rights until after the French Revolution. This universal appreciation of the importance of rock-solid property rights provided a firm foundation for the investments and innovation that industrialization would require.

The early years of William III's reign were a time of government paranoia, much of it justified. The regime attempted to ensure allegiance by imposing various oaths of loyalty, but found they only ensured *de facto* allegiance, that could disappear if James II invaded – in any case several bishops, including the Archbishop of Canterbury William Sancroft,[9] refused to take them and became 'non-jurors'. The Toleration Act 1688 gave toleration to (primarily Whig) Nonconformists, but refused it to Catholics, who by another Act were prohibited from living within ten miles of London – in 1700 this Act forced the young Alexander Pope and his family to move to Berkshire. In general, the power of Nonconformism was far greater than during the Restoration and sexual licence correspondingly less; the Society for Promoting Christian Knowledge was founded in 1698.

William III fought serious wars with James directly in Scotland and Ireland, while, in England, the Habeas Corpus Act was suspended for a time, the second Earl of Clarendon was imprisoned for several months in 1689, as was the centrist Earl of Marlborough[10] in 1692 (whose correspondence with James II had been made illegal by the

---

8. Anthony Ashley Cooper (1621-83). 1st Baron Ashley from 1661, 1st Earl of Shaftesbury from 1673. MP for Tewkesbury and Wiltshire, 1640, 1653-59, 1660-61. Chancellor of the Exchequer, 1661-72, Lord Chancellor, 1672-73, First Lord of Trade, 1672-76, Lord President of the Council, 1679.

9. William Sancroft (1617-93). Archbishop of Canterbury, 1678-91.

10. John Churchill (1650-1722). 1st Earl of Marlborough from 1689, 1st Duke of Marlborough from 1702. MP for Newtown, 1679. Ambassador to France, 1685. Captain-General of the British Army, 1702-11.

Correspondence with Enemies Act 1691). Press censorship was more severely enforced than before 1688 until the Licensing Act was allowed to lapse in 1695, bringing nominal press freedom. Plots against William III's life in 1694 and more doubtfully in 1696 were betrayed by informers. Only after the 1697 Treaty of Ryswick did the security situation improve and national life return to its pre-1688 level of liberty and creativity. William III's own financial position was regularized by the Civil List Act 1697, making a generous regular allowance available for the Court.

For most of William III's reign Britain was at war. Thus, William III could not have followed the practice of Charles II and James II, living off ordinary revenues voted at the beginning of his reign and calling Parliament only when something special was needed. Instead, he and his Parliaments levied much heavier taxes than the English people had grown used to in the benign latter years of Charles II's reign and resorted to heavy borrowing to make up the inevitable deficits. In this, he was immeasurably helped by his experience of Dutch practice, where the state had been almost continuously at war since 1567 and had adopted a system of heavy taxes, funded debt and a quasi-official central bank to deal with the wars' financing needs. By 1688, the Dutch economy was beginning to buckle under the strain – one reason why William was so keen to gain control of the much larger and financially under-borrowed English state – but Dutch financing techniques were to prove invaluable to both William and his successors.

The Convention Parliament of 1689 was determined not to repeat its 1685 predecessor's generosity, funding James II's peacetime government throughout his reign. Accordingly, it abolished the unpopular Hearth Tax and voted only excise duties (which had greatly increased with the Restoration's trade boom) for the whole of William's reign, with customs duties only for three years (later extended to four years). Even William III's peacetime revenues were insufficient.

Then, in 1692, a Whig-dominated Parliament imposed the Land Tax at 20% on the deemed income from land and other assets (essentially a primitive income tax on unearned income from fixed assets) which raised about £2 million annually, effectively doubling the country's tax capacity (it contributed 42% of total revenues during the Nine Years' War).[11] The 1692 land valuations were never revised, but from 1697 a quota system was installed, whereby each area was assigned a quota of land tax payable and local worthies were assigned to collect it. The tax was renewed annually until 1798, when it was made permanent and capitalized.

---

11. Carruthers, *City of Capital*, p. 70.

The Land Tax reduced taxation on thriving areas of increasing population, commerce and finance, while imposing heavy taxation on agricultural land, mostly owned by Tories. Its organization reflected the Whigs' heavy bias in favour of the 'monied interest' and against landholders. It was a major stimulus for the creation immediately following its passage of the long-term government bond market (interest from which escaped the tax). Later, it was a useful boost to industrialization, since industrial assets were mostly not subject to it, subsidising them compared to agriculture. On the other hand, in 1694 Charles Davenant[12] wrote a pamphlet warning that it could cause a collapse in land values leading to national bankruptcy; this was a reasonable fear in its early years.

The years of war brought further Treasury creativity in creating new taxes. In 1694 the Stamp Duty was instituted (similar to that attempted for the American colonies in 1765) by which legal documents were subjected to a compulsory stamp, the amount varying according to the type and value of the document – the tax raised about £50,000 annually initially. In 1712, the tax was extended at a rate of one penny per sheet to newspapers; this tended to suppress the low-end press and restrict publications to relatively wealthy readers. In 1696, the Land Tax was balanced by the Window Tax, in force for the next 155 years, which added to the Land Tax a tax on structures that avoided the dwellings of the poorest. That tax was criticized by sentimental Victorians as 'damaging the health of the people' because the tax resulted in buildings with poor ventilation, but given the state of public health before 1851, the complainers would have done better to have installed some drains!

The Whigs of this period, and up to 1760, were wedded to mercantilism, far more so than the relatively pro free trade Tories (as they had been when passing the Trade with France Act 1678 at a time when Britain and France were at peace). Hence, the Plantation Trade Act 1695 was a substantial tightening of the Navigation Acts, which noted in its preamble the 'great abuses being committed ... by the artifice and cunning of ill-disposed persons'. It now required that all imports and exports from England and its possessions must be carried in English

---

12. Charles Davenant (1656-1714). Tory MP for St Ives and Great Bedwyn, 1685-87, 1698-1701. Commissioner of the Excise, 1678-89, Secretary to Commission for Union with Scotland, 1702-3, Inspector-General of Imports and Exports, 1703-14. Author of *On the Ways and Means of Supplying the War* (1694).

Iron, Steam and Finance, 1689-1720 143

ships with three quarters English crew. It also gave colonial governors and their appointees the same rights of inspection as customs officers in England and forced them to post a bond to ensure their compliance. Admiralty courts were instituted and colonial customs officers were only to be recruited from those born in England. By this Act, the protectionist system in force for most of the eighteenth century (which was much resented in New England) was introduced.

The last years of William III were happier. The Whig Junto was ejected from office in 1699-1700, then the January 1701 election produced a substantial majority for the Tories, after which the Act of Settlement 1701 was passed, providing that the Elector of Hanover (whose mother was the granddaughter of James VI and I) would eventually succeed Queen Anne as George I. During 1701, it became clear after the death of the Spanish king Charles II that Louis XIV would claim the succession for his grandson. Furthermore, when James II died in September 1701, Louis recognized his thirteen-year-old son as King James III. Consequently, further war seemed imminent. The general election of November 1701 gave the Whigs a majority in Parliament. However, in March William III died and the succession passed to Queen Anne, who was strongly Anglican and leaned towards the Tories.

Dutch Finance

Initially, the Nine Years' War (1688-97) was financed by tax increases and short-term debt. The fifteen years beforehand, with booming trade in taxable commodities and cautious fiscal management, allowed considerable capacity for both. However, with larger forces than England's previous foreign wars and campaigns in Ireland and Scotland, the war ran through money at an unprecedented rate. Before 1688, this would have caused national bankruptcy, because lenders were unwilling to lend long term to a monarch who had personal liability but was mortal. With Parliament now involved yearly in the nation's finances, and potential lenders and bankers represented in Parliament, the rights of potential bondholders were more solidly protected.

By 1693, despite the Land Tax, the country was in fiscal crisis. Parliament's solution by the Government Life Annuities Act, 1693 was to escrow some new excise duties for 99 years to secure a new £1 million tontine, the first large long-term borrowing ever attempted in England. Investors subscribed only £108,100 to the tontine, the failure presumably a result of the absurd structure, which incentivized knocking off other

144 *Forging Modernity*

bondholders.[13] However, the Act also provided for life annuities, paying 14% annually, which proved more satisfactory and they were fully subscribed – the (presumably older) person providing the money did not have to be the annuitant, so wealthy people could nominate their grandchildren, who would (the various unpleasant early modern diseases permitting) continue to receive 14% payments long after grandpapa's death.

The following year, the state raised £970,000 through two issues of annuities: the first on one, two or three lives; and a second through selling fixed 96-year annuities to replace life annuities. It also raised £1 million through the Million Lottery,[14] which was well received, given the public's propensity for gambling. (The Million Bank was founded to manage the lottery distributions, issuing shares in return for lottery tickets; it later bought up the 99-year reversions to life annuities that were sold between 1698 and 1702, swapping some of them unprofitably for South Sea stock in 1720. The bank survived until 1796, when the annuities ran out.) Even here, the public's appetite was limited; a Malt Lottery in 1697 failed, although a burst of lotteries in 1711 would raise £7.1 million.

These long-term issues and lotteries all suffered from illiquidity. Although government debts were transferable, there was no established market in the various complex annuities and lottery entitlements, which were almost impossible to value. This had been a problem even in the short-term commercial debt market, where bills of exchange were not fully transferable (unlike in the Netherlands) until the Bills of Exchange Act 1704. Josiah Child had remarked twenty years earlier on the advantage given to Dutch trade by their transferability.

The government's solution to the liquidity problem was not the sale of long-term fixed interest bonds, as would have been natural, but the establishment of a monopoly central bank, the Bank of England, which in return for its charter, which expired in 1705, and the exclusive right to hold government cash balances and issue bank notes, bought £1.2 million of long-term bonds, bearing 8% interest. The Bank financed itself by issuing £1.2 million of common stock, which was taken up within ten days.

---

13. Carruthers, *City of Capital*, p. 75. Under a tontine, annual debt service payments are made to an ever-decreasing number of bondholders, so that the last person standing gets the entire debt service to himself.

14. A project of Thomas Neale (1641-99). FRS 1664. MP for Petersfield, Ludgershall and Stockbridge, 1668-88 (Tory), 1689-99 (Whig). Master of the Mint, 1686-99.

Iron, Steam and Finance, 1689-1720

The Bank of England was the project of the Scottish projector, William Pateron.[15] It gained traction when it was taken up by the Whig Junto's Charles Montagu,[16] who took charge of the nation's finances until 1699. It was set up by the Bank of England Act 1694 (also known as the Tonnage Act). The Bank's first governor was Sir John Houblon (1632-1712),[17] a lifelong Whig who had sat on the City of London Grand Jury 'worth a million of money' that, very questionably, had acquitted Shaftesbury of High Treason in 1681.[18] The Bank thereafter remained a bulwark of the Whig party with many Dissenting shareholders. A Whig government gave it a banking monopoly in 1708 and another Whig government after 1714 allowed it to take over the management of government debt.

The formation of the Bank of England had short-term importance as an example of how to use joint-stock companies to sell government debt. The Tories attempted to match Whig fundraising success with a Land Bank in 1696 but failed because that year specie was exceptionally tight because of the impending recoinage. The Bank of England enlarged its capital in 1697, providing another £1 million of long-term financing. The following year a New East India Company was formed, opposing the generally Tory East India Company and eliminating its monopoly, and providing £2 million in long-term government financing.

The great majority of subscribers to these new financings came from the 'monied interest' – the merchant community domiciled in London and the Home Counties, with a substantial percentage coming from London's Huguenot and Jewish communities. Very few of the traditional rich – notably the peerage – subscribed, nor did the Tory landed gentry; those peers who did subscribe were almost all either government ministers or favourites of William III. This concentration of holders in the 'monied interest' went down in the further issues up to 1720, but the traditional pools of wealth outside London only became major holders

---

15. William Paterson (1658-1719). Scottish merchant, banker, promotor and co-founder of the Bank of England, as well as the (catastrophic) Scottish Darien scheme and union of Scotland with England.

16. Charles Montagu, (1661-1715). 1st Baron Halifax from 1700, 1st Earl of Halifax from 1715. MP for Maldon and Westminster, 1689-1701. Commissioner of the Treasury, 1692-94, Chancellor of the Exchequer, 1694-99, First Lord of the Treasury, 1697-99, 1714-15. Poet and leading member of the Whig Junto.

17. Sir John Houblon (1632-1712). Governor of the Bank of England, 1694-97. Lord Mayor of London, 1695-96.

18. P.G.M. Dickson, *The Financial Revolution in England: A Study in the Development of Public Credit, 1688-1756* (London: Macmillan, 1967), p. 55.

of government bonds in the 1740s and 1750s, when the returns were lower and market manipulation less.[19]

By 1700, the state had funded its needs for the Nine Years' War, with total debt outstanding of £14.2 million, but at a fearful cost – the annual debt service charge was 8.8% of the principal amount.[20] With the hindsight of three centuries, it would seem that the simplest way for the government to lengthen maturities would have been to make modest issues of medium-term (five to seven years' maturity) bonds, then scale up as investor demand appeared. The new bonds would have been easy to value and trade, so a liquid secondary market would have developed naturally. Once the secondary market developed, the debt's cost should have been no higher than the 5% per annum prevalent in the mortgage market – after all, the Netherlands in 1700 had an overall debt cost of little over 4%.[21]

The funding method the government chose, using tontines, lotteries, annuities and new joint-stock companies, was far more expensive, but provided much greater returns for the intermediaries and 'monied interest' investors involved. Walpole refinanced some of this expensive debt by a five-per-cent perpetual bond in 1717, establishing the forerunner of Consols; this could usefully have been done a quarter of a century earlier. Those who watched Wall Street's over-complex financial juggling in the years before 2008 might agree with the Tory squires who believed that a sharp-dealing 'monied interest' was taking advantage of dozy Whig ministers at public expense.

The repeated issues for new joint-stock companies, all of which had some guaranteed income from their holdings of government bonds, helped a secondary share market to develop, located in Jonathan's Coffee House and on Exchange Alley in which Jonathan's was situated. Before 1688, the East India Company had been the only traded share, and its share sales were limited to a tight pool of politically connected investors, since shareholders elected EIC directors who determined the company's policy. (This remained true throughout the eighteenth century, with a contested directors' election involving competing share purchases

---

19. Ibid., pp. 255-60, has details on the subscribers to 1690s issues; the remainder of that chapter discusses the evolution of the bondholder classes up to 1756.

20. Carruthers, *City of Capital*, p. 80.

21. I speak from experience; this was the method I used in Croatia in 1996 and 1997 to develop a medium-term bond market in Croatia's new currency, the *kuna*.

Iron, Steam and Finance, 1689-1720

in 1764.) The Bank of England, the Million Bank, the New East India Company and eventually the South Sea Company broadened the range of investments available, and in 1698 John Castaing[22] published the first daily list of share prices.

The other economic initiative was a major recoinage, begun in 1696. The currency produced by Charles II's milled issue had proved inadequate to the expanding economy, so Montagu appointed Newton as Warden of the Mint to oversee a full recoinage of silver currency. Originally the government intended to raise the coins' face value by one quarter to bring it in line with the higher silver price (Spain's New World mines were less productive than they had been) but Parliament would not approve this, so the recoinage was carried out at the existing silver parity. Initially, the recoinage went very slowly, while existing coins were called in, being reimbursed according to their weight. After Newton took over, the process was mechanised, with 500 men and 50 horses driving the rolling mills and substantial division of labour. Within two years £6.7 million of new coinage had been produced, compared to £3.3 million over the preceding 30 years, with the output reaching £100,000 per working week, more than double the original target rate.[23]

Scotland and Ireland

Scotland and Ireland both suffered from William III's rule. In Scotland, where James VII and II and the Stuarts retained considerable ancestral loyalty, there was resistance in 1689, with the rebels winning a significant victory at the Battle of Killiecrankie before capitulating after defeat at the Battle of Dunkeld. Further resistance was crushed ruthlessly, notably by the 1692 Massacre of Glencoe. The Scottish Act of Settlement 1690 legalised the Presbyterian Scottish Kirk and abolished Scottish Episcopalianism. This led to Whig dominance in Scotland for the next century, but with considerable Episcopalian/Jacobite resistance, which manifested itself in the risings of 1715 and 1745.

Economically, the 1690s were miserable, the coldest decade of the last 750 years. Repeated harvest failures resulting in the 'Seven Ill Years' of widespread famine, killing an estimated 5-15% of the population. In 1695, the Scottish parliament established the Bank of Scotland with capital

---

22. John Castaing (*c.* 1665-*c.* 1725). Huguenot exchange broker. Published bi-weekly, *Course of the Exchange*, from 1698.

23. Thomas Levenson, *Money for Nothing* (New York: Random House, 2020), pp. 57-65, has a good account of the recoinage and Newton's involvement.

148   *Forging Modernity*

of 1.2 million Scottish pounds (£100,000), given a 21-year monopoly to finance Scottish business; it was specifically prohibited from lending to the Scottish government without parliamentary approval and had an English Tory merchant/banker, John Holland[24] as its founder and first governor. As an inducement to invest, foreign shareholders with one share of 1,000 Scottish pounds (£83) were automatically naturalized as Scotsmen.[25] The Bank of Scotland's business focus and lack of central banking operations would make Scottish banking sounder than English, although the 1772 crisis (see Chapter 7) was an exception to this.

The Scottish parliament in 1695 also established the Company of Scotland, with a 21-year monopoly of trade to India, Africa and the Americas, modelled on the Dutch East India Company, and capital of £400,000 raised from investors around Europe, approximately 20% of all the money circulating in Scotland. (Paterson was a leading proponent; it was a largely Whig scheme, matching the Tory Bank of Scotland.)

With Paterson to the fore, the Company decided to establish a Scottish colony at Darien, on the Isthmus of Panama. Five ships with 1,200 colonists set sail from the East Coast port of Leith, sailing round the north coast of Scotland to avoid English warships, and, after a four-month voyage, landed in Darien, christening their settlement 'Caledonia' and its capital 'New Edinburgh'. Alas, the notorious Panamanian fevers wiped out the colony, which was abandoned after only eight months. A second expedition found only a burnt-out and deserted settlement and succumbed within a year to diseases and a Spanish assault. Further expeditions were also failures, and the scheme ended in 1704 with the hanging in Edinburgh of the innocent captain and crew of an English merchant ship.

William III's reign was even more miserable in Ireland. James II had been popular there, restoring some of the property rights of Irish Catholics, appointing Irish Catholic advisers and giving them hope of long-term toleration. After his removal from England, Ireland remained loyal to him, electing a 'Patriot' Parliament that attempted to reverse some more of the Cromwellian land seizures. James II landed in Ireland in 1689 and met with major support. William's regime was hard pressed to defeat him, but it eventually did so at the Battle of the Boyne in

---

24. John Holland (1658-1722). English banker. Founded Bank of Scotland, 1695.
25. This was only a modest inducement in Scotland's impoverished 1690s but by Liverpool's time it gave foreigners cheap access to British nationality, so he abolished the privilege in 1818.

Iron, Steam and Finance, 1689-1720

149

July 1690. The Treaty of Limerick, which ended the war in 1691, was broken by William in subsequent years, during which much of the remaining Catholic property was forfeited to absentee landlords and severe penal laws were introduced and strengthened in the following decade.

By those laws, Catholics were prohibited from sitting in the Irish or English/British Parliaments and, from 1728, prevented from voting; they were also prevented from buying land and in 1704 forced to subdivide their estates on death. (The papacy continued to recognize the Old Pretender as legitimate ruler of Britain until his death in 1766 and allowed him to appoint Irish Catholic bishops, giving a pretext for the penal laws until the 1770s.) The Plantation Trade Act 1695 imposed duties on Irish exports to England, while the Irish were compelled to take English goods duty-free. The Wool Act 1699 prevented Ireland from exporting wool to England or the American colonies; it shut off one of the few areas of Irish comparative advantage. Finally, the Declaratory Act 1719 declared the right of the British Parliament to legislate for Ireland, that its laws superseded those of the Irish parliament and that the British House of Lords would function as the final court of appeal in Irish cases. By 1720, Irish Catholics had little property and few civil rights.

Colonies and Trade

Colonially, the follies of the late 1680s were reflected in the East India Company's poor results in the following decade; the EIC's trade, over £800,000 in 1684, fell to a mere £30,000 in both 1692 and 1695.[26] By suitable application of £60,000 in bribes, Sir Josiah Child, still involved with the EIC although no longer governor, was able to secure a new 21-year EIC charter in 1693. The EIC's business in India was further disturbed by the pirate Henry Every's 1695 seizure of the pride of Aurangzeb's fleet, with around £400,000 in loot. After a mob stormed East India House in 1697, the Whig-allied New East India Company was formed the following year.

The New Company achieved little on India's west coast but had considerable success in China, opening that country further to British trade. Meanwhile, Madras was run by Thomas 'Diamond' Pitt,[27] who

---

26. Keay, *The Honourable Company*, p. 177.
27. Thomas Pitt (1653-1726). MP for Salisbury, Old Sarum and Thirsk, 1689-95, 1710-26. President of Fort St George, 1698-1709. Grandfather of William Pitt (the Elder), Earl of Chatham.

established his family fortunes by buying a diamond which he later sold at an enormous profit to the regent of France and made Madras a highly profitable post trading with the local rulers, by now splitting from Mughal rule. In 1709 the two East India Companies were merged to form the United East India Company and, with peace regained, expansion resumed, with Calcutta, founded in 1690, adding to Bombay and Madras as major centres. By 1720, 15% of British imports were from India, around £900,000 per annum, at last a higher figure than in the early 1680s. Most importantly, in 1716, the EIC had obtained a 'firman' (a grant) from the new Mughal, entitling the company and its servants to trade free of Indian taxes.

In Africa, the Royal African Company lost its legal monopoly in 1689, even though its directors transferred a substantial shareholding to William III. This was regularized by the Trade with Africa Act 1697, which opened the slave trade to all English merchants who were required to pay a 10% levy to maintain the RAC's forts and castles in Africa – the tax was remitted in 1712. The result was the RAC's insolvency in 1708, after which it continued on a reduced scale, transporting slaves until 1731 and wound up in 1750.

Under the new competitive conditions, the volume of slaves carried by British slavers increased – 75,000 by British independent slavers in the decade to 1707 and 23,000 by the RAC.[28] The major recipients were the Caribbean sugar islands, although the North American colonies were growing markets after 1700. By 1712, when the Treaty of Utrecht was being negotiated, the British were the largest slave traders other than Portugal, which supplied slaves to Brazil. Consequently, it made sense to acquire the Spanish *asiento*, a monopoly on supplying slaves to the Spanish empire, for the new South Sea Company. (In the event, the *asiento* was never a true monopoly, because Spanish colonists bought slaves from Jamaica, and it was never very profitable, being suspended in 1739 when the War of Jenkins' Ear against Spain broke out and sold back to Spain for only £100,000 by the 1750 Treaty of Madrid.)

Even though the government was now predominantly Whig and more attractive to the religious zealots of New England, the American colonies showed slower population growth than they had earlier, with total population rising from 210,372 in 1690 to 466,185 in 1720. Population growth was especially sluggish in the 1690s, only 19% over the decade compared to 39% growth in the 1680s. The slave population quadrupled from 16,729 to 68,839 between 1690 and 1720, rising from

---

28. Thomas, *The Slave Trade*, p. 206.

Iron, Steam and Finance, 1689-1720

8% to 15% of the total population, with Virginia and Maryland (tobacco) and South Carolina (rice and indigo) predominating.[29]

Economic Thought

The 1690s marked the beginning of Sir William Petty's 'political arithmetic'. Parliament set up a Public Accounts Committee in 1690 that pulled together the disparate and muddled statistics of government revenue and expenditure. The Treasury in response established its own consolidated budgeting system, the beginning of a budget process that has existed ever since.[30]

Gregory King (1648-1712) obtained a sinecure in the College of Heralds, then, in 1695, joined the government, becoming Commissioner of Public Accounts, where he systematized the collection of economic statistics. King's greatest work, *Natural and Political Observations and Conclusions upon the State and Condition of England*, was completed in 1696 but not published because of the sensitivity of his government position. It set out King's detailed estimates of the population and wealth of England; his demographic breakdown is still used today by historians.

Together with Charles Davenant, King also devised the King-Davenant 'Law', promulgated in Davenant's 1699 *Essay on the Probable Methods of Making the People Gainers in the Balance of Trade*. This law estimates the rise in corn prices from a given shortfall in the harvest: for example, a 40% shortfall in the harvest could be expected to raise corn prices by 280%. The law was derived by close observation and measurement, rather than from highfalutin' theory and it applies only to a closed economic system.

Charles Davenant was the son of the poet and impresario Sir William Davenant. He combined service as Excise Commissioner with poetry in his early life and was a strong Tory in the 1685 Parliament. He lost favour after the Revolution and turned to economic pamphleteering, before returning to Parliament as a Country Tory, sponsored by both Robert Harley[31] and Godolphin, in 1698-1701. His economic writings

---

29. US Census Bureau, *Historical Statistics of the United States, Colonial Times to 1970*, 'Chapter Z: Colonial and pre-Federal Statistics, Series Z 1-19', p. 1168.
30. Deringer, *Calculated Values*, pp. 51-64, details the early misadventures of English public accounting.
31. Robert Harley (1661-1724). 1st Earl of Oxford and Mortimer from 1711. MP for Tregony and New Radnor, 1689-1711. Country Whig who

152   *Forging Modernity*

supported the landed interest, opposed long-term debt, believing it made the country uncompetitive, and favoured financing the war through excise duties on a trade surplus, supplemented by short-term debt. He opposed the Land Tax and the initial proposal for the recoinage of 1696, because of its currency debasement which would have reduced the silver value of rents and other long-term contracts.

Davenant's work was important in focussing policymakers' attention on trade itself rather than the accumulation of 'treasure', as Mun had recommended. By this stage public revenue had increased and it was soon apparent that, provided the state's finances were healthy, it could borrow enormous amounts of money if required. 'Treasure' itself was no longer the critical variable. It remained important to ensure that the volume of trade kept expanding and that its balance ideally remained favourable, since, if these conditions were satisfied, the state's creditworthiness would remain solid. Later, Davenant strongly supported the Tories' doomed attempt in 1713-14 to reopen trade with France.

Another important economic thinker was **Bernard Mandeville**, who immigrated from the Netherlands around 1693 and became a physician and economic writer. He was an early exponent of the division of labour, using watch-making as an example. His greatest notoriety came from his 1714 publication of the *The Fable of the Bees*, which postulated that the consumption of spendthrifts led to economic progress and was later much admired by John Maynard Keynes.[32] Unlike Sir Dudley North, he adopted the belief that: 'Private Vices by the dextrous Management of a skilful Politician may be turned into Publick Benefits' – an early example of the Keynesian bureaucrat fallacy.[33] He is often held to have been an early proponent of the consumer society.

* * *

Scientifically, this period was less productive than that of the Restoration, as the Royal Society was beginning a long quiescence, although Halley

---

        became leader of the Tory Party. Northern Secretary of State, 1704-8, Chancellor of the Exchequer, 1710-11, Lord Treasurer, 1711-14.

32. John Maynard Keynes (1883-1946). 1st Baron Keynes, 1942. Economist. Wrote *The Economic Consequences of the Peace* (1919), *The End of Laissez-Faire* (1926), *A Treatise on Money* (1930) *The General Theory of Employment, Interest and Money* (1936). Headed British delegation to the Bretton Woods Conference, 1944.

33. The idea, promulgated vigorously by Keynes, that wise public-sector bureaucrats know better than the market.

Iron, Steam and Finance, 1689-1720

and Newton produced further important work. Of Royal Society Fellows, Joseph Raphson (FRS 1689) propounded the Newton-Raphson method for finding the solutions to an equation. John Arbuthnot (FRS 1704) was a polymath, physician to Queen Anne, statistician, member of the Scriblerus Club, friend of Jonathan Swift[34] and Pope, noted Tory and inventor of John Bull. Archibald Hutcheson[35] (FRS 1708) invented modern financial analysis. Finally, Brook Taylor (FRS 1712) propounded Taylor's theorem, approximating any curve with a polynomial.

Steps to Industrialization

The unprecedentedly intense and expensive Nine Years' War also produced direct steps towards industrialization. The sharply increased need for flintlock muskets for the army was initially supplied mostly from the Netherlands, since the London gunsmiths, the traditional English suppliers, were more expensive. From 1690, however, at the suggestion of the local MP, Sir Richard Newdigate,[36] the Royal Ordnance started sourcing first guns and then gun parts from Birmingham, where small-scale metalworking had been active since Tudor times.

From 1707, the Royal Ordnance, wishing to avoid undue concentration of manufacturing that could be captured by an enemy, created the 'ordnance system', sub-contracting not only gun manufacturing but manufacturing of gun parts and gun assembly to numerous producers, many of them small, located primarily in Birmingham. From this date, the largest-scale example of Adam Smith's division of labour in British industry was not pin manufacturing, but musket manufacturing.[37] The Birmingham producers became adept at producing gun parts (as well as small-scale, 'toys' metal manufacturing[38]), while the Ordnance coordinated their production and that of assemblers, so the final

---

34. Jonathan Swift (1667-1745). Novelist, satirist, essayist. *Gulliver's Travels* (1726).
35. Archibald Hutcheson (*c.* 1660-1740). FRS 1708. Attorney-General of the Leeward Islands, 1688-1704. Tory MP for Hastings, 1713-27. Lord of Trade, 1714-16.
36. Sir Richard Newdigate (1644-1710). 2nd Bart from 1678. Country Whig MP for Warwickshire 1681, 1689.
37. Priya Satia, *Empire of Guns: The Violent Making of the Industrial Revolution* (New York: Penguin Press, 2018), pp. 30-36, has information on the Birmingham small-arms industry.
38. The term applied by contemporaries to the innumerable small-scale metal objects made by Birmingham manufacturers.

product was produced as economically as possible. The relatively tight manufacturing tolerances required for this were to prove useful in Birmingham's later development of industrial machinery.

The other industrial innovation made possible by the prolonged wars, through their effect on wood and charcoal prices and availability, was the transition into the production of pig iron using coke.[39] **Abraham Darby** (1678-1717) was the son of a prosperous Quaker Staffordshire farmer, with 'cottage industry' sidelines as a nailer and locksmith. He was apprenticed to a maker of malt mills (grinders of malt for beer-making) in Birmingham, then in 1698 he moved to Bristol to become a malt mill maker. In 1702 he was a founder and the first manager of the Bristol Brass Company. There he produced brass pots using moulds made of sand and in 1707 took out a patent for a method of making 'bellied' (wider around the middle) iron pots using sand moulds (the higher temperature of molten iron initially made the moulds crack).

The Bristol Brass Company was itself notable. It stayed in business through several corporate reorganizations until 1833, acquiring patents for copper, brass and zinc smelting. In 1746 one of its partners founded the Warmley Brass Company, the largest brass manufacturing operation in Britain, with 2,000 employees and £200,000 in capital by 1769. Alas, over-expansion led to bankruptcy, though the factory continued operating until 1809.

Meanwhile Darby, with financing from a Bristol merchant, Thomas Goldney, in 1709 moved to Coalbrookdale, which was on the River Severn, had a derelict iron forge, was close to sources of iron ore and located on top of the South Staffordshire coalfield, which had low-sulphur coal. Here he began experimentally to smelt iron using coke. His experiments took several years until he was satisfied with the result, for which he did not take out a patent, presumably knowing of Dudley's and Clerke's earlier efforts. Even now, his coke-smelted iron was not acceptable for wrought iron manufacturers, who continued to use charcoal-smelted iron.

Nevertheless, with Coalbrookdale's considerable advantages, and the continued improvement in the relative economics of coke-based iron smelting, Darby was able to build a substantial and profitable business in 'bellied' iron pots, opening a forge in Dolgellau, Wales. Sadly, in 1717 he died, aged only 39.

---

39. I am indebted, for details in this section, to Emyr Thomas, *Coalbrookdale and the Darbys: The Story of the World's First Industrial Dynasty* (York: Sessions Book Trust, 1999).

Iron, Steam and Finance, 1689-1720

In the capital reorganization that followed his death and that of his wife Mary, a controlling share in the business, worth about £4,000 at this time but mortgaged, passed to the mortgagee Thomas Goldney. The business would have slipped away from the Darby family had not Abraham Darby's eldest daughter Mary married his foreman Richard Ford, who managed the business until his death in 1745, while Goldney and his heir remained in Bristol.

Under Ford, the business expanded, with Bristol remaining its main avenue to markets. In 1722 it began to manufacture iron cylinders for Newcomen engines and in 1729 it started manufacturing iron railway wheels for horse-drawn industrial railways. In 1738, after Abraham Darby II (1711-63), the son of the founder, had come into the business, a new partnership was formed, with the business valued at £16,000.

The business gradually expanded to own sources of coal and iron ore, building a horse-drawn railway to connect the coalfields to the works and, from 1742, using a Newcomen engine to provide supplementary water to allow the furnace to remain in blast year-round. Later, in the 1740s, the business began to manufacture armaments on contract to Bristol dealers, theoretically a problem for a Quaker-controlled operation. Then, around 1750, Abraham Darby II managed to produce coke-fired iron that was acceptable to wrought iron manufacturers. By that time, however, other iron works were using the same process, since the economics of iron smelting had tipped decisively in its favour. The Darbys remained substantial, but never became dominant or truly rich – as Quakers they were socially isolated from the mainstream. When in 1752 Abraham Darby II and his wife, Abiah (1716-94), lived for some weeks at Shrewsbury, a quiet market town of 12,000 inhabitants, Abiah was sufficiently shocked to produce a pamphlet, *A Serious Warning to the Inhabitants of Shrewsbury*, calling for their 'sincere Repentance and Amendment of Life before the Night come upon you'.[40]

Independent of the wars, this period's most important steps to industrialization were taken in steam power. The precursor of this technology, and owner of a patent on it, was **Thomas Savery** (1650-1715), from a gentry background, born in Shilston House, Devon, the grandson of Christopher Savery, MP for Totnes, 1584 and 1593. Savery became a military engineer, rising to the rank of captain by 1702; in 1696 he took out two patents, one for polishing glass and another for a capstan-powered paddle wheel, rejected by the Admiralty. Then, in 1698, Savery produced a pump for removing water from mines, which used two containers

---

40. Ibid., p. 45.

alternately filled with steam and cooled with cold water, with no moving parts, so not technically an 'engine'.

Savery's design appears to have been based on Worcester's 1655 design and resembled that patented by Jerónimo de Ayanz y Beaumont in 1606, but possibly worked marginally better than either and was certainly more vigorously promoted. Savery's pump was slow, relying on a jet of cold water to cool it before a vacuum was created, thus using the engine's steam 'under the most uneconomic conditions possible'.[41] Also, although it could be built relatively small, it suffered from diseconomies of scale, for example, if pumping up a large height, as needed in a mine, it would overheat, build up steam pressure and explode.

Not only did Savery patent his steam pump in 1698, but he obtained a private Act of Parliament, 'Encouraging Thomas Savery's invention for raising water and relating to all sorts of mill work', extending his patent from fourteen years to 35 years, ending in 1733 – he was apparently aware that perfecting the pump to an economic state might require many years and so wanted to take advantage of future developments. Christening the machine, 'The Miner's Friend', he demonstrated it to William III at Hampton Court and to the Royal Society, which elected him a Fellow in 1706. At that time, a Savery pump of 2-4 horsepower (hp) cost between £150 and £200.

Even though Savery marketed the pump adroitly, publishing a pamphlet, *A Description of an Engine to Raise Water by Fire*, sending it to businessmen, and setting up a London workshop in 1702, he sold few of his machines and was forced to close three years later. Fortunately, in 1705 Savery was appointed Treasurer of the Sick and Hurt Commissioners for the Navy, which took him to the port of Dartmouth, where he met Newcomen.

Inaugurating the Steam Age: Thomas Newcomen

The first commercially successful and truly functional steam engine was designed by another Devon man, **Thomas Newcomen** (1664-1729). By doing so, he inaugurated the Steam Age, and has some claim to have been the father of the Industrial Revolution itself, which if accepted would date it from the reign of Queen Anne rather than that of George III.

---

41. Quoted in R.L. Hills, *Power from Steam: A History of the Stationary Steam Engine* (Cambridge: Cambridge University Press, 1989), pp. 16-18.

Iron, Steam and Finance, 1689-1720

Newcomen, himself of gentry ancestry and distantly related to a line of Irish baronets,[42] was an ironmonger and iron fabricator by trade, with a substantial Dartmouth-based business, but a Baptist and thus, in the status-conscious society of Queen Anne, with fewer social connections than Savery. He was, however, a much better engineer with decades of experience of iron fabrication and equally conversant with the workings of Cornish tin mines, the owners of several of which were his clients.

Newcomen appears to have begun experimenting on a steam-driven engine for pumping water from mines about 1703-4, after he inherited the ironmongery business on the death of his father in 1702. We are told by Martin Triewald,[43] later his assistant, that Newcomen began experimenting before meeting Savery, which occurred around 1705-6.

Newcomen's early experiments met with the same problem as Savery's pump – the steam would not cool sufficiently fast to allow the engine to operate at a reasonable pace. However, in one of his experiments, the cylinder was cracked and this allowed a jet of water into the steam immediately, producing a fast and powerful stroke. Newcomen accordingly modified the design to inject a jet of water into the cylinder to produce the required cooling.[44] Unlike Savery's pump, Newcomen's engine had a massive rocking central bar, driving a piston which was pushed into the cylinder by atmospheric pressure – justifying Newcomen's name for it, the 'atmospheric engine'. It was the first truly functional steam engine, quite different to the previous pump designs.

Since it used only atmospheric pressure, Newcomen's engine necessarily had a large cylinder to generate sufficient force to be useful (much of Newcomen's experimental work was bedevilled by scale effects – table-top models did not work properly). Its great advantage over Savery's pump was that it did not build up high pressures and hence was less likely to explode (Queen Anne-era materials and machining technology being what they were). The first Newcomen engines used human agency – a 'plug boy' to open and close valves – but within a

---

42. L.T.C. Rolt and J.S. Allen, *The Steam Engine of Thomas Newcomen* (Hartington: Moorland Publishing, 1977), has invaluable detail on Newcomen's ancestry, his poorly-documented life and the generation and dissemination of his invention. The Irish baronetcy dates from 1623.

43. Martin Triewald (1691-1747). FRS 1731. Swedish merchant, engineer and physicist. Published *A Short Description of the Fire and Air Engine in the Dannemora Mines* in Swedish in 1734.

44. A detailed description of a one-third scale model of the first Newcomen engine in the Manchester Museum of Science is contained in Hills, *Power from Steam*, pp. 20-29.

few years an improvement had made this process automatic. Machining technology was so primitive that the engines' cylinders and pistons fitted each other only to within an inch or so, a problem not solved until John Wilkinson's boring machine of 1774. Thus, a Newcomen engine in action was largely invisible (though hardly inaudible) to an outside observer, being surrounded by a dense fog of escaped steam.

At this point, Newcomen was faced with a difficulty. His engine was quite different from Savery's or any preceding attempt, but Savery's patent could be held to cover it. Proving that it did not would require heavy legal expenditure, for which Newcomen lacked the means. Anyway, a new patent would last only fourteen years, to 1724 if granted in 1710, whereas Savery's patent had been artificially extended to 1733. Accordingly, he came to an agreement with Savery and his machines were marketed under Savery's patent until 1733, giving him protection against others copying his design, as well as the benefits of Savery's earlier marketing work.

Newcomen installed his first engine in 1710 in the Wheal Vor tin mine, controlled by Godolphin, a major Cornish mine owner who was also Lord High Treasurer. This engine was not entirely satisfactory and lasted only four years. The first successful engine, with a 21-in. cylinder, was marketed by Newcomen through Humphrey Potter, Pastor of the Baptist Church at Bromsgrove, and installed at Dudley Castle, in Staffordshire, in 1712, where it worked until at least 1785, pumping water up 51 feet and generating about 5½hp.

Overall, the Newcomen engine was still very thermally inefficient and extremely expensive on coal; thus, its main use was in coal mines, not the tin mines of Cornwall, where coal was expensive. Therefore, its principal early market was in the Midlands and the North, where coal was abundant. To exploit it, after Savery's death in 1715 a public partnership was set up, 'The Proprietors of the Invention for Raising Water by Fire', with capital of about £20,000 and 80 shares outstanding, at least one of which was held by Newcomen. That partnership marketed the engines extensively, through agents around the country and on Wednesday afternoons at the Sword Blade Coffee House in the City.[45] Through dividends, it appears to have made a modest overall profit for its shareholders by the patent's expiry in 1733.

---

45. Rolt and Allen, *The Steam Engine of Thomas Newcomen*, p. 59, quoting the *London Gazette* of 11-14 August 1716. Newcomen may have met Lowther at the Sword Blade.

Iron, Steam and Finance, 1689-1720

One such agent, met through the Bromsgrove Baptist Church, was Joseph Hornblower (1696-1762), together later with his sons, Jonathan (1717-80) and Josiah (1729-1809), who took the technology to the American colonies in 1753. Jonathan's sons, Jonathan and Jabez Carter, would be involved in later advances in steam engine technology from the 1780s.

One early adopter of Newcomen's engines was Sir James Lowther,[46] an immensely wealthy, miserly industrialist and Whig MP with extensive coal mining interests at Whitehaven, Cumberland. (In the 1720s and 1730s Lowther was to buy up Cumberland coalfields, attempting to get a monopoly; he almost succeeded.)

Lowther discussed the problem of removing water from his mines with Newcomen in 1715, which led to a contract in November 1715 for a small (19-in. cylinder) Newcomen engine to be leased from the Proprietors for £182 per annum. The engine proved a success to the extent that Lowther bought it outright in 1727 for £200 and paid another £350 for a licence to operate a second larger engine. Lowther commented to his agent John Spedding:

> We have been very successful from first to last in the timing of things about the Fire Engine, which I should hardly have entered upon if I had not met such a very honest good man as Mr. Newcomen, who I believe would not wrong anybody to gain ever so much.[47]

Despite considerable experimentation, it proved impossible to use Newcomen engines directly to power manufacturing processes, because the single power stroke produced a very irregular motion. Its pump action could, however, be used to provide power for manufacturing indirectly by pumping water past a wheel; this was first done by Martin Triewald at Dannemora, Sweden in 1726.[48]

---

46. Sir James Lowther, 4th Baronet (1673-1755). Independent Whig MP for Carlisle, Cumberland and Appleby, 1694-1702, 1708-22, 1723-1755. Acquired and developed Cumberland coalfields, investing £500,000 over his lifetime; died worth about £650,000. Allegedly rejected for a lordship of the Treasury by Sunderland in 1718 because of his scruffy appearance. Bought one of 80 shares of 'the Proprietors' for £270 in 1721, our only information on its capitalization.

47. Quoted in entry for 'Thomas Newcomen' in A.W. Skempton and M. Chrimes (eds), *A Biographical Dictionary of Civil Engineers in Great Britain and Ireland: Volume 1: 1500-1830* (London: Thomas Telford, 2002).

48. Hills, *Power from Steam*, p. 32.

The Newcomen engine at Dannemora, Sweden, 1726, which was installed by Martin Triewald. Copper engraving by Erik Geringius.

Iron, Steam and Finance, 1689-1720

By the expiry of the Savery patent in 1733, 110 Newcomen engines had been produced and installed. The Newcomen engine, which typically produced 15-20 hp and cost about £1,000, continued in production with only modest improvements being made, by manufacturers in Britain, the future United States and other European countries. Over 1,400 were installed in Britain before 1800, some as late as the 1790s to avoid the Watt patent – three times as many as the Watt engines installed by that date.

James Watt is generally recognized as the progenitor of steam engine technology. With their condensers and rotary motion, his engines were roughly three times as efficient as standard Newcomen engines, and were thus economic for a much wider range of uses. However, although their mechanism differed from the Newcomen mechanism, it was still 'atmospheric' – depending on the pressure of the atmosphere to function. Only with high-pressure engines, developed by Richard Trevithick and Arthur Woolf after 1800 (previous such developments by the Hornblower family having been blocked by the Watt patent), were further developments such as the railways possible – Woolf's 'Cornish Engines' after 1815 being about three times as efficient as Watt's. Overall, it is fairest to give the main credit for steam engine technology to Newcomen. We can then blame the further half-century delay in the Industrial Revolution's economic take-off on the policy mistakes of the Whig Supremacy, the anti-entrepreneurial backlash from the 1720 South Sea Bubble collapse and the failings of early eighteenth century materials and machining technology.

Two Other Important Entrepreneurs

200 Years Ahead of His Time: Sir Ambrose Crowley

Much richer than Newcomen and the Darbys, with an enterprise that, without technological innovations of much significance was in scale and operations the first modern factory, was **Sir Ambrose Crowley.**[49] Crowley was the third in a line of Quaker nail-makers of Stourbridge, Worcestershire, a centre of Midlands nail-making – his grandfather, Ambrose Crowley, had died worth only about £20 but his father, Ambrose

---

49. Ambrose Crowley (1658-1713). Kt 1708. Deputy Governor, South Sea Company, 1712-13. Tory MP for Andover, 1713. M.W. Flinn, *Men of Iron: The Crowleys in the Early Iron Industry* (Winlaton: Land of Oak and Iron, 2019), gives an excellent account of the Crowleys and their enterprises.

Crowley II (1635-1720) began as an ordinary nail-maker, built up a substantial iron works business and died in 1720 worth about £3,000, with a reputation for honesty and benevolence.

Sir Ambrose Crowley (III) apprenticed at an iron works in London from 1673, became a Freeman of the Drapers' Company in 1684, converted to Anglican Toryism and in 1682 opened a nail factory in Sunderland. He offered to his Midlands competitors not to do so on payment of £10,000, a huge sum justified by the lower labour, coal and shipping costs available to him in Sunderland – the principal markets for nails were London itself and the port cities on the East and South coasts, all expensive to reach from the land-locked Midlands.

Crowley undoubtedly knew of the Dudley/Clerke iron-from-coke smelting process – his father was close to Andrew Yarranton, who had partnered Clerke – but he was doubtless also aware of its marginal economics in the 1680s. In Sunderland he could import bar iron from Sweden, which with more wood and lower labour costs than Britain supplied more than half the British market in the early eighteenth century. In the north-east, importing Swedish bar iron through Stockholm or Gothenburg was cheap and efficient, allowing Crowley to avoid market squeezes by English bar iron manufacturers. Indeed, for steel-making, a business Crowley entered later, Swedish 'Oregrounds' bar iron was needed, and no other would serve as well.

To set up nail-making in Sunderland, Crowley imported a few skilled nail-makers from Liège in the Spanish Netherlands, a traditional centre of nail-making, and his workforce by the middle 1680s numbered about 100. Crowley himself remained mostly in London, arranging sourcing of bar iron, marketing the factory's output and setting up a large warehousing operation. By 1688, he was sufficiently well established to petition James II for protection for his skilled ironworkers from Liège, who as Catholics were being harassed by the Sunderland locals. Alas, even though James II granted the petition, it did Crowley no good, since that monarch was overthrown within the year and replaced by governments with bigoted Protestants in the ascendancy.

It is not known what happened then, but it was probably still unpleasant for the foreign ironworkers, for in 1691 Crowley bought land and built a factory for nails and small ironware at Winlaton, four miles west of Newcastle, abandoning his Sunderland factory. (Flinn says the reason Crowley did this, leaving the substantial port and excellent facilities at Sunderland for the rural and less convenient Winlaton is an 'object of speculation' – well, harassment of his Catholic specialist workers in Sunderland by Whig mobs is my speculation!)

Iron, Steam and Finance, 1689-1720

At Winlaton, Crowley eventually set up two factories a mile apart, using water power from the Derwent for the riverside Winlaton Mill, established around 1700. There he forged nails, pots, hinges, wheel-hubs, hatchets and edged goods, making steel to do so. Crowley's plant at nearby Swalwell, purchased in 1707, manufactured swords, anchors and chains. He used mostly bar iron as an input, adding a forge to turn pig iron into bar iron, thereby giving himself additional sources of raw material. Since he did not smelt pig iron, he did not suffer from the relative lack of wood locally – for most other iron manufacturing processes, coal or coal derivatives, plentiful and cheap locally, were already used. Together, the plants employed 1,000 people by Crowley's death and became the largest iron works in Europe.

Crowley, still in London, became active in City politics through the Drapers' Guild and after a knighthood became an Alderman in 1711. As a low-cost supplier of nails and other small items, he obtained his first Navy contract in 1694, after the dominant post-Restoration naval supplier, Robert Foley,[50] related by marriage to the High-Tory Norths, had fallen out of political favour. Crowley quickly expanded to become the Navy's dominant supplier of small ironware by 1697, although he did not obtain his first contract for anchors until 1702 and he never manufactured cannons (his successors did so).

The Crowley Iron Works was the first true industrial enterprise, with integrated production and a mass workforce. It used few new manufacturing techniques, with nail-making by hand as in traditional Midlands 'putting-out' operations. Through its scale and centralization, it achieved better assurance of quality, concentrating production in one works complex, for which it provided all the bar iron, and strictly controlling piecework done by additional nailers in surrounding villages. By this means, its products were of sufficiently uniformly high quality to satisfy the Navy, and Crowley ironware became well-renowned in the trade for a century.

The *Law Book of the Crowley Iron Works*, drafted by Crowley, included detailed operating instructions for management of a large industrial installation over 300 miles from his Greenwich headquarters, with a hierarchical management structure, a system of committees reporting to a council responsible to Crowley for operations, and checks and

---

50. Robert Foley (1651-1702). Tory MP for Grampound, 1685. He married Sir Dudley North's sister, Anne (d. 1717) and was a cousin of Philip Foley (1648-1716), son of Thomas Foley, who transferred all his ironworks in the Midlands to him in 1668 and 1669 for £60,000.

Sir Ambrose Crowley's house in Greenwich – with a warehouse, and headquarters of the logistics empire. Artist unknown; plate from Charles Knight, *Old England: A Pictorial Museum*, vol. 2 (James Sangster and Co., 1845).

balances to ensure against theft and inferior work. The *Law Book* also included provisions for an insurance scheme, the 'Poor Fund' to pay for many of his workers' social needs. Crowley himself maintained his father's high Quaker standards of probity in his business dealings and was an 'enlightened' employer.

As a major creditor of the government, Crowley was involved with Harley in the South Sea Company debt conversion of 1711, receiving some £52,000 of South Sea stock in exchange for debts owed to him and becoming Deputy Governor of the company. He was elected Tory MP for Andover in 1713 but died before he could take the oath. His works and warehouses of finished goods were worth over £100,000 at his death and he had £56,000 in South Sea stock and other assets. His son, John, was briefly a Tory MP and a secret Jacobite donor before his early death in 1728, while his son-in-law, Sir Hynde Cotton, third baronet (1686-1752), was a noted Tory MP from 1708 to 1752, as was Cotton's son until 1780.

The Crowley Iron Works remained in the Crowley family until the 1780s (though the peace after the Treaty of Utrecht of 1713 and Crowley's death limited further expansion) and continued in business well into the nineteenth century, declining only after 1815. Interestingly, its workforce was predominantly politically Tory until the 1780s, turning Radical and Chartist only after the Crowley family sold it.

Crowley's brother-in-law, Sampson Lloyd (1664-1724), another Quaker, founded an iron slitting mill in Birmingham around 1698, which became Birmingham's largest manufacturer of nails, using water-powered technology; his younger son, Sampson Lloyd, in 1765 founded Lloyds Bank.

Deals, Deals, Deals: Sir Humphrey Mackworth

Sir Humphrey Mackworth[51] enjoyed a career that epitomizes this period, combining finance, mineral extraction, Tory politics and religious exhortation. The son and grandson of parliamentarian squires who sat in the Protectorate Parliaments, he was educated at Magdalen College, Oxford and the Middle Temple, being called to the Bar in 1682. As 'Comptroller of the Middle Temple', he was knighted by Charles II at the age of 26 and in 1686 made an excellent marriage, to Mary, the daughter and heir of Sir Herbert Evans, of Neath, whose estate in West Glamorgan was rich in coal mines. (Mackworth inherited the estate in 1696.)

Mackworth revived both the estate's collieries and its copper smelter and in 1697 opened negotiations to purchase the Esgair Hir lead and silver mines in Cardiganshire. This he accomplished with a massive publicity campaign, stock issue and lottery to invest in the 'Welsh Potosi', forming the Mine Adventurers' Company combining all his mineral holdings, which finally received its charter in 1703, with the Duke of Leeds as chairman. Several of the other directors were acquainted with Mackworth through the Society for Promoting Christian Knowledge, of which he had been a founder in 1698. However, Mackworth's plan to combine extraction and energy businesses by using his coal deposits to assist in mining and smelting copper, lead and silver elsewhere was uneconomic. Unlike Crowley, he had paid insufficient attention to seventeenth century logistics, so his business foundered on Wales' lack of decent roads or canals – moving coal 50 miles across the Welsh mountains to smelt Esgair Hir's metals was far too expensive and unreliable.

---

51. Humphrey Mackworth (1657-1727). Kt 1683. Tory MP for Cardiganshire and Totnes, 1701, 1702-8, 1710-13. Founder, Society for Promoting Christian Knowledge, 1698. Deputy Governor, Mine Adventurers' Company, 1698-1711, Governor, 1720-21.

Mackworth entered Parliament as a High Tory in 1701. He was an active member, introducing bills for poor relief and the encouragement of mining, as well as publishing several, well-received, high-church theological tracts. Meanwhile, the Mine Adventurers ran into difficulties, attempting to raise capital in 1707 by a foray into banking, which was foiled by the Bank of England Act 1708. In 1709 the Mine Adventurers declared bankruptcy, and a House of Commons Committee in 1710 disclosed several unsavoury details of Mackworth's activities in its financing. The Whig Defoe wrote:

> Such a fraud has not been practised for some ages in any nation circumstanced with so many unmerciful particulars, wheedling in widows and orphans, and all kinds of unwary people – covering the cheats of management with all the cunning of a 20 years' artifice – lotteries, insurances, funds, loans, interests, ingraftments, banks, and a hundred more shams above ground, besides all their subterranean frauds ... then, to whiten this devil, it has been defended by pious shams, pretences of religion, writing books of meditations, and the like.

Nevertheless, the fall of the Whigs and Mackworth's return to Parliament in 1710 prevented any further proceedings against him, with an Act restructuring the Mine Adventurers passed in 1711. In 1713 Mackworth formed the Mineral Manufacturers' Company with a further share issue, largely to force the Mine Adventurers' management to make peace. This was so successful that in the 1720 bubble he staged a coup and resumed the governorship of the Mine Adventurers, as well as attempting unsuccessfully to float a Welsh Copper Company. After being forced out of the Mine Adventurers in 1721 and losing on South Sea shares, he spent his remaining years in mostly fruitless litigation, dying in 1729 effectively insolvent, his debts exceeding his assets of around £14,000.

Not all Mackworth's litigation was fruitless. In 1715 he did a deal with the childless, wealthy but indebted, Cornish MP, John Praed,[52] under which he would pay £4,000 of Praed's debts while Praed's great-niece and heir would marry his younger son, William, who would assume Praed's name. The lady objected, so William married someone else but after Praed's death in 1717 litigation continued until 1733 when the Praed estates were secured for William, who duly assumed the Praed name and became Tory MP for St Ives.

---

52. John Praed (*c.* 1657-1717). Tory MP for St Ives, 1708-13.

Mackworth's elder son, Herbert, who developed both coal and copper interests further, was Tory MP for Cardiff Burghs from 1739 to 1765, while William's son and grandson, also copper miners and later bankers, were both Tory MPs for St Ives. Thus, the family tradition of mixing business and politics was maintained for a century. In the following generation, Winthrop Mackworth Praed (1802-39) dropped the business for a successful career in poetry but kept the politics, becoming a Tory MP between 1830 and 1832 and from 1835 to 1839. He held the position of Secretary of the Board of Control in Peel's brief 1834-35 ministry.

Economic and Infrastructure Development

The coal industry continued to develop steadily, though the new industrial uses were still modest compared to the heating coal used in London and elsewhere. Coal exports from Newcastle and surrounding ports, an annual average of 478,000 metric tons over 1660-64 and 545,000 metric tons over 1685-88, had increased only moderately to 895,000 metric tons in 1720-24,[53] although there was evidence of acceleration. Secondary sources of coal such as the Staffordshire coalfields were being developed, while the use of Newcomen engines in mine pumping began to allow for an increase in production from deeper seams.

Agriculturally, these years saw a continued increase in productivity, and the halting of population decline around 1700. The 1690s were a period of dearth, with average grain prices at Eton College rising from 31.4s per quarter in the peaceful 1680s to 44.9s, a rise of 43% and especially bad harvests in the cold years of 1695 to 1697. The following two decades were better, with average prices of 33.5s and 37.2s, respectively, despite the persistence of war.[54]

The most notable new technique, at least in Norfolk and Suffolk, was the cultivation of turnips, a useful crop for refreshing soil that had been overcultivated and a way of replacing the traditional 'three-field system'. Whereas around 1660 only 1-2% of Norfolk farmers had grown turnips, by the 1680s 20% were doing so and by 1720 that percentage had risen to

---

53. Mitchell (ed.), *British Historical Statistics*, Table IV-1, pp. 240-41.
54. Ibid., Table XIV-16, pp. 754-55. Mitchell gives figures here in decimal shillings, and for the bread prices referred to in Chapter 8 and 9 in decimal (old) pence; I have kept Mitchell's figures rather than converting them into the pennies and farthings in which the eighteenth century dealt.

over 50%. The experiments of Viscount Charles 'Turnip' Townshend,[55] designing the 'Norfolk' four-course crop rotation system, occurred mostly after 1720.

Also important were the agricultural improvements of Jethro Tull (1674-1741), who, after travelling in France and Italy, invented a horse-drawn seed drill in 1701 that sowed the seed in neat rows, increasing crop yields per acre by up to threefold. He published a treatise *Horse-hoeing Husbandry* in 1731 and later invented a drill plough to sow wheat and a turnip drill. His seed drill further improved agricultural productivity, applying the post-Restoration scientific approach and inventiveness in agriculture.

This period also saw heavier investment in infrastructure, improving Britain's appalling main roads. The turnpike movement installed 'turnpike' tolls on the major roads, the proceeds of which were used to repair and improve them. The first such provision had been made by the Road Repair (Hertfordshire, Cambridgeshire and Huntingdonshire) Act 1663, which had provided for a turnpike on the Old North Road at Wade's Mill in Hertfordshire, the proceeds being used for road repair. Defoe celebrated it in his *Tour Through the Whole Island of Great Britain*:

> That an Act of Parliament was obtained about 30 years since [actually 60], for repairing the road between Ware and Royston, and a turnpike was erected for it at Wade's-mill, a village so called, about a mile and half beyond Ware: This proved so effectual, that the road there, which was before scarce passable, is now built up in a high, firm cause way; the most like those mentioned above, of the Romans, of any of these new undertakings. And, though this road is continually work'd upon, by the vast number of carriages, bringing malt and barly to Ware, for whose sake indeed, it was obtained; yet, with small repairs it is maintain'd, and the toll is reduced from a penny, to a half-penny, for the ease of the country, and so in proportion.[56]

The second such Act of 1695 provided for a turnpike at Wymond-ham in southern Norfolk, to repair and improve the road to nearby

---

55. Charles Townshend (1674-1738). 2nd Viscount Townshend from 1687. FRS 1706. Ambassador to the Netherlands, 1700-11, Northern Secretary, 1714-16, 1721-30, Lord Lieutenant of Ireland, 1717, Lord President of the Council, 1720-21.

56. Defoe, *A Tour Through the Whole Island of Great Britain*, Vol. 2, p. 260.

Iron, Steam and Finance, 1689-1720

Attleborough – Norfolk being an important agricultural county and a Whig haven. The Appropriation of Certain Moneys Act 1697 then provided for fingerposts to be installed at each cross-highway. Further Turnpike Acts were passed in the following decades. An Act of 1707 for a section of the London to Chester road was the first to have trustees who were not Justices of the Peace and brought local resources to bear on top of the turnpike tolls. Each trust required a separate Act of Parliament but, over the following century, Britain's trunk roads were greatly improved and high-speed coaches introduced so that road travel times in 1800 were generally well below half those of 1700. (For example, the travel time by coach from London to Manchester declined from 90 hours in 1700 to 24 hours in 1787.[57])

As important for the future Industrial Revolution was the completion of the Aire and Calder Navigation, a canalization of the Aire and Calder rivers to form a single 34-mile canal from Wakefield to Leeds, achieved by the construction of sixteen locks. The scheme was authorized by Act of Parliament in May 1699 and financed by wool merchants and other tradesmen in Leeds and Wakefield, with a total cost of around £25,000. The initial work was completed in 1704 and tolls made it generally profitable, with the freight in the early years being woollen goods from Leeds, Wakefield, Halifax and Bradford, while raw wool and corn from Lincolnshire and East Anglia travelled the other way.

The Aire and Calder Navigation did not lead to an immediate spate of similar projects but, in its finance from local interests and its long-term benefits to local industry, it foreshadowed the major canal enterprises. It is still in operation, carrying petroleum products rather than coal.

In London, the surging growth in trade led to the creation of Britain's first major commercial dock, the Howland Wet Dock, constructed downstream of Southwark and opened in 1700. The dock, the largest in Europe, was built on land given by the Howland family of Streatham to their daughter on her marriage to the Marquess of Tavistock,[58] the grandson and heir of the Whig Duke of Bedford. Bedford secured the necessary parliamentary approval in 1696, while part of the dock's total cost of £12,000 came from the successful Wells shipping family of

---

57. Dan Bogart, an associate professor of Economics, University of California, Irvine, 'The Turnpike Roads of England and Wales', available at: https://www.campop.geog.cam.ac.uk/research/projects/transport/onlin eatlas/britishturnpiketrusts.pdf (accessed 19 February 2021).
58. Wriothesley Russell (1680-1711). Marquis of Tavistock from 1694, 2nd Duke of Bedford from 1700.

Rotherhithe. The dock proved its worth in the Great Storm of 1703, which ships moored within it survived, and later in the century became the centre of the whaling trade under the aegis of the South Sea Company.[59]

Finally, this period saw the construction of no fewer than three lighthouses on Eddystone Rocks, an especially dangerous reef twelve miles south-south-west of Plymouth Sound. The first lighthouse, an octagonal wooden structure, was begun by Henry Winstanley[60] in 1696 and completed in 1698, despite Winstanley's capture by the French during construction. ('We are at war with England, not with humanity,'[61] said Louis XIV on returning him.) That structure quickly needed repair and was replaced by a dodecagonal stone structure which was, alas, swept away along with Winstanley and five other men in the Great Storm of 1703. A third structure, wood around a brick and iron core, was then completed in 1709, to shine for nearly 50 years, until it caught fire in 1755, killing its 94-year-old keeper.

Political and Financial Developments after 1702

Anne's succession and the Tories' natural popularity produced a massive Tory majority at the July 1702 election necessitated by the new reign. Nevertheless, Anne, through the influence of her Whiggish confidante, Sarah, Duchess of Marlborough,[62] appointed a mixed government.

Anne's reign, like that of William III, was marked by a prolonged war with France, necessitating unprecedentedly heavy government borrowing, but there was none of the paranoia and suspicion that marked the earlier years of William III's reign. The Jacobite claimant was now an unknown Catholic youth, while Anne was a well-liked, indisputably legitimate Stuart, with mildly Tory Anglican sentiments, 'the Church of England's glory',[63] that fitted well with those of her subjects. Despite the continuation of the destabilizing triennial parliamentary system,

---

59. Details of this and other later London docks are given in Peter Stone, *The History of the Port of London* (Barnsley: Pen and Sword History, 2017).

60. Henry Winstanley (1644-1703). Painter, engineer, merchant. Built two Eddystone Lighthouses, 1696-1703.

61. Trinity House, 'Eddystone Lighthouse' https://www.trinityhouse.co.uk /lighthouses-and-lightvessels/eddystone-lighthouse (accessed 24 October 2022).

62. Sarah Jennings (1660-1744). Married John Churchill, 1677. 1st Duchess of Marlborough from 1702.

63. From the lyrics of the Vicar of Bray: 'When Royal Anne became our queen, the Church of England's glory ...'.

Iron, Steam and Finance, 1689-1720 171

her governments were both more solid and better, with the moderate Godolphin in overall charge until 1710, with parliaments evenly balanced after 1705, and then a Tory regime with a landslide majority under the experienced Harley and the brilliant Bolingbroke.

The principal legislative achievement of the Godolphin government was union with Scotland, which passed through both Parliaments in 1706 and came into force on 1 May 1707. Since England had acquired a large expensive debt through its wars, and Scottish investors had lost heavily from the Darien scheme, an Equivalent was paid to Scotland to compensate Scotland for its share of the tax burden from England's debt. After complex discounted cash-flow calculations in which Paterson (for Scotland) and Davenant (for England) were heavily involved, this Equivalent was fixed at £398,085, which was paid with interest over the next few years and went mostly to Scottish investors in the Darien scheme, for which Paterson but not England bore a heavy responsibility.

The union had a considerable economic effect and contributed much to eventual industrialization. Already in the 1720s, Defoe noted that Galloway and Glasgow had benefited substantially from union, catching up with the more economically dynamic parts of England. With the Scottish Enlightenment providing additional intellectual backing for the Industrial Revolution's economic policies, and Glasgow, Paisley and such industrial behemoths as the Carron Iron Works fully participating in it, Scotland was to give important additional strength to its development.

The other legislation of great long-term importance was the Copyright Act 1709. Before 1695, publications had been licensed by the Stationers' Company, a printers' guild, and publishers had owned the copyright, although authors had been able to get copyright protection by royal decree. Then, with the expiry of the Licensing Act in 1695, there was no copyright. By the new Copyright Act, books already published had a copyright of 21 years, vested in the author, while books published after its passage had a copyright of fourteen years, extendible for a further fourteen years if the author was still alive. Later restrictions on imports of foreign pirated editions gave authors solid intellectual property in their work, an important extension of property rights.

As well as founding the South Sea Company, thereby solving an acute short-term debt problem, the Tory government of 1710-14 had several other achievements. The Treaty of Utrecht, signed by Britain in April 1713, ended a generation of war, though minor conflicts continued thereafter. The Tories attempted to use the peace to sign a trade treaty with France in 1713-14 (trade with France had been prohibited since

1689) but the anti-French, mercantilist Whigs put up a ferocious opposition. Despite a well-argued campaign from the aged Davenant, the treaty was defeated in the Commons in 1713 and then Anne's death and the Whigs' accession to power ended the possibility of such a treaty until Pitt's trade treaty of 1786.

The main task of government after the Treaty of Utrecht was to reduce the cost of government debt and spending in general and put it on a sustainable basis. The Tories' solution was the Usury Act 1713 which reduced the maximum allowable rate of interest from 6% to 5%, from September 1714. The preamble to the Act expressed the Tory view of the previous quarter-century of war and chicanery, principally financed through the Land Tax on the landowners, while the 'monied interest' had grown fat through dubious financial dealings:

> WHEREAS the reducing of interest to ten, and from thence to eight, and thence to six in the hundred, hath, from time to time, by experience been found very beneficial to the advancement of trade, and improvement of lands: and whereas the heavy burden of the late long and expensive war hath been chiefly born by the owners of the land of this kingdom, by reason whereof they have been necessitated to contract very large debts, and thereby, and by the abatement in the value of their lands, are become greatly impoverished: and whereas by reason of the great interest and profit which hath been made of money at home, the foreign trade of this nation hath of late years been much neglected, and at this time there is a great abatement in the value of the merchandises, wares, and commodities of this kingdom, both at home and in foreign parts, whither they are transported: and whereas for the redress of these mischiefs, and the preventing the encrease of the same, it is absolutely necessary to reduce the high rate of interest of six pounds in the hundred pounds for a year to a nearer proportion with the interest allowed for money in foreign states ...

Modern free market economists will scoff at the Usury Act; by setting so low a maximum rate of interest, it prevented the free market in money from operating, denying loans that economically ought to be made. Certainly, the earnest Whigs and Peelites who repealed the usury laws in 1854 thought so.

However, the capital market of 1854 was well developed, with a gold standard, interest rates set by the market and vast liquidity in 3% Consols,

Iron, Steam and Finance, 1689-1720

the principal market benchmark, selling close to par. The market of 1713 was very different. A rootless 'monied interest' had taken over the capital markets, pushing up interest rates and making huge profits thereby, while the landed gentry paid most of the cost of this through the burdensome Land Tax. It certainly seemed as if the 'monied interest' might force interest rates to a permanently high level, causing major long-term economic damage and ruining the gentry. The Usury Act 1713 was an attempt to prevent this and together with other actions, it worked. Over the next 40 years, long-term government borrowing rates halved, with the creation of 3% Consols in 1751. Another war in the short term might have caused untold financial damage, preventing even prime credits from borrowing and causing national bankruptcy, but preventing another war in the short term was the Tories' most cherished policy objective.

After the emergence of country banks after 1750, the Usury Act had a distorting effect on the capital market. Banks could not lend legally at more than 5%, and beyond well-established fees, the usual tricks used to raise the true rate of interest above the nominal rate were themselves illegal. This prevented the emergence of a 'junk bond' market in domestic securities in times of speculation and possibly limited banks from long-term loans to emerging industrial and railroad enterprises. On balance, the Usury Act may have inhibited industrial innovation, but it ensured that such innovation happened on a financially sounder basis, financed mostly by equity.

The period 1688-1720 was one of steady naval progress, although administration suffered from the absence of Charles II, James II and Pepys. The victories of Barfleur and Cape La Hogue in 1692 and Vigo in 1702 and the capture of Gibraltar in 1704 were offset by the loss of Sir Cloudesley Shovell[64] and four ships of the line in 1707, which struck rocks off the Scilly Isles because of bad weather and the lack of accurate longitudinal readings.

It had become clear that trade was Britain's life-blood and that protecting trade was the principal function of the Navy. Moreover, the Tory party had become increasingly identified with a 'blue-water' policy seeking to advance British trade and colonization, relegating land war in Europe to a lower priority. The Longitude Act 1714, providing a variable prize of up to £20,000 (equivalent to £7 million today) for the first successful means of accurately determining a ship's longitude, thus

---

64. Cloudesley Shovell (1650-1707). Kt 1689. Whig MP for Rochester, 1695-1701, 1705-07. Captain, 1677, Rear Admiral, 1690, Vice Admiral, 1694, Admiral, 1702, Admiral of the Fleet, 1705.

symbolized both Tory blue-water strategy and national confidence in scientific and technological advances.

In August 1714, everything changed. The much-loved Anne died, having at the last moment deprived Bolingbroke of the reins of power and given the Lord High Treasurership to the cross-party Duke of Shrewsbury. Shrewsbury ensured a smooth transition under the Act of Settlement 1701 to George I, who unlike William III decided to work only with Whigs (as did George II).

The War of the Spanish Succession was more glorious than its predecessor but even more expensive. With the precedents available and the capable Godolphin in charge, it proved somewhat easier to finance. In the war's early years, the government financed itself mostly with irredeemable 99-year annuities, raising around £8 million by that means at around 6.5% per annum in 1704-8.

Then, in 1708, the Bank of England's charter was extended to 1729, and a further £2.9 million of financing was provided to the state, of which £400,000 was a loan from the Bank and the additional £2.5 million raised through a Bank stock issue. The most pernicious feature of the Bank of England Act 1708 was that it confirmed the Bank's monopoly of joint-stock banking throughout England and Wales, providing that no private bank in the country could have more than six partners.

This provision was to have a major effect on England's embryonic banking system; over the next century no substantial banks would be created in England. Thereby, the English banking system, which had already been warped by the excessive profitability of dealing in government issues after the mid-1690s, was distorted for more than a century. The existing goldsmith bankers in London, dealing in government bonds, shares and foreign exchange, flourished but remained limited in size and lacking in knowledge of the new manufacturing sector or domestic commerce in general.

Conversely, the scrivener-bankers, who had specialized in mortgage financing and taking deposits from country gentry, failed to develop in London, since dealing in government securities and quasi-government dividend-paying stocks was more profitable than the complex and expensive business of mortgage lending, at rates below those available on government bonds.

In 1709, since competition had proved to wreck the profitability of both East India Companies, a merger was consummated to form the United East India Company, providing another £1.2 million in financing. Now both major joint-stock companies were Whig-dominated, the danger of which was shown in 1710, when the Bank of England attempted

Iron, Steam and Finance, 1689-1720

to stage a run on short-term government debt after Anne decided to replace the final Whig-dominated Godolphin ministry by the Tories under Harley. In any case, Godolphin's magic touch had run out in 1710, when his lottery and 32-year annuities came only at the appalling cost of 9% per annum.

To combat the financing problem and that of the chartered companies' Whiggishness, in 1711 the new Tory government resorted to the 'project' of a scrivener-turned-banker, John Blunt.[65] Blunt was secretary of an unofficial bank, the Hollow Sword Blade Company, founded in 1691 and acting as a bank under its sword manufacturing charter. The company had undertaken a small but profitable debt-equity swap with the government in 1704 and had invested in forfeited Jacobite lands in Ireland.

With government sponsorship, Blunt formed the South Sea Company, to trade with the South Seas (the Caribbean and southwards) taking advantage of the *asiento* contract to supply slaves to the Spanish dominions that ministers expected to secure from the peace negotiations at Utrecht. The South Sea Company's formation enabled the government to refinance no less than £9.2 million in discounted short-term debt into long-term debt bearing 6% interest, raising that amount through a share issue. Following this success, the Hollow Sword Blade Company began to issue banknotes, violating the Bank of England's monopoly further.[66]

By 1712, the government had borrowed £16.8 million through joint-stock companies, compared to £12.1 million through annuities and £11.5 million through lottery loans.[67] Through Godolphin's efforts and the South Sea financing, the overall annual cost of the debt had been reduced from 8.8% in 1700 to 6.8% in 1712, although this was still well above the Netherlands' cost of borrowing of close to 4%.

Economically, the British financial system was stabilized by two 1717 initiatives. The first serious debt reform was Robert Walpole's scheme dealing with all the public debt except the long annuities, which not only invented the Sinking Fund (albeit not properly secured against revenues) but also refinanced £9.5 million of lottery and annuity debt

---

65. John Blunt (1665-1733). 1st Bt 1720. Scrivener. Secretary, Hollow Sword Blade Company from *c.* 1702. Managing Director, South Sea Company, 1711-21.

66. Since the Newcomen engine was marketed through the Sword Blade Coffee House, it is likely that the Hollow Sword Blade Company organized the funding of about £20,000 for the engine's Proprietors in 1715.

67. Carruthers, *City of Capital*, pp. 76-79, gives the details of the joint-stock company financings.

176 *Forging Modernity*

into 5% perpetual bonds, the first fixed interest debts issued by the Treasury and the ancestors of Consols.[68]

Later that year Newton established what became an effective gold standard. Newton's report to the Treasury of 21 September 1717 addressed the question of the proper relationship between the price of gold and silver, and why silver was shipped in bulk to India. He recommended a devaluation of the gold parity, so that a guinea should be worth 21s 6d, setting the 22-carat gold price at £3 17s 10½d per ounce, the standard that prevailed (with intervals for the Napoleonic wars and World War I) until 1931. Newton intended to allow for a bi-metallic system, with silver valued at 5s 2d per ounce, but in practice silver continued to leave the country (it being worth relatively more in the East, as it had been for the previous 200 years) so Newton's system became a *de facto* gold standard, maintained without change until 1797.

In discussing the government's attempts to reduce its debt costs, and the shenanigans with the South Sea Company, we are indebted to the last of this period's economic thinkers, Archibald Hutcheson, effectively the inventor of modern securities analysis. Hutcheson was of Ulster ancestry, trained as a barrister and as a Tory supporter of James II became Attorney-General of the Leeward Islands, a dangerous job since this was the apogee of pirate activity. Despite being accused of Jacobitism, he returned to London in the late 1690s and resumed his legal practice, becoming a 'man of business' for the second Duke of Ormonde.[69] With the Tory Ormonde appointed Lord Warden of the Cinque Ports in 1712, he arranged for Hutcheson to be elected as an independent-minded Tory for Hastings.

Hutcheson travelled in Europe in early 1714, ingratiating himself with the future George I, and was hence appointed a Lord of Trade on George I's accession, as an apparently reliably Hanoverian Tory who could serve alongside George I's favoured Whigs. Alas, Ormonde's impeachment as a Jacobite in June 1715 ruined Hutcheson's prospects and, from his resignation in January 1716 onwards, he used his mathematical skills in the service of the Tory opposition.

Hutcheson's first contribution to financial analysis was contained in his 1718 *Present State of the Public Debts and Funds*, in which he analysed the movements of national debt since the Treaty of Utrecht, using several

---

68. Dickson, *The Financial Revolution in England*, pp. 83-87.
69. James Butler (1665-1745). 2nd Duke of Ormonde from 1688. Lord Lieutenant of Ireland, 1703-7, 1710-13. Captain General of the British Army, 1711-14. Lord Warden of the Cinque Ports, 1712-15. Title forfeit, 1715.

spreadsheet calculations and sensitivity analyses. Hutcheson estimated that the National Debt had been increased by £11.8 million over the five years since Utrecht, although nearly half of this increase stemmed from the decline in interest rates to 5% having increased the value of the 99-year annuities.

This was the central problem to be solved by the South Sea scheme two years later: the irredeemable annuities could be refunded in lower-cost debt only by increasing the principal amount of debt to compensate for the reduced interest rate. Exchanging them for South Sea shares at a premium would solve the problem and bring Britain's debt costs down to a reasonable level without excessive increase in debt principal – at the cost of substantial losses to holders of irredeemable annuities and chaos in the capital markets generally.

In 1719, the Sunderland[70]/Stanhope[71] faction running the Whig government came up with a wizard wheeze to reduce the burden of the National Debt involving the South Sea Company, still run by Blunt but now dauntless in its Whiggery. The principal problem was the high rate of interest payable on the irredeemable annuities created during the war, particularly those 99-year long annuities created by conversion from the ultra-expensive 1690s financings. A debt conversion for these would have to offer an impossibly high premium, removing the benefit of their conversion. Hence, it was decided to tempt annuity holders by offering South Sea stock, which with its apparently lucrative trade concessions offered large speculative gains.

In 1719, therefore, as a first trial the South Sea Company offered holders of the 1710 lottery (payments on which ran until 1742) the chance to convert into South Sea stock at 11.5 years' purchase (£1,150 for each £100 of annual payments on the lottery.) In the event, £94,330 per annum was exchanged and the necessary stock sold at 114%, giving the South Sea Company a profit of £242,240, reducing the Treasury's debt interest payments by about £9,000 annually (until 1742) and giving it an

---

70. Charles Spencer (1675-1722). 3rd Earl of Sunderland from 1702. MP for Tiverton, 1695-1702. Southern Secretary of State, 1706-10, Lord Lieutenant of Ireland, 1714-17, Lord Privy Seal, 1715-16, Northern Secretary of State, 1717-18, Lord President of the Council, 1717-19, First Lord of the Treasury, 1718-21.

71. James Stanhope (1673-1721). 1st Viscount Stanhope from 1717, 1st Earl Stanhope from 1718. MP for Newport, Cockermouth, Wendover and Aldborough, 1702-17. Commander-in-Chief, Spain, 1708-11. Southern Secretary of State, 1714-16, Northern Secretary of State, 1716-17, 1718-21, First Lord of the Treasury, 1717-18, Chancellor of the Exchequer, 1717-18.

178 *Forging Modernity*

additional loan of £544,142.[72] Win-win-win. The temptation to repeat the process on a much larger scale was irresistible.

The government and the South Sea Company did this the following year. In January 1720 Blunt proposed to James Craggs,[73] Postmaster General, and John Aislabie,[74] Chancellor of the Exchequer, that SSC make an offer for £13.3 million (valued at 20 years' purchase) of 99-year annuities, £1.7 million (valued at fourteen years' purchase) of 'short' (1742) annuities and £16.5 million of 5% government stock, almost all created under Walpole's 1717 scheme. After a short bidding war between SSC and the Bank of England, the proposal was authorized in April, on condition that the company pay the extraordinary sum of £7.5 million to the government for undertaking it. Copious bribes, in the form of fictitious allocations of a total of £500,000 of stock, were spread around the government, George I's mistresses and anyone else who seemed useful.

The proposal relied on SSC stock price rising; if a holder of £100 per annum in annuities was prepared to accept £2,100 in the form of seven shares of SSC stock valued at £300 per share, SSC would have another fourteen shares to sell in the market. Hutcheson returned to the fray when the proposal was before Parliament, with a pamphlet of 20 March, *Some Calculations Relating to the Proposals Made by the South-Sea Company, and the Bank of England, to the House of Commons*. With the SSC share price around £200 per share when Hutcheson published, he analysed all the possible sources of income for the company and determined by discounted cash-flow analysis that the SSC would need an annual profit of £3.3 million from the South Sea trade to justify that price. Since the greatest annual profit from that trade had been around £100,000, the shares were clearly overvalued, even at £200. Thus, those exchanging their annuities for SSC shares were deluding themselves. In this pamphlet, Hutcheson had invented modern stock analysis; it was not a discipline much used for the next 200 years.[75]

---

72. Figures from Dickson, *The Financial Revolution in England*, pp. 87-89.

73. James Craggs the Elder (1657-1721). Whig MP for Grampound, 1702-13. Postmaster General, 1715-20.

74. John Aislabie (1670-1742). Harleyite Tory then Whig MP for Ripon and Northallerton, 1695-1721. Treasurer of the Navy, 1714-18, Chancellor of the Exchequer, 1718-21. Son, William Aislabie (1700-81) was Tory MP for Ripon, 1721-81.

75. Hutcheson's work and its importance are discussed in Levenson, *Money for Nothing*, pp. 191-200.

Exchange Alley in 1720 where Garraway's is on the left. Painting by Edward Matthew Ward.

Hutcheson's calculations were ignored. Three offers were made to government bondholders and four subscriptions sold to the public, at prices up to £1,000 per share before the whole structure cracked at the beginning of September. By this stage about 80% of the long and short annuities and 85% of the redeemable stock had been exchanged for SSC shares, swelling its capital to some £37 million. By October, SSC's stock was trading below £200; during 1721, after its cashier, Robert Knight, had fled to Antwerp[76] with the company's records, it fell below par.

Re-enter Robert Walpole, who had rejoined the government only at the end of April and spent the summer at his estate in Norfolk. On his return to London in September, he took charge, first attempting unsuccessfully to 'ingraft' SSC stock with that of the Bank and the East India Company, then moving in Parliament to protect those ministers he wanted to protect (not including Aislabie and Craggs) and ensure that the highly favourable (to the government) exchanges into SSC

---

76. Antwerp was then in the Austrian Netherlands, with no extradition to Britain. The government is believed to have paid the governor of the Austrian Netherlands £50,000 to keep him there. (Dickson, *The Financial Revolution in England*, p. 112.) Knight returned to London only after Walpole's fall in 1742.

shares were not reversed by Parliament (which was achieved by a vote of 232 to 88 on 20 December). Then, after a series of stormy hearings, the estates of South Sea directors, Knight and his deputy, Aislabie and Craggs were confiscated, producing around £2 million to satisfy SSC creditors. By that time Stanhope and Craggs had died and Sunderland retired, allowing Walpole to become First Lord of the Treasury and effectively Prime Minister.

Further adjustments were made to the debt exchanges' terms over the next few years, as assets appeared and the SSC's debts to the Bank and the government were extinguished. In the end, holders of long annuities got SSC stock worth about three quarters of their' annuities' value (assuming the SSC stock sold around par, which it did after 1723) and received about two thirds of their previous income. Holders of short annuities lost half their capital and more of their income (but extended that income beyond 1742) and holders of redeemables also lost half their capital and half their income.[77] By 1733, most of the SSC stock was segregated into old and new annuities, allowing holders to receive a steady income as they had previously on their government annuities, with only around 15% of the capital devoted to *asiento* and other trading.

This relatively satisfactory result contrasts with that of the Mississippi Scheme in France, where holders of Banque Royale banknotes and stock were wiped out. It was the closest Britain ever came to default after 1672 but in the end, while the South Sea Bubble remained a byword for financial chicanery, its effect on Britain's debt service was on balance salutary, removing the excessively expensive obligations that had been entered into by the 'monied interest' manipulators of the 1690s. The SSC managers and the ministers concerned are remembered as crooks and dupes, but they were no more so than the financiers of the 1690s, and the effect of their gigantic, ground-breaking bubble, once resolved, was considerably less damaging to Britain's long-term solvency. Through it, the annual cost of the outstanding irredeemable annuities was reduced from £1.073 million in 1718 to £212,000 in 1722.[78]

One other legal result of the speculative frenzy was the Bubble Act 1720. Even though SSC stock had been soaring in April and May, the company was dismayed by the frenzy of other money-making schemes that sought funding, most of them scams. Hence, in June Parliament passed the Bubble Act, making it an offence without parliamentary consent to act as a corporate body or to divert an existing corporate

---

77. Ibid., pp. 185-86.

78. Mitchell (ed.), *British Historical Statistics*, Table XI-2, p. 578.

Iron, Steam and Finance, 1689-1720

charter for unauthorized ends. The key test case came on 17 August, when the Lords Justices issued writs of *scire facias* ('make known') seeking their annulment against three companies: the English Copper Company, the Royal Lutestring Company and the York Buildings Company, with another against the Welsh Copper Company (Sir Humphrey Mackworth's entry in the Bubble stakes) the following day.[79]

The result was salutary against the offending companies but damaging to the British economy in both the short and long term. In the short term, it brought the first crack in the SSC's stock price, as market confidence was dented. In the long term, the Bubble Act hampered corporate formations for the next century until it was repealed in 1825, although it was invoked infrequently. Certain inefficiencies resulted from this; for example, Britain had only two assurance companies, the Sun Fire Office (formed in 1710) and the London Assurance Company (formed earlier in 1720) until 1824, when a third, the Alliance Assurance Company was formed by special Act of Parliament under Rothschild tutelage.

The Bubble Act was probably only a modest barrier to industrialization for decades but by the 1780s several industrial companies were large enough to have benefited from incorporation. For example, the elder Sir Robert Peel's Peel, Yates & Co. textile manufacturing partnership, established in 1772, was very substantial, but was dissolved when Peel retired in 1817. Wedgwood, formed in 1759 but incorporated only in 1895, was also a partnership that could have benefited from incorporation. Probably the greatest loser by the Bubble Act was Boulton & Watt, formed in 1775 but starved of the capital needed to exploit steam engine technology quickly; incorporation and an active market in its shares could have helped speed its expansion and thereby the Industrial Revolution.

* * *

In this period, war, Empire-building and finance dominated the political economy, while the scientific, intellectual and economic progress towards industrialization slowed somewhat. Critically, the industrial advances of Newcomen and Darby did not lead to further developments in the short term. I shall suggest below that an underlying reason for the delay in further innovation rested, not on a sudden lack of inventiveness on the part of British engineers, but on a change in the political and ideological climate, from strongly favourable to industrial innovation between 1660 and 1714 to somewhat hostile from 1714 to 1760. In addition, the bursting of the South Sea Bubble in 1720 undoubtedly

---

79. Dickson, *The Financial Revolution in England*, p. 149.

dampened entrepreneurial spirits and the availability of risk-taking finance for decades thereafter. The Whigs who ruled after 1714 were connected primarily with the London-based 'monied interest', making finance and colonial exploitation appear the best roads to serious wealth for ambitious young men. Nevertheless, the additional geopolitical strength and financial resilience Britain gained during this period would build a capital base that could finance industrialization once the nation's full attention returned to it.

6

The Industrial Revolution Takes a Whig Nap, 1721-60

The Whigs Take Control

After George I's arrival in 1714 a Whig ministry took over, led initially by Montagu (now Earl of Halifax) and after his death by Walpole and Townshend. They lost a faction fight in early 1717, being succeeded by Sunderland and Stanhope, but the Whigs remained firmly in charge until a new Tory-oriented King was finally able to lever the Duke of Newcastle[1] out of office in May 1762. Twice Tory hearts leaped: in 1727 when George I died and his son, who had favoured the opposition, succeeded to the throne; and in 1742, when Walpole fell after 21 years in office. On both occasions the Tories were thwarted; George II kept Walpole in office in 1727 and in 1742 turned only to Whigs who had opposed Walpole, with few Tories admitted to the ministry. This prolonged, exclusive one-party rule, since christened the 'Whig Supremacy',[2] was bad for British politics, for the country, and for the burgeoning Industrial Revolution.

---

1. Thomas Pelham-Holles (1693-1768). 1st Duke of Newcastle-on-Tyne from 1715, 1st Duke of Newcastle-under-Lyne from 1756. Lord Chamberlain, 1717-24, Southern Secretary of State, 1724-48, Northern Secretary of State, 1748-54, Leader of the House of Lords, 1748-56, 1757-62, Prime Minister, 1754-56, 1757-62, Lord Privy Seal, 1765-66.
2. The title of Basil Williams' 1939 volume of the Oxford History of England covering this period. He twice stood. unsuccessfully for Parliament as a Liberal.

184 *Forging Modernity*

Walpole was the principal figure in these four decades. He set the parameters of Whig rule and his successors, Henry Pelham[3] and Pelham's brother, Newcastle, had both spent decades as Walpole's subordinates and carried on many of his policies. Walpole's primary interest was social and political stability. If you had told Walpole that, through a different set of policies, he could have set off the Industrial Revolution decades earlier and so contributed to vastly better living standards in his grandchildren's time, at the cost of social instability while he ruled, he would have declined the bargain. 'Let sleeping dogs lie' may be apocryphal as a Walpole quotation; it was the central principle of his rule.

The main Whig objective after 1714 was to cement in place both the Hanoverian dynasty and their own rule. To this end, they passed legislation that both lowered the political temperature and repressed the lower orders, who outside London were still primarily Tory, thereby reducing the likelihood of serious unrest. This legislation had the side-effect of reducing the social mobility and innovativeness of British society, slowing the Industrial Revolution, so that, for example, Newcomen's 'atmospheric engine' remained the technological frontier in steam power for two generations.

George I, advised before his arrival by a tendentious and dishonest *Impartial History of Parties* by the former Whig Lord Chancellor, Lord Cowper,[4] dismissed his Tory ministers and replaced them with Whigs immediately on his arrival in England in September 1714. However, those Tory ministers had been elected by a massive landslide majority of around 354 seats to 148[5] in the election of autumn 1713, less than a year earlier. Consequently, George I's coronation in October was marked by widespread and well-supported riots across the country, accompanied by such cries as 'Sacheverell for Ever! Down with the Roundheads!' The

---

3. Henry Pelham (1694-1754). Younger and more intelligent brother of Newcastle. MP for Seaford and Sussex, 1717-54. Secretary at War, 1724-30, Paymaster of the Forces, 1730-43, Prime Minister and Chancellor of the Exchequer, 1743-54.

4. D.B. Horn and Mary Ransome (eds), *English Historical Documents: Volume X: 1714-1783* (London: Eyre & Spottiswoode, 1969), pp. 194-97. William Cowper (1665-1723). 1st Baron Cowper from 1706, 1st Earl Cowper from 1718. MP for Hertford and Bere Alston, 1695-1705. Lord Keeper of the Great Seal, 1705-7. Lord Chancellor, 1707-10, 1714-18.

5. 'The Parliament of 1713' on the History of Parliament online website, available at: https://www.historyofparliamentonline.org/volume/1690-1715/parliament/1713 (accessed 23 September 2022).

new Whig government attempted to bring the ringleaders to London (safely Whig) for prosecution but were prevented from doing so by (mostly Tory) local magistrates.

George I removed 25 Tory Privy Councillors by October 1714, and the Whigs indulged in a wholesale purge of the justiciary throughout the country, creating what Linda Colley called a 'gangland' quality of political life in these crucial early months of the new reign.[6] (Bolingbroke foresaw the futility of Toryism after 1714 but made it worse by becoming the Pretender's Secretary of State, justifying the Whigs in proscribing the ablest Tory politician of his generation.)

In the general election of January-March 1715, the Tories held most of their broad-franchise county seats and many of the larger boroughs but were decimated in the small boroughs where ministerial influence could run rampant. The new Parliament contained an estimated 341 Whigs to 217 Tories,[7] a reversal achieved before the 1715 Jacobite rebellion had taken place, which allowed the Whigs to purge and harry further. The Whig majority was smaller than the freely elected Tory majority of 1713, and, according to Colley, the Tories would continue to receive a majority of votes cast in elections through the 1730s, but it was sufficient to cement Whig rule.

Immediately, in the new Parliament (and before the 1715 rebellion) the Whigs passed the Riot Act 1714 (passed in March 1715, to come into force on 1 August of that year). The Act empowered local officials to order the dispersal of any group of more than twelve people 'unlawfully, riotously and tumultuously assembled together' ('to read the Riot Act') and anyone remaining gathered one hour later was guilty of a felony without benefit of clergy, punishable by death. The Riot Act was used to quell disturbances on many occasions over the next 200 years, the last being at Birkenhead in 1919. It was a highly successful piece of legislation, but inevitably, in a one-party state with Whig attitudes to dissent from the lower classes, it was abused to quell legitimate opposition.

The Papists Act 1715 required Catholics – mostly Tory-inclined – to register their properties, so that a discriminatory tax could be applied to them.

---

6. Linda Colley, *In Defiance of Oligarchy: The Tory Party, 1714-60* (Cambridge: Cambridge University Press, 1982), p. 183.

7. 'The Parliament of 1715' on the History of Parliament online website, available at: https://www.historyofparliamentonline.org/volume/1715-1754 /parliament/1715 (accessed 23 September 2022).

The Septennial Act 1716 extended Parliament's life to seven years, including (constitutionally very doubtful) for the Parliament then in being, which consequently lasted until 1722. This allowed the permanent Whig government far more flexibility in timing elections, and for 20 years impeded the opposition from organizing support in the country with any chance of success.[8]

The Transportation Act 1717 streamlined the system of transportation to the American colonies for criminal activity. Previously, transportation sentences had frequently been evaded, but the combination of colonial demand for cheap indentured servants and the wish to send undesirable elements with Tory/Jacobite sympathies safely across the Atlantic made the Whigs tighten up the system. The Act made a sentence of seven years mandatory, with fourteen years for offences otherwise punishable by death – an estimated 50,000 convicts were transported to the American colonies over the six decades of its operation.

The Artificers Act 1718 'prevented the destruction of our home manufactures by transporting and seducing our artists to settle abroad'.[9] It provided for a fine of £100 and three months' imprisonment for the (presumably, foreign) seducer, while 'artificers' living abroad for more than six months, after a warning from the British Ambassador, would lose their British nationality, have all their lands and goods forfeited, and be incapable of receiving a legacy or gift. The Artificers Act 1718 and its derivatives were repealed by the more free-market Liverpool administration in 1824. It no doubt seemed sensible protectionism to the Whigs who passed it, but it worked both ways, inhibiting 'artificers' from travelling abroad to learn foreign techniques.

The Taxation Act 1722 imposed a special tax assessment of £100,000 on Catholics, in addition to requiring them to pay double the normal rate of Land Tax; like the Oaths Act of the same year, it reflected Whig paranoia and imposed additional burdens on some Tories. Conversely, the Qualification for Employments Act 1726 and the Indemnity Act 1727 removed most of the barriers to public employment of (mostly Whig) Nonconformists.

---

8. Cf. Linda Colley, *In Defiance of Oligarchy* and J.H. Plumb, *The Growth of Political Stability in England, 1675-1725* (London: MacMillan, 1967) for a more detailed discussion of the impact of the Septennial Act.

9. Sir William Blackstone, *Commentaries on the Laws of England*, 4 vols (Oxford: Clarendon Press, 1765-70), Vol. 2, p. 160. By 'artists' Blackstone means 'artificers' or workmen with special skills.

The Industrial Revolution Takes a Whig Nap, 1721-60   187

The most notorious Whig assault on the poorer working classes was the Criminal Law Act 1722 ('the Black Act') passed in May 1723. An outbreak of rural crimes, such as poaching, mostly around Windsor Great Park and in Hampshire, was used, under the pretence that the criminals were Jacobites, to produce a sharp tightening of the penal laws. The Black Act made it a hanging offence to be caught in with a blackened face near a royal park. Other capital offences included deer hunting, fishing, hunting hares, destroying fish ponds, destroying trees, killing cattle or setting fire to corn. As E.P. Thompson demonstrated,[10] during the severe penal climate of the Whig Supremacy this Act had a chilling effect, since common working-class misdemeanours could be turned into capital offences.

Finally, the Whigs passed two 'reforms' of the 1601 Poor Law, making it more penal. These were the Poor Relief Act 1722 and the Workhouse Test Act 1723. By the former legislation, all applications for relief had to be confirmed with an overseer as well as with a local Justice of the Peace, supposedly in order to reduce fraudulent claims. The Workhouse Test Act provided that a person who wanted to receive poor relief had to undertake the 'workhouse test' whereby he entered a workhouse and undertook a set amount of work. Under these two Acts, between 1723 and 1750, over 600 workhouses were built. The Acts marked a substantial deterioration in the quality of life of the poorest, increasing the downside risks of unsuccessful entrepreneurship for entrepreneurs from the lower classes.

The Workhouse Test Act's punitive principle was removed by the Relief of the Poor Act 1782, (Gilbert's[11] Act) which re-organized poor relief on a county basis and (until 1834) removed the compulsory element in workhouse provision, using workhouses only for the elderly, feeble-minded and others unable to care for themselves, and giving 'outdoor relief' to the able-bodied.

The Poor Law 1601 had greatly reduced the risk for working people of taking entrepreneurial risks and failing. There was still debtors' prison to consider, and many people spent a portion of their lives therein, but

---

10. E.P. Thompson, *Whigs and Hunters: The Origin of the Black Act* (London: Allen Lane, 1975), details in depth the activities that led up to the Act's passage and its effect on working-class life thereafter.

11. Introduced by Thomas Gilbert (1719-98). MP for Newcastle-under-Lyme and Lichfield, 1763-94. Land agent of 2nd Earl Gower, brought in on his interest, so supported North and after 1784 Pitt governments in which Gower served in the Cabinet. Chairman of Ways and Means, 1784-94.

at least poor relief was available to tide families over until new work could be found or a recession ended. Between 1723 and 1782, in districts where workhouses operated, that partial protection was removed, and business failure became more likely to lead to destitution.

Finally, the Whigs' social priorities and the reaction of the labouring classes to their repression were indicated by the passage of Gin Acts in 1732, 1735, 1737, 1741, 1742 and 1750, all attempts to control outbreaks of drunkenness among the lower orders.[12]

Demographics and Economic Statistics

Despite the punitive attitude of the Whigs towards subversion, the Whig Supremacy was not a time of irredeemable misery for the labouring classes. On the contrary, because of population restraint since 1650 and increasing productivity in agriculture, as well as Walpole's two decades of peace, grain prices were relatively low and living standards in England correspondingly high. The price of grain at Eton College, which had been 31.4s per quarter on average in 1680-89, rose sharply during the following decades dominated by war, then declined gradually to 33.9s in the 1720s, bottoming out at 29.1s in the 1730s and 28.2s in the 1740s, before a mild rise to 34.4s in the 1750s as population increase and renewed war took hold.[13] Allen has working-class living standards peaking around 1725 and beginning a slow decline thereafter, although remaining well above the levels of the mid-seventeenth century.[14]

Demographically, these years contain a mystery. The population of England and Wales, which had bottomed out around 1690 and increased slowly thereafter, took a turn upwards around 1730 and then accelerated gradually. The ten-year rate of population increase, which had been negative in the decade to 1729, rose to 3-4% in the 1730s and 1740s, then 5-6% in the 1750s and 1760s and 9-10% in the 1770s and 1780s (so in the last periods population growth was almost 1% annually). Cumulatively, the population of England and Wales was 20% greater in 1760 than in 1700 and increased another 25% by 1790.[15]

---

12. Excised spirits consumption peaked at 7,955,000 gallons in 1742 and fell to 2,639,000 gallons by 1780; see John Rule, *The Vital Century: England's Developing Economy, 1714-1815* (London: Longman, 1992), p. 130.

13. Mitchell (ed.), *British Historical Statistics*, Table XIV-16, pp. 754-55.

14. Allen, *The British Industrial Revolution in Global Perspective*, Figs 2.1 and 2.6.

15. Mitchell (ed.), *British Historical Statistics*, Table I-1, pp. 7-8.

The puzzle is to determine why this happened. The year 1730 is far before the Industrial Revolution had any impact and living standards and grain prices do not suggest any reason why the gently declining population trend before 1690 should have reversed itself with increasing determination, becoming strongly upwards around 1770. Economic historians describe the population trend, but offer no real explanation for it, beyond suggesting that it appears to have derived, not from better health or increased fertility but from a decline in the age of marriage, though this became marked only after 1750.[16]

An examination of Irish population history suggests one possible explanation. Ireland suffered a devastating famine in 1740-41, which reduced its population by about 15%. Following that disaster, Irish population increased more rapidly than English, so that the population of Ireland in 1744 of around 2.1 million had increased to 4.5 million by 1790, an annual growth rate of 1.65%, much more rapid than in England, with population growth continuing to increase rapidly until around 1830, after which increased emigration and the 1840s famine caused a decline that lasted through the rest of the nineteenth century.[17] In Ireland, apart from a measure of recovery from the seventeenth century's troubles, we have one well-accepted explanation: the potato. By allowing the impoverished Irish rural population to produce around 2.5 times more calories per acre than cereal crops, potato cultivation allowed the generally landless Irish population to grow far larger than it could previously have done, reaching its Malthusian limit in the 1840s disaster.

A similar effect from potato growing appears to have occurred in England, primarily affecting the landless or almost landless rural population, and concentrated in relatively few counties. The potato began to be adopted by poorer farmers at the end of the seventeenth century, with its adoption varying by region, the less wealthy and cooler/wetter northern regions being prominent, and Lancashire already growing substantial amounts of potatoes by the 1690s. By the mid-eighteenth century, potato cultivation formed a substantial part of agricultural output in Lancashire, Yorkshire and the north Midlands, primarily the coal-producing regions, while further south it was rare or non-existent except in the market-garden areas around London.[18] It was only in

---

16. Rule, *The Vital Century*, Table 2.2, p. 15.

17. Mitchell (ed.), *British Historical Statistics*, Table I-1c, p. 8.

18. Redcliffe Salaman, *The History and Social Influence of the Potato* (Cambridge: Cambridge University Press, 1949), ch. XXV.

the 1790s, a later period of high grain prices and dearth, that potato growing became general throughout the country. By 1801, according to the Census, 25% of the arable land of Lancashire, 20% of Cheshire, 11% of Middlesex, 9% of West Yorkshire and 8% of Cumberland was under potatoes.[19]

It was these areas of potato cultivation whose population appears to have grown fastest. Emma Griffin has Lancashire, Surrey and the West Riding of Yorkshire, as the fastest growing counties between 1761 and 1801 – all these counties were substantially potato-growing by the time of Arthur Young's[20] tour of England in the 1760s. (Cheshire and Middlesex were also towards the top of Griffin's list.) Conversely, Norfolk and Suffolk, areas of large agricultural output and population with little potato culture, grew in population only slowly.[21]

In summary, therefore, we have a doubly productive new crop, the potato, introduced on a widespread basis in the north of England, as in Ireland. The result in both places was a much more rapid growth in population. One can imagine that, for the poorer rural inhabitants, earlier marriage seemed more feasible with youthful vigour easily surmounting the heavy labour of substantial potato growing. These new households will have had considerable spare labour available, which will have welcomed cottage labour, 'putting out' opportunities from textile businesses that were expanding rapidly, albeit in a very labour-intensive fashion, without much new technology or mechanical power. The new opportunities in textiles, followed by the Industrial Revolution, saved the potato-growing areas of northern England from sharing Ireland's later fate.

Agriculturally, the Whig Supremacy saw a rapid increase in productivity, in terms of both labour and land. Land productivity of wheatfields increased by 0.42% per annum, a total of 18% between 1720 and 1760, while labour productivity in agriculture also increased by about 0.46% per annum, a total of 20% between 1720 and 1760.[22] This was not due to enclosure, which gathered momentum again through

---

19. Overton, *Agricultural Revolution in England*, p. 103.
20. Arthur Young (1741-1820). Farmer and writer. Wrote *Tours* through England, Wales and Ireland (1768-77) and *Travels in France* (1792) opposing French Revolution.
21. Emma Griffin, *A Short History of the British Industrial Revolution* (Basingstoke: Palgrave, 2010), Fig. 4.1, p. 57.
22. Overton, *Agricultural Revolution in England*, Table 3-10, p. 85.

The Industrial Revolution Takes a Whig Nap, 1721-60

parliamentary action only after 1760, but probably to the more general adoption of improvements such as the 'Norfolk' farming system, Jethro Tull's seed drill and Joseph Foljambe's iron plough, patented in 1730.

With agricultural productivity increasing while population growth was slow before 1740, prices declined, while agriculture's increased competitiveness allowed Britain to become an agricultural exporter, with wheat exports peaking at an average of 460,000 quarters per annum in the decade 1745-54.[23] After 1760, as the population increased domestic consumption increased also, making Britain once again a net importer of cereals.

With coal usage increasing in homes, industrial uses beginning to proliferate but inland transportation still very slow and expensive, the Whig Supremacy was a period of important diversification in coal sources throughout Britain. Moreover, the minimum economic size of mines increased; the minimum economic output from a pre-Newcomen mine was hundreds of pounds in value, whereas by the 1740s mines with Newcomen engines needed to have ten times that output.[24]

Coal exports from Newcastle and surrounding ports increased only from an annual average of 895,000 metric tons in 1720-24 to 1,108,000 metric tons in 1756-60, a rate of increase of only 0.6% per annum. However, the Newcastle region by 1756-60 represented only a small portion of total British coal output, which averaged 4,520,000 metric tons.[25] Other important sources included Scotland (an annual average of 900,000 metric tons in 1756-60), Yorkshire (500,000 metric tons average), Staffordshire (250,000 metric tons average), Lancashire (200,000 metric tons average) and the Midlands coalfields (180,000 metric tons average). With coalfields outside Newcastle increasing their output, coal users could increasingly source coal locally.

Table 6.1 summarizes the behaviour of GDP, prices and population over the entire period from 1701 to 1831.[26] The figures cover only the area of 'Great Britain', i.e. England, Wales and Scotland. Irish data is extremely sketchy for the eighteenth century and including Ireland only for the period after 1801 would hugely distort the statistics. In general,

---

23. Mitchell (ed.), *British Historical Statistics*, Table III-16, p. 221.

24. Jacob, *The First Knowledge Economy*, p. 72.

25. Mitchell (ed.), *British Historical Statistics*, Table IV-1, pp. 240-41, and Table IV-3, p. 247. Table IV-3 begins only in 1750, unfortunately.

26. Davenant's work on economic statistics took place in the 1690s, so some economic data is available from that time.

192   *Forging Modernity*

we can say that Irish population almost quadrupled from 1740 to 1840, while output failed to keep up, with little industrialization outside Ulster. Ireland, poor in 1740, was even poorer per capita by 1840, indeed at subsistence level, which Scotland had left behind after the 1690s famine and England and Wales far exceeded throughout the period.

Of the three sets of original data included here, the population figures are the most reliable. The first Census took place only in 1801 but considerable work has been done by backwards extrapolation using parish registers so that the population figures for England are reliable. The figures for Scotland and Wales are less reliable before 1801 but form only a modest percentage of the whole.

For price data, I have used Mitchell's figures of consumer prices, joining the two series by using the 1791 figure, which is included in both series. Because so much of the economy was agricultural, prices jump about from year to year; prolonged wars raise them, as in 1701-11 and 1791-1811, while individual years of agricultural dearth such as 1741 also give them an upwards blip. 'Nominal' output data contains considerable 'noise' from this source; 'real' figures also reflect genuine shortages of agricultural output in years of dearth such as 1741 and 1801.

The least reliable series is that for GDP, a concept unknown before the 1930s. When I began this work in 2017, I used the series contained on the website, MeasuringWorth, which appeared to match the qualitative impressions of contemporaries and indeed the quantitative estimate made by Lord Liverpool in 1822, of national income of £250-£280 million. MeasuringWorth has since changed its estimates, raising the 1820 figure by around 50%, making it incompatible with Liverpool's income estimate and showing rapid growth during the war years and slow growth in the 1820s, both highly implausible based on contemporary impressions. I have therefore used MeasuringWorth's 2017 figures (which do not differ much from their current ones before 1780).

The figures in this table are no more than indicative; the qualitative factors I discuss in each chapter should illuminate this quantification, rather than the other way around.

I shall examine the results in Table 6.1 briefly for each period. For this period, we can see an upswing in real per capita GDP, reflecting increased welfare, from the low point of 1711 at the end of the long and debilitating war. (As mentioned above, the 1741 figure is anomalous due to the agricultural dearth in that year.) That can probably be explained by increasing agricultural productivity, in an era of peace when Britain is agriculturally more than self-sufficient. Living standards in the 1730s are high, the highest since the late Middle Ages 'Merrie England' period

The Industrial Revolution Takes a Whig Nap, 1721-60

Table 6.1
Great Britain GDP, Real GDP and GDP per Capita, 1701-1831

Year	GDP (£m)	Price Index	Real GDP (£m)	Population	Real GDP per capita (£)
1701	60.8	74.1	82.0	6.533	12.55
1711	63.0	100.0	63.0	6.932	9.08
1721	65.4	74.1	88.2	7.167	12.31
1731	67.8	65.2	103.9	7.013	14.82
1741	70.3	80.0	87.8	7.244	12.12
1751	72.9	66.7	109.2	7.626	14.33
1761	79.5	69.7	114.1	7.980	14.30
1771	108.6	79.3	136.9	8.371	16.36
1781	143.0	85.3	167.7	9.011	18.61
1791	191.7	89.7	213.7	9.827	21.75
1801	257.0	155.7	165.0	10.545	15.65
1811	334.0	145.4	229.7	11.970	19.19
1821	322.0	99.7	323.0	14.092	22.92
1831	480.0	95.3	503.7	16.261	30.97

Sources: 1. For GDP, http://www.ukpublicspending.co.uk/year_spending_1841UKm_16mcln# ukgs302.
2. For population and prices, see Mitchell (ed.), *British Historical Statistics*, Tables I-2, I-3 and XIV-2/3. Scottish population estimates before 1801 are taken from: https://1841census. co.uk/1570-1750-estimated-population/ (accessed 16 September 2021).

of 1470-1500. Then later the gradual increase in population and the renewed wars suppress any further improvement. Only after 1760 does output begin to outpace population growth significantly; that period occupies the next chapter.

The Commercial Society

The England of the 1720s had come a long way since the Restoration. Daniel Defoe's *A Tour Through the Whole Island of Great Britain*, published between 1724 and 1726, set out the commercial and industrial activities of each region, demonstrating how market-oriented the society had become. The England of Defoe is not yet industrialized (he does not mention Coalbrookdale or Newcomen) yet trades and industries of all kinds flourish throughout the country, and the populace is highly attuned to markets, both local and international.

Near Cambridge, Defoe visited Stourbridge Fair:

> which is not only the greatest in the whole nation, but in the world; nor, if I may believe those who have seen them all, is

the fair at Leipsick in Saxony, the mart at Frankfurt on the Main, or the fairs at Nuremburg or Augsburg, any way to compare with this fair at Sturbridge.[27]

The fair was divided into two main streets, one for retail customers and the other for wholesale transactions, with a central square for the wool business called the Duddery where:

> there have been sold one hundred thousand pounds worth of woollen manufacturers in a week's time. ... Here are clothiers from Halifax, Leeds, Wakefield in Yorkshire, and from Rochdale, Bury etc. in Lancashire, with vast quantities of Yorkshire cloths, kersies, pennistons, cottons, etc. with all sorts of Manchester ware, fustians and things made of cotton wool; of which the quantity is so great, that they told me there were near a thousand horsepacks of such goods from that side of the country.[28]

Textiles

Even at this stage, before any significant technological improvements in the industry, the West Riding of Yorkshire and to a lesser extent Lancashire had become centres of textile manufacturing. The work was done on the 'putting out' principle, with workers in their cottages, and textile factors collecting the goods and making payment for them on a piecework basis.

Defoe describes Halifax, the centre of the wool textile business at this time, which Defoe believed to have 100,000 inhabitants. Manufacture of kerseys for army uniforms had expanded rapidly since the 1688 Revolution and:

> they have entered on a new manufacture which was never made in these parts before ... the manufacture of shalloons of which they now make, if fame does not bely them, a hundred thousand pieces a year in this parish only, and yet they do not make much fewer kersies than they did before.

One dealer in the parish sold £60,000 worth of kerseys annually, 'and all to Holland and Hamburgh'.[29] Between Halifax and Leeds: 'every way to the right hand and the left, the country appears busy, diligent

---

27. Defoe, *A Tour Through the Whole Island of Great Britain*, Vol. 1, p. 94.
28. Ibid., Vol. 1, p. 96.
29. Ibid., Vol. 3, pp. 71-73. Shalloons are worsted coat linings.

The Industrial Revolution Takes a Whig Nap, 1721-60   195

and even in a hurry of work... the villages are large, full of houses, and those houses thronged with people, for the whole country is infinitely populous.' Leeds is then the market for the cloth where: 'you see ten or twenty thousand pounds value in cloth, and sometimes much more, bought and sold in little more than one hour'.[30]

Defoe also describes the cotton trade in Manchester as 'very much increased within these thirty or forty years beyond what it was before', and indicated its spread beyond Manchester itself to the surrounding villages. As with wool textiles, cotton textile manufacturing was carried on through a 'putting-out' system.

During the Whig Supremacy, the textile industry expanded rapidly. Cotton fabric 'calico' imports from India since the Restoration had created a demand among the rich and middle classes, as well as among trading partners on the Continent. Then, in 1720, under pressure from the woollen industry, the protectionist Whigs passed the Woollen etc. Manufactures Act 1720, which prohibited not only the import of patterned cotton fabrics, but also their domestic production. This limited Indian exporters to plain cloth and raw cotton wool, thereby beginning Britain's assault on the Indian textile sector.

Naturally, British entrepreneurs sought to copy Indian patterns and backward-engineer Indian manufacturing techniques. The damp climate of Lancashire proved especially suitable for cotton spinning, but initially it was impossible to produce fine cotton thread of sufficient strength. The Lancashire textile manufacturers, therefore, took to mixing a cotton 'warp' with a 'weft' of linen, improving the fabric's strength, albeit in coarse quality. In 1735, by the Woollen etc. Manufacturers Act 1735 (note the extra 'r'), Parliament exempted cotton/linen mixes manufactured domestically from the prohibition against patterned fabrics, allowing the domestic cotton/linen industry to expand. By continuing to prohibit the production of pure cotton patterned fabrics, this legislation may well have delayed the full emergence of Lancashire cotton spinning until Arkwright secured its reversal in 1774.

For English textiles, raw cotton could be obtained from the Ottoman Empire, much closer than India, and wool was readily available in England. Raw cotton imports for processing by the English industry totalled 1.76 million pounds in weight in 1714 and had doubled to 3.82 million pounds by 1755, the last peacetime year before 1760.[31] Broadcloth milled in the West Riding of Yorkshire increased from 29,000 pieces in

---

30. Ibid., Vol. 3, pp. 79-80.
31. Mitchell (ed.), *British Historical Statistics*, Table VI-1, p. 330.

1727 (the first year available) to 57,100 in 1755; so wool was on a similar upward trajectory.[32] This doubling of output in both wool and cotton items brought roughly a doubling of the region's workforce.

The first significant technological advance in textiles was the flying shuttle, patented by John Kay (1704-79) in 1733. This allowed the shuttle to be passed through the loom automatically, meaning that a broadcloth loom could be worked with one operator and no longer required a second to catch the shuttle. (The machine was relatively cheap, so 'putting out' was still more efficient than factory labour.) This roughly doubled weaving capacity but disrupted the workforce balance between weaving and spinning – only one weaver per loom was required but each loom used the spun cotton of five spinners. Kay charged a patent fee of 15s per annum for his shuttle but was unable to enforce his patent. In 1747 he left England for France, where his shuttle was widely adopted and the state agreed to pay him a pension equivalent to £100 a year; however, this seems to have fallen into abeyance at some point for he died in penury.

A solution to the spinning/weaving imbalance was patented in 1738 by John Wyatt (1700-66) and Lewis Paul (c. 1700-59), who produced a roller spinning machine similar in principle to Arkwright's 1769 water frame. The first such machine, powered by two donkeys, was set up in 1741 by Wyatt and Paul in a tiny cotton mill in Birmingham, with ten female workers; this went bankrupt the following year, as the machinery proved fragile. They then licensed the machine to Edward Cave,[33] the quite wealthy Tory publisher of *The Gentleman's Magazine*, who set up the water-powered Marvel's Mill in Northampton, which grew to 100 staff by 1745. After Cave died in 1754 the mill passed to his brother and nephew but was never very profitable (the prohibition against patterned cotton fabrics remained in force and Cave as a well-known Tory could not usefully lobby the Whig Supremacy for its elimination) and closed spinning operations by 1761.

Entrepreneurs

One foretaste of the future, though its technology was imported from Italy, was Lombe's Mill silk-throwing works at Derby, designed by George Sorocold,[34] Britain's first nationally known civil engineer. In 1692,

---

32. Ibid., Table VI-12, p. 351.
33. Edward Cave (1691-1754). Established *The Gentleman's Magazine*, 1731.
34. George Sorocold (1668-1738). Civil engineer specializing in water projects. Built Derby waterworks, 1692, Derby silk mill, 1704, and Lombe's Mill, 1718-21.

Sorocold had designed Derby's first waterworks, using a water wheel to pump water through four miles of elm pipes constructed using a boring machine which he had developed and later patented. He built the first silk mill in Derby on the instructions of Thomas Cotchett in 1704, copying machines already used by the Dutch spinners; the mill was unsuccessful. In later life, he built atmosphere engines, iron forges and improved the drainage of mines.

Lombe's Mill. It was a Whig Supremacy silk 'throwster's mill' that used imported technology. Print by J. Walker & J. Storer.

Then, in 1718, John Lombe (1693-1722) returned from Italy after a visit of industrial espionage and obtained a patent in the name of his elder half-brother, Thomas Lombe, for the efficient Italian silk-throwing equipment, invented a century before.[35] The Lombes instructed Sorocold to build a mill, which was completed in 1721. Lombe's Mill was powered by a 50-ft water wheel, and had 10,000 spindles, with 25,000 spinning wheel bobbins, nearly 5,000 star wheels, over 9,000 twist bobbins and 46,000 winding bobbins. From 1732, Lombe's Mill used a steam engine to pump hot air round the works, to dry the silk thread. Lombe's Mill employed around 300; it was Britain's first full-scale textile factory.

Defoe visited it on his way through Derby:

> Here is a curiosity in trade worth observing, as being the only one of its kind in England, namely a throwing or throwster's mill, which performs by a wheel turn'd by the water, and though it cannot perform the doubling part of a throwster's work, which can only be done by a handwheel, yet it turns the other work, and performs the labour of many hands. Whether it answers the expense or not, that is not my business. The work was erected by one Sorocule, a man expert in making mill work, especially for raising water to supply towns for family use.

---

35. Lombe's Mill is described in Mantoux, *The Industrial Revolution in the Eighteenth Century*, pp. 198-201. According to Mantoux, the silk-throwing machinery used therein was described in a treatise published in Padua in 1621.

Defoe then goes on to relate how Sorocold fell under the mill wheel and was thrown backward by it, but miraculously survived without injury.[36]

Lombe's Mill provided a foretaste of industrialization, resembling Richard Arkwright's Cromford cotton mill a half-century later. Moreover, Sir Thomas Lombe[37] died in 1739 worth £120,000, suggesting that the mill's technological advantages were genuine. The problem was the high cost of obtaining raw silk, since it could not be produced in Britain for climatic reasons and the Italian suppliers banned its export.[38] As Lord Liverpool was to remark in 1820, silk manufacture was profitable in Britain only because of high protectionist duties – the Spitalfields silk weavers, who operated from home without heavy machinery, were protected by legislation in 1773 and their skill died out once trade was freed. Lombe's Mill, which obtained its technology through industrial espionage rather than invention, was thus largely a false start in industrialization.

Another silk entrepreneur of this period was Charles Roe (1715-81) although his greater success came later in the metals business. Roe, the youngest son of a Derbyshire vicar, was educated at Macclesfield Grammar School and went into the specialized Macclesfield button industry (Macclesfield buttons were covered in silk). Then he bought a small silk-spinning mill there in 1743 and in 1748, during the year he was Mayor of Macclesfield, he built a larger silk mill modelled on Lombe's Mill, Lombe's patent having run out. From that point on, Macclesfield became a centre of the British silk industry.

Presumably having discovered that profits in the silk business were mediocre, Roe diversified into copper mining, beginning at Coniston in the Lake District in 1756 and in 1758 building a copper smelter on Macclesfield Common, using modest local coal deposits. Here he minted copper halfpennies until the 1790s (before the 'cartwheel' copper coinage of 1797, low-denomination coinage was scarce – producing copper coinage was legal, whereas counterfeiting silver or gold was not). Then, in 1764, he obtained from the Bayly family a 21-year lease for Parys Mountain in Anglesey, where in 1768 he changed the face of British copper production, discovering 'The Great Lode' which provided

---

36. Defoe, *A Tour Through the Whole Island of Great Britain*, Vol. 3, p. 29.
37. Thomas Lombe (1685-1739). Kt 1727. London merchant. Sheriff of City of London, 1727. Obtained patent on Italian silk-throwing machinery, 1718, awarded a further £14,000 when patent ran out in 1732.
38. Anthony Calladine, 'Lombe's Mill: An Exercise in Reconstruction', *Industrial Archaeology Review*, Vol. 16, no. 1 (1993), pp. 82-99, pp. 87-88.

The Industrial Revolution Takes a Whig Nap, 1721-60

the bulk of the country's copper supply for the next 40 years. In 1774 he formed the Macclesfield Copper Company with fourteen other partners, which became one of the country's largest copper and brass producers, specializing in copper sheathing for the Navy.

Equally important to Britain's industrial future was Thomas Boulsover (1705-88). The son of a farmer/cutler from Langley, Yorkshire, Boulsover was apprenticed to a Sheffield cutler. He set up as a free cutler in Sheffield and his business modestly prospered, taking on several apprentices. In 1743, while repairing the decorative handle of a knife made of copper and silver, he overheated it, causing the two metals to fuse. When he experimented further, he discovered that it worked equally well with a thin layer of silver on a thick ingot of copper, producing a result with a similar appearance and properties to pure silver.

Boulsover accordingly set up a factory to make buttons of the new 'Sheffield Plate' as well as buckles, spurs and small snuff boxes. The business prospered and Boulsover moved to progressively larger premises, although competition appeared, since he had not patented his process – Matthew Boulton was producing 'Sheffield Plate' in Birmingham in the 1760s. In 1759, Boulsover bought land and began rolling high-quality steel, discovering that cast steel gave a much better edge than the traditional product of hammered steel. His business survived his death, managed by his heirs until 1887.

The Whig Supremacy was not short of exciting opportunities for able and greedy young men, though few involved the decades-long slog needed to produce a viable and innovative industrial company. Finance was still quietly lucrative; the National Debt was expanding while interest rates declined under the sound tutelage of Walpole and Henry Pelham, making debt-trading profitable. In America and the West Indies, a well-organized slave trade had opened opportunities to make large fortunes from tobacco and sugar plantations. In India, the collapse of the Mughal Empire opened staggering opportunities for the young, clever and sometimes unscrupulous. Robert Clive[39] and William Watts[40] both made fortunes far beyond the dreams of most mere industrialists.

---

39. Robert Clive (1725-74). 1st Baron Clive of Plassey (Ireland) from 1762. MP for Mitchell and Shrewsbury, 1754-55, 1761-74. Commander-in-Chief, India, 1756-60, 1765-67.

40. William Watts (c.1721-64). Commander of EIC fort at Kozimbazar; played central role in Plassey campaign, 1757, and was rewarded with £114,000. Daughter, Amelia (1750-70), married Charles Jenkinson, 1st Earl of Liverpool.

One example of the temptation under the Whig Supremacy for ambitious non-elite people to seek opportunities outside Britain was William Stephens (1731-1803), the illegitimate son of a schoolmaster, educated at Exeter Free School, who in 1746 went to Portugal where his uncle was a merchant. Stephens signed on as an apprentice, but his uncle's business failed and he was taken on as a partner by another successful merchant. After the Lisbon earthquake of 1755, Stephens saw the needs for building materials and discovered he could make more lime by shipping anthracite waste (culm) from England than from scarce local wood. The business struggled, with several shipments captured by the French and near bankruptcy in 1762, but Stephens' developing friendship with the Portuguese prime minister, Sebastião José de Carvalho e Melo (1699-1782), first Marquês de Pombal, enabled the business to survive and Stephens to call his three younger brothers and a sister to join him.

Then in 1769, Stephens was given control of the disused royal glass works, together with a tax exemption and an interest-free loan. He persuaded Pombal to raise the duty on imported glass and with both his glass and lime businesses became wealthy. He was an enlightened employer, opening schools for his employees' families, establishing a sickness and pension system and closing the local taverns. When Pombal lost power in 1777, Stephens secured the favour of the new sovereign, Maria I, and her son, Regent John VI, who ruled after she became mentally unstable in 1792. His brother took over the glass works after his death in 1803, after which it was ceded back to the Portuguese government.

Stephens was a great business talent, who prospered in a backward economy by using tax exemptions and tariff protection; he would surely have become a successful and modernising industrialist in Britain.

Science and Thought

One major technological advance resulted from the Longitude Act 1714. The Act's £20,000 prize stimulated innovation in two unrelated areas: astronomical observation and calculation (which produced a lunar method of determining longitude) and the design and fabrication of increasingly accurate clocks. John Harrison (1693-1776), born into an artisan family in Foulby, Yorkshire, began designing and building clocks, initially of wood, around 1713. In the 1720s, he built three long-case clocks, the most accurate in the world, inventing the grasshopper escapement. In 1730, attracted by the Longitude prize, he began building

The Industrial Revolution Takes a Whig Nap, 1721-60   201

his first sea-going clock (which had to be not only accurate but unaffected by the ship's movement). He was lent £200 in by the clockmaker, George Graham (1675-1751), the surviving partner of Thomas Tompion, and backed by another Tory remnant of the Restoration period, Edmond Halley, still Astronomer Royal, who procured him £500 funding from the Longitude Board.

Harrison built his first sea clock, H1, over the next five years and travelled to Lisbon with it in 1736, where it predicted the ship's true position accurately. With another £500 from the Longitude Board, Harrison produced H2 and H3 but was unable to test them properly because the War of the Austrian Succession made the possibility of their capture by Spanish ships too dangerous. Finally, Harrison produced a watch, H4, the first marine chronometer, which was tested on a run to Kingston, Jamaica in 1761. The Board refused to grant Harrison the prize because it (without Halley, who had by then died) thought the results were an accident. Eventually, Harrison received £10,000 in 1765 and another £8,500 in 1773, after some help from George III, although the Longitude Prize was never formally awarded.

Captain James Cook[41] used a copy of Harrison's chronometer on his second and third long sea voyages, reporting complete satisfaction with it, and chronometers gradually came into use throughout the Royal Navy, although the lunar calculation method of determining longitude also remained popular. For the Industrial Revolution, the most important outcome of Harrison's work were the advances he made in precision engineering and the use of new materials.

The Royal Society largely succumbed to eighteenth-century slumber during this period, with one exception: it instituted the world's oldest surviving scientific award, the Copley Medal. This originated as a bequest of £100 from the Tory MP Sir Godfrey Copley,[42] 'in trust for the Royal Society of London for improving natural knowledge'. The Royal Society, having deliberated for two decades, instituted the Copley Medal in 1731, which spread beyond the usual upper-class dilettantes to include

---

41. James Cook (1728-79). Merchant navy, 1747-55, RN from 1755, Master from 1757. Wolfe credited Cook's maps of the St Lawrence river for his success at Quebec in 1759. Surveyed Newfoundland, 1762-67. First Pacific voyage, 1768-71, mapping the east coast of Australia and discovering New Zealand. Commander, 1771, second voyage, 1772-75. Captain, 1775, third voyage 1776-79. He discovered Hawaii and was killed there by the natives.
42. Godfrey Copley (c.1653-1709). 2nd baronet from 1678. FRS 1691. Tory MP for Aldborough and Thirsk, 1679-81, 1695-1709.

Harrison in 1749 and the Philadelphia printer, Benjamin Franklin,[43] in 1753 and has since become a scientific prize awarded globally, second only to the Nobel Prize in prestige. However, the Royal Society had few new Fellows of note; with the exception of John Smeaton,[44] its most notable Fellow was probably the Reverend Thomas Bayes (1701-61), FRS 1742, whose theorem, a formula for determining the likelihood of a particular outcome, was presented to the Royal Society in 1763, after Bayes' death.

Economically, the most notable figure was the Irish/French economist, Richard Cantillon.[45] Cantillon was an associate of John Law. He speculated successfully in the Mississippi Company, sold early and made enemies by collecting his debts in 1719-20, which may have led to the burning of his London house and his death in 1734. He postulated the Cantillon effect, whereby an increase in the money supply causes localized price rises and speculation; he also identified and named the concept of the entrepreneur. His work was first published in 1755, after his death, but influenced the French Physiocrats and also Adam Smith and Jean-Baptiste Say.

Scotland and Ireland

Scotland flourished during the Whig Supremacy, as the economic effects of the Act of Union took hold. Most notable were the infrastructure-creating efforts of Field Marshal George Wade,[46] appointed Commander-in-Chief, Scotland in 1725. Wade directed the construction of 250 miles of roads through the Highlands, plus 30 bridges, including the Tay Bridge. Like most sharp improvements in infrastructure from a low base, this had a catalytic effect on the Scottish economy, integrating it

---

43. Benjamin Franklin (1706-1790). Postmaster General of British America, 1753-74, Speaker of the Pennsylvania Assembly, 1764. US Postmaster-General, 1775-76. US Minister to France, 1779-85. President of Pennsylvania, 1785-88.
44. John Smeaton (1724-92). FRS 1753. Copley Medal, 1759. Eddystone Lighthouse, 1755-59.
45. Richard Cantillon (1680s-1734). Made his fortune in Law's Mississippi scheme, 1716-20. Probably murdered in London, 1734. *Essay on the Nature of Trade in General* (1755)
46. George Wade (1673-1748). Whig MP for Hindon and Bath, 1715-48. Colonel, 1703, Major General, 1714, Commander-in-Chief, Scotland, 1725-40, Lieutenant General, 1727, General, 1739, Field Marshal, 1743, Commander-in-Chief, 1744-45.

The Industrial Revolution Takes a Whig Nap, 1721-60   203

with the effective commercialism that had taken effect in most of England and producing the preconditions for later industrialization. The Scottish banking system also flourished, with the Royal Bank of Scotland founded in 1727 and numerous provincial banks in the following decades.

Whereas the 1715 Jacobite rebellion had major support in both Scotland and England and failed mostly because of poor leadership, the rebellion of 1745 received far less support in Scotland and enjoyed almost no active support in England. Wade's infrastructure helped the Duke of Cumberland[47] to overcome the rebels at the battle of Culloden in 1746. After that, despite Cumberland's draconian punishment of the rebels, subsequent remedial measures in the Highlands and the active recruitment of Highlanders into the British army eliminated further rebellions.

Following Culloden, Scotland's increasing prosperity and intellectual ferment came to flower in the 'Scottish Enlightenment', a flowering in marked contrast to the intellectual somnolence that the Whig Supremacy produced in England. Scotland had four universities,[48] compared with England's two and the early eighteenth century saw their rapid development, with Edinburgh's medical faculty, for example, becoming recognised as world-class. Notable intellectual clubs were formed, such as the Political Economy Club in Glasgow and the Select Society in Edinburgh, established in 1754 and including Adam Smith and David Hume[49] among its members. In Glasgow, Joseph Black,[50] physicist and chemist, was a major intellectual influence and mentor for James Watt.

Ireland and the American colonies had contrasting fates under the Whig Supremacy, owing to their differing political affiliations. Ireland, full of Tory-inclined Catholics deprived of the franchise and subordinated to England by the Declaratory Act 1719, was used as a test bed for dodgy Whig financial engineering during the 1720s,

---

47. Prince William, Duke of Cumberland (1721-65). Second surviving son of George II. Major General, 1742. Fought at Dettingen, 1743. Lieutenant General, 1743. Fought at Fontenoy, 1745, and Culloden, 1746. Commander-in-Chief, 1745-57. Negotiated installation of Rockingham ministry with George III, 1765.

48. In chronological order: St Andrews (1413), Glasgow (1451), Aberdeen (1495), Edinburgh (1582).

49. David Hume (1711-76). Philosopher, historian, political theorist. *An Enquiry Concerning Human Understanding* (1748), *The History of England* (1754-62).

50. Joseph Black (1728-99). Scottish physicist and chemist; discovered magnesium, latent heat, specific heat and carbon dioxide.

204 *Forging Modernity*

when a Wolverhampton ironmonger, William Wood, was permitted to introduce £100,000-worth of small-denomination, lightweight, copper coinage on Ireland. 'Wood's Halfpence' was memorably denounced by Jonathan Swift:

> If a madman should come to my shop with a handful of dirt raked out of the kennel, I would pity or laugh at him; and if Mr. Wood comes to demand any gold or silver, in exchange for his trash, can he deserve or expect better treatment?[51]

The government was forced to withdraw the coinage and compensate Wood with a pension.

The Irish famine of 1740-41 cannot fairly be attributed to government error. The winter of 1739-40 was exceptionally cold, affecting the stored potato crop (which was already important, though not so dominant as later). The year 1740 was also exceptionally dry, preventing corn from growing and pushing Irish grain prices to record highs. As a result, famine hit Ireland in 1740-41, killing between 13% and 20% of the population, a higher proportion than the Great Famine of a century later. The government's relief efforts were substantial by 1740 standards but inadequate for the scale of the disaster. Nevertheless, with most of the population landless and forbidden education in Protestant schools, Ireland remained poor and undeveloped, on an entirely different economic track (outside the Protestant-settled parts of Ulster) from the more prosperous and commercial England and southern Scotland.

Ulster began moving ahead. Notably, it was ahead of the British mainland in canal development. The anti-Whig Irish parliament set up a Commission for Inland Navigation for Ireland in 1729, which was needed because of the lack of non-absentee property owners who could fund such improvements. The commission immediately authorized planning and construction of the Newry Canal, to connect Lough Neagh via the River Bann to the Irish Sea at Carlingford, allowing coal from the Tyrone coalfields (which had been opened in 1723) to be shipped to Dublin. Work began on the canal in 1731 and the canal, 19.4 miles long with thirteen locks, was opened to shipping in 1742, fifteen years before Lancashire's Sankey Canal. While the Tyrone coalfields were

---

51. Jonathan Swift, *Draper's Letters* (1724-25). William Wood (1671-1730) had previously attempted to float his iron works in the South Sea Bubble. He purchased the commission for making Irish coinage from the King's mistress for £10,000 and intended to increase his profit by debasing or counterfeiting his own coinage.

The Industrial Revolution Takes a Whig Nap, 1721-60

never very successful, owing to their difficult geology, the Newry Canal, widened into a ship canal in 1769, was generally profitable, though its went through several vicissitudes – the canal was privatized in 1829, re-nationalized in 1901 and closed in 1966.

A second canal, the Lagan Canal from Belfast to Lough Neagh, was authorized in 1755 and initially opened in 1763. It proved to be unsatisfactory until a second canal was dug and opened in 1794; it was 27 miles long and the final £62,000 needed was provided by the absentee Marquess of Donegall.[52] Both canals were modestly profitable. However, the private, local investment model pioneered by James Brindley's Grand Cross canals, probably impracticable in Ireland, would produce both more lucrative canals and a better economic 'multiplier' from their development.

Colonies, Trade and Slavery

During the Whig Supremacy, the natural tendency of the American colonies towards independence was benign, because the New England colonies, the most politically active, were Nonconformist and naturally sympathetic to radical Whiggism, with a purely nominal monarchy and no established Church. Even so, the friction increased after the Iron Act 1750, designed to prohibit iron manufacture in the colonies, and the Currency Act 1751, designed to prevent Colonial banks from issuing paper money, which was inflationary and damaging to British merchants. Both Acts were ineffective but annoyed the colonists.

Further south, this was the apogee of the British-generated slave trade, with the African American population of the future United States almost quintupling from 68,839 in 1720 to 325,806 in 1760, about 85% of them in Maryland and the future Confederate States. In 1760 African Americans represented 20.4% of the population of the future United States, close to their peak proportion.[53]

---

52. Arthur Chichester (1739-99). 5th Earl of Donegall (Ireland) from 1757, 1st Baron Fisherwick (UK), 1790, 1st Earl of Belfast (Ireland) 1790, 1st Marquess of Donegall (I) 1791. Independent MP for Malmesbury, 1768-74, turning Pittite in 1790. Educated at Westminster School and Trinity College, Oxford.

53. US Census Bureau, *Historical Statistics of the United States, Colonial Times to 1970*, 'Chapter Z: Colonial and pre-Federal Statistics, Series Z 1-19', p. 1168.

One harbinger of the future was the Molasses Act 1733, which imposed a tax of six pence per gallon on imports of molasses from non-British colonies – it was passed primarily to provide protection for the British sugar colonies, rather than to raise revenue. This was highly unpopular in the American colonies but, since the British government was Whig, opposition was limited to widespread smuggling and evasion. The evasion of the Act, the profits made by the smugglers and the corruption of local officials, nevertheless, produced a contempt for parliamentary legislation, which when combined with political opposition after 1762 would have explosive effects.

The Whig Supremacy saw the transformation of Britain's position in India. The EIC's acquisition of a firman from the Mughal emperor had signalled the Mughal Empire's decline; under Muhammad Shah (Mughal Emperor, 1719-48) that decline accelerated. The turning point was the 1739 sack of Delhi by Nader Shah of Persia, looting the immense Mughal store of treasure. From that point, subsidiary rulers, notably the Hindu Mahrattas of central India, asserted their independence, and Mughal power became intermittent.

EIC textile imports from India increased only modestly after 1720; even at the peak in 1725-29, average import volume was below the free trading 1680-84 level, because of the Woollen etc. Manufactures Act 1720. However, EIC private traders, using the Mughal firman to trade tax-free within India, began to make immense fortunes, often with the help of local rulers seeking revenge against their neighbours. Then, with resumption of the war against France in the 1740s, Madras became vulnerable to attack from the neighbouring French trading post at Pondicherry. The French captured Madras in 1746; it was returned to Britain by the 1748 Treaty of Aix-la-Chapelle. From 1750, the EIC forces in India were gradually increased, from 3,000 men in 1750 to 23,000 in 1763.

The turning point came in 1756-57, when the subsidiary Nawab of Bengal died and was succeeded by his grandson, Siraj-ud-Daulah, ambitious, inept and strongly anti-British. Siraj-ud-Daulah first captured the British trading post at Kozimbazar (commanded by William Watts), then the major EIC post at Calcutta, imprisoning the defenders in the notorious 'Black Hole of Calcutta'. After a relief force, accompanied by a fleet from England, was sent from Madras, Siraj-ud-Daulah was defeated with 60,000 men by 3,000 British troops under Robert Clive at the Battle of Plassey on 23 June 1757 (part of Siraj-ud-Daulah's force defected to the British, suborned by Watts). With further victories against the

The Industrial Revolution Takes a Whig Nap, 1721-60 207

French later in the war, the EIC increasingly dominated India, though the crucial political transition came after 1760.

There was similar British hegemony of the transatlantic slave trade. By one estimate, British ships carried 200,000 slaves across the Atlantic in the 1740s, of which 63,000 were destined for the American colonies, and a similar number in the following decade.[54] The remainder were destined for the Caribbean islands, with a few carried by the South Sea Company to Spanish colonies before its *asiento* ended in 1750. Fortunes were made in Liverpool, Bristol and Glasgow; so also in Newport, Rhode Island, which dominated the trans-shipment business between the British outposts in the Americas. The West Indian sugar trade was much more profitable than the slave trade itself, with sugar imports to Britain averaging £1.4 million annually in 1751-60, over 15% of total imports.[55]

It is appropriate at this point to address the question of how much the abominable evil of slavery financed the Industrial Revolution. There is no question that it played a major role in the growth of the British Empire, the country's other major global achievement during these centuries. Without slavery and the slave trade, both the American and more especially the West Indian colonies would have been much less profitable and their development correspondingly slower and more tentative. Furthermore, revenues from tobacco and sugar plantations, mostly worked by slave labour, played a primary role, perhaps at its peak 20% of state revenues, in enlarging Britain's fiscal capacity and therefore its economic and geopolitical power.

The connection with industrialization is less direct. Lucrative off-market opportunities for self-enrichment in slave plantations and India diverted scarce resources of talent and entrepreneurship from the lengthier and more difficult work of industrial advance – this appears to have been particularly true during the Whig Supremacy. Conversely, the money derived from West Indies trade greatly enriched Liverpool merchants, for example, and therefore provided much of the finance for the industrial development of Lancashire's textile sector and country banking system. We should not make too much of this. Slave-related trade was a central activity for only a few of Britain's wealthy merchants and merchants were only one among many sources of finance for industrialism. As for industrialists themselves, few had any background

---

54. Thomas, *The Slave Trade*, pp. 264-65.
55. Mitchell (ed.), *British Historical Statistics*, Table IX-7, p. 463.

208   *Forging Modernity*

in or connection with slave-related businesses, nor did their revenues and profits depend significantly on such businesses, until the US cotton trade exploded in importance after independence.

Political Developments, 1721-60

After Walpole had cemented himself in power, his skill in financial management and in keeping Britain out of wars usefully increased the country's prosperity and reduced its debt costs. His solution of the South Sea crisis reduced interest rates payable on most National Debt from 5% to 4% in 1728-30. Britain's credit standing was also improved by the Sinking Fund he established in 1726 – although the fund lacked the protection against 'raids' of Pitt's later 1786 scheme, this nevertheless increased confidence in Britain's ability to service its debts.

Through the years of peace and reduction in debt service costs, Walpole was able to reduce the Land Tax rate from 4s in the pound to 3s in 1728, 2s in 1731 and finally 1s in 1732, although this final reduction was reversed the following year on the failure of his Excise Scheme (an attempt to impose new excise duties on wines and tobacco and establish a system of bonded warehouses in order to reduce smuggling). Politically, the Land Tax reductions softened the opposition of the Tory country gentry, although the Excise Scheme cost him some Whig support, some of whom went into opposition at the 1734 election.

Walpole's political position weakened after 1734, with the rise of a combined Whig/Tory 'Patriot' opposition, the death of Queen Caroline[56] in 1737, and the outbreak of war over his opposition in 1739 (which forced him to return the Land Tax to 4s in the pound). He lost office in January 1742, after a near-defeat in the 1741 election. Nevertheless, his long period of peace and sound fiscal management had reduced National Debt charges by 39%, from £3.31 million in 1721 to £2.03 million in 1741.[57]

The Tories had hoped to share power in 1742, but a new almost purely Whig government was formed and the Tories remained in opposition, their position being markedly weakened by the 1745 Jacobite rebellion, which stigmatized the party as unpatriotic, even though active support for the Pretender in England was minimal. From then until 1760, Tory

---

56. Caroline of Ansbach (1683-1737). Wife of George II from 1705. Major intellectual and political influence; ally of Walpole.
57. Mitchell (ed.), *British Historical Statistics*, Table XI-2, p. 578. The year-end in both cases is 29 September.

The Industrial Revolution Takes a Whig Nap, 1721-60

support appeared less than it was; many ambitious young politicians, notably, Charles Jenkinson[58] and Simon Harcourt,[59] worked with the Whigs (for example, in the notably expensive 1754 Oxford election),[60] even though their ancestral connections were Tory and they would revert to Toryism after 1760.

After a brief interlude, Henry Pelham took power, remaining in office at the head of Whig governments until his death in 1754 and following Walpolean policies of sound finance. Elections in 1747 and 1754 (shortly after Pelham's death) produced massive Whig majorities and Tory decline. The 'Patriot' Whigs led by William Pitt[61] 'the Elder' remained an important parliamentary grouping, brought into acquiescence with Pelham's rule by Pitt's 1746 appointment as Paymaster of the Forces.

Pelham's most notable achievement was his reform of British public finances, helped by the Whigs' cosmopolitan and City connections. The expansion of the War of the Austrian Succession from 1744 caused a gaping financing requirement, with deficits rising from £2.4 million in 1744 to £4.8 million in 1748. These needs were met by tender-offer bond financings led by the brilliant Jewish City financier, Sampson Gideon,[62] who

---

58. Charles Jenkinson (1729-1808). 1st Baron Hawkesbury from 1786, 1st Earl of Liverpool from 1796. Tory MP for Cockermouth, Appleby, Harwich, Hastings and Saltash, 1761-86. Secretary to the Treasury, 1763-65, Secretary at War, 1778-82, President of the Board of Trade, 1786-1804.

59. Simon Harcourt (1714-77). 2nd Viscount Harcourt from 1727, 1st Earl Harcourt from 1749. (Grandson of Simon Harcourt, (1660-1727). 1st Baron Harcourt from 1711, 1st Viscount Harcourt from 1721. Tory MP for Abingdon, Bossiney and Cardigan, 1690-1710. Solicitor General, 1702-7, Attorney General, 1707-8, Lord Keeper of the Great Seal, 1710-13, Lord Chancellor, 1713-14.) Governor to the Prince of Wales (the future George III), 1751-59. Ambassador to Mecklenburg-Strelitz, 1761, Ambassador to Paris, 1768-72. Lord Lieutenant of Ireland, 1772-76.

60. Covered in R.J. Robson, *The Oxfordshire Election of 1754* (Oxford: Oxford University Press, 1949).

61. William Pitt (1708-78). 1st Earl of Chatham from 1766. Grandson of Thomas 'Diamond' Pitt. MP for Old Sarum, Seaford, Aldborough, Okehampton and Bath, 1735-66. Paymaster of the Forces, 1746-55, Southern Secretary of State, 1756-57, 1757-61, Leader of the House of Commons, 1756-61, Prime Minister, 1766-68, Lord Privy Seal, 1766-68. Father of William Pitt the Younger.

62. Sampson Gideon (1699-1762). Sephardic Jewish son of Hamburg-born West India merchant Rowland Gideon, who became probably the first Jewish Freeman of the City of London in 1698. Profited from South Sea speculation, then became specialist in government finance, advising

helpfully supported government bonds in the 1745 panic. Nevertheless, even with Gideon's distribution aimed at City financial interests, the base of investors for government bonds had broadened steadily and now included both traditional and commercial wealth-holders.

After 1748, Pelham realized that a longer-term solution must be found, so he involved the Tory financial expert, Sir John Barnard.[63] The final scheme in 1751, the implementation of which was again led by Gideon, refinanced all the government's 4% and 5% debt into a new 'Consolidated Loan' bearing interest at 3½% until 1757 and 3% thereafter, the famous 3% Consols. Consols would be the basis for British financing of future wars – most notably, the Napoleonic wars – until 1914-18 . They also became the principal quasi-liquid holding of the British public, far more important than shares.

After 1751, when the government wanted to finance a war, instead of issuing 5% bonds, it issued 3% Consols at perhaps 60% of the 'par' principal amount, which would then give a 5% (i.e. 3%/60%) running yield. Since all wars were temporary, people who bought 3% bonds at 60% would make generous 5% yields during the war, then a large capital gain afterwards, when yields dropped to 3% and the bonds returned to par. The government could find buyers even in bad war years, provided (as was the case) that there was confidence that Britain would later repay its debts.

So it turned out: not only did investors enjoy strong yields, they also made big capital gains when peace came – 21 percentage points in six years after the bottom in 1762 as the Seven Years' War (1756-63) ended, 33 percentage points in ten years after the wartime bottom in 1782 as the American War of Independence (1775-82) ended, and 32 percentage points in the twelve years after 1812. In all three cases, the investor profits from Gideon's scheme were to provide substantial finance for the Industrial Revolution.[64]

Pelham's friendship for Gideon led him to sponsor the Jewish Naturalization Act 1753, which allowed Jewish people to become naturalized British citizens and enabled them to buy land, vote and

---

the Pelhams, and inventing Consols. Son created a baronet in 1759. Died worth at least £350,000.

63. Sir John Barnard (1685-1764). Kt 1732. Marine insurer. Tory MP for City of London, 1722-61. Sponsored Stock Jobbing Act 1733, 'Sir John Barnard's Act', prohibiting stock jobbing; fortunately, the Act's enforcement was inadequate. Lord Mayor of London, 1738-39.

64. See Martin Hutchinson and Kevin Dowd, 'The Apotheosis of the Rentier: How Napoleonic Finance Kick-Started the Industrial Revolution', *Cato Journal* (Fall 2018).

The Industrial Revolution Takes a Whig Nap, 1721-60   211

enjoy other privileges that were still barred to many Catholics and Nonconformists. Given that only the very richest Jews (like Gideon) could avail themselves of this Act, it was thought by Tories to be a free handout to the Whigs' wealthy City backers. The outcry against the Act caused the government to repeal it hurriedly in the following year. Jews were finally given full privileges of citizenship in 1858, after the repeal of the Test Act against Nonconformists (1828) and Catholic Emancipation (1829).

Pelham also alienated public opinion when, on the advice of the second Earl of Macclesfield,[65] he switched Britain's calendar from the Julian to the Gregorian system, thereby eliminating eleven days from the Michaelmas quarter of 1752 – i.e. 2 September 1752 was followed by 14 September. Astronomically, this was a correct and necessary reform; economically, it was a rip-off (as Tories gleefully pointed out) since tenants were forced to pay a full quarter's rate for only 81 days – as with many Whig Supremacy enactments, the working classes were the primary sufferers. On the other hand, Pelham's British Museum Act 1753, establishing the British Museum benefited primarily the educated.

Following Pelham's death, the political climate began to change. Newcastle took over and won the 1754 election but lacked Pelham's quiet competence and was beleaguered by the Patriot Whigs led by Pitt when Britain drifted into war again in 1756. Then, after a short-lived coalition between Pitt and the nonentity, the fourth Duke of Devonshire, the Pitt-Newcastle administration was formed, which brought massive victories and lasted beyond George II's death in October 1760. The Pitt-Newcastle administration contained several hidden Tories like George Grenville,[66] and was both more open and more populist than previous Whig administrations.

Renewed Progress towards Industrialization

In the late 1750s Britain's progress towards industrialization began to gather momentum. One sign of renewed progress came at Coalbrookdale. Abraham Darby II had perfected the coke-fired process for making pig iron around 1750, and in 1754-55 he undertook a major expansion north

---

65. George Parker (1697-1764). 2nd Earl of Macclesfield from 1732. Whig MP for Wallingford, 1722-27. Astronomer. FRS 1722. President of the Royal Society, 1752-64.

66. George Grenville (1712-70). MP for Buckingham, 1741-70. Treasurer of the Navy, 1756, 1756-62, Leader of the House of Commons, 1761-62, 1763-65, Northern Secretary of State, 1762, First Lord of the Admiralty, 1762-63, Prime Minister and Chancellor of the Exchequer, 1763-65.

of Coalbrookdale, constructing the Horsehay furnace, which could produce 22 tons of iron per week. The following year, after a further infusion of capital, another blast furnace was constructed on the same site, while railways connecting the furnaces to nearby coal mines were also used for transporting the coal to the Severn for downstream sales. Two more furnaces were built at Ketley, Shropshire between 1757 and 1758 – the Seven Years' War proving very good for iron demand and sales prices.[67] Despite a complex series of lawsuits, by the time of Abraham Darby's death in 1763, his technical know-how had been translated into a very substantial business, although still only a moderate fortune.

Other developments were John Wilkinson's 1757 establishment of a blast furnace near Brosely, on the other side of the Severn from Coalbrookdale, and the founding of the Carron Iron Works and Josiah Wedgwood's pottery, both in 1759. The major technological and economic advances of those institutions date from after 1760.

Also in 1759, Francis Egerton, third Duke of Bridgewater, obtained an Act of Parliament for the construction of the Bridgewater Canal, from the Duke's coal mines at Worsley to Manchester, which would be completed in 1761. (An Act of Parliament was necessary because the canal needed to assert compulsory purchase rights along its length to compel landowners – duly compensated – to allow its passage.) The canal, designed by James Brindley, cost a total of £168,000 and was built within a year of the final agreement of the route in a second 1760 Act of Parliament. Extensions to Liverpool and Runcorn on the River Mersey were added later, after another Act of Parliament in 1762, increasing the long-term cost to £300,000 and the canal's total length to 39 miles.

The Bridgewater Canal was unique among the major canals in being financed almost entirely by the duke with a little help from his bankers. It was built on a lavish scale, with a broad gauge (almost fifteen feet) and including an underground dock within the duke's coal mine, a containerization system for loading coal at the mine and offloading it at the destination, a water supply pumped from the mine and the famous Barton Aqueduct carrying the canal 112 yards across the River Irwell. The total cost of the initial phase

The Opening of the Bridgewater Canal by Ford Madox Brown, showing a Pre-Raphaelite view.

---

67. Thomas, *Coalbrookdale and the Darbys*, pp. 45-58.

The Industrial Revolution Takes a Whig Nap, 1721-60　　213

was £16,800 per mile, five times that of the other early canals. The Bridgewater Canal halved the price of coal in Manchester and inspired the later spate of canal building.

Technically, the Bridgewater was mainland Britain's second canal (ignoring the Aire and Calder of 50 years earlier). The first was the Sankey Canal from the Haydock coal mines to St Helens, authorized in 1755 as Sankey Navigation, to widen and deepen the brook of that name, but completed in 1757 as an eight-mile canal, which cost £18,600 and was financed by Liverpool businessmen.[68]

James Brindley, the designer of the Bridgewater Canal, can properly be regarded as the father of Britain's Industrial Revolution canal system. He was born to a farming family in rural Derbyshire, had little education beyond that from his mother, then he was apprenticed to a wheelwright in Macclesfield. After his apprenticeship, he set up as a consulting engineer in Leek, Staffordshire, designing several water-driven mills and an ingenious water-wheel-driven pumping system for the Wet Earth Colliery at Clifton, Lancashire. He also attempted improvements to Newcomen's steam engine, but his wooden cylinders proved a technological dead-end!

Brindley's expertise in water engineering led him into canal projects. The first person to consult him was the second Earl Gower, for what would become the Trent and Mersey Canal; this project was not pursued at that point because of the cost. Then Gower introduced him to Bridgewater, and the rest is Industrial Revolution history. (Gower had married Bridgewater's sister and his land agent, Thomas Gilbert, was the brother of John Gilbert,[69] the manager of Bridgewater's affairs, with whom Brindley worked on the canal.)

Already before 1760, with the encouragement of Gower, Brindley planned a Grand Cross canal system, to link the Trent, Mersey, Severn and Thames rivers; his work on that scheme belongs to the next chapter.[70] During his work on the Bridgewater Canal he invented 'puddling', a technique for mixing clay, sand and water to produce a waterproof bottom for canals – he demonstrated this technique, messily but successfully,

---

68. J.R. Ward, *The Finance of Canal Building in Eighteenth-Century England* (Oxford: Oxford University Press, 1974, pp. 26-27.

69. John Gilbert (1724-95). Agent to Bridgewater from 1758, to Duke of Devonshire from 1770s.

70. Nick Corble, *James Brindley: The First Canal Builder* (Cheltenham: The History Press, 2005), gives a useful account of Brindley's life, though he focusses more on the Bridgewater Canal than on the Grand Cross canals.

A portrait of James Brindley. Brindley's Grand Cross canal system turbocharged the economy. Painting by Francis Parsons.

before a Select Committee of the House of Commons in 1762, while promoting the extension to Bridgewater's canal.[71]

Finally, the 1750s saw the early work of John Smeaton. He was recommended by Macclesfield as the engineer for rebuilding the

---

71. Ibid., p. 82.

The Industrial Revolution Takes a Whig Nap, 1721-60

Eddystone Lighthouse, which had been destroyed by fire in 1755. He produced a stone building in the shape of an oak tree and pioneered 'hydraulic lime' a form of mortar which set under water, completing the lighthouse in 1759; as 'Smeaton's Tower', it remained in operation until 1877, when it was discovered that the rock underneath it was eroding. Also, in 1759, he developed the Smeaton coefficient, a central concept in fluid dynamics, which greatly added to the efficiency of the water wheels used in industrialization and was eventually used by the Wright Brothers in developing the first successful aeroplane.

After 1760, Smeaton like Brindley became heavily involved in engineering works, including canal development, though he was used more on the geographically peripheral canals like the Forth and Clyde rather than the Midlands canals that were Brindley's home territory – he was brought in on the Birmingham and Fazeley Canal after Brindley's death. He also advised on building several bridges and harbour works and Smeaton's Viaduct over the River Trent. As a mechanical engineer, he made modest improvements in Newcomen's steam engine, though his work was overtaken by James Watt, and designed several windmills and water mills. He was a peripheral member of the Birmingham Lunar Society.

* * *

The year 1759 was the 'Year of Victories', in which Great Britain became a superpower and at the end of which Horace Walpole wrote: 'Our bells are worn threadbare with ringing for victories.'[72] In that year also, the Industrial Revolution began accelerating towards fruition on several fronts. On 25 October of the following year, George II died, and shortly afterwards the one-party Whig Supremacy ended.

---

72. *The letters of Horace Walpole, Earl of Orford: including numerous letters now first published from the original manuscripts* (London: R. Bentley, 1840), p. 489.

7

The Tory-Assisted Take-off, 1761-83

Political Developments, 1760-70

The accession of George III made a big difference to British political life. He had been brought up in a household oriented towards the Tory opposition because of his father, Frederick, Prince of Wales, who died in 1751 and had the usual hostile Hanoverian son-father relationship with his father, George II. Then, at the instigation of his mother, Princess Augusta, George, the new Prince of Wales, gained a moderate Tory governor, Earl Harcourt, and a strongly Tory tutor, James Stuart, Earl of Bute,[1] who would become prime minister in May 1762.

Consequently, George was brought up on the ideals of Bolingbroke's *On the Idea of a Patriot King*. Bolingbroke postulated a Tory party revived with the help of the king, which would root out the corruption of the Whig Supremacy and re-establish Tory foreign policy (the blue-water strategy), economic policy (orientation to the provinces and reduced dependence on City financiers), social policy (greater opportunities for provincial gentry, tradesmen and the working classes) and Church policy of strong support for Anglicanism. The idea of the patriot king also owed a lot to the historical legend of Anglo-Saxon King Alfred, extolled by Thomas Arne[2] in a 1740 masque commissioned by Frederick, Prince of Wales, whose rousing finale, 'Rule, Britannia', was a fine exposition of Tory 'blue-water' foreign policy.

---

1. John Stuart (1713-92). 3rd Earl of Bute from 1723. Tutor to George, Prince of Wales, from 1751. Keeper of the Privy Purse, 1760-63. Northern Secretary of State, 1761-62, Prime Minister, 1762-63.
2. Thomas Arne (1710-78). *Masque of Alfred*, featuring 'Rule, Britannia' (1740), *Artaxerxes* (1762).

The Tory-Assisted Take-off, 1761-83

George III, only 22 when he succeeded, saw himself as a patriot king; the first two decades of his reign involved a series of political difficulties generated by this self-image. Nevertheless, over George III's reign, his governments remained primarily Tory, but became more capable and less corrupt, culminating in the successes of William Pitt the Younger and Liverpool.

The Tory rejoicing at his advent was immense; Arne's opera, *Artaxerxes*, first performed three months before the apotheosis of Bute, extolled Artaxerxes/George III:

> *Live to us, to Empire live,*
> *Great Augustus, long may'st thou*
> *From the subject world receive*
> *Laurel wreaths t'adorn thy brow!*

The political changes after George III's accession took a few years to occur and were not total. Bute entered the government as Northern Secretary of State in March 1761 and took over as prime minister in May 1762, with the final removal of Newcastle. The principal short-term policy change made by Bute was to sue for peace; the financial costs of Pitt's drive for national glory had become too great to bear.

In negotiating the peace treaty, the question came up of whether Britain should return to France the vast empty wastes of Canada or the valuable sugar island, based on a slave economy, of Guadeloupe. Bute, much to the fury of the commercially-minded Whigs, chose to keep Canada, since he correctly recognized that the long-term, indeed indefinite, benefit to Britain and its American colonies of removing the French from Canada far exceeded any possible sugar income from Guadeloupe. Two hundred and fifty years later, one can bless that decision, even though it made it easier for the American colonies to seek independence.

The Tories Bute brought into power included Shelburne[3] and Jenkinson in junior offices (North[4] had joined as a Lord of the Treasury in 1757). However, some Tories he appointed to top jobs were not

---

3. William Petty (1737-1805). 2nd Earl of Shelburne from 1761, 1st Marquess of Lansdowne from 1784. MP for Wycombe, 1760-61. (Great-grandson of Sir William Petty.) First Lord of Trade, 1763, Southern Secretary of State, 1766-68, Home Secretary, 1782, Prime Minister, 1782-83.

4. Frederick North (1732-92). Lord North from 1752, 2nd Earl of Guilford from 1790. MP for Banbury, 1754-90. (Great-grand-nephew of Sir Dudley North.) Lord of the Treasury, 1757-65, Chancellor of the Exchequer, 1767-82, Prime Minister, 1770-82, Home Secretary, 1783.

ready for prime time – Sir Francis Dashwood,[5] the Chancellor of the Exchequer, had previously been known as the founder of the Hellfire Club; as Chancellor he introduced a highly unpopular Cider Tax. Even though the new government signed the Treaty of Paris making peace with France and Spain, press hostility was extreme (the press was almost all Whig, having been bribed by the Whigs for the previous half century) and was rallied to action by John Wilkes, a radical journalist and former protégé of Dashwood who was disgruntled at not receiving office.[6]

Bute, a timid soul, resigned in April 1763, but in eleven months had broken the one-party state and installed new Tories throughout government. From this point, although the Whigs regained full control briefly in 1765-67 and 1782-83, most governments contained a healthy admixture of Tories and Tory policies were frequently, although not always, followed. Most important economically, policies no longer favoured London, slave-enabled economies and the Whiggish 'monied interest'. Instead, provincial towns, emerging manufacturing districts and rural areas gained a voice in policy and were able to further their interests. Together with structural changes in finance (country banks) and infrastructure (canals) this set off the Industrial Revolution.

Bute was succeeded by George Grenville, whose Toryism was blighted by an excessively imperious manner with the King, who grew to hate him so much that he dismissed him in 1765 in favour of the Whig Marquess of Rockingham.[7] Rockingham lasted a year, encouraging the disaffected among the American colonists by repealing Grenville's Stamp Act 1765, to be succeeded by a Whig-dominated coalition led initially by Chatham

---

5. Francis Dashwood (1708-81). 2nd baronet from 1724, 11th/15th Baron le Despencer from 1763. MP for New Romney and Weymouth and Melcombe Regis, 1741-63. Chancellor of the Exchequer, 1762-63, Master of the Great Wardrobe, 1763-65, Joint Postmaster General, 1765-81. Founded Hellfire Club, 1755.

6. John Wilkes (1725-97). Radical journalist and politician. Founded anti-government newspaper, *The North Briton* (1762). Most famous for his battle against the use of general warrants. MP for Aylesbury and Middlesex, 1757-64, 1768-69, 1774-90. High Sheriff of Buckinghamshire, 1754-55. Sheriff of London, 1771-72, Lord Mayor of London, 1774-75. For more on Wilkes and Dashwood, see Eric Towers, *Dashwood: The Man and the Myth* (London: Inner Traditions, 1987).

7. Charles Watson-Wentworth (1730-82). 2nd Marquess of Rockingham from 1750. Prime Minister, 1765-66, 1782.

The Tory-Assisted Take-off, 1761-83

and later, as Chatham's health declined, by the Duke of Grafton[8]. This coalition changed its nature substantially in December 1767, becoming more Tory, with the advent of Gower and other followers of the (largely Tory, unusually for his family) fourth Duke of Bedford.[9]

Granville Leveson-Gower, second Earl Gower was born in 1721, heir of the first Earl Gower the sole Tory to enter the predominantly Whig governments in 1742 after Walpole's fall. An immensely wealthy landowner in Staffordshire, Shropshire and Yorkshire after he succeeded his father in 1754, Gower took a strong personal interest in technological developments that could enable him to improve his estates. In 1748, he married Lady Louisa Egerton, sister of the third Duke of Bridgewater, who brought further lands as her dowry; Bridgewater on his death in 1803 would leave the bulk of his estates to Gower's son.

Gower encouraged James Brindley, instructing him with a retainer of £100 per annum to survey the route for the future Trent and Mersey Canal (for which, because of the cost, he did not want to be the sole investor) then introducing him to Bridgewater. After the first phase of the Bridgewater Canal had been completed, the technological problems solved and a demonstration proved, Gower helped Brindley and the local entrepreneur Josiah Wedgwood to put together investor groups and parliamentary authorisation for the Staffordshire and Worcestershire and the Trent and Mersey Canals, the first two of Brindley's Grand Cross scheme, both of which were authorised and the finance raised in 1766. Gower was the catalyst for this central development of the early Industrial Revolution, and intimately involved in its details.

Gower made other direct contributions to industrialization. In 1764, he formed a partnership, Earl Gower & Co., with Thomas and John Gilbert as partners, to develop the coal, lime and ironstone resources of his estates around Lilleshall, Staffordshire. First, the partnership built the 5½-mile Donnington Wood Canal, to connect Gower's coalfields at Donnington Wood with the Wolverhampton-Newport Turnpike, where the coal would be sold from a wharf; this was completed in 1768. Two

---

8. Augustus Fitzroy (1735-1811). 3rd Duke of Grafton from 1757. MP for Boroughbridge and Bury St Edmunds, 1756-57. Secretary of State for the Northern Department, 1765-66, First Lord of the Treasury, 1766-70, Prime Minister, 1768-70, Lord Privy Seal, 1771-75, 1782-83.

9. John Russell (1710-71). 4th Duke of Bedford from 1732. Married Gower's sister, Gertrude, as his second wife, 1737. First Lord of the Admiralty, 1744-48. Southern Secretary of State, 1748-51, Lord Lieutenant of Ireland, 1757-61, Lord Privy Seal, 1761-63, Lord President of the Council, 1763-65.

Granville Leveson Gower, 2nd Earl Gower, was a catalyst of the Industrial Revolution. Painting by Edward Fisher.

branches connected the canal with the limestone quarries at Lilleshall and Pitchstone; since both quarries were around 40 feet below the main canal, a tunnel and system of pulleys was used for one and a system of seven locks for the other. The canal was later connected to other local canals, including the Shropshire Canal in 1790.

The Tory-Assisted Take-off, 1761-83

Initially, Earl Gower & Co. acted primarily as lessor of the various works – the Donnington Wood iron works was constructed by lessees in 1785, with £2,000 financing from Gower – but in 1792 the partnership bought the Donnington iron works and began operating it directly, being replaced by the Lilleshall Company in 1802, in which Gower's second son, first Earl Granville (1773-1846), became a partner. Lilleshall expanded during the nineteenth century and remained in business until its nationalization in 1951.

Gower served as Lord Privy Seal in 1755-57. In 1763, before Bute's fall, Gower was recommended to him as Southern Secretary of State by Henry Fox, Bute's Leader of the House of Commons saying: 'He is of a humour and nature the most practicable; and if any man could do the office of southern secretary without either quarrelling with Charles Townshend or letting down the dignity of his own office, he would.'[10]

Gower returned to government in 1767, adding a Tory flavour to the Grafton ministry, and solidifying its expertise in economic and industrial matters. He remained through the North ministry until 1779, being a noted hard-liner on dealing with the Americans, but resigned in disgust at North's vacillations. He was invited four times to become prime minister by George III over the next four years but turned the king down each time.

Then, in December 1783, Gower was the most important sponsor of Pitt's sudden emergence. He opened the House of Lords debate on 17 December and made a powerful speech against Charles James Fox's India Bill, describing its motivation as 'the amazing patronage that would be acquired to the Minister by the new arrangement'.[11] The Bill was defeated that evening by 95 votes to 76, causing the Fox-North coalition to resign. Then, as Lord President of the Council (which he became on 19 December), he was the keystone member of Pitt's initial

---

10. Gower's entry in the Dictionary of National Biography. Henry Fox (1705-74). 1st Baron Holland from 1763. (Father of Charles James Fox [1749-1806], arch-rival of Pitt the Younger.) MP for Hindon, Windsor and Dunwich, 1735-63. Secretary at War, 1746-55, Southern Secretary of State 1755-56, Paymaster of the Forces, 1757-65, Leader of the House of Commons, 1762-63. Charles Townshend (1725-67). Chancellor of the Exchequer, 1766-67. Not quarrelling with the peppery Townshend was presumably a required qualification for Gower because of Townshend's campaign to increase taxes on the American colonists, the Southern Secretary's responsibility.
11. J. Debrett, *The Parliamentary Register*, Vol. 14, House of Lords, 17 December 1783, p. 69.

Cabinet, seen by North as forming a coalition with Pitt rather than merely serving in his government: 'the Coalition between the present First Lord of the Treasury and the Lord President is a coalition of shreds, of ends and remnants; a coalition of small parts of parties, but not of the parties themselves.'[12]

Gower was in office for the first eleven years of Pitt's ministry, pushing it in a Tory direction, in which he was joined after 1786 by Jenkinson. His influence was significantly increased by his former land agent, Thomas Gilbert, serving from 1784 to 1794 as chairman of the House of Commons' Ways and Means Committee.

After being created Marquess of Stafford in 1786, Gower retired in 1794, when posts were needed for the Portland Whigs. At his death, the marquess was the fifth richest man in Britain, with a net worth of £2 million, showing that traditional landowners who developed their holdings could still outpace the new industrialists financially.

Throughout his tenure in office, Gower brought his colleagues an understanding of the incipient process of industrialization, and of the national economy beyond London, which was to prove invaluable to both North and Pitt, both economically capable but lacking Gower's hands-on industrial development expertise.

A second increasingly important figure on the economic side in governments until 1804 was **Charles Jenkinson**, father of the future prime minister, Lord Liverpool. Jenkinson, cousin to an ancestrally Tory line of Oxfordshire baronets, the first four of whom were MPs, entered top politics as Bute's private secretary in 1761, then became one of two secretaries to the Treasury under Grenville, where he designed the Stamp Act, before losing office with Grenville. However, he had now been befriended by George III and so played an increasingly important back-room role even when not officially in office.

As a Lord of the Treasury in the late 1760s Jenkinson befriended North, then was an increasingly important communications link between the king and North throughout North's period in office, becoming Secretary at War in 1778. After North fell, Jenkinson played a supporting role in the manoeuvring that brought Pitt to power. He was made President of the Board of Trade in 1786, where he remained until 1804, co-operating with Matthew Boulton on a notable coinage scheme and acquiring the barony of Hawkesbury in 1786 and the earldom of Liverpool in 1796.

---

12. Ibid., Vol. 12, House of Commons, 22 December 1783, p. 479.

Jenkinson played a substantial role in economic policy under Grenville, and then again after 1767, as Lord of the Treasury in 1767-73 and thereafter as a major advisor to the king and North. Out of office in 1782-84 and initially resisted by Pitt, he was an even more important economic policymaker from 1786 onwards, pulling Pitt's government towards Toryism, to which it was firmly attached after 1787, and providing a sceptical 'grown-up in the room' voice to Pitt and his other, young, Adam Smith acolytes, all thirty years younger than Jenkinson.

Jenkinson and North both derived their economic policies from the Oxfordshire School of economic thought. They were influenced by Adam Smith, author of *An Inquiry into the Nature and Causes of the Wealth of Nations* (1776), but unlike Pitt were not wholehearted acolytes of Smith's free trade theories, believing, for example, that customs duties were important elements in financing British governments. As President of the Board of Trade, Jenkinson was to have a direct influence on the Industrial Revolution; in these earlier years he was one of several facilitators of the process.

America, India and Ireland

The political transition after 1760 benefited the British people and the Industrial Revolution but had a major ill-effect on relations with the American colonies. The most politically active segment of those colonies, in New England, was rooted in seventeenth-century Puritanism and overwhelmingly Whiggish – it found the first Tory government in half a century intolerable. The government attempted to ease the colonists' grievances by passing the Currency Act 1764, lifting the 1751 Act's prohibition on colonial currencies, though their legal tender status was only restored by the Currency Act 1773. Then the Sugar Act, 1764, reduced duties on sugar and the American Dominions (Trade with) Act 1765 removed protectionist duties on timber and coffee to encourage colonial products. However, the revenue-raising Stamp Act 1765, while going out of its way to appease colonial sentiment, was bound to cause difficulty, as was the Quartering Act 1765, providing for colonial assemblies to provide housing for British troops stationed in North America.

Then the Rockingham government's folly in repealing the Stamp Act before it came into effect, accompanying that repeal with misleading and inflammatory rhetoric, immensely strengthened the minority of radical separatists in New England. The Rockingham government made matters worse by passing the Declaratory Act 1766, which to the more

224 *Forging Modernity*

paranoid Americans seemed analogous to the Whig Declaratory Act 1719 that had subjugated Ireland.

Whether a solution to the conundrum, 'No Taxation Without Representation', that involved giving the colonies representation of say 40 seats at Westminster might have succeeded is unknowable. In any case, it was not tried. The less militant colonists in the middle and southern states eventually followed their New England brethren and radicals corrupted the process through such stunts as the Boston Tea Party. On this side of the pond, the North government was over-confident of its ability to quell an American rebellion. The first shot was heard in April 1775 and the American colonies were lost.

In the long run, separation was probably unavoidable. Both Britain and the colonies had a future of increasing wealth and power (although the contradictions between emergent industrialization and slave-driven agriculture would end in a conflict in the United States far more deadly than the War of Independence). In any case, American independence had little effect on Britain's trajectory of industrialization, beyond partially removing an alternative means of self-enrichment through slave-driven agriculture that had distracted the ambitious. Lord Mansfield's[13] Somersett decision of 1772, forbidding slavery in England, also helped here in beginning to make fortunes from slave-driven agriculture socially unacceptable.

This period also saw developments in India that, while initially benefiting Britain and the East India Company, in the long term may have been economically as well as morally damaging. Thanks to Robert Clive, the EIC in August 1765 signed the Treaty of Allahabad with the Mughal Emperor Shah Alam II, obtaining the *diwani* (tax collection) rights for Bengal, Bihar and Orissa in return for an annual cash subsidy. Thereby, the Company assumed administrative control of provinces with a population of 20 million people, twice that of Britain. From them the Company received a net tax revenue of about £1.6 million per annum after expenses, which it converted into exports of Indian cloth and other goods for sale in Europe, and silver to buy tea from China.

This had several effects. In the short term, the EIC proved incapable initially of replacing the Mughal government structure in the provinces it now controlled; its administrative chaos led to the Bengal famine of 1770, one of the worst in India's history. In the longer term, British

---

13. William Murray (1705-93). 1st Baron Mansfield from 1756, 1st Earl of Mansfield from 1776. MP for Boroughbridge, 1742-56. Solicitor General, 1742-54, Attorney General, 1754-56, Lord Chief Justice, 1756-88.

The Tory-Assisted Take-off, 1761-83

control of India was exercised in the interests of the growing Lancashire textile industry. Exports of finished Indian cloth to Britain had been sharply restricted by the Woollen etc. Manufactures Act 1720; over the next century Lancashire would increasingly come to use American slave-grown cotton rather than Indian cotton. These restrictions tended to impoverish India, while providing excess rents to Lancashire textile manufacturers, which through machinery were competitive with any alternative in the world. In the very long term, this over-developed Britain's textile sector and led to the twentieth-century depression of much of northern England.

India's economic position improved once the polyglot Warren Hastings became Governor of Bengal in 1772 and consolidated EIC rule in India as Governor-General from the following year. There were no more major famines, and India began to benefit from its links with British technological and economic prowess, while the Duty on Cotton Stuffs etc. Act 1774 lifted the prohibition on exporting patterned Indian fabrics to Britain. Since Hastings conducted business primarily in India's languages,[14] there was no separate caste of Indians capable of dealing with British bureaucracy; that arose in the next century from the misguided 'reforms' of Lord William Bentinck[15] and Macaulay. Hastings left a record of enlightened administration in India seldom subsequently equalled; the impeachment proceeding brought against him between 1788 and 1795 by a Whig parliamentary mob was a serious blot on Pitt's administration. (He was subsequently totally exonerated by the House of Lords.)

In Ireland, the early 1760s were quiet years, as the Whiggish management of earlier years continued under a series of absentee lords lieutenant. Then both George, Marquess Townshend (Lord Lieutenant, 1767-72) and the Tory Harcourt (Lord Lieutenant, 1772-76) resided in Ireland and were determined to increase London's control of it, while Harcourt's attempt to conciliate Irish opinion by imposing a 10% tax on the rents of absentee landlords was killed by opposition in London. The

---

14. Warren Hastings (1732-1818). Governor, then Governor-General of the Presidency of Fort William, 1772-85. He spoke Bengali, Urdu and Persian fluently.

15. Lord William Bentinck (1774-1839). Whig MP for Camelford, Nottinghamshire, King's Lynn and Glasgow, 1796-1803, 1812-14, 1816-28, 1836-39. Governor of Madras, 1803-7, Major General, 1805, Lieut. General, 1811. Commanded British forces in Sicily 1811-14. Governor-General of India, 1828-35.

main bones of contention were the punitive Declaratory Act 1719 and the tariffs maintained against Irish exports, especially linen.

When in 1775, London imposed an embargo on Irish exports to the rebel American colonies, Irish parliamentary opinion, which tended to support the colonists, coalesced into an Irish Volunteers movement, which although initially founded to defend Ireland, in practice later formed a nucleus of opposition to British rule. Their slogan, 'Free trade or a Speedy Revolution', showed their early reading of Adam Smith and their determination to be rid of British protectionism. The situation became dangerous and was not helped by Harcourt's feeble successor, the second Earl of Buckinghamshire (Lord Lieutenant 1776-80).

The North government, beleaguered on several fronts, was forced in 1780 to give Ireland free exports to the Empire and Turkey through the Levant Company.[16] Then, in 1782, further Irish agitation and the second Rockingham government produced the Repeal Act 1782, which repealed the Declaratory Act and allowed the Irish parliament to legislate independently. From then until the Act of Union in 1801 Ireland enjoyed a high degree of independence except in foreign policy.

Economic Developments, 1760-83

The political revolution at George III's accession helped to kick-start the Industrial Revolution. The most significant datum is the rate of patents filed; having averaged 5.7 patents per annum in the first half of the eighteenth century and ticked up to 9.2 per annum in the 1750s, they more than doubled to 20.5 per annum in the 1760s, increasing further to 29.4 per annum in the 1770s and nearly doubling again to 47.7 per annum in the 1780s.[17] The Industrial Revolution, which had been largely in abeyance from 1720 to the early 1750s, showed modest signs of life in the late 1750s, then gathered momentum from 1760, becoming inexorable and world-changing over the next 30 years.

As well as a doubling in patents, the 1760s saw a trebling in parliamentary enclosures, the number of Enclosure Acts rising from 117 in the 1750s to 393 in the 1760s and then rising further to 640 in the 1770s, dropping back thereafter.[18] The procedure for carrying out enclosures was regularized and streamlined by the Inclosure Act 1773. This change

---

16. See Ronald M. Knowles, *Political and Economic Impact of the American Revolution on Ireland* (Irish Septs Association, 2004).

17. Mitchell (ed.), *British Historical Statistics*, Table VIII-23, pp. 438-39.

18. Overton, *Agricultural Revolution in England*, Table 4.5, p. 151.

The Tory-Assisted Take-off, 1761-83

marked a sharp increase in the capital intensity of agriculture, caused by the steady population growth, which was leading grain and land prices to rise above their 1740s lows – grain prices at Eton college, which had averaged 28.3s per quarter in the 1740s rose to 34.4s per quarter in the 1750s, 37.9s per quarter in the 1760s and 44.4s per quarter in the 1770s.[19] Land productivity growth continued in this era, albeit at a slower level of around 0.2% per annum as more marginal land was brought into production. Labour productivity growth in agriculture continued somewhat faster, at around 0.3-0.4% per annum, and grain exports declined, balancing imports by the early 1780s.[20]

One agricultural novelty was selective breeding, developed by Robert Bakewell (1725-95), although it spread more widely through being publicized after 1783. Bakewell, the son of a prosperous tenant farmer, inherited the farm in 1760, when he began to experiment with breeding livestock selectively, seeking favourable characteristics by allowing mating only deliberately and specifically and by inbreeding to exaggerate the characteristics he was seeking. He bred both the New Leicester sheep and the Dishley Longhorn cattle and formed the Dishley Society in 1783 to propagate his ideas and market his output. Partly through selective breeding, the average weight of oxen sold at Smithfield market increased from 370 pounds in 1710 to 800 pounds by 1795, that of calves from 50 pounds to 150 and that of sheep from 38 pounds to 80.[21]

Working-class living standards declined somewhat, though the beginnings of industrialization offset the rise in grain prices, but land values and rents rose steadily, increasing the profit from enclosures and thereby the productivity of agricultural land. This process would reach extreme levels of misery in the Highland Clearances of the 1810s and 1820s to make way for sheep. (Gower's Whig son, the first Duke of Sutherland, was married to the hereditary Countess of Sutherland and the Sutherland estate had the largest-scale clearances during this period.) However, in more central areas, with other employment opportunities available, it was disruptive rather than destructive to working-class living standards.

In Ireland there were few such alternatives available. Population pressure from this period onwards caused a decline in Irish living standards that led to unrest in the 1770s and serious impoverishment

---

19. Mitchell (ed.), *British Historical Statistics*, Table XIV-16, pp. 754-55.
20. Overton, *Agricultural Revolution in England*, Table 3-10, p. 85, and Mitchell (ed.), *British Historical Statistics*, Table III-16, p. 221.
21. Mantoux, *The Industrial Revolution in the Eighteenth Century*, pp. 165-66.

228   *Forging Modernity*

thereafter. It also led to the beginnings of Irish migration to England for better employment opportunities, with Irish 'navigators' being especially prominent in canal construction.

Coal prices in several substantial cities declined during this period after the creation of nearby canals; in cases such as Liverpool, Birmingham and Manchester prices halved once the link was made. Hence, coal production continued to accelerate, from an average of 4,520,000 metric tons per annum in 1756-60 to 7,550,000 metric tons per annum in 1781-85, a volume increase of 2.1% annually, or 1.4% annually per capita. The fastest volume increases came in the Staffordshire coalfields, by 3.3% annually to an annual average of 575,000 metric tons in 1781-85, and the Lancashire coalfields, by 3.1% annually to an annual average of 412,000 metric tons in 1781-85.[22] Thus, the Sankey, Bridgewater, Staffordshire and Worcestershire, Trent and Mersey and Birmingham Canals delivered large economic dividends to their local coalfields.

By the end of this period, the Industrial Revolution was in full swing, thanks primarily to Brindley's Grand Cross canals. The statistics of Table 6.1 show this. The periods 1761-71 and 1771-81 showed similar growth in per capita GDP, at 14.4% and 13.8%, respectively. Both 1761 and 1781 were war years, although in both cases the war was shorter and less destructive than that of 1701-13 or 1793-1815. Hence, it appears that a slow growth in per capita GDP began around 1760, beyond a simple recovery from the war, with a further acceleration in the remaining peace years of the early and middle 1770s. The opening of Brindley's canals, bringing new efficiencies of goods transportation, form an obvious explanation for such a pattern.

Great Minds

Two pre-eminent thinkers laid foundations that were essential to the Industrial Revolution's future, codifying what had previously been known only in outline and thereby providing a firm grounding for subsequent generations of businesses: they were Sir William Blackstone and Adam Smith.

Sir William Blackstone, unlike his great seventeenth-century predecessors a firm Tory, was the great codifier of English common law in his 1765-70 *Commentaries on the Laws of England*. Even after Hale's work, common law continued to depend on precedent. It is therefore

---

22. Mitchell (ed.), *British Historical Statistics*, Table IV-3, p. 247, with interpolation for the 1781-85 Staffordshire and Lancashire figures.

The Tory-Assisted Take-off, 1761-83

fair to say that before Blackstone's time it was uncertain and depended on the affiliation of the judge administering it and whether one of the parties had 'influence'. As Blackstone's work quickly became regarded as definitive (in the American colonies also, where English common law was incorporated into the laws of the United States), it prevented many legal disputes, allowing an educated laymen to determine fine points of law for himself through its pages. It thereby added certainty to the English legal system, making it far more user-friendly and greatly reducing the legal risk of entrepreneurship and business transactions generally.

In economics, Adam Smith's *Wealth of Nations* was even more important. Many of the ideas advocated by Smith had been advanced by Petty, North, Davenant or Cantillon, but he assembled them into a rigorous and detailed system with an enormous mass of supporting evidence, in a way his predecessors had not. Smith's explanation of the 'division of labour', for example, was clearer and more complete than his predecessors' and gave rise to a great deal of experimentation among factory owners and managers, since it offered them a demonstration that if they could improve the organization of the workflow, tangible benefits might follow.

Smith's exposition of the 'Invisible Hand' theory countered Mandeville's thinking and strengthened free-market ideas but, at the same time, was inimical to globalization – it was an Oxfordshire School view, which would have been echoed by Sir Dudley North, and contrary to the Whig shibboleth of the next century's unilateral free traders:

> by preferring the support of domestic to that of foreign industry, ... he intends only his own security; and by directing that industry in such a manner as its produce may be of the greatest value, he intends only his own gain, and he is in this, as in many other cases, led by an invisible hand to promote an end which was no part of his intention.[23]

Smith was already well-known for his 1759 work, *The Theory of Moral Sentiments*, so *The Wealth of Nations* won immediate attention. Accordingly, North awarded Smith in January 1778 a sinecure as Scotland's Commissioner of Customs worth £600 per annum,[24] a substantial

---

23. Adam Smith, *An Inquiry into the Nature and Causes of the Wealth of Nations*, 3 vols (London: W. Strahan and T. Cadell, 1776), Bk 14, ch. 11.

24. Ian S. Ross, *The Life of Adam Smith* (Oxford: Oxford University Press, 1995), ch. 19. Smith at this time was a Rockingham Whig; he became effectively a Pittite in the late 1780s.

supplement to his academic salary. Regrettably, the financial strains of the American war prevented North from putting into effect many of Smith's (and Sir Dudley North's) ideas. Nevertheless, North imposed several taxes that had been proposed by Smith, in particular, taxes on manservants and on property sold at auction in the 1777 Budget and an inhabited house duty and a malt tax in the 1778 Budget.[25]

Smith was famously influential on Pitt's administration, the first economist who had a major effect on day-to-day economic policies without himself being an important economic policymaker. Pitt, Dundas[26] and the younger members of Pitt's Cabinet were lucky enough to enjoy several dinner seminars in the 1780s with the great man. There is a nice story of Smith turning up late to dinner at Dundas' house in Wimbledon in 1787, with Addington,[27] Grenville[28] and Wilberforce[29] present, and apologizing for his tardiness, to which Pitt responded: 'No, we will stand till you are first seated, for we are all your scholars.'[30] Indeed they were, all of them except the Scot Dundas (presumably Smith's natural London contact) aged 30 or less, a quarter of a century younger than the economist.

The Whigs were initially sceptical of Smith's work – Fox said that half the book could be omitted 'with much benefit to the subject'. However, by around 1800 the younger Whigs had adopted it and used it to criticize from a generally Radical direction the Oxfordshire School statesmen who ran the country.

---

25. John Rae, *Life of Adam Smith* (London: Macmillan & Co., 1895), p. 294.
26. Henry Dundas (1741-1811). 1st Viscount Melville from 1802. Lord Advocate of Scotland, 1775-83, Home Secretary, 1791-94, Secretary for War and Colonies, 1794-1801, First Lord of the Admiralty, 1804-5.
27. Henry Addington (1757-1844). 1st Viscount Sidmouth from 1805. MP for Devizes, 1784-1805. Speaker of the House of Commons, 1789-1801, Prime Minister and Chancellor of the Exchequer 1801-4, Lord President of the Council, 1805, 1806-7 and 1812, Lord Privy Seal, 1806, Home Secretary, 1812-22.
28. William Grenville (1759-1834). 1st Baron Grenville from 1790. MP for Buckingham and Buckinghamshire, 1782-90. Speaker, 1789, Home Secretary, 1789-91, Foreign Secretary, 1791-1801, Prime Minister, 1806-7.
29. William Wilberforce, 1759-1833. Tory MP for Kingston-upon-Hull, Yorkshire and Bramber, 1780-1825. Leader in the movement to abolish the slave trade and slavery. Close friend of Pitt the Younger.
30. Rae, *Life of Adam Smith*, p. 405.

Country Banks

Domestically, one important economic change that began in the 1750s and accelerated after 1760, assisted by the reorientation of economic life towards provincial centres and playing a major role in the Industrial Revolution hereafter, was the rise of country banks.

Clayton & Morris, which had emerged from a scrivener's practice, had set the pattern for country banks in the Restoration period, providing mortgage loans and deposit facilities to the rural gentry but playing little role in the London and international money markets. After 1688, with the growth of London as a financial centre and the inordinate profitability of the government bond markets, successors to Clayton & Morris did not appear.

Instead, banking became dominated by London houses, mostly descendants of the goldsmith bankers, who were experienced in dealing with government finances and the markets. Over time, they divided into City firms, who specialized in international trade and financial market manipulation, and West End houses, who specialized in holding the cash and managing the financial affairs of the high aristocracy. This left a gap in provision for provincial financial needs, both of landowners below the very largest and for businesses that were naturally local in extent.

The equivalent of this London dominance did not occur in Scotland, where there was no Bank of England quasi-monopoly, and regional banks appeared after 1707. In England the Bank of England Act 1708, providing that no private bank could have more than six partners, prevented the emergence of joint-stock banks with limited liability like the Bank of Scotland (1695) and the Royal Bank of Scotland (1727). Since the Bank of England did not open branches until 1826, this also left the provinces starved of financial services.

Although a few country banks had been founded earlier, such as Smith's of Nottingham, founded in 1688, the growth of country banking began after 1750, with the early examples mostly deriving from country attorneys, the successors to the seventeenth-century scriveners, active in the conveyancing and mortgage businesses. Such attorneys were key organizers in gathering money for infrastructure developments such as turnpike roads, river improvements and, from the 1760s, canals and managing the funds generated from such enterprises. They also had the connections through their clients, typically prosperous local tradesmen rather than the gentry, to capitalize small but substantial businesses like the early country banks.

232   *Forging Modernity*

With the new businesses formed through expansion of local infrastructure or development of new industries, formation of a country bank was a natural development, since the close-knit local networks and speed of communication gave such banks an immense advantage in both getting business and assessing credit, compared to their distant London brethren. It also helped if one or more shareholders were active in local government, while landholding partners gave a new bank (whose partners had unlimited liability) a very real substance.

Beyond the scrivener/attorneys, the most common country bank shareholders were those in wholesale trade, who already had substantial financing needs and a credit network among their business counterparties. For example, ten of the fourteen Liverpool country banks originated in merchant houses,[31] although in that case many of their mercantile interests involved overseas rather than domestic trade, with a particular emphasis on Caribbean sugar plantations. One early example of such a combination was the Newcastle-on-Tyne house of Bell, Cookson, Carr and Airey, formed in 1755 with three merchants and an attorney as partners, £2,000 in capital and assistance from a London banker, George Campbell, who had helped to re-form Coutts bank in 1753.[32]

Within the wholesale category, an especially fruitful source of shareholders was the textile trade, expanding before 1760 and more rapidly after it. This growing business gave rise to both profits that could be invested in banking and demand for financial services, mainly to finance inventories and receivables rather than for capital investment. In a typical textile wholesale business, the proprietor would undertake prolonged journeys selling the wares he had available, and the ability to finance such sales and the lengthy period before the goods could be delivered was critical. The need for banking services extended well beyond textiles; Pressnell says that 'the Stuckeys, supplying corn, salt and timber to much of the west country, rank as really outstanding bankers of the most unassailable virtue',[33] while the significant Manchester bank, Jones, Loyd & Co., was founded in 1771 by tea importers.[34]

---

31. L.S. Pressnell, *Country Banking in the Industrial Revolution* (Oxford: Oxford University Press, 1956), p. 49.
32. Ibid., p. 118.
33. Ibid., p. 53. Stuckey & Co. was established at Langport, Somerset, in 1772 and later connected through common partners with banks in Bridgewater, 1804, and Bristol, 1806, with branches at Wells and Taunton. Dawes and Ward-Perkins, *Country Banks of England and Wales*, vol. 2, pp. 311-12. It became a joint-stock bank in 1826.
34. Pressnell, *Country Banking in the Industrial Revolution*, p. 51.

Among the most significant country banks was Taylors & Lloyds of Birmingham, founded in 1765 with £6,000 capital by John Taylor, Birmingham's leading button maker and the Quaker Birmingham ironmaster, Sampson Lloyd,[35] son of the Sampson Lloyd who had founded the ironmaster business and nephew of Sir Ambrose Crowley.

Gurney's Bank, Norwich. This was a typical successful country bank, which later merged into Barclays.

Another highly significant country bank was John & Henry Gurney, founded by two Quaker brothers in Norwich in 1770; this became an extremely profitable institution, with many local correspondents forming a local network, greatly enriching the Gurney family, who became proverbially wealthy.[36] In 1800, Gurney's supplied the capital for the leading London discount house that became Overend, Gurney & Co., which failed spectacularly in 1866. More successfully, Gurney's was also the Quaker nucleus for Barclays Bank, into which it was merged in 1896.

The remittance business resulting from an agency for one of the two major fire assurance companies could also become a reliable basis for banking. So could the business of tax collection, especially for land and stamp taxes, which were especially dilatory in being paid to the Exchequer; there were about 50 such collectors in the late eighteenth century, with total balances owing to the Exchequer of over £650,000 in 1780, and still over £374,000 in 1819.[37] Country bank notes were frequently used for tax payments, though in times of distress like 1772 and 1793, the wiser tax collectors were selective in the houses whose notes they would accept. This became an exceptionally lucrative business during the Napoleonic wars with the expansion of Revenue demands and the rise in interest rates; it contracted severely after

---

35. Sampson Lloyd (1699-1779). Bought Town Mill with his brother, 1725. Partner in the bank was John Taylor (1704-75), Birmingham's leading button maker, who left £200,000 on his death.
36. For example, Gilbert and Sullivan, *Trial by Jury* (1873): 'At length I became as rich as the Gurneys / An incubus then I thought her / So I threw over that rich attorney's / Elderly, ugly daughter.'
37. Pressnell, *Country Banking in the Industrial Revolution*, pp. 58-60. Joseph Berwick, a draper of Worcester, and Samuel Worrall of Bristol both established banks on this foundation.

234 *Forging Modernity*

Waterloo and may have been a significant contributor to the country banks' 1825 difficulties.[38]

Country banks cleared their payments and ensured their liquidity through a correspondent relationship with a London bank, while they provided more convenient and 'high-touch' banking services for their local clients. As the country banks proliferated, rather than existing London banks acquiring their agency business, new specialist banks were formed for the purpose, often with one or more country banking partners. (London banks that existed primarily to serve a single large country bank were said disapprovingly to have a 'pig-on-pork' relationship with it, through one such 'pig-on-pork' bank was Barings, founded in London and Exeter in 1762.) One such multi-correspondent bank formed in 1773 became Pole Thornton, whose failure in December 1825 is said to have caused the failure of 38 of its country bank correspondents.[39]

Country banks relied on their London correspondents as lenders of last resort in times of difficulty, keeping reserves with them when money was plentiful, using the well-developed London system of bills of exchange. Bills of exchange were central to the country banking system, in introducing local trading businesses as new customers for a country bank, when they required that bank's bills discounting service. Bills of under 60 days' maturity were discountable at the Bank of England, and therefore acceptable by most London banks; those of longer maturity were handled by specialized London bill brokers, which proliferated during the years of the American and Napoleonic wars.

Over time, country bankers began to open branches, especially after the 1797 suspension of cash payments made their £1 and £2 notes an attractive instrument for retail customers. Branches were concentrated in rural rather than industrial areas, since although there were fewer investment opportunities in rural areas, there was a wide ability to collect deposits (through the small banknotes mechanism, for example). In 1784, 112 of 119 country banks had only one office, by 1798, 298 of

---

38. Ibid., p. 74. Country bank bankruptcies remained in single digits throughout the war years, except for fifteen bankruptcies in 1810 and 1812; there were then sixteen bankruptcies in the first year of peace of 1814, 21 in 1815 and 35 in 1816.

39. L. Neal, 'The Financial Crisis of 1825 and the Restructuring of the British Financial System', *Federal Reserve Bank of St Louis Review* (May/June 1998), pp. 53-76.

The Tory-Assisted Take-off, 1761-83

312 had one office only, but by 1813, 761 banks had a total of 922 offices licensed to issue bank notes.[40]

The principal function of the country banker was to provide means of payment, transfer and remittance, a vital function to early industrial companies in an era when specie was scarce (as it was before the recoinage of 1816-17). Bankers initially issued interest-bearing promissory notes, payable on a certain date, as had the earlier scriveners; these promissory notes were often used as an investment for liquidity balances. Then, as their solidity and their customers' familiarity with them grew, banks increasingly issued non-interest-bearing bank notes payable on demand, which circulated as currency and, from 1782, by law bore a Revenue stamp. By another 1787 law, the minimum denomination for such notes was £5; then after that law was removed in 1797, £1 and £2 notes circulated widely, as well as smaller denominations from some banks when coinage was especially scarce[41] – such notes were particularly used by large factories to pay workers' wages. This was made all the more possible because, except in times of acute credit scarcity, country banks' notes mostly traded at par (unlike U.S. local banks' notes after the Second Bank of the United States de-chartering in 1836)– even notes of banks from distant towns could be cleared by the local bank through its London correspondent.

Both Sir Francis Baring[42] and Henry Thornton[43] wrote pamphlets in the 1790s saying that demand notes were unsound (since communication speeds meant country banks could not secure liquidity immediately) and recommending that they be prohibited, but they were so popular that this was done only in 1826, for notes of £1 and £2 but not larger denominations. By 1810, at least £20 million of country bank notes were

---

40. Pressnell, *Country Banking in the Industrial Revolution*, p. 126.
41. Notes below £1 denomination were prohibited in 1808.
42. Pressnell, *Country Banking in the Industrial Revolution*, p. 140. Francis Baring (1740-1810). 1st Baronet from 1793. Shelburneite (i.e. Tory until 1790, then conservative Whig). MP for Grampound, Wycombe and Calne, 1784-90, 1794-1806. Founder with two brothers of Barings Bank in London and Exeter, 1762.
43. Henry Thornton (1760-1815). MP for Southwark, 1782-1815. Joined the bank of Down & Free of London in 1784 which later became Pole Thornton. Leader of the Clapham Sect of evangelical reformers seeking the abolition of the slave trade and sponsor of William Wilberforce. In 1802 wrote *An Enquiry into the Nature and Effects of the Paper Credit of Great Britain*, later recognized as a foundation text of monetary economics and reissued in 1939 with an introduction by Friedrich Hayek.

in circulation, of which £2 million were from Scotland.[44] The country bank note issue declined after 1815, but increased substantially in the 1823-25 bubble, with the volume of new country bank notes stamped increasing from £4.7 million in 1823 to a peak of £8.8 million in 1825, although this was still less than the £11.8 million of new notes stamped in 1813, for example.[45] As well as their financial value to the issuing bank, country bank notes acted as an advertisement, acting to 'give a sort of éclat to the establishment' as one country banker put it in 1832.[46]

As well as issuing notes, country banks took deposits, paying interest at 3-4%, from local individuals, generally in fairly substantial amounts – there were few interest-bearing deposits of less than £20 and most were above £100. Country banks also took deposits from local businesses, charities, executors for deceased and bankrupt estates and local government bodies, which together normally formed a large part of their total deposit obligations. Finally, country banks served local retail and institutional customers by acting as agents for their investments, advising them on investing surpluses in Navy bills and East India bonds (which might well yield more than the statutory 5% through trading at a discount), clipping coupons on bonds and stocks, and sending them for payment through their London correspondents.

Country banks retained reserves of hard cash as a reserve for their notes. Opinions varied as to how large that reserve should be, with many estimates suggesting one fifth of the notes outstanding and Alexander Baring (to the House of Commons in 1819) suggesting a reserve as high as a third. There was general agreement that country banks needed smaller reserves than London ones and, in practice, even sound country banks maintained cash reserves of less than a tenth of their total deposits and notes outstanding,[47] although Stuckey's, for example, increased its

---

44. Pressnell, *Country Banking in the Industrial Revolution*, p. 146, discusses the range of estimates for this figure, which went as high as £32 million.
45. Ibid., Table XVI, p. 188. Notes once stamped remained outstanding until they were redeemed for gold or fell apart, so the outstanding amount in any year was a multiple of the number of new notes stamped.
46. Quoted in ibid., p. 157.
47. Quoted in ibid., p. 194. Alexander Baring (1774-1848). 1st Baron Ashburton from 1835. MP for Taunton, Callington and Thetford, 1806-35. Moderate Whig, breaking from the Whigs after Grey had barred him as a parvenu from his 1830 government. Second son of Sir Francis Baring. Partner in Baring Brothers & Co., 1807-30, where he became the world's leading banker ('the Fifth Great Power') by 1820. President of the Board

The Tory-Assisted Take-off, 1761-83

reserve ratio to a fifth or more in times of crisis. Overall, payments were made in cash, Bank of England notes, country bank notes, bank drafts and bills of exchange.

Country banks made loans from (i) their own capital (ii) outside resources (acting as loan brokers like the old scriveners) and (iii) deposits taken from the public and notes issued to them. Subscribed capital was generally quite small, normally under £10,000, although the Exchange Bank of Bristol, founded in 1764, had £18,000 of capital, all but £2,000 paid in immediately. Some of that capital was devoted to immediate expenses such as premises and the remainder was invested in a liquid form such as 3% Consols. Generally, at this period, the annual profit was paid out to partners; no additional reserves were normally held until after the 1825 crisis, although specific anticipated losses were reserved against. However, the partnerships carried unlimited liability for their partners, and wealthier partners often left substantial sums on deposit with the bank, generally at three months' notice and bearing a good (though below 5%) rate of interest. Conversely, partners could borrow from the bank, a flexibility liable to abuse.

Overall, as well as providing services to private individuals and institutions, country banks provided a wide range of services to nascent industrialization, which would have been greatly hindered by their absence. Discounting bills of exchange, and thereby providing liquidity, was often the main introductory service, but paying wages to workers in local banknotes (which would be immediately acceptable at par in the local area) and providing receivables financing through discounting were all common. In addition, the country banker might provide inventory and other financing through overdraft facilities to the business' owners, generally secured by promissory notes, often for double the amount of the loan facility, or by mortgages, which were highly illiquid but represented a claim on an asset of real value. However, many bankers, for example, Jones, Loyd of Manchester, a well-run bank in an industrial region, refused to take mortgages as security after 1815.[48] In addition, country banks provided executor and trustee services when a proprietor died, facilitating the continuance of the business after his death.

The one area where country bank participation in local industries was very limited was long-term financing of fixed assets by 'subprime loans', 'junk bonds' or equity, all of which would have placed excessive

---

of Trade, 1834-35. Negotiated Webster-Ashburton Treaty with the United States, 1842. Opposed Repeal of the Corn Laws, 1846.

48. Pressnell, *Country Banking in the Industrial Revolution*, p. 308.

238 *Forging Modernity*

strains on banks' liquidity and credit skills – with high-risk long-term lending also being heavily discouraged by the Usury Act limiting interest rates payable to 5%. Country bankers frequently acted as agents for local capital raising, especially for infrastructure investments such as turnpikes, canals and land enclosures, where they had even better contact networks than the local scriveners that preceded them. The rise of country banks, often acting as treasurers of local schemes, was a major facilitator of the post-1760 booms in infrastructure as well as of the Industrial Revolution.

More directly, there were several country banks that were set up by partners in mining or industrial enterprises and deeply engaged in their financing; the inevitable conflicts of interest involved sometimes led to bankruptcy, even if the industrial company survived. For example, Gibbons & Timmins, of Wolverhampton, established in 1782, was closely connected with Fereday of Bilston, an iron works; in the post-war slump of 1816, it was forced to close due to financial pressure on the iron works.[49] Some large industrial companies were connected with several banks; for example, the Bristol Brass Company had £70,000 in banking facilities from five Bristol banks between 1763 and 1768, when it was forced into a merger with the Warmley Brass Company.[50] In 1788, the Lancashire calico printers, Livesey, Hargreaves & Co., with 800 employees, went bankrupt, taking with them their bank, William Allen & Co. of Manchester, which had been founded in 1771 as the first bank in Manchester and had become increasingly involved in their business.[51] On a more positive note, Wright & Co. of Nottingham, founded in 1761, provided considerable financial help to Sir Richard Arkwright[52] in his early expansion.

A successful example of industrial financing was the Truro bank, Praed & Co., established in 1771 by four partners experienced in copper mining, two of them, Sir Humphrey Mackworth Praed[53] and William

---

49. Ibid., p. 326.
50. Ibid., p. 328. One of the founders of the Bristol Brass Company was Abraham Darby; the Warmley Brass Company, formed in 1746, was the largest in England, but was in financial difficulty; the Bristol Brass Company's loans appear to have allowed it to compete in a price war with Warmley and then absorb its business.
51. Pressnell, *Country Banking in the Industrial Revolution*, p. 91. In the same work, p. 336, Presnell gives a partial figure of Livesey, Hargreaves' short-term accommodation bills of £94,787.
52. Pressnell, *Country Banking in the Industrial Revolution*, p. 337.
53. Humphrey Mackworth Praed (1718-1803). MP for St Ives and Cornwall, 1761-68, 1772-74. Partner in Praed & Co., Truro from 1771.

The Tory-Assisted Take-off, 1761-83

Praed,[54] grandson and great-grandson of Sir Humphrey Mackworth. Praed & Co. lent heavily to the Cornish copper-mining industry, financing its Boulton & Watt pumping engines once Watt had produced a clearly superior model in 1776, as well as financing Boulton & Watt itself for a short period in 1781. Brunt[55] claims this makes Praed & Co. equivalent to a modern venture capitalist; it certainly made it integral to the expansion of Cornish copper mining. Praed & Co. flourished, to declare bankruptcy only after a 'run' in 1846, even then paying depositors in full.

There were two economically damaging banking crises during or just after this period, though only one significantly involved English country banks. The first, the Ayr Bank crash of 1772, concerned a Scottish bank, Douglas Heron & Co. based in Ayr, a town with a population of 4,000, which in only three years from its foundation with a nominal capital of £150,000 and no fewer than 131 partners had issued banknotes and bills of exchange unbacked by real transactions totalling £1.2 million, discounted through a London broker, Neal, James, Fordyce and Down. Parliament had attempted to restrict Scottish banks' over-issue of banknotes by the Bank Notes (Scotland) Act 1765 but the general problem remained.

When Neal, James, Fordyce and Down failed, due to unsuccessful East India Company speculations (shorting the shares) by its managing partner, Alexander Fordyce, the market in Scottish bills of exchange seized up.[56] This brought down the Ayr Bank, with around 40% of all Scottish banking assets, and 21 other smaller, mostly Scottish, banks, as well as causing a Europe-wide liquidity crisis that lasted for a year. However, because of the unlimited liability of the partners and the inclusion among them of several Scottish dukes, Ayr Bank creditors were eventually repaid in full, though it took many years.

The Ayr Bank crash shows that the "free banking" lack of a central bank and freedom from the six-partner rule did not make Scottish banks much sounder than English banks. This had been forgotten by

---

54. William Praed (1747-1833). Tory MP for St Ives and Banbury, 1774-75, 1780-1808. Chairman, Grand Junction Canal Co. from 1790. Partner, Praed & Co., Truro, from 1771, Praed & Co., London, from 1802.

55. Liam Brunt, 'Rediscovering Risk: Country Banks as Venture Capital Firms in the First Industrial Revolution', *Journal of Economic History*, Vol. 66, no. 1 (2006), pp. 74-102.

56. Details of the crash and a discussion of the economic principles involved are contained in Tyler Beck Goodspeed, *Legislating Instability: Adam Smith, Free Banking and the Financial Crisis of 1772* (Cambridge, MA: Harvard University Press, 2016).

240 *Forging Modernity*

the crisis of 1825-26, when the Scottish banking system, sound for a half a century because of memories of the Ayr Bank debacle, was held up by Lord Liverpool as an example to the English and as a condemnation of the atomized English country banking system.[57] The Ayr Bank crash also caused Adam Smith in *The Wealth of Nations* published four years later to propound the real bills doctrine: that bills of exchange were only sound if representing real trade transactions – this became a shibboleth of monetary policy for the next two centuries.

The second major banking crisis was that of 1793. By this stage, following a canal-building boom in 1789-92, there were around 280 country banks, some without solid business foundations – in the opinion of *The Times* (17 April 1792): 'The Country Banks have enormously increased, are increasing and ought to be diminished.'[58] When war came in February 1793, the prices of canal bonds and other securities crashed, trade was badly disrupted and country banks got into severe difficulty, although a £5 million issue of exchequer bills in May 1793 provided liquidity to the money market. Henry Thornton's contemporary estimate was that 58 country banks failed, with a concentration in Liverpool and Bristol and total losses of around £6 million. However, many of them subsequently reopened their doors. A parliamentary committee of 1797 found only 22 country bank failures over those four difficult years, of which sixteen took place in 1793 itself.[59] Credit conditions remained very tight until the suspension of cash payments in February 1797, after which country banks flourished, with their small denomination notes widely used as a local transaction mechanism.

The banking crash of 1825 left many people including Lord Liverpool convinced that country banks were unsound. His Country Bankers Act 1826 allowed for the creation of joint-stock banks and prohibited country banks from issuing £1 and £2 notes, the increase in which had fuelled much of the 1825 speculation. Given the full gold standard and the ample available specie by 1826, the prohibition of small-denomination

---

57. See Lord Liverpool's letter to the Bank of England, 13 January 1826, quoted in Martin Hutchinson, *Britain's Greatest Prime Minister: Lord Liverpool* (Cambridge: The Lutterworth Press, 2020), Appendix, p. 418.

58. Quoted in Pressnell, *Country Banking in the Industrial Revolution*, p. 108. The phraseology referred back to John Dunning's famous motion of April 1780 about the powers of the Crown.

59. Ibid., Appendix 28, pp. 546-47. Also, in ibid., p. 45, Thornton wrote to Pitt on 1 March 1793, 'I am sorry to have to add that all the banks of Liverpool or all but one have stopped payment'; and in ibid., p. 444, parliamentary committee estimate.

The Tory-Assisted Take-off, 1761-83

notes was probably desirable, while the creation of larger joint-stock banks did not immediately prove fatal to the smaller partnerships.

In retrospect, the unsoundness of the country banks is less clear, although the demise of Pole Thornton, not itself a country bank, can be regretted. Sir Matthew White Ridley, MP for Newcastle-upon-Tyne, 1813-36, told the House of Commons in June 1828 that before the crisis there had been 770 country bankers, 63 had failed to reopen at once, but 23 resumed, paying 20s in the pound (100%); of the remainder, 31 were arranging their affairs and hoping to pay 20s; the average dividend so far on the failures of 1825-26 was 17s 6d in the pound (87.5%).[60]

During the full gold standard period, before 1797 and after 1821, and knocking out the fly-by-night operations, there were a couple of hundred solid country banks, all run independently by different partner groups. Since there was no centralized credit training, each country bank did business in its own way, with its own specialties. Provided an entrepreneur was not so eccentric as to set up his business where there was no local expertise, there were probably half a dozen country banks he could talk to within a day's horse ride, each of them doing business differently. Even as a working man, he could probably get an introduction to one of them, or more if he needed it – these people were regarded as superior tradesmen, not socially grand like the later London merchant bankers.

The result was that, in the country banking system, many entrepreneurs obtained finance and a vast range of small businesses were able to discount their receivables, which was what most of them needed. No 'groupthink' was possible, no fashionable ideas quelled the eccentrics – the bankers were not fashionable. If an idea could work, and could be begun on a modest scale, the chances were that it could be financed. The localism and pluralism of England's country banking system made it a major contributor to the Industrial Revolution, which has not been sufficiently recognized. Alas, in the later nineteenth century, the banking system became more conservative, oriented towards larger businesses and far less available to small entrepreneurs.

Canals

This period also saw the first great surge in canal building, which brought economic benefits that sparked the Industrial Revolution. The Duke of Bridgewater had completed the initial stage of his canal in

---

60. Ibid., p. 491.

1761, demonstrating the economic effect a canal could have, by halving the price of coal in Manchester, and deriving a large profit for his own coal mines. Other great landowners took note, but so did non-ducal businessmen, who realized that the cost of a local canal was well within the financial reach of local merchants and industrialists if they banded together, while the benefits of a canal for heavy goods transport as an alternative to horse-drawn haulage over muddy roads were potentially immense. Like the earlier Aire and Calder Navigation but on a much greater scale, this surge in canal building was driven largely by the needs of local tradesmen and industrialists, with country banks assisting in the financing, both directly and indirectly through finding and stimulating local investors.

The economic benefits of canals for transporting heavy goods were simple. Given the roads of this period (half a century before Thomas Telford and John McAdam improved them), the maximum load for a horse-drawn cart was about two tons and that required two men to lever the cart out of innumerable potholes or rescue it when it ran off the road.[61] Progress would be slow, at best. However, a canal narrowboat could carry 50 tons of goods, and required the same horse and the same two men, one to guide the barge and the other to tend the horse. Canals were therefore potentially about 25 times as productive as road transport for heavy goods such as coal. This was a revolutionary advantage, far more than in most pre-1810 steam-engine applications other than pumping water.

There were three great surges in canal building: the period of roughly 1766-77 (before the American War of Independence), the late 1780s, before the Napoleonic wars, and 1816-25, after they ended (finance was expensive and difficult to obtain during wartime). Of the three surges, this first one saw the highest profitability and the greatest economic effect since (as one would expect) the best projects were attempted first. Conversely, the 1816-25 surge of canal building suffered from poor economic returns because the economic lives of its investments were artificially curtailed by the coming of the railways. This first surge was therefore by far the most economically important of the three, with the most important and profitable canals all receiving parliamentary authorization between 1766 and 1770.

---

61. Some heavy goods transportation was by wagons with eight horses; these may have saved somewhat on people per ton carried, but not on horses per ton.

The first of the new canals to get parliamentary approval were the Staffordshire and Worcestershire and the Trent and Mersey, both approved in May 1766 by the same Act of Parliament. James Brindley was heavily involved in the engineering of both canals; they were part of his Grand Cross scheme to link the Trent, Mersey, Severn and Thames rivers. He was also involved in the design of the Birmingham Canal, the Coventry Canal, the Oxford Canal (also part of his Grand Cross scheme) and the Leeds and Liverpool Canal, though he died in 1772 before most of those canals were finished.

Brindley knew that, unlike the Bridgewater Canal, sponsored by an immensely wealthy duke, the canals in his Grand Cross scheme were much longer and would be financed mostly by local tradesmen of limited means; hence, they should lack the Bridgewater Canal's luxury features. The routes of Brindley's later canals were designed to follow the contours of the land, producing longer, more winding canals but with fewer viaducts and tunnels, both very expensive with limited eighteenth-century digging equipment. He also designed them with only a 7-ft width, rather than the Bridgewater Canal's fifteen feet, making them single-track thoroughfares for 'narrowboats', under seven feet wide and up to 70 feet long (Brindley's locks were 72 feet in length).

Even though several portions of Brindley's canals were replaced later, to shorten the route or to allow boats to pass each other, his canals continued profitably in use into the twentieth century, demonstrating the soundness of their design and the immense economic benefits they brought. Brindley's Grand Cross canals, with their immense cost advantage over preceding technologies, created for the first time a national transportation network, so heavy raw materials could reach the new factories while heavy goods sourced anywhere in the industrial Midlands could be transported cheaply both nationally and, through the ports, internationally.

Brindley never became rich, receiving a few hundred pounds per annum from each canal he advised on, though his coal holdings under Kidsgrove Hill on the Trent and Mersey rewarded his family after his death. Moreover, his last years, dashing around the Midlands on horseback from canal to canal, may have been stressful enough to shorten his life. Nevertheless, he has an even better claim than James Watt to rank as the father of the Industrial Revolution.

The **Staffordshire and Worcestershire Canal** appears to have been sponsored partly by Gower, the largest landowner in Staffordshire and the principal sponsor of the simultaneously approved Trent and Mersey. Its capital was £70,000 initially, with an additional £30,000 callable;

244 *Forging Modernity*

apart from two peers, about a quarter of the shareholders were landed gentry and just over half were tradesmen, mostly from Wolverhampton and Kidderminster.[62] The canal was 46 miles long, linking the River Severn at Stourport with the Trent and Mersey Canal at Haywood Junction. It had 43 locks, 31 taking it up 292 feet from the Severn to a ten-mile summit before the remaining twelve locks took it down to Haywood Junction. It followed natural contours, minimizing artifacts (aqueducts, tunnels etc.) but making it longer than necessary – its cost per mile was £2,168, the lowest of the early canals.[63] The canal was completed by 1771, albeit with a modest cost overrun, and opened to traffic in 1772, carrying coal from nearby mines to the iron works of John Wilkinson and Abraham Darby III and pottery from Staffordshire to Bristol's international shipping trade.[64] It was an immediate financial success, profitable into the twentieth century, by 1828 paying a dividend of £40 on each £100 share (for which £140 was paid up) and selling at £800 per share.[65]

Plans had been drawn up for the **Trent and Mersey Canal** by Brindley with Gower's funding and encouragement before 1759, but nothing further was done because Gower did not want to finance it alone. Wedgwood became interested in 1761 and with Gower worked to secure broad-based local financing. When the canal was authorised in 1766, £66,900 of the authorized share capital of £130,000 had been subscribed. By further Acts of Parliament of 1770, 1775 and 1776, another £166,000 was borrowed, making a total debt and equity capital of £296,000.

Peers put up only 7% of the equity, but Samuel Egerton of Tatton Park, Cheshire, put up £42,750 of the loan capital and landed gentry, including Egerton, held 39% of the shares and 46% of the loan capital. In Staffordshire £140,000 of the share and loan capital was raised but only £19,300 in the Potteries.[66] (The Wedgwood family, who contributed £6,000, were nothing like as rich in 1766 as they later became, but Josiah

---

62. Ward, *The Finance of Canal Building in Eighteenth-Century England*, p. 29.
63. Charles Hadfield, *The Canal Age* (New York: Praeger, 1969), Appendix III, p. 211.
64. This is confirmed in Anon, *An Address to the Public on the New Intended Canal from Stourbridge to Worcester with the Case of the Staffordshire and Worcestershire Canal Company* (1786).
65. W.T. Jackman, *The Development of Transportation in Modern England*, 2 vols (Cambridge: Cambridge University Press, 1916), Vol. 1, p. 425.
66. Ward, *The Finance of Canal Building in Eighteenth-Century England*, pp. 28-29.

The Trent and Mersey Canal. It is peaceful, 7 feet wide, and it changed the world. Image by Elliott Brown.

Wedgwood cut the first sod of soil at the massive celebration on 26 July 1766.) Samuel Egerton (1711-80) was a second cousin of Bridgewater and a Tory MP for Cheshire from 1754 until 1780, described by the 'Public Ledger' in 1779 as: 'A very wealthy country gentlemen, and a Tory in principle. He votes constantly with Government when he attends Parliament and professes a great veneration for Lord North.'[67]

The Trent and Mersey Canal was 93 miles long, from Preston Brook, where it meets the Bridgewater Canal, to the River Trent at Derwent Mouth in Derbyshire. It offered two huge advantages to pottery manufacturers like Wedgwood. First, it greatly reduced the cost of transporting Cornish china clays, which had recently been discovered near St Austell. Second, it enabled potters to avoid the large pottery breakages from road transport – the roads round Burslem were notorious because potters dug them up for the clay, an essential ingredient.

---

67. Entry for Samuel Egerton in L. Namier and J. Brooke (eds), *The History of Parliament: The House of Commons, 1754-90* (Woodbridge: Boydell & Brewer, 1964).

246 *Forging Modernity*

By 1771, when Wedgwood's Etruria factory opened, most of the canal had been built to Preston Brook, as had the eastern section from Burslem to the Trent. At Kidsgrove Hill, near Stoke-on-Trent, the canal passed through the 2,880-yard Harecastle Tunnel, boatmen propelling their crafts by foot, lying on their backs. The canal's economics were helped by the fact that Kidsgrove Hill proved to consist largely of coal, which was mined by the Golden Hill colliery, partly owned by Brindley. Moreover, since Kidsgrove stood at the canal's high point, the steam engine pumping out the mine supplied the necessary water to the canal. Even with this tunnel, the canal's cost was a relatively modest £3,213 per mile.[68]

The canal was constructed by Brindley to follow the land's contours; it therefore swings a long way south to meet the Staffordshire and Worcestershire Canal and the later Coventry Canal, before swinging back north to meet the Trent. The full canal was opened in 1777; like the Staffordshire and Worcestershire, the Trent and Mersey Canal was immediately financially successful, paying off its bonded debt, and at the 1825 peak sold for £4,000 per £200 share, paying an annual dividend of £150. The canal was profitable until World War I.[69]

The **Birmingham Canal** was authorized by Parliament in February 1768, with sponsorship from Matthew Boulton and the Lunar Society, to run from Birmingham to the Staffordshire and Worcestershire Canal near Wolverhampton, on a Brindley plan which was largely level but meandering, with branches to Ocker Hill and Wednesbury, where there were coal mines. Five hundred shares of £140 were subscribed for a total of £70,000, with 23% of the shares bought by manufacturers. The cost overrun to an eventual cost of £112,400, or £4,091 per mile, was covered by short-term loans and subventions from running profits.[70] The first stretch was to Wednesbury, whereupon the price of household coal in Birmingham halved overnight; the full canal of nearly 23 miles with 30 locks was completed in 1772, just before Brindley's death. There were two separate terminals in Birmingham, as well as a branch to Boulton's

---

68. Hadfield, *The Canal Age*, p. 211. C.S. Forester's *Hornblower and the Atropos* gives an excellent account of Hornblower propelling a boat through the Sapperton Tunnel (3,817 yards) on the Thames and Severn Canal in December 1805.

69. Jackman, *The Development of Transportation in Modern England*, Vol. 1, p. 424.

70. Ward, *The Finance of Canal Building in Eighteenth-Century England*, p. 30.

The Tory-Assisted Take-off, 1761-83

Soho Manufactory; the canal enabled Birmingham's metalworking industries to serve export markets directly. Smethwick Hill turned out to be too soft for tunnelling, so locks were built; it also proved difficult to ensure adequate water feed to Smethwick Hill, so two Watt engines were installed in 1778 and 1779 to ensure full-time operation.[71]

The Birmingham Canal borrowed another £121,400 from 1784 to 1798 to construct the Birmingham and Fazeley Canal, providing a more direct link to the Coventry Canal; this money was repaid between 1800 and 1819.[72] With this additional leverage and new asset, the canal's £140 shares were already selling at £900 in 1792 and were divided into eighths for greater convenience; by 1828 an eighth-share was selling for £300, while dividends were 100% on the original £140 shares.[73]

Those first three canals were all remarkable success stories; the remainder even in this early period were less so, because they ran out of money during construction, suffering long delays before their completion. The **Coventry Canal** was authorized by a separate Act in 1768 with 500 shares of £100, half of which came from Coventry businessmen.[74] Since the canal runs 38 miles north from Coventry to the Trent and Mersey Canal at Fradley Junction, the initial capital was clearly inadequate, being only £1,316 per mile of canal. Brindley was again hired to construct the canal but was fired within a year when the canal ran out of money – his construction standards were allegedly too high. Construction ceased in 1771, by which time the canal had reached Atherstone colliery. Further loan capital of £37,500 was not raised until 1786, and the canal was completed and connected to the Trent and Mersey in 1790. Still, the canal's long-term profitability was good; by 1834 the £100 shares stood at £610 and paid a dividend of 44% during the 1820s.[75]

The first Scottish canal, the **Forth and Clyde Canal** had a still more chequered history. Also authorized in 1768, the canal had capital of £150,000 in £100 shares, with an additional £50,000 callable if

---

71. One of the Smethwick engines, now in the Birmingham Science Museum, is the oldest operational steam engine.
72. Ward, *The Finance of Canal Building in Eighteenth-Century England*.
73. Jackman, *The Development of Transportation in Modern England*, Vol. 1, pp. 423-24.
74. Ward, *The Finance of Canal Building in Eighteenth-Century England*, p. 31.
75. Jackman, *The Development of Transportation in Modern England*, Vol. 1, p. 423.

248 *Forging Modernity*

necessary, to run 35 miles from the River Carron at Grangemouth to the River Clyde at Bowling. A large portion of the investment was put up by the immensely rich Tory MP Sir Lawrence Dundas (1710-81), who had made a fortune of some £900,000 through contracting to the British Army at Culloden and again during the Seven Years' War. As MP for Newcastle-under Lyme in 1762-68, he was doubtless aware of the Staffordshire projects.[76] Work on the canal, with Smeaton as engineer, began in 1771 and, after a hiatus, by 1775 had reached to within six miles of the Clyde, when it ran out of money and construction stopped. Eventually, it received a grant of £50,000 from the barons of the Court of Exchequer in Scotland, from the proceeds of forfeited Jacobite estates; with this money the last portion was finished in 1790.

Even though this canal had a branch to Glasgow, and by the 1820s ran passenger steamboat trips, it was never very profitable – for one thing, the links to the sea were not especially valuable, since canal boats could not survive in the rough North and Irish Seas. The shares rose only to £160 by 1829, and the annual dividend was only 6¾%.[77] The canal was sold to the Caledonian Railway in 1867.

The **Oxford Canal** was the final link in Brindley's Grand Cross scheme – it provided the link to the Thames. It was authorized by Parliament in 1769, sponsored by the company's chairman, Sir Roger Newdigate, the Tory MP for Oxford University, a country gentleman with large landholdings in Warwickshire and Middlesex, who wrote after George III's accession: 'Men must love peace, men proscribed and abused for 50 years should be presented with fools' caps if they make ladders for tyrant Whigs to mount by.'[78]

The canal's initial capital was £150,000 in £100 shares, but only £122,300 was taken up; a further attempted share issue of £30,000 in 1775 raised only £18,900; the gap was filled by loans of £70,000 in 1775-79 and £60,000 in 1786-90. The largest subscriptions came from Oxford and villages along the canal's route, with clerical Oxford dons subscribing

---

76. Entry for Sir Lawrence Dundas in Namier and Brooke (eds), *The History of Parliament: The House of Commons, 1754-90*.

77. Jackman, *The Development of Transportation in Modern England*, Vol. 1, p. 426.

78. Entry for Sir Roger Newdigate in Namier and Brooke (eds), *The History of Parliament: The House of Commons, 1754-90*. Roger Newdigate (1719-1806). 5th Bt from 1734. MP for Middlesex and Oxford University, 1742-47, 1751-80. Legacy endowed Oxford University's Newdigate Prize for English Verse Composition, 1806.

The Tory-Assisted Take-off, 1761-83

13% of the shares and £35,000 of the loan capital.[79]

The canal's route runs 78 miles, from the Coventry Canal at Hawkesbury Lock to Oxford, where it connects with the Thames; its construction was supervised by Brindley until his death. The canal reached Banbury in 1778, where construction ceased for lack of funds. Construction from Banbury to Oxford continued in 1786 on the cheapest possible basis, incorporating part of the River Cherwell, and the canal was finally opened in Oxford on 1 January 1790. It was highly profitable for its first fifteen years, until the Grand Junction Canal's main section was opened in 1805 – apparently, already in 1790 Newdigate was receiving as annual income the entire amount of his initial investment.[80] The canal was still quite profitable in 1829, paying a 32% dividend with a share price of £670 per £100 share.[81]

Roger Newdigate was a Tory MP for Oxford, the chairman of the Oxford Canal, and endowed the Newdigate Prize. Painting by Arthur Devis.

Finally, the **Leeds and Liverpool Canal** was the most ambitious of all these early schemes and the longest canal in Britain, given parliamentary authorization in May 1770 on plans drawn up by the ubiquitous Brindley for a 109-mile canal with a 14-ft width, at a cost of £259,777. The parliamentary authorization specified capital of £260,000, plus another £60,000 callable if necessary. The initial issue was undersubscribed, but the sale of 1,919 shares of £100 was notable for a high 36% subscription

---

79. Ward, *The Finance of Canal Building in Eighteenth-Century England*, pp. 32-33.
80. Jackman, *The Development of Transportation in Modern England*, Vol. 1, p. 425, note says that: 'In 1790 the papers mentioned a certain baronet who was receiving annually as profits the full amount of his investment in a navigation.' There may have been another such baronet, but Newdigate is my educated guess. Prizes for English Verse Composition don't fund themselves!
81. Ibid., Vol. 1, p. 426.

by merchant 'capitalists'. Almost half the initial shareholders came from Yorkshire's Aire Valley, with other large investments from Liverpool.

The Yorkshire side of the canal reached from Leeds to Gargrave (four miles north-west of Skipton) by 1777; the Lancashire side was built from Liverpool to Wigan by 1781, when the money ran out with a total of 61½ miles built. Work resumed in 1790, proceeding along a more southerly route in Lancashire and financed by an issue of a further 697 shares of £100 par value at prices of £160 and £180, by borrowing £442,154 on mortgage by 1822 and by setting aside toll income.[82] The 1,640-yard Foulridge Tunnel, costing £40,000 alone, was completed in 1796, opening the canal across the Pennines from Leeds to eastern Burnley. The canal was then lengthened in several stages, with the main canal opened in 1816 and final completion in 1820, at a cost of £1.2 million, or £9,449 per mile. The canal was quite successful financially despite its huge cost; by 1829, the £100 shares were selling at £470 and paying a dividend of 18%.[83] With its access to coal mines, limestone kilns and factories, it was central to Lancashire's textile industry once steam-powered factories became common.

Eminent Industrialists

The Industrial Revolution manifested itself in the careers of five important industrialists, beginning around 1760 and extending through this period: they were Josiah Wedgwood, John Roebuck, John Wilkinson, Richard Arkwright and Matthew Boulton. The rise in patent activity, the surge in infrastructure spending and the sudden efflorescence of the country banking system all indicated that around 1760, something changed; the careers of these five individuals launched Britain fully into industrialization in all its facets. In addition, we should include a sixth, Samuel Whitbread, whose career began significantly before 1760, though it took off in 1761 when he bought out his partner. Finally, there was Wilkinson's 'Copper King' collaborator, Thomas Williams, whose business activity involved little more than being a clever lawyer, but who ended up richer than most of this group.

The sudden appearance of these industrial giants indicates that Walter Rostow's 'take-off' of the Industrial Revolution occurred, not

---

82. Ward, *The Finance of Canal Building in Eighteenth-Century England*, pp. 33-36.
83. Jackman, *The Development of Transportation in Modern England*, op. cit. Vol I p 426

The Tory-Assisted Take-off, 1761-83

in 1783, as Rostow postulated,[84] but nearly two decades earlier, largely sparked by the first canal boom. As I have suggested, it was nurtured by underlying political and economic conditions stretching back for over a century. Whether the political transition of 1760 directly catalysed industrialization can be questioned. More likely, it had been latent for half a century, had begun to appear in Queen Anne's time, but had been dampened by the takeover of the authoritarian and London-centred Whigs in 1714.

Samuel Whitbread (1720-96) was the seventh of eight children of a prosperous Nonconformist family in Cardington, Bedfordshire (his father was Bedfordshire's Receiver of Land Tax). In 1736, he was apprenticed with a London brewer for the large fee of £300. In 1742, in partnership with Thomas Shewell, he invested £2,600 from an inheritance in two small breweries. With Whitbread the managing partner, they bought the derelict King's Head brewery in Chiswell Street in 1750 and specialized in the single product of porter.

Demand for the brewery's porter was strong; Whitbread invested in the latest brewing equipment and, in 1761, bought out Shewell for £30,000, by which time his capital in the business was £116,000. The business continued to expand; by the 1780s, it was the largest brewery in the world, producing 202,000 barrels of porter in 1796. Brewing is estimated to have represented 8% of Britain's GDP in 1770, declining to 6% of an expanded GDP in 1810.[85]

The brewery acquired in 1785 a purpose-built, Boulton & Watt steam engine, the Whitbread Engine, one of the first rotary engines. James Watt himself demonstrated the engine when George III and Queen Charlotte visited the brewery in 1787.[86] Whitbread was worth over £1 million by his death in 1796, the richest of the six industrialists profiled here.

Whitbread entered politics in 1768 as an independent MP for Bedford, for which he sat, with a short gap, until 1790; he also sat for Steyning from 1792 until 1796. He generally supported North's and Pitt's ministries,

---

84. See Walter W. Rostow, 'The Stages of Economic Growth', in *Economic History Review*, Vol XII, no. 1 (1959), p. 5. Rostow dates the take-off at 1783.

85. Figures from Rule, *The Vital Century*, p. 130.

86. Jay Brooks, 'Historic Beer Birthday: Samuel Whitbread', in Brookston Beer Bulletin, 30 August 2020, available at: https://brookstonbeerbulletin. com/historic-beer-birthday-samuel-whitbread/ (accessed 19 June 2021). Whitbread's sales volume was over twice that of the Thrale brewery, which peaked at 96,000 barrels when sold to Barclay, Perkins in 1781.

Josiah Wedgwood invented modern marketing. Print and etching by George Salisbury Shury.

thus he was a Tory, unlike his Radical Whig son who dissipated much of his fortune.[87] He was an early supporter of the abolition of slavery.

Whitbread was the only one of the six profiled here whose business was based in London. It grew through scale, modern equipment and specialization, together with the increasing size of London itself (and the poisonous nature of most of London's water!). Despite Whitbread's own Toryism, the business gained early traction during the London-oriented Whig Supremacy, which may have assisted it by its plethora of Gin Acts discouraging gin drinking. The size, specialization, technology and branding of Whitbread's business were all beyond that feasible previously, making Whitbread's success and wealth an important facet of the Industrial Revolution's emergence.

The career of **Josiah Wedgwood** (1730-95) shows that there was more to industrialization than a new power source. His potteries employed primarily traditional production methods, yet, through sophisticated design, marketing and distribution, they achieved global market penetration and consumer salience that had not previously been possible. Wedgwood's innovative design and marketing were as important to industrialization and modernity as James Watt's condenser; they showed the way for the mass consumer society of the nineteenth and twentieth centuries.

The Wedgwood family had been potters for several generations – the first was Josiah's great-great-grandfather, Gilbert Wedgwood (1588-1678), who established a crude pottery, fuelling the kilns with local coal and using the exceptionally suitable clay around Burslem, Staffordshire. Gilbert's son, Thomas, bought the Churchyard Works at Burslem and

---

87. Entry for Samuel Whitbread in Namier and Brooke (eds), *The History of Parliament: The House of Commons, 1754-1790*.

The Tory-Assisted Take-off, 1761-83

he, his son and his grandson, further Thomases, established a modest family business (with profits of less than £40[88] per annum) making low-quality black pottery with a speckled design until Thomas died in 1739, nine years after the birth of his eleventh child, Josiah. The successful Wedgwood potters were their cousins, Aaron, Thomas and Long John, working at the higher end of the market and selling to London directly, with annual profits well into three figures.

As a child, Josiah was educated to bare literacy and numeracy. He then learned pottery in the Churchyard Works run by his elder brother, Thomas (1716-73), along the lines of his ancestors. A bout of smallpox made him unable to work a potter's wheel, so he decided to concentrate on design. In 1754, he joined the established high-quality pottery of Thomas Whieldon (1718-95), where he developed several new designs. Finally, in 1759, he dissolved his partnership with Whieldon and established his own pottery in Burslem, renting the small Ivy House pottery works from Thomas and Long John, to specialize in high-quality ware.

Throughout his career Josiah was a diligent and careful experimenter and he had already developed green and yellow glazes that appeared to beat the competition, but his first real breakthrough came some months after establishing the Ivy House works, when he developed a new translucent glaze for cream pottery that finally allowed it to appear truly cream-coloured, rather than off-white like other glazes. Then he encountered John Sadler and Guy Green of Liverpool, who in 1756 had patented a transfer printing process, whereby engraved images could be imprinted on pottery; together with Josiah's new glaze this allowed for spectacular effects. The port of Liverpool also offered links to a new and growing market in the American colonies, not yet recalcitrant but exponentially increasing their purchases of English luxury goods.

After an initial loss of a cargo to French privateers, Wedgwood established the Liverpool mercantile connections that gave him a leading position in satisfying the colonials' demand for fine earthenware. Another Liverpool connection was Thomas Bentley (1731-80), from a gentry background with intellectual interests, who from 1768 until his death in 1780 was his partner and manager of his London sales operation. With increasing prosperity, in 1764 Wedgwood married his third cousin, Sally, from the wealthiest (country banking and cheese

---

88. Bryan Dolan, *Wedgwood: The First Tycoon* (London: Penguin, 2004), discusses the economics of the very modest Wedgwood family pottery business, and the more substantial, higher-quality one of Josiah's cousins.

254   *Forging Modernity*

factoring, set to inherit £20,000) branch of the extended Wedgwood family.

Wedgwood's big break was an order in 1764 for a full set of tableware with the family crest from Sir William Meredith,[89] an independent-minded MP. Meredith's patronage marked Wedgwood's entry into a better class of business; it was followed by other orders from the aristocracy, notably, Gower. Then in 1765 came an invitation to submit samples for a dinner service for Queen Charlotte.[90] Not only did Wedgwood win the order, he charmed the queen, who allowed him to term himself, 'Potter to Her Majesty' and to market copies of her dinner service as 'Queen's Ware'.

From this point, Wedgwood's prosperity was assured, provided that through skilful marketing, of which he was a pioneer, he could keep the aristocracy interested in his wares. His next coup was to copy the Etruscan pottery in the collection of Sir William Hamilton,[91] a 'coffee table' book on which had just been published, and market reproduction Etruscan tableware, complete with authentic-looking ancient glazes, to the super-luxury market. He also built a new and larger works and a house for himself next to the planned Trent and Mersey Canal, calling them 'Etruria'. With the addition of a magnificent West End showroom managed by Bentley, Wedgwood's leading position in the pottery business was assured and he expanded the pottery market towards decorative rather than merely utilitarian pieces.

Wedgwood's position was further bolstered by an order he received in 1773 to make a 952-piece, 'Green Frog' dinner set for Empress Catherine the Great of Russia. This service contained pictures of over 900 English country scenes painted over the course of a year by a hired team of painters. Wedgwood conceived the clever scheme of putting the set on display (before it went to St Petersburg) in his London showroom, where

---

89. William Meredith (1725-90). 3rd Bt from 1752. MP for Wigan and Liverpool, 1754-80. Entered Parliament in 1754 as a Tory, then supported Bute, served as a junior Lord of the Admiralty under Rockingham and became a Privy Councillor under North.

90. Charlotte of Mecklenburg-Strelitz (1744-1818). Married George III, 1761. Queen of Great Britain, 1762-1801, of United Kingdom, 1801-18.

91. William Hamilton (1730-1803). KB 1772. MP for Midhurst, 1761-65. British Ambassador to Naples, 1764-1800. Published *Collection of Etruscan, Greek and Roman Antiquities from the Cabinet of Honorable William Hamilton* (1767). Later the husband of Emma Hamilton, who became the mistress of Horatio Nelson.

The Tory-Assisted Take-off, 1761-83

the aristocracy came to see and criticize the portrayals of their stately home parks.

In another display of entrepreneurship, Wedgwood sent an associate to the back country of the Carolinas, still occupied by Cherokee Native Americans, on an arduous journey costing over £600 to obtain five tons of pure white kaolin, with which he could make Chinese-style porcelain. After further experimentation, by adding barium sulphate he produced 'jasperware', an opaque pottery stained through the clay that proved unique and extremely popular. The romantic story of the kaolin's origin made excellent marketing copy.

In later years, Wedgwood mastered the technical challenge of copying the 'Portland Vase', a blue-and-white glass vase from the first century AD of exceptional workmanship, bought first by Sir William Hamilton and then by the third Duke of Portland.[92] He also became active in the movement for abolition of the slave trade, befriending William Wilberforce and Thomas Clarkson[93] and producing the slave medallion in support of abolitionism, 'Am I not a man and brother', for distribution by the Society for the Abolition of the Slave Trade – doubtless, this was also useful brand marketing among the rising middle-class Evangelical community.

In 1796, Wedgwood died worth £600,000, by far the leading pottery producer in Britain, with nearly 80% of his production exported in the peacetime 1780s. His life demonstrated four key elements of many modern businesses: original scientific research and development; large-scale production; aggressive and thoughtful marketing; and a concentration on luxury goods that carried high profit margins. As much as any inventor of steam engines, Wedgwood, a chemical innovator and inventor of much of the modern array of marketing techniques, was a key builder of our world.

Like Wedgwood's pottery works, the Carron Iron Works was also founded in 1759, by **John Roebuck** (1718-94), the son of a prosperous Sheffield cutlery manufacturer. Roebuck, with an early interest

---

92. William Henry Cavendish-Bentinck (1738-1809). 3rd Duke of Portland from 1762. MP for Weobley, 1761-62. Lord Chamberlain, 1765-66, Lord Lieutenant of Ireland, 1782, Prime Minister, 1783 and 1807-9, Home Secretary, 1794-1801, Lord President of the Council, 1801-5, Minister without Portfolio, 1805-6.

93. Thomas Clarkson (1760-1844). Founder of the Committee on Abolition of the Slave Trade, 1787, introducing William Wilberforce to the problem. Also helped found worldwide Anti-Slavery Society, 1825.

256 *Forging Modernity*

in chemistry, studied at Edinburgh and Leiden, both more oriented towards practical subjects than Oxford or Cambridge. After graduating as a doctor of medicine, he set up practice in Birmingham, carrying out scientific experiments in his spare time. He devised a better means for extracting refined gold and silver from ore and then established a specialist laboratory, acting as consulting chemist to local manufacturers. In 1749, he built a factory for producing sulphuric acid, using lead condensing chambers, thereby reducing production costs by around three quarters – this is believed to have been the world's first substantial chemical works.[94] However, he omitted to patent the technique (an attempt to get a Scottish patent was rejected by the court in 1771) so over time he was undercut by other manufacturers, although the works remained profitable.

Carron in Stirlingshire was his next venture. With his brother, Ebenezer, and other partners, he used the Darby's process for producing pig iron with coke and himself introduced numerous process improvements, including in 1762 the conversion of cast iron into malleable iron using a hollow pit-coal (rather than coke) fire. In 1764, the Board of Ordnance granted Carron a contract to provide armaments, and Roebuck became a Fellow of the Royal Society.

Roebuck also owned a colliery at Bo'ness that supplied coal to Carron, but it flooded so severely that its Newcomen pumping engine could not keep up. Roebuck contacted James Watt, taking over his debts and financing the application for his 1769 patent and the development of his engine, the first example of which was built at Carron. By 1772, Roebuck was in financial difficulty from the costs of his flooded coal mine which Watt's engine could not solve, so Roebuck was forced to sell his shares in the coal mine, Watt's engine (to Matthew Boulton), the sulphate production plant and Carron to satisfy his creditors. He devoted the remainder of his life to farming, manufacturing alkali and pottery.

At Carron, the death of Ebenezer Roebuck in 1771 caused quality control problems and Carron lost its Royal Navy contract in 1773. A new manager, Charles Gascoigne (1738-1806), improved quality control and produced a new gun, the carronade, shorter, much lighter and quicker to load than a conventional cannon; these were an immediate success in the Royal Navy from their adoption in 1779 and remained in service until the 1850s. Carron's reputation for quality then became such that Wellington wanted only Carron guns in the Peninsular army – by 1814 Carron was Europe's largest iron works, employing 2,000 men.

---

94. F. Crouzet, *The First Industrialists: The Problem of Origins* (Cambridge: Cambridge University Press, 1985), p. 35.

The Tory-Assisted Take-off, 1761-83 257

Roebuck, an amiable man, did not end up rich, but he was important because he was both an entrepreneur and a scientific innovator, playing a significant role in the development of three quite separate industrial technologies.

John Wilkinson, known as 'Iron-Mad', was the son of Isaac Wilkinson (1695-1784), an iron-foundry industrialist – albeit one of shaky finances and dubious business ethics. Isaac was apprenticed as a foundryman in Ambrose Crowley's Swalwell iron works around 1710. Then, after 1720, he became a subcontractor to the Little Clifton iron works, near Workington in Cumbria, which was already coke-fired, followed by the charcoal-fired Backbarrow furnace. In 1753 he became operator of the Bersham iron works near Wrexham, Wales, which was gradually taken over by his son, John, after the bankruptcy of their partner in 1759. Isaac sued his son in 1762 and moved to Bristol in 1763, becoming a foundryman in the West Dowlais iron works and then starting the Plymouth iron works, both around Merthyr Tydfil. After further financial difficulties and further lawsuits, he retired to London.

John Wilkinson was educated at a Dissenting academy at Kendal; his sister married the chemist, Joseph Priestley.[95] He was apprenticed to a Liverpool merchant for five years in 1745 and then, in 1755, after marrying a wealthy wife, who died the following year, entered into partnership with his father at the Bersham iron works. With demand strong because of the Seven Years' War, he erected another blast furnace in 1757 at Willey, near Broseley, Staffordshire. He took full control of Bersham in 1761 and erected his largest and most successful blast furnace at Bradley, near Wolverhampton, around 1766, with help from a second wealthy wife. At Bradley he experimented with substituting raw coal for coke in iron manufacture.

Bersham became the centre for Wilkinson's armaments manufacture business, in which his brother, William (1744-1808), became a partner. In 1774 Wilkinson invented[96] a tool for boring iron guns from a solid piece, making them considerably less likely to explode in action. He

---

95. Joseph Priestley (1733-1804). Radical chemist. FRS 1766. *Experiments and Observations on Different Kinds of Air* (1774) propounded the existence of oxygen but within Johann Becher's phlogiston theory. Priestley's main energies were devoted to attacking the Church of England and after 1789 to supporting the French Revolution. Later he emigrated to the United States.

96. Or possibly copied from a similar machine built in 1770 by the Dutch gun-founder, Jan Verbruggen (1712-81), at the Royal Arsenal.

John Wilkinson was nicknamed 'Iron-mad'. His cylinder borer revolutionized steam engines. Painting by Thomas Gainsborough.

The Tory-Assisted Take-off, 1761-83

clamped the solid gun stock to the bench and then, using a water wheel for power, rotated a very hard iron boring tool against it. He attempted to patent this, but the Royal Navy ensured the patent was quashed, though Wilkinson remained a major manufacturer of naval guns. In 1777, at the invitation of the French government, William Wilkinson departed for France to set up a cannon manufacturing works at Indret, near Nantes; from 1779 this manufactured cannon used in the war against Britain and William remained abroad until 1789.

Wilkinson's boring machine, the first machine tool, was also essential for the cylinders of steam engines. He bored the cylinder of Boulton & Watt's first commercial engine in 1776 and gained an exclusive contract for providing cylinders because of the tighter tolerances this method could bring – initially 'the width of a shilling' (one tenth of an inch), subsequently about half that – and the far lower resulting steam leakage. Indeed, without Wilkinson's cylinder boring machine, it is doubtful that steam engines could ever have moved on significantly from the inefficiencies of the Newcomen design.[97]

Wilkinson also saw the potential for steam engines driving machinery; Watt's first rotary engine was installed at Bradley in 1783. Wilkinson invented a reversing rolling mill with two steam cylinders that made the iron rolling process much more economical. In the late 1780s Wilkinson was found to be making unauthorized copies of the patented Watt engines, so Boulton & Watt took their entire manufacture in-house from 1795, using William Wilkinson as an advisor.

Wilkinson was a leader and major shareholder in the construction of the Iron Bridge (the world's first successful such construction) linking the town of Brosely with the Coalbrookdale side of the Severn. The bridge was authorized by Parliament in 1776 and completed in 1779; Abraham Darby III of Coalbrookdale (1750-89) was commissioned to cast and build it. In 1787 Wilkinson also constructed at Brosely the first barge made of iron, the precursor of the following century's shipping and in the following year provided 40 miles of cast-iron water pipes for the city of Paris.[98]

From the late 1770s, Wilkinson, seeing the enormous demand from the Royal Navy for 'copper cladding' the hulls of its fleet, which had

---

97. Simon Winchester, *The Perfectionists: How Precision Engineers Created the Modern World* (London: HarperCollins, 2017), gives an elegant account of Wilkinson's invention and its effects on the Industrial Revolution.

98. It's not clear whether he got paid for these, revolutions being what they are.

first been successfully tried in 1761, diversified into copper. He bought shares in eight Cornish copper mines (where he installed steam engines for more efficient pumping) and invested in the mines and manufacturing interests of Thomas Williams, the 'Copper King' who effectively controlled the Parys Mountain mine in Anglesey. He also acquired a lead mine near Wrexham, Cheshire.

Thomas Williams[99] was born into a minor Anglesey gentry family and became a local attorney. In 1769 he was retained by the Lewis and Hughes families to fight a boundary dispute against the Bayly family, who owned the Parys Mountain copper deposit, on which its lessee, Charles Roe, had the previous year discovered a gigantic lode. The dispute over an obscure will technicality involved the Attorney General and the Solicitor General on opposing sides and, at the end of it in 1778, Williams emerged as the controlling partner in the gigantic Parys deposit, although the Reverend Edward Hughes (1738-1815)[100] continued to collect large royalties from it.

Williams aggressively exploited the deposit and marketed the resulting copper, gaining a bad reputation among fellow businessmen but enabling him to amass a fortune of £500,000 by his death in 1802, by which time the gigantic deposit was nearing exhaustion. As a side-line, he established in 1792 the Chester and North Wales Bank, managed initially by his son, Owen, which continued in business until bought by Lloyds Bank in 1897. Thomas Williams is also said to have invested £70,000 in the slave trade, a major user of copper for chains, manacles and so on.

Wilkinson and Williams set up the Cornish Metal Company in 1785 as a marketing company for copper and copper manufactures, attempting to monopolize Cornish production and compete with the smelters; by 1787 it owned copper inventories worth £500,000. Beginning in 1787, Wilkinson and Williams produced by steam-stamping a copper 'token', halfpenny coinage, 'Willys' and 'Druids'. Beyond the profit between their copper value and coined value, the Willy tokens also acted as advertising, bearing a portrait of Wilkinson. To market the tokens, Wilkinson founded country banks in Holywell in 1790, Broseley in

---

99. Thomas Williams (1737-1802). Conservative Whig MP for Great Marlow, 1790-1802. Sheriff of Anglesey, 1790-91. Boulton called him 'the despotick sovereign of the copper trade'.

100. Hughes' son, William (1767-1852), became Whig MP for Wallingford, 1802-31, and was created 1st Baron Dinorben in 1832. The family seat, Kinmel Hall, bought by Edward Hughes in 1786 but later rebuilt, was known as the 'Welsh Versailles'.

The Tory-Assisted Take-off, 1761-83   261

1800 and possibly Birmingham in 1802 and became a partner of a country bank in Shrewsbury in 1793. His banks also issued notes, as was customary.[101]

By 1796, in another period of high wartime demand, Wilkinson was producing around one eighth of Britain's cast iron. However, by that time he had also become involved in legal disputes with his brother, William, and others. He died in 1808, worth about £130,000 and was buried in an iron coffin. Alas, his fortune never passed to his illegitimate children, conceived in his 70s after both wives had died, being consumed by 20 years of lawsuits instituted by his half-nephew, Thomas Jones.

Richard Arkwright (1732-92) was born in Preston, Lancashire, the youngest of seven children of a tailor. Unschooled, he was taught to read by a cousin, then apprenticed to a barber, setting up shop in Bolton in the early 1750s. Over time he prospered modestly, became a dealer in hair and invented a waterproof dye for periwigs; the proceeds of the dye sales funded his further businesses.

In 1767 Arkwright, possibly having seen the Wyatt/Paul machine in Northampton, hired a clockmaker John Kay,[102] initially to 'make brass rollers for a perpetual motion machine' and then to produce a spinning frame, a machine that produced twisted threads using metal rollers instead of human fingers, the first completed model being powered by horses. Arkwright patented 'his' spinning frame in 1769, which had much higher spinning productivity – the water-powered spinning frames in his later mills could spin 96 threads simultaneously. He also, possibly with Kay's help, invented an improved carding engine, which converted raw cotton to a continuous skein prior to spinning. Since the flying shuttle had roughly doubled the capacity of weaving operations, there was considerable demand for these advances in spinning. Arkwright attempted to control the market through a 'master patent' filed in 1775 but, after several years of hearings, this was denied.

Then, in 1771, Arkwright formed a partnership with Jedediah Strutt[103] and Samuel Need, wealthy hosiery manufacturers, to build the world's

---

101. Dawes and Ward-Perkins, *Country Banks of England and Wales*, Vol. 2, Directory, where the banks are listed by location. I can find no record of Wilkinson bank partnerships in Bilston, Bradley or Brymbo, as is claimed.
102. John Kay of Warrington (*c.* 1735-90). No relation to the inventor of the flying shuttle.
103. Jedediah Strutt (1726-97). Born into farming family. With his brother-in-law, William Woollatt, developed an attachment to the stocking frame (patented in 1759) that allowed production of 'Derby Rib' ribbed stockings. Expanded to eight mills by 1780s where he built workers' housing.

Sir Richard Arkwright. He got the law changed and industrialized textiles. Painting by Joseph Wright of Derby.

The Tory-Assisted Take-off, 1761-83 263

first large water-powered cotton mill at Cromford, which covered both carding and spinning operations and employed 200 people. (Lombe's Mill, on the same river a few miles away, was a useful model.) In 1775, Arkwright built a second larger mill at Cromford, then additional mills at Bakewell and Wirksworth. In 1777 in the mill at Wirksworth he installed a steam engine, the first to be used in a cotton mill (it was not used to drive machinery directly but for pumping, thereby producing year-round water power).

With its water-powered frame, rather than the hand-power of Hargreaves' spinning jenny, Arkwright's mill could spin cotton thread strong enough to allow cloth of pure cotton, rather than the cotton/linen mixture used elsewhere. Old Whig prohibitions needed to be overcome, so Arkwright petitioned Parliament, now run by North's Tory-dominated government, probably with the help of Gower, the local magnate and Lord President of the Council. The result was the Duty on Cotton Stuffs etc. Act 1774, which removed the prohibition on producing printed cotton fabrics from the Acts of 1720 and 1735, creating a new industry and eventually a new world. It also reopened the British market to Indian patterned fabrics, but they were no longer very competitive against British fabrics produced with Arkwright's new machinery.[104]

Arkwright is popularly thought to have invented the factory system, but that ignores the work of Wedgwood, who slightly preceded him, as well as Lombe's Mill, and Ambrose Crowley's integrated iron works with 1,000 employees and a fully-fledged personnel system. Arkwright, while building houses and a pub for his Cromford employees, was less benign than Wedgwood or Crowley, instituting a thirteen-hour day, with the factory gates locked to exclude those late for work. One notable innovation was to invite whole families to move to Cromford, including children, so that by the time of his death two thirds of his employees were children. By 1782, with 5,000 employees spread across several mills, he was probably Britain's largest employer.

Arkwright, a difficult man, eventually bought out his partners. A Church of England Tory, he was knighted in 1786 (an honour not given to Whitbread, Wedgwood or Boulton, the first and last also Tories) and served as High Sheriff of Derbyshire in 1787-88. He died in 1792, by which time he was worth £500,000. Others followed him into textile manufacturing and made even more money.

---

104. For the legislative history, I am indebted to Mantoux, *The Industrial Revolution in the Eighteenth Century*, specifically pp. 229-31 in this case.

Contemporaries deemed Arkwright the 'Father of the Industrial Revolution' – he was singled out as its leader along with Boulton and Watt in an 1820 speech by Lord Liverpool.[105] He was responsible for only a few of the innovations that industrialized the textile sector and did not invent the factory system. Nevertheless, as the first of many truly wealthy textile tycoons, the instigator of the 1774 legislation opening up the patterned cotton fabric industry and a major innovator in a sector that dominated industrial Britain and its economic growth until the 1820s, he deserved the recognition he received.

Arkwright's role is also significant because Birkacre Mill in Lancashire, leased by Arkwright in 1777, was the locus of a serious early outbreak of Luddism in 1779 (Ned Ludd himself, if he existed,[106] was reputed to have broken two stocking frames in that year). With the American war, raw cotton imports had fallen off drastically, so the textile industry was in a severe downturn, and the workers naturally assumed that the new machinery, producing many times the output of hand workers, was to blame for their unemployment. Hence, on 2 October, an unarmed mob of around 2,000 people attacked Birkacre Mill and was beaten off with difficulty, then, on 4 October, the mob, now armed and swollen to 4,000 people attacked the mill again and, despite resistance from around 40 army pensioners, destroyed the machinery and burned down the mill. Arkwright, having lost around £4,000 worth of equipment, abandoned his lease and concentrated production in his other mills.[107]

This was just one of numerous Luddite attacks in Lancashire and Yorkshire during the autumn of 1779, in which ten mills were burned down or their machinery wrecked. It appears to have been the first such series of incidents, although food riots and anti-Catholic riots were quite common (the Gordon Riots in London occurred the following year). It marked the beginning of industrial working-class radicalism, which was to strengthen during the difficult 1790s – before this time the working class outside London had been generally Tory, even when collected in factories as in the Crowley Iron Works.

The Whig response to this unrest was to organize a mass meeting of Yorkshire Whiggery on 30 December 1779, which formed the Yorkshire

---

105. Hansard, *Parliamentary Debates New Series*, Vol. 1, cols 417-22, 16 May 1820.
106. The Ned Ludd story first appeared in *The Nottingham Review* of 20 December 1811.
107. 'Lancashire Past: Birkacre Mill, Yarrow Valley Country Park', available at: https://lancashirepast.com/2020/10/17/birkacre-mill-yarrow-valley-cou ntry-park-near-coppull-and-chorley/ (accessed 3 September 2021).

The Tory-Assisted Take-off, 1761-83

Association under Christopher Wyvill[108] to pressure Parliament. This association and sister associations in other counties were dedicated to parliamentary reform (i.e. pro-Whig gerrymandering) and 'Economical Reform' to reduce the number of sinecures in government, now that so many of them were held by Tories. There was no mention by the associations of improving conditions for industrial labourers, the original cause of unrest.[109]

Two other inventors, James Hargreaves and Samuel Crompton made significant advances in textiles, though neither ended up substantial industrialists.

James Hargreaves (1720-78) was born in Oswaldtwistle, Lancashire and for most of his life was an illiterate handloom weaver and carpenter, the sort of downtrodden working-class operative so thoroughly suppressed by the Whig Supremacy, although he made enough of a living to support thirteen children. Then, in 1764, he invented the spinning jenny, which consisted of eight spindles all rotated by a single wheel (the most that could be controlled by a single operative), increasing eightfold the amount of coarse thread that could be produced and enabling spinners to keep up with John Kay's flying shuttle, which had doubled weaver productivity. He produced and sold jennies locally, then obtained a patent in 1770 and opened a small mill, leaving £7,000 to his heirs on his death in 1778.[110] Even before steam engines and Arkwright's spinning frame, his invention began the process which increased productivity in Britain's textile industry, enabling it to out-compete the world, despite Britain's high labour costs.

Samuel Crompton (1753-1827) was the son of a caretaker at a big house, who, although both literate and accomplished (he earned extra money as a violinist), became a spinner after his father died. Since the jenny could spin only coarse thread, he realized the need for something better, and devoted time and money to perfecting his invention for six years before developing the mule-jenny, a considerably more complex machine, in 1779, which spun the fine thread used in manufacturing muslin. He lacked the money for a patent, relying on other manufacturers to reimburse him; initially he received only £60. The mule was adapted elsewhere and reproduced in iron; in 1812 a survey concluded there were

---

108. Christopher Wyvill (1740-1822). Wealthy radical cleric, secretary of Yorkshire Association, 1779-83.

109. Herbert Butterfield, *George III, Lord North and the People, 1779-80* (London: G. Bell & Sons, 1949), ch. 5.

110. That figure is in Mantoux, *The Industrial Revolution in the Eighteenth Century*, p. 223.

Matthew Boulton was a Birmingham entrepreneur who tried everything till something worked. Artist unknown.

over five million mule spindles in use. Crompton received £500 from manufacturers in 1800 and a parliamentary grant of £5,000 in 1812. Alas, the businesses he started with those funds were unsuccessful, but his last years were alleviated by an annuity of £63 per annum purchased by friends. As with Hargreaves, the long-term effects of Crompton's achievements far exceeded any money he made.

In terms of breadth of achievement, **Matthew Boulton** (1728-1809) was the greatest early industrialist, but he did not die the richest – Whitbread, Wedgwood, Williams and Arkwright all appear to have died richer. Boulton was more of a polymath than most industrialists, with a broad range of scientific and business interests. He tended to invest heavily in projects that appealed to him, many of which failed to produce the hoped-for returns. He was also commercially 'sharp' with a tendency to cut corners; several of his business relationships ended in acrimony.

Boulton's family came from Lichfield (one of his ancestors had been Chancellor of Lichfield Cathedral). His father owned a modest but relatively successful workshop in Birmingham manufacturing buckles. Boulton left school at fifteen, went into the family business and developed a new method of enamelling buckles that proved popular, especially as they were marketed as 'imported from France'. In 1749 he married a wealthy cousin, Mary Robinson, and by the middle 1750s he was running the business – his father retired in 1757 and died in 1759. One marketing coup was to gift a sword to Prince Edward,[111] which resulted in a follow-up order from the future George III.

After Mary died in 1759, Boulton married her sister, Anne, the following year and, in 1764, inherited, through this second marriage, a further substantial fortune. (This marriage was technically illegal,

---

111. Prince Edward (1739-67). Duke of York and Albany from 1760. Younger brother of George III. FRS 1760. Admiral of the Blue, 1766.

The Tory-Assisted Take-off, 1761-83

but possible in a parish where neither party was known, probably with a substantial payment to the celebrant.) In 1761, having formed a partnership with a local merchant, John Fothergill (1730-82), he leased a large house with thirteen acres of land, Soho House and, by 1765, using his wives' and Fothergill's money as well as substantial borrowings, had erected the Soho Manufactory, at a cost of £10,000 for buildings and eventually another £10,000 for equipment.

During the 1760s, Boulton's interest in scientific experimentation was as important as his business development, for he was a prime mover in the Birmingham Lunar Society, which began formal meetings around 1765, and continued in some form until 1813. The society met monthly, on the Sunday nearest the full moon (making night-time travel easier and safer) at the house of one of its wealthier members. Discussion groups of this kind (there were other regional equivalents elsewhere) operated as a transmission mechanism to local industrialists for new scientific ideas and the Scientific Method, and for discussions of the latest economic knowledge. Britain's more open society, compared to most continental European countries, made such transmission mechanisms effective in bridging the gap between theoretical knowledge and its practical application in industry.

The Lunar Society appears to have developed from a friendship between Boulton and the polymath, Erasmus Darwin,[112] which began around 1757-58. Three older mentors who encouraged their investigations were the clockmaker, John Whitehurst,[113] the printer, John Baskerville,[114] and the Philadelphia printer, scientist and statesman, Benjamin Franklin, who travelled to Birmingham in 1758, while the astronomer and geologist, John Michell, the most impressive intellectually of them, was also a member of the gradually coalescing group.

Even before the society took full shape around 1765, there was considerable skills transfer among this group. Baskerville was his era's major proponent of the aesthetics of typology and of design in general, as well as a substantial Birmingham businessman. Whitehurst was a master of clockmaking technology, since Thomas Tompion the principal

---

112. Erasmus Darwin (1731-1802). Physician, natural philosopher, physiologist. FRS 1761. Author of *Zoonomia* (1794-96). Grandfather of Charles Darwin.

113. John Whitehurst (1713-88). Derby clockmaker, geologist. FRS 1779. Stamper of Money Weights, Royal Mint, 1774.

114. John Baskerville (1707-75). Printer and manufacturer of lacquerware items, based in Birmingham. Designed Baskerville typeface in the 1750s.

nexus of tight-tolerance metallurgic engineering, vital to Boulton in the decades ahead. Darwin and Michell were scientific polymaths, who broadened the group's intellectual range, while Franklin, also a scientific polymath, was already a major political figure in the American colonies.

Wedgwood joined the Lunar Society at its formal inception in 1765 – he and Boulton met while Wedgwood was campaigning for the Trent and Mersey Canal – and they quickly discovered interests in common. Wilkinson appears to have taken an interest in it and often attended meetings and James Watt was a frequent correspondent of the society even before he moved to Birmingham in 1773, but Roebuck and Arkwright appear not to have been members, even at a distance. The society gradually broadened after 1765 to attract more members, with Boulton remaining central to the group.

One member at a distance was the radical chemist, Joseph Priestley, but Priestley did not move to Birmingham until 1780 and cannot have participated actively before then. This is important because the Lunar Society changed in nature over the years. At first, it was purely a society of scientific enquiry, with no political affiliations other than mild Toryism – Boulton, Michell and Whitehurst were all Tories, as befitted middle-class provincials with Anglican religious connections. Then later, under the influence of Priestley and to a lesser extent Darwin and Wedgwood as their anti-slavery interests became deeper, the Lunar Society became a hotbed of free-thinking and radicalism, favouring at least the early years of the French revolutionary regime. The split became severe after a Birmingham mob sacked Priestley's house in 1791, forcing Lunar Society members to take sides. Even then Boulton remained firmly committed to public order and the support of Pitt's government (from which he received substantial contracts).

Boulton's first venture in the new Soho works was to expand his metalworking business to silverware and silver plate. The latter, following Boulsover's 1743 invention presented no great problems, but silver had to be assayed and stamped and the nearest Assay Office was in Chester. Boulton and other Birmingham metalworkers petitioned Parliament for a new Assay Office in Birmingham (with opposition from London goldsmiths) and, in 1773, they were successful; assay offices were set up in Birmingham and Sheffield. In the event, the silverware business proved unprofitable, requiring large inventories of increasingly expensive silver, but Boulton remained in the silver-plated dinnerware business.

Still selling to the wealthy, Boulton then got into the ormolu (gold-plated) vase business, following Wedgwood's marketing example in selling a few to Queen Charlotte, and then holding sales at Christie's,

The Tory-Assisted Take-off, 1761-83

the auctioneer. Alas, this business was also unprofitable and alienated Wedgwood, at least temporarily.

In the late 1760s, Boulton sought to increase the water power to his Soho works by buying a steam engine to pump water into the millpond. In 1766 he began correspondence with **James Watt**, meeting him two years later. Watt, the son of a Greenock shipwright and shipowner, trained as an instrument maker in London, before returning to Glasgow and setting up a small instrument-making workshop in Glasgow University. From 1759 for six years, he operated a small business with James Craig selling musical instruments and toys, in 1764 marrying his cousin, Peggy Miller.

In 1763 Watt set out to repair a Newcomen engine owned by the university. His work led to his idea in 1765 to improve the engine's efficiency with a separate condenser and he took out a fourteen-year patent on this in 1769. He then formed a partnership with John Roebuck to construct a full-sized engine to pump out Roebuck's mine. However, he was still unable to make a sufficiently tightly machined cylinder. When Roebuck went bankrupt in 1772, Boulton bought his interest and Watt moved to Birmingham. The full partnership Boulton & Watt was formed in 1775, after Boulton had used his parliamentary influence to extend the life of Watt's patent from 1783 to 1800.

Boulton then introduced Wilkinson's boring machine to the process, allowing Watt to produce a commercially viable engine (albeit still using a beam on the Newcomen principle) in 1776; the first was sold to Wilkinson and the second to the Carron Iron Works. In 1778, Smeaton measured the 'duty' of a Watt engine and found it to be more than three times the 'duty' of a Newcomen engine.[115] Demand for the new engines as more efficient mine pumps was swift, particularly in Cornwall, where Boulton set up a separate sales and engineering office, hampered only by his insistence on receiving a percentage of the coal saved by the engines, leading to endless disputes with customers.

Boulton encouraged Watt to work on a rotary steam engine, that could be used to power machinery and in 1781 Watt came up with a sun-and-planets gear system that achieved this. The first rotary Watt

---

115. Hills, *Power from Steam*, p. 59. The 'duty' of an engine was the amount of water it raised by one foot using one bushel of coal. Watt's engine had a 'duty' of 18,902,136 lbs compared to a standard Newcomen engine's 'duty' of 5,044,158 lbs and a Smeaton-improved atmospheric engine's 'duty' of 9,636,660 lbs. The bushel itself was an uncertain measurement, being 84 lbs in Newcastle and 88 lbs in London.

270 *Forging Modernity*

engine was sold in 1783 to Wilkinson, for use at Bradley, the second to Whitbread. Since the introduction to the market of Watt's rotary engine effectively coincided with the political changes bringing Pitt to power, I will take up the story of Matthew Boulton's later career, and that of the Boulton & Watt partnership, in the next chapter.

Science

Scientifically, this era was notable for the flowering of modern chemistry. Priestley published his ground-breaking discovery on the nature of combustion in 1774 and the Frenchman Antoine Lavoisier published his more theoretically sound analysis four years later. The dawn of a new age was dramatically illustrated by the artist Joseph Wright (1734-1797) of Derby's 1771 masterpiece, painted three years before Priestley published, with full title: 'The Alchymist, In Search of the Philosopher's Stone, Discovers Phosphorus, and Prays for the Successful Conclusion of His Operation, as Was the Custom of the Ancient Chymical Astrologers'.

Wright, who had close connections with the Lunar Society through Erasmus Darwin and painted several of the Midlands industrialists, notably, Boulton and Arkwright, was an artistic devotee of rationalism and science, even when, as in chemistry, the actual scientists had not yet surpassed their alchemical predecessors.

Another major chemist was Henry Cavendish (1731-1810), who in 1766 discovered hydrogen, naming it 'inflammable air' – Lavoisier later gave it its present name. Cavendish, the grandson of the Whig grandee, the second Duke of Devonshire, was educated privately and at Peterhouse College, Cambridge, after which in 1760 he was elected FRS. He led a reclusive life, performing experiments at his London house; in 1798 he performed the 'Cavendish Experiment', based on John Michell's work, discovering that the density of the earth was 5.448 times that of water. He also performed electrical experiments, but did not publish their results, which included Ohm's law and Coulomb's law. Cambridge's Cavendish Laboratory was endowed by a later relative and named after him.

Finally, a Tory counterpart to the Whig-connected Cavendish was the astronomer and geologist John Michell (1724-93), a true polymath and a founder of the Lunar Society. The son of an Anglican clergyman, Michell was educated at Queens College, Cambridge, where he became a Fellow in 1752, and an FRS in 1760, after which he became the Woodwardian Professor of Geology from 1762-67, then left Cambridge to become Rector of St Michael's Church in Thornhill, Yorkshire. Michell's work included *A Treatise of Artificial Magnets* in 1750, which propounded the inverse-square law of magnetic force and proposed several types of artificial magnets. In 1756, following the Lisbon earthquake, he wrote *Conjectures Concerning the Cause and Observations upon the Phaenomena of Earthquakes*, in which he postulated the existence of faults and that earthquakes propagate through the Earth's crust through force waves; he also identified the Earth's crust for the first time. He devised a torsion balance for measuring the Earth's mass – after his death this resulted in the Cavendish Experiment. In 1767, he used statistical analysis to determine the existence of double stars, influencing William Herschel's work. Finally, in a 1783 paper for the Royal Society's *Philosophical Transactions*, he predicted the existence of black holes.

Political Developments, 1770-83

In 1770 North, previously Chancellor of the Exchequer, assumed power at the head of a mostly Tory government that lasted twelve years. His economic principles were not as well-formed as those of the younger Pitt or Liverpool, but on several occasions, he showed himself competent and sound.

The first demonstration of North's economic capability was his reform of the East India Company, carried out by the East India Company Act 1772, helped by Charles Jenkinson, who had become an India expert during the struggle to reappoint Clive to the governorship of Bengal in 1763-64. Since that time, the Bengal famine of 1770 had wrecked the EIC's reputation, while its attempt to administer the tax system of Bengal, together with excessive purchases of China tea, now rotting in warehouses, had wrecked its finances.

The Treasury had lent the EIC £1.5 million, so the Act forbade dividends of more than 6% until that loan was repaid. The Act also elevated Hastings to Governor-General, with responsibility for all the EIC's operations in India. Most importantly, it prohibited EIC officers from undertaking private trade; this had been notoriously lucrative to them in earlier years, but damaged both the EIC's interests and those of the Indian population. Finally, it established a Supreme Court at Calcutta to provide a local application of the British justice system. Overall, the Act brought the EIC more fully under control of the Crown, but the wars of 1778-82 and the political furore surrounding Hastings' return to England showed that more direct control was required, which was imposed definitively by Pitt's East India Company Act 1784.

By the Tea Act 1773, North and Jenkinson attempted to alleviate the problem of the EIC's tea surplus by selling it at a reduced duty to the American colonies; the EIC foolishly combined most of it into one huge shipment later that year and it ended up at the bottom of Boston harbour. The Act and the tea deserved a better fate.

North's most important purely economic legislation was the Corn Act 1773. The rise in the British population from around 1740 had eliminated the grain export surplus, so the trade was approximately in balance, but fluctuating sharply from year to year. Elizabethan laws had forbidden grain speculation, preventing the market from working properly, so North decided to move to a freely traded system, but with exports forbidden and imports allowed once the corn price was above 48s per quarter and the reverse when the price was below that level. While this would make grain on average more expensive for British consumers, it would support agricultural incomes and, through labour market competition, nominal incomes outside agriculture. An additional second-order effect would be to raise the price of land, making it easier for proprietors to mortgage their land (as had the Duke of Bridgewater) to pay for industrial investment – the low land prices of the 1740s had discouraged such ventures.

North's Corn Laws, and Liverpool's forty years later were a product of their Oxfordshire School economic thinking; they were not simply free traders and did not favour ultra-low labour costs as would many disciples of Adam Smith.

North's next important economic action, implemented by Jenkinson, was a major gold recoinage in 1774. By this time, rising silver prices had caused the bi-metallic standard established by Newton to evolve into a pure gold standard, with silver, not recoined since 1696, only circulating in heavily clipped form. Hence, the gold coinage was recoined, with underweight coins being taken only at their weight, and five million troy ounces of new gold guineas and half-guineas were issued. With a modest issue of copper coinage in these years also, the economy's need for specie was satisfied in the short term but, in the longer term, the shortage remained acute until Liverpool's great recoinage of 1816-17.

The North administration's reaction to the Boston Tea Party was to pass the punitive 'Intolerable Acts'. Of these, the most important was the Quebec Act 1774 which guaranteed the practice of the Catholic faith in Quebec, allowed French law to be used in private disputes and provided for its government by a governor and an appointed legislative council. This ensured Quebec's loyalty to Britain when invaded by an American army the following year but provoked an unpleasant outbreak of Presbyterian religious bigotry in Massachusetts, making its support for independence inevitable.

In the same year, important legislation for a relatively new industry was the Life Assurance Act 1774. This introduced the concept of an insurable interest, so that it became illegal to take out life assurance on a third party without a legitimate economic interest in that person's life, while the maximum sum assured would be the amount of that interest. This stopped all the gambling and third-party assassinations that had taken place with the tontines and annuities of the 1690s, making life assurance a respectable investment for the middle classes and widening its scope.

As a belated exit from medievalism, the Colliers and Salters Act (Scotland) 1775 emancipated the Scottish workers in coal and salt mines, who by a 1606 Act had been placed in permanent bondage to their employer. These relics of earlier working relationships were still common in most continental countries except the Netherlands. In the same year, the Erection of Cottages Act 1775 repealed 1588 legislation that had attempted to eliminate squatters by providing that any new cottage must have no less than four acres of land.

Once news of the British defeat by the Americans in the Battle of Saratoga reached England in late 1777, North became less effective, wishing to retire, but prevented from doing so because George III could not find another prime minister who could be relied upon to prosecute the American war vigorously. From then until 1782, as crises multiplied (and Britain's military and naval position was truly perilous in 1779-80, more perilous than it ever became during the Napoleonic wars) decisions were taken effectively by George III, ably assisted by Jenkinson and the chief ministerial 'fixer', John Robinson.[116]

Nevertheless, some further Acts appeared bearing North's reforming stamp. The Papists Act 1778 reduced the penal provisions of the 1698 Act against Catholics, although it still did not give them the right to vote. The Nonconformist Relief Act 1779 permitted Dissenters to preach and teach provided they were Christian and Protestant and loyal to the Crown. The Papists Act was violently unpopular among the more bigotedly Protestant sections of the population and resulted in the highly destructive Gordon Riots of 1780 in London. These were only ended when Jenkinson as Secretary at War finally obtained legal clearance to deploy against the rioters a regiment of regular troops, which he had ordered to march from Canterbury three days earlier when the disturbances first looked threatening.

---

116. John Robinson (1727-1802). MP for Westmorland and Harwich, 1764-1802. Secretary of the Treasury, 1770-82.

274 *Forging Modernity*

After the news of the British defeat at Yorktown reached London, North lingered for a few months but was subjected to a vote of no confidence in March 1782. Rockingham succeeded him, but died in July, and was followed by Shelburne, whose Tory leanings made him unacceptable to the Rockingham wing of the Whigs. Shelburne fell in March 1783, to be succeeded (after another attempt by the king to recruit Gower, who lacked Commons support) by a coalition between North and the leftist Whig, Charles James Fox,[117] under Portland as figurehead, a government hated by the king and distrusted by most of his subjects.[118]

Gower, Jenkinson and Robinson all backed Pitt's assumption of power in December 1783, even though Pitt was an 'independent Whig'. The period of political instability and Whig dominance lasted only 21 months.

It produced several items of legislation. The Civil List and Secret Service Money Act 1782 was a product of the Whig campaign for 'Economical Reform'. It reduced royal patronage by transferring control of the Civil List to the Treasury; it also abolished the Board of Trade, an exceptionally foolish piece of Whiggery that had to be reversed two years later. Then Gilbert's Act, proposed by Gower's former agent, Thomas Gilbert, under Rockingham and passed under Shelburne, liberalized the system of poor relief. Finally, the Stamp Duties Act 1783 imposed a stamp duty of 3d on every registration of births – this made parish registers thoroughly unreliable.

* * *

At the end of 1783, Britain entered a new era politically, with the advent of William Pitt the Younger. A few months earlier, the world had entered a new era technologically, with the delivery of James Watt's first rotary steam engine.

Qualitatively, 1760-83 saw the advent of the country banking system, allowing ordinary people throughout the nation to obtain finance, the first burst of canal building, financed by local share issues rather than through the City of London, the doubling in patent applications after 1760

---

117. Charles James Fox (1749-1806). MP for Midhurst, Malmesbury and Westminster, 1768-1806. Foreign Secretary and Leader of the House of Commons, 1782, 1783 and 1806. Second son of Henry Fox, 1st Lord Holland.

118. I have on my wall a copy of an October 1783 Gillray cartoon, '*BONUS – MELIOR – OPTIME*' ('Good', 'Better', 'Best'), depicting North, Fox and the Devil.

The Tory-Assisted Take-off, 1761-83

and the plethora of new entrepreneurs, carrying out their businesses in ways never seen before. These were all evidence that Britain's economic state had changed fundamentally and was beginning to move forward in new and more productive directions (as also in a negative sense was the first outburst of Luddism in 1779). That fundamental change had been assisted by policy developments stretching back over a century, but the new Tory statesmen, notably Gower, North and Jenkinson, all played important roles in nurturing the embryonic Industrial Revolution.

8

Pitt, Rotary Steam Engines and War, 1784-1806

Political Developments, 1784-94

The political centrepiece of this period was William Pitt the Younger's Budget speech of 17 February 1792,[1] which marked the first occasion on which a prime minister noted the new forces of the Industrial Revolution. After an optimistic forecast of fifteen years of peace, Pitt analysed the preceding decade's progress in government revenues, and the reasons for that progress:

> What is it that has enabled [the energy of the country] to act with such peculiar vigour and so much beyond the example of former periods? The improvement which has been made in the mode of carrying on almost every branch of manufacture, and the degree to which labour has been abridged, by the invention and application of machinery, have undoubtedly had a considerable share in producing such important effects.[2]

Pitt then praised the easy credit conditions (which would lead to difficulties in the following year partly as a result of the outbreak of war) and continued:

> But there is still another cause, even more satisfactory than these, because it is of a still more extensive and permanent

---

1. W.S. Hathaway (ed.), *The Speeches of William Pitt in the House of Commons* (London: A. Strahan, 1817), pp. 338-62.
2. Ibid., p. 357.

William Pitt, the younger, speaking in the Commons. He fought one revolution and led another. Painting by Anton Hickel.

nature; that constant accumulation of capital, that continual tendency to increase, the operation of which is continually seen in a greater or less proportion, whenever it is not obstructed by some public calamity, or by some mistakes and mischievous policy, but which must be conspicuous and rapid indeed in any country which has once arrived at an advanced state of commercial prosperity.[3]

Pitt recognized the existence of the Industrial Revolution and, in the earlier part of his speech, appeared to praise labour-saving machinery as the fount of prosperity. However, he then fell back on his underlying belief in the wonders of compound interest (the foundation of his Sinking Fund) and quoted Adam Smith in support of his thesis that increasing capital intensity, rather than increasing productivity, was the source of Britain's rising prosperity. It is an important distinction; only Liverpool after 1815 finally recognized the true nature of the continuing changes. The Industrial Revolution was mostly caused by new technology, not just more water wheels.

---

3. Ibid., p. 358.

278   *Forging Modernity*

Pitt's assumption of power, with Gower's help and the backing of George III, upended Britain's political system, although only after his solid victory at the 1784 general election was it clear that the change would last. That election result represented a triumph for the country's underlying Toryism and its opposition to most of the existing political class, epitomized by Charles James Fox and, by this stage, Lord North.

Pitt's government remained somewhat Whiggish for a couple of years, attempting to pass parliamentary reform in 1785 and voting to impeach Warren Hastings in 1786. However, with Gower as its senior member, Thomas Gilbert as Chairman of the House of Commons Ways and Means Committee and Jenkinson as President of the Board of Trade from 1786 (though not in the Cabinet until 1791), the government's underlying Toryism soon became apparent. Pitt's own move towards Toryism was signalled by his voting against repeal of the Test Act, a favourite Whig nostrum (since it benefited Nonconformists but not Catholics) in March 1787.

Pitt's life was in many ways tragic. Groomed for leadership by his domineering, elderly (51 when he was born) father, he achieved the pinnacle of power extraordinarily young, then performed in it with remarkable ability. However, the heroic portrayal by Victorian historians of one who achieved everything as a paragon standing alone is wrong; in his early years of power, his fine economic policies owed much to Gower and Jenkinson, both a generation older. Later, apart from the older Dundas, he amassed a solid collection of able colleagues and younger acolytes who helped him to navigate the difficult war years. Yet, he became fundamentally isolated; he rejected the possibility of marriage to Eleanor Eden, daughter of the political and diplomatic careerist, William, Lord Auckland,[4] and in later years descended into illness, alcoholism and debt, dying at 46. Admiration for the statesman should be accompanied by pity for the man.

Pitt quickly showed his economic abilities. He had read *The Wealth of Nations* as a teenager and absorbed its teachings. Even though the national budget was very shaky when he took over, with debt of £243 million against revenue of £13.2 million in the year to October 1784,[5] he

---

4. William Eden (1744-1814). 1st Baron Auckland from 1793. MP for New Woodstock and Heytesbury, 1774-93. Chief Secretary for Ireland, 1780-82, Ambassador to Spain and the Netherlands, 1787-90, Postmaster General, 1798-1804, President of the Board of Trade, 1806-7. Eleanor Eden (1777-1851). Married Robert Hobart, 4th Earl of Buckinghamshire, 1799.

5. Mitchell (ed.), *British Historical Statistics*, Tables XI-1 and XI-7.

took Smith's advice and lowered customs duties on the easily smuggled items of tea, wine, spirits and tobacco. This, together with energetic customs administration, brought in £2 million of additional revenue and stabilized the nation's finances.

Pitt's East India Company Act 1784 solidified the achievements of North's 1772 Act, bringing India under a London-based Board of Control appointed by the king and making the governor-general in Calcutta clearly the superior of the governors of Bombay and Madras. From this point, India came increasingly under direct rule, with the EIC a mere administrative convenience, while additional territories were added by able governor-generals such as Cornwallis,[6] Wellesley[7] and the Marquess of Hastings.[8] The East India Company Act 1793 extended the company's charter for a further 20 years but made few substantive changes.

The EIC continued expanding its areas of control; Francis Light[9] established the island colony of Penang and its capital George Town off the Malay peninsula in 1786 – its population would grow to 20,000 by the time of his death in 1794. In 1792, the era's most famous attempt at eastward expansion took place, with the expedition of George, Earl Macartney[10] to China seeking to open trade. Regrettably, the great

---

6. Charles Cornwallis (1738-1805). KG 1786. Earl Cornwallis from 1762, 1st Marquess Cornwallis, 1792. MP for Eye 1760-62. Lieutenant General, 1777, commanding forces in North America. Surrendered at Yorktown, 19 October 1781. Governor-General of India, 1786-93, 1805. Master of the Ordnance, 1794-98. Lord Lieutenant of Ireland, 1798-1801. Minister Plenipotentiary to France, 1801-2.

7. Richard Colley Wellesley (1760-1842). Earl of Mornington, 1781-99, Marquess Wellesley from 1799. Governor-General of India, 1798-1805, Foreign Secretary 1809-12, Lord Lieutenant of Ireland 1821-28, 1833-34.

8. Francis Rawdon-Hastings (1754-1826). 1st Marquess of Hastings from 1816, Baron Rawdon, 1783, 2nd Earl of Moira from 1793. Colonel, Adjutant-General and amateur actor in the American War, 1774-81. Commander-in-Chief, Scotland, 1803-6, Master-General of the Ordnance, 1806-7, Governor-General and Commander-in-Chief of India, 1812-23, Governor of Malta, 1824-26.

9. Francis Light (1740-94). East India Company from 1765. Superintendent of Penang, 1786-94.

10. George Macartney (1737-1806). 1st Baron Macartney (Ireland) from 1776, 1st Earl Macartney (Ireland) from 1792, 1st Baron Macartney (GB) from 1795. MP for Cockermouth, Ayr Burghs and Bere Alston, 1768-69, 1774-76, 1780-81. Ambassador to Russia, 1764-66, 1767-68, to China, 1792-94, Chief

280   *Forging Modernity*

Emperor Qianlong,[11] by then 82, rejected Macartney's proposal, as would his son, Emperor Jiaqing,[12] reject a similar offer from William, Lord Amherst[13] in 1816. Who knows what might have happened with a different Chinese response? The beginnings of Chinese industrialization? A happier century for China? Perhaps even a better balance between the Chinese and Western economies?

Another major advance of Pitt's early years was the establishment of Australia, initially as a penal colony, to replace the United States as a repository for malefactors. The first fleet led by Captain Arthur Phillip[14] of six transports carrying 775 convicts, three supply ships and two Royal Navy escorts left Portsmouth on 13 May 1787 and arrived at Sydney (named after Pitt's Home Secretary) in January 1788; it had cost £84,000 to equip and send.

The Quebec Act 1791 divided Britain's Canadian settlements into two, Lower Canada, mostly French-speaking Quebec and sparsely populated Upper Canada, now Ontario, giving both parts representative assemblies. The success of this measure was shown in the War of 1812, when both parts fought together against the aggressive United States.

Pitt's 1786 institution of the Sinking Fund by the National Debt Act 1786 seems strange to a modern observer. We are now used to the governments of 'developed' countries borrowing all the money they want, relying on what seems automatic economic growth and inflation to service the debt. In 1786, there was no structural inflation because of the gold standard and politicians could rely only on population increase to raise national output and debt-servicing capacity – the Industrial Revolution was well underway, but it did not reach politicians'

Secretary for Ireland, 1769-72, Governor of Grenada, 1776-79, Governor of Madras (Chennai), 1781-85, Governor of Cape Colony, 1797-98.

11. Qianlong (1711-99). 6th Emperor of the Qing Dynasty from 1735, abdicated 1796 but retained ultimate power. In response to Macartney's embassy, he wrote to George III: 'Our Celestial Empire possesses all things in prolific abundance and lacks no product within its own borders.'

12. Jiaqing (1760-1820). 7th Emperor of the Qing dynasty from 1796. Fifteenth son of the Qianlong. Opposed both Christianity and Western contact.

13. William Amherst (1773-1857). 2nd Baron Amherst from 1797, 1st Earl Amherst from 1826. Ambassador Extraordinary to China, 1816-17, Governor-General of India, 1823-28.

14. Arthur Phillip (1738-1814). Captain, RN 1781. Governor of New South Wales, 1788-92. Rear-Admiral, 1801, Vice Admiral, 1806, Admiral of the Blue, 1814.

consciousness until Pitt's 1792 Budget speech. The government needed to convince investors that the government had the debt under control and might eventually repay it.

The Nonconformist minister Richard Price,[15] a follower of Shelburne, had published in 1771 *Appeal to the Public on the Subject of the National Debt*, advocating a Sinking Fund, by which a relatively small annual fund would compound and eliminate the national debt within 50 years. North had supported this idea but had been unable to apply it because of the American war; Pitt in 1786 set up a Sinking Fund of £1 million per annum which would be invested in Consols and would compound until it had purchased the entire stock of public debt outstanding. Pitt's Sinking Fund had better protections against alienation than had Walpole's of 60 years earlier.

The Sinking Fund worked as advertised until 1792. Then, after 1793, with wartime borrowings, each new borrowing had its own Sinking Fund attached, so that even in 1813, with the Sinking Fund running at £15 million annually, the whole national debt was supposed to be extinguished within 45 years. The additional Sinking Fund payments, together with the practice of issuing 3% Consols at a deep discount when interest rates were high, ballooned the amount of debt issued to fund the Napoleonic wars.

Issuing extra debt for 22 years to pay into a Sinking Fund when the budget was in deficit and the markets unfavourable has since been mocked, but the Sinking Fund added considerably to the belief of investors that the debt would eventually be repaid; the existence even at the worst point of 1813 of a £150 million Sinking Fund to offset against £900 million of public debt was very comforting. Indeed, the reassurance provided by the Sinking Fund may have prevented default in 1797-98, when the budget deficit was 15% of GDP, the Bank of England suspended payment, the Navy mutinied and Pitt's dozy public finance agent, Boyd, Benfield & Co., slid towards bankruptcy. In any case, since the Sinking Fund commissioners bought Consols in the market, the marginal cost of issuing extra Consols to maintain the Sinking Fund was small.

After the end of the war, several factors led Liverpool to abolish the Sinking Fund in stages up to 1824. By around 1820, it was obvious that industrialization was causing national income to grow beyond mere population increase – so even with a gold standard debt could be expected

---

15. Richard Price (1723-91). FRS 1765. Nonconformist minister and mathematician. Demographer, who wrongly believed that the British population was inexorably declining.

to decline as a percentage of national income without additional budget surpluses. In such circumstances, a Sinking Fund appeared less necessary, while taxes were close to their maximum possible level and a further major war seemed increasingly unlikely. Hence, the Sinking Fund was sacrificed to provide the tax reductions of the 1820s and never reinstated.

Pitt's 1786 treaty with France, negotiated by William Eden, was the first trade opening to France since the abortive Tory attempts of 1713-14. It opened the markets of each country to the other's goods, on payment of a 12% duty in textiles, for example. This was highly advantageous to Britain since Lancashire's textile manufacturers, now well on the way to full mechanization, were far more competitive than their French counterparts. In practice, trade with France was in 1787-92 far below what would have been expected given France's size and population. Moreover, because of its adverse effect on the French textile industry, the treaty became highly unpopular in France, poisoning Anglo-French relations after 1789.

As a reforming prime minister, Pitt brought in several items of legislation dealing with the new industrialization. The Chimney Sweepers Act 1788, prohibited the use of chimney sweeps aged less than eight years old, an early example of regulating working conditions. The Protection of Stocking Frames Act 1788 made stealing or breaking textile machinery a felony punishable by seven to fourteen years' transportation – it would be reinforced several times, notably, by the Destruction of Stocking Frames etc. Act 1812. The Stage Coaches Act 1788 was the first piece of stagecoach safety legislation; it stated that no more than six people were allowed to ride on the roof.

To modern eyes, one of the most important political developments of the 1780s was the birth of the anti-slavery movement, first as a campaign to prohibit British participation in the slave trade, then as a campaign to outlaw slavery itself in British possessions. The movement picked up momentum through the activities of Clarkson and Wilberforce in the 1780s, but the first legislation on the subject was sponsored by the Tory Sir William Dolben,[16] who had succeeded Newdigate as MP for Oxford University in 1780. The Slave Trade Act 1788 restricted the number of slaves that could be carried to 1.67 per ton of the ship's burthen and one per ton above 207 tons. This curb on slave overcrowding brought a substantial decline in slave mortality on the Middle Passage in the 1790s. Further attempts were made to abolish the trade, but success came only in 1807.

---

16. Sir William Dolben (1727-1814). 3rd Bt from 1756. MP for Oxford University and Northamptonshire, 1768-74, 1780-1806.

Pitt's Toryism was cemented by the Regency Crisis of 1788-89. George III's descent into 'madness' (or possibly the recurrent disease of porphyria) in November 1788 caused the Whigs to get excited, since the young Prince of Wales (the future George IV) was then firmly in their camp. They demanded an immediate Regency, which they would use to remove Pitt from office. Several ministers, notably, the Lord Chancellor Edward, Lord Thurlow,[17] played a double game, seeking to retain office under a Regency. Pitt delayed, then, when he had finally brought in a Regency Bill in February 1789, the king showed signs of recovery and the Whigs were thwarted. Political lines were hardened by this crisis, with Pitt growing closer to those ministers such as Gower, Jenkinson (now Lord Hawkesbury) and Dundas, who had supported the king and Pitt throughout.

The French Revolution, which began with the storming of the Bastille on 14 July 1789, further shook political alignments. Conservative Whigs like Edmund Burke[18] and Portland were soon repelled by the increasingly radical turn of events, with Burke first speaking against the revolution in February 1790 and publishing his *Reflections upon the Revolution in France* in November. Accordingly, they began to move towards Pitt politically, even though their leaders did not join Pitt's Cabinet until 1794.

Pitt won a second election victory in 1790, slightly increasing his majority to about 340 government to 183 opposition. By this stage, his reputation was assured, as the economy had enjoyed several years of unprecedented progress. His Cabinet was strengthened by the retirement of several mediocre Whigs and their replacement by superior talents such as Dundas, Grenville and Hawkesbury, who joined the Cabinet in 1791.

After Pitt's Budget speech of February 1792, the international situation steadily darkened. France declared war on Austria in April 1792, Prussia and Austria invaded France in August and were soundly defeated at the Battle of Valmy on 20 September. Then, on 21 January 1793, the French government executed Louis XVI, declaring war on Britain on 1 February. The war would last 22 years, with only a year's respite between 1802 and 1803.

---

17. Edward Thurlow (1731-1806). 1st Baron Thurlow from 1778. MP for Tamworth, 1765-78. Solicitor General, 1770-71, Attorney General 1771-78, Lord Chancellor 1778-83, 1783-92.
18. Edmund Burke (1729-97). Whig MP for Wendover, Malton and Bristol, 1765-94. Paymaster of the Forces, 1782, 1783-84. Author of *Reflections on the Revolution in France* (1790).

The outbreak of war completed the process by which many conservative Whigs had been moving towards Pitt's government. The slippery, former Northite, Loughborough[19] replaced the equally slippery Thurlow as Lord Chancellor in January 1793. Then, in July 1794, Spencer,[20] Windham,[21] Portland and Fitzwilliam[22] joined the Cabinet, enlarging it, with only the elderly Stafford (the former Gower) retiring.

This enlargement of the ministry was not a move towards 'liberalism'. It made the government more repressive against the working classes as its new members had pre-1760 Whig attitudes, with only Fitzwilliam having liberal instincts and resigning in March 1795. However, it made the government's Commons majority overwhelming, with the main Foxite rump of the Whigs, supporting peace with France and increasingly committed to parliamentary reform, numbering fewer than 100 members and absenting itself from the Commons for long periods.

Economic Developments

In the period to 1792 the economy's buoyancy was increased by good policy, the ending of the American war and a wealth boost of about £83 million from the rise in 3% Consols' prices from 55 in 1784 to 90 in 1792. Table 6.1 suggests a modest acceleration in GDP per capita growth, from 13.8% in 1771-81 to 16.8% in 1781-91. Per capita real GDP was over 40% higher in 1791 than at the early-century peak of 1731, despite a 40% increase in population, an impressive demonstration of the life-enhancing effects of even the earliest industrialization. The decade was also prosperous for Ireland, where the removal of several British

---

19. Alexander Wedderburn (1733-1805). 1st Baron Loughborough from 1780, 1st Earl of Rosslyn from 1801. MP for Ayr Burghs, Richmond, Bishop's Castle, 1761-69, 1770-74, 1778-80. Solicitor General, 1771-78, Attorney General, 1778-80, Chief Justice of the Common Pleas, 1780-93. Lord Chancellor, 1793-1801.

20. George Spencer (1758-1834). 2nd Earl Spencer from 1783. Lord Privy Seal, 1794, First Lord of the Admiralty, 1794-1801, Home Secretary, 1806-7.

21. William Windham (1750-1810). MP for Norwich, St Mawes, New Romney and Higham Ferrers, 1784-1810. Chief Secretary for Ireland, 1783, Secretary at War, 1794-1801, Secretary of State for War and Colonies, 1806-7.

22. William Wentworth-Fitzwilliam (1748-1833). 4th Earl Fitzwilliam from 1756. Nephew and heir of the 2nd Marquess of Rockingham. Lord President of the Council, 1794, Lord Lieutenant of Ireland, 1794-95, 1806, Minister without Portfolio, 1806-7. Lord Lieutenant of the West Riding of Yorkshire, 1798-1819.

Pitt, Rotary Steam Engines and War, 1784-1806

trade restrictions and the recovery of the Irish parliament's autonomy produced relative peace, progress and contentment.

Technologically, James Watt's rotary steam engine was applied only slowly after its introduction. The principal feature was an increase in trade through Pitt's liberalizing policies. Imports increased from £12.7 million in 1781 to £19.7 million in 1791, while exports rose more rapidly, from £11.3 million to £22.7 million.

Demographics and continuing improvements in agricultural productivity combined to have an economic effect that may have exceeded that of the still limited industrialization. Enclosures accelerated still further, depriving the rural poor of their livelihoods (albeit increasing potato growing) but spreading the coverage of high-productivity modern agriculture, and increasing average farm size – 52% of the tenant farms on the Gower estates were over 200 acres in 1807-13, compared with 32% in 1759-79.[23] Technologically, the most important advance was the drum threshing machine, designed to separate grain from its husks and stalks, patented by the Scottish engineer and millwright, Andrew Meikle (1719-1811), in 1788; he had been working on the design for about a decade. Meikle made little money from his invention and was receiving poor relief by 1809, but its use spread, nonetheless. The threshing machine, particularly when powered by a steam engine, greatly reduced the labour needed in a harvest, further increasing agricultural productivity. The French economist, Jean-Baptiste Say,[24] who visited England in 1814, wrote in *De l'Angleterre et des Anglais*:

> But it is principally the introduction of machines in the arts, which has made the production of riches more economical. There are almost no big farms in England where, for example, threshing machines are not used, by means of which, in a large operation, more work is done in a day than was done in a month by ordinary methods.[25]

The mechanization of agriculture was given a vast boost by the war. Britain was now a major importer of grain, yet the war cut off trade intermittently from its sources in eastern Europe. This brought high

---

23. Rule, *The Vital Century*, Table 3.3, p. 65.
24. Jean-Baptiste Say (1767-1832). French economist. Author of *Traité d'economie politique* (1803) and *De l'Angleterre et des Anglais* (1815). Originator of Say's law. Co-founder of École spéciale de commerce et d'industrie, 1819, the world's first business school.
25. Say, *De l'Angleterre et des Anglais* (Paris: Chez Arthus Bertrand, 1815), pp29-30. Author's translation as no English translation appears to exist.

prices, exacerbated by bad harvests in several years, notably, 1795 and 1800. The high prices, endemic after 1800, brought high profits for landowners, at least in years with decent harvests. Conversely, labour was drained from agriculture by the new industries and by service in the expanded army, navy and militia. Hence, the landowners mechanized, using machines such as Meikle's thresher to increase output while reducing the labour force needed for the harvest. Overall, capital investment in agriculture doubled from 8% of rentals in the 1780s to 16% of rentals in 1801-10.[26] High prices also led landowners to bring marginal land into production.

Coal production continued its rapid expansion from 7,550,000 metric tons in 1781-85 to 12,960,000 metric tons in 1801-5, a rate of increase of 2.7% annually, or 1.9% per capita per annum, significantly faster than the previous period. The Staffordshire (by 3.9% per annum to 1,225,000 metric tons annual output) and Lancashire (5% per annum to 1,100,000 metric tons) coalfields expanded rapidly, but they were joined by the South Wales coalfield, expanding by 5.4% per annum to 1,000,000 metric tons. The growth of these three groups of coalfields reflected the impact of low-cost canal transportation (the Glamorganshire Canal in South Wales opened in 1798).[27]

Economically, the war made the late 1790s the worst period the British economy suffered between the 1640s and the 1940s. Real GDP per capita declined by 28% between 1791 and 1801, as much as in the US Great Depression of the 1930s but from a much lower base. Living standards plummeted, as did real wages (preventing US Great Depression-like levels of unemployment) and 1795 and 1800 were the last years of widespread near-famine in the United Kingdom outside Ireland.

There were several reasons for this decline. The war, which was initially financed mostly by budget deficits, pushed up borrowing costs – Pitt as wartime Chancellor of the Exchequer failed to realize the scale of the problem and was slow in devising new taxation mechanisms to meet the vastly increased government expenditure, which trebled between the fiscal years 1792 and 1797. These deficits caused the price of Consols to fall dramatically, giving the economy a negative 'wealth shock' of about 50% of GDP to the 1797 nadir, making capital both scarce and expensive.

---

26. Rule, *The Vital Century*, Table 3.2, p. 60.
27. Mitchell (ed.), *British Historical Statistics*, Table IV-3, p. 247, with interpolation for the 1781-85 and 1801-5 Staffordshire, Lancashire and Midland output figures.

There was a major credit crisis in 1793, causing a record number of 1,956 bankruptcies,[28] almost twice the previous peak, as the easy money of the pre-war years disappeared. Later, the country's near-insolvency in 1797, suspending gold payments in February, caused a further crisis in confidence, although 1797's bankruptcies were only two thirds of the 1793 level. That crisis of confidence was justified, since the government's 1797 budget deficit was 15.9% of GDP, based on modern calculations, and the deficit remained above 10% of GDP until 1801, except in 1799. Even after the invention of income tax in 1798, yields from the tax were inadequate until its 1803 reform by Addington. Financial conditions were generally more hostile to industry and business in the late 1790s that at any time since the mid-seventeenth century.

The ill effect of huge budget deficits was compounded by Pitt having entrusted the bulk of the government's huge funding needs not to Barings, already solid and flourishing and used by Shelburne at the end of the American war but to Boyd, Benfield & Co., a bank founded only in March 1793 by the Tory Walter Boyd[29] on the ruins of an expropriated Paris operation. Boyd, Benfield made large profits at first but got into severe difficulties in late 1796 as Consol prices relentlessly declined – the stress on bond issue underwriters in the early years of war was an unfortunate side-effect of Gideon's ingenious Consol structure. After two years staggering on with the help of government bailouts, the firm folded in March 1799, after which the government turned to Barings.

Pitt's failure to rely for the government's financial needs on a sound house blots his reputation as a financial manager. Boyd's failure made the country's credit position in 1797-99 even more difficult than was inevitable, damaging market confidence and bringing distress sales of Boyd, Benfield's large government debt holdings.

Inflation and food shortages forced down real wages, with the London bread price rising from 6.3d for a quartern loaf in 1791 to 15.5d

---

28. Ibid., Table XII-20, where I have used the 'Official Statistics' figure throughout.
29. Walter Boyd (1754-1837). Tory MP for Shaftesbury and Lymington, 1796-1802 and 1823-30. Founded Boyd, Ker in Paris, 1785; fled to London, 1792. Founded Boyd, Benfield & Co., 1793. Raised two £18 million loans for government in 1795 but failed on £7.5 million loan in 1796. Partnership dissolved, March 1799; Boyd declared bankruptcy, March 1800. Travelled to France, 1802, to try to rescue French assets; imprisoned until 1814. Recovered some French assets, 1817-21, and discharged debts, 1822. Left around £240,000.

in 1801.[30] Real wages were especially weak in manufacturing, while several poor harvests meant that high prices did not bring farmers the income they needed to expand production. In addition, Ireland had a miserable decade, with poor harvests, the population rising sharply, trade barriers still blocking access to the British market and considerable unrest, culminating in the Irish rebellion of 1798.

The first year of real distress was 1795, with the London price of a quartern loaf at 9.6d. In that year the parish of Speenhamland in Berkshire devised the Speenhamland system of poor relief, which was generally more generous than the 1601 Poor Law's 1s a week. If the 'gallon loaf' (equivalent to two quartern loaves) cost 12d, then the Speenhamland magistrates would subsidize the income of a working man with a wife and two children to 7s 6d per week, compared with the 4s outright allowance under the Poor Law. If the price of the gallon loaf rose to 2s, equivalent to 12d for the quartern loaf (which it did in London in 1800, 1801, 1805 and 1809-13), then the Speenhamland subsistence level for the four-person family would be increased to 13s a week, making subsidy payments far greater than under the Poor Law.

In practice, the Speenhamland system proved expensive and was only feasible for relatively wealthy non-urban parishes in southern England, many of which adopted it, although it was never codified into national law. It also provided perverse incentives, allowing landlords to raise rents and employers to reduce wages, relying on the parish to provide relief. Nevertheless, the Speenhamland system provided a welcome income subsidy to the poor in very difficult times, like the Poor Law, reducing the costs of failure and unemployment.

In nominal terms, foreign trade grew; imports at official values rose from £19.7 million in 1791 to £32.8 million in 1801 and exports (domestic plus re-exports) rose from £22.7 million to £42.3 million. The real-terms performance was less impressive, with real imports declining by 4% during the decade, while real exports rose by 8%. Nevertheless, given the war, the trade performance showed considerable underlying strength.

After 1801, even though the war paused for only a year with the Peace of Amiens, the financial strain diminished substantially. Public expenditure increased, but slightly less than GDP, so declining from 25.5% to 24.8% of GDP between 1801 and 1806. Meanwhile, more

---

30. London bread prices per quartern loaf, in pence, are given in Mitchell (ed.), *British Historical Statistics*, Table XIV-22, p. 770.

effective financial management from Addington and Lord Henry Petty[31] increased public income from 15.3% of GDP to 20.5%, so lowering the public sector deficit from 10.2% of GDP to 4.3% of GDP. The price of Consols also recovered somewhat from the 1797-98 low of around 50%, averaging 61% in 1801 and 62% in 1806, providing a modest positive wealth effect.

Economically, 1801-6 saw a slow recovery, helped by the increasing stability of the financial sector with no further agricultural crises like those of 1795 and 1800. However, living standards in 1806 were still below those of 1781 and far below those of 1791.

Economic Effect of War

Overall, the war had three effects on the British economy, one of which was very detrimental to industrialization. First, the massive spending on war items had a modest Keynesian effect in increasing output. Consumption was increased by borrowing, but the borrowing was raised in a mostly (though not entirely – there was some foreign demand for Consols) closed financial system, so the net stimulative effect of the extra expenditure was small. Second, there was a highly negative effect on industrialization through the capital markets, raising interest rates, reducing confidence and making private sector financing hard to obtain. The sad story below of this period's canals tells its own tale; so also does the slowing of progress in steam engine technology, which did not lead to either the mass adoption of high-pressure engines or viable railways until after the war ended.

Conversely, the war years greatly expanded the 'military-industrial complex', which had spin-off effects in both technology and production methods. The heavy military expenditure had a direct effect in stimulating the process of industrialization, particularly in the iron industries, but as important was the manufacturing effect of that spending. Most of it was devoted to arms, ammunition and equipment produced in unprecedented quantities, revolutionizing technologies, production techniques and know-how in several sectors of the economy.

---

31. Henry Petty-Fitzmaurice (1780-1863). 3rd Marquess of Lansdowne from 1809. Whig MP for Calne, Cambridge University and Camelford, 1802-9. Chancellor of the Exchequer, 1806-7, Home Secretary, 1827-28, Lord President of the Council, 1830-34, 1835-41, 1846-52, Leader of the House of Lords, 1846-52, Minister without Portfolio, 1852-58.

290 *Forging Modernity*

During the Napoleonic wars, the intensity of musket and rifle manufacturing increased markedly. The Royal Ordnance standardized its demand on a somewhat simpler gun design than the previous long 'Brown Bess' musket, which could be manufactured by a wider range of producers. It retained its system of subcontracting manufacturing to private-sector producers and assemblers. Output, centred primarily on Birmingham, soared tenfold from previous early-1780s peaks, to around 700,000 pieces per annum in the last decade of the war, compared with an average combined output of 190,000 guns per year from the fourteen French government-owned works.[32]

Most small arms manufacturing remained hand-crafted, although the level of specialization increased further, but steam engines were introduced into barrel making by the Birmingham firms, Ketlands and Whateleys in 1803. Boulton & Watt also benefited from the massive expansion in gun-making during the war, like most of the Birmingham metalworking complex.

Other than handguns and the Carron output, most military and naval weaponry was manufactured by government-owned arsenals, the largest of which was at Woolwich, and by government-owned dockyards, the largest of which were at Portsmouth and Chatham. In these facilities too, major technical advances occurred. The Royal Arsenal at Woolwich had a maximum manpower of 5,000 in 1815; it manufactured ammunition, field guns and gun carriages as well as containing artillery and engineer personnel within its walled site of more than 100 acres. It was also the main centre for military research, developing Sir William Congreve's[33] rockets, the first of which was produced in 1805, as well as improved gun and gun carriage designs and more efficient explosives, and manufacturing the first marine steam engines in Britain. Its cutting-edge technology with engineering work by Marc Isambard Brunel[34] and manufacturing by Henry Maudslay[35] included the use of steam engines (for a patented planing machine and

---

32. Satia, *Empire of Guns*, p 141.
33. William Congreve (1772-1828). FRS 1811. 2nd Bt from 1814. Tory MP for Plymouth, 1818-28. Demonstrated solid fuel military rockets, 1805.
34. Marc Isambard Brunel (1769-1849). Kt 1841. FRS 1814. Father of Isambard Kingdom Brunel (1806-59). French royalist, left France, 1793. US, 1793-99, acquiring US citizenship. Moved to Britain, 1799, and designed machinery for Portsmouth works. Built Thames Tunnel, 1825-43.
35. Henry Maudslay (1771-1831). Bramah & Co., 1790-97. Developed screw-cutting lathe, 1800, block-making machines for Portsmouth Block Works, 1803-8. Bench Micrometer, 1805. Manufactured marine steam engines

saw mills) and some mass production methods at its Royal Carriage Works, built in 1803.

The government was also a manufacturer of gunpowder, having bought the Royal Gunpowder Mills at Waltham Abbey in 1787. As with gun manufacturing, production was scaled up hugely for the wars, though the mills remained water-powered until the 1850s. Gunpowder was moved from building to building in the process of manufacture, using a flow production method common in modern process industries.

The naval dockyards at Chatham, Portsmouth, Plymouth and Sheerness were also important centres of industrial innovation. In 1802, Maudslay devised the steam dredger, a military invention with immediate non-military benefits in the construction of new harbour works. Within the dockyards, the most important new enterprise was the Portsmouth Dockyard Block Mills, making naval blocks, authorized in 1802 at the request of Sir Samuel Bentham,[36] with a total of 45 machines designed by Brunel and manufactured by Maudsley. The complex was developed between 1803 and 1805, with three production lines, driven by two steam engines and a production that ramped up to 130,000 blocks in 1808 – the world's first example of true mass production. Regrettably, its technology was kept so secret that its manufacturing techniques were not quickly adopted elsewhere – standardization of parts was not universal until the 1850s, while mass production on an assembly line was even further from general adoption.

Another area of military innovation was communication. The Ordnance Survey mapping of England and Wales began in 1790 and was mostly completed in the next two decades. One-inch-to-one-mile maps were published for general use, the first of Kent in 1801; by 1810 most of England and Wales was available. A system of shuttle telegraphs, by which messages could be sent considerable distances in a few minutes, was initiated by France in 1790-95. Britain quickly copied it, with Admiralty systems between London and Deal, Yarmouth and Portsmouth by 1808. Regrettably, an Admiralty economy drive resulted in the system being dismantled immediately after the initial peace in 1814, so that the news

---

from 1815, building HMS *Lightning*, first Royal Navy steam-powered ship, 1823. Thames Tunnel tunnelling shield, 1825.

36. Samuel Bentham (1757-1831). Knight of St George (Russia). Brother of Jeremy Bentham (1748-1832). Served as engineer in Russian forces, 1780-91. Inspector General of Naval Works, 1796-1805.

292   *Forging Modernity*

of Waterloo could not be transmitted by the Deal-London telegraph but reached London in Major Henry Percy's gig.[37]

The huge military spending on procurement disappeared after 1815, leading to severe downsizing for most military contractors and in some cases, such as Brunel, to bankruptcy. With the exception of the Admiralty telegraph,[38] the technologies invented for military use did not disappear and nor did the production and management techniques those contracts had generated.

Steam Engine Developments

Technologically this period's major development was the gradual adoption of Watt-type steam engines, vigorously protected under the Boulton & Watt patent until 1800. Initially, the engines were manufactured outside the Soho works, frequently by Wilkinson, but increasing concern over the Watt patent caused Boulton & Watt to bring manufacturing in-house at a specialized manufacturing facility from 1796: the Soho Manufactory, which used standardized interchangeable parts. Within Soho, new workforce management methods were practised, training workers to specialize in particular operations and even to train their sons up to those operations, thus creating the 'semi-skilled worker' of nineteenth-century engineering.[39]

Since the initial scheme of pricing the engines by the amount of coal saved proved unworkable, Watt in 1783 invented the horsepower (hp), a rate of 33,000 ft-lbs per minute at which a strong horse might work. Engines could then be sold based on their standardized horsepower rating, but a rental pricing was still used, an annual fee of £5 per hp outside London and £6 10s per hp in London.[40] Performance was further improved by using double-acting engines, in which the rods were both pushed and pulled by opposing steam-filled cylinders. The Whitbread engine, installed in 1785, and an engine used to power Boulton's Albion

---

37. An account of Percy's journey is given in Brian Cathcart, *The News from Waterloo: The Race to Tell Britain of Wellington's Victory* (London: Faber & Faber, 2015).

38. Sir Francis Ronalds' (1788-1873) workable electric telegraph was turned down in 1816 by the Admiralty's Sir John Barrow (1764-1848) as 'wholly unnecessary' – this advance had to await the Great Western Railway in 1839.

39. Rule, *The Vital Century*, p. 154.

40. Shena Mason, *Matthew Boulton: Selling What All the World Desires* (Birmingham: Birmingham City Council, 2009), p. 67.

A 1785 Watt rotary engine from Whitbread brewery. Gigantic, but still not very efficient. Image by David Maciulaitis.

Mill in London, grinding wheat at the rate of 150 bushels per hour (although burned down in 1791), were used as demonstrations of what engines could do.

The engines' sales growth was not smooth; many engines worked erratically, as they required local installation and a skilled local 'engineer' to run them, while Boulton & Watt were better at devising complex pricing schemes than at providing after-sales service. Before 1800, 496 Boulton & Watt engines were installed,[41] but this was still only one third of the 1,400 Newcomen engines installed. In 1785 both Boulton and Watt were recognized by election as Fellows of the Royal Society.

In the mid-1780s, Boulton turned his attention to coinage, establishing the Soho Mint, with eight steam-driven presses and a capacity of 500 coins per minute. In 1789, he wrote to Hawkesbury, then President of the Board of Trade:

> In the course of my journeys, I observe that I receive upon an average two-thirds counterfeit halfpence for change at

---

41. Hills, *Power from Steam*, p. 70. Thirty-eight per cent of the engines were for pumping and 62% rotary, mostly for the textile industry.

toll-gates, etc. and I believe the evil is daily increasing, as the spurious money is carried into circulation by the lowest class of manufacturers, who pay with it the principal part of the wages of the poor people they employ. They purchase from the subterraneous coiners 36 shillings'-worth of copper (in nominal value) for 20 shillings, so that the profit derived from the cheating is very large.[42]

Hawkesbury was already a strong proponent of mechanical milling of coins for: 'machines, which act with a given force, can work with more truth and accuracy than the arm of man'.[43] However, Hawkesbury was not yet a member of the Cabinet and in 1790 Pitt's government postponed the question of recoinage indefinitely.

Only after the Bank of England stopped payment in 1797 did Hawkesbury, now Earl of Liverpool (since 1796), act. It was clear that the working classes could not be expected to have faith in government-issued paper money after the hyper-inflation of the American continentals and the French *assignats*. To relieve the huge volume of counterfeit coinage circulating, Liverpool decided to issue a large volume of copper coinage. Since copper from Welsh mines, notably, the Parys deposit, was readily available, the new coinage would have a bullion value close to its nominal value, unlike coinage in 'token' form. This would ensure that public confidence in the currency was maintained and inflation avoided even though high-value payments would be in paper only.

By this time, Boulton & Watt was coining rupees for the East India Company with steam presses at the rate of 30,000 per hour.[44] Accordingly, Liverpool summoned Boulton to London and by a proclamation of 26 July instructed him to strike with his steam presses 500 tons of new penny and two-penny pieces in copper. The pieces would weigh one ounce and two ounces, around the bullion equivalent of their value, also allowing them to be used as weights as well as coinage. The result was some ten million of the 'cartwheel' penny and two-penny pieces, numismatically important, hard to counterfeit and, indeed, beautiful, with the design stamped into the metal rather than raised from it. By coining copper coins at their bullion value and putting no limit on their

---

42. Samuel Smiles, *Lives of Boulton and Watt* (London: John Murray, 1865), quoted on Wikipedia.
43. First Earl of Liverpool, *A Treatise on the Coins of the Realm: In a Letter to the King* (Oxford: Oxford University Press, 1805), p. 227.
44. Charles, 2nd Baron Colchester (ed.), *The Diaries and Correspondence of Charles Abbot, Lord Colchester*, 3 vols (London: J. Murray, 1861), Vol. 1, p. 87.

tender, Liverpool effectively put working-class Britain temporarily onto a copper standard.

Boulton and Watt both retired in 1800 (Boulton died in 1809, Watt lived until 1819). Their business carried on, owned by the Boulton and Watt families but with principal intellectual input from William Murdoch (1754-1839), a partner in the business from 1810 to 1830. The son of a Scottish millwright on James Boswell's[45] estate, Murdoch walked 300 miles to Birmingham in 1777 to seek a job with Watt. He became an engine erector for Boulton & Watt customers in the Cornish mining industry, and invented several steam engine improvements, including the sun-and-planet gear that allowed Watt to produce a rotary steam engine. In 1784, he produced a prototype model steam locomotive, but Watt discouraged him from pursuing the idea (which was in any case impracticable with Watt's low-pressure engines).

Murdoch's discoveries in chemistry included an iron cement, useful in sealing steam engines, and a first attempt at aniline dyes, patented in 1791 but fully developed only in the 1850s. His most important long-term discovery was a process for extracting gas from coal and using it in gas light, which he developed in the early 1790s – his residence at Redruth, Cornwell, was the first to be lit by gas, in 1792. In 1798, he returned to Birmingham and continued his gas experiments, lighting the outside of the Soho Manufactory by gas to celebrate the Peace of Amiens in 1802. Boulton & Watt became leaders in the early gas lighting market but failed to develop their capabilities in street lighting and left the business in 1814.

From 1817, Murdoch led Boulton & Watt into the business of marine engines, carrying out successful trials with the P/S *Caledonia* (a paddle-wheel steamship), built in Scotland in 1815, whose engines the company replaced before selling it to a Danish buyer. Murdoch's career indicates the breadth of industrial experimentation and innovation that had been achieved by this period; the partnership of a creative inventor with a substantial and innovative engineering company was highly fruitful.

The careers of Boulton and Watt were not entirely positive for steam engine development, because of their exploitation of Watt's patent, which Boulton had artificially generalized and extended by 1775 Act of Parliament to 1800 instead of its original termination date of 1783. They made repeated efforts in the 1790s to obtain legislation extending

---

45. James Boswell (1740-95). 9th Laird of Auchinleck from 1782. Landowner, barrister, author of *Life of Samuel Johnson* (1791).

their patent further beyond 1800, thereby perpetuating their iron grip on steam engine technology. Fortunately, these were unsuccessful.

Boulton's aggressive exploitation of this patent buried the work of Jonathan Hornblower Jr (1753-1815) of the steam-engine-building Hornblower family, who in 1781 had patented the first compound steam engine, which achieved more thermal efficiency by having a high-pressure cylinder and a low-pressure cylinder through which the steam successively passed. He was forced by Boulton to abandon production of his invention. His brother, Jabez Carter Hornblower (1744-1814), was also driven out of business in 1799 and thrown into debtors' prison by Boulton's aggressive legal assertion of the Watt patent.

One creative steam engine inventor who lacked Boulton's business savvy and so never achieved financial success was Richard Trevithick (1771-1833). The son of a Cornish mining captain, Trevithick grew up around the steam engines pumping water out of Cornish mines. He began by building high-pressure water engines to work hammers etc., then determined that metallurgy had improved sufficiently to risk building high-pressure steam engines, making his first high-pressure steam engine in 1799. High-pressure engines were far more thermally efficient than Watt's low-pressure engines, and so could be made much smaller. One application this made possible for the first time was locomotive engines.

In 1801, Trevithick made a steam locomotive that carried passengers up Camborne Hill. Then, in 1802, he built a stationary engine at Coalbrookdale, making 40 strokes to the minute with an unprecedented pressure of 145 lbs per square inch. The following year he built a high-pressure engine to power a dredging machine. Then, in 1804, he built a high-pressure steam engine to drive a hammer at the Pen-y-darren Iron Works at Merthyr Tydfil to which wheels were attached so it carried a 10-ton load a distance of ten miles at 2.4mph.

Trevithick's further exploits were less successful. He built an experimental rail locomotive, 'Catch Me Who Can', which ran on a circular track at 'Trevithick's Steam Circus' near Euston at a top speed of 12mph. The Steam Circus may have been a paying proposition, but his attempt from 1805-9 to build a tunnel under the Thames with Cornish miners was a disaster – the Cornish miners were used to tunnelling through rock, not the slushy alluvial deposits of the lower Thames basin. As a result of these failures, Trevithick went bankrupt in 1812.

He then spent several years in South America, building successful engines for mines in Peru, where the altitude was too high for low-pressure engines, before returning to England in 1827. His last project was a 1,000-ft iron column to celebrate the passage of the Reform Bill. Nevertheless, both his high-pressure engines and his steam locomotives were carried on to later critically important success by other men.

After the expiry of Watt's patent, Arthur Woolf (1766-1837) developed a compound steam engine, patented in 1804, using the tighter tolerances developed during his work under Joseph Bramah (see below). His engine was essentially a combination of a Trevithick high-pressure cylinder and a Watt low-pressure condenser. Initially, it became most popular in France and other continental countries, where coal was more expensive than in Britain, but later its usage spread more widely. Woolf thereafter moved to Cornwall and, by combining his compound engine design with the tight engineering tolerances he had learned with Bramah, produced from 1815 stationary compound 'Cornish' engines with a 'duty' of over 50 million pounds, nearly three times the efficiency of Boulton & Watt's low-pressure engines.[46]

This period's other steam application was in marine engines. The first working steamboat appears to have been French, the *Pyroscaphe*, a 40-ft paddle steamer built in 1783 by the Marquis de Jouffroy d'Abbans (1751-1832) on the Saône river but never accepted by the Académie des Sciences because it could not be viewed in Paris. The first practical steamboat was the 56-ft *Charlotte Dundas*, built by William Symington (1764-1831) and launched in January 1803 on the Forth and Clyde Canal, whose chairman was Henry Dundas, now Viscount Melville. Symington was a steam engine designer and colliery manager who had built the first horizontal engine and obtained a patent in 1801, after the expiry of the Watt patent. Regrettably, Melville and the canal company failed to follow up Symington's design while the aged Bridgewater, who had ordered eight replicas of the *Charlotte Dundas*, died without direct heirs later that year.

Robert Fulton (1765-1815), an American engineer, was present at the trials of the *Charlotte Dundas*, then built a steamboat in France which sank in August 1803. After returning to the United States with a Boulton & Watt engine in 1806 and receiving funding from Robert R. Livingston (1746-1813), he built the first commercially successful steamboat the *North River Steamboat* (colloquially known as the *Clermont* after Livingston's estate), which began carrying passengers up the Hudson (North) River from New York to Albany in August 1807, taking 32 hours.

This was the first significant area in which US innovation outpaced British (it used a British-built engine, but of Fulton's design). Its success

---

46. Hills, *Power from Steam*, p. 108.

298   *Forging Modernity*

derived from the greater commercial need on that widely spaced
continent, with huge, broad navigable rivers connecting several of its
population centres. (Paddle steamers were potentially damaging to
the fabric of Britain's narrow canals.) As always, marginal cost/benefit
factors determined the first adoption of a technology that was initially
superior in few cases.

Textiles

The textile industry was now the principal nexus of industrial growth;
its fastest growth in output, at 12.76% annually, came in 1780-90, a true
explosion of economic impact.[47] Over time, many but not all textile
factories moved from water to steam power, installing Watt engines as
a central power source for a wide variety of equipment. The transition
was gradual, and the early experiments were not always successful; the
first steam-powered mill built in 1786 by George and James Robinson at
Papplewick, Nottinghamshire, powered with a Boulton & Watt engine,
failed within a few years.

The industry's further growth was facilitated by the invention in
the United States in 1793 of the cotton gin, a mechanical device that
removed seeds from cotton, by Eli Whitney (1765-1825). This device
made US cotton producers, based on slave labour, more cost-competitive
than Indian and Egyptian competitors, particularly after the Louisiana
Purchase of 1803 more than doubled the potentially available cotton
growing area; raw cotton prices for the British textile industry steadily
declined.

In the 1780s, exports of cotton goods began their spectacular rise,
increasing from £296,000 in 1781 to £1.64 million in 1791. Cloth milled
in the West Riding also rose rapidly from 4.7 million yards in 1781 to 10.6
million yards in 1791. Perhaps most indicative of the industry's strength,
raw cotton imports more than doubled from 11.4 million pounds in 1784,
the first full year of American peace, to 28.7 million pounds in 1791.[48]

Between 1791 and 1806, raw cotton imports doubled again from 28.7
million pounds in 1791 to 58.1 million pounds in 1806, while exports
of cotton goods increased sixfold from £1.6 million to £10.5 million,
representing 25% of the country's total exports by 1806. Yorkshire's

---

47. Rule, *The Vital Century*, Table 4.5, p. 107.
48. Mitchell (ed.), *British Historical Statistics*, Table IX-8 (cotton goods
    exports), Table VI-12 (West Riding milled cloth), Table VI-1 (raw cotton
    imports).

West Riding began to lose its pre-eminence in cloth manufacturing with output there rising only from 10.6 million yards to 16 million yards.[49]

Anecdotal evidence suggests that the 1780s and 1790s were the golden age of the handloom weavers operating from home as part of a network of 'out-workers'. Demand for their output was increasing rapidly, while there was little steam-powered loom weaving in factories. After 1800, that began to change rapidly, and handloom weaving and other 'putting out' production methods became uncompetitive, except initially for highly patterned fabrics.

The principal technological innovator in the textile industry was the Oxford graduate, Tory Anglican clergyman, Edmund Cartwright.[50] His power loom, which sought to automate the weaving process to allow it to keep up with the advances in spinning, was initially patented in 1785, but subsequently refined by Cartwright himself with a further patent in 1789 as well as by several other inventors. Cartwright set up a water-powered mill at Doncaster, and invented a wool-combing machine, but went bankrupt in 1793. His inventions were water-powered. Nevertheless, the principle applied as well to a steam-powered loom. If the difficulties could be ironed out, textile production could be speeded up exponentially using powered machinery rather than hand labour.

Robert Grimshaw (1757-99), of Gorton near Manchester, built Knott's Mill in 1790, which was expected when completed to have up to 500 Cartwright power looms powered by a Boulton & Watt engine. The mill was destroyed by Luddite arson in 1792 and Grimshaw went bankrupt and took his own life in debtors' prison. Cartwright's power loom was improved and modified by others and widely adopted, with 2,400 power looms in operation by 1803. Cartwright himself was awarded £10,000 by the House of Commons in 1809, a serious sum at a time of wartime budget difficulty.

Several entrepreneurs established large, successful textile enterprises. One was Samuel Oldknow,[51] the son of a Nottingham tradesman, who

---

49. Mitchell (ed.), *British Historical Statistics*, Table IX-1 (imports, exports and re-exports), Table IX-8 (cotton goods exports), Table VI-12 (West Riding milled cloth) and Table VI-1 (raw cotton imports).

50. Edmund Cartwright (1743-1823). MA, Magdalen College, Oxford, 1766. FRS 1821. Prebendary of Lincoln Cathedral, 1783. Invented power loom, 1784. Parliamentary grant of £10,000, 1809. His brother, the Radical Major John Cartwright (1740-1824), founded a 600-employee 'Revolution Mill' in 1788 (celebrating the 1688 Revolution) – it went bankrupt in 1795. (Crouzet, *The First Industrialists*, p.76.)

51. Samuel Oldknow (1756-1828). High Sheriff of Derbyshire, 1824.

went into the muslin business in 1779 with a £1,000 loan from a local squire. Then, in 1784, with funding of £3,000 from Arkwright, he leased larger premises in Stockport and within two years had become the largest manufacturer of low-quality muslin in Britain, with 450 employees on the 'putting-out system' recording profits of £17,000 in 1786 and 1787 before the boom subsided. In 1791 Oldknow established a mill at Hillgate in Stockport making better-quality, 120-count muslin, powered by an 8hp Boulton & Watt engine.

Oldknow's Mellor Mill, opened around the same time, was 400 feet long with six floors and employed 2,000 people, 550 of them within the mill; it was the largest cotton mill in the world at the time.[52] The outbreak of war in 1793 pushed Oldknow into difficulties and he first mortgaged mills to Arkwright, then later was forced to sell them, keeping only Mellor, which was never especially profitable, even though it had 10,080 spindles in 1804. At his death in 1828, without direct heirs, Oldknow's debts totalled £206,000, although by then his interests had concentred on agriculture (probably also unprofitable after 1815). After his death, the Arkwright family took over his properties in satisfaction of his debts to them. Oldknow had a positively twenty-first-century reliance on leverage; one is forced to the conclusion that he was not an especially good businessman.

His creditor, Richard Arkwright Jr[53] was an exceptionally good businessman, as well as a strong Tory – his own son, Richard (1781-1832), was Tory MP for Rye, 1813-18 and 1826-30. General William Dyott (1761-1847), on a visit to Richard Jr's younger son, Charles, in 1831, wrote that he was struck by the:

> great difference in the habits and pursuits of the two great cotton-spinners, the Peels and the Arkwrights, the former linking themselves in bonds of marriage with the noble families and living in high life, the latter contenting themselves with rural and domestic engagements with their county neighbours, quite unassuming, unostentatious, though fuller of wealth and riches than the Peels.[54]

---

52. See: https://oldknows.com/mellor-mill.html (accessed 24 September 2021).
53. Richard Arkwright (1755-1843). High Sheriff of Derbyshire, 1801. Worth £3.25 million at his death.
54. Entry for Richard Arkwright in D.R. Fisher (ed.), *The History of Parliament: The House of Commons 1820-32* (Cambridge: Cambridge University Press, 2009).

Sir Richard Arkwright, on his death in 1792 left much of his wealth to his daughter, leaving his son not much beyond the remaining factories. Richard, who had worked in his father's factories from an early age and effectively took them over on his father's retirement in 1783, diversified from textiles in the 1790s, keeping only the Masson and Cromford mills. Masson, of six stories on the Derwent river, was completed in 1783 and powered by water, the single wheel being replaced by a pair in 1801; the mill continued with water-powered production into the twentieth century. Cromford, Sir Richard's first mill, opened in 1771, was converted to other uses in 1840 when the water supply developed problems.

Richard Arkwright Jr bought Consols at a discount, mostly in the 1790s, to become the largest individual holder of Consols in Britain. He founded a country bank, Arkwright & Co. of Wirksworth, Derbyshire (with a branch in Ashbourne), in 1804, in which two of his sons were partners until 1846 and which financed agriculture and coal-mining projects. He lent money directly to the aristocracy, often against mortgage security, with a notable borrower being Georgiana, Duchess of Devonshire.[55] Directly and through foreclosing on loans to the aristocracy, he bought agricultural land, with foreclosure especially fruitful in the depressed periods of the 1790s and the early 1820s.

Arkwright also financed much of the Cromford Canal, completed in 1794 at a cost of £82,000, whose £100 shares were by 1829 standing at £420 and paying a dividend of 18%.[56] His venture capital activities, for example, his loans of some large share of £206,000 to Oldknow, were highly profitable, especially when he could do a debt/equity swap on the borrower's death, as with Oldknow, whose Mellor Mill he kept. He died in 1843 worth £3.25 million, the richest commoner in Britain, more than twice as rich as the elder Sir Robert Peel and nearly as rich as John Jacob Astor in New York, who died in 1848 worth $20 million (£4.1 million).

Another textile manufacturer who died rich was John Marshall[57] of Leeds. Marshall came from a Dissenting background, the son of a linen draper, whose ancestors can be traced back to the early 1600s; in 1787 he inherited a warehouse and £7,500. He heard of John Kendrew's (1748-

---

55. Georgiana Spencer (1757-1806). Married William Cavendish, 5th Duke of Devonshire, 1774.

56. Jackman, *The Development of Transportation in Modern England*, Vol. 1, p. 426.

57. John Marshall (1765-1845). Whig MP for Yorkshire, 1826-30. Sheriff of Cumberland, 1821.

1800) new flax-spinning machine, for which he purchased a licence, and was able to improve it with the assistance of engineer, Matthew Murray (see Chapter 9 below). In 1791 he opened Marshall's Mill in Leeds to spin flax near the partly completed Leeds and Liverpool Canal and gradually expanded it, initially using a Boulton & Watt engine to improve the flow from his water wheel and running 7,000 spindles with up to 2,000 workers. With partners, he opened a further flax mill at Ditherington near Shrewsbury in 1796 at a cost of £17,000, which was the first iron-framed building in the world; he bought out his partners in 1804 on a £64,000 valuation. Late in life, he built a third flax mill, the Temple Works in Holbeck near Leeds, in the Egyptian Revival style with 7,000 spindles and 2,600 employees; this was powered by a 240hp, double-beam steam engine.

Conditions in Marshall's mills were hot and humid (this made the flax easier to work) but he was a relatively benign employer, offering part-time schooling for children. By gaining early technological leadership, specializing primarily in flax and using little leverage, Marshall mitigated the dangerous cyclicality of the early textile industry and left 'between £1.5 million and £2.5 million'.[58]

In Scotland, the first enterprise to use steam-powered looms was John Monteith's at Pollokshaws near Glasgow. The Monteith brothers, John (1760-1803), James (1763-1802) and Henry,[59] were sons of a prosperous handloom weaver who had diversified into lace products. All three sons went into the textile business; James, primarily, as a broker, while John built a steam-powered factory with 200 power looms in 1801. Henry, a graduate of Glasgow University, opened his own textile manufacturing company in 1785 and a second in 1802 manufacturing handkerchiefs. When his brothers died and he took over their businesses in 1804, he was employing 6,000 people, the largest employer in the industry. Henry later became Lord Provost of Glasgow as well as a 'Church and King' Tory MP for Linlithgow.

Finally, we come to the early textile manufacturing family best remembered today, because of the political activities of the grandson, Sir Robert Peel (1788-1850).[60] The founder of the family fortunes was

---

58. 'John Marshall', in the *Oxford Dictionary of National Biography*.
59. Henry Monteith (1765-1848). Tory MP for Linlithgow, 1820-26, 1830-31.
60. Robert Peel (1788-1850). 2nd Baronet from 1830. MP for Cashel, Chippenham, Oxford University, Westbury and Tamworth, 1809-50. Chief Secretary for Ireland, 1812-18, Home Secretary, 1822-27, 1828-30, Prime Minister 1834-35, 1841-46.

Robert 'Parsley' Peel (1723-95), the son of a Lancashire farmer with a grammar school education, who invented the process of roller printing on calico with a characteristic 'parsley' pattern, setting up a calico printing works in 1750. He was always interested in improvements; one of his employees was James Hargreaves, the inventor of the spinning jenny, which he installed in his factory. Then, in 1768, a riot by workers who believed themselves made unemployed by the new technology destroyed the equipment, so Peel moved operations to Burton-on-Trent in Staffordshire, attracted by the new canals, where he built three mills. In 1779, the Luddites struck again, so Peel switched to Arkwright's carding 'engine' and expanded further, ending with 23 mills across northern England (his largest competitor had ten), as well as founding a country bank, Peel, Greaves & Co. (Manchester New Bank) in Manchester in 1790. At his death in 1795, he was worth £140,000,[61] which he divided equally between his eight children, with a coat of arms, *Industria*, featuring a lion holding a cotton spindle.

'Parsley' Peel's strategy pushed the capabilities of hand-powered technology and small production units (easy for a single overseer to manage) as far as possible. His early experience of Luddism probably deterred him from investing massive capital in a single facility, allowing large groups of workers to assemble or relying on unfamiliar technology.

Sir Robert Peel, first Baronet,[62] began his working life in 1772 with £500 from his father, setting up a partnership, Peel, Yates & Co., with his uncle, James Haworth, and William Yates (whose daughter, Ellen, he married in 1783) and establishing a calico-printing works at Bury, with spinning mills nearby supplied by local handloom weavers. The partnership bought its first textile mills in 1780, the Makin Mill in Heywood and the Radcliffe Mill at Radcliffe, both water-powered. In those mills they established a system of acquiring orphans from the workhouses of London, Birmingham and locally, and indenturing them until the age of 21, gaining a largely unpaid and relatively docile workforce of 15,000 employees in 1803, spread between several factories.

---

61. Entry for Sir Robert Peel I in R. Thorne (ed.), *The History of Parliament: The House of Commons, 1790-1820* (Woodbridge: Boydell & Brewer, 1986). I find Thorne's figure of £140,000 at 'Parsley' Peel's death more credible than Wikipedia's £13,000; his 23 factories may have been small but must have added up, and he had also founded a bank.
62. Robert Peel (1750-1830). 1st Baronet from 1800. Tory MP for Tamworth, 1790-1820.

304   *Forging Modernity*

Conditions in Peel's mills were initially abominable but, after a highly critical health report on the Radcliffe Mill from the Salford magistrates in 1784, conditions improved and Peel became a model employer, by the standards of the day. He expanded production to Tamworth, Staffordshire, in the 1790s and bought Drayton Manor there. Peel, Yates imported the first bales of American cotton in 1785 and became Lancashire's largest calico printers after the 1788 collapse of Livesey, Hargreaves. Over time, Peel bought out his partners and in 1817 dissolved the partnership, dying in 1830 worth £1.5 million.

As an MP, Peel was a leader in reform of factory conditions, sponsoring the Health and Morals of Apprentices Act 1802, outlawing the worst child labour abuses and, in 1819, together with Lord Liverpool and helped by the reforming factory-owner, Robert Owen,[63] sponsoring the broader Cotton Mills and Factories Act 1819. He was a great admirer of Pitt and a friend to Liverpool, though despised by Canning,[64] who referred to him as 'fatty Peel'.[65]

Like his father, Sir Robert kept his factory investments dispersed, deriving competitive advantage from market share and extensive use of free 'apprentice' labour rather than from innovation in power systems. His exit from the business in 1817 may have been due to concern about its potential effect on his son's political career.

Iron Works

This period's principal development in the iron industry was the invention by Henry Cort (1740-1800) of a more efficient process for de-carbonizing pig iron, making British bar iron fully competitive with Swedish sources. Cort was funded in building his Fontley Works by a loan of £58,000 from Adam Jellicoe, chief clerk at the Royal Navy's Pay Office, using Pay Office funds. Regrettably, when Jellicoe died in 1789, the Navy wanted its money back, and Cort was forced into bankruptcy.

Cort's process was made to work properly by Richard Crawshay (1739-1810) at his Merthyr Tydfil works, using coke-fired pig iron rather

---

63. Robert Owen (1771-1858). Manchester cotton mill owner. In 1800 bought control of larger mill at New Lanark. Formulated factory legislation with Peel, 1815, then embraced socialism. Emigrated to United States, 1825, and founded socialist community at New Harmony, IN.
64. George Canning, 1770-1827. MP for Newtown, Wendover, Tralee, Petersfield, Liverpool, Harwich and Seaford, 1793-1827. Paymaster of the Forces 1800-1, Foreign Secretary, 1807-9, 1822-27, Prime Minister, 1827.
65. Thorne, *The History of Parliament: The House of Commons, 1790-1820.*

than the traditional charcoal-fired pig iron Cort had used. Crawshay, a Yorkshireman, was apprenticed to a bar iron warehouse owner in 1755, became sole proprietor of the business in 1763 and, by 1770, a leading London merchant of Swedish and Russian bar iron. From 1775, he was the agent for Anthony Bacon's[66] business at Merthyr Tydfil, supplying cannon to the Royal Ordnance – the business was an early user under licence of Wilkinson's cannon-boring process. He became a partner in that business in 1777, while Bacon, as an MP was forced to retire from government contracting in 1782. Crawshay took over the Cyfarthfa Iron Works in partnership in 1786, following Bacon's death, licensing Cort's bar iron production system in 1788, making it work and terminating the partnership in 1791, at which point Cyfarthfa was barely profitable.

Crawshay was a major investor in the Glamorganshire Canal, established in 1790 and opened to Cardiff in 1798 at a cost of £103,000; in 1828 its £100 shares were selling for £153 and paying a dividend of 7.8%[67] – Crawshay gained major cost advantages from it against his competitors. By 1794 he had built eight puddling furnaces, three melting fineries, three balling furnaces and a rolling mill at Cyfarthfa. The Napoleonic wars were very good for his business; he was reputed to be worth £2 million in 1799 and his will in 1810 was proved at £1.5 million. Having both the production and distribution sides of iron manufacturing under his control is probably what enabled Crawshay to become much richer than Wilkinson.

After Crawshay's death, Cyfarthfa was run for a decade by his son-in-law, Benjamin Hall,[68] a prominent Tory MP, rather than by his son, William Crawshay; after Hall's death in 1817, the management of Cyfarthfa passed to Crawshay's grandson, William Crawshay II (1788-1867), who ran it successfully until his death.

Crawshay's great rival in Merthyr Tydfil was Samuel Homfray (1762-1822), who with his brothers founded the Pen-y-darren Iron Works there in 1784. Homfray was the grandson of Francis Homfray (1674-1736) of Stourbridge, who had managed a nail warehouse there for Ambrose Crowley. After founding Pen-y-darren, Homfray then sank £40,000 into the Glamorganshire Canal. In 1804, he won a £1,000 bet with

---

66. Anthony Bacon (1717-86). MP for Aylesbury, 1764-84, voting with government to protect his contracting interests.
67. Jackman, *The Development of Transportation in Modern England*, Vol. 1, p. 426.
68. Benjamin Hall (1778-1817). Son of Chancellor of Llandaff Cathedral, educated at Westminster and Christ Church College, Oxford. Tory MP for Totnes, Westbury and Glamorganshire, 1806-17.

Crawshay as to which of them could first build a steam locomotive – he commissioned Trevithick to build the successful entry though little came of that success.

Homfray also established the Tredegar Iron Works in Monmouthshire in 1800, having married the daughter of the Tory MP, Sir Charles Gould Morgan,[69] who owned the land. With interests in two iron works, he also diversified into country banking with Samuel Homfray & Co. of Monmouth, established in 1810, but dissolved in 1814. In later years he went into politics, becoming High Sheriff of Monmouthshire in 1813 and Tory MP for Stafford, 1818-20.

Another great Welsh iron works fortune was that of Josiah John Guest.[70] Guest was the son and grandson of the controlling shareholders of the Dowlais Iron Company, which, when he took over in 1807, had been operating since 1759 but was financially marginal. Guest modernized the works and made it the largest in Britain, supplying rail for the Stockton and Darlington Railway in 1821 and many subsequent railways, in Germany and Russia as well as Britain. By 1845, the works operated eighteen blast furnaces, employed 7,300 people and produced 88,400 tons of iron each year. Guest became a Whig MP for Honiton and then the new seat of Merthyr Tydfil, helping that borough to gain incorporation in 1837. Dowlais remained in the Guest family until it was merged to form Guest, Keen and Nettlefolds in 1899.

Outside Wales, a major iron works was formed at Butterley, in Derbyshire, where iron ore was discovered in the construction of the Cromford Canal. One of the canal's promotors had been the land agent, Joseph Outram, whose son, Benjamin Outram (1764-1805), founded an iron works with £6,000 in capital in 1790 to take advantage of the iron ore deposits. The iron works was renamed the Butterley Company when outside partners were included in 1793. The outbreak of war expanded annual output to 1,000 tons of pig iron by 1796. Outram was an early advocate of L-shaped tramrails, which Butterley manufactured along with the carriages. Tramways became a major feeder system for industrial goods to the later canals, and Outram predicted in 1799 that railways would become the nation's leading transport system and that they should all have the same gauge to ensure inter-operability.

---

69. Sir Charles Gould Morgan (1726-1806). 1st Bt from 1792. Tory MP for Brecon and Breconshire, 1778-1806. Second son, Charles Morgan Robinson (1792-1875). Created 1st Baron Tredegar in 1859. Tory MP for Brecon, 1812-18, 1830-32, 1835-47.

70. Josiah John Guest (1785-1852). 1st Bt 1838. FRS 1830. Whig MP for Honiton, 1826-31, for Merthyr Tydfil, 1832-52.

After Outram's early death, Butterley continued to flourish, producing the ironwork for Vauxhall Bridge in 1814. It was attacked in the Pentrich rising in 1817, when the rioters attempted to kill the management and seize the works for weapons; the factory agent, George Goodwin faced the rioters down with a few constables. By 1830, Butterley was the largest coal owner and the second largest iron works in the East Midlands; it survived until 2009.

Machine Tools

The advances in machine tools during this period were truly revolutionary. They were mostly the product of two men: Joseph Bramah and Henry Maudslay, both based in London. Having missed out on the previous generation's advances because it lacked water power, London, with the advent of the Watt rotary engine, became again a major centre of technological innovation, particularly for products that sold to wealthy consumers. I shall deal with Bramah in this chapter; Maudslay deserves reference in two chapters.[71]

Joseph Bramah[72] was the second son of a Yorkshire farmer, apprenticed to a local carpenter, who in 1772 walked to London, where he found work with a Mr Allen, installing patented water closets. He solved the problem of toilets freezing in winter by designing a hinged flap sealing the bottom of the bowl, obtaining a patent for this in 1778 and going into business himself; by 1800, he had installed 6,000 water closets and Bramah water closets remained popular through the nineteenth century.

Bramah then went into the lock business, designing his 'Challenge lock', for which he obtained a patent in 1784, and offering a prize of 200 guineas for anyone who could pick or open it. That prize went unclaimed until an American, Alfred Charles Hobbs, succeeded in picking the Challenge lock over 31 days at the 1851 Great Exhibition. Bramah formed a separate company, the Bramah Locks Company, still in business today,[73] but was unable to sell the Challenge lock until he

---

71. John Cantrell and Gillian Cookson, *Henry Maudslay and the Pioneers of the Machine Age* (Stroud: Tempus Publishing, 2002), has a lengthy chapter on Maudslay and another chapter with considerable detail on Bramah and other contemporary engineers. It also has chapters on several of Maudslay's pupils/apprentices.

72. Joseph Bramah (1749-1814). Machine tool pioneer. Inventor of the Bramah Challenge lock and hydraulic press.

73. Company website: http://www.bramah.co.uk/.

308 *Forging Modernity*

could produce the locks in quantity; that awaited the arrival of Henry Maudslay in 1790. The locks business gave Bramah one vitally important insight: the need for far greater manufacturing precision than had previously been available, with parts fully interchangeable and much tighter tolerances in the manufacturing process. It was a crucial lesson of modernity.

Bramah's most important invention was the hydraulic press, patented in 1795, which operated through Pascal's principle,[74] and enabled machinists to scale up the force exerted on an object by pushing on a narrow piston to obtain a much larger force across a broad one. To avoid leakage, both pistons and the apparatus connecting them had to be machined to very fine tolerances, by now a Bramah specialty. The hydraulic press was further developed by William George Armstrong (1810-1900) and is much used today.

Bramah continued as a prolific inventor. He patented improved beer pumps in 1785 and 1793, having a readily available market through the large London breweries. Late in life, he invented an early fountain pen. He moved to Pimlico in 1810 to set up a larger works, employing around 100 people and died in 1814, through catching pneumonia while testing a hydraulic tree uprooter. His sons successfully carried on the business.

As Bramah's business expanded, he trained assistants. He taught Arthur Woolf to machine to close tolerance, enabling him to design and produce his successful compound steam engine. Joseph Clement (1779-1844) also worked briefly for Bramah before his death and then for Maudslay.

Bramah did not gain the riches enjoyed by the Arkwrights, Wedgwood or Crawshay, though he remained comfortably off and his locks business survives today. Nevertheless, with his inventions and the impetus he gave to the machine tool industry (partly through Maudslay), and from the importance he ascribed to tight tolerances and process replicability, he changed the world. The next, more powerful generation of steam engines would not have been possible without him.

Henry Maudslay was the fifth of seven children of a wheelwright in the Royal Engineers, who became an 'artificer' at the Royal Arsenal at Woolwich, where Maudslay himself was apprenticed as a 'powder monkey' in 1783. Within two years, he had been promoted, first to the carpentry department and then to the smithy, where he learned accurate

---

74. Pressure change in a confined incompressible fluid is transmitted throughout the fluid so that the same change occurs everywhere. Blaise Pascal, 1653.

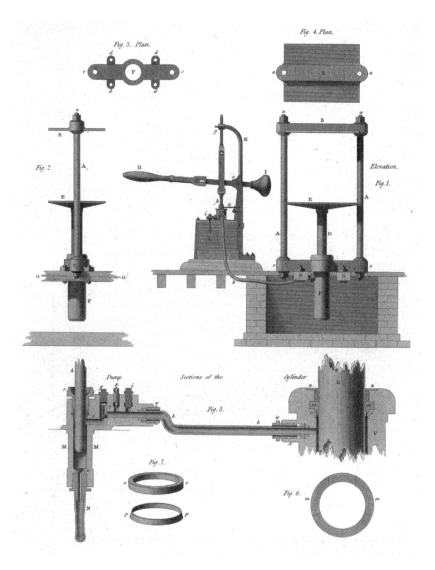

Bramah's Hydraulic Press is one of Joseph Bramah's major contributions to modernity. Engraving by John Farey.

metalworking techniques, producing metal 'trivets' from scrap metal pieces that won admiration. Bramah, looking for an assistant to speed lock production, hired him in 1790 and Maudslay quickly constructed specialized tools and machines that could replicate the complex lock mechanism in quantities, making the locks a cost-effective product for sale.

Henry Maudslay effectively invented the machine tool industry.
Lithograph by Pierre Louis Grevedon.

Maudslay also provided vital assistance on Bramah's hydraulic press, designing a leather cup washer that sealed the cylinder where the piston rod entered it, but offered no resistance when pressure was removed. In general, Maudslay's mechanical ingenuity greatly helped the Bramah workshop's operations. However, in 1797, when Maudslay asked for a raise in wages above his £1 10s per week, Bramah refused, causing Maudslay to leave and set up for himself. Maudslay was 22 years younger than Bramah and ambitious; his departure was probably inevitable and Bramah may have realized this, as his relations with subordinates were generally good.

Maudslay's first innovation in his independent business was the screw-cutting lathe in 1800. This allowed for nuts and bolts to be standardized, with the threads of a standard pitch. Maudslay devoted a considerable portion of his life to screw technology, standardising pitch and thread across his works' output; his pupil, Sir Joseph Whitworth (1803-87), would extend the principle in 1841 to the British Standard Whitworth system, used in most non-metric countries. Maudslay's lathes for screw cutting and other machining purposes were entirely made of metal, giving greater rigidity and accuracy, and they included one or possibly two 'slide rests' that enabled the tool to be held in place while the piece was rotated against it.

Maudslay's other invention of this period was the bench micrometer, developed around 1805, with a screw pitch of 0.01in., which was used to measure down to 0.0001in., a further leap forward in precision. The tool was known as the 'Lord Chancellor' because its decision on a measurement was final. (Lord Eldon,[75] himself from a working-class background, would have been flattered by the comparison!)

With the screw-cutting lathe, the bench micrometer and his improvements in lathe technology, Maudslay is today recognized as the father of machine tool technology. I shall return to his career and his pupils in Chapter 9.

Infrastructure

Much more money was spent on canals during this period than in 1766-77. The cost per mile of this period's canals was far higher, only partly because they were generally 'broad' (fourteen to fifteen feet) rather than 'narrow' (seven feet). The most profitable developments were the completion of Brindley's Grand Cross scheme with the extension of the Oxford Canal to Oxford in 1790 and the completion of the Coventry and the Forth and Clyde Canals – completed canals were proportionately far more profitable and economically productive than half-finished ones.

The profitability and economic effect of this period's canals was however lower. Indeed, this period's investment in canals may have been unprofitable overall – several expensive ones such as the Ellesmere Canal were left uncompleted and others were completed only at the cost of massive stock dilution. That was not entirely the canal planners' fault. After 1793 the country was involved in an unexpected 22-year war(if Pitt did not expect it, canal builders could hardly have done so). A canal

---

75. John Scott (1751-1838). 1st Earl of Eldon from 1821. Solicitor General, 1788-93, Attorney General, 1793-99, Lord Chief Justice, 1799-1801, Lord Chancellor 1801-6, 1807-27.

fully funded in 1791 might well run out of money by 1798, owing to wartime cost inflation, and then be unable to raise the additional capital needed in a market where confidence was low and interest rates had doubled. Some of these unhappy cases were finished after 1815, but were often still only marginally profitable, given their bloated final cost; the ones left unfinished were generally a dead loss.

Even taking account of most of these later canals being built to a 14-ft width rather than Brindley's 7-ft standard, they were inordinately expensive, sometimes costing five or six times as much per mile as Brindley's earlier efforts, with cost increases above the effect of wartime inflation. There appears to have been an inverse 'learning curve', perhaps similar to that causing the exorbitant cost of infrastructure today.

One example (passed by Act of Parliament in May 1783) was the Thames and Severn Canal, to link the local Stroudwater Navigation (from the Severn to Stroud) with the Thames at Lechlade, a distance of 29 miles. This canal, with authorized capital of £130,000 was subscribed mostly from outside the local region; fully 56% of the subscriptions came from capitalists.[76] It was executed in broad (14-ft) gauge, even though the Shepperton Tunnel of 3,817 feet was rendered far more expensive thereby. An additional £104,000 was raised to complete the canal in 1789. This canal was typical of later canals in being financially unsuccessful; its shares were selling at 28% of par by 1828.[77]

The **Grand Junction Canal**, the longest canal of this period and one of the few financially successful ones, was authorized by Parliament in 1793 as an alternative route from the Midlands to London, by-passing the narrow Oxford Canal and reaching the Thames at Brentford, much closer to London. With a length of 109 miles and a 14-ft width, it eventually cost £1.8 million, a cost of over £16,000 per mile. Its initial capital was £500,000 in £100 shares, most of which were bought by landowners and tradesmen along its length. Inevitably, further money was required, and several additional issues of shares and convertible loan notes were carried out, in 1796, 1801, 1803, 1805 and 1811.[78] Despite its cost overruns, the Grand Junction Canal was eventually successful, with the main length opening in 1805, siphoning much of the traffic

---

76. Ward, *The Finance of Canal Building in Eighteenth-Century England*, pp. 64-66.
77. Jackman, *The Development of Transportation in Modern England*, Vol. 1, p. 421.
78. Ward, *The Finance of Canal Building in Eighteenth-Century England*, pp. 43-46.

from the less convenient and more roundabout Oxford Canal. By 1828 its shares were standing at £295 and paying a dividend of 13%.[79]

Thomas Telford[80] was nearly as important an engineer in this period as Brindley in the previous one, albeit in a less concentrated way. Self-taught and beginning as a stonemason, through his wealthy patron, Sir William Pulteney,[81] he became Surveyor of Public Works in Shropshire. There he built some 40 bridges, including an iron bridge at Buildwas that was half the weight of Abraham Darby III's Ironbridge and 30 feet longer. He then became designer of the Ellesmere Canal, which was never finished, and the seventeen-mile Shrewsbury Canal, finished in 1797, which was modestly financially successful. After conducting a highland survey, he built 184 miles of new roads in Scotland and what is now the A5 to Holyhead. Later in life he built the second Harecastle Tunnel on the Trent and Mersey Canal, as well as St Katharine Docks in London and several later canals. After Parliament passed the Church Building Act 1818, he was also commissioned to design a simple rural church that could be replicated many times. He died considerably richer than Brindley and is buried in Westminster Abbey.

Science

In terms of benefit to humanity, the greatest scientific advance was made by Edward Jenner,[82] the son of an Anglican vicar in Berkeley, Gloucestershire. After a good education, Jenner was apprenticed in 1763 to a surgeon in Chipping Sodbury and then studied at St George's Hospital, London. From 1773, he became a doctor in Berkeley with an interest in scientific research, who became an FRS in 1788 after his study of the life cycle of the cuckoo. His greatest discovery came about when noticed that milkmaids appeared not to be susceptible to smallpox. He speculated that their immunity might come from the lesser infection,

---

79. Jackman, *The Development of Transportation in Modern England*, Vol. 1, p. 426.
80. Thomas Telford (1757-1834). Founder and President of the Institute of Civil Engineers from 1818.
81. Sir William Johnstone (1729-1805). 5th Bt from 1794. Changed surname to Pulteney on inheriting the Earl of Bath's estates in 1767. Tory-leaning independent MP for Cromarty and Shrewsbury, 1768-74, 1775-1805. Scottish feudal aristocrat and lawyer, worth over £2 million at his death.
82. Edward Jenner (1749-1823). FRS 1788. *Inquiry into the Variolae Vaccinae Known as the Cow-pox* (1798). Appointed Physician Extraordinary to King George IV, 1821.

cowpox. In 1796 he inoculated an eight-year-old boy with cowpox obtained from the blisters on a milkmaid's hands – 'vaccination' (Latin *vacca* = cow). Since smallpox killed around 10% of the population, his invention saved the lives of more people than any other.

Another scientist whose name resounds today was Sir William Herschel. Herschel, the son of an oboe player in the Hanover Military Band, also joined the band and then moved to England in 1757, joining orchestras in Durham and Newcastle. As a professional musician, he composed 24 symphonies, becoming organist at the Octagon Chapel, Bath in 1766. Herschel's intellectual curiosity led him to astronomy. With his younger sister, Caroline (1750-1848), he took to astronomy in 1773, building his own telescopes and focussing initially on double stars, of which he discovered over 800.

In March 1781, Herschel discovered a new disc which he determined to be a planet beyond the orbit of Saturn, naming it initially, *Georgium Sidus*, after George III. There would be much debate over the name, only settled in 1850 when it became known universally as Uranus.[83] After this discovery, Herschel turned his attention to nebulae, moving to Windsor in 1785 and using two 20-ft telescopes he had built; by 1802 he had discovered over 2,400 such formations. He supplemented his income by making telescopes, the most famous of which was a 40-ft model, completed in 1790, for which he received a subsidy of £4,000 from George III. He also researched sunspots, identifying their cyclicality, discovered two moons of Saturn and two of Uranus, and in 1800 discovered infra-red radiation. In 1820, he helped to found the Royal Astronomical Society.

As eminent was the naturalist and botanist, Sir Joseph Banks,[84] the son of a wealthy Lincolnshire squire and Tory MP, educated at Harrow, followed by Eton and then Christ Church College, Oxford, funding the Cambridge botanist, Israel Lyons (1739-75), to deliver a course of lectures at Oxford in 1764. Having inherited the family lands, he was elected FRS in 1766, then voyaged with Captain Sir Thomas Adams (1738-70) and Lieutenant Constantine Phipps (1744-92) to Newfoundland and Labrador, making his name by publishing a Linnean study of its flora and fauna.

In 1768, Banks was appointed chief of an eight-man scientific team on HMS *Endeavour*, Cook's first voyage to the South Seas, initially to

---

83. I have to believe a world in which the three outermost planets were named George, Louis-Philippe and Hoover would be a better one!

84. Joseph Banks (1743-1820). 1st Bt from 1781. KB 1795. GCB 1815. FRS 1766. President of the Royal Society, 1778-1820.

observe the 1769 transit of Venus across the Sun. The voyage travelled to Brazil, Tahiti, New Zealand and Australia, and Banks identified over 1,300 new species, increasing the known flora of the world by 25%. In 1778, Banks was elected President of the Royal Society, after which he advised the king on Kew Gardens, making it one of the world's foremost botanic collections. He also advised the House of Commons, recommending the colonization of Australia and remaining in constant correspondence with the Botany Bay's first four governors.

Less eminent scientifically, but a polymath with superb self-marketing abilities and administrative skills was the American Sir Benjamin Thompson, Count Rumford.[85] Thompson was born in Woburn, Massachusetts to a well-off local family and educated locally with occasional lectures at Harvard. In 1766, he was apprenticed to a Salem merchant, educating himself further in science and other matters. In 1772, he married a wealthy widow and was appointed major in the New Hampshire militia. When the Revolutionary War broke out, he recruited loyalists, then he deserted his wife and fled to the British lines. He became an advisor in Massachusetts to the governor, General Thomas Gage (1721-87), and to Lord George Germain.[86] He also conducted experiments to measure the force of gunpowder, which were published by the Royal Society and gave him a reputation as a scientist.

From 1785 to 1798, Thompson lived in Bavaria, where he became aide-de-camp and chamberlain to Prince-elector Charles Theodore,[87] reorganizing the military and inventing a nutritious soup for the poor, being rewarded in 1791 with the title of Count Rumford. While there, he undertook his most important theoretical work, on the nature of heat, concluding from observation of cannon-boring machines that it was a form of motion, measuring the mechanical equivalent of heat and inventing the concept of specific heat. In 1796, he invented the 'Rumford fireplace' with a narrower chimney to remove smoking and increase heat retention, which became a great commercial success when he

---

85. Benjamin Thompson (1753-1814). FRS 1779. Kt 1784. Count of the Holy Roman Empire, 1791.

86. George Sackville (Germain from 1769) (1716-85). 1st Viscount Sackville from 1782. MP (Ireland) for Portarlington, 1733-61. MP for Dover and East Grinstead, 1742-61, 1767-82. Army from 1737. Colonel, 1743. Fontenoy, 1745. Major General, 1755, Lieutenant General, 1758. Minden, 1759. Cashiered for cowardice, 1761. Chief Secretary for Ireland, 1750-55, First Lord of Trade, 1775-79, Secretary of State for the Colonies, 1775-82.

87. Charles Theodore (1724-99). Elector Palatine from 1742, Elector of Bavaria from 1777.

returned to London in 1798. He also invented a photometer, to measure the intensity of light, by measuring the intensity of the shadow it cast.

In 1800, with Banks, Rumford founded the Royal Institution, important in developing the next generation of scientific talent, employing Humphrey Davy, Michael Faraday and Friedrich Accum. In 1804, his American wife having died, he married Marie-Anne Lavoisier (1758-1836), the wealthy widow of the guillotined chemist, Antoine Lavoisier. He separated from her after three years but remained in Paris until his death in 1814, endowing a professorship at Harvard University.

Political Developments, 1794-1807

Legislatively, most of the Acts of Parliament of Pitt's second decade were caused by the war. As the war became harsher and conditions more difficult, repressive legislation hardened. The decade was notable for the level of unrest, which took three forms. Political unrest began in 1792, and peaked in 1794-96, as Radicals took heart from activities in France. Then, in 1797, declining real wages in the army and navy brought military unrest with two major navy mutinies and an outbreak of anti-draft rioting. Finally, late in the decade, the continuing decline in real wages brought serious industrial unrest.

Even in the harsh conditions of 1795, the Tories in Pitt's government remained more sympathetic to the poor than their new Whig colleagues. The Poor Removal Act 1795 prevented magistrates from throwing a poor person out of a parish unless they actually applied for relief, while the Relief of the Poor Act 1795 abolished those provisions of the Whigs' repressive 1722 legislation that had prohibited 'outdoor relief' (direct payments to paupers) – the result was the more generous Speenhamland system of poor relief. The government's sympathy for popular hardships, together with the disorganization of the Foxite Whigs, was rewarded in 1796 by a substantial further increase in Pitt's majority with some 417 pro-government and 141 opposition.

The year 1797 was especially difficult, with a French invasion of Wales in February that caused the Bank of England to suspend specie payments, legalized by the Bank Restriction Act 1797. The government's reaction to this change continued with Liverpool's copper coinage scheme, the counterfeiting of which was made high treason by the Counterfeiting Coin Act 1797. Finally, the Militia Act 1797 extended the English militia to Scotland, causing serious disturbances there, including that at Tranent in which the young Hawkesbury was involved.[88]

---

88. See Hutchinson, *Britain's Greatest Prime Minister*, pp 39-40.

Industrial unrest worsened in 1798-99, due largely to inflation, which many employers did not match by corresponding wage increases. The Unlawful Combination of Workmen Act 1799 (followed by another Act in 1800) and the Unlawful Societies Act 1799 drove both the embryonic trades unions and the radical organizing societies underground, as the government feared they would be used through strikes in wartime to overthrow the government. Hawkesbury as Home Secretary tested the provisions of the Combination Acts in 1804 and found it impracticable to prosecute under them; hence, the Acts remained largely dead letters until replaced by new legislation in 1824.

Pitt's own approach to the war reflected the consensus within his Cabinet. He expanded the navy rapidly, doubling the number of frigates in commission, but wasted much of Britain's military strength on an expedition against the slave rebellion in Haiti, which cost £4 million and 100,000 men, most dying of disease.

On land, Pitt relied on assembling vast coalitions to oppose French advances (the First, 1793-97, the Second, 1798-1801, and the Third, 1805-6) but these proved fragile and unable to oppose effectively the strong French armies, with better and more aggressive generals even before Napoleon Bonaparte took over full command of French forces in 1800. (France's population was well over double Britain's in the 1790s, and British economic superiority over France was not then as overwhelming as it later became.) The naval mutinies of 1797 reflected Pitt's financial maladministration; naval pay had not been increased since 1660. Only after Nelson's victory at the Battle of the Nile in August 1798 did British naval strength start to balance French military power.

The Irish rebellion of 1798 scared British public opinion, which saw the country as ripe for French invasion (the most serious attempt at this, Hoche's expedition of December 1796, had been defeated by chance and bad weather). Consequently, Pitt passed through both the Irish and British Parliaments the Act for the Union of Great Britain and Ireland 1800, which came into effect on 1 January 1801. In order to get the Act through, Pitt had promised the Irish that the major offices of state would be open to Catholics (Irish Catholics already had the vote, by an Act of 1793, which was extended to UK parliamentary elections by the Act of Union). Unfortunately, he had not cleared this with the king, so royal objections forced his resignation.

Pitt was succeeded by Addington, the former Speaker of the House, in a government with Liverpool still at the Board of Trade and his son, Hawkesbury, as Foreign Secretary (the family represented around 20% of the Cabinet). Since Napoleon Bonaparte was now First Consul in France and wanted an armistice, Hawkesbury was able to sign the

Treaty of Amiens on 1 October 1801, which produced an interlude of peace lasting until May 1803. Following the peace, Addington dissolved Parliament; he was rewarded by a huge majority of some 467 pro-government to 149 combined opposition, which proved evanescent once war returned. Addington was a better financial administrator than Pitt; his introduction of withholding to the income tax system in 1803 (most notably, on government bond interest) nearly doubled the tax's yield and stabilized Britain's finances.

Once war restarted in May 1803, Pitt returned to the premiership but, without Addington, Grenville or Fox and their supporters, his second government from May 1804 was a weak one. (Grenville had moved towards the Whig opposition, Addington had been alienated by Pitt's manoeuvrings and Fox was vetoed by the king.) Economically, the most important legislation was the Corn Law 1804. The law's main effect was to raise sharply from the previous 1773 Act the price below which corn imports would suffer a heavy duty from 44s to 65s (under the 1815 Corn Law imports were to be prohibited below 80s).

According to modern price statistics for the period, the 1804 legislation raised the price at which heavy duties were imposed by about the 47% inflation between 1773 and 1804, while the 1815 Corn Law reduced the limit by about 2% in real terms. Only with the deflation after the wars ended did the corn price at which imports were freed rise sharply in real terms, by 38% in the decade up to 1825. The Corn Laws were thus skilfully designed to maintain constant real corn prices. Because of high prevailing grain prices the Corn Law 1804 was never invoked until the bumper harvest of 1813.

Hawkesbury said in support of the Bill: 'The best security that the country could have against famine, laying out of consideration the accidents of seasons, against which human precaution is to no avail, is to encourage the farmer to cultivate as much of the soil as he can.'[89] He knew from his father's Board of Trade experience of the dearths of the 1790s that the risks between high and low corn prices were asymmetric. In a situation of 'sticky' international markets, rapidly rising population and uncertain climate it was much better to maximize domestic production than to rely on cheap imports that might not always be available.

Addington returned to government in December 1804, rewarded by the title of Viscount Sidmouth, but resigned six months later over the impeachment of Melville; without him, the government lacked a

---

89. Hansard, *The Parliamentary Debates from the Year 1803 to the Present Time*, Vol. 2, cols 1047-9, 16 July 1804.

Commons majority, especially after the Trafalgar triumph had been followed by the defeats of Ulm and Austerlitz, which destroyed Pitt's Third Coalition. Even had Pitt lived beyond January 1806, the new session of Parliament would probably have seen him defeated. It was this, not doubt of his own abilities, that led Hawkesbury to turn down the prime ministership when the king offered it to him after Pitt's death.

After Hawkesbury's refusal, the Ministry of All the Talents was formed, containing Grenville, Sidmouth and Grey,[90] but with its major talent being Fox at the Foreign Office. Alas, Fox died in September 1806, at which point Grenville as the government's leader asked the king for a dissolution of Parliament, only four years into its term, to increase the ministerial majority, as normally happened. In this case, there was only a small increase in the government's shaky majority, possibly because Lord Henry Petty had in the 1806 Budget increased the income tax rate from 6½% to 10%, the highest then thought possible – subsequent governments would learn not to undertake a large tax increase just before an election!

Nevertheless, the Talents ministry at the end of 1806 appeared stable. It passed one item of legislation of immense long-term significance, the Abolition of Slave Trade Act 1807, prohibiting the slave trade within the British Empire. This was thought likely to lead to the end of slavery itself, but the US Louisiana Purchase of 1803 and Whitney's cotton gin had opened up immense new lands that could profitably grow cotton, providing a large new market for slaves. It was only in the 1820s, when Britain had once again attained financial stability, that abolition of slavery itself, which to British statesmen of that period required slaveholders to be bought out by the government, became practical politics.

Abolition of the slave trade, accepted immediately by all British political groups, had an important effect in furthering industrialization. It became clear that there would soon be no avenues to wealth from exploiting slave labour, which together with exploiting Britain's Indian possessions had been a major source of enrichment in the eighteenth century. Hence, entrepreneurial energies could mostly be devoted to industrial development, working within the constraint of relatively high-cost British labour rather than profiting primarily from workforce exploitation. After 1815 alternative means of enrichment would arise,

---

90. Charles Grey (1764-1845). 2nd Earl Grey from 1807. Whig MP for Northumberland 1786-1807. First Lord of the Admiralty, 1806, Foreign Secretary and Leader of the House of Commons, 1806-7, Reform Bill Prime Minister, 1830-34. Inspired a teabag!

in finance and the growth of international trade caused by improved communications.

The Talents government did not long survive its slave trade abolition triumph. It attempted to issue an order allowing Catholics to serve in the top ranks of the British army without informing the king, who was now almost blind. When called on this and asked to promise no further such shenanigans, the government resigned, and Eldon and Hawkesbury were called to Windsor to form a new government. They did so under the nominal leadership of Portland, who immediately called another general election. He was rewarded with a thumping majority of 384 government supporters to 218 opposition; Catholic emancipation was highly unpopular among the British electorate. The last long and most successful period of Tory government had begun.

9

Liverpool's Policies Lead to Modernity, 1807-30

The Liverpool Legacy

We end with the Tory governments that took office in March 1807 and continued until their final defeat in November 1830. In economic policy, the dominant influence was Robert Banks Jenkinson, second Earl of Liverpool, first among equals in the governments of Portland and Perceval, then prime minister with unchallenged control over economic policy until his stroke in 1827, then dominating the economic thinking of his successors, Canning, Goderich[1] and Wellington.[2]

As well as capable economic policy, the period was notable for the remarkable broadening of the Industrial Revolution, from engines

---

1. Frederick John Robinson (1782-1859). 1st Viscount Goderich from 1827, 1st Earl of Ripon from 1833. MP for Carlow and Ripon, 1806-27. President of the Board of Trade, 1818-23, 1841-43, Chancellor of the Exchequer, 1823-27, Secretary of State for War and Colonies, 1827, 1830-33, Prime Minister, 1827-28, Lord Privy Seal, 1833-34, President of the Board of Control, 1843-46.

2. Arthur Wellesley (1769-1852). 1st Viscount Wellington from 1809, 1st Duke of Wellington from 1813. MP (Ireland) for Trim, 1790-97, MP for Rye, Tralee, Mitchell, and Newport, 1806-9. Chief Secretary for Ireland 1807-9, Master-General of the Ordnance, 1818-27, Prime Minister, 1828-30, 1834 (briefly), Foreign Secretary, 1834-35. Army, 1787, Major-General, 1802. Assaye, 1803. Lieutenant General, 1808, General, 1812, Field Marsal, 1813. Portugal and Spain, 1808, 1809-14. Waterloo, 1815.

Robert Banks Jenkinson, 2nd Earl of Liverpool presided over the Industrial Revolution's flowering. Painting by Thomas Lawrence.

and textiles at its start to almost the whole range of human endeavour by its end. Scientific enquiry had been practised in Britain at the highest level for a century and a half; this period was notable for an acceleration in the application of scientific enquiry to industrial problems, with the professionally educated scientists less distinguishable than in earlier periods from the skilled working men tinkering with existing techniques. The full-scale industrial research laboratory was still decades away, but many entrepreneurs of this period came close to replicating its techniques and were rewarded by notable, albeit not always lucrative, technological advances. The Industrial Revolution thereby matured to its full, overwhelming strength.

Liverpool both understood the Industrial Revolution and followed economic policies close to ideal for its development. The political revolution that took place after November 1830 caused an accelerating drift away from those policies, while the unlucky railway accident that killed William Huskisson[3] in 1830 removed Liverpool's principal economic acolyte. With the opening of the Liverpool and Manchester Railway, that year also marked the end of an era in British industrial development. After 1830 the Industrial Revolution was self-sustaining, was more developmental than revolutionary and was no longer confined to Britain.

It is extraordinary that Liverpool has been given so little respect from subsequent historians, for his achievements were remarkable.

---

3. William Huskisson (1770-1830). Tory MP for Morpeth, Liskeard, Harwich, Chichester and Liverpool, 1796-1802, 1804-30. PC 1814. First Commissioner of Woods and Forests, 1814-23, President of the Board of Trade, 1823-27, Secretary of State for War and Colonies, 1827-28. Killed by Stephenson's 'Rocket' at the opening of the Liverpool and Manchester Railway.

Liverpool's Policies Lead to Modernity, 1807-30

He designed the financial attrition strategy that defeated Napoleon; he led the UK through the take-off stage of the industrial revolution; he inherited a daunting fiscal situation that included a debt/GDP ratio of 250%, implanted the austerity measures needed to put this ratio onto the path leading to later Victorian prosperity; he reformed the currency; he pushed through the return to the gold standard; he promoted both the Corn Laws and free trade; and he successfully managed the 1825 financial crisis and pushed through subsequent reforms that put the British banking system onto a stable trajectory that lasted a century.

Liverpool's diffident, understated personality made him underrated by most contemporaries, and the political revolution that followed his death led to him being derided by Whig historians. Both contemporaries and historians erred; there is every case for rating Liverpool as one of Britain's greatest leaders. The Industrial Revolution was already well under way when he achieved high office, but the combination in his era of optimal policy and fast-paced innovation and social change was unequalled elsewhere.

Political and Economic Developments, 1807-15

The Portland government was weak, largely because of the conflicting ambitions and inexperience of its senior members: Hawkesbury (second Earl of Liverpool from December 1808) at the Home Office, Canning at the Foreign Office, Castlereagh[4] at War and the Colonies and Perceval at the Exchequer. Nevertheless, the government achieved much: a successful expedition against Denmark's fleet, the Orders in Council, which blockaded Napoleon's Empire and, most importantly, the beginning of the Peninsular War campaign – Sir Arthur Wellesley's modest expedition to Portugal in 1808 and his return there in 1809, with a defensive victory at Talavera for which he was created Baron Wellington. However, the Fifth Coalition against Napoleon was no more successful than the previous four and led to the disastrous Walcheren Expedition, where a strong British force sent to the Belgian coast succumbed to fever. Finally, Canning's unchecked ambitions produced a plot to replace Portland and fire Castlereagh, which led to the government's fall and a duel between Canning and Castlereagh in September 1809.

---

4. Robert Stewart (1769-1822). Viscount Castlereagh from 1796, 2nd Marquess of Londonderry from 1821. Chief Secretary for Ireland, 1798-1801, President of the Board of Control, 1802-6, Secretary for War and Colonies 1805-6, 1807-9, Foreign Secretary 1812-22.

The Orders in Council were passed in November 1807 to match Napoleon's Berlin and Milan Decrees, issued over the previous year. The orders had a serious effect on trade with the United States, largely because President Jefferson enacted an embargo preventing US exporters from trading with Britain. There was a short-term effect on the textile industry's raw cotton imports, which fell from 75 million pounds in 1807 to 44 million pounds in 1808, but then rebounded; a similar effect was caused by the War of 1812, which caused raw cotton imports to fall from 92 million pounds in 1811 to 51 million in 1813.[5] Both effects were transitory, whereas the combined effect on French trade of the Orders in Council and the British capture of all France's West Indian colonies by 1810 was severe.

In the following 1809-12 government, Liverpool deferred the leadership again to Perceval. Canning and Castlereagh were ruled out because of their duel, Liverpool became Secretary for War and the Colonies, Wellesley (Wellington's brother) became Foreign Secretary and the nonentity Richard Ryder[6] took over the Home Office. This government, weak initially, gradually strengthened as Perceval and Liverpool worked effectively together. Liverpool devised a strategy of steady moderate pressure against Napoleon's financially rickety Empire, which began to work as Wellington's successful Peninsular campaigns culminated in the victory at Salamanca in July 1812. Napoleon made a disastrous decision to invade Russia in June (and the French army finally retreated from Russian soil in December the same year). Early in 1812 Castlereagh succeeded Wellesley at the Foreign Office and Sidmouth returned to government, making it a very strong one but, alas, Perceval was assassinated on 11 May.

The Slave Trade Felony Act 1811 was an important additional step towards the abolition of slavery; it made trading in slaves a felony. With the Royal Navy's West Africa Squadron instituted in 1808 and Perceval an evangelical opponent of the trade, the British slave trade was mostly wiped out during these years, although foreign traders continued in action. Various provisions were written into the 1815 Treaty of Vienna by which Continental powers promised to abolish the trade; those promises were only slowly and intermittently kept.

---

5. Figures from Mitchell (ed.), *British Historical Statistics*, Table VI-1.
6. Richard Ryder (1766-1832). MP for Tiverton, 1795-1830. Home Secretary, 1809-12.

Liverpool's Policies Lead to Modernity, 1807-30

The Destruction of Stocking Frames etc. Act 1812 was a response to the Luddite outbreaks early that year, which resulted from the trade disruption and high food prices caused by the embargoes and a bad 1811 harvest. The Act added machine breaking to the list of felonies punishable by death, a provision repealed in 1814 and never enforced in practice. In introducing the Act in the Lords, Liverpool said:

> the present interposition of Parliament is called for, not by the distresses of the workmen, but from a conspiracy against the machinery, which has regularly exhibited itself at all times when machinery has been employed to the disuse of manual labour. We have found penal statutes necessary for the protection of every successive kind of machinery.[7]

The Bullion Committee pointed the way forward for the British economy and public finances. It was set up in 1810, following a series of letters in the Whig *Morning Chronicle* by the political economist, David Ricardo,[8] and chaired by the moderate Whig, Francis Horner,[9] other members included Henry Thornton, William Huskisson and Alexander Baring. It sought to determine whether the high price of gold was due to shortage of gold supply or excess coinage of paper money. (In practice it appears to have resulted from both causes.) The Committee was unaware that its report came at a time of maximum gold supply strain.

Annual global gold production in 1800 was about 600,000 ounces, of which 400,000 ounces came from Latin America, having risen only 0.5% annually, about in line with world output, in the eighteenth century. Gold output did not rise much further during the next fifteen years of global warfare, while demand for gold rose sharply, to pay British troops in the Peninsula and French troops throughout Europe. Only after 1823 did Russian production from the Ekaterinburg mines produce a sharp upsurge in global gold production. Gold production increased markedly later in the nineteenth century, to 1.4 million ounces in 1846, before the California discoveries, then to a peak of fifteen million ounces annually in the 1890s. Over the nineteenth century, new gold supply rose at 3.3%

---

7. Hansard, *Parliamentary Debates from the Year 1803*, Vol. 21, cols 1082-83, 5 March 1812.

8. See p. 129, note 60..

9. Francis Horner (1778-1817). Whig MP for St Ives, Wendover and St Mawes, 1806-12, 1813-17. One of the founders of the *Edinburgh Review*.

annually, well above the annual rise in real world GDP of 1.8%.[10] The gold standard was thus not unduly deflationary.

The Bullion Committee concluded that issuing excess paper money beyond the value of gold held had the same effect on the price of gold as currency debasement. Since the suspension of cash payments in February 1797, the Bank of England had raised the amount of its notes outstanding from £11 million in 1796 to £21.2 million in May 1810, causing the gold value of the currency to decline, even though efficiency improvements in banking had increased the velocity of money.

The committee then affirmed that a change in the gold parity would be a breach of faith. The suspension of cash payments in gold by the Bank of England should be ended as quickly as possible without waiting for the war's end. No more than two years should be allowed for the Bank of England to adjust and the country banks' issue of notes should be quickly ended thereafter, returning the country to a gold standard at the pre-war parity. The alternative would be a potentially devastating loss of confidence in Britain's ability to meet its obligations.

In practice, as Liverpool knew, resuming cash payments before the war ended would be economically and militarily suicidal. The budgetary strain of maintaining a substantial force in Portugal and providing subsidies to the Portuguese government was too great, as was the need for specie to support Wellington. However, the committee's general conclusions governed his policy after the war.

Liverpool appeared to be Perceval's inevitable successor in 1812 but, thanks to an adverse Commons motion, was subjected to three weeks of uncertainty while Wellesley, Canning, Moira, Grenville and Grey attempted unsuccessfully to form governments. With Sidmouth as Home Secretary, Castlereagh as Foreign Secretary, the underrated Vansittart at the Exchequer and only Canning missing, Liverpool then won a larger majority (419 to 239) at the 1812 election than had Portland in 1807, helped by timely relaxation of the restrictions on Dissenters.[11]

Following Napoleon's defeat in Russia, in 1813 Liverpool and Castlereagh assembled the Sixth Coalition against him, which after Wellington's victory at Vitoria in June won the Battle of Leipzig in October and forced Napoleon to abdicate in April 1814. Napoleon's

---

10. Sources: for gold supply: Website Info.goldavenue.com; for GDP: Wikipedia, 'Gross World Product'.

11. By the Places of Religious Worship Act 1812, which repealed the Five Mile and Conventicle Acts and updated the registration system for Dissenting chapels.

return from Elba the following year was unsuccessful, largely because the fiscal and strategic advantage of Britain's well-organized economy against Napoleon's economically chaotic France was now overwhelming, despite France having twice Britain's population.

The East India Company Act 1813 extended the company's charter until 1833, but repealed its commercial monopoly, except for the tea and opium trade with China. The controls on British missionary activity were also relaxed, and the company undertook to promote Indian education.

Of more importance to entrepreneurs was the Insolvent Debtors (England) Act 1813, which set up a court system by which those imprisoned for debt could reach a settlement of their obligations. It was the beginning of relief from the draconian debtors' prison system, reducing the downside risks of entrepreneurship.

The Wages etc. of Artificers Act 1813 abolished the provision of the 1563 Statute of Artificers rendering a tradesman who had not undergone a seven-year apprenticeship subject to prosecution. It was an important step in freeing and modernising the labour market.

Liverpool's first business in the 1815 session, even before the crisis caused by Napoleon's return from Elba, was to pass the Importation Act 1815, known colloquially as the Corn Law. This followed the pattern of the 1773 and 1804 Corn Laws but raised the price below which corn imports would be prohibited to 80s per quarter – prices were so much higher than in 1773 that 1815's 80s was closely equivalent to 1773's 48s. In addition, the Act was extended to Ireland, giving Ireland protection against dumping of foreign corn and encouraging it to become a granary for the English market.

Thomas Malthus[12] had demonstrated in 1814 that a moderate Corn Law had two advantages. First, with imports prevented when grain prices were low, the country would be more self-sufficient in time of war since the maximum possible amount of land would be kept in cultivation. Second, the Corn Law's effect on forcing up wages would ensure that British labour was relatively high-cost compared with that of foreign countries, which would encourage the substitution of labour by machinery. This effect was a major contributor to Britain's industrial advancement.

---

12. Thomas R. Malthus (1766-1834). Cleric and political economist. Author of *An Essay on the Principle of Population* (1798), a work which appears increasingly prescient. His views on the Corn Laws appeared in *Observations on the Effects of the Corn Laws* (1814).

Conversely, Jean-Baptiste Say noted that high British taxation and the gigantic government debt raised the cost of labour and everything else in Britain and depressed the profits of business and commerce; he believed British goods would be uncompetitive in Europe once the European economies had recovered from the war.

Liverpool in his speech introducing the bill made the point that manufactured goods were protected, so that moderate protection of agriculture merely balanced the scales – free trade in agriculture would actively discourage it. The price of a quartern loaf, if corn prices were 80s per quarter, would be about 1s (12d), which consumers should see as a reasonable price. He also deprecated Say's point about British labour being too expensive:

> The success of our manufactures does not depend on cheapness of labour, but upon capital, credit and fuel. The importance of this latter article is clearly shown by the thriving establishments of manufactories in those countries where coal is plentiful; our great excellence in machinery gives us likewise a decided superiority. Cheapness of labour is, therefore, a secondary consideration, and we have the evidence of the manufacturers themselves at the bar of the House with regard to the Orders in Council, that they consider cheapness of labour as comparatively of little consequence. As to the labourers themselves who are employed in manufactures, I have no doubt that if they had to choose between cheapness of bread and a reduction in wages, and bread at its present price with their present wages, they would not hesitate to prefer the latter.

Later in the speech, Liverpool pointed out the Corn Law's advantage to agricultural workers:

> I must however observe that the agricultural labourer, who has not the same means of making his complaints known as the labourers of other classes, is fully entitled to your attention, as the distress of that class of persons must be a serious evil to the country.

He ended by observing that, if agriculture was reduced in extent owing to free trade:

> fifty years might be necessary to replace us in our present situation. A great and alarming evil might thus be produced

by rejecting the Bill and discouraging and diminishing agriculture, by rendering us dependent upon foreign nations for a supply which they might withhold or increase the price of at pleasure, whilst by passing the Bill, encouragement and support would be given to the agriculture of the country, tending to the material increase of our resources, and consequently, of our prosperity.[13]

In the event, the price of corn averaged 78s per quarter in the five years to summer 1820, suggesting the Corn Law had been appropriately designed, while Irish corn exports to England expanded to 350,000 quarters in 1820. Then the deflation caused by the return to gold brought a sharp fall in the corn price in 1820-22.

Although fiscal management remained good, the strain on the British economy imposed by the war increased in 1807-14. The government's demands reached a peak in 1814, when public spending totalled 34% of GDP, a level unequalled until the twentieth century and unsustainable in an economy still only modestly above subsistence level. Nevertheless, the budget deficit never reached 1790s peaks, reaching 11% of GDP in 1813, well below the 15.9% of GDP registered in 1797, dropping back sharply with the peace, to 6.2% of GDP in 1815 and 0.6% of GDP in 1816. Consols' prices also remained above their 1797-98 low of around 50%, bottoming at an average of 59% in 1812, but the heavy financing needs of 1813 made Liverpool and Vansittart's job very difficult until the news of the victory at Vitoria arrived in July.

The decade 1807-16 saw further economic growth, accelerating after a poor harvest in 1811 to over 2% per annum, with living standards in 1816 near the peak of 1791. Food prices were very high until 1813 because of Napoleon's Milan Decree embargo, which also caused bankruptcies to peak at 2,483 in 1811, about a quarter above the 1793 figure.[14] The poor 1811 harvest caused the London bread price to peak at 17d per quartern loaf in 1812[15] and brought the most serious outbreak of Luddite frame-breaking riots. The years 1813-15 were years of full employment and high grain prices but 1815 saw political riots in London against the Corn Laws.

---

13. Hansard, *Parliamentary Debates from the Year 1803*, Vol. 30, cols 175-86, 15 March 1815.
14. Mitchell (ed.), *British Historical Statistics*, Table XII-20, where I have used the 'Official Statistics' figure throughout.
15. London bread prices per quartern loaf, in pence, are given in ibid., Table XIV-22, p. 770.

330   *Forging Modernity*

Conversely, this was an excellent decade for agriculture, which, despite increased labour shortages due to industrialization and military needs, by adoption of labour-saving equipment like Meikle's threshing machine saw an increase in the acreage planted by 1813 to the highest seen before World War II. This would cause trouble after peace came as prices declined and foreign competition reappeared.

Coal production continued to expand rapidly as steam engines proliferated, from an annual average of 12,960,000 metric tons in 1801-5 to 24,800,000 metric tons in 1826-30, an increase of 2.6% annually, or 1.8% per capita per annum, slightly slower than before, reflecting the greater maturity of the coal industry and coal usage. The fastest expansion came from the Lancashire coalfields, whose output quadrupled from 1,100,000 metric tons per annum in 1801-5 to 4,500,000 metric tons in 1826-30, an annual growth rate of 5.8%. That reflected the extraordinary growth of the Lancashire-based textile industry and its wholesale conversion to steam power.[16]

Britain's economy was now qualitatively different from any other in the world and from its own state thirty years earlier. In *De l'Angleterre et des Anglais,*[17] Say said:

> At last human labour, which has rendered the high cost of consumer goods so expensive, is in no circumstances replaced so advantageously, as by steam engines, improperly called 'fire-pumps' by some. There is no work which cannot be reached to be executed by them. They go to the mills, weaving cotton and wool; they brew beer, they cut crystals. I have seen them embroider muslin and beat butter. At Newcastle, at Leeds, I have seen moving steam engines dragging after them carts of coal; and nothing is more surprising, at first sight, for a traveller, than to meet in the country long convoys which advance by themselves and without the help of any living being.
>
> Everywhere steam engines are prodigiously multiplied. There were no more than two or three in London thirty years ago, there are thousands at present. There are hundreds of them in the large manufacturing towns; one sees them even in the countryside, and industrial works could not be sustained profitably without their powerful help. But they must have

---

16. Ibid., Table IV-3, p, 247, with interpolation for the 1801-5 Lancashire output figures.
17. Say, *De l'Angleterre et des Anglais*. Author's translation.

Liverpool's Policies Lead to Modernity, 1807-30   331

abundant coal, that combustible fossil which Nature seems to have reserved to supplement the exhaustion of forests, the inevitable result of civilization. Thus, one could, with the help of a simple mineralogical map, trace an industrial map of Britain. There is industry everywhere there is coal in the ground.

Even before 1815, technological progress was accelerating, helped by the 'military-industrial complex'. Late in the war, the government built a single armaments factory, at Enfield, but output from this did not exceed 25,000 pieces annually before the war ended, although the Royal Small Arms Factory became the major British small-arms producer later. Conversely, getting new private businesses funded was difficult while the war's drain on the financial markets remained. Interest rates were high and the country banks, as issuers of banknotes, had easier and more lucrative games to play than the difficult work of financing small businesses. Nevertheless, the Napoleonic wars' economic effect differed from that of previous wars, in that there were now many well-established industrial businesses, who could finance themselves provided market conditions were not too difficult.

The stock market's silent transition from gambling casino to a serious place to raise finance was emphasized by the prosecution of the Great Stock Exchange Fraud of 1814. This was an extraordinary scheme, concocted by the independent Radical MP, Andrew Cochrane Johnstone,[18] his nephew, Thomas, Lord Cochrane[19] (also an MP, for Westminster) and Lord Cochrane's financial advisor, Richard Gathorne Butt, to defraud government bond investors by spreading a false rumour on 21 February 1814, when the outcome of peace negotiations with Napoleonic France was still highly uncertain, that Napoleon had been killed and the Allies had obtained a complete victory.

The Cochranes' associate, Charles Random de Berenger, arrived at the Ship Inn in Dover that morning, posing as Colonel de Bourg,

---

18. Andrew Cochrane Johnstone (1767-1833). MP for Stirling Burghs and Grampound, 1791-97, 1807-8, 1812-14. Governor of Dominica, 1797-1803. Expelled from House of Commons after fraud conviction and absconding, 1814.

19. Thomas Cochrane (1775-1860). Marquis of Maranhão (Brazil) from 1824, 10th Earl of Dundonald from 1831. Radical MP for Honiton and Westminster, 1806-18. Royal Navy Captain 1801, struck off Navy list, 1814, restored as Rear Admiral by Whigs, 1832, Vice Admiral 1841, Commander-in-Chief, West Indies and North America, 1848-51, Admiral, 1851. Vice Admiral in Chilean Navy, 1818-22. Admiral in Brazilian Navy, 1823-25.

aide-de-camp to Lord Cathcart,[20] with a forged letter to the Port Admiral at Deal to be transmitted by telegraph to London. This was done, and Lord Cochrane sold £139,000 government bearer bonds called 'Omniums' that morning, while Cochrane Johnstone sold £241,000 and Butt sold no less than £392,000. Assuming an average profit of around five percentage points on the fraud,[21] Lord Cochrane cleared £7,000, Cochrane Johnstone £12,000 and Butt £19,600.

The Cochranes had an old-fashioned view of market integrity; had they carried out their fraudulent scheme in 1712, they would doubtless have suffered no penalties and been the toast of the Kit Kat Club.[22] In 1814 the Committee of the Stock Exchange launched an investigation, discovered that £1.1 million of government bonds had been sold on 21 February which had been purchased only the previous week, and referred the matter to the High Court. The conspirators were sentenced on 21 June to £1,000 fines, twelve months of prison time and an hour in the public pillory. Lord Cochrane was also stripped of his naval rank and expelled from the Order of the Bath. The 1814 prosecution of the Cochranes was an important step in the professionalization of the capital markets.

Infrastructure

The first three decades of the nineteenth century saw major advances in infrastructure. The Napoleonic wars accustomed government and engineers to larger projects, and that expertise was adapted in peacetime, while, after 1815, private sector finance was readily available. Not all the infrastructure was well directed; the Thames Tunnel was a notable misfire. Canal investments of this period were uniformly financial disasters because the canal network had already been built to its economically optimal level and the next technological advance in

---

20. William Schaw Cathcart (1755-1843). 10th Lord Cathcart (Scotland) from 1776, Viscount Cathcart from 1807, Earl Cathcart from 1814. General, 1812. PC 1798. Ambassador to St Petersburg, 1812-20, serving with the Army of Liberation, 1812-14.

21. A. Aspinall (ed.), *The Letters of King George IV, 1812-30*, 3 vols (Cambridge: 1938), Vol. 1, p. 407, note 1, gives the rise in Omnium that morning as 5½ percentage points, from 27½ to 33. ('Omnium' referred to the partly-paid bonds of the latest Consols issue.)

22. Whig drinking and dining club, *c.* 1699-1720, portraits of whose members now have their own room in the National Portrait Gallery, Establishment Whiggery being what it is.

the form of the railways would shorten their economic lives. However, the availability of finance in large quantities and the success of earlier infrastructure investments spread infrastructure investment far beyond canals.

In London, the period saw major expansion of dock facilities. Trade volumes had been expanding continuously during the eighteenth century, more rapidly in the latter decades as industrialization took root, with cargo tonnage rising from 234,639 in 1751 to 620,845 in 1794.[23] There had been no major wet dock built around London since the Howland Wet Dock of 1700. The major expansion had come in West Indian trade for which London's pre-eminence had been threatened by the construction of seven docks between 1717 and 1785 in Liverpool, now the principal port for transatlantic commerce.

In 1796 a parliamentary Select Committee examined the matter and asked for research to be done, with a second committee under Hawkesbury in 1799 examining the results. The committee recommended the building of a canal across the Isle of Dogs and the ensuing West India Dock Act 1799 created a West India Dock Company with capital of £500,000 to construct a dock for West Indies trade on the Isle of Dogs, on the north side of the river. This was done, at an eventual cost of £1.4 million, with Pitt laying the foundation stone in 1800 and the docks opening in August 1802, presided over by Addington. A southern extension of the West India Dock was opened in 1829.

The canal across the Isle of Dogs was funded by the City of London and completed in 1805, but turned out to save little time, because of the necessity to de-rig the ships and have them pulled through the canal by horses. In 1829, the City of London sold the canal to the West India Dock Company for storage.

A second dock scheme, sponsored by merchants doing business with neither the West nor the East Indies, passed through Parliament in 1800, and resulted in the London Dock at Wapping, also on the north side of the river, closer to the City of London than the West India Dock. That scheme, with a gigantic tobacco warehouse measuring 752 feet by 160, attracted Addington to lay the foundation stone in 1802, but not Pitt to its opening in January 1805.

Following the success of the West India Dock, the East India Company obtained parliamentary authorization in 1803 for an East India Dock

---

23. British History Online: 'The West India Docks: Introduction', available at: https://www.british-history.ac.uk/survey-london/vols43-4/pp247-248 (accessed 18 November 2021).

A Fish Dinner at the Brunswick Hotel, East India Dock. Illustration by Richard Doyle, from *Punch*, 1849.

also on the north side of the river, but further down it at Blackwall. The foundation stone was laid in February 1805 and the dock opened in July 1806. Being more isolated, the dock included a brickworks but also the Brunswick Hotel, constructed exactly on the meridian line opposite Greenwich, which became famous for its fish dinners. The Commercial Road, which opened in 1806, was built to connect the West and East India Docks to Whitechapel and eventually Aldgate.

On the south bank of the river, several smaller ventures combined to create the Surrey Docks, primarily for Baltic timber, beginning in 1807 and taking over the Howland Wet Dock (now known as the Greenland Dock) in 1810.

The Regent's Canal Dock was an offshoot of the Regent's Canal project, which connected the eastern terminus of the Grand Junction Canal at Paddington with the river between the London and West India Docks. The eight-mile canal was begun in 1812 and completed in 1820, with the dock at its eastern terminus to transfer cargo from seagoing vessels to barges.

Finally, the St Katharine Dock, just east of the Tower of London and west of the London Dock, was authorized by Parliament in 1825 with the merchant/economist Thomas Tooke[24] as chairman and designed by Telford. It opened in two stages in 1828 and 1829, specializing mainly in Indian tea and New Zealand wool.

Further docks were built in the Victorian era, but the main body of London's dockland was constructed within this 30-year period, to take advantage of the enormous increase in trade. All these London docks were built by the private sector, the only early public-sector investment being the failed canal across the Isle of Dogs.

Outside London, the major development was the rapid improvement of the road network led by John Loudon McAdam.[25] After making a modest fortune as a merchant in New York, McAdam returned to Britain in 1783 and after periods in Ayr and Falmouth, in 1815 became surveyor of the Bristol Turnpike Trust, where he invented 'Macadamization', a system of road building with crushed stones of around 0.75-in. diameter bound with gravel on a firm base of larger stones and given a raised camber in the middle to ensure proper drainage.

Macadamization was the greatest improvement in road construction since Roman times. McAdam published two treatises on road building in 1816 and 1819, appeared before a parliamentary committee in 1823 and became Surveyor General of Metropolitan Roads from 1827. British roads were rapidly brought up to this new standard, ensuring that journey speeds on trunk roads in 1830 were more than triple those of 1700. Macadamization was also adopted worldwide, a notable early example being the US National Road completed in 1837. The modern term 'tarmac' (tar-bound McAdam) reflects McAdam's memory.

This period also saw the power of steam applied to the drainage of the Fens. Wind-powered pumping engines had proved insufficiently

---

24. Thomas Tooke (1774-1858). Economist and businessman. Governor of the Royal Exchange Corporation, 1840-52. Author of *A History of Prices and the State of Circulation, from 1792 to the Present Time*, 6 vols (1838-1857).

25. John McAdam (1756-1836). Born in Ayr, Scotland, moved to New York in 1770 and made his fortune as a merchant and contractor. Returned to Scotland, 1783, became trustee of Ayrshire turnpike. Surveyor of Bristol Corporation, 1804, and Surveyor of Bristol Turnpike Trust, 1815. Surveyor-General of Metropolitan Roads, 1827. Wrote *Remarks on the Present System of Road-Making* (1816) and *Practical Essay on the Scientific Repair and Preservation of Roads* (1819).

336   *Forging Modernity*

powerful, but the first steam-powered fen drainage installation was at Pode Hole in Lincolnshire, where the engineer, Benjamin Bevan,[26] surveyed the local Deeping Fen and oversaw the installation in 1825 of two pumping engines, a 60hp engine made by Fenton & Murray and an 80hp engine by Butterley. These were completely successful, continuing in operation until 1925 and were followed by further engines around the Fens, bringing the full drainage that had eluded the fourth Earl of Bedford 200 years earlier.

The Gas Lighting Explosion

This period's other major infrastructure development was gas lighting. William Murdoch had lit his Cornwell residence by gas in the 1790s and lit Boulton & Watt's Soho Manufactory by gas in 1802, but Boulton & Watt was only one of the pioneers in gas lighting, leaving the business in 1814. The principal advances in further gas light development were made by the German-born entrepreneur, Friedrich Albrecht Winzer/Winsor,[27] the German scientist, Friedrich Accum,[28] and the engineer, Samuel Clegg.[29]

London's gas street lighting was inaugurated by Winsor, who lit half of Pall Mall in 1807. Winsor had come to Britain in 1799 and was attracted by the wood gas illumination pioneered in Paris in 1802 by Philippe Lebon (1767-1804); he acquired a British patent for coal gas illumination

---

26. Benjamin Bevan (1773-1833). Engineer and surveyor. Principal engineer, Grand Junction Canal.
27. Friedrich Albrecht Winzer/Winsor (1763-1830). Born in Brunswick, moved to Britain, 1799. Acquired patent for French wood gas system, 1803. Patented coal gas lighting in 1804. Lit one side of Pall Mall, 1807. Founded Gas, Light and Coke Company, 1812, forced out of management. Died in Paris.
28. Friedrich Accum (1769-1838). Lecturer on chemistry and minerology attached to Royal Institution, 1801-3. Isolated iodine and devised process for its production, 1811-14. Director of Gas, Light and Coke Company, 1812, overseeing construction of first gasworks. Author of *System of Theoretical and Practical Chemistry* (1803), *Description of the Process of Manufacturing Coal-Gas* (1815) and *A Treatise on Adulterations of Food and Culinary Poisons* (1820). Returned to Germany, 1821, lectured and wrote in Berlin.
29. Samuel Clegg (1781-1861). Invented lime purifiers for town gas and patented gas meter, 1818. Chief Engineer, Gas, Light and Coke Company. Subsequently involved in unsuccessful ventures including atmospheric railway.

Gas lighting in Pall Mall that lit up a new age. Engraved by Thomas Rowlandson, 1807-09.

in 1804. With the help of Accum as chemist, he then produced the illuminations in Pall Mall as a demonstration. He applied to Parliament for a corporate charter (still necessary under the Bubble Act) and, after several attempts, obtained one for the Gas, Light and Coke Company in April 1812. The new company was capitalized at the huge sum of £1 million, divided in 80,000 shares, a sign of the impressive strength of the London capital market, even in wartime.

Friedrich Accum was an impressive scientific polymath. The son of a German Jewish officer who converted to Christianity, Accum was apprenticed to an apothecary, moving to England and another apothecary in 1793, where he devised a method of producing sugar from beets in 1799. Then, he became a professional lecturer on chemistry and mineralogy, attached to the Royal Institution in 1801-3 and then independent. In 1803 he published the first chemistry textbook in English that integrated the Lavoisier system of oxygen combustion, after which he isolated the element iodine and devised a process for its production. During these years, he became involved in gas production, assisting Winsor in his illumination of Pall Mall, then becoming a director of the Gas, Light and Coke Company in 1812.

Accum published the first handbook on coal gas production, *Description of the Process of Manufacturing Coal-Gas*, in 1815, providing basic information that was used to proliferate gas lighting installations across the country over the next decade. Accum himself was unfortunately unable to remain in England to receive the plaudits. In 1820, he published the first significant work on food adulteration, *A Treatise on Adulterations of Food and Culinary Poisons*, an important guide to a future in which food would be industrially manufactured for consumption in big cities. Alas, he was foolish enough to include the names of prominent London manufacturers who had adulterated food and was forced to leave the country. He moved to Berlin, where he became a professor and published further works before he died in 1839.

Samuel Clegg received a scientific education under John Dalton, then apprenticed at Boulton & Watt. Having learned the basics of gas lighting, he introduced it into the textile industry, equipping Willow Hall Mills at Sowerby Bridge, Yorkshire, with gas lighting in 1805. He developed a wet-liming process to purify gas (a serious safety issue in the early years) and joined the Gas, Light and Coke Company as chief engineer in 1812.

In 1818, he patented a water meter to enable users to measure the consumption of gas, which became widely used and led to the beginnings of domestic gas lighting. Over the next decades, he became an independent gas lighting contractor, based primarily in Birmingham, and was active by 1825 in providing gas lighting in Chester, Bristol, Birmingham, Worcester and Kidderminster. His subsequent engineering ventures in Portugal and in railway construction were less successful – he was involved in the atmospheric railway system, which proved to be sub-optimal. In old age, he worked as a government advisor and with his son, Samuel, in writing a treatise on the manufacture of coal gas, published in 1850.

The Gas, Light and Coke Company proved successful, lighting Westminster Bridge in 1813 and then setting up several gasworks around London, eventually becoming the nucleus of British Gas plc. Since there were initially few economies of scale in gas manufacture and supply, there was a rapid adoption of gas lighting technology, with gas companies being localized, hundreds of them appearing – the principal scarce resource being skilled gas engineers, such as Clegg and the three Malam brothers, John, James and George, who were responsible for over 50 gas establishments by 1846.

The first big gas lighting boom, lighting most British towns with a population of 10,000 or more, took place between 1818 and 1825 with a total capital investment of around £3.15 million, mostly through chartered companies, forming around 10% of the capital raised in

Liverpool's Policies Lead to Modernity, 1807-30

the stock market boom of the early 1820s. In London alone, some 300 miles of gas mains were in use by 1823. Factory lighting was the most attractive sector of the business since street lighting contracts with local municipalities were not very remunerative.[30] Thus, gas lighting had gone from prototype to near-universality within 30 years,

Science

The rapid science-driven adoption of gas lighting demonstrates the more important role scientific investigation was coming to perform in the industrialization process. The Royal Society early in its life had been a pioneer in practical experimentation, then after 1700 it had settled down into upper-class dilettantism. This now began to change; the Royal Society became more intellectually serious and once again attached to technological advance, although neither Friedrich Accum nor other gas lighting pioneers were ever recognized by it. However, other learned societies such as the Royal Institution grew up, enlarging the scientific community and increasing its salience for industrial innovation.

Three towering minds made this an exceptionally fertile period of scientific discovery, with two making important technological advances.

John Dalton[31] was the least technologically involved of the three and the most isolated from mainstream society. The son of a Quaker weaver, he entered the workforce at age ten and was thereafter largely self-taught. In 1793, he was appointed teacher of mathematics and natural philosophy at the 'Manchester Academy', a Dissenting higher education institution. After considerable work on colour blindness and gas diffusion, in 1803, he developed the atomic theory and published a table of atomic weights, the key discovery for which he is famous. In 1810, he was invited by Humphrey Davy to accept a Fellowship in the Royal Society but turned the offer down. He remained a private teacher in Manchester, given a modest pension by Grey's Whig government in 1833, although he was awarded honorary membership of both the French and United States Academies of Sciences. Dalton's work was of immense long-term importance to both chemistry and physics but had little short-term effect on industrial technology.

---

30. Statistics on the gas industry from M.E. Falkus, 'The British Gas Industry before 1850', *Economic History Review*, Vol. 20, no. 3 (1967), pp. 494-508.
31. John Dalton (1766-1844) Inventor of the atomic theory, and pioneering researcher into colour blindness.

Humphrey Davy[32] was born in deeply rural Cornwall, the son of a woodcarver, and educated at the grammar schools in Penzance and later Truro but, unlike the equally humbly born Dalton, he was inclined to Toryism. After studying chemistry under a physician, in 1798, he joined the Pneumatic Institution at Bristol, where he experimented on nitrous oxide, noticing its anaesthetic properties and nicknaming it 'laughing gas'. While in Bristol, he became friendly with the poets, William Wordsworth (1770-1850), Robert Southey (1774-1843) and Samuel Taylor Coleridge (1772-1834), all with national reputations and moving politically towards Toryism.

In March 1801, Davy left Bristol for an assistant lectureship at the Royal Institution in London. There he utilized the most powerful battery then known for a course of lectures on 'Galvanism', which was immensely successful and followed by a series on agricultural chemistry. During these lectures he put forward the thesis that mankind was no longer just the observer of natural forces but could control them and use them for his own ends. In 1802, he passed the battery's current through a thin strip of platinum, creating the first arc light, which he improved in 1806, although it was still several decades before this discovery was competitive with gas lighting.

Davy was a pioneer in electrolysis, using the 'voltaic pile' battery to split common compounds, thereby isolating new elements. By this technique, in the years after 1807, he isolated, 'discovered' and named nine of the periodic table's 92 naturally occurring elements. His 1808 paper, *On Some Chemical Agencies of Electricity*, was fundamental to future chemical research.

In 1812, Davy left the Royal Institution, married, was knighted and the following year, after damaging his eyesight, took on Michael Faraday as his assistant. In 1813, he and Faraday travelled to France (still at war with Britain) to be awarded a medal from Napoleon, after which he continued to Rome and Mount Vesuvius, where he collected volcanic crystals.

On his return to Britain, Davy investigated the causes of the Felling mine disaster of 1812 and developed the Davy miners' safety lamp,

---

32. Humphrey Davy (1778-1829). Kt 1812. FRS 1804. 1st Bt from 1818. Lecturer, Royal Institution, 1801-12. President, Royal Society, 1820-27. Discovered sodium, potassium, barium, calcium, strontium, magnesium, boron, chlorine and iodine. Invented arc lamp in 1806 and Davy miners' safety lamp, 1815. Author of *Elements of Chemical Philosophy* (1812).

Liverpool's Policies Lead to Modernity, 1807-30   341

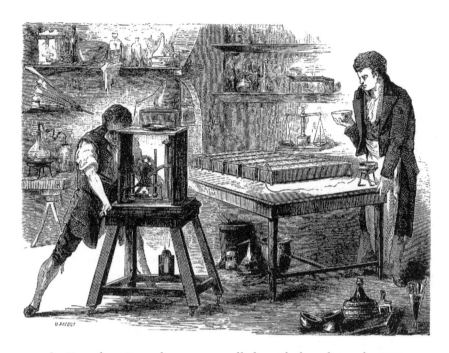

Sir Humphrey Davy decomposing alkalis with the voltaic pile, 1807.
Engraving by Louis Fiuler.

unveiled in 1815, which used metal gauze to prevent the flame from reaching the atmosphere. He then did considerable work on defining acids and bases. In 1820, he became President of the Royal Society, in succession to Sir Joseph Banks. He resigned in 1827 when a series of strokes caused him to retire. He died in 1829 in Switzerland. Before then, he had become a founding fellow of the Zoological Society, which established the London Zoo in 1826, with other founders including Lansdowne, Peel and Sir Stamford Raffles.[33]

Of this period's three notable scientists, Davy's work had the most substantial and immediate effect in industrial technology, helping to create a chemical industry that was to dominate the second stage of industrialization. His lecturing and networking at the highest levels of British science, politics and society notably assisted the propagation and acceptance of his ideas.

---

33. Thomas Stamford Raffles (1781-1826). Kt 1817. FRS 1817. Governor-General of the Dutch East Indies, 1813-16. Founded Singapore, 1819.

342   *Forging Modernity*

Michael Faraday,[34] was the son of a Newington blacksmith, like Dalton largely self-educated and apprenticed to a London bookseller at fourteen. At the end of his apprenticeship in 1813, he attended a series of Davy's lectures, took 300 pages of notes and was taken on as Davy's assistant. After accompanying Davy to France, he worked further on electrolysis, identifying benzine, conducting experiments on the diffusion of gases and formulating laws of electrolysis.

Faraday's greatest work was done in electromagnetism during the 1820s at the Royal Institution. In 1821, after discussions with Davy, he designed the first electric motor. He then formulated laws of electromagnetic induction, the principles behind the motor and the dynamo; these were later put into mathematically rigorous form by James Clark Maxwell (1831-79) as Maxwell's equations. Finally, in 1831, Faraday designed the first dynamo, by which motion could be used to generate electricity. From this work, the electric power industry of the 1870s onwards was germinated.

Faraday remained in London and more involved with society than Dalton, giving annual Christmas Lectures for children, but religious principles prevented his accepting honours or taking as active a social and political role as had Davy. Nevertheless, by living a generation longer than Davy, he became a towering figure to the Victorians and his work had the greatest long-term influence of the three.

Brunel and Maudslay

Besides Maudslay, the principal industrial innovator emerging from the Napoleonic wars military-industrial complex was **Mark Isambard Brunel**. The second son of a prosperous Norman French farmer, Brunel became a cadet in the French Navy, before declaring Royalist sympathies after the Revolution and fleeing to the United States. There he got involved in a forerunner of the Erie Canal and submitted a design for the US Capitol. He then took US citizenship in 1796, after which he was appointed Chief Engineer of the City of New York.

After a dinner conversation in 1798 during which Brunel learned of the Royal Navy's difficulties in manufacturing pulley blocks, he designed a set of block manufacturing machines and re-emigrated to England, arriving in March 1799 with a letter of introduction to the First

---

34. Michael Faraday (1791-1867). FRS 1824. Assistant to Davy, 1813. Lecturer, Royal Institution from 1821. Discovered laws of electrolysis and electromagnetic induction. Invented electric motor, 1821; dynamo, 1831.

Lord of the Admiralty. That year, he met Maudslay and married Sophia Kingdom (1775-1855), an English lady whom he had met in France. Among their children was Isambard Kingdom Brunel (1806-59).

After completing the Portsmouth Block Works with Maudslay, Brunel continued to benefit from military patronage. In 1806, he designed the first large steam-powered circular saw, examples of which, built by Maudslay, he installed at Woolwich and Chatham dockyard, with another in his own sawmill factory in Battersea.[35] Then, having seen the pitiful footwear of Sir John Moore's troops returning through Portsmouth from Corunna in 1809, he built a shoe factory at Battersea, with sixteen machines, operated by 25 disabled military veterans, which by 1812 could produce 400 pairs of military boots per day (all of them straight, without left-foot and right-foot variants, to reduce the number of lasts needed). Brunel's mass-produced boots were used in the last stages of the Peninsular War and at Waterloo.

Alas, when peace came, Brunel had a stock of 80,000 unwanted pairs of boots, inventory control not being his strong point. This, combined with a disastrous fire in 1814 which consumed the Battersea sawmill and an abortive venture into the tinfoil business, bankrupted Brunel and sent him into debtors' prison in 1821, from which he was rescued by a £5,000 grant from the Liverpool government, conditional on him agreeing to remain in Britain.

The principal activity of the remainder of Brunel's life was the construction of the Thames Tunnel. There was no Thames crossing downriver of London Bridge at this time, nor could there be above-ground, because shipping using the river and the immense docks complex being constructed during these years would be impeded. So, a tunnel was necessary. Trevithick's attempt to build one between 1805 and 1809 had failed disastrously, after which the Brunels, father and son, took up the challenge.

In 1818 Brunel patented a tunnelling shield, a revolutionary technology that could advance tunnel construction while avoiding the danger of flooding; the shield for the Thames Tunnel would be built at Maudslay's engineering works in Lambeth. A plan was produced in 1823, a Thames Tunnel Company was formed in 1824, with 4,000 shares of £50 par value (a total of £200,000) and a public share offering in that year's bull market to investors, including Wellington, and construction

---

35. Details of Brunel's Battersea operations are given in Colin Thom, 'Fine Veneers, Army Boots and Tinfoil: New Light on Marc Brunel's Activities in Battersea', *Construction History*, Vol. 25 (2010), pp. 53-67.

344   *Forging Modernity*

began in February 1825. Alas, despite the tunnelling shield, the tunnel repeatedly flooded. It was not completed until 1843, after a £247,000 government grant from the Whig Treasury in 1834. Although wide and high enough to accommodate carriages, the tunnel was only opened for pedestrian use and was a financial disaster, having cost a total of £634,000. It was sold to the East London Railway in 1865 for £200,000 and converted into a rail tunnel.

Marc Isambard Brunel and his son were both engineering geniuses of surpassing quality, but neither of them had much business sense. The Thames Tunnel was typical of some of Isambard's more ambitious projects in that insufficient attention was paid to its economics. Without the possibility of transporting goods beneath the Thames, or connections to a transportation network, the Thames Tunnel was never going to recoup its costs, even had its construction not been a 20-year nightmare, fraught with disasters and supremely unpleasant working conditions.

Beyond his work on Brunel's Thames Tunnel shield, the second half of Maudslay's career was as productive as the first. In 1807, he patented the first table-sized steam engine, which eliminated the rocking beam, common since Newcomen, and made the engine entirely self-contained, allowing it to be used in such applications as printing works, where fire was a risk. These engines, with powers between 1.5hp and 40hp, became a staple of the Maudslay workshop's output for the next 50 years. His engineering business expanded steadily to around 80 workers by 1810, when he moved to a new works at Lambeth, where he expanded further, taking into partnership around 1820 a promising young Admiralty draughtsman, Joshua Field.[36] Maudslay was the first to realize the importance of accurate plane surfaces for guiding tools and, with the assistance of Joseph Whitworth, produced standard steel planes so smooth they adhered to each other, separable only by sliding.

Maudslay's precision engineering and his interest in steam power later led his workshop to specialize in marine engines. His first marine engine of 17hp was built in 1815 and fitted to the *Richmond*, a Thames steamer. In 1823, he built the engine for the *Lightning*, the first steamer commissioned into the Royal Navy, and in 1829 he built a 400hp

---

36. Joshua Field (1786-1863). FRS 1836. Joined Henry Maudslay's workshop about 1808 and became his partner around 1820. Co-founded Institute of Civil Engineers, 1817, President, 1848. Built engines for SS *Great Western*, 1838.

engine for the steam paddle-sloop HMS *Dee*, the largest marine engine completed to that time; HMS *Dee* served in the Royal Navy until 1871.

Maudslay's workshop was notable for training younger engineers who would later become major figures; these included: Joseph Clement (1779-1844; Maudslay workshop, 1814-17); Richard Roberts (1789-1864; Maudslay workshop, 1814-16); David Napier (1788-1873; Maudslay workshop, 1814-16); Sir Joseph Whitworth (1803-87; Maudslay workshop, 1825-28); and James Nasmyth (1808-90; Maudslay workshop, 1829-31).

Maudslay's business continued until 1904, with his sons, Thomas Henry (1792-1864) and Joseph (1801-61), and Joshua Field initially in charge. His great-grandson, Walter H. Maudslay, founded an early automobile company, Maudslay Motors, the family's engineering reputation doubtless helping sales.

Of Maudslay's followers, two, Joseph Clement and **Richard Roberts**, had important achievements before 1830. Roberts, first, has been termed the most important mechanical engineer of the nineteenth century. After leaving Maudslay in 1816, he returned to the north of England (he had originally moved to London in 1813 to escape a militia call-up) and set up as an engineer in Manchester, with his lathe in the bedroom, driven by his wife on a big wheel in the basement.[37] Soon he developed a range of machine tools, most notably a gear cutter, a back-geared lathe that could handle work up to six feet long and a planing machine, one of which was sold to Maudslay in 1825 or 1826. In 1818, he designed the first gas meter for the Manchester Police Commissioners.

In 1821, Roberts moved to larger premises, partnered with Thomas Sharp (1779-1841) and turned his attention to textile machinery. In 1822, he took out a patent for a power loom, vastly improved from existing looms because it used precision all-metal manufacturing techniques; by 1825, the firm was producing about 4,000 power looms a year. Then, in March 1825, he took out a patent on a self-acting spinning mule, which greatly reduced the number of spinners needed; since the preceding winter had seen massive strike action in the industry, this too was very popular with manufacturers – the design's 1830 modification was in widespread use until 1927.

After 1830, the firm diversified into locomotive building, but became unprofitable and was dissolved in 1852. Roberts died in straitened circumstances in 1864. Nevertheless, his advances in machine tools and textile machinery set the patten for industry for the rest of the nineteenth

---

37. Cantrell and Cookson, *Henry Maudslay and the Pioneers of the Machine Age*, p. 55.

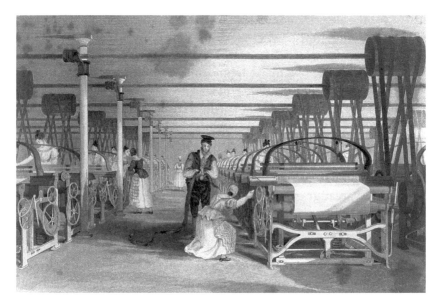

The Roberts power loom was Richard Roberts' 1822 ultimate in textile technology. Engraving by T. Allom, J. Tingle.

century. The manufacture of machine tools remained a business with low capital requirements, in which former toolmakers could become small manufacturers and modestly prosper.[38]

Clement's major pre-1830 achievement was important only in the very long term; he was chosen by Charles Babbage[39] to build his Difference Engine. He had set up an independent works in Newington, London, where he made several improvements to the lathe and became renowned as a draughtsman; in later years he specialized in building organs.

Babbage, a superlative mathematician, had graduated from Trinity College, Cambridge and was elected FRS in 1816, at the age of only 25. He worked on the principles of computation and their mechanical expression, in 1822 designing an automated difference engine to compute

---

38. Crouzet, *The First Industrialists*, p. 87.
39. Charles Babbage (1791-1871). FRS 1816. Mathematician, inventor and engineer. Inherited £100,000, 1827. Lucasian Professor of Mathematics, Trinity College, Cambridge, 1828-39. Invented the Difference Engine and the Analytical Engine (never built), mechanical ancestors of the computer, and along with Ada Lovelace developed the logic behind computer programming.

Liverpool's Policies Lead to Modernity, 1807-30

navigational, gunnery and other mathematical tables. His pamphlet explaining this possibility was discussed at a Treasury Board meeting presided over by Liverpool on 1 April 1823, after which a £1,700 grant was awarded to Babbage for the work.

Clement assisted him in building the first prototype, designing several complex machine tools for the purpose. However, despite receiving a further £15,000 in government funding (Wellington was also a strong supporter of the Difference Engine), Babbage and Clement fell out in 1831, so the prototype was never completed. Babbage went on to design an Analytical Engine, in its principles the first computer, working with Ada, Countess of Lovelace,[40] on its programming, but that too was never completed and the unimaginative Peel[41] cut off funding in 1842.

While of enormous importance for the very distant future, the Babbage engines were too advanced, given early nineteenth-century engineering tolerances. Even had they been successfully built, their practical use would have been limited without major further scientific and technological development.

Textiles

By this period, the textile industry was mature and progress was by expansion with fewer technological breakthroughs. There were already 2,400 power looms in operation in 1803; that number expanded to 14,650 by 1820 and then soared to 55,500 by 1829, with Roberts' 1822 loom providing a major upward impetus. In 1807, there were already large textile companies using steam-driven machinery, although the cost advantages of steam over water power were not compelling for works located by a good water source; for example, the Quarry Bank Mill remained water-powered throughout the nineteenth century.

The most important technological innovation was the Jacquard loom, invented by the French weaver and merchant, Joseph Marie

---

40. Ada Byron (1815-52). Countess of Lovelace from 1838. Daughter of George Gordon Byron, 6th Baron Byron. Devised much of the logic for Babbage's analytical engine.

41. As early as 1823, Peel had written to John Wilson Croker: 'I should like a little previous consideration before I move in a thin house of country gentlemen, a large vote for the construction of a wooden man to calculate tables from the formula x^2+x+41.' (Peel letter to Croker, 8 March 1823, quoted in *The Correspondence and Diaries of John Wilson Croker*, 3 vols. [London: John Murray, 1884], Vol. 1, p. 263.)

Jacquard (1752-1834), in 1804. This used a system of punched cards to allow a power loom to make intricately patterned fabrics; the highly ingenious invention was an inspiration for Babbage's analytical engine. Interestingly, instead of allowing Jacquard to patent the machine, the statist Napoleonic regime declared the design public property in 1805, rewarding Jacquard with a pension of 3,000 francs (£120) per annum plus a royalty of 50 francs on each loom sold until 1811. The Jacquard loom only penetrated the British market significantly after 1815, but an 1836 estimate[42] was that 7,000-8,000 Jacquard looms were in action in Britain. The adoption of the Jacquard loom, with its ability to weave complex patterns, brought about the final decline of the handloom weaver.

Raw cotton consumption increased from 73 million pounds in 1807 to 248 million pounds in 1830, with the fastest growth in the 1820-25 boom. In 1830 80% of raw cotton imports came from the United States, reflecting the cost advantages of the southern states' slave-driven production. The domestic wool clip increased only moderately, from 100 million pounds to 120 million, but raw wool imports also increased, from 11.7 million pounds in 1807 to 32.3 million in 1830, little of which was yet from Australasia.[43] Textile prices began to decline as production efficiency increased; the average value of cotton piece goods exported declined from 11.73d per linear yard in 1821 to 7.62d in 1830.[44] Despite declining prices, exports of cotton goods increased robustly from £10.3 million in 1807 to £19.4 million in 1830.[45]

After 1800, home-based methods in both spinning and weaving became uneconomic. Their practitioners took decades to disappear, immiserated by ever-declining piecework rates paid by the mills for which they worked. While textile factory employment increased from 93,000 in 1807 to 185,000 in 1830, the number of handloom weavers also increased somewhat, from 188,000 to 240,000 as patterned

---

42. *Manchester Guardian*, 14 December 1836, quoted in Manchester Science and Industry Museum, 'Programming Patterns: The Story of the Jacquard Loom', available at: https://www.scienceandindustrymuseum. org.uk/objects-and-stories/jacquard-loom (accessed 3 December 2021).
43. Mitchell (ed.), *British Historical Statistics*, Tables VI-2, VI-3, VI-6 and VI-7.
44. Ibid., Table XIV-19.
45. Ibid., Tables IX-2, IX-8 and IX-11. There are discontinuities in the tables, so the 1807 and 1830 figures may not be precisely comparable.

fabrics benefited from handloom work. After 1830, handloom weaver employment finally declined, to only 43,000 by 1850 as Jacquard power looms became universal.[46] By the early 1840s, the remaining handloom weavers earned wages below subsistence levels, with the depressed 1830s and early 1840s leaving them fewer alternatives than in the prosperous 1820s. Poor communications, sticky local labour markets and the downward mobility of wages slowed the mechanization of the textile industry, weakening its long-term position and vindicating Malthus and Liverpool's 1814-15 view that long-term prosperity lay in high wage rates not low ones.

Textile entrepreneurs with substantial successful businesses included Samuel Greg (1758-1834) of the Quarry Bank Mill in Cheshire, Kirkman Finlay (1773-1842) in Glasgow, Adam and George Murray in Manchester and, in woollens, Benjamin Gott (1762-1840) of Leeds, who used both steam power and power looms to become a millionaire by his death.

James McConnel (*c.* 1768-1831) and John Kennedy (1769-1855) were the founders of McConnel and Kennedy of Manchester; in 1797, they built a steam-powered mill, the Old Mill, adjacent to the Murray Mills in Ancoats, Manchester, which was powered by a 16hp Boulton & Watt engine. The Long Mill, powered by a 45hp Boulton & Watt engine was added in 1803, which became one of the first gas-lit mills when a gas-making plant with six gasometers was added in 1809. The Sedgewick Mill, the largest in the complex was built in 1818-20; it was eight stories high and seventeen bays long, the tallest cast-iron structure in the world, and was powered by a 54hp Boulton & Watt engine with a 24-ft flywheel. The company was then the largest employer in Manchester with 1,500 employees; after Kennedy retired in 1826, it traded as McConnel and McConnel, remaining in business until 1959. Kennedy was a leading initial sponsor of the Liverpool and Manchester Railway and a judge at the 1829 Rainhill Trials.

A different sector of the textile business was mechanized by John Heathcoat,[47] the son of a Derbyshire farmer who was apprenticed as framework knitter. He became a frame-smith with a good local reputation, and over 1804-9 took out several patents for several, progressively

---

46. Ibid., Table VI-36.

47. John Heathcoat (1783-1861). Whig MP for Tiverton, 1832-59. Inventor of bobbin net lace-making machine, 1809. See: https://www.knitting together.org.uk/behind-the-scenes/the-people/john-heathcoat-1783-1861/ (accessed 17 June 2022).

improved, 'bobbin net' machines for making lace, the most complex of all textile machinery.[48] He set up a factory in Loughborough in partnership and, by 1816, they had 55 lace-making frames in operation. In 1816, seventeen armed rioters attacked the factory, destroying frames worth close to £10,000. Heathcoat and his partners responded by relocating to Tiverton, Devon, building a mill that used both water and steam power to drive 300 lace-making machines and building a steam plough that sank without trace in a muddy field. Heathcoat became Whig MP for Tiverton from 1832, serving alongside Lord Palmerston;[49] the business continues today and in 2020 made the fabric for the landing parachute of NASA's *Perseverance* Mars rover.

The textile tycoon best remembered today was more famous as a social reformer. Robert Owen was born in Montgomeryshire, Wales, the sixth child of a saddler, ironmonger and postmaster. He was apprenticed to a Lincolnshire draper at the age of ten, then, around 1790, he borrowed £100 from his elder brother to enter the business of manufacturing spinning mules, becoming manager of the Piccadilly Mill in Manchester. In 1795, he left Manchester and with partners set up the Chorlton Twist Mill in Chorlton, Lancashire, which he would sell in 1809. In 1799, he married Ann Caroline Dale, whose father owned the large New Lanark Mills, which were water-powered, had been established by David Dale (1739-1806) in 1785 and now had around 2,000 employees. Owen and his partners bought out Dale for £60,000 and Owen became manager of New Lanark in January 1800.

Owen tested various philanthropic ideas, generally successfully, on New Lanark employees, of whom around 500 were children. His philanthropy did not extend to paying employees in cash, rather than using the 'truck' system at a company store, but it did extend to an eight-hour day, instituted in 1810. In 1813 he published *A New View of Society* and bought out his partners, replacing them with philanthropic investors, including Jeremy Bentham,[50] who were prepared to accept a lower than

---

48. He said in 1836: 'The single difficulty of getting the diagonal threads to twist in the allotted space was so great that, if now to be done, I should probably not attempt its accomplishment.'

49. Henry John Temple (1784-1865). 3rd Viscount Palmerston (Irish) from 1802. MP for Newport, Cambridge University, Bletchingley, Hampshire South and Tiverton, 1807-65. Secretary at War, 1809-28. Turned Whig, 1830. Foreign Secretary, 1830-41, 1846-52, Home Secretary, 1852-55, Prime Minister 1855-58, 1859-65.

50. Jeremy Bentham (1747-1832). Founder of utilitarianism, much admired by radical Whigs. Now stuffed in University College, London.

Liverpool's Policies Lead to Modernity, 1807-30

normal return on their investment. He supported the Liverpool/Peel Cotton Mills and Factories Act 1819, had several meetings with Liverpool, and his book was circulated round the Cabinet by Sidmouth.

After 1817, Owen turned to cooperative socialism, selling New Lanark in 1825 and moving to the United States, where he set up a cooperative in New Harmony, Indiana. The cooperative failed, but Owen remained active until his death, proselytising his ideas.

Owen's economic ideas were poor and he was only a moderately successful businessman. His attempts to improve working conditions were pioneering in what had become a low-wage industry with mostly low skill levels and a high proportion of child labour.[51] The resistance of other 'sweatshop' manufacturers in the industry meant that the 1819 legislation was only moderately successful. Further legislation followed after 1830 and working conditions in the industry improved only gradually.

One exception to the textile industry's unattractive working conditions was in lace-making. Heathcoat's patent expired in 1823 and, since acquiring a lace-making machine was within the financial capacity of a working man, many in Nottingham obtained such machines, so that in 1829 two thirds of the lace-makers were former framework knitters. Even though the 1830s brought overcapacity and price-cutting, lace-making remained profitable and attractive to the small operator at least up to the 1851 census.[52]

Chemicals, Paper and Printing

One final winner from the textile industry's expansion began by bleaching cloth, then by 1830 created the world's leading chemical company. Charles Tennant (1768-1836) was born into a large Ayrshire farming family and apprenticed to a handloom weaver. (He was mentioned as 'wabster Charlie' in a poem of Robert Burns [1759-96], *Letter to James Tennant of Glenconner* [1786].) He soon saw that primitive bleaching methods restricted the cloth industry (cloth was drenched in urine and laid out in the sun for up to eighteen months) so in 1788 he

---

51. Textile manufacturing spawned other industries that were not low-skilled. One of my ancestors, married in 1856, was a moulder, the son of a spindle-forger, both based in Oldham, Lancashire, primarily serving the textile industry. As skilled operatives, they and their families lived comfortably.

52. Crouzet, *The First Industrialists*, p. 87.

Charles Tennant's St. Rollox Chemical Works, 1831 is the future in one picture. Painting by David Octavius Hill.

acquired bleaching fields and experimented, gaining a patent in 1798 for a mixture of chlorine and lime, then developing a bleaching powder, patented the following year.

In 1797, with four partners, Tennant opened his first chemical factory at St Rollox, near Glasgow, taking control of the works in 1800 and by 1803 producing 9,200 tons of bleaching powder per year. He also, with the chemist, Charles Macintosh,[53] established an alum works at Hurlet, Renfrewshire. He gradually expanded into other chemicals, notably, soda ash, using the Leblanc process at St Rollox in 1825, and sulphuric acid at Carnoustie around 1830. After 1825, he became active in the development of railways, realizing their potential for moving chemicals and other bulky goods, being mainly responsible for extending the railway system into Glasgow. By 1830, St Rollox was the world's largest chemical factory, covering 100 acres with 250,000 square feet of floor space, although with only 1,000 employees, reflecting the business' capital intensity. After Tennant's death, the Tennant chemical business continued to expand, producing one of Britain's greatest industrial

---

53. Charles Macintosh (1766-1843). FRS 1823. Invented in 1823 'mackintosh' waterproof fabric, which included naphtha from coal tar distillation.

fortunes, until it became the core of Imperial Chemical Industries by merger in 1926.

The chemical industry also sprouted elsewhere. The proliferation of gasworks after 1812 led to chemical works to make use of the coal tar by-product, for example, the Bonnington works near Edinburgh, established by George Dixon Longstaff (1799-1892) in 1822. By 1830, the Bonnington works produced naphtha (used in the Mackintosh process for waterproof coats), creosote, pitch and lampblack, as well as sulphuric acid, hydrochloric acid, magnesium carbonate and sodium sulphate. The works was taken over by Tennant's in 1847.

By 1830, the chemical industry, generally thought of as a driver of the 'second' Industrial Revolution after 1880, was already substantial, diversified and highly profitable in Britain.

The paper industry also began its nineteenth-century evolution in these years. Paper continued to be made primarily from rags, the supply of which increased with the textile sector's development (wood pulp was not introduced until 1843). However, in these years, a continuous-flow paper-making machine was developed. The original design had been patented by a French inventor, Louis-Nicolas Robert (1761-1828), in 1798, but the design was bought and developed by the London stationers, the Fourdrinier brothers, Henry (1766-1854), and Sealy (1773-1847), and given an English patent in 1801. The Fourdriniers financed the machine's development, mostly undertaken by the engineer Bryan Donkin (1768-1855), but despite patent protection they were unable to recover its development cost and declared bankrupt in 1812. They were voted £7,000 in compensation by a parliamentary committee in 1837.

Donkin, the son of a Northamptonshire land agent, became a bailiff for the Duke of Dorset, where he met John Smeaton, who advised him to apprentice with John Hall (1765-1836), an established engineer in Dartford with whom he remained associated in several ventures – Hall and Donkin married sisters. In 1802, he moved to Bermondsey, forming the Bryan Donkin Company, still in business today, and began work on what became the Fourdrinier paper-making machine. By 1810, he had made and installed eighteen machines and by 1851 he had produced 200, the machine having become the industry standard.

In 1812, in association with Hall, Donkin set up a canning factory at Bermondsey, the first to use tinned iron containers for food canning; this became a successful business through Admiralty orders. He also went into the gas valves business, where he set several standards. In later life, Donkin advised Telford and Marc Brunel on their projects and consulted with Babbage to resolve differences with Clement. Then, in 1857-59, the business, now run by his sons, built the first working difference engine, exhibited at the Paris Exposition in 1862. Donkin was elected FRS in 1838.

Finally, the world was changed forever by the invention of Friedrich Koenig (1774-1833) – the steam-powered printing press. Koenig was born in Germany, apprenticed to a printer and soon realized the scope for improving printing presses, which had barely changed since Gutenberg's day. He made a prototype press around 1803, found no financial backing in Germany and so moved to England in 1807. Assisted by the engineer, Andreas Bauer (1783-1860), and with financial backing, they patented a machine by 1810 and by 1812 had a rotary printing machine that could produce 800 pages per hour.

Their presses caught the eye of John Walter, owner/editor of *The Times*,[54] who ordered two machines with a printing speed of 1,100 sheets per hour; these were delivered in 1814 and the first copy of *The Times* to be printed by steam appeared on 29 November 1814. *The Times'* circulation, around 5,000 at that time, grew to 40,000 by 1850 as it became the most influential newspaper in Britain. Koenig and Bauer fell out with their London backer and moved to Würzburg, Bavaria, in 1817, where they set up a factory in an old monastery and remain in business today. Their invention, like many products of the Industrial Revolution, caused a fundamental change in British life, as daily newspapers began to reach a mass market.

Political and Economic Developments, 1816-30

With the prestige gained by having beaten Napoleonic France, the Liverpool government remained in office until Liverpool suffered a debilitating stroke in February 1827. Before then, he had won three more elections. In the 1818 election, after a difficult post-war recession, his majority was reduced by about half, to 332 government supporters to 239 opposition. In 1820, after a further sharp economic recession in 1819, followed by disturbances, including the Cato Street Conspiracy to assassinate the Cabinet, the position was approximately maintained, although in Liverpool's view the Radicals gained significantly at the expense of conventional Whigs. In 1826, after six mostly prosperous years, the government's position improved by at least 20 seats, giving the

---

54. *The Times*, founded in 1785 by John Walter (1738-1812). It was initially Radical but became Whig as circulation expanded after 1814. Son, John Walter II (1776-1847). Manager/editor of *The Times* from 1803.

Tory governments of the late 1820s a substantial stable majority, only a little less than in 1812-18, until defections from both wings of the party weakened it.[55]

After the war ended, there were two nasty recessions in 1816-17 and 1819-20. The first was caused by severe post-war readjustment and the harvest failure of the 'Year Without a Summer'. The second recession, which lasted less than a year, can be put down to government policy – the deflation needed to return to the gold standard. Overall, the British economy continued to grow haltingly and by 1820 had attained the living standards of 1791. Bankruptcies, which had peaked at 2,701 in 1816, about 10% above the 1811 figure, had a secondary peak of 2,043 in 1819.

With two recessions, the post-war period was notable for industrial and other unrest. In the industrial districts, there were unemployment riots in the summer of 1816 and the Pentrich riots of 1817 attacking the Butterley works appeared the precursor of a nationwide uprising. Then, after a period of quiescence, 1819 saw unrest in Birmingham, followed by the 'Peterloo' mass meeting in Manchester, broken up with fatal (albeit limited) results by the local magistrates. In London, there were two outbreaks of primarily political unrest, the Spa Fields riot of December 1816 and the 'Queen Caroline' unrest of 1820-21, between which there was a conspiracy to murder the Cabinet, the Cato Street Conspiracy, organized by some of the instigators of the earlier Spa Fields riot.

Liverpool's fiscal policy, implemented by the admirable Vansittart, was highly restrictive, not helped by the Whig-led parliamentary rebellion to abolish income tax in 1816. The budget was balanced in 1818, just three years after the war ended, and the 1819 legislation for the return to gold brought a further addition of taxation. By the early 1820s, the budget was running a considerable surplus and taxes could be remitted, much to the joy of Vansittart's successor from January 1823, the bombastic and feeble Robinson.

To Liverpool's ministers, this post-war period was that of maximum danger, in which ministerial feebleness or ineptitude could have led to a pre-revolutionary situation such as that in 1789-93 France. That no such thing happened is largely down to Liverpool's firm handling of

---

55. Thorne (ed.), *The History of Parliament: The House of Commons, 1790-1820*, and Fisher (ed.), *The History of Parliament: The House of Commons, 1820-32*. Fisher does not give the helpful estimates of post-election party strengths that Thorne does.

unrest and the highly effective system of informers set up by Sidmouth, an underrated Home Secretary.

Post-war legislation by the Liverpool government had a modernizing flavour, as the government recognized the social and economic changes that were rapidly taking place. The Coinage Act 1816 authorized a complete recoinage of Britain. It was Liverpool's homage to his father, Charles Jenkinson, who had been the nation's leading coinage expert, directing the 1774 recoinage and in 1805 publishing *Coins of the Realm*, the definitive work on the subject. The Act defined the price of one troy pound of standard gold at 44½ guineas and limited silver coins' legal tender status to 40s. Once the Bank of England resumed gold payments in 1821, it put Britain definitively on the gold standard. This recoinage finally solved the eighteenth-century problem of inadequate quantities of silver coinage, minting 'old head' George III coins that set the standard for the following 155 years until decimalization. It also differed from previous recoinages in taking old coins for exchange (if genuine) at their face value rather than at their bullion value; this cost the Exchequer £500,000 but was an important buttress of ordinary people's property rights.

The Consolidated Fund Act 1816 merged the British and Irish treasuries, with Britain taking over Irish debt. At this time, although Ireland had more than half the population of England and Scotland combined, it produced only one fifteenth of the revenue, an indication of its poverty, illustrating how the lack of well accepted property rights throughout Irish society prevented Ireland from developing industrially.

Economically, the most important legislation was the Savings Bank Act 1817. This established Trustee Savings Banks, administered by trustees, which could invest only in government securities and deposits at the Bank of England and which would, hence, provide an absolute haven for savings, secure from the vagaries of the loan market. Trustee Savings Banks were to last until the 1980s; even by 1825, they had total deposits of £13.3 million, 4.5% of GDP and one third of the stock exchange's market capitalization. One important provision was that a savings bank holding of up to £30 would not make the holder ineligible for poor relief – an important incentive toward saving. With the country banks in trouble as a result of the post-war deflation of 1813-25, the Trustee Savings Bank movement was an essential alternative home for working-class savings, a key necessity for innovation to occur among ordinary people.

A century before Keynes, the Poor Employment Act 1817 was Keynesian in its approach – it allowed for the issue of up to £5 million of Exchequer Bills (about 1.5% of GDP) to carry out public works and thereby employ the poor. It also set up the Exchequer Bills Loans Commission to administer such loans, a body that, as the Public Works Loans Board, existed until 2020. The Act was designed for sharp recessions such as those of 1816-17 and 1819-20, of a type not seen in the pre-industrial era. To the extent that its application was limited to those recessions, it was genuinely beneficial – the problem would arrive when the principle was applied by Keynes and his followers more widely.

The Church Building Act 1818, provided £1 million towards the building of new Church of England churches in industrial areas (it was followed by another £0.5 million grant in 1823). To Liverpool, this was the most important Act of his administration;[56] such churches would, it was hoped, civilize the otherwise very unpleasant industrial areas and provided a focal point for working-class self-improvement. In practice, the nineteenth century was to show that function being more effectively exercised by the Methodists, partly because the Church of England did not give sufficient priority to endowing and staffing these new churches. Still, it cannot be denied that organized religion, of whichever denomination, was an important civilizing influence in the new industrial areas, many of which lacked basic amenities.

The Cotton Mills and Factories Act 1819, referred to above, limited the hours worked by children in cotton mills and regulated their welfare; it was the first effective factory legislation. It was modified further by the Cotton Mills Regulation Act 1825, which established a maximum twelve-hour day for children under sixteen. The Steamboat Act 1819, another harbinger of the future, compelled all passenger-carrying steam vessels to be registered and inspected annually by a competent engineer.

The major economic policy decision was the return to gold, legislated for in 1819 by the Resumption of Cash Payments Etc. Act 1819. This provided for the Bank of England to resume cash payments on or before 1 May 1821 and from that date put Britain back on the gold standard, at the same parity as before 1797. During the 1840s when Peel was revered, this was referred to as 'Peel's Act' but Peel was merely the head of a Commons committee enquiring into what should be done, with the more senior Harrowby[57] chairing an equivalent committee in the Lords, both under guidance from Liverpool. The actual legislation was

---

56. See Hutchinson, *Britain's Greatest Prime Minister*, p. 252.
57. Dudley Ryder (1762-1847). 2nd Baron Harrowby, 1803, created Earl of Harrowby, 1809. MP for Tiverton, 1784-1803. Paymaster of the Forces, 1791-1800, Treasurer of the Navy, 1800-1, Foreign Secretary, 1804-5,

358   *Forging Modernity*

designed and implemented by Liverpool, with advice from Vansittart and Huskisson.

Prices in 1813 were almost double the pre-war level and this had a marked deflationary effect, with prices falling some 40% in the decade up to 1824. Industrially, the return to gold had two effects: it made borrowing very expensive in real terms in the decade after the war, causing entrepreneurs to finance almost entirely with equity, and it brought bountiful returns to the holders of Consols, which in turn produced a plethora of investible capital by the early 1820s and a massive economic boom.

In May 1820, Liverpool inaugurated one of the most important economic policy reversals in British history: he instituted a move towards free trade that persisted until the Cobden-Chevalier Treaty with France in 1860, which marked its apogee and the beginning of its slide into self-defeatism. On 16 May, in response to a petition from Birmingham manufacturers, Liverpool issued the following encomium on machinery:

> I will take the opportunity of telling you that, next to the spirit of her people, England is indebted for her commercial power and greatness to the inventions which this people have made in machinery. It has given, as it were, legs to the lame and sight to the blind: it has inspired the dull with enterprise, and to the enterprising has given additional energy; it has placed the country, in spite of all its disadvantages, on a level with the most favoured nations, and has enabled its merchants, who pay a heavy price for labour, to compete with other nations, who pay but a trifle for it.[58]

Ten days later, in response to a motion on free trade by Lansdowne, Liverpool took a careful, case-by-case approach, pointing out that some industries were more vulnerable than others:

> The cotton manufacture, for instance, in which we have acquired so great a superiority over other nations, need not fear any thing from an abolition of all protection. I believe also –although the woollen manufacturers are not of that

---

Chancellor of the Duchy of Lancaster, 1805-6, Minister without Portfolio, 1809-12, Lord President of the Council, 1812-27.

58. Hansard, *Parliamentary Debates New Series*, Vol. 1, cols 417-22, 16 May 1820.

opinion – that if all the protecting laws which regard the woollen manufacture were to be repealed, no injurious effect would thereby be occasioned. But with respect to silk, that manufacture in this kingdom is so completely artificial, that any attempt to introduce the principles of free trade with reference to it, might put an end to it altogether. I allow that the silk manufacture is not natural to this country; I wish we had never had a silk manufactory; I allow that it is natural to France; I allow that it might have been better had each country adhered exclusively to that manufacture in which each is superior; and had the silks of France been exchanged for British cottons. – But I must look at things as they are; and when I consider the extent of capital, and the immense population (consisting I believe of above 50,000 persons) engaged in our silk manufacture, I can only say, that one of the few points in the noble marquis's speech in which I totally disagree with him, is the expediency, under existing circumstances, of holding out any idea that it would be possible to relinquish the silk manufacture, and to provide for those who live by it, by parliamentary enactment.[59]

Nevertheless, Liverpool agreed overall with the principle of free trade and set up a parliamentary committee to address areas where trade might be freed. Over the next several years, not only were various protectionist duties reduced or eliminated, notably by Robinson's Budgets of 1823-25, but the Navigation Acts were amended to reduce their protection of British shipping. The move towards freer trade stalled after Liverpool's death – the Whigs, despite their commitment to free trade, introduced few such measures in their 1830-41 period of power, partly for budgetary reasons – but the Peel government of 1841-46 pushed the idea further, as did its successors.

As the decade turned, so did the economy. The sharp depression of 1819-20 gave way to a sustained economic upturn. The period from 1821 until the financial crash of December 1825 saw the fastest economic growth yet seen. GDP per capita grew at over 3% annually between 1821 and 1826, a figure which includes the modest economic downturn after the financial crash. Real wages outside agriculture reached unprecedented levels, as employers facing robust demand were unable to cut wages sufficiently to match the fall in prices. With increasing GDP

---

59. Ibid., Vol. 1, cols 565-94, 26 May 1820.

360   *Forging Modernity*

and re-financings in 1823-24 reducing debt interest, public spending including debt interest also declined from 18% of GDP to just under 14% of GDP in 1826 – Liverpool had halved the fiscal 'take' of the state over his period in office.

After 1820, even as the overall economy grew at an unprecedented rate, corn prices fell far below the 80s per quarter equilibrium of the 1815 Corn Law and farmers who had borrowed heavily during the wars to expand and modernise production found themselves in severe difficulty. The bottom of the agricultural depression came in early 1822, after which prosperity elsewhere brought a halting recovery, though corn prices never returned to their 1815 level.

The first half of the nineteenth century was a period of substantial growth in both land productivity (up 0.9% per annum) and labour productivity (up 0.69% per annum) in agriculture, but the post-war cutback in land usage and low prices slowed mechanization. Overall, the agricultural workforce increased from 1 million to 1.1 million between 1800 and 1850, albeit more slowly than population, while the horse population in agriculture increased more rapidly, from 0.7 to 1.0 million. The change in agricultural economics was also reflected in enclosures, which were high in 1810-19 but dropped sharply after 1820.[60]

Some of the large wartime agricultural profits were re-deployed intelligently into industrial and mining investments. For example, John Crichton-Stuart, second Marquess of Bute (1793-1848), inherited in 1814 a large and liquid landed estate from his grandfather, including major land holdings in south Wales. In 1817, he began surveying the Glamorgan coalfields, consolidating his local land holdings as he did so and expanding the Welsh coal-mining industry during the 1820s. Between 1822 and 1848, he also developed the Cardiff docks area, opening the new Bute Dock in 1839 at a cost of £350,000. His activity in both areas brought him huge debts of £494,000 at his death, although his assets greatly exceeded that value, and their profitability developed further, so that in the 1870s his grandson and heir was claimed (probably incorrectly, given the rise of American fortunes) to be the richest man in the world.

The quality of the 1820s boom is described in the standard study of the Industrial Revolution: Arthur Gayer, W.W. Rostow and Anna Jacobsen Schwartz's *The Growth and Fluctuation of the British Economy, 1790-1850*:

---

60. Overton, *Agricultural Revolution in England*, Table 3.10, p. 85 (productivity), Table 3-22, p. 126 (horses/men population), p. 151 (enclosures).

The character of the (1822-26) cycle as a whole, however, can be distinguished from earlier cycles by the scale and the scope of new private investment. There was an increase in railways construction, new docks were built, and what appears to be the greatest building boom until the forties [the 1840s] took place. Gas-light, insurance, building, trading, investment, provision companies, in addition to many others, were formed on a large scale. These, the fluctuations of foreign government and mining issues and the fabulous Stock Exchange boom and crash (1824-25) impart to these years their unique character.[61]

Other than the move towards free trade, there was no sharp policy break between the repression of 1815-19 and the supposed 'liberal Toryism' of 1822-30. Canning's advent at the Foreign Office after Castlereagh's suicide in 1822 made little difference to economic or industrial policy, in which he had little interest. The main change came from improving economic conditions and the consequent decline in unrest. Sidmouth's watchful Home Office policy was no longer necessary and Peel, succeeding him in early 1822, made his reputation by a programme of legal reform, finally undoing repressive legislation passed by the Whigs a century earlier.

The Importation Act 1822 and the Importation of Corn Act 1828 were modifications of the 1815 Corn Law. The 1822 Act added a provision, allowing the ports, once opened by a price above 80s, to remain open until the price dropped to 70s, with a sliding scale duty of up to 12s. The 1828 Act was passed by Wellington's government. Liverpool's retirement in 1827 had deprived the nation of a more liberal alternative designed by Liverpool and Huskisson. It allowed corn imports at prices above 52s, with a maximum duty of 34s, declining to 1s when the corn price reached 73s. In practice this sliding scale of duty was too steep, did not work well and led to shenanigans among corn importers. The 1828 Act was still more protectionist than North's 1773 Act, which had set a price of 48s at which the ports would be fully opened (1828 prices overall being only about 5% above those of 1773).[62]

Three Acts of 1823-25 revolutionized labour relations. The Masters and Servants Act 1823 codified the punishments for employees

---

61. Gayer, A., W.W. Rostow and A.J. Schwartz, *The Growth and Fluctuation of the British Economy, 1790-1850*, 2 vols (Oxford: Clarendon Press, 1953), Vol. 1, p. 185.

62. See Mitchell (ed.), *British Historical Statistics*, Table XIV-2 and XIV-3.

breaching their employment contracts, allowing for imprisonment with hard labour for up to three months. The number of cases brought under this legislation rose as industrialization wore on – there were more than 10,000 prosecutions under it between 1858 and 1875.[63] Then the Combinations of Workmen Acts of 1824 and 1825 first repealed all previous anti-combination legislation and then, when a massive wave of strikes had shown this to be too liberal, made illegal all combinations except those for wages and working hours. This legislation remained in effect until 1871 and was probably the optimal industrial relations balance, allowing collective bargaining but not mass secondary picketing.

The Weights and Measures Act 1824 was the first full codification of British weights and measures, standardizing them on what became known as the Imperial system. As Maudslay had demonstrated with screw threads, such standardization was essential to enabling mass production with replaceable parts.

Inevitably, the boom of 1821-25 was too good to last – Liverpool warned against excessive speculation in the House of Lords in March 1825. Furthermore, the London merchant banks took advantage of the easy monetary conditions of 1822-24 to issue Latin American bonds, without knowing which Latin American countries were creditworthy, or even in existence.[64]

The financial crisis of 1825, the first crisis of a cyclical industrial economy unrelated to war, had begun in the late spring. The Bank of England's bullion reserves declined from £10.1 million in January 1825 to £7.3 million in April to £4.4 million in July, a grossly inadequate monetary base for a gold standard economy with an 1825 GDP of around £386 million. Instead of raising interest rates as gold flooded out of its vaults in the first half of 1825, the Bank of England kept monetary policy easy, buying government bonds to replace the gold it lost, without raising interest rates. It thereby allowed the bubble to inflate further – by the fourth quarter of the year, many country banks were in trouble, having issued too many notes and made too many souring loans and investments. Even in late summer, when its gold reserves seemed likely to disappear, the Bank did not significantly raise interest rates to attract

---

63. See S. Naidu and M. Yuchtman, 'How Green Was My Valley? Coercive Contract Enforcement in Nineteenth-Century Industrial Britain', June 2010, available at: https://www.eco.uc3m.es/temp/ms_paper_draft _june_2010_submission.pdf (accessed 29 September 2022).
64. The fictitious country of Poyais issued a £300,000 bond issue in 1822.

Liverpool's Policies Lead to Modernity, 1807-30

gold back into the country; only in December, when the crisis was in full swing, did its discount rate reach 5%.

The first signal that something was seriously wrong came on 24 October when the merchant Samuel Williams, with large American business, stopped payment. Then, on 10 December the major private bank, Pole Thornton, was forced to close its doors. Because of Pole Thornton's extensive network, this failure directly caused the failure of 38 country banks.

The climax of the crisis came on 16 December, when the Bank of England came close to stopping gold payments (according to Tooke, its gold reserves bottomed out at £1,027,000 on 24 December, slightly below the nadir of February 1797 – without so serious a crisis to excuse it, and in an economy more than 50% larger).[65]

Once the immediate crisis was over, Liverpool, most helped by Robinson and Bexley (the former Vansittart), designed a programme of banking reform, which became the Country Bankers Act 1826. By this Act, the restriction of country banks to six partners was removed, and joint-stock banks were also allowed to be formed, which could issue notes if based more than 65 miles from London. Country banks were also prohibited from issuing notes below £5 in denomination, while the Bank of England agreed to open agencies in provincial centres.

This Act had the effect over time of 'consolidating' the banking business, until by 1918 only a 'Big Five' clearing banks were left outside London. Industry itself was also 'consolidating' – by that time natural economies of scale had eliminated the small operators in many sectors. Over time, the London merchant banks took more interest in industrial companies, but they had a bias towards size and never provided much venture capital (also, the banks' persona came across as snooty and difficult for an entrepreneurial working man even to approach, let alone deal with[66]). The disappearance of the country banks was thoroughly bad for Britain's innovation and industrial development, but Liverpool's 1826 legislation should not be given sole blame for this – Peel's highly restrictive 1844 Bank Charter Act was at least equally responsible.

The December 1825 financial crash led to only a short-lived recession, after which growth resumed. In 1830 the Whig historian, Macaulay, no

---

65. Thomas Tooke, *A History of Prices and the State of the Circulation from 1793 to 1837*, 6 vols (London: Longman, 1838-57), Vol. 2, p. 185, note.
66. I can attest to this personally, having worked for one – Hill Samuel & Co. Ltd, in 1973-79 – although it was less snooty than most.

364   *Forging Modernity*

admirer of the Tory governments then in power almost continuously for 47 years, wrote: 'We might with some plausibility maintain that the people live longer because they are better fed, better lodged, better clothed and better attended in sickness, and that these improvements are due to that increase in national wealth which the manufacturing system has produced.'[67]

The year after Macaulay wrote, real GDP per capita, a reasonable measure of living standards, was 42% higher than at the pre-war peak of 1791 and more than double that of the nadir in 1801 or the pre-industrial peak of 1731. Real GDP per capita rose rapidly in 1826-31, although part of that was recovery from the 1826 downturn. A bad harvest in 1829 raised prices and caused unrest, but progress in living standards continued throughout the 1820s, while prices continued a gentle decline.

Fiscally, the period 1826-31 saw substantial budget surpluses in 1828-30, preceded and followed by modest deficits, with recession and mismanagement – Robinson's in 1827, Whig in 1831 – being responsible for both. Rapidly increasing GDP decreased the burden of debt further, with public spending including debt interest declining further to 11% of GDP in 1831. The Whigs were left a healthy and easily manageable fiscal legacy.

External trade saw substantial increases between 1821 and 1825, followed by a recession in 1826, with growth resuming thereafter. Overall, based on official values, imports rose substantially in 1821-31 from £30.8 million to £49.7 million, while exports and re-exports rose somewhat less, from £51.4 million to £71.4 million. Bankruptcies were low in 1821-25, but spiked to 3,301, 22% above the 1816 figure, in the bubble-bursting year of 1826.

After Liverpool's stroke and a hiatus of 53 days, Canning took over. However, possibly deliberately, he had alienated most of Liverpool's Cabinet and so he formed a mixed Tory-Whig government. Canning died after only 119 days in office, to be succeeded by the feeble Robinson (now Viscount Goderich). Goderich quailed at meeting Parliament for the 1828 session and so was succeeded by Wellington, at the head of a Tory government, which included the Canningites only until Huskisson's resignation (accompanied by other Canningites) after four months.

With a rather smaller majority Wellington carried on, with Peel leading the House of Commons. Their decision the following year to

---

67. T.B. Macaulay, *Edinburgh Review*, 1830, quoted in Roger Osborne, *Iron Steam & Money: The Making of the Industrial Revolution* (London: Pimlico Press, 2014), p. 343.

pass the Roman Catholic Relief Act 1829 lost them the support of the opposite 'Ultra-Tory' wing of the party, after which the government was on shaky ground, with both wings of the party missing, despite the Tories having gained a near-landslide majority under Liverpool in 1826.

The next blow was the death of George IV in 1830, which necessitated a general election without adequate preparation. In this, the Tories lost only around 20 seats but, with 60 of those returned being 'Ultras' and maybe 30 Canningites, the Wellington government no longer had a majority. Wellington opened negotiations with the Canningites, but the admirable Huskisson, their leader, was killed on 15 September 1830, after which Palmerston, the next-ranked Canningite, sold out to the Whigs for a promise of the Foreign Secretaryship. Accordingly, when Wellington met Parliament, his government was defeated by 29 votes on the civil list on 15 November 1830.

Steam: Boats, Trains and Carriages

This period's central technology, taking over transportation and many other sectors, was the steam engine. By 1807, Trevithick and Woolf had already removed the power-to-weight-ratio constraints of low-pressure Watt engines by developing high-pressure engines that provided more power and compound engines with multiple cylinders, that also increased the motive power produced. The main developments were in practical applications of those advances.

The year 1807 saw Robert Fulton's *North River Steamboat* begin passenger service up the Hudson River. Despite the success of the *Charlotte Dundas* in 1803, commercial steamboat service did not begin in Britain until 1812 when the *Comet* of engineer Henry Bell (1767-1830) began thrice-weekly service on the Clyde, between Glasgow, Greenock and Helensburgh. Bell's service was not commercially successful, and the *Comet* was wrecked in 1820, with Bell dying in poverty.

The first successful Thames steamboat service between London and Margate began in 1815 with the Margate Steam Packet Company. Service was frequent and profitable, but various boiler explosions and fires led to the Steamboat Act 1819. Liverpool travelled by Thames steamer on his visit to Walmer Castle in 1823, by which time the service had become a well-accepted way of travelling from London to the Kent and Essex coasts.

US steamboat technology and usage advanced faster than in Britain, with Fulton's first Mississippi steamer, the *New Orleans*, launched at Pittsburgh in 1811, the first steamboat with a high-pressure engine,

366   *Forging Modernity*

the *Comet*, in 1813, and the first classic Mississippi steamboat with two decks, a high-pressure engine and a stern paddlewheel, the *Washington*, launched at Wheeling, Virginia, in 1816, making the trip from New Orleans to Louisville in 25 days in 1817.

Militarily, steamboat technology scored a triumph in the Anglo-Burmese War of 1824-26, when the East India Company's single paddle-steamer gunboat, the 60hp *Diana*, built in Kidderpore in 1823 and commanded by Frederick Marryat,[68] achieved great success against the Burmese warship *praus*, whose elite oarsmen fell exhausted and vulnerable after a few hours of being chased up the fast-flowing Irrawaddy River by the *Diana*'s inexorable paddle wheels. Indeed, the *Diana* was so successful that the Burmese government insisted on acquiring it in the peace settlement.

Ocean-going ships represented a significant additional technological problem, primarily because of the fuel requirements for a transatlantic voyage. The SS *Savannah*, built in the eponymous Georgia city, became the first steamboat to cross the Atlantic in 1818, but only 11% of her journey was carried out under her engines, and she was wrecked off Long Island in 1821, bankrupting her developers. The first full transatlantic steamboat crossing did not occur until 1838, at which time Isambard Kingdom Brunel's *Great Western* and the *Sirius*, built by Robert Menzies of Leith, raced each other to achieve the feat – the *Sirius* won.

The first commercially viable steam locomotive was built by the Newcastle-born engineer, **Matthew Murray** (1765-1826). After apprenticeship to a smith, Murray, in 1789, went to work for the flax manufacturer, John Marshall, where he invented an improved machine for flax spinning, which he patented in 1793. Then, in 1795, Murray set up in Leeds, in an engineering and machine-making partnership that became Fenton, Murray and Wood, with Murray in charge of the engines department.

The firm's customers were initially mostly textile mills, but Murray concentrated on making improvements to steam engines that increased their power and reduced their weight, inventing a slide valve and an automatic furnace damper. He made engines with tighter tolerances than Boulton & Watt, the leading manufacturer; indeed, Boulton & Watt's Murdoch visited him to gain competitor information. In 1802, Murray

---

68. Frederick Marryat (1792-1848). FRS. Navy from 1806, Commander, 1815, Captain, 1824, left Navy, 1830. Author of *Mr Midshipman Easy* (1836) and *The Children of the New Forest* (1847).

patented a hypocycloidal mechanism and his hypocycloidal engine of 1805 is the third oldest engine now working, after the Smethwick engine and the Whitbread engine, both built by Boulton & Watt. He also supplied a steam engine for the Portsmouth Dockyard Block Mills and cylinder-boring machines for the dockyards.

In 1812, Fenton, Murray and Wood supplied to Middleton Colliery, near Leeds, the first commercially viable locomotive, named *Salamanca* after Wellington's victory. It had a 4-ft 1-in wheel gauge and two cylinders, drawing itself along the railway by a rack and pinion arrangement. It was followed by the *Prince Regent*, *Lord Wellington* and *Marquis Wellington* in 1813-14. The Middleton Colliery's wagon-railway, leading towards the city of Leeds and a mile in length, had been built in 1758 and was the first railway to be authorized by an Act of Parliament. *Salamanca* transported coal for six years until its boiler blew up in 1818, allegedly because its safety valve had been tied down.

After *Salamanca*, Murray diversified into marine engines, making a twin-cylinder marine engine that was pirated by Francis Ogden, the US consul at Liverpool, with copies used to power Mississippi paddle steamers. Then, in the late 1820s, after Murray's death, the firm returned

'The collier' with Salamanca – the first commercially successful locomotive. Illustration by R. & D. Havell.

368   *Forging Modernity*

to the railway business, becoming a major supplier of engines, first, to the Liverpool and Manchester Railway and, then, to Isambard Brunel's Great Western Railway before going out of business in 1843.

Two other engines of this period merit attention. At Wylam Colliery near Newcastle, *Puffing Billy*, completed in 1813, was the first engine to use friction with iron rails to propel itself; it and a twin, *Wylam Dilly*, pulled coal along the colliery's five-mile railway until 1830. They had a boiler pressure of 50 lbs per square inch and a top speed of around 5mph.

The second independently developed engine was the 1814 *Blücher* (named after the Prussian Field Marshal), the first of several engines developed at the Killingworth Colliery by **George Stephenson** (1781-1848). *Blücher* was modelled on Murray's *Lord Wellington*; like *Puffing Billy* it used the wheels to propel itself on the Killington Colliery's eight-mile railway and was the first engine to have the 4-ft 8½-in. wheel gauge that became standard. Other engines in the next few years included the *Wellington*, the *My Lord*, the *Killington Billy* and *The Duke*, which was sold to the Kilmarnock and Troon railway in Scotland, where it also carried coal.

Stephenson was the son of an illiterate fireman at Wylam Colliery, who supported himself with various colliery jobs while gaining literacy and a night-school education. After a few months in Scotland, in 1811 he became engineer at Killington Colliery, where he repaired the pumping engine. As well as railway engines Stephenson designed a miners' safety lamp, roughly simultaneously with Humphrey Davy; the two lamps differed in design, but Davy's prominence caused his lamp to be used nationally, except in the Newcastle area.

Stephenson was hired to build the eight-mile Helton colliery railway in 1820, again on a 4-ft 8½-in. gauge. Then, on 19 April 1821, parliamentary approval was obtained for the 25-mile Stockton and Darlington Railway,[69] and Stephenson and his 18-year-old son, Robert (1803-59), were put in charge of its construction in January 1822. Stephenson recommended an alteration in the route, for which parliamentary approval was gained in May 1823, and the line ordered two engines from Stephenson's works in Newcastle.

---

69. An earlier bill had been defeated by thirteen votes in 1819 because the railway was to run through Lord Chancellor Eldon's estate. In old age, Eldon would also (unsuccessfully) oppose Isambard Kingdom Brunel's Great Western Railway, which was planned to run through another of his estates in Oxfordshire.

Liverpool's Policies Lead to Modernity, 1807-30

After Stephenson had built the first iron railway bridge across the River Gaunless, on 27 September 1825 the line was opened. Stephenson's engine, *Locomotion No. 1*, covered the 8½ miles from Shildon to Darlington in two hours at a top speed of 15mph, pulling 21 coal waggons with up to 600 passengers riding on the coal. It then returned to Stockton, covering the 25 miles in three hours seven minutes, with only one injury, a passenger who fell off the coal, after which a celebratory dinner was enjoyed and free coal was distributed to the poor.

In its early years, the Stockton and Darlington was primarily a coal railway; its passenger-carrying operations were limited to horse-drawn coach transport. In 1833 the coach companies were bought out and a passenger railway service began. After several expansions and modernisations, the railway was bought by the North-Eastern Railway in 1863.

Six months before the Stockton and Darlington's debut, Mrs Harriet Arbuthnot,[70] the well-connected diarist, had made a different railway investment:

> There is a railway going to be made between Liverpool and Manchester which promises to answer immensely. We have 10 shares in it for which we gave £3 a piece and which are now worth above £58 each and they are expected to be worth above £100. I am very fond of these speculations and should gamble greatly in them if I could, but Mr. Arbuthnot does not like them, and will not allow me to have any of the [South] American ones as their value depends on political events and he thinks in his official situation it would be improper.[71]

Mrs Arbuthnot got in on the ground floor – the Arbuthnots were one of the 96 initial London shareholders of the Liverpool and Manchester Railway with a total of 844 shares of the 4,233 issued. (She doubtless later blessed her husband's admirable caution with respect to Latin American securities!) Her diary entry was dated 16 March 1825; the

---

70. Harriet Arbuthnot (1793-1834). Second wife of Charles Arbuthnot (1767-1850). MP for East Looe, Eye, Orford, St Germans, St Ives and Ashburton, 1795-96, 1809-31. Joint (Senior) Secretary to the Treasury, 1809-23, First Commissioner of Woods and Forests, 1823-27, 1828, Chancellor of the Duchy of Lancaster, 1828-30.

71. Francis Bamford and the Duke of Wellington (eds), *The Journal of Mrs Arbuthnot, 1820-1832*, 2 vols (London: Macmillan & Co. Ltd, 1950), Vol. 1, p. 382.

370   *Forging Modernity*

Liverpool and Manchester Railway Company had been formed in 1823, with George Stephenson appointed its principal engineer in June 1824. Its first attempt to get parliamentary authorization in 1825 failed (largely through opposition by the second Marquess of Stafford, owner of the competing Bridgewater Canal) and it gained authorization only in May 1826, with Stafford granted 1,000 shares.

The line, 31 miles long, was built over three years, with the most difficult section being a bog, Chat Moss, into which 70,000 cubic feet of spoil was dumped to provide a firm foundation, on which rails were laid on wooden trestles. Most of the line was designed for steam traction, though the urban portions at each end initially used cable traction, as the parliamentary authorization did not allow steam engines running through the cities. In October 1829 the Rainhill trials were held on a one-mile stretch of railway, to select between ten locomotives, of which five actually made it to the trials:

- *Cycloped*: entered by a technological traditionalist; it was powered by a horse on a treadmill.
- *Perseverance*: designed by Timothy Burstall (1776-1860) of London; it had a vertical boiler but was underpowered.
- *Sans Pareil*: built by Timothy Hackworth (1786-1850), superintendent of the Stockton and Darlington Railway; it was an antiquated design, but was bought by the Liverpool and Manchester Railway and ran until 1844.
- *Novelty*: designed by the Swedish John Ericsson (1803-89) and John Braithwaite (1797-1870) was the world's first tank engine (with the water carried on board, rather than in a tender).[72] It managed a speed of 28mph at Rainhill and claimed a speed of 64mph in another trial but had recurring boiler problems. Ericsson later designed the US Navy's first screw-driven frigate, the USS *Princeton* in 1843. Braithwaite later designed the first steam fire engine.
- *Rocket*: designed by George and Robert Stephenson, was the only engine to complete the trials averaging 12mph with a top speed of 30mph. The Stephensons were given the contract to produce locomotives for the Liverpool and Manchester Railway. *Rocket* was in service on the railway until 1834,

---

72. This is true for railway engines, but Goldsworthy Gurney's steam carriage was also effectively a tank engine.

Liverpool's Policies Lead to Modernity, 1807-30   371

then on Lord Carlisle's[73] private railway in Brampton, Cumberland, until 1840. It was quickly superseded in design by *Northumbrian* and *Planet*, both built by the Stephensons and introduced in 1830.

Following the Rainhill trials and the completion of the Liverpool and Manchester Railway, which unlike the Stockton and Darlington had two parallel tracks, its Grand Opening on 15 September 1830 was honoured by the presence of Wellington, the prime minister, Huskisson, the MP for Liverpool, who was now 60 and ailing but had risen from his sick-bed to attend, and Mrs Arbuthnot accompanying Wellington:

> At 10 o'clock in the morning on the 15th, we set off on our unlucky expedition to the railroad. We were a party of 12 people in three carriages and went at once to the yard, where a magnificent car of carved and gilt wood with scarlet cloth awning, capable of holding about 40 people, was waiting to receive us. We started almost immediately amidst the enthusiastic shouts of many thousand spectators. I don't think I ever saw a more beautiful sight than at the moment when the car attached to the engine shot off on its journey, that part of the railway being cut deep thro' the rock and the sides, far above our heads, being covered with people waving their hats and handkerchiefs.
>
> We little anticipated the miserable accident which was to put an end to all our hilarity. We went sixteen miles in about 40 minutes and then stopped at a large tank to take in water. We had at times gone at the rate of 30 miles an hour, and at other times had slackened our pace that other engines, drawing the rest of the party (which consisted of 800 people) and were on the other line of the railway, might pass and be passed by our engine for the Duke's amusement and that he might see them work. We had performed it with the utmost success, every arrangement was perfect, and we were in the highest spirits enjoying the excursion and really glorying in the magnificent work, which is a triumph of human genius over every sort of natural obstacle.
>
> While we stopped for water many of the gentlemen chose to get out and walk about, though the directors had particularly

---

73. George Howard (1773-1848). 6th Earl of Carlisle from 1825. Lord Privy Seal, 1827-28.

The Liverpool and Manchester Railway, showing the Duke's Train Being Prepared on 15 September 1830. Artist unknown.

requested that nobody would. All at once there was a cry that an engine was coming. Mr. Huskisson, who had at that moment been talking to the Duke and me, left us to get into the carriage. He got alarmed at seeing the engine coming, lost his head and, while he was hesitating, was caught by it, thrown down and the engine passed over his leg and thigh, crushing it in the most frightful way.

It is impossible to give an idea of the scene that followed, of the horror of every one present, or of the piercing shrieks of his unfortunate wife, who was in the car. He said scarcely more than 'It's all over with me. Bring me my wife and let me die.' Lord Wilton, who was by him and has studied anatomy and surgery, instantly and with the greatest skill applied a tourniquet to his thigh; he was lifted on a door and put into the car which had contained the music, was attached to one engine and instantly sent on towards Manchester, we remaining in the road. The engine was forced on at its utmost speed and, in less than 20 minutes, reached Eccles, 10 miles off, where he was taken out and carried to the house of Mr Blackburne, the clergyman. Every possible assistance was procured for him, but all in vain! The surgeon said that, if amputation were attempted., he would die under the operation. Violent spasms came on and he died at 9 o'clock at night, the accident having happened at ½ past eleven in the morning.[74]

It was truly an accident that changed history. As Mrs. Arbuthnot remarked: 'If it had not been for the unfortunate accident which destroyed all our pleasure, it would have been the most delightful week I ever passed.'[75]

Without the accident, the joint triumph of the day would presumably have cemented the relationship between Huskisson and Wellington, bringing Huskisson back into the government. That would have given Wellington enough extra Commons votes to survive the meeting of Parliament two months later, allowing a continuation of the great Tory governments of 1783-1830. Huskisson was ailing and would not have remained in the government long, but he would not have needed to; most of the Ultra-Tories had forgiven Wellington by the following spring, and he would then have had a solid Commons majority. Mrs Arbuthnot's happiness (she was a fine Tory) and, in my view, the long-term happiness of the country were wrecked irretrievably by that miserable railway accident, which coincided with the apotheosis of Britain's Industrial Revolution.

To illustrate what the change in government meant for industrialization, we should look at road transport, the third area of steam-powered transportation that flourished in this period. Here the central figure is **Sir Goldsworthy Gurney** (1793-1875). Gurney came from a gentry family in Cornwell and, after an education at Truro Grammar School, took a medical qualification and bought a practice in 1813. He moved to London in 1820 and became a professional scientific lecturer, developing an oxy-hydrogen blowpipe in 1823. He began working on steam engines in 1825, developing the blastpipe, which used steam to increase the flow of air through a steam engine's chimney, thereby greatly increasing the power-to-weight ratio over a conventional steam engine.

In 1825-28, Gurney, from his workshop near Regent's Park, patented and manufactured several steam carriages which ran on public roads at up to 20mph, including such notable feats as climbing Highgate Hill.

---

74. Bamford and Wellington (eds), *The Journal of Mrs Arbuthnot*, Vol. 2, pp. 385-86.
75. Ibid., p. 387.

The Gurney Steam Carriage, 1829, which was killed off by a Whig Parliament. Artist unknown.

In July 1829, two months before the Rainhill trials, one of his carriages made the journey from London to Bath and back, at an average speed of 14mph, including stops for fuel and water.

The carriages, which in at least one case included a pair of supplementary steam-driven legs to assist in climbing hills, were highly competitive with contemporary railway technology, and did not suffer from railways' difficulties with gradients. In addition to his carriage, in which engine and boiler were integrated with accommodation for up to 20 passengers, Gurney also a designed a 'steam drag' in which the engine pulled a cart – this was more reassuring for passengers than sitting on top of the boiler.

In 1830, Sir Charles Dance,[76] who had bought three steam carriages from Gurney, began a regular steam-carriage service between Cheltenham and Gloucester, a distance of nine miles; in the four months it was allowed to operate it carried over 3,000 passengers. Then, at the

---

76. The only Sir Charles Dance in the 1832 Debrett is Colonel Sir Charles Webb Dance (1785-1844) who fought at Waterloo. I can find nothing connecting the gallant colonel to the early history of steam motoring but, in terms of age, he is plausible, being 46 in 1831.

insistence of local stagecoach companies, the turnpike trusts began to impose a differential toll of £2 on steam carriages as against 2s for horse-drawn carriages, making the service uneconomic. In 1831, in the new Whig House of Commons, over 60 bills were passed through Parliament, imposing steam-carriage tolls at this or higher levels on various turnpikes throughout England. Consequently, Gurney declared bankruptcy in 1832, with liabilities of £232,000.

A select committee of the House of Commons in 1833-35 examined 'Mr Goldsworthy Gurney's case' and found him entitled to £5,000 compensation (the Whig Chancellor of the Exchequer vetoed the figure first suggested of £16,000) but by then it was too late. He was forced to sell the Cornish castle he had built in his years of prosperity and became a consultant, advising on the ventilation of the new Houses of Parliament and developing the Bude Light, in which oxygen is injected into a flame, as well as the limelight, which became a staple of Victorian theatres. He was knighted by Queen Victoria in 1863, perhaps an indication of Establishment guilt, but the roads of Britain were never again graced by his elegant and efficient steam carriages.

* * *

Britain's legislative environment for industrial innovation changed for the worse in 1830 and the Reform Act 1832 cemented that change in place. From that point, Britain was no longer uniquely friendly to industrialization, while other countries, notably, the United States but also France, Belgium and what was to become Germany, had seen Britain's success and wanted to copy it. From the mid-seventeenth century until 1830, the Industrial Revolution had been a story of unique British success; from that date on, the story is one of first relative and later absolute decline. The Industrial Revolution itself was no longer a revolution by 1830; it was an overwhelmingly powerful ongoing process, that only the worst of policies could have stopped.

10

Epilogue: The Victorians and After

The Industrial Age Goes Global

I have now covered the course of the Industrial Revolution in Britain to 1830 and have demonstrated that superior policy and economic management played a major role in Britain gaining 'first mover' benefits. From 1830, three things changed. First, the Industrial Revolution was no longer revolutionary; it was an ongoing and unstoppable process of industrialization. Second, it was no longer confined mainly to Britain; other countries, notably, France, the United States and later Germany, began industrializing rapidly, achieving an increasing proportion of the world's technological breakthroughs before Britain. Third, the quality of governance in Britain began to decline, so that economic policy, which had been so helpful to industrialization, became increasingly damaging to Britain's industrial and economic position. This final Chapter will examine those three effects, look at the changes in British policy, and draw some conclusions about economically beneficial policies for the future.

The change of government in November 1830 was cemented in place by the 1832 Reform Act, which utterly changed the basis of Britain's parliamentary representation, locking out the party that had been in power for the previous half-century, benignly supervising the Industrial Revolution. Contrary to subsequent legend, it was not a significant move towards democracy. The predominant franchise qualification before the Act had been ownership of a freehold with a rental value of 40s (£2) per annum; the Act changed this to £10, thereby disfranchising much of the working class. However, the Act, drafted by the Radical fringe of the Whig party, also undertook a far more drastic replacement of

Epilogue: The Victorians and After 377

constituencies than had been expected, disfranchising Tory boroughs that had shrunk due to population movements and replacing them with large industrial towns and amorphous Whig/Radical suburbs of the largest cities such as London.

It was not simply a matter of eliminating Old Sarum and Dunwich; the Act also eliminated distinct communities such as Wootton Bassett and Ilchester, replacing them with constituencies that represented mere numbers rather than distinct communities. Thereby, the Act increased the electorate by about 15%, but made it less representative; as the *Poor Man's Guardian* said: 'Our English Whigs extended the franchise to the small middlemen in order the more effectively to keep down the working classes. Of all governments, a government of the middle classes is the most grinding and remorseless.'[1] As in 1780 and on several other later occasions, the Whigs exacerbated working-class discontent by stirring up a popular agitation in 1831-32 in favour of their favourite nostrum of 'parliamentary reform', which actually made the working class's position worse.

Policy also changed after 1830 and, from industrialization's viewpoint, not for the better. The 1830s were inevitably an economically difficult decade, because of the need to finance the railways, which between 1830 and 1845 absorbed a capital of £225 million,[2] around 50% of GDP, far more than the earlier investment in the less capital-intensive textile sector or the cheaper canals. In addition, the Whigs chose this decade to undertake the compensated abolition of slavery, a morally necessary enterprise that took another £20 million out of the London capital market. The market drain from railway investment and abolition of slavery brought an upward pressure to interest rates (despite the prolonged peace, 3% Consols did not exceed their 1824 high price of 91% until 1843) and limited the availability of capital for other investments. Since capital in such quantities was diverted into fixed investment, and profits on the investments took years to arrive, labour's share of the economic pie correspondingly fell, at least temporarily, as shown by the sluggishness of real wages.

Combined with several less than stellar Whig Chancellors of the Exchequer, this made the 1830s an economically miserable decade. Friedrich Engels,[3] writing in 1843-45, wrote of the immiseration of

---

1. Quoted in E.P. Thompson, *The Making of the English Working Class* (London: Victor Gollancz, 1963), p. 821.
2. Mitchell (ed.), *British Historical Statistics*, Table X-6, p. 543.
3. Friedrich Engels (1820-95). Monied Marxist philosopher. Published *The Condition of the Working Class in England* (1845).

the working classes by industrialization, which anti-industrialization writers have since called the 'Engels pause'. On an overall basis for the period from 1790, although the 1790s were a difficult decade, he was wrong; living standards increased substantially. For the period 1830-42, he was correct in that living standards increased very little. Over the 50 years 1791-1841, a calculation stretching from a peak in living standards to a trough, real GDP per capita, an approximate proxy for living standards, rose 31%, or 0.54% per annum, despite the 90% (1.3% per annum) increase in population. Alternatively, over the 30 years 1812-42, real wages rose 38% in agriculture, 77% in building trades and 57% in cotton factories, more than 1% per annum in each case.[4]

It was not just stagnant living standards that made the working classes discontented. Whig social legislation and irresponsible encouragement of unrest should bear much of the blame. Notoriously, the Poor Law Amendment Act 1834 was inspired by the half-baked theories of Jeremy Bentham and by a belief that poor relief under the Poor Law 1601 and the Speenhamland system was impossibly expensive. Under the Act, relief would only be distributed through workhouses, which would be designed on the infamous 'less eligibility principle' under which nobody would go near them if they could possibly avoid it.

In its own terms, the Act was successful. Expenditure on poor relief, which had peaked at £7.9 million in the depression year of 1817 and had already declined to £7 million in 1831, the most depressed year of the 1830s, and £6.3 million in the more normal year of 1833, was reduced to a low of £4 million in 1836.[5] However, the effect on working-class people who lost their jobs or took entrepreneurial risks that failed was catastrophic, as the threat of the workhouse, instead of a period on outdoor relief, hung over entrepreneurial failure.

An additional result of this Act was the rise in 'Chartism', a destructive working-class movement far more damaging than the limited agitation of 1817 and 1819, which only petered out after 1848, when it became obvious that working-class living standards in the big cities were reaching highs never seen before. Beyond Chartism itself, the radicalization and class distrust sown by this iniquitous legislation lasted until after World War II, poisoning labour relations, national politics and entrepreneurial activities alike.

---

4. Mitchell (ed.), *British Historical Statistics*, Table II-25 (wages), Table XIV-3 (prices).

5. Ibid., Table XI-9, p. 605. The year end is 5 January, so the 1834 figure refers essentially to the calendar year 1833.

Epilogue: The Victorians and After

The advent of Sir Robert Peel's government in 1841 should have changed matters, since it brought back the party that had shepherded industrialization. His 'Tamworth Manifesto' of 1834 contained little of substance on economic matters; its main purpose was to suggest that Peel's 'Conservatism' differed from the Toryism of Pitt, Liverpool and Wellington. In practice, Peel, the son of a very wealthy textile manufacturer, favoured cheap labour and unrestricted imports, rather than the high wages and moderate protectionism of Liverpool.

Peel moved in his favoured direction in 1842, substantially weakening the Corn Laws and re-introducing income tax, giving himself a revenue platform to move towards full free trade. In the short term, income tax broadened the tax base, making the task of government finance easier, when the interest on Napoleonic war debt was still more than all the remaining government expenditure put together.[6] In the very long term after 1914, high rates of income tax held back the economy, more than offsetting the benefit from lower or zero tariffs.

Peel next attempted to rethink Liverpool's banking reform of 1826, with the Bank Charter Act 1844. This sharply restricted note issuance by country banks, setting an overall fixed limit on note issuance by all banks, including the Bank of England. In practice, it was impossibly restrictive, having to be suspended three times in its first 22 years of operation, in 1847, 1857 and 1866. By restricting one of the country banks' most lucrative operations, the issuance of local banknotes, it also led to consolidation in the banking system, by 1918 approaching the current oligopoly. By this consolidation, and the tight-money conditions produced by the Act, the ability of local entrepreneurs to raise capital was sharply restricted, setting new barriers to business formation.

Peel's background in low-wage manufacturing became vitally important in 1846, when he repealed the Corn Laws. He had been convinced by the intellectual case for free trade and by the persistent agitation of the Anti-Corn Law League, a largely urban, middle-class body. Then, when Ireland suffered the first onslaught of its potato famine, with the 1845 crop blighted, he decided that the solution to Ireland's problems lay in free imports of cheap corn. (In reality, this 'solution' was counterproductive; the starving potato growers had no cash to buy cheap corn, and removing protection killed the substantial Irish corn-growing sector, nurtured by Liverpool through the Corn Laws.)

---

6. Ibid., Table XI-4. In the year to 5 January 1843, total expenditure was £55.1 million, of which debt charges were £29.6 million.

380   *Forging Modernity*

Repeal of the Corn Laws did nothing useful for Ireland. It also did nothing for the agricultural workers that still formed over a third of Britain's workforce – their wages declined to match the decline in their employers' purchasing power. Conversely, repeal brought a surge in the purchasing power of urban workers, by about 20% for both building workers and cotton factory workers over the decade 1842-52.[7] A rise in living standards that was already resuming after 1842 became a windfall surge, spuriously validating unilateral free trade policies in the minds of an expanding portion of the electorate.

In terms of trade, repeal of the Corn Laws opened British markets to the corn growers of eastern Europe, but not yet to those of the United States. Liverpool had scoffed in 1822 at the idea that US corn could be competitive with British, because of transportation costs and time taken to cross the Atlantic. The advent of steamships and, more particularly, of US railroads radically changed the situation. British farming remained generally competitive during the 1850s and 1860s, as overall population and wealth increase caused demand to rise. However, with the US Midwest competitive as a supplier of corn and increasingly (with refrigerated box cars invented in 1878) of meat, and Argentine beef becoming available shortly thereafter, British agriculture went into a prolonged depression after 1873 that only the two world wars alleviated.

The dogmatism of the Victorian free trade movement is illustrated by the Sugar Duties Act 1846, which removed all duties on sugar, which had previously protected the producers in the British Caribbean, whose cost structure had already been adversely affected by the abolition of slavery. Doubtless, it provided cheaper sugar for the industrial workers who were uppermost in Peel's mind, allowing low-end wages to be further squeezed. It also opened sugar producers in the British Caribbean to competition from Brazil and other countries where slavery was still practised, thereby increasing the global market share of slave-produced sugar. The impoverishment of the British Caribbean, the huge destruction of wealth involved and its inhabitants' miserable reaction in such events as the Jamaican Morant Bay rebellion of 1865, were entirely preventable consequences of this legislation, a product of free trade fanaticism.

The 1840s also saw the political radicalization of business. While the first industrial entrepreneurs, such as Crowley, Boulton and Arkwright, had been generally Tory, with only the Nonconformists among them tending towards Whiggery, there had been a gradual drift leftwards since

---

7. Ibid., Table II-25 (wages), Table XIV-3 (prices).

Epilogue: The Victorians and After

the 1790s as the industrial workforce abandoned its natural Toryism. Nevertheless, in the 1820s, there were still plenty of Tory industrialists – naturally enough since the government was Tory and favoured industry.

Then, after 1830, industrialists' support began to swing, not to the incorrigibly snobbish mainstream Whigs, but to their Radical wing. There were several reasons for this development. After the 1832 Reform Act, there were many naturally Radical parliamentary seats in industrial areas and down-market London suburbs ideally suited for an industrialist, preferably with some local connection (the other alternative, some non-resident sprig of the nobility with Radical leanings, generally proved intolerable to the local electorate). Also, many industrialists were 'governmentalist' – they supported whatever government was in power, in the hope of lucrative contract opportunities.[8] As the Whigs with their Radical and Irish allies almost monopolized power between 1830 and 1874, 'governmentalism' drove industrialists towards supporting them. Finally, after 1846 the larger export-oriented manufacturers became Radical and committed to extreme versions of free trade, because it gave promise of opening international markets, while cheap food enabled them to squeeze wages.

On the other side, while the Conservatives under Peel remained reliably pro-business, the 1846 split drove the managerial Peelites towards the Whigs and, within the Conservatives, elevated aristocrats like Lord George Bentinck,[9] the fourteenth Earl of Derby[10] and Benjamin Disraeli,[11] whose approach to politics was anathema to the modernizing Toryism of Liverpool-era manufacturers.

---

8. I met that word in Croatia in early 2000 after Socialists had won elections in both Croatia and Chile, where the Croatian-Chilean billionaire, Andronico Luksic (1926-2005), had major assets. When I commiserated with Luksic's Croatian representative on his losing two elections in two weeks, she responded: 'Mr Luksic is a governmentalist. He is in favour of whatever government is in power at any time, in the countries where he does business.'

9. Lord George Bentinck (1802-48). Whig (to 1834) then Conservative MP for King's Lynn, 1828-48. Leader of the Conservative Party, 1846-48.

10. Edward Smith-Stanley (1799-1869). Lord Stanley from 1834, 14th Earl of Derby from 1851. MP for Stockbridge, Preston, Windsor and North Lancashire, 1822-44 (Whig until 1834, Tory from 1841). Chief Secretary for Ireland, 1830-33, Secretary of State for War and Colonies, 1833-34, 1841-45, Leader of the Conservative Party, 1846-68, Prime Minister 1852, 1858-59, 1866-68.

11. Benjamin Disraeli (1804-81). 1st Earl of Beaconsfield from 1876. MP for Maidstone, Shrewsbury and Buckinghamshire, 1837-76. Conservative

382   *Forging Modernity*

Disraeli should bear a major share of the blame for British policy-makers' turning away from policies that fostered industrialization. In his novel, *Sybil*, he followed Charles Dickens[12] in appealing to the intellectual middle classes by painting a bleak and inaccurate portrait of industrial Britain. Still worse, he betrayed the history of his own party by portraying Liverpool as the 'Arch-Mediocrity', a cheap and unjustified slur that has bedevilled British history writing ever since. As a politician, he favoured an anti-economic coalition of the landed aristocracy and the working classes against industrialization, ignoring the traditional gentry and tradesmen who had formed the bulk of Tory support for two centuries. His Second Reform Act expanded the urban bias of the franchise, leaving the county franchise at a restricted level until the Third Reform Act seventeen years later. Finally, as Prime Minister he granted trades unions legal privileges they should not have been permitted, which took over a century to reverse, while he did nothing about the economic decline caused by unilateral free trade policies, painfully obvious by his last years in power.

The 1850s were the high tide of the British industrial economy, when relative strength, absolute strength and living standards are considered together.[13] Although the United States, ahead of other competitors, was catching up fast, Britain was still the world's strongest industrial power, measured by output of various industrial goods, and it was still enjoying rapid economic growth. Urban living standards had leaped with Corn Laws repeal, and with the exception of the agricultural workforce, living standards were continuing to improve rapidly – though poor urban sanitation meant that diseases like cholera were rampant (the Great Stink of 1858 finally led to progress here).

Furthermore, in the 1850s the British industrial economy was still highly innovative – the demonstration by Sir Henry Bessemer[14] of his steel process at Cheltenham in 1856 is just one example, while the greatest

---

   Leader in the Commons, 1849-76. Chancellor of the Exchequer, 1852, 1858-59, 1866-68, Prime Minister 1868, 1874-80.

12. Charles Dickens (1812-70). Novelist. Author of, *inter alia*, *Oliver Twist* (1839), *Hard Times* (1854) and *Great Expectations* (1861).

13. See, for example, Ben Wilson, *Heyday: The 1850s and the Dawn of the Global Age* (New York: Basic Books, 2016), for a discussion of this era.

14. Henry Bessemer (1813-98). Kt 1879. FRS 1879. Invented Bessemer process for manufacturing steel, demonstrated at British Association, Cheltenham, 24 August 1856.

Epilogue: The Victorians and After

achievements of Isambard Kingdom Brunel, such as the *Great Eastern*, date from this period, as does the first transatlantic telegraph cable. Government policy was still largely favourable to industry – Aberdeen, Palmerston and Derby, prime ministers for most of the decade, were free-marketers who generally understood the needs of an industrial economy.

For example, the Joint Stock Companies Act 1856, passed by Palmerston's first government and only slightly modified by his second government with the Companies Act 1862, gave ordinary people the ability to set up a company with limited liability without an Act of Parliament. It was an enormous fillip to industrial entrepreneurship, limiting the potential personal loss from activity conducted through a company and thereby reducing the risk that had previously arisen from the unlimited-liability partnership form of association, whereby a partner with substantial outside assets (for example, a landed estate) could jeopardize his entire fortune.

On the other hand, the Locomotives on Highways Act 1861 provided that any road locomotive could travel at a maximum of 4mph and must be preceded by a man with a red flag no less than 60 yards in front. Gurney's road carriages were long gone, and this Act eliminated the unfair toll differential imposed on them. However, it hampered the development of a British automobile industry until its repeal in 1896, a decade after Karl Benz had produced the first functioning internal-combustion-engine automobile, thereby granting a substantial lead to German, French and American competitors.

Britain's free trade movement of the 1840s and 1850s was largely unilateral, but Britain's global influence was still so great that other countries, some through the German *Zollverein*, also reduced their tariffs, though only occasionally to zero. Britain's repeal of the Navigation Acts in 1849 theoretically brought full free trade in shipping, but other countries' restrictions similar to the US Jones Act of 1920 meant that worldwide shipping was never truly free. The culmination of this free trade movement was the Cobden-Chevalier Treaty of 1860, providing for full free trade between Britain and France, and leading to the introduction of cheap 'Gladstone claret' in British groceries. The United States was also relatively free trading at this time; the Tariff of 1857, spearheaded by the much-maligned President James Buchanan, was moderate in its incidence, being like previous tariffs a compromise between Northern protectionists and Southern free traders.

Regrettably, the era of globalist free trade instituted by Cobden-Chevalier would last only a year. The US Lincoln administration raised

384 *Forging Modernity*

tariffs twice, in 1861[15] and 1862, and further tariff increases were enacted regularly, culminating in the ultra-protectionist McKinley tariff of 1890, with a 50% average rate, enthusiastically supported by Andrew Carnegie seeking to protect his steel business from British and now German competition. Germany, united in 1871, increased its tariffs sharply in 1879.[16] Thereafter, it pursued a policy of protectionism, seeking to draw smaller countries into its sphere of influence, which was to continue through the Nazi economic order of the late 1930s. France also increased her tariffs after her defeat of 1871, passing a protectionist tariff law in 1892.[17]

These tariffs reversed the initial beneficial effect of free trade on the British economy. Even from 1861, and more particularly from the late 1870s, Britain was not competing on a 'level playing field' but was allowing foreign companies to export freely to British and colonial markets, while British-made goods were increasingly blocked from foreign domestic markets. The effect of this could be seen most clearly in steel, where Britain had invented the Bessemer process technology, but British producers remained small-scale and relatively high cost, while US and later German and even French producers were able to build greater efficiencies and economies of scale behind high tariff walls. From around 1870 on, the statistics show it clearly: the British economy went into relative decline, indeed, in some respects, into absolute decline.

It took a remarkably long time for any rational response to this phenomenon to appear. Even as early as the Overend, Gurney & Co. crash of 1866 it was clear that something was going wrong in British economic development, with the provincial financial centres no longer financing new enterprises, but after the financial crash of 1873, the British economy's senescence in both agriculture and industry was plain for all to see. David Cannadine[18] has documented in detail the

---

15. The first Morrill Tariff was passed on 3 March 1861, before the inauguration of President Lincoln but after the withdrawal of Southern representatives from Congress had removed the free trade forces.
16. The German tariffs of 1879 had duties of 15-30% for industrial goods but was notable for imposing tariffs on grain and agricultural products, protecting the inefficient farmers of eastern Germany from US competition.
17. The Méline tariffs of 1892 ended the period of relatively free trade between Britain and France begun by the Cobden-Chevalier Treaty. It is regarded as the most important piece of economic legislation of the Third Republic.
18. In David Cannadine, *The Decline and Fall of the British Aristocracy* (New Haven, CT: Yale University Press, 1990).

Epilogue: The Victorians and After

travails of the traditional landed classes after 1873, while Correlli Barnett[19] half a century ago recounted with gloomy relish the increasing uncompetitiveness of British industry. For any economically thoughtful statesman, such as had abounded a century earlier, both the problem and the potential solution should have been obvious.

Given that Disraeli started his career as a protectionist, it might have been expected that he would have taken up that banner again in old age, certainly after Germany's 1879 tariff, but he failed to do so. William Gladstone,[20] a dogmatic free trader, more interested in solving the Irish question (which he could have done had he taken it up earlier, when he had a majority, rather than in 1886, when he did not), could not perhaps have been expected to act. Salisbury,[21] in early life an admirer of the Liverpool ministry and its policies, could certainly have acted any time after 1887, when he had the protectionist Joseph Chamberlain[22] in his party. As it was, it fell to Chamberlain himself, in 1903, when the Tory government was already on the way out, to propose a scheme of Imperial Preference that was by that stage crying out for implementation. A party split prevented action at that time, after which nothing was possible until after World War I.

The period 1870-1914 marked the beginning of Britain's relative economic decline. Per capita economic growth, which had averaged 1.56% annually between 1830 and 1870, despite already sub-optimal economic policies, dropped sharply to 0.72% annually from 1870 to 1913, with a tendency to slow still further during the latter years of

---

19. In Correlli Barnett, *The Collapse of British Power* (New York: William Morrow & Co., 1972), and subsequent sequels.

20. William Ewart Gladstone (1809-98). MP for Newark, Oxford University, South Lancashire, Greenwich and Midlothian, 1832-95. President of the Board of Trade, 1843-45, Secretary of State for War and the Colonies, 1845-46, Chancellor of the Exchequer 1852-55, 1859-66, 1873-74, 1880-82, Prime Minister 1868-74, 1880-85, 1886, 1892-94.

21. Robert Gascoyne-Cecil (1830-1903). 3rd Marquess of Salisbury from 1868. Conservative MP for Stamford, 1853-68. Secretary of State for India, 1866-67, 1874-78, Foreign Secretary, 1878-80, 1885-86, 1887-92, 1895-1900, First Lord of the Treasury, 1886-87, Lord Privy Seal, 1900-2, Prime Minister, 1885-86, 1886-92, 1895-1902.

22. Joseph Chamberlain (1836-1914). Liberal (to 1886) then Liberal Unionist MP for Birmingham and Birmingham West, 1876-1914. Mayor of Birmingham, 1873-76. President of the Board of Trade, 1880-85, President of the Local Government Board, 1886, Colonial Secretary, 1895-1903.

386   *Forging Modernity*

that period.[23] That halving of long-term economic growth, in a period when global growth was generally rising through the intensification of industrialization, was a sign of how far British policy had strayed from the optimal path.

One sign of the free market at work after 1870, as British economic growth slowed, was the expansion of the City of London's role in international finance. Ever since 1817-18, with Barings' recovery loans to Louis XVIII's France, the City had played a leading role in cross-border lending but, after 1870, that role sharply expanded, with the City taking on advisory as well as lending roles in much of Latin America. Australian and South African mining booms saw equity issues as well as debt expand markedly, with the merchant banks becoming fully involved in domestic corporate finance only from Barings' sponsorship of the Guinness stock flotation in 1886. The Barings' bail-out of 1890, when Argentine lending led to that luckless bank's first collapse, slowed the City's risk appetite in Latin America. However, by the Edwardian era emerging market lending was again in full swing. Overall, Britain's overseas investment earnings increased from an average £45.5 million, 4.4% of GDP in 1870-74, to £146.7 million, 9.1% of GDP in 1910-13[24] – a doubling in relative importance that represented the increasing financialization of Britain's economy.[25]

Apart from Britain's unilateral free trade policy, a significant cause of the decline in economic growth was the trades union legislation embodied in Gladstone and Disraeli's Trades Union Act 1871 and Employers and Workmen Act 1875. A Royal Commission set up by Derby's Conservative government in 1867 had recommended continuing the existing restrictive legislation. However, the Gladstone government adopted the minority position, put forward by the workers' representative on the commission under instruction from the Trades Union Congress, and not only legalized trades unions but gave their funds immunity from lawsuits. Then Disraeli's government in 1875 abolished all potential criminal law liability for union activity, hoping that the legislation would 'gain and retain for the Conservatives the lasting affection of the

---

23. Figures are for the United Kingdom as a whole (including Ireland) taken from Mitchell (ed.), *British Historical Statistics*, Table XVI-6 (real GDP at 1900 prices) and Table I-3 (population).
24. Ibid., Tables XVI-4 and XVI-15.
25. The British financial sector's development after 1815 is covered in David Kynaston, *The City of London*, 4 vols (London: Chatto & Windus, 1995-2002).

Epilogue: The Victorians and After

working classes'.[26] Naturally, the legislation did nothing of the kind. Instead, fuelled by socialist agitation, it led to ever more violent strikes, first in 1887 and then a near General Strike in 1911-12 which paralyzed the economy.

From this point on, industrial innovation could only be carried out with the consent of the unions, thereby becoming very difficult. The result, in area after area of the economy, was to lock in the work methods of 1871 and prevent either increases in productivity or mergers, so that companies in traditional industries became thoroughly ossified. Only in wholly new industries (such as automobiles and aircraft, for example) could new working methods be used. Even in some of these, such as telephony and electric power, productivity was hobbled by an entirely unnecessary structure of state ownership.

At the end of the century, socialism also became an inhibiting factor in industrial innovation. With industry increasingly dominated by substantial, established companies, it became less and less possible for an ambitious working man to think of bettering himself through entrepreneurship, although industrial management remained open to him – there were few MBAs until the 1960s. Conversely, new avenues of self-betterment opened up through trades unions, friendly societies and other non-market opportunities. The first socialist MP, Keir Hardie,[27] did not win a seat until 1892 and the Labour party (formally established in 1900) was not a serious contender for power until 1918. Nevertheless, anti-capitalist attitudes were already well established in the working class before then. (The intelligentsia had become anti-capitalist even earlier, spurred by the French Revolution, but their influence among potential industrial innovators was limited.)

Even more important in slowing growth than socialism in the workforce was the increasing trend towards public and municipal ownership in new industries. The Telegraph Act 1868, passed by the first government of the ineffable Disraeli, provided for the state to take over electric telegraph companies, thereby preventing the emergence of a private sector equivalent to the US Western Union. This nationalization was carried out in 1870, for a price of £10 million.

---

26. Robert Blake, *Disraeli* (London: Faber & Faber, 1966), p. 555.
27. James Keir Hardie (1856-1915). Elected independent MP for West Ham South, 1892. Formed Independent Labour Party, 1893. Lost seat, 1895. ILP MP for Merthyr Tydfil, 1900-15. Chairman of the Independent Labour Party, 1894-1900, 1913-14, Chairman of the Labour Party, 1906-8.

The Tramways Act 1870 allowed for private operation of tramways, but only on 21-year concessions from local authorities, with the local authorities having the right to take over the line at depreciated value of assets, with no valuation of the business itself, at the end of that time – the so-called 'scrap-iron clause' which prevented investment in upkeep and maintenance in the later years of the concession.

The invention of the telephone in 1876 produced a couple of embryonic telephone companies in Britain before 1880. In that year a court judgement (*Attorney General* v. *Edison Company of London Limited*) declared that a telephone was a telegraph, within the meaning of Section 4 of the Telegraph Act 1868, so private companies had to obtain a 31-year licence from the Post Office, which in practice undertook the development of the telephone system itself. It was this decision that produced the appallingly backward and inefficient British telephone system of the 1970s.

The Electric Lighting Act 1882 allowed for electric lighting companies to be set up but, again, as with tramways, with local authorities having the right to provide their own electric light or to purchase the companies' assets at depreciated value after 21 years. This discouraged the formation of substantial long-term power companies but led to a crazed stock exchange bubble in the 1880s for fly-by-night companies. The collapse of this bubble, which was followed by regulations requiring companies to operate under seven-year orders from the Board of Trade, slowed the development of electric power in Britain. Progress was further stunted by several later Acts, one of which in 1926 created the Central Electricity Board, a public body which could choose which power stations were allowed to supply power. The full nationalization of the industry in 1947 was a final step in retarding its development.

The first radio broadcast in Britain, of Dame Nellie Melba singing, was made in 1920 sponsored by the *Daily Mail*; further such broadcasts were promptly banned at the insistence of the Post Office. A public sector monopoly was set up by the Post Office in 1922, financed by licence fees on all those buying radio sets; this became the British Broadcasting Corporation in 1926. Private sector broadcasting was not permitted until the 1950s and the compulsory licence fee has continued to this day.

Overall, these Acts, most of which were uncontroversial when they passed as they applied to small, new industries, gave local authorities or the Post Office monopoly control of some of the most dynamic new sectors of the economy – the arbitrary legal decision which doomed the British telephone service for the next century being especially egregious.

Epilogue: The Victorians and After 389

As they related to sectors from which dynamic growth and change might be expected, these Acts were more economically damaging than the Attlee[28] government's nationalizations of the late 1940s, which related to old or even moribund industries.

Looking back from the twenty-first century, we can recognize that the Whigs were proud of the corporations established by their Municipal Corporations Act 1835. We can also recognize that their Post Office reforms around 1840 had made that institution a model of efficiency and rapid service (though adding additional functions to it sapped that efficiency). Nevertheless, we must still shake our head at this hugely damaging state-monopolist legislation from statesmen who claimed to believe in capitalism.

Direct taxation, in modern times so severe a brake on economic growth, played little role in the 1870-1914 slowing of British growth, because it did not become a serious factor even at the end of the period. The success of nineteenth-century economic growth in reducing the burden of Napoleonic war debt (even though little of it was paid down), and of the late Victorians in keeping Britain out of European wars, meant that, even after the costly Boer War, government debt was only 30% of GDP in 1914, an eighth of its relative level a century earlier.

As a result, both the massive dreadnought naval rearmament programme and the beginnings of old age pensions and national insurance were financed in the years leading up to the war without a huge increase in either income tax rates or the overall burden of taxation. In 1913, gross public income was £189 million, 8.9% of GDP of £2,133 million, while the top combined rate of income tax and super tax in the 1914 Budget, even after several increases from 1909 on, was 12.9% (2s 7d in the pound).[29]

World War I inevitably brought a sharp lurch for the worse in British economic policy. Only 28% of the war was financed through taxation, a considerably lower percentage than in the Napoleonic wars or World War II. At the same time, the government's free trade proclivities and the

---

28. Clement Attlee (1883-1967). 1st Earl Attlee from 1955. MP for Limehouse and Walthamstow West, 1922-55. Chancellor of the Duchy of Lancaster, 1930-31, Lord Privy Seal, 1940-42, Secretary of State for Dominion Affairs, 1942-43, Lord President of the Council, 1943-45, Deputy Prime Minister, 1942-45, Prime Minister, 1945-51.

29. Mitchell (ed.), *British Historical Statistics*, Table XI-3 (revenue), Table XVI-4 (GDP); Finance Act 1914 (tax rates).

profligate spending of the post-war Lloyd George coalition unbalanced the fiscal system so badly that, even though Britain's debt/GDP ratio after 1919 was well below that of 1815, top rates of income tax/super tax after 1919 were far more intrusive and damaging to the economy (at 50% in 1925, to pick a random example), impeding the accumulation of the modest capital stakes that can fuel entrepreneurship or act as 'angel' investments.

One reversion to pre-1846 policy came with the Corn Production Act 1917, introduced to alleviate the problem that Liverpool had identified in introducing the 1815 Corn Law, insufficient corn production in wartime. The 1917 Act not only banned imports at low corn prices, but guaranteed the prices paid to farmers through government subsidy. Even though it was extended by the Agriculture Act 1920, supposedly with four years notice required for its abolition, a sharp decline in corn prices in early 1921 led the unprincipled and incompetent Lloyd George government to panic at its potential cost and repeal the Act with immediate effect.[30] A return to the Corn Laws would have been both more effective and cheaper.

Despite the war's losses, the Conservative post-war governments were determined to return to the gold standard. Keynes had estimated in 1923 that returning to gold at the pre-war parity would result in the pound being 8%-10% overvalued. Stanley Baldwin[31] in 1923 proposed a solution for this: a 10% Imperial Preference tariff that would go some way (but not the whole way) towards equalizing the tariff regimes between Britain and its trading partners. Regrettably, he felt the need to call an election before implementing this, which he lost.

Winston Churchill,[32] as Chancellor of the Exchequer tasked with the gold standard's implementation in 1925, had campaigned as a

---

30. I am indebted to Edith H. Whetham, 'The Agriculture Act, 1920 and Its Repeal: The "Great Betrayal"', for this account; available at: https://www.bahs.org.uk/AGHR/ARTICLES/22n1a3.pdf (accessed 20 February 2022).

31. Stanley Baldwin (1867-1947). 1st Earl Baldwin of Bewdley from 1937. MP for Bewdley, 1908-37. President of the Board of Trade, 1921-22, Chancellor of the Exchequer, 1922-23, Prime Minister, 1923-24, 1924-29, 1935-37, Lord President of the Council, 1931-35.

32. Sir Winston Churchill (1874-1955). KG 1953. MP for Oldham, Manchester NW, Dundee, Epping and Woodford, 1900-64. President of the Board of Trade, 1908-10, Home Secretary, 1910-11, First Lord of the Admiralty, 1911-15, 1939-40, Chancellor of the Duchy of Lancaster, 1915, Minister of Munitions, 1917-19, Secretary of State for War, 1919-21,

Epilogue: The Victorians and After

Liberal in 1923 against the tariffs that would have made it less painful. Nevertheless, Churchill went ahead, but the government did nothing significant to reduce public spending, so the pound remained overvalued and Britain in a recession for the remainder of the 1920s. The overvalued pound and high direct tax rates of the late 1920s were devastating to British entrepreneurship in a period when the United States was forging ahead.

The 1930s were a different story. Britain left the gold standard in 1931. The following year Neville Chamberlain[33] by the Ottawa Agreement finally implemented the 10% Imperial Preference tariff that should have been imposed half a century earlier, and Britain's unilateral free trade self-destruction was at an end. The result was an economic recovery that has been little celebrated but that by some measures was the most rapid Britain ever experienced, with GDP rising 24%, or 3.2% per annum per capita, between 1932 and 1938. It was also a period of exceptional technological innovation, with radar, rayon, broadcast television, the Spitfire, the 1938 Lagonda V-12, the jet engine and the first primitive electronic computer all British and dating from the decade 1933-43.

One additional reason for the 1930s boom: housing was extremely cheap by today's standards, especially around London. Eighty per cent of houses sold for less than £750 (equivalent to roughly £150,000 today) and interest rates were also low. The housing market for building, purchases and rentals was still almost free from bureaucracy and restrictions, and low interest rates and economic recovery resulted in a suburban housing boom, with 365,000 houses built in Britain in 1936, a figure matched since only briefly in 1965-69.[34] The removal of cheap housing, and its translation since 1990 into extremely expensive housing, is one of many reasons for the British economy's further relative decline since the 1930s.

    Colonial Secretary, 1921-22, Chancellor of the Exchequer, 1924-29, Prime Minister 1940-45, 1951-55.

33. Neville Chamberlain (1869-1940). MP for Birmingham Ladywood and Birmingham Edgbaston, 1918-40. Postmaster-General, 1922-23, Minister for Health, 1923, 1924-29, Chancellor of the Exchequer, 1923-24, 1931-37, Prime Minister, 1937-40, Lord President of the Council, 1940.

34. Mitchell (ed.), *British Historical Statistics*, Table VII-5, p. 390. The peak of the Macmillan boom in 1954 was only 348,000 units, mostly inferior council flats, as were those of the late 1960s – the average British new build has halved in size since the 1920s.

Post-Industrial or Post-Britain?

World War II ended the recovery. Since it was accompanied by a demonization of 1930s political figures, notably, Chamberlain, the architect of economic recovery and was followed by Clement Attlee's Labour government, it ended it definitively. Top rates of income tax went above 90% almost continually until 1979, while food rationing persisted until 1954. The Town and Country Planning Act 1947 imposed a vast bureaucracy on any building project, which is still in place, while the Furnished Houses (Rent Control) Act 1946 destroyed the private rental sector until its partial repeal in the late 1980s. In fairness, Attlee had never seen the British economy at its best except for a brief period in the late 1930s when he was in opposition; even in his youth, between 1900 and 1914 it was sluggish and un-entrepreneurial.

Equally damaging to Britain's post-war economy was the 1944 Bretton Woods Conference between Britain, the United States and the communist Soviet Union, which set out the post-war economic order. Keynes was the chief British negotiator and he hated Imperial Preference, partly for 'not invented here' reasons. (He had lost influence in the Treasury and its lucrative insider-trading opportunities[35] during Chamberlain's peacetime tenure.)

Consequently, at Bretton Woods he agreed to the Roosevelt administration's intolerable demand that Britain abandon Imperial Preference, cutting Britain off from her main international markets, and condemning the country to relative impoverishment throughout the 1970s. He also pushed for an international currency 'bancor' that was never going to be acceptable to the United States and set up a spurious system of post-war international financial institutions, the IMF and the World Bank, that took away much emerging market advisory work which had been highly lucrative to London's merchant banks before 1914. Finally, Keynes agreed to a system of rigidly fixed exchange rates, with the pound at an overvalued $4.03, and negotiated an inadequate post-war loan from the US government.

A negotiator with Britain's true economic interests at heart would not have allowed chimerical new schemes of international finance to dominate the conference but would have focussed like a laser on Britain's

---

35. See Robert Skidelsky's 3-volume biography of Keynes (London: Viking, 1983, 1992 and 2000), footnotes in which detail Keynes' net worth at various points of his life. These can be correlated with his official positions, while the text outlines his unexpected loss of investment mojo in the 1930s. Insider Trading was not illegal in the UK until 1980.

Epilogue: The Victorians and After

three crucial interests: the preservation of Imperial Preference, the largest possible post-war loan, perhaps from J.P. Morgan and the private sector, and the ability to engineer an immediate sterling devaluation.[36]

In 1946, William Morris, Lord Nuffield,[37] of Morris Motors was planning a massive export drive to take over the US market for small cars. British automobile production at that time benefited from a sectoral protection – the McKenna duties on luxury goods first imposed in 1915, levying a 33% import tariff on automobiles – but suffered from the British horsepower tax, first imposed in 1920, of an annual £1 per horsepower which pushed British production towards small and underpowered cars. The combination of the two taxes and low production volumes made cars twice as expensive in Britain as in the United States. Morris Motors' export drive for the US market, concentrated on small cars, would benefit from much lower labour costs but suffer from lower British production volumes and from British steel being 40% more expensive than supplies to US manufacturers. A devaluation such as finally occurred in September 1949 was necessary to make it work.[38] Alas, despite Nuffield's brilliance his US market ambitions were stillborn – the devaluation came too late, after raging US post-war automobile demand had tapered off into recession.

After 1951, Britain settled into a generation of quasi-socialist mediocrity, with Imperial Preference abandoned and the empire seeking independence. Its economic inefficiency was worsened by the failure of the 1952 'ROBOT' scheme to move to a floating exchange rate and the consequent series of exchange rate crises, with the insane maintenance of tight exchange controls until 1979 devastating investment decisions throughout the economy. Then, in 1960-61, entry to what became the European Union appeared to Harold Macmillan[39] (whose 1938 *The*

---

36. See Benn Steil, *The Battle of Bretton Woods: John Maynard Keynes, Harry Dexter White, and the Making of a New World Order* (Princeton, NJ: Princeton University Press, 2019).

37. William Morris (1877-1963). FRS 1939. 1st Bt from 1929, Baron Nuffield from 1934, Viscount Nuffield from 1938. Founder of Morris Motors, 1919, which by 1926 represented 42% of British car manufacture.

38. The post-war plans and possibilities for Morris Motors are set out in *Fortune* magazine, July 1946, 'Morris Motors Ltd.', pp. 89-95, 219-228.

39. Harold Macmillan (1894-1986). 1st Earl of Stockton from 1984. MP for Stockton-on-Tees and Bromley, 1924-29, 1931-64. Secretary of State for Air, 1945, Minister of Housing and Local Government, 1951-54, Minister of Defence, 1954-55, Foreign Secretary, 1955, Chancellor of the Exchequer, 1955-57, Prime Minister, 1957-63.

Middle Way advocated massive nationalization and abolishing the Stock Exchange – as his nanny said, 'Mr Harold is a dangerous pink') as a solution to Britain's problems. In reality, it threw away Britain's traditional advantage of access through relationships with the former colonies to raw materials and cheap manufacturing labour, gaining little in return.

With over 50 million people on a small island, the British economy in 1960 was already service-oriented, with a large, if declining, manufacturing sector, and lacked self-sufficiency in foodstuffs, energy or raw materials. Accordingly, its natural trading partners were countries with abundant raw materials, energy and cheap food. Britain had such trading partners, in the countries of the Commonwealth, both the white-dominated dominions and the ethnically varied but impoverished remainder.

Without Imperial Preference Britain had little remaining structure in place to take advantage of those relationships. However, the trading relationships with the newly independent former colonies remained and an enlightened Britain could have focussed on them. Europe, heavily protectionist and dominated by manufacturing and hopelessly inefficient and expensive agriculture, was an unattractive partner. The EU marriage arranged in 1961-73 was a hopeless *mésalliance*.

Britain's economic policy took a modest upturn after 1979 with the advent of Margaret Thatcher.[40] On the plus side, her privatizations, trades union legislation, reductions in top tax rates and modest deregulations were helpful to entrepreneurship and produced an improvement in economic growth from the previous dismal levels. On the negative side, her 'reform' of the City of London, undertaken while its real capital base had been reduced to midget levels by the inflation and sluggish markets of the 1970s, left its great names horribly vulnerable to the larger and more aggressive houses of Wall Street.[41] The reform was Whiggish in principle, demolishing Britain's barriers to entry while other countries

---

40. Margaret Thatcher (1925-2013). Baroness Thatcher from 1992. MP for Finchley, 1959-92. Secretary of State for Education and Science, 1970-74, Prime Minister, 1979-90.

41. Inflation hits banks especially badly, because their assets are almost all denominated in nominal terms, so their 'real' capital shrinks. My own first employer, Hill Samuel, had more capital than the major Wall Street houses Goldman Sachs or Salomon Brothers in 1972; by the time 'deregulation' came in the 1980s, it was an underpowered midget and one of the first victims.

Epilogue: The Victorians and After

kept theirs up; it was also remarkably ill-timed, leaving the centuries-old British houses no chance of survival.

Since Thatcher's departure, Britain has drifted further from the policies that produced industrialization. One barrier to entrepreneurship has been the inexorable rise of regulation, particularly in the environmental area and with respect to 'climate change'. Large established organizations have teams of people lobbying to ensure that regulations are moulded in their favour; entrepreneurs do not. The huge cost of environmental regulation is therefore borne by entrepreneurs and by those who are prevented from entrepreneurship by the density of the regulatory thicket. Add to this the cost of unnecessarily expensive energy, for example, as environmental activists prevent Britain from fracking its abundant natural gas resources.

The persistently ultra-loose monetary policy has kept interest rates below the rate of inflation, so that the outstanding stock of perpetual 2½% Consols[42] were redeemed in 2015, even though in today's fiat currency world with its inevitable inflation their real return to investors (and cost to the government as issuer) is far lower than when Pelham introduced them. The persistent ultra-low interest rates, set at an artificial level as if GOSPLAN were managing the British economy,[43] have had two adverse effects. First, they have stifled productivity growth, which grew only 5.6% or 0.39% per annum, in the fourteen years 2007-21, a rate that would have been considered inadequate 250 years earlier, or at any time in the quarter-millennium in between. Second, they have encouraged excessive investment in housing, which since the 1980s has been the main British form of saving. This has reduced British living standards through high house prices, starving the more productive sectors of the economy of capital, while failing, because of excessive planning restrictions, to increase the housing supply sufficiently to prevent the endless price spiral.

In Britain, a third barrier to entrepreneurship and innovation has been the Blair[44] government's destruction of constitutional structures

---

42. The 3% Consols introduced in 1757 were refinanced in 1888 by Consols bearing a 2½% interest rate from 1902.

43. By setting the price of money persistently far below a market level, monetary authorities are operating the same artificial price system, sending incorrect signals to buyers and sellers, as the central planning agency, GOSPLAN, in the pre-1991 Soviet Union.

44. Tony Blair (1953-). KG 2022. MP for Sedgefield, 1983-2007. Prime Minister, 1997-2007.

that had stood for centuries or even millennia and their replacement by badly designed modernism. Scottish and Welsh devolution have subjected those polities to perpetual socialism, as well as in Scotland's case to significant uncertainty about whether the country will split from the United Kingdom. The abolition of the traditional House of Lords in 1998 and its replacement by a body of 'Tony's cronies', appointed life peers, vastly increased the political system's fascination with fashionable leftist nostrums and eliminated its long-standing roots in the permanent interests of the country and its people. The replacement of the traditional Lord Chancellor presiding over the judicial House of Lords, an office created in AD 604, and its replacement by a 'Supreme Court', controlled by the legal left, removed the protections traditional English law gave to property and individual rights. Subordinating British Courts to the European Court of Human Rights, effective in 1998, subjected British citizens and businesses to yet another layer of unaccountable 'woke' jurisdiction.

With the changes since 1990, despite the Thatcher trades union reforms and lower top income tax rates, the British economic, legal and social environment has again become generally more unfriendly to the kinds of innovation that bring industrial and economic progress. One can argue whether it is freer today than in the era of socialism and wartime controls of around 1950 but, either way, today's Britain is very far from entrepreneurial renewal.

Possible Future Policies

The final question is which of the policies that brought the Industrial Revolution should be re-adopted today in Britain and what beneficial effect they might have. Some few of those policies are still in effect (the Scientific Method is still in place, though assailed from time to time), while others (the profitable empire) are gone for ever. Still, there are several of the Industrial Revolution's central principles that have been abandoned; their re-adoption would serve Britain very well indeed.

The most important of these principles is that the rights of private property should be sacrosanct. We theoretically live in a capitalist system, in which private property is the basis of most transactions, yet its rights are never mentioned, except to be attacked and evaded. Read any of Liverpool's economic speeches, or those of Pitt, and you will see that property rights were of the utmost importance to both men and to their contemporaries, far more important than any other economic principle. Their demotion, to be violated by unelected bureaucrats and

Epilogue: The Victorians and After

large corporations, is the principal reason why the British economy works far less well now than it did 200 years ago. The main intellectual damage to this principle was done in the nineteenth century, aided by Charles Dickens, in particular. By 1900 property rights were already regarded as thoroughly suspect – in *A Man of Property* (1906) by John Galsworthy,[45] Soames Forsyte is not a sympathetic figure.

Second, and related to the first, the principle of individual freedom, in economic matters but also more widely, has been eroded particularly since 1900. The two world wars were largely to blame; during them the British public grew used to extreme restrictions on their freedom. Unforgivably, many of those restrictions, notably, exchange controls, remained in place for decades after the wars, while other freedoms, notably, that of speech have been sadly eroded in the last 30 years. Innovation is only possible if the oddballs, the eccentrics, those who do not conform to the norm, are able to think different thoughts, discuss them freely and pursue those thoughts in their garages. British individual freedom was developed after the Restoration; it is impossible in a society with rigid speech codes, whether of Puritans or of 'woke' militants.

The third change needed for a new Industrial Revolution is a mass repeal of regulations. The original Industrial Revolution was almost unregulated, with the government undoing mediaeval regulations such as the Statute of Artificers that limited labour and other markets. This situation was already changing before 1830, when the first Factory Acts regulated such areas as child labour where the workers' bargaining power was inadequate and had led to abuse. The trickle of regulations became a flood after 1906, when the Fabian enthusiasts who supported the 1906-15 Liberal government applied their regulatory zeal across the economy. Just as Blackstone codified English common law, making its implications clear and unambiguous to all, so regulations must be drastically pruned back and a new Blackstone must nail down their precise meaning and implications.

World Wars I and II naturally worsened this tendency, and the arrival of environmentalism has made it still worse, adding regulations of incalculable but invisible cost, thereby, together with artificially low interest rates, slowing productivity growth close to zero. Large companies can deal with this environment, using their lobbying power to evade the worst regulations, but small businesses cannot, and are

---

45. John Galsworthy (1867-1933). Novelist and playwright. Author of the multi-volume *The Forsyte Saga*, first published under that title in 1922; *A Man of Property* (1906) is the first volume.

differentially harmed by the regulatory jungle. Even without a full return to the free market, an abandonment of such expensive regulatory follies as 'net zero' and their replacement by a carbon tax, if necessary, would greatly improve Britain's micro-economy, although without a full return to principles of property rights and individual freedom that improvement would be only partial.

Another essential to a revival of the Industrial Revolution in Britain is a return to sound money and a decent savings climate. The negative real interest rates of the last 25 years are death to savers and encourage speculation and leverage, both of which divert money away from industrial innovation into get-rich-quick schemes. They also cause the market to become excessively 'financialized', pushing the most able into financial speculation rather than industry. If we cannot return to a gold standard, Britain must at least return to an environment in which the financial system holds short-term rates well above the rate of inflation, encouraging savings and discouraging financialization and leverage.

The labour-saving innovations that made the Industrial Revolution were the product of expensive labour and policies such as mass colonization that increased wage rates. The cheap labour policy instituted with the repeal of the Corn Laws has been intensified since the Blair era by excessive immigration, both legal and illegal, promoted by the cheap labour lobby. This damages British culture, but more importantly, it degrades British living standards and dilutes the scientific genius, technological innovation and entrepreneurship that allow British and human advances to continue. As technological sophistication advances, it increases demand for high-skill but not low-skill labour; it is utterly perverse to import mass quantities of the latter.

Finally, the most difficult Industrial Revolution era policy to reproduce is the decentralization of decision making about investment and finance that characterized it. The country banks of that era were distributed all over the country and each had its distinct operating methodology; there was no centralized training for country bankers. In our own day, the big banks form an oligopoly, while private equity sources, apparently diverse, have a remarkable uniformity of training and thought processes, so that unusual ideas or people are unlikely to get financing. Higher interest rates, by reducing the pull of asset-generating businesses, might diversify those sources' hiring even as it reduced their number, but the financial environment of 1760-1826, with country banks and local share issues, may have been unique and irreproducible.

* * *

Epilogue: The Victorians and After

Overall, there are several policy improvements that could be made to restore entrepreneurship and innovation in the British economy and increase the country's prosperity. Our conclusion should not be to cavil, but simply to marvel at the concatenation of policy and social factors that allowed Britain to produce an economic change that did more than any other to improve the human condition. To the statesmen, thinkers and innovators who engineered this wonder we, whether British or just human, should be forever grateful.

Bibliography

A. Primary Sources

Aspinall, A., (ed.), *The Letters of King George IV, 1812-30*, 3 vols (Cambridge: Cambridge University Press, 1938)

———, and E. Anthony Smith (eds), *English Historical Documents: Volume XI: 1783-1832* (Oxford: Oxford University Press, 1959)

Bacon, Francis, *Novum Organum Scientiarum* (Antwerp: Wijngaerde, 1620)

Bamford, Francis, and the Duke of Wellington (eds), *The Journal of Mrs Arbuthnot, 1820-1832*, 2 vols (London: Macmillan & Co. Ltd, 1950)

Bank of England, Minutes of the Court of Directors, available via the Bank's website: www.bankofengland.co.uk

Blackstone, Sir William, *Commentaries on the Laws of England*, 4 vols (Oxford: Clarendon Press, 1765-70)

Bullion Committee, *Report from the Select Committee on the High Price of Gold Bullion* (London: J. Johnson & Co. and J. Ridgway, 1810)

Clarendon, Edward, Earl of, *The Life of Edward Earl of Clarendon*, 3 vols, (Oxford: Clarendon Press, 1759)

Coke, Sir Edward, *Institute of the Lawes of England*, 4 vols (Clarke, 18th edn, 1797 [1628-44])

Colchester, Charles, 2nd Baron, (ed.), *The Diaries and Correspondence of Charles Abbot, Lord Colchester* (London: J. Murray, 1861)

Debrett, John, John Stockdale and John Almon, *The Parliamentary Register; or, History of the Proceedings and Debates of the House of Lords and House of Commons*, 77 vols (London: 1780-1803)

Defoe, Daniel, *A Tour Through the Whole Island of Great Britain*, 3 vols (London: 1724-26)

Fortescue, Sir John, *The Difference between an Absolute and Limited Monarchy* (London, W. Bowyer, 1714)

———, *In Praise of English Law* (Company of Stationers, 1616)

Fuller, Thomas, DD, *History of the Worthies of England* (London: J.G.W.L and W.G., 1662)

The Gentleman's Magazine, Vol. 79, Pt 1 (January-June 1809)

Hansard, T.C., *The Parliamentary Debates from the Year 1803 to the Present Time* (1803-20)

———, *The Parliamentary Debates New Series: Commencing with the Accession of George IV,* (1820-30)

Hathaway, W.S., (ed.), *The Speeches of William Pitt in the House of Commons* (London: A. Strahan, 1817)

Horn, D.B., and Mary Ransome (eds), *English Historical Documents: Volume X: 1714-1783* (London: Eyre & Spottiswoode, 1969)

Jennings, Louis, (ed.), *The Correspondence and Diaries of John Wilson Croker,* 3 vols. (London: J. Murray, 1884)

Malthus, Thomas, *An Essay on the Principle of Population* (London: J. Johnson, 1798)

Marx, K., and F. Engels, *Collected Works* (Moscow: Progress Publishers, 1980)

Mitchell, B.R., (ed.), *British Historical Statistics* (Cambridge: Cambridge University Press, 2011)

Morris, Christopher, (ed.), *The Illustrated Journeys of Celia Fiennes, 1685-c.1712* (London: Macdonald & Co., 1982)

Mun, Thomas, *England's Treasure by Forraign Trade* (London: Grismond, 1664)

North, Sir Dudley, *Discourses upon Trade* (Basset, 1691; Wokingham: Dodo Press repr., 2009)

North, Roger, *Life of the Honourable Sir Dudley North, Knight* (London: John Whiston, 1745)

Ricardo, David, *On the Principles of Political Economy and Taxation* (London: J. Murray, 1817)

Say, J.B., *De l'Angleterre et des Anglais* (Paris: Chez Arthus Bertrand, 1815)

Smith, Adam, *An Inquiry into the Nature and Causes of the Wealth of Nations,* 3 vols. (London: W. Strahan and T. Cadell, 1776)

The State of the Nation at the Commencement of 1822, Considered under the Four Departments of the Finance, Foreign Relations, Home Department, Colonies and Board of Trade (London: John Hatchard & Son, 1822)

Sully, Maximilien de Bethune, duc de, *Memoires des sages et royalles oeconomies d'estate domestiques, politiques et militaires de Henri le Grand* (Amsterdam: 1638)

B. Secondary Sources: Europe, Economic Theory and General

Abu-Lughod, Janet, *Before European Hegemony: The World System,* AD *1250-1350* (New York: Oxford University, 1989)

Allen, Paul, *Philip III and the Pax Hispanica, 1598-1621: The Failure of Grand Strategy* (New Haven, CT: Yale University Press, 2000)

Appleby, Joyce, *The Relentless Revolution: A History of Capitalism* (New York: Norton, 2010)

Baer, Marc, *The Ottomans: Khans, Caesars and Caliphs* (New York: Basic Books, 2021)

Bibliography

Bavel, Bas van, and Auke Rijpma, 'How Important Were Formalized Charity and Social Spending before the Rise of the Welfare State?: A Long-run Analysis of Selected Western European Cases, 1400-1850', *Economic History Review*, Vol. 69, no. 1 (2016)

Cameron, Euan, (ed.), *Early Modern Europe: An Oxford History* (Oxford: Oxford University Press, 1999)

Clark, Christopher, *Iron Kingdom: The Rise and Downfall of Prussia, 1600-1947* (Cambridge, MA: Harvard University Press/Belknap, 2006)

Cook, Harold J., *Matters of Exchange: Commerce, Medicine and Science in the Dutch Golden Age* (New Haven, CT: Yale University Press, 2007)

Crafts, Nicholas, and Terence C. Mills, 'Six centuries of Economic Growth: A Time-Series Perspective', *European Review of Economic History*, Vol. 21, no. 2 (2017), pp. 141-58

Drelichman, Mauricio, and Hans-Joachim Voth, *Lending to the Borrower from Hell: Debt, Taxes and Default in the Age of Philip II* (Princeton, NJ: Princeton University Press, 2014)

Elliott, Sir John, *Imperial Spain, 1469-1716* (London: Edward Arnold, 1963)

Evans, R.J.W., *Rudolf II and His World: A Study in Intellectual History, 1576-1612* (Oxford: Oxford University Press, 1973)

Frohman, Larry, *Poor Relief and Welfare in Germany from the Reformation to World War I* (New York: Cambridge University Press, 2008)

Grayling, A.C., *The Age of Genius: The Seventeenth Century and the Birth of the Modern Mind* (London: Bloomsbury, 2016)

Häberlein, Mark, *The Fuggers of Augsburg: Pursuing Wealth and Honor in Renaissance Germany* (Charlottesville: University of Virginia Press, 2012)

Harris, Ron, *Going the Distance: Eurasian Trade and the Rise of the Business Corporation, 1400-1700* (Princeton, NJ: Princeton University Press, 2020)

Hobsbawm, Eric, *The Age of Revolution: Europe 1789-1848* (London: Weidenfeld & Nicolson, 1962)

Hoffman, Philip, G. Postel-Vinay and J.-L. Rosenthal, *Dark Matter Credit: The Development of Peer-to-Peer Lending in France* (Princeton, NJ: Princeton University Press, 2019)

Howard, Douglas A., *A History of the Ottoman Empire* (Cambridge: Cambridge University Press, 2017)

Israel, Jonathan I., *The Enlightenment that Failed: Ideas, Revolution, and Democratic Defeat, 1748-1830* (Oxford: Oxford University Press, 2019)

Jacob, Margaret C., *The First Knowledge Economy: Human Capital and the European Economy, 1750-1850* (Cambridge: Cambridge University Press, 2014)

Kuhn, Thomas S., *The Structure of Scientific Revolutions* (Chicago: University of Chicago Press, 1962)

Maddison, Angus, *The World Economy: Historical Statistics* (Paris: OECD, 2003)

Marshall, Peter, *The Mercurial Emperor: The Magic Circle of Rudolf II in Renaissance Prague* (London: Pimlico, 2007)

Mexia, Pedro, *The Historie of All the Romane Emperors*, tr. W. Traheron (London: Matthew Lownes, 1604)

Monod, Paul K., *The Power of Kings: Monarchy and Religion in Europe, 1589-1715* (New Haven, CT: Yale University Press, 1999)

Murphy, Antoin E., *The Genesis of Macroeconomics: New Ideas from Sir William Petty to Henry Thornton* (Oxford: Oxford University Press, 2009)

Norrhem, Svante, and Erik Thomson (eds), *Subsidies, Diplomacy, and State Formation in Europe, 1494-1789* (Lund, Sweden: Lund University Press, 2020)

Onnekink, David, and Gijs Rommelse, *The Dutch in the Early Modern World* (Cambridge: Cambridge University Press, 2019)

Pitts, Vincent J., *Henri IV of France: His Reign and Age* (Baltimore: Johns Hopkins University Press, 2012)

Pomeranz, Kenneth, *The Great Divergence: China, Europe, and the Making of the Modern World Economy* (Princeton, NJ: Princeton University Press, 2000)

Rady, Martyn, *The Habsburgs: To Rule the World* (New York: Basic Books, 2020)

Rae, John, *Life of Adam Smith* (London: Macmillan & Co., 1895)

Ricardo, David, *The Principles of Political Economy and Taxation* (London: J.M. Dent, 1911)

Richards, John, *The Mughal Empire* (Cambridge: Cambridge University Press, 1993)

Roberts, Andrew, *Napoleon the Great* (London: Allen Lane, 2014)

Schama, Simon, *The Embarrassment of Riches: An Interpretation of Dutch Culture in the Golden Age* (London: Collins, 1987)

Sharman, J.C., *Empires of the Weak: The Real Story of European Expansion and the Creation of the New World Order* (Princeton, NJ: Princeton University Press, 2019)

Siemann, Wolfram, *Metternich: Strategist and Visionary* (Cambridge, MA: The Belknap Press, 2019)

Smith, Pamela H., *The Business of Alchemy: Science and Culture in the Holy Roman Empire* (Princeton, NJ: Princeton University Press, 1994)

Stasavage, David, *States of Credit: Size, Power and the Development of European Politics* (Princeton, NJ: Princeton University Press, 2011)

Steil, Benn, *The Battle of Bretton Woods: John Maynard Keynes, Harry Dexter White, and the Making of a New World Order* (Princeton, NJ: Princeton University Press, 2013)

Stein, Stanley J., and Barbara H. Stein, *Silver, Trade and War: Spain and America in the Making of Early Modern Europe* (Baltimore: Johns Hopkins University Press, 2000)

Vittorio, Antonio di, (ed.), *An Economic History of Europe* (London: Routledge, 2006)

Vries, Jan de, *The Economy of Europe in an Age of Crisis, 1600-1750* (Cambridge: Cambridge University Press, 1976)

Bibliography

405

Vries, Jan de, and Ad van der Woude, *The First Modern Economy: Success, Failure and Perseverance of the Dutch Economy, 1500-1815* (Cambridge: Cambridge University Press, 1997)

Whaley, Joachim, *Germany and the Holy Roman Empire*, 2 vols (Oxford: Oxford University Press, 2012)

Wilson, Peter H., *Heart of Europe: A History of the Holy Roman Empire* (Cambridge, MA: The Belknap Press, 2020)

C. Secondary Sources: Britain

Beckett, J.V., *The Aristocracy in England, 1660-1914* (New York: Blackwell, 1986)

Bindoff, S.T., (ed.), *The History of Parliament: The House of Commons, 1509-1558* (Woodbridge: Boydell & Brewer, 1982) (available online)

Bown, Stephen, *Merchant Kings: When Companies Ruled the World, 1600-1900* (New York: Thomas Dunne Books, 2009)

Butterfield, Sir Herbert, *George III, Lord North and the People, 1779-80* (London: G. Bell & Sons, 1949)

Cannadine, David, *The Decline and Fall of the British Aristocracy* (New Haven, CT: Yale University Press, 1990)

———, *Victorious Century: The United Kingdom, 1800-1900* (London: Allen Lane, 2017)

Carlos, A., L. Neal and K. Wandschneider, 'The Origins of National Debt: The Financing and Re-financing of the War of the Spanish Succession', paper presented at the IEHA annual meeting, Helsinki, 2006

Carruthers, Bruce C., *City of Capital: Politics and Markets in the English Financial Revolution* (Princeton, NJ: Princeton University Press, 1996)

Cathcart, Brian, *The News from Waterloo: The Race to Tell Britain of Wellington's Victory* (London: Faber & Faber, 2015)

Colley, Linda, *Britons: Forging the Nation, 1707-1837* (New Haven, CT: Yale University Press, 1992)

———, *The Gun, the Ship, and the Pen* (New York: Liveright Publishing, 2021)

———, *In Defiance of Oligarchy: The Tory Party, 1714-60* (New York: Cambridge University Press, 1982)

Corble, Nick, *James Brindley: The First Canal Builder* (Cheltenham: The History Press, 2005)

Dalrymple, William, *The Anarchy: The Relentless Rise of the East India Company* (London: Bloomsbury, 2019)

Dawes, Margaret, and C.N. Ward-Perkins, *Country Banks of England and Wales* (Canterbury: Chartered Institute of Bankers, 2000)

Dickson, P.G.M. *The Financial Revolution in England: A Study in the Development of Public Credit, 1688-1756* (London: Macmillan, 1967)

Fara, Patricia, *Life after Gravity: Isaac Newton's London Career* (Oxford: Oxford University Press, 2021)

Feiling, Sir Keith G., *The Second Tory Party, 1714-1832* (London: Macmillan, 1938)

Fisher, D.R., (ed.) *The History of Parliament: The House of Commons, 1820-32* (Cambridge: Cambridge University Press, 2009) (available online)

Floud, Roderick, Jane Humphries and Paul Johnson (eds), *The Cambridge Economic History of Modern Britain: Volume 1: 1700-1870* (Cambridge: Cambridge University Press, 2014)

Forester, C.S., *Hornblower and the Atropos* (London: Michael Joseph, 1953)

Fox, Harold G., *Monopolies and Patents: A Study of the History and Future of the Patent Monopoly* (Toronto: University of Toronto Press, 1947)

Gayer, A., W.W. Rostow and A.J. Schwartz, *The Growth and Fluctuation of the British Economy, 1790-1850*, 2 vols (Oxford: The Clarendon Press, 1953)

Gleick, James, *Isaac Newton* (London: Vintage, 2003)

Goodman, Ruth, *The Domestic Revolution: How the Introduction of Coal into Victorian Homes Changed Everything* (New York: Liveright Publishing, 2020)

Guldi, Jo, *Roads to Power: Britain Invents the Infrastructure State* (Cambridge, MA: Harvard University Press, 2012)

Hadfield, Charles, *The Canal Age* (New York: Praeger, 1969)

Hayton, D., and E. Cruikshanks (eds), *The History of Parliament: The House of Commons, 1690-1715* (Woodbridge: Boydell & Brewer, 2002) (available online)

Henning, Basil D., (ed.) *The History of Parliament: The House of Commons, 1660-1690* (Woodbridge: Boydell & Brewer, 1983) (available online)

Hilton, Boyd, *A Mad, Bad, & Dangerous People?: England, 1783-1846* (Oxford: Oxford University Press, 2006)

Jackman, W.T., *The Development of Transportation in Modern England*, 2 vols (Cambridge: Cambridge University Press, 1916)

Keay, John, *The Honourable Company: A History of the East India Company* (London: HarperCollins, 1991)

Kinkel, Sarah, *Disciplining the Empire: Politics, Governance, and the Rise of the British Navy* (Cambridge, MA: Harvard University Press, 2018)

Knight, Roger, *Britain against Napoleon: The Organization of Victory, 1793-1815* (London: Penguin, 2013)

Knowles, Ronald M., 'Political and Economic Impact of the American Revolution on Ireland', Irish Septs Association, 2004

Macaulay, Thomas B., *The History of England from the Accession of James the Second*, 5 vols (London: Folio Society, 2009)

Macfarlane, Alan, *The Origins of English Individualism: The Family, Property and Social Transition* (Oxford: Basil Blackwell, 1978)

Marriott, Sir James A.R., *The Life and Times of Lucius Cary, Viscount Falkland* (London: Methuen, 1907)

McKendrick, Neil, John Brewer and J.H. Plumb, *The Birth of a Consumer Society: The Commercialization of Eighteenth-Century England* (London: Europa Publications, 1982)

Melton, Frank, *Sir Robert Clayton and the Origins of English Deposit Banking, 1658-1685* (Cambridge: Cambridge University Press, 1986)

Bibliography

Mortimer, Ian, *The Time Traveller's Guide to Restoration Britain* (London: Vintage, 2017)

Namier, L., and J. Brooke (eds), *The History of Parliament: The House of Commons, 1754-1790* (Woodbridge: Boydell & Brewer, 1964) (available online)

O'Brien, Patrick K, 'The Political Economy of British Taxation, 1688-1815' *Economic History Review*, Vol. 41, no. 1 (1988), pp. 1-32

Overton, Mark, *Agricultural Revolution in England: The Transformation of the Agrarian Economy, 1500-1850* (Cambridge: Cambridge University Press, 1996)

Plumb, J.H., *The Growth of Political Stability in England, 1675-1725* (London: MacMillan, 1967)

Pressnell, L.S., *Country Banking in the Industrial Revolution* (Oxford: Oxford University Press, 1956)

Pryor, Francis, *The Fens: Discovering England's Ancient Depths* (New York: Apollo, 2019)

Roberts, Andrew, *The Last King of America: The Misunderstood Reign of George III* (London: Viking, 2021)

Rodger, N.A.M., *The Command of the Ocean: A Naval History of Britain, 1649-1815* (New York: W.W. Norton, 2004)

Rule, John, *The Vital Century: England's Developing Economy, 1714-1815* (London: Longman, 1992)

Sack, James, *From Jacobite to Conservative: Reaction and Orthodoxy in Britain, c. 1760-1832* (Cambridge: Cambridge University Press, 1993)

Salaman, Redcliffe, *The History and Social Influence of the Potato* (Cambridge: Cambridge University Press, 1949)

Scott, Jonathan, *How the Old World Ended: The Anglo-Dutch-American Revolution, 1500-1800* (New Haven, CT: Yale University Press, 2019)

Sedgwick, Romney, (ed.), *The History of Parliament: The House of Commons, 1715-1754* (Woodbridge: Boydell & Brewer, 1970) (available online)

Slack, Paul, *The English Poor Law, 1531-1782* (Cambridge: Cambridge University Press, 1990)

Smart, William, *Economic Annals of the Nineteenth Century: Volume 1: 1801-1820* (London: Macmillan & Co., 1910)

———, *Economic Annals of the Nineteenth Century: Volume 2: 1821-1830* (London: Macmillan & Co., 1917)

Stone, Peter, *The History of the Port of London: A Vast Emporium of Nations* (Barnsley: Pen and Sword History, 2017)

Thompson, E.P., *The Making of the English Working Class* (London: Victor Gollancz, 1963)

———, *Whigs and Hunters: The Origin of the Black Act* (London: Allen Lane, 1975)

Thorne, R.G., (ed.), *The History of Parliament: The House of Commons, 1790-1820* (Woodbridge: Boydell & Brewer, 1986) (available online)

Thrush, A., and J.P. Ferris (eds), *The History of Parliament: The House of Commons, 1604-29* (Cambridge: Cambridge University Press, 2010) (available online)

Towers, Eric, *Dashwood: The Man and the Myth* (Wellingborough: Crucible Press, 1986)

Uglow, Jenny, *In These Times: Living in Britain through Napoleon's Wars, 1793-1815* (New York: Farrer, Straus and Giroux, 2014)

———, *The Lunar Men: Five Friends Whose Curiosity Changed the World* (New York: Farrer, Straus and Giroux, 2002)

Valentine, Alan, *Lord North*, 2 vols (Norman: University of Oklahoma Press, 1967)

Vaughn, James, *The Politics of Empire at the Accession of George III* (New Haven, CT: Yale University Press, 2019)

Vries, Peer, *State, Economy and the Great Divergence: Great Britain and China, 1680s-1850s* (New York: Bloomsbury, 2015)

Ward, J.R., *The Finance of Canal Building in Eighteenth-Century England* (Oxford: Oxford University Press, 1974)

Weil, Rachel, *A Plague of Informers: Conspiracy and Political Trust in William III's England* (New Haven, CT: Yale University Press, 2013)

Williamson, J.G., 'Why Was British Growth So Slow during the Industrial Revolution?', *Journal of Economic History*, Vol. 44, no. 3 (1984), pp. 687-712

Wilson, Ben, *Heyday: The 1850s and the Dawn of the Global Age* (New York: Basic Books, 2016)

D. Secondary Sources: Trade, Finance, Industrialization and Industrialists

Allen, Robert G., *The British Industrial Revolution in Global Perspective* (Cambridge: Cambridge University Press, 2009)

Anon., *The mystery of the new fashioned goldsmiths or bankers their rise, growth, state, and decay, discovered in a merchant's letter to a country gent., who desired to bind his son apprentice to a goldsmith* (1676), repr. 'The New-Fashioned Goldsmiths', *Quarterly Journal of Economics*, Vol. 2, no. 2 (1888), pp. 251-62

Ashton, T.S., *The Industrial Revolution 1760-1830* (Oxford: Oxford University Press, 1948)

Ashworth, William J., *The Industrial Revolution: The State, Knowledge and Global Trade* (London: Bloomsbury, 2017)

Bagust, Harold, *The Greater Genius?: A Biography of Marc Isambard Brunel* (Hersham: Ian Allen, 2006)

Barnett, Correlli, *The Collapse of British Power* (New York: William Morrow & Co., 1972)

Beckert, Sven, *Empire of Cotton: A Global History* (New York: Knopf, 2014)

Bibliography

Brunt, Liam, 'Rediscovering Risk: Country Banks as Venture Capital Firms in the First Industrial Revolution', *Journal of Economic History*, Vol. 66, no. 1 (2006), pp. 74-102

Buchanan, Angus, *Brunel: The Life and Times of Isambard Kingdom Brunel* (London: Continuum, 2001)

Calladine, Anthony, 'Lombe's Mill: An Exercise in Reconstruction', *Industrial Archaeology Review*, Vol. 16, no. 1 (1993), pp. 82-99

Cantrell, John, and Gillian Cookson, *Henry Maudslay and the Pioneers of the Machine Age* (Stroud: Tempus Publishing, 2002)

Coffman, D'Maris, Adrian Leonard and Larry Neal, *Questioning Credible Commitment: Perspectives on the Rise of Financial Capitalism* (Cambridge: Cambridge University Press, 2013)

Crouzet, François, *Capital Formation in the Industrial Revolution* (London: Methuen, 1972)

———, *The First Industrialists: The Problem of Origins* (Cambridge: Cambridge University Press, 1985)

Dawson, Frank, *John Wilkinson: King of the Ironmasters* (Cheltenham: The History Press, 2012)

Deringer, William, *Calculated Values: Finance, Politics and the Quantitative Age* (Cambridge, MA: Harvard University Press, 2018)

Dolan, Bryan, *Wedgwood: The First Tycoon* (London: Penguin, 2004)

Falkus, M.E., 'The British Gas Industry before 1850', The Economic History Review, Vol. 20, no. 3 (1967), pp. 494-508

Flinn, M.W., *Men of Iron: The Crowleys in the Early Iron Industry* (Winlaton: Land of Oak and Iron, 2019)

———, *Origins of the Industrial Revolution* (London: Longmans, 1966)

Goodspeed, Tyler Beck, *Legislating Instability: Adam Smith, Free Banking and the Financial Crisis of 1772* (Cambridge, MA: Harvard University Press, 2016)

Griffin, Emma, *A Short History of the British Industrial Revolution* (Basingstoke: Palgrave, 2010)

Hatfield, John, and Julia Hatfield, *The Oldest Sheffield Plater* (Huddersfield: Advertiser Press, 1974)

Hills, Richard L., *Power from Steam: A History of the Stationary Steam Engine* (Cambridge: Cambridge University Press, 1989)

Hutchinson, Martin, *Britain's Greatest Prime Minister: Lord Liverpool* (Cambridge: The Lutterworth Press, 2020)

———, and Kevin Dowd, 'The Apotheosis of the Rentier: How Napoleonic Finance Kick-Started the Industrial Revolution', Cato Journal (Fall 2018)

King, P.W., 'Dud Dudley's Contribution to Metallurgy', *Historical Metallurgy*, Vol. 36, no. 1 (2002)

———, 'Sir Clement Clerke and the Adoption of Coal in Metallurgy', Transactions of the Newcomen Society, Vol. 73, no. 1 (2001), pp. 33-52

Kynaston, David, *The City of London*, 4 vols (London: Chatto & Windus, 1995-2002)

Levenson, Thomas, *Money for Nothing* (New York: Random House, 2020)

Mantoux, Paul, *The Industrial Revolution in the Eighteenth Century* (London: Jonathan Cape, 1928)

Mason, Shena, *Matthew Boulton: Selling What All the World Desires* (Birmingham: Birmingham City Council, 2009)

Naidu, S., and N. Yuchtman, 'How Green Was My Valley? Coercive Contract Enforcement in Nineteenth-Century Industrial Britain', June 2010, available at: https://www.eco.uc3m.es/temp/ms_paper_draft_june_2010 _submission.pdf

Neal, Larry, *The Rise of Financial Capitalism: International Capital Markets in the Age of Reason* (New York: Cambridge University Press, 1990)

——, 'The Financial Crisis of 1825 and the Restructuring of the British Financial System', *Federal Reserve Bank of St Louis Review* (May/June 1998), pp. 53-76.

Nevell, Michael, 'Power and Innovation: Excavating Pre-1806 Steam Engines in the Manchester Area', *International Journal of the History of Engineering and Technology*, Vol. 88, no. 2 (2019), pp. 204-24

Osborne, Roger, *Iron, Steam & Money: The Making of the Industrial Revolution* (London: Pimlico Press, 2014)

Pistor, Katharina, *The Code of Capital: How the Law Creates Wealth and Inequality* (Princeton, NJ: Princeton University Press, 2019)

Ridley, Matt, *How Innovation Works: And Why It Flourishes in Freedom* (New York: HarperCollins, 2020)

Roberts, Jenifer, *Glass: The Strange History of the Lyne Stephens Fortune* (Chippenham: Templeton Press, 2003)

Rolt, L.T.C., and J.S. Allen, *The Steam Engine of Thomas Newcomen* (Hartington: Moorland Publishing, 1977)

Ross, Ian S., *The Life of Adam Smith* (Oxford: Oxford University Press, 1995)

Rostow, Walter W., *The Stages of Economic Growth: A Non-Communist Manifesto* (Cambridge: Cambridge University Press, 1960)

Russell, Ben, *James Watt: Making the World Anew* (London: Reaktion Books, 2014)

Satia, Priya, *Empire of Guns: The Violent Making of the Industrial Revolution* (New York: Penguin, 2018)

Selgin, George, *Good Money: Birmingham Button Makers, the Royal Mint, and the Beginnings of Modern Coinage, 1775-1821* (Ann Arbor, MI: Independent Institute, 2008)

Skempton, A.W., and M. Chrimes, (eds), *A Biographical Dictionary of Civil Engineers in Great Britain and Ireland: Volume 1: 1500-1830* (London: Thomas Telford, 2002)

Smith, Dorothy B., *A Georgian Gent & Co.: The Life and Times of Charles Roe* (Ashbourne: Landmark Publishing, 2005)

Tennant Group, *Enterprise: An Account of the Activities and Aims of the Tennant Group of Companies First Established in 1797* (London: Adprint Limited, 1945)

Bibliography

Thom, Colin, 'Fine Veneers, Army Boots and Tinfoil: New Light on Marc Brunel's Activities in Battersea', *Construction History*, Vol. 25 (2010), pp. 53-67

Thomas, Emyr, *Coalbrookdale and the Darbys: The Story of the World's First Industrial Dynasty* (York: Sessions Book Trust, 1999)

Thomas, Hugh, *The Slave Trade: The Story of the Atlantic Slave Trade, 1440-1870* (New York: Simon & Schuster, 1997)

Tooke, Thomas, *A History of Prices and the State of the Circulation from 1793 to 1837*, 6 vols. (London: Longman, 1838-57)

Trinder, Barrie, *Britain's Industrial Revolution: The Making of a Manufacturing People, 1700-1870* (Carnegie, 2013)

Veevers, David, 'Before Empire', *History Today*, Vol. 70, no. 10 (2020)

Ventura, J., and H.J. Voth, 'Debt into Growth: How Sovereign Debt Accelerated the First Industrial Revolution', NBER Working Paper No. 21280, 2015

Vialls, Christine, *Coalbrookdale and the Iron Revolution* (Cambridge: Cambridge University Press, 1980)

Winchester, Simon, *The Perfectionists: How Precision Engineers Created the Modern World* (London: HarperCollins, 2017)

Index

1688 Revolution 69, 103, 104, 110, 126, 137, 139, 140

Abbott, Robert 111
Aberdeen, George Hamilton-Gordon, 4th Earl of 383
Abolition of Slave Trade Act 1807 319
Accum, Friedrich 316, 336, 337, 338
Act for the Settlement of Ireland 1652 99, 124
Act of Settlement 1662 100, 125
Act of Settlement 1701 143, 174
Act of Union with Ireland 226, 317
Act of Union with Scotland 65, 202
Adams, Captain Sir Thomas 314
Addington, Henry see Sidmouth, Viscount
Agricultural Revolution 16, 87, 110, 190 226, 227, 360
Agriculture Act 1920 390
Aire and Calder Navigation 169, 213, 242
Aislabie, John 178, 179, 180
Aix-la-chapelle, Treaty of 206
Albert, Archduke of the Spanish Netherlands 65
Albion Mill 292
Alfred the Great, King 216
Allahabad, Treaty of 224
Allen, Robert 17, 66, 109, 188
Allen, William & Co., bank 238
Alliance Assurance Co. 181
Amboyna massacre 58, 89
American Dominions (Trade with) Act 1765 223
American War of Independence 210, 230, 242, 264, 273, 281, 284, 287

Amherst, William, 1st Earl 280
Amiens, Peace of 288, 295, 318
Amsterdam 17, 57, 61, 62, 70, 101
    Amsterdam Stock Exchange 58
Amsterdam, New see New York
Analytical Engine 347, 348
Andros, Edmund 122
Anglo-Burmese War 366
Anglo-Dutch War
    Fourth 58, 62
    Second 118, 121
    Third 107, 118
Anne of Orange, Princess and Regent 57
Anne, Duchess of York 105
Anne, Queen 82, 105, 116, 138, 139, 143, 153, 156, 157, 170, 172, 174, 175, 251
Anti-Corn Law League 379
Antwerp 17, 57, 179
Appropriation of Certain Moneys Act 1697 169
Appropriation of Revenue Act 1700 108
Arbuthnot, Harriet 369, 371, 373
Arbuthnot, John 153
Arkwright & Co., bank 301
Arkwright family 300, 308
    Arkwright, Richard III MP 300
    Arkwright, Richard junior 300, 301
    Arkwright, Sir Richard 7, 10, 24, 195, 196, 198, 238, 250, 261-66, 268, 270, 300, 301, 303, 380
Armstrong, William George 308
Arne, Thomas 217
    Artaxerxes (opera) 217
Artificers Act 1718 186
Artificers Going Abroad Act 1824 186

414   *Forging Modernity*

Ashburton, Alexander Baring, 1st Baron 236, 325

Assignats, French paper money 16, 41, 294

Astor, John Jacob 301

Asturias, Spain 34

atmospheric railway system 338

Attlee, Clement, 1st Earl 389, 392

Attorney General v. Edison Company of London Limited 388

Auckland, William Eden, 1st Baron 278, 282

Augsburg, Peace of 1555 47

Augusta, Princess 216

Aurangzeb, Mughal Emperor 119, 120, 149

Austen, Jane xii

Austerlitz, Battle of 319

Australia 280, 315, 386

Austria 16-18, 21, 45, 50, 52, 55, 283
 Austrian East India Company 54
 Austrian Netherlands 52, 62, 65, 162
 Austrian Succession, War of the 48, 201, 209

Avon, River 111, 126

Ayanz y Beaumont, Jeronimo de 33, 130, 156

Ayr Bank (Douglas Heron & Co.) 239, 240

Babbage, Charles 346, 347, 348, 353

Bacon, Anthony 305

Bacon, Francis Viscount St. Alban 4, 5, 47, 59, 79, 85, 86, 90, 104, 125, 133

Bahamas 90, 122

Bakewell, Robert 227

Baldwin, Stanley, 1st Earl Baldwin of Bewdley 390

Bank Charter Act 1844 363, 379

Bank of England 16, 144, 145, 147, 174, 175, 178, 231, 234, 237, 281, 294, 316, 326, 356, 357, 362
 Bank of England Act 1708 11, 166, 174, 231

Bank of Scotland 147, 148, 231
 Bank Notes (Scotland) Act 1765 239

Bank Restriction Act 1797 316

Banks, Sir Joseph 314, 315, 341

Banque Royale 38, 41, 180

Barbados 90, 102, 121, 122

Barclays Bank 233

Barebone's Parliament 100

Baring, Alexander *see* Ashburton, 1st Baron

Baring, Sir Francis 235

Barings bank 234, 287, 386

Barnard, Sir John 210

Barnett, Corelli 385

Barton Aqueduct 212

Baskerville, John 267

Bastiat, Frederic 40

Bauer, Andreas 354

Bavaria, Duchy 44, 51, 315, 354
 Prince-elector Charles Theodore of 315

Bayes, Rev. Thomas 202

Bayly family 198, 260

Becher, Johann Joachim 49

Bedford, Francis Russell, 4th Earl of 88, 94, 336

Bedford, John Russell, 4th Duke of 219

Bedford, William Russell, 1st Duke of 169

Bedford, Wriothesley Russell, 2nd Duke of 169

Belgium *see* Austrian Netherlands

Bell, Cookson, Carr and Airey, bank 232

Bell, Henry 365

Bench Micrometer 311

Bengal 26, 206, 224, 225, 271

Bengal Famine 1770 14, 224, 271

Bentham, Jeremy 350, 378

Bentham, Sir Samuel 291

Bentinck, Lord George 381

Bentinck, Lord William 225

Bentley, Thomas 253, 254

Benz, Karl 383

Berenger, Charles Random de 331

Berkeley, Sir William 122

Berlin decree 324

Bermuda 90, 122

Bessemer, Sir Henry 382, 384

Bevan, Benjamin 336

Bill of Rights 1689 3, 138

Bills of Exchange Act 1704 144

Birkacre Mill 264

Birmingham 153, 154, 165, 196, 199, 228, 233, 246, 247, 256, 261, 266-69, 290, 295, 303, 338, 355, 358
 Birmingham and Fazeley Canal 215, 247
 Birmingham Canal 228, 243, 246, 247
 Birmingham Lunar Society 215, 246, 267

Index 415

Black Death 2
Black, Joseph 203
Blackstone, Sir William 4, 228, 229, 397
Blair, Sir Tony 395
Blücher, locomotive 368
Blunt, John 175, 177, 178
Boer War 389
Bohemia, Kingdom of 44, 45
Bolingbroke, Henry St. John, 1st
    Viscount 105, 171, 174, 185, 216
Bombay 118, 119, 150, 279
Bonnington chemical works 353
Boston, Massachusetts 89, 122
    Boston Tea Party 224, 272
Boswell, James 295
Boulsover, Thomas 143, 189
    Sheffield Plate 199
Boulton and Watt 8, 117, 181, 251, 259,
    269, 270, 290, 292-300, 302, 336, 338,
    349, 366, 367
Boulton family 266
    Boulton, Anne Robinson 266
    Boulton, Mary Robinson 266
    Boulton, Matthew 8, 10, 199, 222,
    246, 250, 256, 263, 264, 266-70, 293-
    96, 380
Bourbons, family 32
Boyd, Benfield 281, 287
Boyd, Walter 287
Boyle, Robert 104, 133, 134
    Boyle's Law 133
Boyne, Battle of the 148
Brahe, Tycho 46, 135
Braithwaite, John 370
Bramah, Joseph 297, 307-10
    Bramah Challenge Lock 307
    Bramah Locks Company 307
    Bramah water closets 307
    Bramah's hydraulic press 308, 310
Brand, Hennig 49
Brandenburg, Electorate 44, 54
Brazil 30, 58, 102, 114, 115, 120, 150,
    315, 380
Bretton Woods Conference 1944 392
Bridgewater, Francis Egerton, 3rd Duke
    of 17, 212, 213, 219, 241, 245, 272, 297
    Bridgewater Canal 212-14, 219, 228,
    241, 243, 245, 370
Briggs, Henry 86

Brindley, James 10, 24, 61, 205, 212-15,
    219, 228, 243, 244, 246-49, 311-13
Bristol 83, 117, 131, 154, 155, 207, 238,
    240, 244, 257, 338, 340
    Bristol Brass Company 154, 238
    Bristol Turnpike Trust 335
British Broadcasting Corporation 388
British Gas plc 338
British Museum Act 1753 211
British North America 89-91, 99, 121,
    150, 223
British Standard Whitworth system 311
Bruges, Belgium 31
Brunel, Isambard Kingdom 343, 366,
    368, 383
Brunel, Marc Isambard 290-92, 342-
    44, 353
Brunel, Sophia Kingdom 343
Bubble Act 1720 180, 181, 337
Buchanan, U.S. President James 383
Buckingham, George Villers, 1st Duke
    of 79
Buckingham, George Villiers, 2nd Duke
    of 112, 113
Buckinghamshire, John 2nd Earl of 226
Bullion Committee 325
Burgundy, Dukedom of 44, 55
Burke, Edmund 283
Burns, Robert 351
Burslem, Staffordshire 132, 245, 246, 252
Burstall, Timothy 370
Bute, James Stuart, Earl of 216-18, 221, 222
Bute, John Crichton-Stuart, 2nd
    Marquess of 360
Butt, Richard Gathorne 331
Butterley Company 306, 336, 355

Cabal ministry 107
Cabot, John 68
Cabot, Sebastian 68
Cadiz, Spain 31, 33
Calcutta 150, 206, 271, 279
    Black Hole of Calcutta 206
California 25
    California gold mines 325
Cambridge University 134, 256, 270,
    314, 346
Cambridgeshire 88
Campbell, George 232

Canada 37, 42, 90, 217, 280
canals 10, 11, 17, 127, 165, 205, 212, 213, 215, 218, 219, 228, 231, 238, 241-50, 289, 298, 303, 306, 311-13, 333, 377
Cannadine, David 384
Canning, George 304, 321, 323, 324, 326, 361, 364
Canningites 364, 365
Cantillon, Richard 39, 129, 202, 229
  Cantillon Effect 202
Cardiff 305
  Cardiff docks 360
Carew, Thomas 92
Caribbean islands 42, 89, 90, 99, 114, 121, 150, 175, 207, 232, 380
Carlisle, George Howard, 6th Earl of 371
Carnegie, Andrew 384
Caroline of Ansbach, Queen 208
Caroline of Brunswick, Queen 355
Carron Iron Works 171, 212, 255, 256, 269, 290
Cartwright, Edmund 299
Castaing, John 147
Castile, Spain 29
Castlereagh, Robert Stewart, Viscount 323, 324, 326, 361
Cathcart, General Earl 332
Catherine of Braganza, Queen 116, 119
Catherine the Great, Czarina 8, 37, 254
Catholic Church 19, 28, 29, 34, 41, 42, 53
Catholics 47, 55, 57, 65, 89, 96, 99, 100, 104, 129, 138, 140, 148, 149, 162, 185, 186, 203, 264, 272
Catholic Emancipation 137, 211, 273, 317, 320, 365
Cato Street Conspiracy 354, 355
Cave, Edward 196
Cavendish, Henry 270
  Cavendish Experiment 270
  Cavendish Laboratory 270
Chamberlain, Joseph 385
Chamberlain, Neville 391, 392
Chancellor, Richard 68
Chandler, Prof. Alfred D. ix
Charles I, King 56, 67, 79, 82-84, 89, 91-93, 97
Charles II, King 13, 16, 47, 86, 103, 104, 106-08, 110, 114, 116-19, 125, 128, 132, 133, 137, 139, 141, 147, 165, 173
Charles II, King of Spain 32, 33, 143

Charles III, King of Spain 22, 32, 33
Charles IV, King of Spain 32, 33
Charles IX, King of France 35
Charles V, Holy Roman Emperor 29, 46, 53
Charles VI, Holy Roman Emperor 48
Charles VII, Prince-Elector of Bavaria 48
Charlotte Dundas, steamship 297, 365
Charlotte of Mecklenburg-Strelitz, Queen 251, 254, 268
Chartism 378
Chatham, naval dockyard 290, 291, 343
Chatham, William Pitt, 1st Earl of 209, 211, 217-19
Chester and North Wales Bank 260
Child, Sir Josiah 119, 144, 149
Child's Bank 113
Chimney Sweepers Act 1788 282
China 5, 23, 25, 26, 58, 85, 89, 108, 149, 224, 279, 280, 327
  China tea 116, 117, 271
chocolate 15, 106, 114, 117
Chorlton Twist Mill 350
Church Building Act 1818 313, 357
Church of England 92, 105, 170, 357
Churchill, Winston 390
Churchman, Walter 117
Churchyard Works, pottery 252, 253
Cicero, Marcus Tullius 92
Civil List Act 1697 141
Civil List and Secret Service Money Act 1782 274
Civil War, English 3, 6, 65, 68, 69, 72, 74, 84, 88, 91, 93, 97, 102, 118, 130, 135
Clarendon, Edward Hyde, 1st Earl of 13, 72, 91, 93, 96, 103, 104, 106, 107, 133, 139
Clarendon, Henry Hyde, 2nd Earl of 105, 140
Clarkson, Thomas 255, 282
Clayton & Morris, bank 110-13, 231
  Clayton, Robert 111-13
  Morris, John 111, 113
Clegg, Samuel 336, 338
Clement, Joseph 308, 345-47, 353
Clerke, Sir Clement 131, 132, 154, 162
  Clerke, Talbot 131
Clive, Robert 1st Baron 199, 206, 224, 271
coal 20, 21, 25, 26, 33, 34, 42, 53, 61, 74-76, 80-83, 94, 131, 154, 155, 158, 159, 162, 163, 165, 167, 169, 189, 191,

Index

417

198, 204, 212, 213, 219, 228, 242-44, 246, 250, 256, 257, 269, 273, 286, 297, 301, 307, 328, 330, 331, 360, 367-69
coal gas 295, 336-38
coal tar 353
Coalbrookdale 21, 131, 137, 154, 193, 212, 259, 296
Coalition, Fifth 323
Coalition, First 317
Coalition, Second 317
Coalition, Sixth 326
Coalition, Third 317, 319
Cobden-Chevalier Treaty 358, 383
Cochrane Johnstone, Andrew 331
Cochrane, Admiral Thomas Lord 331
Coinage Act 1816 356
Coke, Sir Edward 83, 84
Colbert, Jean-Baptiste 20, 32, 38, 42, 43, 132
Coleridge, Samuel Taylor 340
Colley, Linda 185
Colliers and Salters Act (Scotland) 1775 273
Cologne, Electoral Bishopric 44
Columbus, Christopher 115
Combinations of Workmen Acts 1824 and 1825 362
Comet steamship 365
Comet steamship (U.S.) 366
Commercial Road 334
Commission for Inland Navigation for Ireland 204
Companies Act 1862 383
Company of Scotland 148
Congreve, Sir William 290
Consolidated Fund Act 1816 356
consols 9, 13, 41, 146, 172, 173, 176, 210, 237, 281, 284, 286, 289, 301, 329, 358, 377, 395
Continentals, American paper money 16, 294
Convention Parliament 1660 102, 106
Convention Parliament 1689 129, 138, 141
Cook, Captain James 201, 314
Copley, Godfrey, 2nd Bart. 201
Copley Medal 201
Copyright 8, 51, 171
Copyright Act 1709 171
corn laws 18, 272, 318, 323, 327, 329, 360, 361, 379, 380

Corn Act 1773 272, 256
Corn Law 1804 318
Corn Law 1815 318, 327, 328
Corn Production Act 1917 390
Importation Act 1822 361
Importation of Corn Act 1828 361
Cornwall 102, 269, 295, 297, 336, 340, 373, 375
cornish china clays 245
Cornish engines 18, 161, 297
Cornish Metal Company 260
cornish mining industry 157, 158, 239, 260, 295, 296
Cornwallis, Charles, 1st Marquess 279
Correspondence with Enemies Act 1691 141
Corrupt Practices Act 1695 139
Cort, Henry 304
Cotchett, Thomas 197
Cotton Mills and Factories Act 1819 304, 351, 357
Cotton Mills Regulation Act 1825 357
Cotton, Sir Hynde, 3rd Bart. 164
Council of State, 1653 96, 100, 130
Council of State, 1659 102
Counterfeiting Coin Act 1797 316
country banks 9, 11, 14-16, 105, 114, 173, 207, 218, 231-41, 242, 250, 253, 260, 261, 274, 301, 303, 306, 326, 331, 356, 362, 363, 379, 398
Country Bankers Act 1826 363
Court of Wards and Liveries 13
Coutts Bank 113, 232
Coventry Canal 243, 246, 247, 249, 311
Cowley, Abraham 92
Cowper, William 1st Earl 184
Craggs, James 178, 179
Craig, James 269
Crawshay, Richard 304-06
Crawshay, William 305
Crawshay, William II 305
Criminal Law Act 1722 187
Cromford Canal 301, 306
Cromford mill 198, 263, 301, 213
Crompton, Samuel 265, 266
Crompton's mule-jenny 265
Cromwell, Oliver Lord Protector 65, 89, 93, 96, 98-102, 108, 111, 124, 148
Cromwell, Richard 102
Cromwell, Thomas 76

Crowley family 164, 165
  Crowley, Ambrose I 161
  Crowley, Ambrose II 126, 162
  Crowley, Sir Ambrose 137, 161-65, 233, 257, 263, 305, 381
Crowley Iron Works 163, 164, 263, 264
  Law Book 163
Cugnot, Nicolas-Joseph 41
Culloden, Battle of 203, 248
Cumberland, William Duke of 203
Currency Act 1751 205
Currency Act 1764 223
Currency Act 1773 223
Cycloped, locomotive with horse 370
Cyfarthfa Ironworks 305

Daily Mail, newspaper 388
Dale, David 350
Dalton, John 338, 339, 340, 342
Danby, Earl of *see* Leeds, 1st Duke of
Dance, Sir Charles 374
Dannemora, Sweden 159, 160
Danzig 113
Darby family 155, 161, 256
  Darby, Abiah 155
  Darby, Abraham I 20, 131, 154, 155, 181
  Darby, Abraham II 155, 211, 212
  Darby, Abraham III 244, 259, 313
  Darby Ford, Mary 155
Darcy, Mr. (Jane Austen) xii
Darien project 148, 171
Darwin, Erasmus 267, 268, 270
Dashwood, Sir Francis 218
Davenant, Charles 126, 142, 151, 152, 171, 172, 229
Davenant, Sir William 151
Davy, Sir Humphrey 316, 339-42
  Davy miners' safety lamp 340, 368
de la Court, Pieter 60
Declaratory Act 1719 149, 203, 224, 226
Declaratory Act 1766 223
Dee, John 46, 69
Deeping Fen 336
Defoe, Daniel 19, 166, 168, 171, 193-95, 197, 198
Denmark 323
Derby 134, 196, 197, 270
Derby, Edward Smith-Stanley, 14th Earl of 381, 383, 386

Descartes, René 40, 59
Destruction of Stocking Frames etc. Act 1812 7, 282, 325
Devonshire, Georgiana, Duchess of 301
Devonshire, William Cavendish, 2nd Duke of 270
Devonshire, William Cavendish, 4th Duke of 211
Diana, steamship 366
Dickens, Charles 382, 397
difference engine 346, 347, 354
Dishley Society 227
Disraeli, Benjamin, 1st Earl of Beaconsfield 381, 382, 385-87
Ditherington, flax mill 302
Dolben, Sir William 282
Dolgellau, Wales 154
Donegall, Arthur Chichester, 1st Marquess of 205
Donkin, Bryan 353, 354
  Bryan Donkin Company 353
Donnington Wood Canal and Ironworks 219
Dowlais Iron Company 257, 306
Down Survey 125
Downing, Sir George 90
Drake, Sir Francis 69
Dreadnought, battleship 389
Drogheda, massacre 99
Dudley 61, 131, 158
  Dudley, Dudd 82, 83, 126, 130-32, 154, 162
  Dudley, Edward Sutton, 5th Baron 82
  Tomlinson, Elizabeth (mother of Dudd Dudley) 82
Dundas, Henry *see* Melville, 1st Viscount
Dundas, Sir Lawrence 248
Dunwich, mostly underwater Parliamentary constituency 377
dutch auction 58
Dutch East India Company (VOC) 26, 37, 43, 57, 58, 62, 69, 89, 90, 119, 148
dutch finance 105, 108, 139, 143
Dutch Water Line 59
Dutch West India Company (GWC) 58, 62
Duty (steam engine) 269, 297
Duty on Cotton Stuffs etc. Act 1774 225, 263

Index

Dwight, John 132
Dyott, General William 300

Earl Gower and Company 219
East India Company 10, 13, 26, 57, 69, 74, 78, 79, 88, 98, 101, 106, 117, 145, 146, 149, 150, 174, 179, 224, 236, 239, 271, 279, 294, 327, 333, 366
  New East India Company 145, 147, 149, 150
  East India Company Act 1772 271,279
  East India Company Act 1784 271, 279
  East India Company Act 1793 279
  East India Company Act 1813 327
  East India Dock 333, 334
East London Railway 344
Economical reform 265, 274
Eddystone lighthouses 170, 215
Eden Treaty 1786 282
Eden, Eleanor 278
Edgehill, Battle of 86, 93
Edinburgh 148, 203, 256, 353
Edward, Duke of York and Albany 266
Egerton, Samuel 244
Ekaterinburg mines 325
Eldon, John Scott, 1st Earl of 311, 320
Electric Lighting Act 1882 388
Elers brothers 132
Elizabeth I, Queen 35, 37, 46, 64, 65, 68, 70, 72, 76, 79
Elizabeth of Bohemia, Queen 47
Ellesmere Canal 311, 313
Embargo, U.S. 324
Employers and Workmen Act 1875 386
enclosures 87, 226, 227, 238, 285, 326
Engels, Friedrich 377, 378
English Copper Company 181
'Equivalent' 171
Erasmus, Desiderius 92
Erection of Cottages Act 1775 273
Ericsson, John 370
Esgair Hir lead and silver mines 165
Estates-General 38, 39, 44
Etruria factory 246, 254
Eugene, Prince 48
Euler, Leonhard 5, 49
European Court of Human Rights 396
European Union 393
Evans, Sir Herbert 165

Evelyn, John 119
Every, Henry 149
Exchange Bank of Amsterdam 58
Exchange Bank of Bristol 237
Exchequer Bills 240, 357
Excise Scheme 208

Fahrenheit, Dante Gabriel 59
Falkland, Lucius Cary, 2nd Viscount 91-93
Faraday, Michael 316, 340, 342
fens 88, 335, 336
Fenton, Murray and Wood 336, 366, 367
Ferdinand I, Holy Roman Emperor 46
Ferdinand II, Holy Roman Emperor 28, 47, 48
Ferdinand III, Holy Roman Emperor 48
Ferdinand VI, King of Spain 32
Fereday of Bilston, ironworks 238
Field, Joshua 344, 345
Fielding, Henry 105
Finlay, Kirkman 349
First Stadtholderless Period 56, 60, 61
Fitzwilliam, William Wentworth-Fitzwilliam, 4th Earl of 284
Flamsteed, John 133, 134, 135
Fleury, Cardinal 39, 41, 42
Flodden, Battle of 72
Flores, Battle of 51
Floud, Roderick xi, xii
flying shuttle 196, 261, 265
Foley, Philip 127
Foley, Robert 163
Foljambe, Joseph 191
Fontley Iron Works 304
food adulteration 338
Ford, Richard 155
Fordyce, Alexander 239
Forsyte, Soames (Galsworthy) 397
Fortescue, Sir John 3, 67, 68, 70, 84, 96
Forth and Clyde Canal 215, 247, 297, 311
Fothergill, John 267
Fourdrinier, Henry and Seely 353
  Fourdrinier paper-making machine 353
Fox, Charles James 164, 230, 274, 278, 318, 319
Fox, Henry, 1st Baron Holland 221
Fox-North coalition 221
Fox's India Bill 221

framework knitters 7, 18, 37, 349, 351

France xii, 2, 3, 5, 6, 10, 13, 16, 17, 20, 22, 23, 27, 34, 35–44, 45, 47, 50, 51, 53, 54, 57, 59, 60, 62, 63, 65-67, 69, 74, 90, 104, 106, 107, 109, 118, 132, 138, 142, 150, 152, 168, 170, 171, 180, 196, 206, 217, 218, 259, 266, 282-84, 291, 297, 316, 317, 324, 327, 331, 340, 342, 343, 354, 355, 358, 359, 375, 376, 383, 384, 386

 French East India Company 37, 43

 French Wars of Religion 29, 35, 36

 French West India Company 42

Francis I, Holy Roman Emperor 48

Francis II, Holy Roman Emperor 48

Francis II, King of France 35

Franklin, Benjamin 202, 267

Frederick Henry, Stadtholder 56

Frederick II, King of Prussia 48, 49

Frederick V, Elector Palatine 47

Frederick, Prince of Wales 216

Fronde 6, 43

Fry, Vaughan and Co. 117

Fugger family 30, 32, 46, 48, 53

 Fugger, Jakob 'the rich' 53

Fuller, Thomas 72

Fulton, Robert 297, 365

Furnished Houses (Rent Control) Act 1946 392

Gage, General Thomas 315

Galen 86

Galsworthy, John 397

Garraway's Coffee House 115, 116, 179

Garway, Thomas 115, 116

gas lighting 24, 295, 336-40

gas meter 345

Gas, Light and Coke Company 337, 338

Gascoigne, Charles 256

Gauss, Carl-Friedrich 49

Gayer, Arthur 360

general election (1690) 138, (1701) 143, (1702) 170, (1713) 184, (1715) 185, (1734) 208, (1741) 208, (1747) 209, (1754) 211, (1784) 278, (1790) 283, (1807) 320, (1812) 326, (1818) 354, (1820) 354, (1826) 354, (1830) 365

Genoa 70

 Genoese banks 30

Gentleman's Magazine 196

George I, King 139, 143, 174, 176, 178, 183, 184, 185

George II, King 57, 174, 183, 211, 215, 216

George III, King 10, 105, 139, 157, 201, 216, 217, 221, 222, 226, 248, 251, 266, 273, 278, 283, 314, 356

George IV, Prince Regent and King 139, 283, 365

Germany 52, 306, 354, 375, 376, 384, 385

 German freedoms 45

Gibbons & Timmins, bank 238

Gideon, Sampson 209, 210, 211, 287

Gilbert, John 213, 219

Gilbert, Thomas 187, 213, 219, 222, 274, 278

 Gilbert's Act 1782 187, 274

Gilbert, William 69

Gin Acts 188, 252

Gini coefficient 39

Gladstone claret 383

Gladstone, William 385, 386

Glamorganshire Canal 286, 305

Glasgow 171, 203, 207, 248, 269, 302, 349, 352, 365

Glencoe, Massacre of 147

Godolphin, Sidney Earl of 138, 151, 158, 171, 174, 175

Godoy, Manuel 33

Gold Standard xi, xii, 15, 16, 172, 176, 240, 241, 272, 280, 281, 323, 326, 355-57, 362, 390, 391, 398

Golden Hill colliery 246

Goldney, Thomas 154, 155

goldsmiths 70-72, 80, 107, 108, 113, 114, 127, 128, 174, 231, 268

Goodman, Ruth 74, 75

Gordon Riots 264, 273

GOSPLAN, Soviet planning agency 395

Gott, Benjamin 349

Gower, Granville Leveson-Gower, 2nd Earl 10, 23, 213, 219-22, 227, 243, 244, 254, 263, 274, 275, 278, 283-85

Gower, John Leveson-Gower, 1st Earl 219

Gower, Louisa Egerton, Countess 219

Grafton, Augustus Fitzroy, 3rd Duke of 219, 221

Graham, George 201

Grand Cross canal system 10, 61, 205, 213, 214, 219, 228, 243, 248, 311

Grand Junction Canal 249, 312, 334

Index

Grand Remonstrance 93
Granville, Granville Leveson-Gower, 1st Earl 221
Graunt, John 126
Great Bedwyn, parliamentary constituency 79
Great Eastern, steamship 383
Great Exhibition 1851 307
Great Fire of London 1666 111, 115, 126, 133
Great Level, Cambridgeshire Fens 88
Great Stink of 1858 382
Great Stock Exchange Fraud of 1814 331
Great Stop of the Exchequer 107, 108, 113, 114
Great Storm of 1703 170
Great Tew circle 91-93
Great Western Railway 368
Great Western steamship 366
Green, Guy 253
Greenwich Observatory 134, 135
Greg, Samuel 349
Grenville, George 211, 218, 222, 223
Grenville, William, 1st Baron 230, 283, 318, 319, 326
Gresham College 133
Gresham, Sir Thomas 70, 73
Grey, Charles, 2nd Earl 319, 326, 339
Grimshaw, Robert 299
Grotius, Hugo 59
Guadeloupe 42, 217
Guericke, Otto von 49
Guest, Josiah John 306
Guest, Keen and Nettlefolds 306
Guinea coast 118
Guinea Company 101
Guise family 35
Gurney family 233
Gurney, John & Henry, bank 233
Gurney, Sir Goldsworthy 373-75
Gurney steam carriages 373, 374, 383
Gustavus Adolphus, King of Sweden 47, 56

Habeas Corpus Act 1679 108, 140
Habsburgs, family 29, 30, 32, 44-46, 48, 50, 52, 55
Hackworth, Timothy 370
Haiti 42, 317
Hale, Sir Matthew 84, 228

Halifax, Charles Montagu, 1st Earl of 145, 147, 183
Halifax, Yorkshire 169, 194
Hall, Benjamin 305
Hall, John 353
Halley, Edmond 126, 133, 135, 152, 201
Halley's Comet 135
Hamilton, Sir William 254, 255
handloom weavers 7, 18, 265, 299, 302, 303, 348, 349, 351
Hanover, Electorate 44, 314
Hanse towns 53
Harcourt, Simon, 1st Earl 209, 216, 225
Hardie, James Keir 387
Harecastle Tunnel 246, 313
Hargreaves, James 263, 265, 266, 303
Harley, Robert, 1st Earl of Oxford 151, 164, 171, 175
Harrison, John 200-02
Harrowby, Dudley Ryder, 1st Earl of 357
Harvard University 89, 315, 316
Harvard Business School ix
Harvey, William 86
Hastings, Francis Rawdon, 1st Marquess of 279
Hastings, Warren 225, 271, 278
Hawkesbury, Lord see Liverpool, Earls of
Hawkins, Sir John 115
Haworth, James 303
Health and Morals of Apprentices Act 1802 304
Hearth Tax 128, 141
Heathcoat, John 349-51
Helton colliery railway 368
Henley-on-Thames 132
Henry II, King 64
Henry II, King of France 35
Henry III, King of France 35
Henry IV, King of France 29, 35-37, 41-43
Henry the Navigator, King of Portugal 30
Henry VIII, King 3, 16, 67, 70, 72, 84, 108
Herschel, Caroline 314
Herschel, William 49, 271, 314
Heylyn, Peter 101
HMS Dee, steamship 345
Hoare's Bank 113
Hobbes, Thomas 59, 124, 125
Hobbs, Alfred Charles 307
Hoche, General Louis Lazare 317

Holbeck, flax mill 302
Holland, John 148
Holland, Netherlands province 55, 57-59, 72, 194
Hollander paper making windmill 62
Hollow Sword Blade Company 175
Holmes, Admiral Sir Robert 118
   Holmes's Bonfire 118
Holy Roman Empire xiii, 2, 3, 6, 7, 12, 13, 20, 23, 27-30, 34, 44-54, 56, 62, 63, 74, 106, 109
Homfray, Francis 305
Homfray, Samuel 305, 306
   Homfray, Samuel & Co., bank 306
Hooke, Robert 130, 132-34
   Hooke's Law 134
Hooker, Richard 92
Hornblower family 161, 296
   Hornblower, Jabez Carter 296
   Hornblower, Jonathan 159
   Hornblower, Jonathan, jr. 296
   Hornblower, Joseph 159
   Hornblower, Josiah 159
Horner, Francis MP 325
Houblon, Sir John 145
House of Commons 45, 93, 166, 172, 178, 214, 221, 222, 236, 241, 274, 277, 278, 284, 299, 315, 319, 326, 357, 364, 373, 375
House of Lords 7, 93, 108, 149, 221, 225, 325, 357, 362, 396
Howland family 169
Howland Wet Dock 169, 333
Hudson's Bay Company 89
Hughes, Rev. Edward 260
Huguenot community 35, 36, 38, 138, 145
Hume, David 203
Hundred Years War 67
Hungary 45, 48, 50, 52
Huskisson, William 322, 325, 358, 361, 364, 365, 371-73
Hutcheson, Archibald 153, 176-79
Huygens, Christiaan 59, 132

Iberian Union 29
Ilchester, constituency wrongly disfranchised in 1832 377
Imperial Chemical Industries 353
Imperial Diet 44, 45

Imperial Preference 385, 390-94
Imperial system of weights and measures 362
Importation Act 1815 *see* Corn Laws
Inclosure Act 1773 226
Income Tax 76, 98, 141, 287, 318, 319, 355, 379, 389, 390, 392, 396
Indemnity Act 1727 186
India 14, 18, 25, 26, 43, 88-90, 118-20, 150, 195, 199, 206, 224, 225, 279
Indret, French arsenal 259
Insolvent Debtors (England) Act 1813 327
International Monetary Fund 392
Interregnum 3, 19, 27, 72, 95-98, 103, 104, 106, 111, 117, 126, 130, 135
Ireland 16, 18, 64-66, 77, 78, 96, 99, 138-40, 143, 147-49, 175, 189, 190-92, 202-05, 225-27, 284, 288, 327, 356, 380
Irish famine of 1740-41 189, 204
Irish famine of 1845-49 189, 379
Irish Rebellion, 1641 65
Irish Rebellion, 1798 288, 317
Iron Act 1750 205
Iron Bridge 259, 313
Isabella Clara Eugenia, Princess 65
Italy 18, 44, 45, 52, 168, 196, 197
Ivan IV 'the Terrible' Czar 68
Ivy House pottery works 253

Jacobites 6, 147, 164, 170, 175, 176, 185-87, 203, 208, 248
Jacquard, Joseph Marie 348
   Jacquard loom 347, 348
Jahangir, Mughal Emperor 26, 88
Jamaica 101, 121, 122, 150, 201, 380
James II, King 57, 104, 105, 108-10, 114, 117-22, 128, 129, 133, 137, 138, 140, 141, 143, 147, 148, 162, 173, 176
James Stuart, Old Pretender 138, 143
James VI and I, King xii, 20, 26, 41, 47, 64, 65, 70, 79, 84, 88, 90, 98, 143
Jamestown, Virginia 89, 115
Japan 5, 23, 25, 26, 58, 89
Jefferson, Thomas U.S. President 140, 324
Jellicoe, Adam 304
Jenkinson, Anthony 68
Jenkinson, Charles *see* Liverpool, 1st Earl of

Index

Jenkinson, Robert Banks *see* Liverpool, 2nd Earl of
Jenkinson, Sir Robert, 1st Bart. 101
Jenner, Edward 313
Jesuits' Bark 135
Jewish community 30, 101, 145
Jewish Naturalization Act 1753 210, 211
Jiaqing Emperor 280
John III Sobieski, King of Poland 48
John of Gaunt, Duke of Lancaster 30, 65
John VI, Regent and King of Portugal 200
Joint Stock Companies Act 1856 383
Jonathan's Coffee House 116, 146
Jones Act (U.S.) 383
Jones, Loyd, bank 232, 237
Jones, Thomas 261
Joseph I, Holy Roman Emperor 48
Joseph II, Holy Roman Emperor 48, 54
Jouffroy d'Abbans, Marquis de 297

Kahlenberg Mountain, Battle of 48
Karlowitz, Treaty of 48
Kay, John 196, 265
Kay, John of Warrington 261
Kendrew, John 301
Kennedy, John 349
Kepler, Johannes 46
Ketlands, Birmingham 290
Kew Gardens 315
Keynes, John Maynard 1st Baron 38, 130, 152, 356, 357, 390, 392
Kidderpore 366
Kidsgrove hill 243
Killiecrankie, Battle of 147
Killington Billy, locomotive 368
Killington Colliery 368
Kilmarnock and Troon railway 368
King, Gregory 126, 151
    King-Davenant Law 151
King's Head brewery 251
Kinsale, Battle of 65
Kit Kat Club 332
Knight, Robert 179
Knox, John 65
Koenig, Friedrich 354

La Rochelle, Siege of 38
Labour Party 387
Lagan Canal 205

Lancashire 189, 190, 250, 264, 304
    Lancashire coalfield 191, 228, 286, 330
    Lancashire textile industry 22, 194, 195, 207, 225, 238, 282, 330
Lancaster, James 88
Land Bank 1696 145
land tax 41, 97, 128, 141-43, 152, 172, 173, 186, 208, 251,
Lansdowne, Henry Petty-Fitzmaurice, 3rd Marquess of 289, 341, 358
Lansdowne, William Petty, 1st Marquess of 217, 274, 281, 287
Laud, Archbishop William 92
Lavoisier, Antoine, comte de 40, 270, 337
    Lavoisier, Marie-Anne, comtesse de 316
Law, John 38, 39, 202
Lebon, Philippe 336
Lee, William 37
Leeds 169, 194, 195, 250, 301, 302, 330, 349, 366, 367
Leeds and Liverpool Canal 243, 249, 250, 302
Leeds, Thomas Osborne, 1st Duke of 107, 108, 138, 165
Leeuwenhoek, Antoine van 59
Leeward Islands 122, 176
Leibniz, Gottfried 49, 133, 134
Leiden, university 256
Leipzig, Battle of 231
Leopold I, Holy Roman Emperor 48, 49
Leopold II, Holy Roman Emperor 48
Lerma, 1st Duke of 27, 31
Levant Company 127, 226
Levellers 96
Liège, Austrian Netherlands 162
Life Assurance Act 1774 273
Light, Francis 279
Lilleshall, Staffordshire 219, 220
    Lilleshall Company 221
Limerick, Treaty of 149
Lincoln, U.S. President Abraham 383
Lisbon, Portugal 201
    Lisbon earthquake 1755 200, 271
List, Friedrich 51
Liverpool (port) 207, 212, 213, 228, 232, 240, 250, 253, 257, 333, 367, 371
Liverpool and Manchester Railway 322, 349, 368-72

Liverpool, Charles Jenkinson, 1st Earl of 209, 222, 223, 271-75, 278, 283, 293, 294, 316, 317, 356

Liverpool, Robert, 2nd Earl of ix, 7, 14-16, 18, 23, 42, 68, 70, 78, 101, 115, 186, 192, 198, 217, 222, 240, 264, 271, 272, 277, 281, 304, 316-29, 343, 347, 349, 351, 354-65, 379-82, 385, 390, 396

Livesey, Hargreaves & Co. 238, 304

Livingston, Robert R. 297

Lloyd George, David 65, 390

Lloyd, Sampson 165, 233

Lloyd, Sampson the younger 165, 233

Lloyd's of London 116

Lloyds Bank 165, 233, 260

Locke, John 59, 97, 140

Locomotion No. 1, locomotive 369

Locomotives on Highways Act 1861 383

Lodève textile factory 42

Lombe's Mill 196, 197, 198, 263
 Lombe, John 197
 Lombe, Sir Thomas 197, 198

London 10, 11, 15, 17, 20, 39, 52, 53, 55, 66, 69-71, 73-76, 78, 81, 82, 101, 102, 107, 110, 115, 122, 127, 132, 133, 135, 140, 153, 156, 162, 163, 167, 176, 179, 184, 185, 189, 202, 218, 225, 226, 230, 251-54, 257, 264, 269, 270, 273, 279, 287, 288, 293, 294, 303, 305, 307, 308, 313, 316, 329, 330, 336, 338-40, 342, 345, 346, 353, 355, 365, 369, 373, 377
 London Assurance Co. 181
 London Bridge 343
 London Docks 169, 313, 333-35
 London, Great Fire of 133
 London Zoo 341
 London, City of 8, 58, 70, 80, 95, 98, 105, 107, 108, 114, 116, 126, 128, 145, 163, 174, 182, 231, 233, 234, 236, 239, 268, 274, 337, 386, 394
 London merchant banks 241, 362, 363, 392

Long Turkish War 46

Longitude Act 1714 173, 200

Longstaff, George Dixon 353

Lord Wellington, locomotive 367

Loughborough see Rosslyn, 1st Earl of

Louis IX, King of France 67

Louis XIII, King of France 36, 41

Louis XIV, King of France 10, 12, 20, 36, 38, 43, 114, 138, 143, 170

Louis XV, King of France 22, 39

Louis XVI, King of France 39, 31, 283

Louis XVIII, King of France 40, 386

Louisiana 42

Louisiana Purchase 298, 319

Lovelace, Ada, Countess of 347

Lowell, Francis Cabot 22

Lowther, Sir James, 4th Bart. 159

Ludd, Ned 7, 264

Luddism 7, 264, 275, 299, 303, 325, 329

Luther, Martin 47

Lyons silk industry 37

Lyons, Israel 314

macadamization 335

Macartney, George, 1st Earl 279

Macaulay, Thomas Babington, 1st Baron 111, 225, 363, 364

Macclesfield 198, 213
 Macclesfield Copper Company 199

Macclesfield, George Parker, 2nd Earl of 211, 214

Machine de Marly 11, 12

Macintosh, Charles 352

Mackworth, Herbert 167

Mackworth, Sir Humphrey 165, 166, 181, 239

Macmillan, Harold, 1st Earl of Stockton 393, 394

Madras 43, 119, 149, 150, 206

Madrid, Spain 31

Madrid, Treaty of 1750 150

Magdeburg, Sack of 99

Magna Carta 108

Mainz, Electoral Bishopric 44

Makin Mill, Heywood 303

Malam, John, James and George 338

Malt Lottery 1697 144

Malthus, Thomas 100, 327, 349

Manchester 194, 195, 212, 213, 228, 232, 237, 238, 242, 299, 303, 345, 349, 350, 355

Manchester Academy 339

Mandeville, Bernard 60, 129, 152, 229

Mansell, Sir Robert 80, 81

Index

Mansfield, William Murray, 1st Earl of 224
Margaret of Austria, Queen of Spain 28
Margate Steam Packet Company 365
Maria I, Queen of Portugal 200
Maria Theresa, Archduchess of Austria 32, 48
Marlborough, John Churchill, 1st Duke of 140
Marlborough, Sarah, Duchess of 170
Marquis Wellington, locomotive 367
Marryat, Captain Frederick 366
Marshall, John 301, 302, 366
    Marshall's Mill, flax mill 302
Martinique 42
Marx, Karl 51, 52
Mary I, Queen 73
Mary II, Queen 57, 105, 138, 139
Mary, Queen of Scots 65
Mary Stuart, Duchess of Orange 56
Maryland 89, 122, 151, 205
Massachusetts 89, 121, 272, 315
Massacre of St. Bartholomew 35
Masson cotton mill 301
Masters and Servants Act 1823 361
Matthias, Holy Roman Emperor 46
Maudslay, Henry 290, 291, 307-11, 342-45
    Maudslay, Joseph 345
    Maudslay Motors 345
    Maudslay, Thomas Henry 345
    Maudslay, Walter H. 345
Maurice of Orange, Stadtholder 55, 56
Maurice, Prince 118
Maximilian I, Holy Roman Emperor 46, 55
Maxwell, James Clark 342
    Maxwell's Equations 342
McAdam, John 242, 335
McConnel, James 349
    McConnel and Kennedy 349
McCulloch, John 129
McKenna Duties 393
McKinley tariff (U.S.) 384
Medici family 53
    Medici, Catherine de, Queen of France 35, 36
    Medici, Marie de, Queen of France 36
Meikle, Andrew 285, 286, 330
Melba, Dame Nellie 388

Mellor mill 300, 301
Melville, Henry Dundas 1st Viscount 230, 278, 283, 297
Menger, Carl 51
Menzies, Robert 366
Meredith, Sir William 254
Merrie England 2, 66, 192
Merthyr Tydfil 257, 296, 304-06
Metternich, Klemens von 50, 54
Mexico 30
Michell, John 267, 268, 270
Middleton Colliery 367
Midlands coalfield 191
Milan Decree 7, 324, 329
Militia Act 1797 316
Million Bank 144, 145
Million Lottery 144
Milton, John 71
Mine Adventurers Company 165, 166
Mineral Manufacturers Company 166
Mississippi paddle steamers 365, 366, 367
Mississippi Scheme 38, 39, 42, 180, 202
Mitsui trading house 26
Molasses Act 1733 206
Mompesson, Sir Giles 79-81, 93, 94
Monck, George, 1st Duke of Albemarle 102, 111
Monied Interest 142, 145, 146, 172, 173, 180, 182, 218
Monteith, John, James and Henry 302
Montgolfier brothers 41
Moore, General Sir John 343
Morant Bay rebellion 380
Morgan, J.P. & Co., bank 393
Morgan, Sir Charles Gould 306
Moriscos 28
Morris, William, 1st Viscount Nuffield 393
    Morris Motors 393
Mughal Empire 5, 23, 26, 88, 89, 119, 150, 199, 206, 224
Muhammad Shah, Mughal Emperor 206
Mun, Thomas 32, 98, 99, 152
Municipal Corporations Act 1835 389
Murdoch, William 295, 336, 366
Murray, Adam and George 349
Murray, Matthew 302, 336, 366-68
Muscovy Company 57, 68, 69
My Lord, locomotive 368

Nader Shah of Persia 206
Nantes, France 259
Nantes, Edict of 36, 43, 138
Napier, David 345
Napier, John 86
Napoleon Bonaparte 6, 7, 40, 41, 44, 317, 323, 324, 326, 327, 329, 331, 340, 348
Napoleonic Wars 15, 16, 40, 48, 52, 176, 210, 233, 234, 242, 273, 281, 290, 305, 331, 332, 342, 354, 379, 389
Nasmyth, James 345
National Debt 11, 176, 177, 199, 208, 281
National Debt Act 1786 280
Naturalization of Jews Act 1753 210
Navigation Acts 72, 98, 99, 142, 359, 383
Neal, James, Fordyce and Down 239
Need, Samuel 261
Nelson, Admiral Horatio 317
Netherlands xiii, 2-4, 6, 16, 17, 19, 21-23, 27, 29, 30, 34, 38, 40, 43, 54, 55–63, 70, 74-76, 88, 96, 97, 99, 122, 136, 138, 144, 146, 152, 153, 175, 273
Neumann, Caspar 135
New Harmony, cooperative 351
New Lanark Mills 351
New Orleans steamship 365
New River Company 80
New Soap patent 83, 93
    Society of Soapmakers of Westminister 83
New York 122, 297, 301, 335, 342
Newbury 72
Newbury, First Battle of 93
Newcastle, Thomas Pelham-Holles, 1st Duke of 183, 184, 211, 217
Newcastle-on-Tyne 20, 74, 75, 81, 162, 167, 191, 232, 241, 314, 330, 366, 368
Newcastle-under-Lyme 248
Newcomen engine 21, 137, 155, 157-61, 167, 184, 191, 213, 215, 256, 259, 269, 293
Newcomen, Thomas 24, 156-59, 161, 181, 193, 344
Newdigate, Sir Richard, 2nd Bart. 153
Newdigate, Sir Roger, 5th Bart. 248, 249, 282
Newport, Rhode Island 207
Newry Canal 204
Newton, Northamptonshire revolt 88
Newton, Sir Isaac xi, 16, 47, 85, 104, 133, 134, 147, 153, 176, 272

Nicolls, Colonel Richard 122
Nieuwpoort, Battle 56
Nile, Battle of the 317
Nine Years War 132, 138, 139, 141, 143, 146, 153
Norman Conquest 2
North family 127, 163
    North, Sir Dudley 127-30, 152, 229
    North, Frederick Lord 139, 217, 221-24, 226, 229, 230, 245, 251, 263, 271-75, 278, 279, 281, 361
North River Steamboat 297, 365
North-Eastern Railway 369
Northumbrian, locomotive 371
Norwich 233
Nottingham 114, 231, 238, 299, 351
Novelty, locomotive 370

Oaths Act 1722 186
Ogden, Francis, U.S. Consul 367
Old Sarum, constituency justifiably disfranchised in 1832 377
Oldknow, Samuel 299-301
Omnium, partly-paid Consols 332
Orders in Council 323, 324, 328
Ordnance Survey 291
Ordnance system 153
Oregrund ('Oregrounds') bar iron 162
Orleans, Regent Philippe d' of France 38
Ormonde, James Butler, 2nd Duke of 176
Ottawa Agreement 391
Ottoman Empire 5, 23, 25, 26, 48, 115, 195
Outram, Joseph 306
    Outram, Benjamin 306
Overend, Gurney & Co. 233, 384
Owen, Robert 184, 304, 350, 351
    Owen, Ann Dale 350
Oxford Canal 243, 248, 249, 311, 312
Oxford election 1754 209
Oxford University 82, 124, 133-35, 165, 248, 256, 282, 299, 314
Oxfordshire School of Economic Thought 91, 92, 127, 223, 229, 230, 272

P/S Caledonia, steamship 295
Palatinate, Electorate 44
Pall Mall 336
Palmerston, Henry Temple, 3rd Viscount 350, 365, 383
Papin, Denis 130

Index

427

Papists Act 1715 185
Papists Act 1778 273
Paris 11, 17, 34, 37, 41, 52, 124, 259, 297, 316, 336
Paris Exposition 1862 354
Paris, Treaty of 1763 218
Parliament of 1685 109, 114, 128, 137, 151
Parliament, Model 66
Parys Mountain 198, 260, 294
Pascal's principle 308
Patents 10, 33, 37, 51, 62, 79-84, 117, 132, 154, 191, 196-99, 226, 250, 253, 256, 259, 261, 265, 274, 285, 290, 295-97, 299, 307, 308, 336, 338, 343-45, 348, 349, 351-54, 366, 367, 373
  see also New Soap patent, Savery patent, Venetian patent statute 1474, Watt patent
Paterson, William 148, 171
Patriot King 105, 216, 217
Patriot Whigs 208, 209, 211, 152
Paul, Lewis 196
Peasants Revolt 2
Peel family 300
  Peel, Ellen Yates 303
  Peel, Greaves & Co., bank 303
  Peel, Robert (Parsley) 303
  Peel, Sir Robert, 1st Bart. 181, 301, 303, 304, 351
  Peel, Sir Robert, 2nd Bart. 18, 167, 172, 302, 341, 347, 357, 359, 361, 363, 364, 379-81
  Peel, Yates & Co. 181, 303
Pelham, Henry 184, 199, 209-11, 395
Penang 279
Peninsular War 256, 323, 324, 343
Penn, William 96, 97, 122
Pentrich rising 307, 355
Pen-y-darren ironworks 296, 305
Pepys, Samuel 118, 173
Perceval, Spencer 7, 321, 323, 324, 326
Percy, Major Henry 292
Periodic Table 340
Perseverance, locomotive 370
Perseverance, Mars rover 350
Persia 68, 206
Peterloo massacre 355
Petty, Sir William 124-26, 133, 137, 151, 229
Philip II, King of Spain 22, 27, 29, 30, 32, 34, 35, 46, 53, 55

Philip III, King of Spain 27-30, 32, 33, 65
Philip IV, King of Spain 32
Philip V, King of Spain 32
Philip the Good, Duke of Burgundy 55
Phillip, Captain Arthur 280
Phipps, Lieutenant Constantine 314
Phlogiston Theory 49
Physiocrats 39, 202
Piccadilly Mill 350
pieces of eight 34
Pinkie, Battle of 65
Pitt, Thomas "Diamond" 149
Pitt, William the elder see Chatham, 1st Earl of
Pitt, William the younger 23, 139, 172, 208, 217, 221-23, 225, 230, 271, 274, 276-87, 294, 311, 316-19, 333, 396
Planet, locomotive 371
Plantation Trade Act 1695 142, 149
Plymouth, Massachusetts 89
Pneumatic Institution, Bristol 340
Pode Hole, Lincolnshire 336
Pole Thornton, bank 234, 241, 363
Pombal, Marques de 200
Pondicherry 206
Poor Employment Act 1817 356
Poor Law 1536 76
Poor Law 1601 2, 19, 72, 76-78, 125, 187, 288, 378
Poor Law Amendment Act 1834 19, 77, 187, 378
Poor Man's Guardian 377
Poor Relief Act 1722 187
Poor Removal Act 1795 316
Pope, Alexander 116, 140, 153
Portland Vase 255
Portland Whigs 222
Portland, William Cavendish-Bentinck, 3rd Duke of 255, 274, 283, 284, 320, 321, 323, 326
Portsmouth 280, 290, 291, 343
  Portsmouth Dockyard Block Mills 291, 343, 367
Portugal 30, 42, 69, 89, 119-21, 150, 200, 323, 326, 338
Post Office 388, 389
potatoes 23, 100, 189, 190, 204, 285, 379
Potosi silver mine 28, 30, 120
Potosi silver mine, Welsh 165
power loom 299, 302, 345-49

Praed & Co, bank 238, 239
  Praed, Sir Humphrey Mackworth 238
  Praed, William 239
Praed, John 166
Praed, William Mackworth 166, 167
Praed, Winthrop Mackworth 167
Prague 46
presbyterians 65, 95, 96
Pressnell, Leslie S. 232
Price, Richard 281
Pride's Purge 95
Priestley, Joseph 257, 268, 270
Prince Regent, locomotive 367
Prince Rupert's Land 123
property rights 6, 8, 9, 32, 33, 35, 40, 41,
  51, 59, 69, 96, 100, 101, 139, 140, 148,
  171, 356, 396-98
Protection of Stocking Frames Act
  1788 282
Protectorate parliaments 100, 101, 125
Prussia 51, 54, 283
Public Accounts Committee 109
Public Works Loans Board 357
Puckle's Machine Gun 82
Puffing Billy, locomotive 368
Pulteney, Sir William 313
Pym, John 93
Pyroscaphe, steamship 297

Qianlong Emperor 280
Quarry Bank Mill 347, 349
Quartering Act 1765 223
Quebec 37, 272
  Quebec Act 1774 272
  Quebec Act 1791 280
Quesnay, Francois 39

Radcliffe Mill 303
Raffles, Sir Stamford 341
railways 14, 21, 24, 155, 161, 212, 242,
  289, 306, 333, 352, 361, 374, 377
Rainhill Trials 349, 370, 371, 374
Raleigh, Sir Walter 69, 115
Raphson, Joseph 153
Ravenscroft, George 132
Real Bills doctrine 240
Reform Act 1832 139, 297, 375, 376, 381
Reform Act 1867 382
Reform Act 1884 382

Regency Crisis 283
Regent's Canal and Dock 334
Reinheitsgebot beer purity law 51
Relief of the Poor Act 1795 316
Repeal Act 1782 226
Restoration settlement 69, 84, 96, 103
Resumption of Cash Payments Etc. Act
  1819 357
Ricardo, David 129, 325
Richelieu, Cardinal 36, 37, 40, 42, 43, 47
Ridley, Sir Matthew White 241
Riot Act 1714 185
Ripon, Frederick Robinson, 1st Earl of
  355, 359, 363, 364
Road Repair (Hertfordshire,
  Cambridgeshire and
  Huntingdonshire) Act 1663 168
Robert, Louis-Nicholas 353
Roberts, Richard 345
  Roberts power loom 345-47
Robinson, George and James 298
Robinson, John 273, 274
ROBOT scheme of free exchange rates 393
Rochester, Laurence Hyde, 1st Earl of
  104, 105, 113, 128, 138
Rocket, locomotive 370
Rockingham, Charles Watson-
  Wentworth, 2nd Marquess of 218,
  223, 226, 274
Rodger, N.A.M. 5, 118
Roe, Charles 198, 260
Roe, Sir Thomas 66
Roebuck, Ebenezer 256
Roebuck, John 250, 255-57, 268, 269
Rolfe, John 115
Roman Catholic Relief Act 1829 see
  Catholic Emancipation
Roosevelt, U.S. President Franklin D. 392
Rosée, Pasqua 115
Rosslyn, Alexander Wedderburn, 1st
  Earl of 284
Rostow, Walter 250, 360
Rothschild, Nathan Meyer 181
Rouen, France 37
Royal Adventurers into Africa 118, 121
Royal African Company 121, 150
Royal Arsenal, Woolwich 290, 308
  Royal Carriage Works, Woolwich
  Arsenal 291

Index

Royal Astronomical Society 314
Royal Bank of Scotland 203, 231
Royal Exchange 116
Royal Gunpowder Mills 291
Royal Institution 316, 337, 339, 340, 342
Royal Lutestring Company 181
Royal Navy 6, 117, 201, 256, 259, 280, 304, 342, 344, 345
Royal Observatory 132
Royal Ordnance 153, 256, 290, 305
Royal Small Arms Factory 331
Royal Society 47, 85, 104, 124, 125, 130, 132-35, 152, 153, 156, 201, 202, 256, 271, 293, 315, 324, 339, 341
Rudolf II, Holy Roman Emperor 45, 46, 47, 69
Ruhr coalfield 53, 61
Rumford, Benjamin Thompson, Count 315, 316
 Rumford fireplace 315
Rump Parliament 95, 96, 99, 100, 102
Rupert of the Rhine, Prince 49, 101, 102, 104, 117, 118, 121, 123, 133
Russell, William 128
Russia 8, 37, 45, 68, 69, 254, 305, 306, 324, 325, 326
Ryder, Richard 324
Rye House Plot 128
Ryswick, Treaty of 139, 141

Sackville, George Germain, 1st Viscount 315
Sadler, John 253
Salamanca, Battle of 324
Salamanca, locomotive 367
Salisbury, Robert Gascoyne-Cecil, 3rd Marquess of 285
Sancroft, Archbishop William 140
Sankey Canal 204, 213
Sans Pareil, locomotive 370
Saratoga, Battle of 273
Savery, Christopher MP 155
Savery, Thomas 8, 130, 155-57
 Savery patent 8, 40, 130, 156, 158, 161
Savings Bank Act 1817 9, 356
Saxony, Electorate 44, 49, 126, 194
Say, Jean-Baptiste 40, 202, 285, 328, 330
 Say's Law 40
Schwartz, Anna Jacobsen 360

Scientific Method 4, 5, 26, 47, 85, 104, 124, 133, 267, 396
Scotland 64-66, 74, 77, 99, 113, 138, 140, 143, 147, 148, 171, 191, 192, 202-04, 229, 231, 236, 239, 248, 273, 295, 302, 313, 316, 356, 368, 396
 Scottish Act of Settlement, 1690 147
 Scottish coalfield 75
 Scottish Enlightenment 171, 203
 Scottish Parliament 148, 171
Screw-cutting Lathe 310, 311
scriveners 70-72, 111, 112, 174, 175, 231, 232, 235, 237, 238
Sedgewick Mill 349
Selden, John 84, 92
Septennial Act 1716 186
serfdom 2, 3, 12, 16, 49, 51
Seven Ill Years 147
Seven Years War 43, 48, 210, 212, 248, 257
Seville, Spain 28-31, 33
Shaftesbury, Anthony Ashley Cooper, 1st Earl of 140, 145
Shah Alam II, Mughal Emperor 224
Sharp, Thomas 345
Sheffield 199, 255, 268
Shelburne see Lansdowne, 1st Marquess of
Sheldon, Archbishop Edward 92
Shepperton Tunnel 312
Shewell, Thomas 251
ship money 97
Shovell, Admiral Sir Cloudesley 113
Shrewsbury 155, 185, 261, 302
Shrewsbury Canal 313
Shrewsbury, Charles Talbot, 1st Duke of 174
Shropshire 212, 219, 313
Shropshire Canal 220
Sidmouth, Henry Addington, 1st Viscount 230, 287, 289, 317-19, 324, 326, 333, 351, 356, 361
Sidney, Algernon 128
sinking fund 175, 208, 277, 278, 281, 282
Siraj-ud-Daulah 206
Sirius steamship 366
slave trade 30, 31, 58, 101, 120, 121, 150, 199, 205, 207, 255, 260, 282, 319, 320, 324
Slave Trade Act 1788 282

Slave Trade Felony Act 1811 324
Smeaton, John 202, 214, 215, 248, 269, 353
   Smeaton coefficient 215
   Smeaton's Tower 215
   Smeaton's Viaduct 215
Smethwick Hill 247
   Smethwick Engine 367
Smith, Adam 14, 26, 79, 99, 125, 127, 129,
   153, 202, 203, 223, 226, 228-30, 240,
   272, 277, 279
Smith's of Nottingham, Bank 114, 231
Smithfield market 227
Society for Promoting Christian
   Knowledge 140, 165
Soho Manufactory 247, 267-69, 292,
   295, 336
Soho Mint 293
Somers, John 1st Baron 107
Somerset, Edward Seymour 1st Duke
   of 73
Somersett decision 224
Song Dynasty 25
Sorocold, George 196, 197
South Carolina 151
South Sea Company 38, 147, 150, 164,
   170, 171, 175, 177, 178, 180, 207, 208
   South Sea Bubble 13, 128, 137, 144,
   161, 166, 176-78, 180, 181
South Staffordshire coalfield 154
South Wales coalfield 286
Southey, Robert 340
Sovereign of the Seas, ship 102
Soviet Union 392
Spa Fields meetings 355
Spain xii, 2, 3, 6, 13, 20-23, 27–35, 36, 41,
   42, 45, 46, 50, 51, 53-58, 62-67, 69, 72,
   74, 101, 106, 107, 109, 120, 121, 147,
   150, 218
Spanish America 30, 34, 114, 115, 121,
   150, 175, 207
Spanish Netherlands see Austrian
   Netherlands
Spanish Succession, War of the 6, 32, 48,
   132, 174,
Spedding, John 159
Speenhamland system of poor relief 288,
   316, 378
Spencer, George, 2nd Earl 284
spinning frame 261, 265

spinning jenny 263, 303
Spinoza, Baruch 59
SS Savannah steamship 366
St Paul's Cathedral 134
St. Katharine Dock 313, 335
St. Rollox chemical works 352
Stafford, 1st Marquess see Gower, 2nd Earl
Stafford, 2nd Marquess see Sutherland,
   1st Duke of
Staffordshire 10, 132, 154, 158, 213, 219,
   243, 244, 248, 252, 257, 303, 304
Staffordshire and Worcestershire Canal
   126, 219, 228, 243, 246
Staffordshire coalfields 167, 191, 228, 286
Stage Coaches Act 1788 282
Stamp Act 1765 218, 222, 223
Stamp Duties Act 1783 274
Stamp Tax 142
Stanhope, James, 1st Earl 177, 180
Statute of Artificers 1563 73, 327, 397
Statute of Labourers 1351 2, 18
Statute of Monopolies 1624 81, 95
Steamboat Act 1819 357, 365
Stephens, William 200
Stephenson, George 368-71
   Stephenson miners' safety lamp 368
Stephenson, Robert 368, 370, 371
Stock Exchange 58, 331, 332, 356, 361,
   388, 394
Stockton and Darlington Railway 21,
   306, 368-71
Stourbridge Fair 193
Strafford, Thomas Wentworth, Earl of
   84, 92
Stroudwater Navigation 312
Strutt, Jedediah 261
Stuckey & Co., bank 232, 236
Suckling, Sir John 92
Sugar Act 1764 223
Sugar Duties Act 1846 380
Sully, Maximilien de Bethune, duc de
   37, 43
Sumitomo trading house 26
Sun Fire Office 181
Sunderland 162
Sunderland, Charles Spencer, 3rd Earl of
   177, 180, 183
Sunderland, Robert Spencer, 2nd Earl of
   137, 138

Index

431

Surat 88, 119
Suspension of Cash Payments, 1797 234, 240
Sutherland, Elizabeth, Duchess of 227
Sutherland, George Leveson-Gower, 1st Duke of xii, 227, 370
Swalwell works 163, 257
Sweden 47, 56, 159, 160, 162
Swift, Jonathan 153, 204
Switzerland 44, 49, 341
Sybil, novel 382
Sydenham, Thomas 135
Sydney, Thomas Townshend, 1st Viscount 280
Symington, William 297

Talavera, Battle of 323
Tamworth Manifesto 379
Tariff of 1857 (U.S.) 383
Taxation Act 1722 186
Taylor, Brook 153
Taylor, John 233
Taylors and Lloyds, bank 233
Tea Act 1773 271
Telegraph Act 1868 387
Telford, Thomas 242, 313, 335, 353
Tennant, Charles 351, 352
  Tennant chemical business 352, 353
Tenures Abolition Act 1660 13, 15, 106
Test Act 129, 211, 278
Thames, River 213, 243, 248, 249, 296, 312, 344, 365
Thames and Severn Canal 312
Thames Tunnel 296, 332, 343, 344
Thatcher, Margaret Baroness 394-96
The Alchymist, painting 270
The Duke, locomotive 368
The Times 240, 354
Thirty Years War 3, 6, 30, 32, 46, 48, 51-53, 55, 74, 99
Thomas, Hugh 30
Thompson, E.P. 187
Thornton, Henry 235, 240, 325
Thünen, Johann Heinrich von 50
Thurlow, Edward, 1st Baron 283, 284
Tokugawa shogunate 26
Toleration Act 1688 140
Tom Jones, novel 105
Tompion, Thomas 132, 134, 201, 267

Tonnage Act 1694 145
Tooke, Thomas 335, 363
Tory party 10, 23, 91, 101, 103-06, 108, 109, 114, 122, 126, 127, 134, 137, 138, 145, 146, 148, 151, 153, 162-67, 170-76, 183-86, 196, 201, 203, 208-10, 216-19, 221-23, 225, 228, 245, 248, 249, 252, 263, 264, 268, 270, 271, 274, 275, 278, 282, 283, 287, 299, 300, 302, 305, 306, 314, 320, 321, 340, 355, 361, 364, 365, 373, 377, 379-82, 385
Tower of London 82
Town and Country Planning Act 1947 392
Townshend, Charles 221
Townshend, Charles 2nd Viscount 168, 183
Townshend, George 1st Marquess 225
Trade with Africa Act 1697 150
Trade with France Act 1678 109, 142
Trades Unions 317, 382, 387, 394, 396
  Trades Union Act 1871 386
  Trades Union Congress 386
Trafalgar, Battle of 319
Tramways Act 1870 388
Tranent riot 316
Transportation Act 1717 186
Tredegar Ironworks 306
Trent and Mersey Canal 213, 219, 228, 243-47, 254, 268, 313
Trevithick, Richard 161, 296, 297, 306, 343, 365
  Trevithick's Steam Circus 296
Triennial Act 1694 139
Trier, Electoral Bishopric 44, 51
Triewald, Martin 157, 159, 160
Trinidad 115
Trustee savings banks 9, 356
Tull, Jethro 168, 191
Turenne, Marshal 56
Turgot, Anne-Robert Jacques 39
Tyrone coalfield 204

U.S. Capitol 342
U.S. National Road 335
Ulm, Battle of 319
Ulster 65, 66, 176, 192, 204
Ultras 365
United States 16, 22, 34, 45, 51, 84, 88, 224, 229, 235, 280, 297, 298, 324, 339, 342, 348, 351, 375, 376, 380, 382, 383, 391-93

United States, Second Bank of the 235
Unlawful Combination of Workmen Act 1799 314
Unlawful Societies Act 1799 314
Uranus 314
USS Princeton, steam frigate 370
Usury Act 1713 172, 173, 238
Utrecht, Treaty of 124, 150, 164, 171, 172, 175-77
Uztáriz y Hermiaga, Luis Jerónimo de 32

Vaccination 314
Valmy, Battle of 281
Valois, Marguerite de, Queen of France 35
Vansittart, Nicholas, Lord Bexley 44, 326, 329, 355, 358, 363
Vaughan, Stephen 72
Venetian Patent Statute 1474 81
Venice 26, 70, 81, 132
Versailles palace 11, 114
Vervins, Treaty of, 1598 29
Victoria, Queen 375
Vienna 17, 18, 46, 48, 52
Vienna Stadt Banco 52
Vienna, Treaty of 1815 324
Virginia 69, 89, 90, 99, 121, 122, 151, 366
Vitoria, Battle of 326
Vyner, Sir Richard 107

Wade, Field Marshal George 202
Wages etc. of Artificers Act 1813 327
Walcheren Expedition 323
Wales 64-66, 77, 113, 154, 165, 174, 188, 191, 192, 257, 291, 316, 350, 360
Wallenstein, Albrecht von 51
Waller, Edmund 92
Walpole, Horace 215
Walpole, Sir Robert 14, 146, 175, 178-80, 183, 184, 188, 199, 208, 209, 219, 281
Walter, John II 354
Warmley Brass Company 154, 238
Wars of the Roses 2
Washington steamship 366
Waterloo, Battle of 44, 234, 292, 343
Watt family 295
Watt, James 6, 23, 203, 215, 243, 251, 256, 268, 269, 293, 295
  Watt engine 4, 24, 239, 247, 256, 259, 269, 293, 295, 297-300, 302, 349, 365, 367

Watt patent 6, 161, 259, 269, 292, 295-97
Watt, Peggy Miller 269
Watt rotary engine 22, 117, 251, 259, 270, 274, 285, 292, 293, 307
Watts, William 199, 206
Wedgwood family 132, 181, 244, 252, 254
Wedgwood, Aaron 132, 253
Wedgwood, Gilbert 252
Wedgwood, Josiah 10, 24, 132, 181, 212, 219, 244-46, 250, 252-55, 263, 266, 268, 269, 308
Wedgwood, Long John 132, 253
Wedgwood, Sally 253
Wedgwood, Thomas 132, 252, 253
Weights and Measures Act 1824 362
Wellesley, Richard, 1st Marquess 279, 324, 326
Wellington, Arthur Wellesley, 1st Duke of 256, 321, 323, 324, 326, 343, 347, 361, 364, 365, 367, 371, 373, 379
Wellington, locomotive 368
Welsh Copper Company 166, 181
West India Dock 333
West India Dock Act 1799 333
West Riding, Yorkshire 190, 194, 195, 298
Western Union Company 387
Westminster Abbey 313
Westphalia, Treaty of 44, 45, 47, 50
Wexford, massacre 99
Whateleys, Birmingham 290
Wheal Vor tin mine 158
Whieldon, Thomas 253
Whig martyrs 128
Whig party 10, 11, 19, 40, 103, 105-07, 109, 110, 122, 126, 128, 129, 132, 134, 137-43, 145-50, 159, 162, 166, 169, 170, 172, 174-77, 182, 217-19, 222-25, 227, 229, 230, 235, 248, 252, 263-65, 270, 274, 278, 283, 284, 306, 316, 318, 323, 325, 339, 344, 350, 354, 355, 361, 363-65, 374-78, 380, 381, 389, 394
Whig Supremacy 9, 161, 183-215, 216, 251, 252, 265
Whitbread, Samuel 250-52, 263, 266, 292
Whitbread, Samuel II 252
  Whitbread Engine 251, 270, 292, 293, 367
White Mountain, Battle of 30, 47

Index

433

Whitehurst, John 267
Whitney, Eli 298, 319
Whitworth, Sir Joseph 311, 344, 345
Wilberforce, William 230, 255, 282
Wilkes, John 218
Wilkins, John 124
Wilkinson, Isaac 257
Wilkinson, John 10, 158, 212, 244, 250,
    257-61, 268-70, 292, 305
Wilkinson, William 257, 259
Wilkinson's cylinder boring machine
    158, 259, 269
Willem-Louis of Nassau 56
William I "the Silent," Stadtholder 55
William I, King of the Netherlands 57
William II, Stadtholder 56
William III, King and Stadtholder 56, 57,
    100, 104, 105, 138-41, 143, 145, 147-50,
    156, 170, 174
William IV, King 139
William IV, Stadtholder 57
William V, Stadtholder 57
Williams, Samuel & Co., merchant 363
Williams, Thomas, "Copper King" 250,
    260, 266
Willow Hall Mills 338
Willys and Druids tokens 260
Winchcombe, John 72, 73
Winchester palace 114
Windham, William 284
windmills 61, 62, 63, 215
Window Tax 142
Winlaton, near Newcastle 162, 163
Winsor, Friedrich Albert 336, 337
Winstanley, Henry 170
witch burnings 46
Wittelsbach family 48

Wolverhampton-Newport Turnpike 219
Wood, William 204
    Wood's Halfpence 204
Wool Act 1699 149
Woolf, Arthur 4, 161, 297, 308, 365
Wootton Bassett, constituency wrongly
    disfranchised in 1832 377
Worcester, Edward Somerset, 2nd
    Marquess of 33, 130, 156
Wordsworth, William 340
Workhouse Test Act 1723 187
World Bank 392
World War I 176, 246, 380, 385, 389, 397
World War II 330, 378, 380, 389, 392, 397
Wren, Sir Christopher 114, 133, 134
Wren, Matthew 133
Wright & Co, bank 238
Wright brothers 215
Wright, Joseph of Derby 270
Wyatt, John 196, 261
Wylam Colliery 368
Wylam Dilly, locomotive 368
Wyvill, Christopher 265

Yarranton, Andrew 83, 126, 127, 162
Yates, William 303
Year Without a Summer 355
York Buildings Company 181
Yorkshire 189, 190, 194, 195, 199, 200,
    219, 250, 264, 270, 298, 306, 307, 338
    Yorkshire coalfield 191
Yorktown, Battle of 274
Young, Arthur 190

Zheng He, Admiral 25
Zollverein, German 50, 51, 54, 383
Zoological Society 341

Also by Martin Hutchinson:

Britain's Greatest Prime Minister

Lord Liverpool

Britain's Greatest Prime Minister: Lord Liverpool unpicks two centuries of Whig history to redeem Lord Liverpool (1770-1828) from 'arch-mediocrity' and establish him as the greatest political leader the country has ever seen.

In the past, biographers of Lord Liverpool have not sufficiently acknowledged the importance of his foremost skill: economic policy (including fiscal, monetary and banking system questions). Here, Hutchinson's decades of experience in the finance sector provide a more specialised perspective on Liverpool's economic legacy than most historians are able to offer.

From his adept handling of unparalleled economic and social difficulties, to his strategic defeat of Napoleon and unprecedented approach to the subsequent peace process, Liverpool is shown to have set Britain's course for prosperity and effective government for the following century. In addition to granting him his rightful place among British Prime Ministers on both domestic and foreign policy grounds, Hutchinson advances how a proper regard for Liverpool's career might have changed the structure and policies of today's government for the better.

'Martin Hutchinson, one of the rarest of Wall Street's birds of plumage – a true original thinker – here makes the persuasive case that the greatest of Britain's prime ministers is a man whose name perhaps few Americans have ever heard. This splendid, erudite, fast-moving biography assures Lord Liverpool of the recognition he so richly deserves.' – **James Grant**, Founder and Editor of *Grant's Interest Rate Observer*

Published 2020

Hardback ISBN: 978 0 7188 9563 1
Paperback ISBN: 978 0 7188 9564 8
PDF ISBN: 978 0 7188 4821 7
ePub ISBN: 978 0 7188 4822 4

You may also be interested in:
Silas Burroughs, the Man who Made Wellcome

American Ambition and Global Enterprise
by Julia Sheppard

Silas Burroughs arrived in London from America in 1878 and proved himself an exceptional entrepreneur, taking the pharmaceutical business by storm. He was the brains and energy behind Burroughs Wellcome & Co. With his business partner Henry Wellcome he created an internationally successful firm, the legacy of which can be found in the charity the Wellcome Trust, yet few now remember him and the impact he made in his short lifetime.

A consummate salesman, Burroughs was also an astute businessman, with new ideas for marketing, advertising and manufacturing: his writings describe sales trips around the world and the people he met. He was also a visionary employer who supported the eight-hour working day, profit-sharing, and numerous social and radical political movements, including the single tax movement, free travel, Irish Home Rule and world peace. In this first biography of Burroughs, Julia Sheppard explores his American origins, his religion and marriage, and his philanthropic work, as well as re-evaluating the dramatic deterioration of his relationship with his partner Wellcome.

> *'the definitive biography of Silas Burroughs, the dynamic young American behind one of Victorian Britain's most successful (yet fraught) business partnerships.'* –
> **Christine Macleod**, University of Bristol

Julia Sheppard FRHistS graduated in history from the University of Newcastle upon Tyne and has spent her career working with military and medical archives. As Head of Research and Special Collections at the Wellcome Library, she was instrumental in the acquisition of Burroughs's papers, and he has fascinated her ever since. Her previous publications include *British Archives: A Guide to Archive Resources in the United Kingdom*. She was recently Chair of the British Records Association.

Published 2022

Hardback ISBN: 978 0 7188 9598 3
Paperback ISBN: 978 0 7188 9599 0
PDF ISBN: 978 0 7188 9600 3
ePub ISBN: 978 0 7188 9601 0